INTERACTIONS

INTERACTIONS

Teaching Writing and the Language Arts

Leif Fearn
San Diego State University

Nancy Farnan
San Diego State University

Houghton Mifflin Company   Boston • New York

Senior Sponsoring Editor: Loretta Wolozin
Development Editor: Lisa Mafrici
Editorial Development: Bruce Cantley
Senior Project Editor: Kathryn Dinovo
Manufacturing Manager: Florence Cadran
Marketing Manager: Jay Hu

Cover design: Diana Coe/ko Design Studio
Cover image: Garth Evans, *Warren St. #34,* 1998.

Copyright © 2001 by Houghton Mifflin Company. All rights reserved.

No part of this work may be reproduced or transmitted in any form or by any means, electronic or mechanical, including photocopying and recording, or by any information storage or retrieval system without the prior written permission of Houghton Mifflin Company unless such copying is expressly permitted by federal copyright law. Address inquiries to College Permissions, Houghton Mifflin Company, 222 Berkeley Street, Boston, MA 02116-3764.

Printed in the U.S.A.

Library of Congress Catalog Card Number: 00-133845

ISBN: 0-395-95965-9

3456789-MP-08 07 06 05 04

To teachers who believe that
all **children can become** *effective* **thinkers and writers**

BRIEF CONTENTS

CONTENTS

PREFACE

We welcome you to *Interactions: Teaching Writing and the Language Arts.* This is a book about meanings—definitions, clarifications, and explanations. It's about words, the communicative arts, the language arts. We invite you into our book as an active participant. We assume, because you are reading this, that you have a commitment, as we do, to the literacy development of children and adolescents.

All of our reasons for writing this book center on helping to ensure that children develop literacy skills that will enable them to thrive, not merely survive, on the life paths they choose for themselves. After years of teaching in our own classrooms and working with teachers in theirs, we know that in the hands of committed educators, the ideas presented in these sixteen chapters will help all youngsters become increasingly literate and able to use language in powerful ways. That's why we wrote this book.

Our approach is collaborative. As we wrote the book, we were aware of our readers—aware that you are as integral a part of the life on these pages as we are. In Chapter 1, "The Language Arts and This Book," we make the unambiguous statement that this book needs you. We've organized the chapters around the idea that the book is a conversation in which the authors have collaborated and in which we all now participate together. The chapters are meant to be explicit and clear, informative, and, above all, useful to you, the educators who will directly implement intentional instruction in classrooms with some of the most important people on the planet, children and young adolescents.

Approach and Key Concepts

Interactions is a comprehensive, forward-looking book about teaching writing and the language arts. It draws on a research foundation and acknowledges seminal work that has influenced where we are today in our understandings about literacy development. It takes a close look at accepted theories that help us understand the why's of learning, curriculum, and instruction. Based on sound theories and the research that tests them, we make direct and specific connections to effective classroom practices. Those practices are what this book is about: curriculum and instruction that have clear and measurable effects on student learning and achievement.

The cornerstone concept of the book is the idea of *interactive* language arts. The book describes the powerful key for literacy learning that lies in the interactions between writing and the other language arts. This book is unique in that it places writing at the center of the language arts. As we look out from that center, three of the book's distinguishing concepts emerge:

1. Writing has a powerful role in children's literacy development.
2. Instruction that takes advantage of the natural interactions between writing and the language arts actively supports the literacy learning of all children.
3. Writing is a discipline to be taught and learned. Based on this concept, we describe comprehensive, multifaceted writing instruction with objectives, activities designed to meet the objectives, and assessments used to determine growth and development and to inform subsequent instruction.

We call this *balanced writing instruction*—instruction in which writing is taught intentionally and purposefully and is designed to ensure that all students become increasingly effective writers. We return to these pivotal concepts a bit later in the Preface and in detail throughout the book.

The Organizational Scheme

Interactions is organized around three major sections: foundations, balanced writing instruction, and teaching to the interactions between writing and the language arts.

Part I: Getting Started

The two chapters in this part present concepts that are foundational to the book, including an explanation of what we mean when we say, "The book needs you." Because it's important to set out clear definitions, we begin Chapter 1, "The Language Arts and This Book," by defining the term *language arts*, and, along with that, we take a historical look at literacy instruction. We discuss why it is so important to design instruction that ensures young learners will be successful, meaning that they not only increase their literacy skills but also develop a powerful and authentic sense of their own competence regarding their skills and expertise. Also in Part I we discuss the meaning of the term *interactive* and explain how to operationalize it for instruction.

Three other major concepts are critical to understanding fully the ideas in this book: *learning*, *creativity*, and *intentional instruction*. In Chapter 2, "Foundations of the Interactive Language Arts," we explain the cognitive foundations of learning on which the book rests (attention, perception, and memory) and discuss how teachers' knowledge of learning helps them understand the interactive relationship between teaching and learning. This discussion is based on the premise that it's virtually impossible to teach effectively without understanding learning. We also look closely at the relationship between writing and creativity. We explore the role of creative thinking skills in teaching and learning and, particularly, the overt and specific role that creative thinking plays in all writing, where writing is defined as the construction of ideas and images through print. Finally, we discuss the power (and necessity) of direct, intentional instruction and how such instruction supports a curriculum designed around creative thinking and writing.

Part II: Interactions: Teaching in a Balanced Writing Program

This is the curricular heart of the book, and here the focus is on teaching writing. The chapters detail three basic areas of content that comprise balanced writing instruction: craft, processes, and genres. Like the three largest and strongest limbs of a mature tree, each of these three components of balanced writing instruction supports branches that nurture the whole.

Chapters 3 through 6 are about craft in writing. In Chapter 3, "Thinking About Craft in Writing," we carefully define the writer's craft, along with its multiple branching elements, each of which is critical to writing well. Then, in Chapters 4 through 6, we describe those elements and provide specific instructional ideas for teaching sentencing, paragraphing, and mechanical control—all within the context of children's own writing. We also describe how to teach the craft of writing through the various modes of discourse and Short Cues. Chapters 4 through 6 are, respectively, "Teaching Craft: Sentences," "Teaching Craft: Mechanical Control," and "Teaching Craft: Paragraphs, Modes of Discourse, and Short Cues."

Chapters 7 and 8 take a close look at writing processes. At the heart of these chapters is the seemingly simple statement that *writing is process. Process* here refers to the mental procedures that comprise the act of writing, procedures that are complex and unique to the writer. What do we know about writing processes? How do they work? What can we learn about writing processes from practicing writers? You'll notice that in each of these questions, the word *process* is plural. That's because there is no such thing as one writing *process*, for either novice or experienced writers. Writing is comprised of multiple elements that interact fluidly with one another as writers write. This idea is captured in Chapter 7, "Thinking About Processes in Writing," in the iterative model of interactive writing process. As in other chapters, we quickly make the connection between the explanations and models to classroom practice—because that's what teachers do.

Chapter 8, "Teaching and Learning Writing Processes," deals more specifically with instruction, beginning with a rationale for teaching writing processes and describing ways to help youngsters become familiar with their own processes. The chapter includes a section on helping children become increasingly effective writers through participation in Writers' Workshops, where direct and functional feedback support the revision and editing processes.

Chapters 9 and 10 describe the third component of a balanced writing program: the genres. In Chapter 9, "Thinking About Genres in Writing," we explain the meaning of the word *genres* in writing context. We explore how an understanding of each genre, with its distinctive features and purpose, informs writing instruction across the various types of writing. Chapter 10, "Teaching and Learning the Genres," focuses on instruction. It describes in detail numerous instructional processes through which young writers can learn to write short fiction, reports of information, persuasive pieces, poetry, biographies, autobiographies, and various kinds of technical writing.

Thus far in Part II, the chapters have described the teaching of writing through a balanced, comprehensive writing curriculum. The last two chapters in this part focus, respectively, on technology and writing and on a critical element in any curriculum, assessment. Chapter 11, "Technology and Writing," explores the effects of technology on not only how we write, but also on what we write. It examines the increasing role of networked discourse and provides specific examples of the infusion of technology into teaching and learning. Through these examples, we invite you to take a look at actual classrooms where technology is being used to support children's use of inquiry and collaboration and the development of their skills in the communicative arts.

Finally, in Chapter 12, "Assessment in Balanced Writing Instruction," we discuss what assessment means and what makes it an important part of any curriculum. We attempt to answer the question of what we broadly, as a profession, value in students' writing and how we can create assessments to measure what we value. In addition, we describe five kinds of writing assessment systems, and analyze each one in the context of the purpose for assessment and the audience for which the results are intended. A major message of this chapter is that teachers have a significant role to play in assessment and can better serve students, their families, the administration, and the larger public if the assessment possibilities are well understood.

Part III: Interactions: Teaching Writing and the Language Arts

This part of the book turns to the writing-language arts interactions. Woven throughout the book, not only in Part III, you will find attention to the critical interactions that take place between writing and both oral language and listening. Chapters 13 through 16 describe, respectively, the powerful writing-reading, writing-spelling, and writing-vocabulary interactions and provide numerous instructional ideas in each that are designed for the explicit purpose of developing young learners' literacy and language arts skills. Chapter 13, "Writing-Reading Interactions," describes, among other things, how children develop what Holdaway referred to as a *literacy set* (1979) and the writing-reading interaction in Book Clubs. Chapter 14, "Writing-Spelling Interactions," explores research in spelling and examines why we teach spelling, what words children need to learn, and how to ensure that students retain the spellings that have been the target of instruction. Chapter 15, "Writing-Vocabulary Interactions," also explores research, with a focus on what we know about vocabulary development. In addition, it describes how writing-vocabulary interactions highlight the necessity for instructional ideas that lead to the recall of words rather than mere recognition of words.

The final chapter in Part III, and in the book, features the MaxiLesson, a comprehensive lesson design that highlights the interactions among the language arts. Its core is a larger piece of writing, often a genre, and in each lesson there is attention to writing processes, organization, craft, the relationships between form and function, and, as appropriate, spelling or vocabulary, or both. MaxiLessons offer a coherent way to organize the language arts curriculum and average approximately thirty to forty-five minutes. Chapter 16, "MaxiLessons: Highlighting Writing and the Interactive Language Arts," describes several MaxiLessons and their design.

Special Features

At the beginning of the Preface, we mentioned that as we wrote, we were aware of the fact that our book needs you, the reader. In our overview of the book's three parts, we explained the basic organizational scheme within which we worked. It's a scheme we created with readers in mind, repeatedly asking ourselves if what we were constructing would provide a logical structure around which to build the content. We asked ourselves a similar question with each chapter, our objective always being to make the text accessible and enhance each reader's understanding of the ideas presented. Toward that end, each chapter has its own organizational structure and devices threaded throughout:

- **Before You Read.** Each chapter begins with a list of prereading statements and questions that serve as a preparatory mind-set for reading the chapter, an expectation for the content you will encounter. Good readers have an expectation for what they will read, as well as a purpose for reading. The "Before You Read" sections are designed to address the expectations and purposes. As you read, look for answers and explanations related to the items in "Before You Read."

- **Review and Reflection**. Each chapter contains several "Review and Reflection" sections that contain questions and statements designed to cause review and reflection of the preceding content. Expert readers reflect on what they've read, and our intent with these sections is to support readers as they engage in the best processes of highly literate individuals.

- **Instructional Scenarios**. Instructional scenarios are extended descriptions of authentic classroom practices relevant to the chapter's content. Each is presented as it has occurred in classrooms where teachers and students are engaged in teaching and learning. They take us directly into classrooms and illustrate how the instructional ideas presented in a chapter look when they are applied with young learners.

- **ESL Sections**. All children require sound instruction to support their learning. However, children who are learning English as a second language (ESL) require special emphases and sometimes adjustments in content and procedures as support for their literacy development. These children are developing literacy skills at the same time that they are learning a new language. In each chapter, instruction is highlighted that specifically addresses the needs of children who are learning English as a second language.

- **Action Research.** Action research is classroom research designed to lead to an action—that is, to revise a way of delivering instruction, adjust content being taught, and better meet the needs of children through continuously refined curriculum and instruction. It begins with a question, a problem, and ends with results that inform classroom practice. We welcome readers to conduct action research with their students and contact us about their successes and questions.

- **A Summary.** Each chapter contains a summary of the main points presented. The summary brings closure to the chapter and, more than that, gives readers another opportunity to reflect on the content presented.

- **Figures, Tables, and Glossary.** We've used some helpful comprehension devices throughout the chapters. Figures and tables help make information more accessible. We've also used italics and boldface throughout the text in order to highlight ideas and key terms we felt were especially important and worth noting. Terms in boldface are defined in a handy end-of-text Glossary.

- **Resources for Further Investigation**. In this section, at the end of the text, we have annotated resources that over the years we have found interesting and helpful. It is organized into five sections: "Writers on Writing," "On the Writing Act," "Teaching Writing and the English Language Arts," "What Writers Read," and "The Internet." In all, there are fifty-two resources that we hope readers will find relevant, informative, and perhaps even compelling.

Supplemental Materials

Accompanying the book are two sets of supplemental materials: the *Instructor's Resource Manual (IRM)* and a Web site.

The IRM was written specifically as support for instructional use of the text. It contains a brief synopsis and overview of each chapter, a chapter outline, and key ideas found in the chapter. In addition, for each chapter, selected references have been included, along with annotations. The discussion topics that accompany each chapter could also be used as questions (or statements to prompt reflection) on an examination.

Sample syllabi are included in the IRM as models of how university courses might be structured around the text. Blackline masters are also provided and can be made into overhead transparencies for classroom use.

The book's Web site is a dynamic resource that we anticipate will evolve as materials are added and revised. It provides such resources as questions to guide possible action research projects, links to other relevant sites, access to selected articles, and additional chapter-by-chapter information.

It is our intention that readers find these resources useful and supportive of their work in both preservice and in-service settings.

Audience and Contexts for Using the Book

As we conceptualized and wrote this book, we had a clear vision of its audiences. Both of us teach in teacher preparation programs and are aware of the need to help preservice teachers develop a high level of knowledge and expertise in teaching writing and the language arts. For that reason, this book is for all instructors of literacy and language arts who teach in teacher credentialing programs and their students. Both of us also teach in graduate programs and are aware of the desire of in-service teachers to refine what they do, read and study, and reach ever-greater understandings about children's literacy development. For that reason, this book is appropriate as a text in graduate programs for in-service teachers who are studying writing, language arts, and literacy. In the *Instructor's Resource Manual* we have provided several ways to use the book: for the teaching of writing and language arts in both ten- and fifteen-week courses.

It is our experience that all teachers, as reflective practitioners, consistently seek to use theories of teaching and learning to refine their work, engage in practices that are informed by research, and develop an increasing repertoire of ideas for instruction that will meet the needs of all their students. Based on our own teaching experiences and those of teachers with whom we've worked, it is our belief that all teachers would find this text supportive of their commitment to student learning.

The Heart of the Matter

At the heart of this book lie three propositions. We use the word *proposition* in the sense of essential ideas put forth, ideas that are foundational to the book.

Proposition 1: Writing is the center of the language arts curriculum.

Children often begin writing before they read. They begin manipulating symbols, called letters, that represent sounds and, collectively, ideas. Their first attempts at writing, referred to as emergent writing, occur through drawing and scribbling and then through invented and then temporary spellings as they begin constructing meaning with the symbols of language. Throughout the book, we describe not only how writing helps children access the world of print, but how writing interacts with other language skills to further children's literacy development. The concept of interactions is captured in our second proposition.

Proposition 2: The language arts are interactive language skills, and it is through these interactions that literacy is best developed.

Part I of the book describes the concept of interactions. In Part II the concept is evident as, throughout the chapters, instructional processes highlight ways in which all the language arts work naturally together, that is, interact, to support children's literacy development through the writing curriculum. It is in Part III, however, Chapters 13 through 16, that we spend concentrated time discussing the interactions between writing and the other language arts. Fundamental to this book is the concept of helping children develop their language arts skills by teaching with and to the interactions.

Proposition 3: Writing is a discipline and, as such, can be taught, learned, and assessed.

The word *discipline* here refers to the content of learning, as in the discipline of history or science or mathematics. Because writing is a discipline, it contains content that can be taught and learned. Teaching writing is central in this book. There is ample evidence that instruction, not mere promotion of writing, is necessary if students are to increase their writing and literacy skills. There is ample evidence that writing is better taught than caught. Much of this book is about *teaching* writing.

These propositions raise some major questions, all of which we answer in the book:

- What do we mean by interactions?
- What does it mean to teach to the interactions?
- Why place writing at the center of a language arts curriculum?
- What do we mean by instruction?
- Does the idea of intentional writing instruction violate writing process?
- Does the idea of intentional writing instruction violate creativity in writing?
- What makes writing creative?
- If there is "creative" writing, is there also noncreative writing?
- What does balanced, comprehensive writing instruction look like?

We invite you to read this book to find answers to these questions and others of your own. Also, we urge you to use this book as a resource. Do not feel bound by the linear arrangement of chapters. For example, you might want to begin with Chapters 1 and 2, then move to Chapter 12 to find out about assessment in writing and the role it plays in a balanced writing program. From there, you might want to go back to Chapter 3. The point is that this book is yours to use in whatever way you choose. We've described some possible ways to use the text in the *Instructor's Resource Manual* by providing several different course outlines that we've developed around the book.

Acknowledgments

Before you begin Chapter 1, we'd like to share with you our acknowledgment of people who have contributed either directly or indirectly to the book. They are our colleagues, friends, and mentors. Some of them we have known for years, some only since we began the first draft of *Interactions*. All of them, however, made significant contributions to the book's development, and we want them to know how much we appreciate them. They asked the right questions, helped us refine and clarify important concepts, and taught the lessons. They are the Writers' Haven writers, especially Betty Abell Jurus and Jerry Hannah; Kathleen Foster; Elizabeth Goldman; Suzanne Jackson; Patricia R. Kelly; Robert E. McCabe; Anne Perry; Ellen Phaneuf; Diane Rocha; and all the teachers who have participated over the past decade in our Writing Institute for Teachers. At Houghton Mifflin, we particularly acknowledge Loretta Wolozin for listening; and Bruce Cantley, Lisa Mafrici, and Nancy Benjamin for their guidance. We thank the text's reviewers for their careful reading, critical insights, and encouragement. They are Judith Cape Craig, Ph.D.; Joanne Galli-Banducci, University of California, Davis; Rosemary G. Palmer, Boise State University, Idaho; and MaryEllen Vogt, California State University, Long Beach.

And finally, we thank the muse whose subtle presence made collaboration successful and painless.

INTERACTIONS

PART I

Getting Started

1 The Language Arts and This Book

BEFORE YOU READ

- What is meant by the term *language arts*?
- Why should teachers be knowledgeable about the history of literacy instruction?
- For whom was this book written?
- What are the principles that support the book's fundamental ideas?
- What can readers expect to find in the book?

This book is about writing as the anchor in a language arts program. But what are the **language arts?** Where did the term *language arts* come from? What can we learn from the history of language arts and literacy instruction, and why is it important for teachers to be knowledgeable about the roots of literacy and language arts instruction? In this chapter, we examine those questions and provide a road map of what you can expect to find as you travel with us into the world of curriculum and instructional ideas in writing and the language arts.

Defining the Language Arts

Language arts is an umbrella term that over the past fifty years has been used to describe curriculum in reading, writing, speaking, listening, literature, problem solving, **semantics,** critical thinking, grammar, vocabulary, spelling, and history of the English language. After studying major curriculum reports, textbooks, histories of American education, and journals, Whitman (1973) puts the beginning of the "language arts movement," as he calls it, shortly after World War II.

Today we typically use the phrase *language arts* to refer to the four language skills of reading, writing, speaking, and listening. In *The Literacy Dictionary*, Harris and Hodges (1995) define *language arts* as those curriculum areas dedicated to improving the four language skills. They also define it as the communication arts, for which language is the "common denominator" (p. 133).

But once we define the term, what do we do with it? Do we think of language arts as a content area? What exactly do we mean when we say we are teaching a language arts lesson? Is it a time when we teach reading, writing, speaking, and listening as separate subjects? Or, as many books and articles suggest, do we teach the language arts by somehow putting them together? Would that mean we teach a little bit of reading, writing, speaking, and listening all at the same time? Or is the emphasis on reading? Or on writing?

What typically occurs during language arts time is not reading instruction and often it isn't writing either, at least not something that could be described as a writing program. Speaking and listening tend to be woven throughout the language arts period, not necessarily intentionally and purposefully, but often as a natural consequence of classroom interactions and activities. Language arts time also tends to include language study (parts of speech), journals or other freewriting activities, skill sheets associated with editing, paragraph analysis, work on thematic units, and perhaps read-alouds. The point is that reading and language arts, including writing, are often segregated in a curricular sense. This is not a new phenomenon. Let's take a look at the historical precedent for the separation of reading from the rest of the language arts curriculum.

REVIEW AND REFLECTION

1. If your teachers used the term *language arts* in their teaching, based on what you observed and experienced as a K–12 student, how do you think they defined *language arts?*
2. From what you've observed and experienced, both as a student and after you left the K–12 system, what is most commonly taught during the time called *language arts?*

A Historical Look at Literacy Instruction

The separation of reading from the rest of the curriculum goes back to colonial America, where reading and writing were two separate "Rs," often taught in different schools by different teachers. Reading instruction encompassed the study of letters, syllables, and words, in that order; writing instruction was considered more advanced and was begun only *after* children could read. And even then,

A hornbook. Hornbooks were replaced by the *New England Primer*, published by the Puritans in 1690.
© Bettmann/CORBIS

A page from the *New England Primer*.
© Bettmann/CORBIS

writing focused primarily on penmanship and careful transcriptions of what others had already written. Reading instruction was a high priority because of the importance attached to the ability to read religious writings.

The first books in colonial America were hornbooks, wooden boards printed with the alphabet, some words, and some religious concepts. Words and letters were printed on sheets of paper, and transparent coverings made from hammered sheets of cow's horn were affixed to the board to protect the lesson sheet, hence the name hornbook.

Reading instruction had primacy in the curriculum in order to transmit strict religious and moral values to children. Childhood was not a carefree time of fun and comfort. Life was hard and often short, and the colonists believed it was necessary for children to learn how to live obedient and righteous lives. The path to salvation required a serious mind, strict discipline, and knowledge of religious tenets. Writing was considered much less important than reading, and it was certainly not considered important for girls to learn to write because writing was necessary only for work outside the home or in college.

The *New England Primer* provided reading instruction that began with smaller units of language, letters and the alphabet, moving to the study of one-, two-, three-, and four-syllable words and then to brief sayings and prayers. It wasn't until the mid-1700s that materials were printed specifically for children's enjoyment and instruction. These materials, called *chapbooks,* were sold for pennies by peddlers who were called *chapmen.* The stories were crudely written versions of fairy tales and nursery rhymes. Bernice Cullinan, an expert on children's literature, tells us that these early chapbooks did serve two vital functions. They "created a readership for later books published for children" and "perhaps even more important, they preserved many fairy tales and nursery rhymes for later and better retellings" (Cullinan, 1989, p. 645).

How History Informs Us

The history of the **literacy** curriculum gives us a perspective on where we've been and how that history has influenced where we are today. Without a historical view, each idea, theory, and instructional suggestion seems unique and new. Without it, we are denied the foundational knowledge that allows us to make decisions as informed practitioners.

Although we are always learning and refining what we do, there are some important concepts and theories that have informed educators for decades, if not centuries, and they provide a valuable context for where we are today. For example, before the turn of the twentieth century, several concepts emerged that we've built on to create today's vision of curriculum and instruction. Two of those concepts are (1) a student-centered curriculum, based on a child's natural development and attributed to Johann Pestalozzi (1746–1827), designer of what has become the modern elementary curriculum, and (2) an emphasis on individual differences in an activity-oriented curriculum, attributed to Friedrich Froebel

(1782–1852), designer of the idea of kindergarten. In 1899, John Dewey published *School and Society,* in which he espoused, among other things, active learning, as opposed to a read-recite-test setting dominated by teacher lecture, in a child-centered environment. These theories continue to resonate in conversations of student-centered environments in which learners use prior knowledge and new information to construct their understanding.

By the mid-twentieth century, voices were clamoring for a "return to the basics" because of fears that American education was on a steep slope to destruction. In 1955, Rudolf Flesch, in *Why Johnny Can't Read,* jumped into the fray with a call for a renewed emphasis on phonics and basic instruction in reading and writing. He argued that American education had lost its rigor and was on a serious decline. This fire was fueled by the Russians' launching in 1957 of the satellite *Sputnik,* which sent the American public into a panic regarding the teaching of science and math.

In the 1950s and 1960s, the concern over reading was called the "great debate." In the 1990s, we had what has been called the "reading wars." We've argued about whether children were actually learning to become literate, questioned curriculum and methods of instruction that lead to that outcome, and debated methods and outcomes. Interestingly, the concerns of the 1990s were similar to those raised in the 1950s and 1960s.

The history of reading and writing is an important subject for educators because without a historical context, our ability to make informed professional decisions is compromised. Nelson and Calfee's *The Reading-Writing Connection* (1998) provides an excellent overview of the history of reading and writing.

REVIEW AND REFLECTION

1. Why is a historical perspective on literacy teaching important for teachers today?
2. Give a specific example of how a historical perspective on literacy teaching could affect your thinking about teaching and learning today.

For Whom Did We Write *Interactions?*

One of our favorite books is Gary Paulsen's *The Winter Room.* It's about a family living on an eighty-seven-acre farm in the northernmost part of Minnesota, adjacent to a thick forest. As Paulsen describes it, "The woods are tight all around the farm" (p. 10), with its white wooden farmhouse that has four rooms downstairs and two bedrooms upstairs. One of the downstairs rooms is what today would be called the living room, but the family calls the winter room because in it sits the wood stove, which they gather around in the evening to reminisce and spin stories, warm their fingers and toes, and carry out a family tradition of togetherness before bedtime. We experience life on this farm through the eyes of the narrator, an adolescent boy named Eldon, who, along with his older brother, Wayne, lives on the farm with their parents and two uncles and has experiences that can move readers to laugh out loud and sometimes cry.

For Leif, the book conjures up familiar experiences because he was raised on a Pennsylvania farm with a farmhouse not too unlike that in *The Winter Room.* For Nancy, that farm and farmhouse, and the cycle of life whose momentum comes from changing seasons, offered a foray into a different world with new cultural trappings. For both of us, the book was compelling. We laughed, felt the pathos, and relished the images Paulsen's words painted.

It might seem that we digress from the question this section of the chapter promises to answer: For whom did we write this book? But Paulsen takes us directly to the answer. In Chapter 1, his writing gives readers a peek at the rich, sensory milieu of life on the farm. But he also acknowledges that the book itself can't provide the smells, sounds, and sights of the farm: "If books could have more, give more, be more, show more, they would still need readers, who bring to them sound and smell and light and all the rest that can't be in books. The book needs you" (p. 3).

We say the same thing: This book needs you. It needs your previous and current experiences, your purposes for reading, your openness to ideas and new learnings. It also needs your commitment as an individual and professional educator to teaching and learning, and to young learners and their literacy development.

We've tested the contents of this book with preservice teachers, who are just beginning their professional preparation, and with experienced teachers, many of whom we've worked with in their classrooms. For those of you who are preparing to be teachers, the book may be one of your first opportunities to think about the relationship between teaching and **learning,** how to teach writing effectively, how to teach in a way that fully engages your students and highlights interactions between writing and the language arts, and how to ensure that your students will become highly literate individuals able to function productively in the world outside school.

If you are in your early years as a classroom teacher or if you're an experienced teacher, some, and perhaps even much, of what you read in this book may be affirming. There are classrooms across the country, and at every grade level, in which the work teachers do with children, adolescents, and young adults is absolutely thrilling. Students are positive, engaged, and productive. The teachers share with students a vision for learning that makes it seem important, sometimes even urgent. Their students see the vision. They talk about what they are learning in class, and they talk about it after class. One of these wonderful teachers once reported to us that she overheard several of her students at a basketball game discussing their plans to stage a scene from *Macbeth* in her class. The learning didn't stop when the bell rang at the end of class. Students in classrooms with exemplary teachers experience some of the best education in the world.

Teaching is about learning. Learning is at the center of everything teachers think and do, and for that reason the very best educators are themselves always learning. They read books like this one, attend professional conferences, spend time and energy (and money) to participate in the collegial atmosphere of graduate study, attend staff development sessions in their schools and districts, and work daily with other teachers to share their best ideas and practices. Because you bring to this book a desire to read and learn, we fully expect that it will offer you new ways of thinking and point to new practices.

So we'll say it again: This book needs *you.* We invite you to read through it with your own experiences, purposes, and needs in mind. As closely as we can approximate it, we would like the book to represent a conversation among professionals who are committed to the same objective: the literacy development and success of the children, adolescents, and young adults with whom we work.

What Is the Purpose of the Book?

Based on work in many classrooms across the country, as well as on general knowledge about human nature, it is clear that children and adolescents come to school with a desire to be successful. They have every hope that the day will go smoothly, that they will be liked and appreciated by those around them, and that whatever they do that day will result in feelings of competence and well-being.

Over forty years ago, Robert White (1957) wrote about this phenomenon, which he called **competence theory.** "To be competent," he said, "means to be sufficient or adequate" (p. 121). In order to explain the concept fully, he traced its evolutionary importance, explaining that human beings have always tried to understand their environment and the effect they can have on it. In fact, their survival depended on it. Competence in the environment meant that humans were familiar with and able to manipulate the environment to their benefit. Unsuccessful humans failed to understand their environment and how they could influence it to ensure their survival, whether that meant understanding which berries were edible and which were poisonous, or having an effect on the environment that resulted in a successful hunt or avoiding becoming prey.

Our immediate, day-to-day survival might not be as dependent on competence in the same way as it was for early humans, but it does have an effect on whether we thrive. White (1957) describes a child's developing sense of competence in this way: "In learning to be competent, the child reaches out to the friendly and useful aspects of the world, and lays the foundation for what may become enduring interests" (p. 120). White also relates confidence and **self-esteem** to competence, and he points out the fallacy in a common rhetoric associated with self-esteem: that if we're just nice enough and kind enough to youngsters, their self-esteem will "improve." Although White notes that self-esteem may be somewhat related to "what others think about us," its strong root is "in our own experiences of competence" (p. 122).

Colvin and Schlosser (1997–1998) interviewed middle school students and found that less effective readers and writers have very little confidence in their ability to succeed. Their work with these students led them to conclude that teachers can have a powerful effect on students' developing sense of competence. Teachers, however, must do more than simply tell students they are good. Rather, Colvin and Schlosser suggest the following:

- Teachers must believe their students can be successful and send that direct message to them. But that is not enough.
- Students must have clear evidence that they are able, potent, and competent—that is, successful. According to Bandura's (1986) theory of self-efficacy (which means, literally, "the self is able"), an individual's confidence to do a task directly affects his or her performance. Success helps learners develop confidence and feelings of competence.
- Students' successes must emerge from challenging learning environments. Tasks that are too easy send students a message that they are not able. However, when students face a challenging task, they must be able to accomplish it. This is what Vygotsky (1986) had in mind when he described his theory of the **zone of proximal development.** Productive learning, he said, occurs just beyond what a learner currently can do alone, but definitely can do given teacher guidance and support—what is called *scaffolding.* Here, choosing appropriate curriculum and instruction is an important key for learning.

We can speculate on what makes young learners feel competent in school. Certainly one way that children experience school as a place where they can be successful is to encounter realistic expectations that they are able to meet or exceed. What are the expectations of school? There are many, of course, and not all of them have to do with academics. Many center on social and interpersonal success. However, much of what determines whether students will find success in school involves academic performance. But academic performance by itself may not be sufficient.

You may have firsthand experience with the fact that a "good job" or "nice try" may not be enough to persuade a student that she has, in fact, done well. What is critical is *the individual's own perception of success,* which comes from effective performance on tasks he or she finds challenging and engaging, on tasks in which the learner has an investment and which provide him or her with tangible evidence of accomplishment.

The fundamental purpose of this book is to provide a way of thinking about curriculum and instruction in writing and the language arts that students will experience as challenging and engaging. The writing program this book presents supports youngsters in their growth and development as thinkers and writers. It engages them in learning through the authentic interactions between writing and the language arts. It is designed to ensure that young learners, with expert help and guidance from their teachers, will not only become increasingly literate, but will experience their increasing literacy in ways that make them feel competent and potent.

Some children seem to have been persuaded at a tragically young age that it is impossible for them to be successful in school. They may not approach every day with a desire to be successful because that desire has long since been squelched as unrealistic. Often it seems to their teachers and parents that they don't even try to succeed. When individuals believe absolutely that they cannot fulfill an expectation, meet a goal, or accomplish a task, they do what many adults do: find success in other ways.

If their school experiences tell them that they cannot accomplish a task or meet a goal, they will avoid what makes them feel unsuccessful and incompetent and find other things to occupy their thoughts and their time.

We believe passionately that one purpose for education is to ensure that all youngsters grow up to have a meaningful and productive life both inside and outside school. The content of this book focuses on a critical ingredient in a meaningful and productive life. *The book is about ensuring that young learners are able to function with a high degree of literacy and are competent users of all the language arts.*

REVIEW AND REFLECTION

1. How would you explain the relationship between self-esteem and competence?
2. Why do some learners shy away from even trying to do or learn certain things?
3. What can teachers do to ensure that students view themselves as competent learners?

What Can You Expect to Find as You Read *Interactions*?

Overview of the Book

In Part I, "Getting Started," we explain what we mean by thinking interactively about the language arts and when we say that this is a way of thinking that places writing at the heart of the language arts program. We describe the nature of the interactive language arts, discuss cognition and learning in the context of language arts instruction, and describe the relationship between teaching and learning and the role of creative thinking skills in both.

Everything in this book rests on what we know about learning, which is where all of our thinking about teaching must start. That's why we begin in Part I with discussions of critical knowledge about learning. With that as a foundation, we move into Parts II and III, where the focus is on what we know about what learning means for teaching.

Part II focuses specifically on teaching in a balanced writing program. We describe the three major elements in a comprehensive and balanced writing program: craft, processes, and genres. The chapters alternate between foundational information on, for example, craft in writing (Chapter 3) and specific applications for teaching craft in writing (Chapters 4 and 5). Chapter 6 presents background information on larger main ideas. Chapters 7 and 8 look directly at writing processes and teaching applications related to writing processes. Also in Part II we discuss the form and function relationship (genres) in writing, the role of technology in writing (Chapter 11), and the nature and process of assessment (Chapter 12).

Part III examines the interactions between writing and the language arts. We describe the specific interactions—between writing and reading, writing and spelling, and writing and vocabulary development—and describe how those interactions lead to specific classroom instruction.

What You Will Find in the Chapters

Every chapter begins with a brief section entitled Before You Read, with questions to think about as you read. Good readers have purposes in mind before they read. They also have schema or background for what they will find in a text. These chapter beginnings are designed to give readers an idea of what they will find in the chapter, providing opportunities to set purposes for the reading and begin the chapter with background for what will follow.

You will notice that each chapter contains portions of text written in *italics*. These italicized phrases and sentences highlight particularly important ideas. Likewise, throughout the text there are terms in boldface print, which are then defined in the Glossary at the back of the book. Other pedagogical features are integral to the chapters. These features are there to make teaching and learning come alive. They include, where appropriate, references to language arts performance standards, Instructional Scenarios that take readers into classrooms to hear teachers' and students' voices during actual lessons, and samples of student writings. Also, throughout each chapter we have included sections called Review and Reflection. They contain statements and questions that relate to topics and concepts found in the preceding pages and provide an opportunity to pause, review, and reflect on what you just read. These sections are most often found at the end of major chapter sections.

Some common strands are threaded through all the chapters in Parts II and III. We do not have separate chapters for topics such as **second-language learners** and working with **diverse** populations of students, including students with **special needs.** Instead, we have woven those topics as appropriate throughout the chapters, and you'll find icons that signal those topics in the text. It seemed artificial to separate, for example, discussions about students learning **English as a second language** from discussions about curriculum and instruction.

Similarly, it was artificial to separate oral language development and listening, both critical language and communication skills, from the other language arts. All the language arts are rooted in language and communication; to treat them instructionally as discrete pieces is unnatural and counterproductive to language development. Because much of language learning and development, and communication, are auditory, we explicitly draw attention to the role of oral language and listening throughout the writing-language arts program. The focus is on the *interactions.*

Still another strand woven throughout several chapters focuses on implications for instruction across the content areas. Writing and the language arts, and thus language and communication, do not exist in isolation from the rest of the curriculum. As appropriate, therefore, we make connections between writing and the other curriculum areas.

Finally, the instructionally oriented chapters include short- and long-term lesson plans as models for instructional planning. The short-term plans may focus on one week's worth of lessons on a topic, and the long-term plans may suggest planning ideas for up to three to six weeks. These were designed as prototypes only, as ways of thinking about instructional planning around particular concepts and instructional objectives. And in Chapter 16, we show how **MaxiLessons** can be designed to plan for students' achievement in the whole of the language arts program.

As you read this book, we encourage you to keep in mind the overview described in this chapter, and we also encourage you to keep in mind your own purposes and expectations for reading a language arts text. This book needs you and your skills and expertise to bring the ideas and activities in it alive in classrooms in order to ensure that all students have a chance to be counted among the most literate individuals on the planet.

2 Foundations of the Interactive Language Arts

BEFORE YOU READ

- What is the role of teaching in learning?
- What does *interactive language arts* mean?
- What is creative writing?
- What cognitive processes are critical for learning?
- What does practice do?

The Nature of Interactive Language Arts

The language arts are complementary; that is, they are dynamically tied to each other by their common foundation and purpose. The foundation is language, and the shared purpose is communication. The descriptor in the first sentence of this paragraph punctuates the interactive relationship that occurs when we use language to communicate through the language arts. That is why in this book, **interaction** is the key term we use to describe the relationships between and among the language arts.

When we write, for example, we don't pull all of our language skills together for the purpose. Each part of writing is a situation-specific interaction with all other language arts.

Consider vocabulary as an example. How do we know words? What is it that makes a word part of the enormous bank from which we select one to do just the right work in a sentence? Is there a list of words somewhere in our memory—a mental list—to which we have access, sort of like a dictionary but not alphabetized?

Let's say we're writing a story, and there is a character whom we want to move across the room in a certain way that will display the character's personality. We might first write this: *The man walked slowly across the room, an air of arrogance about him.* Then it hits us. We delete a lot of what we wrote and add just the right word. Now it reads: *The man swaggered across the room.* We didn't find the new verb by scanning through an alphabetized list or, say, a list of verbs. Nor did we look up *arrogant* and search a list for synonyms.

No, *swagger* comes strutting into our story because it resides in a category, waiting to add the sneer that fits the image intended. And the words didn't become a category because they were studied in isolation or inserted in artificial sentences to satisfy a homework assignment. They fell into a category that fit an image. The category has lots of words in it for people who need it for talking or reading or writing. For people who don't need the category, there aren't many words.

For example, how many words do you have for that white stuff fluttering down late on a crisp winter afternoon when the sky seemed ice-blue just moments before? If you're from Ohio and Pennsylvania, as we are, you have one word: *snow.* For most of us, it snows hard or softly. The light snow is powder if you ski and leaden when it's wet. Sometimes it sticks, and sometimes it doesn't. Sometimes it snows so hard and for so long in places like Cedar Falls, Iowa, that cars fly flags from their radio antennas to signal other drivers at corners where the drifts are so high the drivers can't see cars coming the other way. To us, it's all snow.

But there are folks who live north of Churchill, inland from Canada's Hudson Bay, who have words for each kind of snow. There are people who live near Irkutsk in Siberia, along the banks of Lake Baikal, who study for an academic degree with a specialization in snow. These people become experts in the mechanics of building on frozen tundra and snow packed so hard over so many eons under so much pressure that when they understand how to use it, the snow will support buildings of steel and concrete. Those folks in Canada and Siberia have words for what the rest of us call snow because their lives are spent on snow. They can walk on an ice floe and read its stability two miles away from reflections off the clouds.

Let's go back to *swagger* as the verb that describes the man. There are only three reasons for knowing that word. First, we need to know the word if it pops up in a line of print we're reading. Although context will make it a verb so we can continue reading even if we don't know the word, the word's specific meaning gives us the textured image the writer intended when (s)he selected it. Second, we are writers, and we need just the right verb that will describe the character. And third, we're talking to someone about the man, and our oral need is the same as our writing need.

These are the three reasons for needing to know the word, and every one is an interaction between knowing words and other language arts: reading, writing, and talking, respectively.

So how do we know words? We know *cold* because we know all sorts of temperature words that are both like and unlike *cold.* We know synonyms and antonyms, not mere definitions, but relationships between and among the words so that *chilly* can be used when it's not cold, it's not cool, and the situation we're describing is not comfortable. The words are useful precisely because they're in a category. And the existence of the category and the words within it is a direct reflection of language need. The need creates the words and the categories, and the words and categories interact with each of the language arts they serve. *Interaction* is the image on which this book rests. Readers who would call *interaction* an idea would not be wrong, but we want readers to *see* the interactive image.

Seeing the Interaction

Because this book is about *interactions* between and among the language arts, the key focus is the interaction itself. When two entities are *interactive*, the focus is the *interaction*, not either of the entities. The focus on the interaction between writing and spelling, then, is on how writing and spelling mutually affect one another's development and practice. The instructional focus is on young writers writing well because writing and spelling represent a natural and progressively automatic way of recording and communicating in language.

Our focus is on the *interactive* relationships between writing and the other language arts. Our spelling example is precisely the point. In this book, writing is the foundation of language arts instruction, and spelling, as well as the other language arts, interacts in support of language development and communication.

We explore here a way of thinking about teaching the language arts. This book is not a collection of theories and ideas that cumulatively represent an activities-based language arts program. Rather, it is a focus on the natural interactions between and among the arts in the language arts, where the interactions, not the arts, result in progressively more effective language users.

For example, there is evidence that direct instruction in the conventions of punctuation does not result in better writers (Dahl & Farnan, 1998). Is that because there is no relationship between punctuation knowledge and writing well? That's unlikely. The effectiveness of writing is closely tied to the writer's use of meaning markers (capital letters and punctuation marks) on which readers depend for meaning construction. Might the evidence be the result of students not writing enough to discover how to punctuate and to practice what they discover? That's unlikely too. When young writers write, they practice and habituate what they're writing. If their writing is inaccurately punctuated, they're practicing writing that is inaccurately punctuated. The result is that they become increasingly automatic at writing inaccurately punctuated prose. The problem is not insufficient practice.

We would argue that the reason that teaching punctuation rules does not result directly in better writing is that punctuation instruction and writing are rarely *interactive*.

Use the apostrophe to show singular and plural possessive in the following sentences.

1. The birds nests had fallen from the trees branches.
2. Roberts shoelaces were broken, and he had to call Kevins mothers aunt for another pair.

An activity like the one above is commonly used in the context of writing instruction, but rarely does the instruction highlight for young writers that punctuation *is* part of writing, that writing works *because,* in part, it is punctuated properly. Therefore, effectiveness increases when we make *writing* the instructional context for punctuation.

> Thinking and writing as we punctuate properly.
>
> 1. Write a sentence in which the word *birds* is used as a plural possessive.
> 2. Write a sentence in which you use the names of at least one person as a singular possessive.

The interaction between punctuation and writing is similar to the legs on a table. Remove a leg, and the table doesn't work. Remove writing from punctuation instruction, and the punctuation doesn't get better.

What about reading? Everyone seems to agree that young writers write better because they read a lot, and reading a lot is directly associated with writing well. Maybe young writers who don't write well need to read more. Consider three questions:

1. Do we find that good readers are also good writers?
2. Do we find that good writers are also good readers?
3. Does the relationship between reading and writing occur because there are certain children who are likely to be both good readers and good writers?

The three questions are very different. The answer to questions 2 and 3 is clearly yes. The answer to question 1 is trickier. It seems that good writers tend to be good readers, but good readers aren't necessarily good writers.

What do the questions and answers have in common? The first tries to put reading and writing together, as though they are somehow apart and we want to see if, by viewing them as connected, the reading influences the writing.

The second question and answer fails because merely reversing the order doesn't change the inaccuracy of the premise that if we somehow relate reading and writing better in lessons, youngsters will learn them more effectively. To relate reading and writing that way isn't much different from trying to do some writing in gym class because the principal said all the students have to write in every period. The third explanation is not useful because it speaks to a dynamic that instruction cannot control.

Reading does not get suddenly connected to writing through good instruction. Reading and writing both demand enormous information about language and how language works, how to manage or control language, and how to use language to make meaning. Reading and writing are natural and critical *interactions* within the language arts. Spelling and vocabulary development are naturally and critically interactive with one another and with both writing and reading.

A reading-writing interaction. © 1994. Jeffrey Myers, Stock Boston. All rights reserved.

We've created an image of the interactive language arts with writing at the center, as the anchor in the language arts curriculum. If Figure 2.1 represented a naturally occurring compound in nature, we would say that the strength of the whole depends on the interactions among the elements. That's the point here too. It's the interactions, not the separate language arts. The interactions all reside in the language of ideas and images, which learners construct with words and sentences. That too represents a critical interaction that is illustrated in the figure. Given the image, it's reasonable to wonder what the interactions can look like in classrooms.

REVIEW AND REFLECTION

1. What distinguishes the concept of interaction from connections, or integration, among the language arts?
2. What do we mean when we say that the language arts are connected by a common foundation and purpose?
3. Give an example of what we mean by interactions in the language arts.

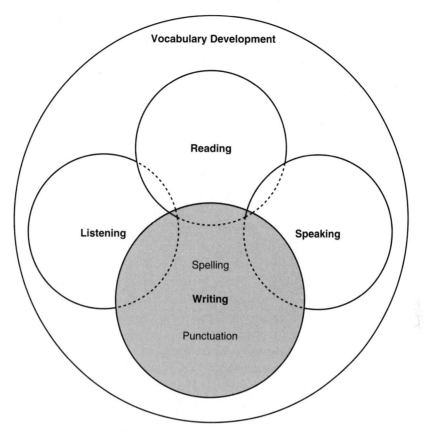

FIGURE 2.1   Model of Interactive Language Arts

Cognition and Learning in the Language Arts

To **cognize** is to discover immediately, to have awareness, to rediscover, to **recognize** information in various forms, to comprehend, to suddenly understand (Meeker, 1969, p. 7). To cognize is to "see" in the sense that someone exclaims, "Oh, I *see!*" Someone *sees* because he or she has either a preliminary or early sense of something or a more mature, more thorough sense after studying a while. In the first case, we say that we *recognize* someone when what we're really saying is that we have made a connection between what we remember and what we're seeing now. We had a sense of the person before (we connected the voice, the aroma, the image, a mannerism with a person), and now we sense a connection again. We *recognize* the person. We cognized before; now we cognize again.

In the second case, we have a more thorough sense of something after studying it. We may have understood the nature of sentences well enough to get through high school. Then in college we're confronted with the fact that the sentence isn't an arrangement of parts in the linear string we had learned earlier in our formal education. Now we *recognize* that our sentence represents a sense of its own, a feeling of wholeness that occurs when we write. It isn't the result of trying to make subjects rub against verbs. Instead, it's a sound, a linguistic feeling, a seemingly natural connection between and among kinds of words that make our sentence right—not because we were thinking about verbs and "complete thoughts," but because we were painting a word picture. Ahh, a *re cognition.*

Cognition and the *re cognition* are the individual's experiences. One person cannot cognize for another. No one's *re cognition* can be transferred to someone else. Cognition is what a person does for himself or herself. It is learner behavior. This business of cognition is fundamental to everything associated with learning. Learning doesn't occur in its absence.

Teaching is about making cognition and recognition happen. How is it that interactive language arts instruction causes cognition and recognition to happen?

Begin with a simple figure that contains much of what we know about schooling. Figure 2.2 shows that teachers are responsible for doing things that the public and its representatives define as teaching. It also shows that teachers are responsible for causing students to show the extent to which the teaching is reflected in their performance.

The language of school, clearly reflected in administrative observations of novice and seasoned teachers, and even reflected in the language of educational criticism and defense, is focused on what teachers do to cause students to perform on tests of various sorts. Virtually everything we do in schools is about what teachers do. That isn't necessarily bad, but where is the *learning* in the scenario?

The Relationship Between Teaching and Learning

Part of the interaction in the interactive language arts program is the relationship between what teachers do—teach and assess—and what students do—actively learn. In other words, teaching the language arts is necessary but not sufficient.

Teaching Behaviors	Indicators of Having Learned
Telling what to do (content)	Tests of achievement
Explaining how	Assessment of progress
Showing what and how	Recitations by students
Promoting appropriate behaviors	Collections of student work
Illustrating with examples	Performing by students
Providing resources and purpose	
Facilitating progress	
Prompting activity	
Guiding activity	

FIGURE 2.2   A Traditional Conception of Teaching and Learning

The very best teaching possible is necessary, but even that is insufficient. If teaching were both necessary and sufficient, it would be technologically possible, as well as far less expensive, to put the best language arts instruction on CD-ROMs from which every student could learn. But the CD-ROM that shows the very best teaching accomplishes only teaching, and even the very best teaching does not ensure learning.

Interactive language arts thinking, planning, and instruction rest on several basic principles about learning. We know that people tend to learn what they do, not necessarily what they are taught. We also know that people learn something from everything they do. Given that, there are three outcomes possible when teachers teach:

- Students learn what their teachers teach.
- Students learn variations on and sometimes inaccurate applications of what teachers teach.
- Students learn things contrary to what teachers planned to teach.

Take those basic principles and outcomes into the classroom and see what they can mean. That students learn what they do, not necessarily what they are taught, is apparent in the first grade when the teacher teaches an onset rime (*l-ake*), and a student doesn't "get" it, in the sense of being able to generalize to (*r-ake*). The teacher taught a critical lesson about phonemic awareness that is supposed to generalize to an understanding of how the print system works, but the student learned that she didn't learn reading that day. That she learns something from every lesson is clear because she learned something that day. It just wasn't what the teacher taught. It was what the student did.

Now for the outcomes. If that first grader had learned the **onset-rime** pattern the teacher taught that day, she would be closer to understanding part of how reading works. If she learned that the (*ake*) pattern *always* reads (*lake*), she would have learned an inaccurate application of what the teacher thought he taught. In the third instance, while the teacher intended to teach a print principle, what the student may have learned is that reading isn't within her six-year-old capacity.

Take that example into a classroom where the teacher's objective is for students to learn to think in and write sentences. The teacher directs everyone to write a sentence. Everyone writes something because every first grader wants to please the teacher. The teacher asks several students to read their sentence aloud, praises the work of most, and reminds those who wrote nonsentences that their sentences must be "complete."

With a partner, make a list of possibilities in response to each of the following three questions. The focus now is on the students, not the teacher. In case you're curious, the scenario happens precisely the way it was described, even in the first grade.

1. If the students learned what the teacher taught, what did the students learn?

2. What variations on what the teacher taught could the students have learned?

3. What could the students have learned that is contrary to what the teacher intended to teach?

Did you say that given what the teacher taught, students might have learned something about complete sentences? If so, how would they have learned that? Did you say that students might have learned that writing is fun, that writing occurs in sentences, and that the students are good at sentence writing? How would they have learned those things? Finally, did you say that students might have learned that they don't understand the idea of *complete* in sentences? How might they have learned that? The real questions here are:

- What were the students paying **attention** to?
- What meanings are students likely to make?
- What are students likely to remember?
- What big pictures (concepts) are they likely to construct?
- What influence is this lesson likely to have on students' ability to write a story or autobiographical incident?

We might all agree that what the teacher did in that scenario isn't teaching, good or otherwise. But what the teacher did is what teachers do. The point is that there are various possible outcomes, most of which aren't associated with what the teacher had in mind, which, we presume, had something to do with learning to write good sentences.

Interactive language arts instruction seeks not only to teach the language arts properly, but to ensure that students *learn* the interactive language arts. That means the instruction has to be conducted so that the teaching ensures that most, if not all, students learn what the teacher teaches. That is the reason for this entire conversation about cognition in the context of interactive language arts instruction.

Return now to Figure 2.2, which shows "teaching" on one side of discussions about school and "having learned" at the other. If instruction is to ensure learning, there has to be something called *learning* in the equation. The learning occurs between "teaching" and "having learned." If learning is ensured, it must occur *because* of what the teaching does. Between the "teaching" and the "having learned," for purposes of this discussion, are the cognitive processes. We ensure learning by making certain our instruction promotes cognition.

Paying Attention

What does it mean to ensure that instruction promotes cognition? Think back to a second grade where the teacher placed the following addition "problem" on the board: $3 + 5 = (\ )$. One group of seven year olds remembers that 8 is the number that finishes the "number sentence," so they raise their hands. Another group knows they could get to the right number by counting on their fingers, which they start to do immediately. A third group of second graders raise their hands with their best guess. The teacher knows which children know, which ones would know if given enough time, and which ones are guessing. She reinforces addition fact memory by calling on children in the first group. She praises the hard work of the second group, and she works with the third group by explaining again the addition fact on the board, urging that third group of children to notice how the numbers relate to one another. The teacher understands the relationship; some children do not.

What is the problem here? The teacher did yesterday exactly what she is doing today, and she'll do it again tomorrow until everyone gets it—that is, realizes there is a relationship between numbers and signs.

The problem in the example is not that some second graders aren't as good at arithmetic as others are. It is that the group that doesn't know doesn't get much more knowledgeable very rapidly or efficiently. That they do "get it" eventually is but marginal fortune, given that the teacher has to move ahead into subtraction and multiplication, to say nothing of second-grade probability and statistics, measurement, algebra, logic, and problem solving before the year is done. It's common to hear educators say that the point of arithmetic instruction, or any other instruction, is the child, not the book, so the pace is unimportant. But what happens to the children is what one of our mothers used to say from her Pennsylvania Dutch heritage: "The hurrier I go, the behinder I get." If those second graders don't "get it" on a reasonable pace, they're behind, and they get behinder every year.

What to do? The children need to *pay attention* to how numbers and signs work in addition. Simply remembering the addition facts isn't paying attention to relationships between and among numbers and signs. Counting on their fingers is closer to coming to understand those relationships eventually, but that is painfully slow and inefficient. And guessing, as an alternative to knowing, is merely avoiding arithmetic thinking.

Here's a basic fact about learning: *People learn what they attend to.* And by *attention* we mean concentration. Attention is also selective—by the learner. Learners decide to pay attention for one or more of the following reasons:

- They know that if they concentrate, their uncertainty will be reduced.
- They know that if they concentrate, they will be able to do something they think is important.
- They know from their own experience that concentration is itself rewarding.

Teachers have very little to do with making children pay attention, but they have everything to do with the three reasons that learners attend. *When teachers emphasize what learners do, they focus on learners' understanding.* **Direct instruction** teachers, teachers who leave nothing to chance, capitalize on the intrinsic value of attention.

The teacher who uses the cognitive process known as attention in the addition lesson in the second grade gets away from number facts as quickly as possible. After two or three addition fact lessons, plus work with Unifix Cubes, pop beads, or tiddlywinks, the teacher poses the sort of problem that causes young arithmetic learners to concentrate on relationships between and among numbers and signs. The teacher writes on the board: $\square + \square = 8$, then asks, "How many ways can you fill in the boxes?"

Go ahead, admit it. You read that line and immediately thought of two possibilities. Right? More than two? There's a certain intrigue associated with it. It is compelling.

Now allow yourself ten seconds of concentration on the teacher's direction. How many ways can you fill in the boxes? We'll be quiet while you concentrate.

So what were you concentrating on during those ten seconds? No, not arithmetic.

If you got past the first five or six possibilities, you started actively and deliberately to concentrate on making additive relationships. You are probably a whole lot better at it than second graders, but think about this. How long do you think it will take before second graders who deliberately concentrate on additive relationships between and among numbers for a few minutes every day figure out that there's a system here and they can understand it? More quickly then they do when they guess? More quickly than they do when they memorize every possible addition fact? More quickly than they do when they laboriously count every addend?

The teacher knows the importance of ensuring that second graders pay attention and concentrate on the right content. The right content is *not* addition facts. It is how numbers act in the presence of an addition sign.

Every teaching activity in an interactive language arts program ensures that students pay attention to the right content. Later chapters elaborate on the nature of the right content, but to make the point here, consider the right content for paragraph learning. It is *main idea*. If students understand main idea, they understand paragraphing, for both writing purposes and organizational purposes. Although a lot of other attributes are often instructionally associated with paragraphs—some architectural, some having to do with the number and nature of sentences—the only attribute of paragraph that *defines* paragraph is main idea. To come to know the concept of paragraph, young writers must pay attention to, concentrate on, main idea.

Perception

Perception means "making meaning." It occurs when learners make their own meanings based on new stimuli (e.g., a vocabulary word) and prior knowledge. *Perception is construction of meanings by learners.* It is something that learners do. Teachers cannot teach perception. Meanings belong to the learner because the learner constructs them.

Does that mean that all meanings are equally good because learners construct them? Certainly not! Teachers provide the vocabulary word for young writers' consideration, and teachers cause young writers to pay attention to the right information so that meaning making is possible. And when young writers make their own meanings, teachers listen to those meanings and guide the quality of the constructions.

Here's a scenario. The new word for the fourth graders to learn is *rapid*. The teacher directs the children to find *rapid* in their desk dictionary, write the definition, and write a sentence that contains the word *rapid*. Now the question is, Did everyone learn the word *rapid* from this exercise?

It's a good bet that the children know how to use a dictionary, and they know the dictionary definition of the word. But they used the word in their own sentence, you may say, and that shows they know the word on their terms. Our reply is for you to think how many words you studied that way that you began using in your everyday oral and written language. Make a list of words you use regularly that you learned from the vocabulary pages of *Readers Digest* or from your preparation manual for the SAT. Short list?

What the young learners do in the example, widely referred to as vocabulary instruction, has little at all to do with knowing words or, for that matter, vocabulary *instruction*. It has to do with fourth graders finding words and using meanings that are not their own.

Another teacher writes the word *rapid* on the board and places a small numeral 1 above it. Then the teacher asks for some more words that would fit in column 1 with *rapid*. The teacher next writes a small 3 on the board maybe two feet to the right of *rapid* and asks if there is a word that is the opposite of *rapid* that can be written in that column. Someone usually knows one: *slow*. The task now is to come up with words for both columns.

1	3
rapid	
quick	
fast	

What are they doing? They're certainly paying attention to the key word (*rapid*), and they're paying attention to *rapid* in context with words that fit into *rapid*'s meaning world. They, not the teacher, are "rubbing words against each other" to achieve meaning context, and it's the meaning context that allows people to "own" words for subsequent use. There isn't just one meaning; there are lots of meanings that relate to one another. Clever teachers conduct such a word continuum twice each week and put them on the **Word Wall** (Cunningham, 1991).

Memory

Every child in every classroom is learning something all the time. If it stopped there, everyone would have to learn it all again every time it was experienced. At the least, that would be inefficient. If this were characteristic of all learning, everyone's entire learning capacity would be consumed with accommodating every experience as if it were a new one. No one would ever get anywhere.

But it doesn't work that way. Just about everything we learn gets recorded somewhere in our mental apparatus in a form that some people call instances of **memory,** or "engrams" (Lashley, 1974). Because sensory images and instances of learning are at least routinely, and maybe even always, stored in memory and most learning is based on mental constructions that include new stimulation and **prior knowledge,** one key to deliberate learning is access to and use of prior knowledge—that is, what we already know. Most five year olds, for example, know something about writing; they have writing prior knowledge. Much of direct writing instruction in the kindergarten will be based on this prior knowledge. What they learn each day in the kindergarten becomes part of their accumulation of knowledge about writing, so every day they become cumulatively more writing literate. But this all depends on what they remember about writing each day.

Direct writing instruction must ensure memory. We plan each day's teaching on the assumption that everyone remembers what they learned yesterday.

We teachers have a surprising amount of influence on what young learners remember and the extent to which they can access and use what they remember. Memory is not a matter of chance, nor is it a talent at which some are very good while others are not. We influence students' memory of what we teach because we understand several principles about memory:

- People remember what they pay attention to. If the material is compelling, young learners pay attention. Concentration promotes memory. For example, if young writers concentrate on arrangements of letters in words, they are more likely to remember how words are spelled.

- People's active memory capacity for unpracticed stimuli is between five and seven items (Miller, 1956). Young writers just learning to handle sentences, for example, are faced with spelling, capitalization, punctuation, main idea (purpose for the sentence), legibility, the teacher's definition of sentence, and whatever else is on the child's mind. That is too much unpracticed stimuli to handle at once. The young writer will almost certainly forget most of it. That is why so much of the early sentence writing occurs in this book as formal oral language. Young writers can commit their memory capacity to main idea, and when that is clear and practiced, they can put it on paper while remembering other matters.

- People remember material better when it is chunked into familiar and manageable categories. For spelling, a familiar category is chunks of letters (*le tt ers*), though not necessarily syllables.

- Remembering is but part of the process. Access to memory is also critical. Storing learned information is important, but it is irrelevant if stored information cannot be accessed. In early writing, access can be promoted as young writers use oral language to rehearse and review the sounds and constructive properties of sentences. (This will become clearer in Chapter 4.)

- The ability to access the memory store is increased when learners' storage is in a form with which they are familiar (their own constructed meanings). The link between unfamiliar stimuli and automaticity is thoughtful practice. The more that young learners work thoughtfully with what they are to remember, the higher the probability is that access to memory will be automatic. For example, young learners who work with relationships between numbers and signs, rather than merely memorize number facts, and do that regularly as oral and written practice will come to remember number facts automatically.

Conceptualization

Conceptualization is not about teaching concepts; it is about building, or constructing, concepts. Teachers do not teach concepts; learners build concepts on the basis of information they learn through their own work and their teacher's work.

Transfer

The concepts young learners construct are useful to the extent that they are able to generalize them to understanding new situations. Those second grade arithmetic learners, for example, are in a position to use what they learned about solving addition equations with unknowns when early algebraic thinking comes into the curriculum later in the year.

Automaticity

With sufficient practice, learning becomes automatic. **Automaticity** is critical in all highly complex behaviors and operations because there are so many parts that have to work together. For example, young writers cannot both write well and find writing reinforcing until they can focus their attention on the purpose for their writing, and that occurs fully only when mechanical details occur correctly because they are automatic.

Consider a complex behavior with which we're all familiar. At the age of sixteen, or a little before, most of us learned to drive. In a parking lot, we learned to hold the steering wheel, push the gearshift to the right position, lift our left foot as we pressed our right foot, look at three mirrors, and focus straight ahead, all unpracticed behaviors and all at the same time. Each of the little behaviors or skills was relatively simple to learn, but that wasn't driving. Driving required doing them all at once.

We "did" the behaviors. We practiced them, and in due time, each of the behaviors became increasingly practiced, or automatic, so we could do more and more of them simultaneously while keeping our focus on driving. Eventually we became sufficiently practiced (automatic) with all of the individual driving skills that we could drive, while solving unpracticed problems and even responding to emergencies.

That is what we have to accomplish in the interactive language arts. Young writers, for example, must achieve sufficient automaticity that they can deliberately focus on the point of the message they are constructing while their sentence writing, paragraph organizing, punctuating, spelling, and word finding skills occur virtually automatically.

Summary of Cognitive Processes

Good teaching causes young learners to pay attention, promotes learner meaning making, and helps young learners construct and use concepts. Good teaching causes both storage in memory and access to memory. And it promotes the kind of practice that leads to automatic application of new learnings. *Teachers teach and monitor; learners learn. We ensure learning by planning teaching around specific learning processes.*

REVIEW AND REFLECTION

1. What are the roles of cognition and recognition in learning?
2. Explain the following phrase: Teaching and learning are not the same thing.
3. Give an example that illustrates student learning, but not of what the teacher believed he was teaching.
4. What elements of cognition are necessary to ensure learning?
5. Give an example of a lesson that ensures learning by focusing on cognition.

Using Creative Thinking Skills in Teaching and Learning

We all believe that creativity is the magic elixir, the basic ingredient without which education is merely ordinary. But what is this business we call creativity? Creativity is skills. Creativity depends on knowledge. Creativity is what happens when people put their preparation together with their courage and some idea about what they're trying to accomplish. Creativity is a way of looking at the world.

The classic and still widely accepted definitions of creativity center on the organization and reorganization of knowns (Hyman, 1964; Torrance, 1965). There are also classic definitions that imply that the result of creative effort must be productive (Parnes, 1972). No one speaks of creativity as waiting around for something to happen, nor do they talk about creativity in terms of either having it or not having it. Findlay and Lumsden (1988) define creativity as a process of formulating problems or advancing novel and appropriate solutions. In his conception of creativity, Csikszentmihalyi (1996) defined creativity as "a process by which a symbolic domain in the culture is changed. New songs, new ideas, new machines are what creativity is about" (p. 8).

Whether the conception of creativity comes from researchers in the field, creative luminaries, or people who study creative people, creativity is conceptualized in one or more of the following ways:

- Because creativity is often hard work, it demands *effort.*
- Because creativity is purposeful, it results from *preparation.*
- Because creativity does not occur in an intellectual vacuum, it requires *knowledge.*
- Because creativity means difference, it requires *courage.*

An enormous amount of research has isolated these characteristics of creativity. Barron's work (1976) is illustrative. His research strategy was to assemble highly productive, creative individuals (from such diverse practitioners as architects, musicians, physicists, visual artists, and chemists) for retreats over several days, survey how they did their work, and then conclude from those results what creative people do when they behave creatively. From those sources, he found patterns of effort, preparation, knowledge, and courage.

He found specific skills and inclinations as well, and these kinds of skills and inclinations have been described by many others in the field of creativity research (Guilford, 1962; Torrance, 1979; Williams, 1972):

- Creative people think of multiple possibilities. Researchers have called this **fluency.**
- Creative people view problems or questions from more than one perspective. Researchers have called this **flexibility.**
- Creative people embellish on problems and questions. Researchers have called this **elaboration.**
- Creative people wonder about and ponder the world around them. Researchers have called this **curiosity.**
- Creative people often find that they have developed something they hadn't thought of or seen before. Researchers have called this **originality.**

These skills and inclinations, along with effort, preparation, knowledge, and courage, seem to capture the essential nature of creativity and creative behavior. Fearn (1976) arranged those into a scheme in three dimensions of creativity:

1. Collecting data or information (Knowledge, Fluency, Flexibility)
2. Managing data or information (Perseverance, Elaboration, Ordering Chaos)
3. Being unique (Courage, Originality, Curiosity, Imagination)

How do these skills, inclinations, and demands play out in an interactive language arts program? Remember that learning is what occurs because of teaching but before testing. Thus, creativity represents a way to learn.

It is the third grade, about midyear. Ms. Cornell is teaching paragraphs and directs her third graders to read and speculate on the main idea of the paragraph design on the board.

> Dan searched and searched. He looked down . . . Then he went . . .
>   Suddenly he saw . . . He ran . . . Dan was pleased . . .

As the third graders read the first sentence and five subsequent sentence stems on the board, they are speculating, or wondering (*curiosity*), and their wondering is focused on the essential attribute of every paragraph—the main idea. How many times do you think third graders might have to focus on main idea in paragraphs before they begin to understand what main idea is and what it means in paragraphs?

As the children respond to Ms. Cornell's direction, they offer more than one possibility (*fluency*). As young learners hear more than one idea, they can become increasingly inclined to try more than one possibility on their own. They also become increasingly inclined to appreciate more than one possibility.

What do you think is the main idea of the prospective paragraph in the activity above? Is it a young boy looking for a lost pet, or something along those lines? If everyone in the room volunteered that idea, or variations on the theme, the multiple ideas would constitute *fluent* thinking. But what if one youngster suggested that the character is an adult, like her dad who is working on his master's degree at State U., and he's searching in the library for a certain book? That would be a different perspective, a *flexible* idea, dependent on that student's accumulated general knowledge. In that room, lots of children participated in *fluent* thinking, and one, because she saw a different view, thought *flexibly*. Lots of children were *curious* because every suggestion resulted from wondering about what the main idea might be. In that one writing activity, in response to one direction from the teacher, a variety of third graders participated in one or more of three different kinds of creative behaviors. Some observers might call Ms. Cornell's activity by the term **creative writing.**

Creativity and Writing

In this book we define the creativity in "creative writing" as *what writers do when they write.* The behaviors or operations defined as creative thinking skills that we see so far in Ms. Cornell's third grade are fluency, originality, and flexibility. That is why Ms. Cornell's paragraph instruction can be called *creative* writing.

Very early in the year, Ms. Cornell wanted to ensure that her students understood some basic notions about sentence thinking and writing. So what she did early in the year was ask her third graders to think of a sentence that contained the idea of an old man. She emphasized that they were to use the *idea* of old man rather than specifically that term. She said that they were certainly allowed to use the words *old man,* but they could just as well use the idea without the words. (See Chapter 4 for a more complete explanation of sentence instruction.)

The students understood quickly enough because the first sentence volunteered was, *My grandfather puts on a tie every day.* There was laughter around the room when Roger used *codger.* Someone said, "Roger the codger," and everyone else started to laugh. Ms. Cornell allowed some of the mirth, but she cut it off when it got silly.

Notice the creativity in Ms. Cornell's sentence thinking and writing activity. She provided an idea and directed the students to write a sentence that contains the idea. Her direction ensured that every third grader who participated in the activity would think *elaboratively. Elaboration* is a creative thinking skill that means to add onto, to embellish, to extend. Writing is fundamentally elaborative, for most writing begins with a small idea that develops over time.

Then Ms. Cornell directed the third graders to think of a sentence that contains not only the idea of an old man but something about the weather too. "Think of one sentence that contains both ideas," she said. Again the children read many sentences they had written in their minds. Again the young writers elaborated on the teacher's direction. However, this time the children had two ideas they had to arrange in a sentence. The instructive idea here is *arrange.* Creative people arrange and **organize;** they find order. The sentence that Ms. Cornell's third graders wrote in response to her direction reflects organizational thinking. Ms. Cornell's third graders wrote creatively again because her direction caused creative thinking applied to writing.

Are you beginning to suspect that just about everything young writers do can be defined within the range of the various creative thinking skills? So far you're right. So far, we have posed two writing tasks—one at the sentence level and the other with paragraphs—and both have caused the third graders to think creatively.

Now, still in the same writing lesson that emphasizes thinking and writing at the single-sentence level, Ms. Cornell adds to the complexity: "Think of a sentence that contains the ideas of old man and weather, and this time I want the idea of vehicle in your sentence too." She offered several examples to make sure the children knew what *vehicle* means; after mentioning airplane, car, skateboard, and motorcycle, they understood well enough to do the thinking.

This exercise was harder for the third graders than the other activities, but about half of the children raised their hand immediately and read sentences they had written in their minds. Most of the sentences sounded something like this: *My grandpa drove his car to the store in the rain.* As several children read their sentences, others in the room figured out what the task demanded, and they raised their hand too. The creativity demands of this task were *elaboration* and *ordering chaos.*

That afternoon Ms. Cornell brought her third graders back to the writing area for a follow-up on the morning session. She wrote the three morning cues on the board (*old man, vehicle,* and *weather*) and put a number beside each idea:

old man—3

vehicle—2

weather—1

"Think of a sentence that contains the three ideas in this order," she said. "Make weather the first of the three ideas to appear in your sentence. Make vehicle the second of the three ideas to appear in your sentence, and make old man the last of the three ideas. Remember, one sentence, three ideas, in the order on the board." This sentence thinking and writing task is highly demanding.

One student read the sentence she wrote in her mind: *The rain was very hard when the car crashed with the old man driving.* Ms. Cornell remarked that that is a sentence, and the ideas are in the right order for the activity. Then she went on.

Does that feedback trouble you? What the student wrote isn't a very elegant English sentence, but notice the task: to think and write a sentence by arranging three ideas. The student followed the direction: she arranged the ideas and elaborated on the arrangement to make a sentence. The direction did not call for elegance. Ms. Cornell said it is a sentence. It is.

Another student offered her sentence: *The foggy night made it hard for the car's lights to shine far enough ahead for my grandpa to see.* Ms. Cornell acknowledged that sentence and several more that fit the direction. She said that everyone had done a good job with this very hard sentence thinking and writing task, and they would return to it again the next day. Within the next few days, Ms. Cornell will show the third graders how the sentence thinking and writing activity is related to the kinds of problems they run into every day with their authentic writing (see Chapter 4).

Ms. Cornell caused an important creative thinking skill to occur that afternoon. Third graders, when faced with the three ideas (old man, weather, vehicle), invariably put the old man in the subject position, that is, first, in their sentences. Most people do that when one of the ideational options is a character. Later Ms. Cornell took the old-man-as-subject-in-the-first-position away and forced the young writers to think of an alternative. The children had only two options: (1) keep the old man as the subject, but at the *end* of the sentence, or (2) make something other than the old man the subject of the sentence. In both cases, they have to look at something in a new way. When the children were not allowed to use the character as the subject at the beginning of the sentence, they had to rethink the arrangement and use the ideas in ways that did not seem automatic to them. They had to think about the old man in a different way. That's *flexible* thinking. That's creative writing.

In the three scenarios, Ms. Cornell caused her third graders to use *fluency, flexibility, elaboration, organization,* and *curiosity* in three writing lessons on two areas of craft instruction.

Everything in these scenarios has focused on one of the three dimensions of **balanced writing instruction: craft.** Each craft lesson promoted one or more creative thinking skills. The creative thinking is the learners' action, what they do. What is important is that the children are active learners, and the activity here is creativity applied to writing.

It's also important to note that the creativity of the children occurred not by chance or hope but because of Ms. Cornell's instruction. She knew that if she posed the directions in certain ways, she would promote certain kinds of creative behaviors. There is a direct relationship between what the teacher cues or directs and what learners do.

There is also a direct relationship between what learners do and their performance on assessments. Assessments often include sentence-writing performance as one criterion among several associated with writing. Ms. Cornell's third graders have performed sentence thinking and writing for months. They have worked with sentencing directly and systematically in the context of writing in various genres and in isolated craft lessons, and the children have always attended deliberately because of the creative thinking caused by the instructional processes. The teacher's instructional processes have promoted a variety of thinking and writing actions at the sentence level, and the inevitable result will be reflected in the students' writing performance.

In this situation, there is a direct relationship between what teachers do and what learners do, and what learners do is reflected in the assessment of their performance. This is a curricular model that emphasizes learning as the most critical component.

REVIEW AND REFLECTION

1. What is "creative" writing, and how do we know if young writers are writing creatively?
2. What is "noncreative" writing, and how do we know if young writers are writing noncreatively?
3. Why do you think there is no mention in the creativity literature of time pressure compromising creativity?

Creative Thinking Skills and Cognitive Processes

The critical elements of cognition do not happen merely because we want them to happen, and they aren't merely the result of something called **motivation.** Young learners decide to pay attention because the stimulation or the lesson compels them. Creative thinking is compelling. Learners find that when they commit themselves to elaborating on an idea, they can produce something that is different from what everyone else produces, and their sentence works, and it is theirs.

They also find, because of the oral emphasis, that there are lots of ways to solve the problem of constructing ideas in sentences. As they manipulate ideas, make new sentences, and hear others, they increasingly make or construct for themselves the larger meaning of sentence.

E S L It is vitally important that children who are learning English as a second language come to know the sound of an English sentence and have opportunities to try out the patterns and the sounds. In a first-grade classroom, Jésus listens to his peers "read" their oral sentences about rain. Gabriele says, *I see the rain on the* *street.* Marcus reads the sentence from his mind: *Rain is good for plants.* Belinda raises her hand and says, *I like to play in the rain.* After hearing several sentences, Jésus raises his hand. He "reads," *I like the rain.* Jésus is constructing his own sentence not because he knows that he has used a pronoun subject, verb, and direct object, but because he is learning the sound of the sentence in a new language. ■

It is critical that all language learners (and that means all children) learn to construct their ideas in the syntax of a standard English sentence. The oral component of this construction is critical because the oral component is the sound of the sentence. They do not plan what they say and write based on the understood need for subjects, verbs, and objects in their sentences. Rather, they plan around what for them are automatic understandings of how the language looks and sounds. *Their main avenue to developing a sense of sentence is writing, whether mental or physical, managing ideas, and hearing alternative ideas.*

The Role of Direct or Intentional Instruction

Let's say for purposes of overgeneralized discussion that there are two kinds of teachers in your school: those who make things happen and those who wait for things to happen. People whose teaching style appears very direct and systematic teach actively and directly, and people who tend to wait for things to happen in the classroom often expect students to discover what they need to learn. So what we're talking about here is more a continuum from one kind of teaching to another. Nevertheless, we're going to use the two categories for our discussion because they help us clarify a point here.

In the following items, rate yourself on each item with a number between 1 and 5, where 1 means you think you are more like the direct instruction teacher and 5 means you are more like the indirect instruction teacher. Use 2 and 4 to show that you lean in one or the other direction. Do not use 3.

_____ Direct instruction teachers tend to call themselves teachers. Indirect instruction teachers tend to call themselves facilitators of learning.

_____ Direct instruction teachers tend to decide what they will teach. Indirect instruction teachers tend to allow students' apparent need to dictate what they will teach.

_____ Direct instruction teachers tend to have a sense of the content in a course of study and the sequence in which they will teach that content. Indirect instruction teachers tend to plan curriculum on the basis of what comes up each day.

_____ Direct instruction teachers tend to expect that everyone will participate in every lesson. Indirect instruction teachers tend to expect that all learners

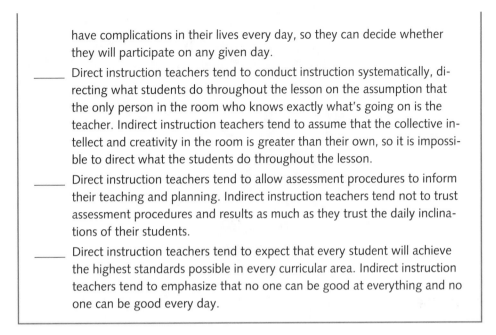

have complications in their lives every day, so they can decide whether they will participate on any given day.

_____ Direct instruction teachers tend to conduct instruction systematically, directing what students do throughout the lesson on the assumption that the only person in the room who knows exactly what's going on is the teacher. Indirect instruction teachers tend to assume that the collective intellect and creativity in the room is greater than their own, so it is impossible to direct what the students do throughout the lesson.

_____ Direct instruction teachers tend to allow assessment procedures to inform their teaching and planning. Indirect instruction teachers tend not to trust assessment procedures and results as much as they trust the daily inclinations of their students.

_____ Direct instruction teachers tend to expect that every student will achieve the highest standards possible in every curricular area. Indirect instruction teachers tend to emphasize that no one can be good at everything and no one can be good every day.

How did you rate yourself? If your total is near 30, you perceive yourself in the indirect instruction range. If your total is near 15, you perceive yourself more like a direct instruction teacher. A direct instruction teacher tends to lean toward lower numbers on the items, but much of what direct instruction means can point toward low numbers during one portion of the day and high numbers during another. Furthermore, being a direct instruction teacher can mean low numbers during one portion of a lesson and high numbers during another portion of the same lesson. That's why the idea of a continuum is more accurate than thinking of two separate categories that describe most teachers in one way or the other. Also, it is important to understand that this isn't like a magazine survey from which you begin to wonder if you are okay. There is no implication here that either direct or indirect instruction is a preferable style.

The purpose of this discussion is to specify some differences between direct and indirect instruction in writing and to clarify the circumstances under which a more direct instructional style can be productive, and perhaps even necessary.

A *Reading Today* article ("Read*write*now!," 1998) provides an example of how a direct instruction teacher thinks. The article was about summer reading programs that took place in fifty states in which children read and wrote in a journal for thirty minutes every day. Direct instruction teachers would never suggest that reading and writing for thirty minutes every summer day is not useful, but they might ask some questions:

- What do the children write in their journal?
- Is there an audience for their journal writing?

A teacher teaches reading. © Elizabeth Crews

- Do the children get any writing instruction that is informed by the way they write in their journals?
- Do their journals get better through the year?
- Does their writing get better as the year rolls along?
- Is there a goal in the writing program—a goal that is reflected in literacy expectations for the end of the year?
- Does the teacher measure the writing performance of every young writer on regular occasions during the year?
- Do the students' writing performances inform the teacher's subsequent instruction?

There are other questions we could ask. Do second-grade teachers know how a second grader should write in November, March, and June? Does a third-grade teacher know how a third grader should write in November, March, and June, and are the third-grade expectations calibrated to show that third graders write measurably better than second graders?

Teaching Purposefully

Direct instruction doesn't leave what young writers (and young historians, scientists, mathematicians, and artists) learn to chance. Direct instruction teachers tend to let young learners in on how historians and mathematicians think, how scientists explore the world, and how experienced writers think as they write.

It is not uncommon to hear the following statement: "If students write enough, mechanical correctness will eventually take care of itself." Direct instruction teachers, on the other hand, let young writers in on the systems for how writing works, the various formats, procedural knowledge, and conventions. Let's explore this concept a bit using the example of teaching a comma.

It is not uncommon for third-grade teachers to teach the various uses of the comma. It is also not uncommon for the comma to be an instructional focus in the fourth, fifth, and sixth grades as well. It is not uncommon for middle school teachers and high school teachers to be teaching the comma, still. And yet, a distressing number of the best high school graduates still use the comma clumsily when they are upper-division university students and even graduate students.

Now there are only about five or six high-frequency uses for the comma in most writing, and all of them are seen in sentences that young writers are able to write before they are finished with the fourth or fifth grade. The reason for this lack of understanding of how to use the comma can be gleaned from university students' self-reports. Many report that they had never been told exactly how to use the comma and that they had been told to get their ideas out on paper and take care of the punctuation later. Many also report that their teachers have always given them two grades—one for content and one for mechanics—and the content grade was invariably the one that ended up on the report card.

From the students' self-reports, we can draw three conclusions: (1) they weren't given clear directions about how to use commas, (2) their teachers believed they would gradually learn on their own, and (3) the students weren't paying attention, which may be true for some students. We can draw one inescapable conclusion: *mechanical correctness does not result from merely writing a lot.*

This is where direct instruction enters the conversation. Throughout the language arts, to say nothing of the larger curriculum, an indirect approach toward teaching can result in some serious misconceptions by children and adolescent learners. In the larger curriculum, it is dangerously late in the educational process when students come to understand the nature of history. They tend to have learned the chronologies found in history books, but many have little or no sense of the voices of history, the problem of lack of availability of primary sources, and an essential sense of what historians do. It's the same in science. High school science students, and even university science students, confuse the method of science with the laboratory reporting format, assuming the latter is the former. The assumption is that if history and science students read enough history and participate in enough laboratory demonstrations, they will eventually figure out what history and science are.

Direct instruction teachers let young writers in on the systems for how writing works, the various formats, procedural knowledge, and conventions.

To illustrate a direct instruction application in the fifth grade, a direct instruction teacher introduces the autobiographical incident. This is the first one of the year. It occurs on the second day of the second week of the fifth grade.

"I want you to make a list," Mr. Marsh tells the class. "I want you to remember a time when something good happened in your life. It can be a special meal with your family, a time when you did something you're proud of, or something you did that made someone else feel good. Think now.

"You don't have to think of the best thing that has ever happened in your life. We will do several of these lists and writings every month during the year, so pick out something now that you can write about today." He then provides the following directions:

1. In a word or short phrase, write the name of the event or happening.
2. Write a word or phrase that tells where the event happened.
3. Write the names of some of the people who were there.
4. Write a sentence about what happened just before your event.
5. Write a sentence about what happened right after your event.
6. Make a list of other people who could have had an experience similar to yours.
7. Write a word or phrase that tells how the experience made you feel.

Mr. Marsh directs everyone in the room to rank-order what they wrote: "Put the number 1 beside the item you think is the most important if you were going to tell someone about what happened. Put the number 2 beside the item that you think is the next most important. Put the number 3 beside the next most important, and so forth until you have every item on your list numbered." He gives them a couple of minutes to think about their items.

Mr. Marsh now prompts the writing: "I want you to use your list to write as much as you can, as well as you can, about the event or happening. You may use the items on your list in any order you choose. You may also ignore items on your list, and you may use information you don't have on your list. But I want you to write as much as you can and as well as you can for ten minutes."

Mr. Marsh's agenda for the year is to include autobiographical incidents among the variety of genres that his fifth graders will write. (See Chapters 9 and 10 for more on autobiographical incidents.) His plan is for every fifth grader to write two autobiographical incidents each week during the school year because he wants his students to finish the fifth grade with an autobiography of at least sixty pages that reflects at least sixty incidents.

Notice that Mr. Marsh didn't assume that if the fifth graders write often enough about their lives, they would eventually come up with something autobiographical. Instead, he taught them how to think in, organize, and draft autobiographical incidents. He taught *intentionally;* he didn't leave students to figure out the genre by chance.

Indirect instruction teachers do not necessarily leave the autobiographical incident to chance. However, direct instruction teachers tend to approach the genres and all learning in a systematic fashion, from which young writers can personalize according to their needs and experiences. Indirect instruction teachers, on the other hand, are more inclined to prompt the fifth graders to write about something they remember, and the teachers assume that authenticity will carry the day.

If we were talking about drawing, we would know the indirect instruction teacher because she would tend to promote lots of drawing every day. A direct instruction drawing teacher would teach young artists to manage light and shadow and then promote the practice in drawing to make the skills automatic. As young artists become automatic with the skills and techniques, they concentrate on their message and medium. *Direct or* **intentional instruction** *rests on the belief that if teachers do the right things with the right students on the right schedule for the right amount of time, everyone will learn, and nearly everyone can progress toward, in this case, the ability to write well.*

This book is oriented to intentional instruction, and creativity is an important element in the intentional instruction process. Every discussion of content assumes that teachers *can* know what to teach, to whom, when, and under what circumstances; to assess young writers' performance; and to redesign instruction on the basis of the assessment.

REVIEW AND REFLECTION

1. Some educators believe that direct instruction and creativity are at odds with one another. How would you argue an opposite view?
2. Describe the basic difference or differences between direct and indirect instruction.

Nature and Role of Practice

Mastery of any high-level literacy skill requires concentrated and thoughtful **practice** over a protracted period of time (Anderson, 1980, p. 235). There are at least four questions in that sentence about practice:

- What is **"mastery"**?
- What is "concentrated"?
- What is "thoughtful"?
- How long is "protracted"?

Practice is the mediator between where we are before we learn something and where we are when we have learned it so thoroughly that we no longer have to think about it deliberately. Let's get that nailed down with an example.

It's early in the third grade. The children have come a long way in their writing, and the teacher has begun to notice that they need a lot of corrective feedback about those pesky nonsentences they write that begin with *because*. The teacher wants to call the nonsentences **"fragments,"** but he knows third graders won't understand the term any better than he did when he was in the third grade, or the eighth, which was years before he began to figure it out.

So he directs the children one morning to think of a sentence that begins with the word *although*. "Don't put the sentence on paper," he tells them. "Just write the sentence in your head, and listen to what it sounds like." He waits five seconds. "Now write your sentence from your mind onto your paper." As they write, he roams around the room, peering over the shoulders and making a mental note of the children who write the sentence rather than only the opening clause.

After a minute, he asks for readers. He calls on one of the children who has a sentence. The third grader reads: *Although it isn't dark, I have to go inside.* The teacher thanks Ralma for her sentence and repeats it several times, each time making an exaggerated production out of the sounds in the sentence—the sound of two parts, two pieces, two sounds:

Although it isn't dark

I have to go inside.

He repeats the first part and asks what has to come next. Everyone chants the second part. "Boys and girls," he says in an animated way, "listen to the two parts in Ralma's sentence." He repeats the sentence, again exaggerating the sounds of the two parts, and continues, "Everyone, read your sentence, and make sure it has two parts. If it doesn't have two parts, add the second part."

There follow several readings of sentences, each exemplifying the sound of the complex sentence. The teacher reinforces the sound. When he has listened to several sentences, he asks, "How will the person who reads your sentence know where one part ends and the second part begins?" Someone always raises her hand and triumphantly says, "It's the comma!" The teacher agrees and says, "Everyone, make sure you put a comma in your sentence to show readers where the first part ends and the second part begins."

The third graders write a similar sentence that day and several more the following day. Then the teacher directs them to think of a sentence in which *because* is the first word. It takes half the time it took in the first lesson for the third graders to notice that the sentence has the same sound (two parts) and one comma to tell readers where the first part ends and the second part begins. "Boys and girls, when we write a sentence that begins with *because* or one of those other words we've worked with, we have to make sure there is a second part in the sentence. Always listen for the second part when *because* is the first word."

The lesson has been taught, and the third graders have learned it. But that's only the beginning. If young writers have to think consciously about that sentence every time they begin one with the word *because,* they will never write **complex sentences** automatically. How do we go from the children's having learned the sentence to their being able to write the sentence automatically? That's what practice is for.

What's vital here is to remember that the children learned to think in and write this kind of sentence in their own minds with their own writing. They did not learn the sentence from a worksheet with someone else's writing. The first principle of practice is that *people learn to do what they do.* If we want young writers to think in and write complex sentences, they must think in and write complex sentences under instructional direction that ensures that they learn the sentence properly. If, on the other hand, they discriminate between sentences and nonsentences on worksheets, they learn how to discriminate between sentences and nonsentences on worksheets.

People learn what they do, and practice makes permanent, so if young writers practice thinking and writing in complex sentences, their ability to think in and write complex sentences will become permanent. If they practice discriminating between someone else's sentences and nonsentences on a worksheet, their ability to do that will become permanent. If the objective in the complex sentence lesson is to promote complex sentence *writing,* it is clear that the students must think in and write complex sentences, and many of them, regularly, over protracted time, in the context of their own writing, both isolated and authentic.

It is important to remember the second basic principle of practice: *in spite of what everyone says, practice does not make perfect; instead, practice makes permanent.* When we connect the first principle about practice (that people learn to do what they do) with the second principle (that practice makes permanent), we have the proper image of practice. Clearly, *what* people practice is what becomes permanent.

Now it's the eighth grade. The teacher values students' literacy and commits a full third of all reading/language arts, or English, time to writing. Every student has a portfolio and is responsible for writing in at least three genres every day. The students write between twelve and fifteen pages (three thousand to four thousand words) every week, in a variety of genres (e.g., fiction, poetry, autobiography, and persuasion) and across the curriculum (e.g., biography, report of information, and research). Their attitudes toward writing and their own ability to write are good. They enjoy writing and look forward to writing every day.

The picture is good if we accept the proposition that the more students write, the better they will become as writers. But if we accept the basic principles of practice, we have to ask how well the students write and how much better they are getting each week. It turns out that at least half of the students in that eighth grade do not write very well at all. Many have serious problems with staying on the topic throughout a single piece. Some have serious mechanical problems. Five write nonsentences (fragments) regularly. Two of those also seem to have little idea about where sentences begin and end, so they don't use periods and capital letters properly. Many do not spell words correctly that they should spell correctly. Only nine students organize their work in paragraphs. Five students do not understand how to write dialogue.

If we accept the basic principles of practice, we believe that writing a lot causes each young writer to make increasingly permanent the writing he or she practices. Therefore, the five students who write nonsentences are writing a lot of nonsentences and making their nonsentences progressively permanent.

Nothing in this description of practice suggests that practice makes perfect or that young writers get better at writing merely because they write a lot. Students become increasingly better writers because they practice a lot of *good* writing. They become better writers every day because the teacher knows what they need to get better, and the teacher teaches those kinds of things systematically, directly, and every day.

What Is Mastery?

In this book, *mastery* means automaticity. Learners are automatic with end marks, for example, when they are able to commit their deliberate attention to the image or idea about which they are writing. The young writers have achieved mastery with end marks when they use end marks properly and automatically, even in the earliest drafts.

The problem with writing is that there are too many aspects or elements going on simultaneously for young writers to handle all of them deliberately. Early in the learning process, then, most young writers focus deliberately on sentence development and lose focus on their purpose. Then they focus on purpose and lose focus on punctuation. They focus on spelling the words correctly and forget where they are in the sentence. They focus on sentences and lose focus on the main idea in their paragraph. If young writers do not practice their way to automaticity with the mechanical, syntactic, and organizational aspects of writing, they can never effectively put their full attention on their topic, their purpose, their agenda. *In the absence of automaticity, or mastery of the aspects of writing, which occurs through practice, writing is forever a labor of divided attention and frustration.*

Concentrated and *thoughtful* practice emphasizes the student's ability to think, create, and exercise self-discipline. Consider a practice worksheet that requires complex sentence writing; each student is to write ten complex sentences for homework (e.g., "Write a sentence in which the first word is *while.*") No one knows how many complex sentences a novice has to write in order to master complex sentences, but it's very likely more than one and almost certainly fewer than a million. On the first night, everyone writes ten. If everyone writes five or six for homework two nights a week and four in class every day, there will be about ten per day, or thirty per week. Now we're beginning to see the possibility of mastery.

What Is Meant by *Protracted* Time?

Students who have a complex-sentence lesson on Tuesday and complex-sentence homework Tuesday evening, followed by a complex-sentence lesson Wednesday and complex-sentence homework Wednesday night, have had two lessons and two practice sessions. If it all stops there and the teacher goes on to compound sentences, few students will master either complex or **compound sentences.**

Protracted time, with respect to practice, means sufficient time for young writers to achieve automaticity with particular skills—in this case, associated with the larger writing task. As young writers achieve automaticity with an increasing number of skills directly associated with authentic writing, the larger task of writing becomes increasingly automatic, and that leaves the young writer's mind free to concentrate on the point of the writing.

The time needs to be spread over weeks and months, even years. It just won't do to give a paragraphing lesson in the fall and assume that paragraphs are "done" for the year, no matter how concentrated the lessons might be. Young writers master the idea of paragraph as an organizational structure by writing paragraphs for organizational purposes perhaps every day for years. There are many experienced writers who claim, for example, that they have to read good sentences and practice writing good sentences every day because it takes a lifetime to master sentence writing. That's what *protracted time* means.

This doesn't mean, however, that we teach the same things year after year to our students. It means that as students achieve automaticity, they are continually practicing at ever-increasing levels of sophistication. For example, the vast majority of students should not be taught end punctuation year after year. That should be automatic at around second or third grade. Then, youngsters add to their repertoire the increasingly sophisticated structures of sentencing such as compound and complex sentences. The concept of paragraphing should be mastered somewhere in the middle to upper elementary grades, but as students move up the grades, they should practice paragraphing in increasingly complex structures of the genres.

The nature of practice, then, includes thoughtful concentration by the young writer over extended time. Practice is the mediator between what young writers learn and what they master. The result of thoughtful, concentrated practice over protracted time is automaticity, and automaticity is critical in any complex human behavior, such as writing. Without automaticity, young writers are never able to focus their attention on the ideas and images they are trying to create with their writing.

Practice is everything. It is the joy that comes from being free of the tedium, free to focus on connecting the character with the setting, the argument with the rationale, knowing that the words are spelled properly and the sentences work.

REVIEW AND REFLECTION

1. What is the role of practice in learning?
2. Does all practice ensure learning? Explain why it does or does not.
3. If someone said to you, "Practice makes perfect," what might you say in response?

A Summary: Foundations of Interactive Language Arts

The foundation of interactive language arts is language. The focus is the relationships between and among the language arts. These interactions are very important. We are not suggesting that the language arts are related; we're saying that the language arts are interrelated because they are dependent on one another.

Instruction in the language arts must accommodate not merely *what* to teach, but how to teach in such a way that young writers learn. It is clearly not sufficient to teach well because people do not necessarily learn what they are taught. Interactive language arts instruction focuses on what young writers do when they learn. That focus includes specific learning behaviors, some of which are creative.

In the interactive language arts, teachers make things happen that lead inexorably to learning. And part of intentional instruction is intentional practice on the part of young writers.

Intentional instruction in the interactions, and sufficient practice by young writers, lead to mastery, which is demonstrated by young writers' progressive ability to perform quality writing skills and behaviors automatically so they can focus their attention on the larger purposes of writing as communication. Instruction, learning, and practice are the foundations that make the interactions work, and the interactions produce people who can use their language effectively.

PART II

Interactions: Teaching in a Balanced Writing Program

3 Thinking About Craft in Writing

BEFORE YOU READ

- What do you think about when you see the word *craft* in a discussion about writing?
- What do you think craft might entail?
- What do you think the role of craft is in writing well?
- What is there about craft that you think you have learned to use well?
- Chapters 4, 5, and 6 explain the ideas in this chapter for classroom use.

Writing Is a Craft

Winston Churchill is said to have credited his formal education for having taught him how to write an English sentence. Notice that he *didn't* say he learned to be creative in school or that his teachers moved him toward being a lifelong writer. He said that in his formal education experience he learned how to write a sentence. As we describe the balanced writing program, you'll see in this chapter just why Churchill's statement is so important.

What We Mean by *Craft*

While driving near Kennebunkport, Maine, we noted a sign posted on the side of a building:

SHOP FOR RENT

We got to talking about whether the sign meant that this was a place in which one could shop for rent, or if it were a shop that was for rent. Was *shop* a verb, or was it a noun? Was *rent* a verb or was it a noun? If *shop* were the verb, then this would have been a place where people could find places to rent—that is, where they could "shop" for rentals. If *shop* were a noun, on the other hand, then the sign was meant to signal passersby that the place (the shop) could be rented. We eliminated the possibility that people who lived on the south coast of Maine posted signs about rent shopping and decided the intended meaning was that a shop was available to be rented.

   We share this anecdote primarily as a humorous diversion based on a frivolous reading of a sentence printed on a sign. (Of course, the sentence on the sign was abbreviated, with the verb understood.) The wording on that sign, however, is symptomatic of what we mean when we refer to craft in writing instruction and the interactions between writing and the other language arts.

A Definition of Craft

Writing is about recording, whether for ourselves or for others. We write because we have something to say, something to remember, something we want others to know. The writing is a record of what we think and/or see. It appears in ideas and images. The record works because it is crafted effectively. By *craft* we mean the *effective* use of language to record ideas and images.

   When *ideas* are written, they can be thought again by the writer, or they can be thought by readers for whom the ideas are new or variations on the familiar. When *images* are written, they can be seen or heard or felt again by the writer, or they can be experienced by readers for the first time or again as variations on what they experienced before.

   Writing can be described in those ways. We write *ideas* and *images,* and we write to *record* and *communicate.* There are interactions between recording and communicating, of course. The recording can be for the writer alone, as in getting it down so I won't forget or getting it down so I can reexperience it. Just as clearly, the recording can be for communicating. People write about their awe while driving across southern Utah. What they write is a record, but if they write well enough, their journal is more revealing of their awe than are the photographs they took along the way. While the writing is a record, it is also a communication. The quality of the communication is directly related to how effectively the writing is constructed. The construction is what we mean by *craft.*

   There are also interactions between images and ideas. A chapter in a chemistry textbook about optical crystallography describes ideas associated with the wave normal and the biaxial indicatrix, but the text also seeks to create images of a plane perpendicular to a wave normal. And a fiction writer paints visual pictures (images) of characters and environments, all the time trying to make a point about a value system or explore a way to think about coming to know. Ideas and images interact in writing, as do recording and communicating.

It is important that the ideas and images work. Writing is supposed to do what the writer intends for it to do. If a writer intends to create an idea that is similar to the one in his mind, then the writing works if readers end up with the idea. If the writer's intent is to paint a picture similar to the one he sees and such an image appears in readers' minds, the writing works. The concept of when writing works, and how we know, is a key idea that we discuss further in Chapters 7 and 8.

Now go back to that shop for rent in Maine, or the place in Maine where one can shop for rent. There was an idea intended in the simple wording. We think the intended message was about a place for rent—a shop one could rent. However, the writing didn't work very well. Readers first had to consider the other possible meaning (*shop* as verb, not noun) and make sense by assuming the higher-probability meaning. Readers didn't get the idea from the reading; they got the idea by using their prior knowledge. When we're teaching craft, we're teaching for clarity and precision.

The Craft and the Grammar

A major part of balanced writing instruction is the act of constructing or crafting language. Craft isn't so simplistic as what some call "grammar," for the sign about rent doesn't violate any grammatical construction. It just isn't clear. Although craft includes the ability to use basic grammatical elements and structures, that ability is insufficient for writing well.

There is a reason that the evidence shows little, if any, relationship between teaching grammar and writing well (Hillocks, 1986), and the reason is deceptively simple. It's obvious that people who write well handle sentences expertly, and in doing so they use nouns, verbs, and **modification.** That translates into what appears to be a reasonable, but flawed, generalization: to write well, young writers must know how to handle sentences and, therefore, nouns, verbs, and modifiers. Then there occurs another great leap sideways. Given that good writers handle sentences and their parts adroitly, it follows that we should teach sentence parts to young writers so they too will write well.

The reasoning fails entirely because although good writers *can* handle nouns, verbs, and modifiers adroitly, that isn't *why* they write well. Furthermore, being armed with grammatical knowledge is almost completely unrelated to writing ability because no one who writes well (or ill, for that matter) uses that ability as any sort of template for sentence writing. Put another way, writers certainly use nouns, verbs, and the rest of what we associate with grammar, but they don't use that ability as a guide when they write.

We're *not* arguing against teaching subjects and predicates, or direct objects and pronouns. We're simply urging teachers not to be surprised and frustrated when young writers don't write appreciably better as a result of their learning to define and find sentence parts. They will write better because they know how to think in and write sentences, not because we teach them how to name and find what's in sentences. Craft is thinking in and writing good sentences.

It's related to bicycle riding, playing the piano, and chemistry. We don't ride and play better, or "do" chemistry better, because we know how bicycles, music, and the Periodic Table are constructed, but some people who ride, play, and conduct experiments eventually learn how those three are constructed. Knowing the constructive properties isn't why people ride, play, and do chemistry well. Knowing how a sentence is constructed isn't why we write good ones either.

Craft is not merely knowing that a sentence contains a subject, a predicate, and something *complete*. The concept of the *incomplete* thought is too abstract for seven- or ten-year-old children. "Because I'm tired" is a thought but not a sentence. "Be careful, or you could get injured" is a thought expressed in a sentence. There are sentences, and there are nonsentences. Defining a sentence as a *complete* thought has no utility for young writers.

Craft is knowing how to think in and write sentences so they work. It isn't understanding vague distinctions between whole and partial thoughts or knowing about adverbs. It's adding texture to a verb so it reaches off the page and takes readers on a leisurely afternoon walk in the forest. Of course, good writers use a word such as *meander* and eliminate the need for the adverb. To craft the language means knowing that the right word is better than the nearly right word with a modifier.

The Craft and the Mechanics

Craft also isn't so simplistic as what some call "mechanics." The generic mechanics are certainly necessary in writing well, but craft is more than that. All sorts of people satisfy grade-level expectations on mechanics standards and do not write well because the mechanical conventions do not by themselves produce good writing.

Craft in Proper Perspective

Craft is the part of writing that makes it possible for readers with the requisite prior knowledge to interact effectively with writers. Reading experts have defined reading as a transaction between readers, a text, and a context (International Reading Association, 1988). If writers craft the language well, readers know the ideas and images the writers intended when they wrote the piece. Writers create what Rosenblatt (1978) called a blueprint for meaning, the text.

Everything we've suggested so far about craft is at the level of the single sentence: word selection, word order, and mechanical conventions. Craft is certainly about thinking and writing in sentences, but it is also about thinking and organizing in paragraphs.

Craft is about connections between and among sentences that themselves affect main idea. Craft is about transitions and organizational devices. It is about spelling and capital letters, of course, and word selection that creates the precise idea or image the writer has behind her eyes.

But craft is also about what our favorite writer does to write that paragraph we post on the refrigerator. We post the paragraph because everything in it seems to enhance the main idea, just as a gnarled tree in the distance enhances a beach scene in watercolor. The paragraph on the refrigerator door wouldn't be quite so complete without its third sentence, and the beachscape wouldn't be quite so complete without that gnarled tree. When we teach the craft, we teach young writers to understand how to make the connections that complete the word picture.

Craft is the foundation of writing effectively. It makes writing work. For example, as diverse young writers gain progressive control over the craft, they can begin to record and communicate the experiences and passions that they hold dear. Craft isn't the only part of what writers do that makes writing work, but when writers do everything else right and fail to craft effectively, the writing doesn't work. And if writers craft brilliantly but fail to do the other things that make writing work, the writing still fails.

The Last Sign of Craft

Craft is necessary in writing well, but it is not sufficient. As we explain what we mean by craft, we focus on that special bear they have in Wellesley, Massachusetts. We know about it because there, right along Route 95, was the warning sign:

BOSTON BEAR LEFT

It seems from the sign that the Boston Bear is ahead on the left. On the other hand, the Boston Bear may have left Wellesley. Maybe the Boston Bear left Boston, or all of New England. Where is the Boston Bear?

Of course, we all know the sign isn't about a Boston Bear. We all know the sign warns drivers to bear left to get to Boston from Wellesley along Route 95. We all know that *bear* isn't a noun in that sentence, although we've been drilled relentlessly that a noun is the name of a person, place, or thing, and *bear* is a thing. We just know *bear* is a verb in that sentence. And we know that *left* isn't a verb, although it's a variation on *leave*, which shows action and must be a verb. But in that sentence, we know *left* is an adverb. And we know that no matter that the sentence, as written, shows *Boston* to be an adjective that modifies *bear*, it's a noun. We just know that. Right?

Maybe. It depends on what readers are thinking and doing at the time they're reading the wording on the sign, and it depends as well on readers' prior knowledge. In fact, the readers we're referring to had become completely confused driving in Boston, such that they started for Wellesley from the Boston Common at 4:30 P.M. and by following the signs through Boston arrived back at the Common at 5:40 P.M. These were readers for whom ideas printed as road signs throughout Boston didn't make any sense because they had no prior knowledge relative to Boston. There were two to five lanes of traffic going in every direction all over Boston. When the drivers saw a sign, they had a nanosecond to make sense of it. When the sign's wording suggested something about a bear, for a nanosecond they thought of a bear, and while they considered the humor in the sign, they lost focus and missed the turn.

To craft the language well is to eliminate the nanoseconds of misinformation, confusion, or distraction. It is to use the right words in the right positions for the right reasons. That is what we mean by craft.

REVIEW AND REFLECTION

1. How do you distinguish between craft and grammar?
2. How do you distinguish between craft and mechanics?
3. What is the relationship between how you viewed craft in writing before reading so far in this chapter and how you view craft now?
4. What do you think is the proper perspective for viewing the craft of writing?

What Does Craft Include?

We begin to answer this question by discussing the place of craft in learning to write well. Often it's either stated or implied that spelling, punctuation, usage, and organizational structures are only small parts of the entire writing process and *secondary* to creating text. But how is it that a writer "creates" text if many of the features and the form of the creation are secondary? Asked another way, How does anyone create text if sentences, paragraphs, and mechanical control are not primary in the process? In fact, text itself is constructed of sentences and paragraphs that are all arranged to serve the message. The conventions are part of the message and are integral to the text on which communication rests.

One problem in writing instruction is that teaching the craft of written language has been approached as drill and practice divorced from context or meaning. Far from the narrow, drill-based conceptions that have permeated past discussion of craft instruction, balanced writing instruction rests instead on creative thinking, interactive language processes, and thoughtful practice. Craft is an integral part of writing instruction, and it includes each of the following elements of written language on an age- and skill-appropriate basis throughout the grades: sentences, relationships between and among sentences, paragraphs, relationships between and among paragraphs, and mechanical control.

Sentences

The fundamental element of craft is the sentence. Writing, at least in English, doesn't work in prepositional phrases, compound predicates, nouns, or dependent clauses. *English works in sentences and only in sentences.*

By the word *sentence* we mean the smallest possible sentence of a single word that appears in fiction in response to a character's question, "Have you drawn the bath?" The other character responds, "No." Both characters' lines are sentences.

We also refer to the longer sorts of sentences such as that from Charles Dickens in an 1845 observation of an execution:

> The place of execution was near the church of San Giovanni decollato (a doubtful compliment to Saint John the Baptist) in one of the impassable back streets without any doorway—a street of rotten houses, which do not seem to belong to anybody, and do not seem to have ever been inhabited, and certainly were never built with any plan, or for any particular purpose, and have no window-sashes, and are a little like deserted breweries, and might be ware-houses but for having nothing in them. (Dickens, 1846, in Carey, 1987, p. 313)

How would you characterize this Charles Dickens sentence?

- Is it a "complete" thought?
- Does it have a subject and a predicate?
- If a sixth grader were to write it, how might the teacher describe it?
- If you were Dickens's teacher, what would you suggest to him about improving his writing?

Craft instruction helps young writers understand the nature of the sentence from the beginning. It helps them avoid the pesky run-ons and fragments because compound- and complex-sentence structures, which are often written as run-ons and fragments, are an integral part of the intentional instruction and creative thinking-writing program.

Craft instruction helps young writers understand why one word rather than another one is used in a sentence. When we are teaching sentences, we are also helping young writers understand that subjects can be singular or plural, and if a subject is plural (*the boys*), the predicate has to agree (*play*). If the pronoun is singular (*she*), the predicate has to agree (*plays*). If a noun is plural (*children*), the following pronoun also has to be plural (*they* or *them*).

Craft instruction includes what we typically refer to as *usage.* Young writers write in the usage patterns we teach, and their practice is based on their own thoughtful writing.

Craft instruction at the level of the sentence causes young writers to focus, concentrate, and deliberately attend to the construction of sentences. Often when teachers direct young writers to write a sentence, the youngsters begin with a big letter and hope something happens before they get to the period. They write their sentences as an act of faith. That tends to work often enough for native speakers of English because they've been doing just that with oral language since they were about twelve to eighteen months of age. The problem is that writing is not talk written down, so mere hoping that a sentence means something and fits between the previous one and the next one doesn't lead consistently to well-constructed writing. Craft instruction helps young writers understand the planfulness of writing, and with enough direct instruction in sentences, they will begin to write planful sentences automatically, just as more experienced writers do. (In Chapter 4 we describe this instruction.)

When a writing cue prompts a sentence and young writers have to think *flexibly* or *elaboratively,* or they have to *organize* information, the sentence thinking and writing is creative. It is important to remember what we said above about the sentence: that it is the smallest piece of **whole written language,** not "whole language," but a whole instance of written language. Sentence instruction, then, if it is conducted properly, is not only creative writing; it is also creation of whole and meaningful written language.

Relationships Between and Among Sentences

One of the myriad problems with traditional sentence instruction is that it rarely involves more than one sentence at a time. Although it is true that one sentence is a whole piece of written language, most authentic writing occurs in more than one sentence, and the sentences are related to one another. It is important that young writers master the relationships between and among sentences.

Notice that we said they must master the *relationships* between and among sentences. It is the relationships they must master, not merely several sentences written in a row. Those relationships are what writers call **cohesion**—a sort of joint between sentences that connects sentences. It's the connective tissue that makes readers flow from one sentence to another. (What is the connective "tissue" between the first and second sentences in this paragraph?)

Traditionally, intentional writing instruction begins with the sentence. Then, after several years of single-sentence activities and analyses, the idea of transitional *devices* is introduced, usually about the fifth or sixth grade. We introduce several transitional devices as something new to learn—pronouns, for example. The teacher teaches the word *pronoun* and shows young writers how pronouns can take the place of people's names, and if a person's name is in the first sentence and a pronoun introduces the second sentence, there is a transition.

> The girl went to her room after dinner. There, she worked with her computer until bedtime.

When the fifth graders have used pronouns to affect transitions between pairs of sentences on the worksheet, the teacher introduces the next transitional device for connecting sentences, perhaps words that show sequence (*first, second, next, then*). It all seems quite artificial and apart from authentic thinking and writing.

When sentences are taught directly and creatively as whole pieces of written language, writers typically write more than one sentence, and when they do, they use various transitional devices naturally because they have been using transitions in their oral language for most of their lives. The intentional instruction teacher calls attention to what young writers already know and do naturally, and then uses those transitions in instruction that allows young writers to use their natural transitions deliberately. It's natural, predictable, authentic, and direct. (Chapter 4 explores this instruction.)

REVIEW AND REFLECTION

1. Recall when you were taught sentences and relationships between and among sentences. How did your teachers teach those things?
2. What does it mean when we say that writing is not talk written down? How does that square with what we so often hear: "Just write it the way you'd say it"?
3. The key to intentional sentence instruction is concentration—that is, deliberate attention. How can we get young writers to focus on how they are crafting sentences? How do we get young writers to become increasingly competent at crafting sentences?

Paragraphs

There are a variety of ways to think about paragraphing. The paragraph can be conceptualized as a way to segment text. It can be a form of punctuation that signals various shifts in the flow of discourse, an indented initial sentence, for example (Nystrand, 1986). Partridge (1973) defined the paragraph as a division of discourse beyond the sentence, a collection or natural series of sentences that have a unity of purpose. For instruction, Savage (1998) defined the paragraph in terms of multiple sentences, all related to a central idea. Sebranek, Meyer, and Kemper (1990) wrote that the paragraph focuses on "a specific topic, which can be 'developed' in the form of a story, a description, an explanation, or an opinion" (p. 75).

The paragraph is defined universally in terms that capture the concept of unity of idea or purpose. But notice a subtle difference between definitions that come from writers or writing research (Nystrand, 1986; Partridge, 1973) and those associated with teaching and learning (Savage, 1998; Sebranek et al., 1990). The former conceptualize the paragraph as a division or segmentation of text; the latter conceptualize the paragraph as collections of sentences that form a central idea. The difference, although subtle, is enormous, and it may serve to explain why paragraph writing seems so difficult for young writers.

If we observe experienced writers, we find them writing extended discourse in sentences. They'll certainly segment along the way, but their early divisions, when they draft, are largely for the purpose of attempting to isolate what initially appear to be idea clusters in running text. For experienced writers, it appears that the paragraph is a way to break up the text as they draft. In revision, the paragraph becomes an organizational device.

That is very different from setting out to write paragraphs, especially if there is a specific taxonomy that includes, for example, a thesis sentence, certain kinds of body sentences, and a conclusion sentence. The paragraph is a natural way to organize sentences into authentic arrangements that serve the communication purpose. Viewed in any formulaic terms, the paragraph becomes an artificial template that functions quite apart from the authentic flow of ideas that occurs as writers create text.

In this book, we use Fearn's (1983) definition of paragraph: "a thoughtful way to arrange ideas" (p. 16). Paragraphing therefore occurs in the draft and again as writers revise. This definition suggests that there are two instructional emphases in paragraph instruction:

1. We introduce young writers to the need to think about their developing ideas, even as they are developing the ideas.
2. We introduce young writers to the need to rethink the idea clusters that occurred naturally as they drafted.

It is likely that in the rethinking, young writers will form new paragraph clusters that better reflect their ideas. After all, it is only when the draft is finished that writers can see what the idea clusters are. It was E. M. Forster who said, "How do I know what I think until I see what I say?" (Murray, 1990, p. 101). Of course, that concept wouldn't mean much to ten year olds, but we can make the concept of paragraph real to them. We discuss the specifics of paragraph instruction in Chapter 6, but first explore some fundamental ideas related to paragraphing and paragraphing instruction.

Probably the most fundamental idea related to paragraphing is that the main idea is central to paragraph instruction. Paragraph instruction always includes main idea. Main idea is so fundamental to the paragraph, in fact, that without a main idea, there is no paragraph. All paragraph instruction in this book rests on main idea.

Young writers have to become accustomed to thinking about and noticing main idea. When we read aloud, we need to ask young writers to think about the ideas the writer is developing—for example, "Listen to me read, boys and girls, and try to count the main ideas you hear." Part of the read-aloud experience is children's active participation in how the text itself is developed and organized. As their sensitivity to main idea becomes increasingly automatic, they are increasingly likely to hear the development of their own main ideas.

As young readers and writers read, they need to pay attention to the paragraphs and talk about the main ideas in those paragraphs. They should also notice differences between paragraphs in fiction and trade books and those in their science and social studies books. Young readers and writers should also notice paragraph-like clusters in the stanzas or verses of many poems. The more they notice main ideas in their reading, the more likely they will notice main ideas in their own writing.

Young writers need to find main idea clusters and arrange sentences into those clusters. Intentional and thoughtful writing instruction will engage them in main idea finding and arranging with existing text. Chapter 4 presents some paragraphing lessons that do just that.

Our paragraphing terminology includes what writers do when they paragraph (*segment* as they draft and *rearrange* as they revise) and what they use as the paragraphing device (main idea). The absence of reference to "topic sentence" does not mean that paragraphs do not have a topic sentence. Rather, it means that there are countless good paragraphs that do not have a topic sentence. But all paragraphs, good or otherwise, have a main idea. We teach the concept of main idea because it is both necessary and sufficient for effective paragraphing.

We do not suggest to young writers that paragraphs have certain numbers of certain kinds of sentences. There is nothing we know of in the entire history of written language, in English, or any other language as far as we know, that dictates five sentences per main idea, or three or seven. Nor is there any requirement that a paragraph contain a sentence that compares or contrasts, one that explains, and one that shows cause and effect. There probably aren't 10 percent of the paragraphs in any print you choose, whether book, magazine, or newspaper, that fit any sentence-based formula you can find in a paragraph lesson.

The obvious conclusion is that writers don't write paragraphs in a formulaic manner, and formulaic paragraphs don't appear routinely in any published form. Therefore we ought not teach it to young writers.

But what about the argument that the formula is something like training wheels for novice writers—that until they fully understand the paragraph, the formula is helpful to them? One of the things we know for sure about learning is that learners learn what they do, not necessarily what they are taught. We may think we are teaching them to use paragraphs authentically when we teach a formula, but what they're doing is formulaic. Given that a formula is what they are doing and what they are doing occurs during paragraph instruction, they're learning that a paragraph follows a formula. Young writers, therefore, are learning the wrong information.

We should teach young writers to think in main ideas as they draft and revise. We should teach them to notice main ideas when they read and to think about main ideas as they construct meaning (comprehend) from their reading. We shouldn't teach young writers that they have to have this or that sentence to have a paragraph, but we certainly would never prohibit them from writing a compare-and-contrast sentence when such a sentence would enhance their main idea. (A compare-and-contrast sentence seemed to fit right there in this paragraph, in fact.) We teach young writers that the main idea, not the kind or number of sentences, determines whether there is a paragraph.

REVIEW AND REFLECTION

1. *A paragraph is a thoughtful way to arrange and rearrange ideas in writing.* How would you explain that statement to someone who has not read this chapter?
2. The focus in paragraphs is main idea. How can you identify a main idea if there is no topic sentence?
3. Most writers segment their writing into what they think might be idea clusters as they write, and they organize their writing into more formal paragraphs as they revise. When do you remember doing this in your own writing?

4. *Because it is impossible to know what the main ideas are before there is a sufficient amount of text drafted to be able to see them, it makes sense for young writers to learn how to use paragraphs to organize what they have written.* Do you agree with both parts of that statement? Do you agree with only one? If you disagree with the second part, what should we teach about paragraphing? If you disagree with the first part, when do you think writers know what their idea clusters are?

- -

Relationships Between and Among Paragraphs

It is important for young writers to understand that paragraphs do not occur in isolation. Writers arrange their writing in paragraphs to organize their main ideas in logical sequence so readers can understand writers' ideas and images. The result of paragraph writing isn't an isolated paragraph here and there. It's paragraph after paragraph in a line of coherent meaning development that leaves readers with the whole idea or image.

Paragraphs have to move one to another in much the way sentences do. We teach sentences *and* connections between and among sentences. It is also important to focus on teaching paragraphs *and* relationships between and among paragraphs.

Traditionally, when paragraph instruction works, children learn to write them very well. Then they come to the sixth or seventh grade, and the teacher makes a three-paragraph homework assignment on something they are reading. If they remember what they learned through their formative years, they write three well-formed paragraphs, each with a beginning, a middle, and an end.

The middle school language arts teacher reads the papers, notices the need on many of the papers for transitions from paragraph to paragraph, and plans to spend some portion of the next two weeks on ideational transitions, repeated word transitions, and sequential transitions. The children learned to write artificial paragraphs and now will learn to use transitions artificially.

Instead we should be emphasizing the authenticity of writing and the transitions in good literature. That permeates everything in balanced writing instruction, and it becomes utterly critical at the point at which writing starts to take on bigger meanings.

The big picture in a piece of extended discourse, a larger message, is bigger than one paragraph. It requires that writers make the leap from one paragraph to more than one paragraph, and seamlessly. That's what organization is all about and what *coherence* means.

Seamless is what Gardner (1983) meant by "the fictional dream." It's what we mean when we say a piece of writing hangs together. It's part of what makes a book so compelling that we can't put it down. Although the writing consists of sentences and paragraphs, it nevertheless seems not to have any parts. It's seamless.

The flow from paragraph to paragraph is what language arts teachers call *transitions,* but even transitions, when they're artificial, don't flow well. So when we plan paragraph lessons for balanced writing instruction in the interactive language arts, we plan for more than one paragraph at a time. Essentially, intentional paragraph instruction almost always includes one paragraph, plus something about the previous or the next paragraph.

The simplest way for young writers to practice seamlessness from one paragraph to the next is to write a paragraph plus the first sentence or the main idea of the following paragraph. To get from the paragraph to the first sentence of the next paragraph, they have to think about the connection between the two paragraphs.

The connection is the tissue that moves readers from one idea to the next. It is a sort of trail between the two paragraphs. The transition is a natural connection between the paragraph they write and the following paragraph. The two are connected naturally. Young writers should rarely write a final sentence in their paragraphs. They should invariably leave a way to get to the next paragraph. To leave a way is to make a transition from one paragraph to the next.

Faced with a three-paragraph homework assignment, why didn't they leave two of the three paragraphs open in the first place? Some did, but if they used what they learned about paragraphs before they got to the seventh grade, and what they learned had paragraphs ending with summary or concluding sentences, they couldn't leave two of the three paragraphs open.

Authentic writing doesn't end many of its paragraphs with summary or concluding sentences. Authentic writing is about flow, from the beginning, from word to word, phrase to phrase, sentence to sentence, paragraph to paragraph. The flow is an integral part of all balanced writing instruction.

REVIEW AND REFLECTION

1. Think back to your paragraph writing lessons in elementary, middle, and secondary school, and maybe even university writing classes. Were you taught about five sentences, each with a label? Were you taught "hamburger" paragraphs (bun on the top, meat in the middle, bun on the bottom—dressings as details)? How were you taught to think in and write paragraphs?
2. What word do you use to tell what a sentence is about? (*subject*) What word do you use to tell what a paragraph is about? (*main idea*) What word do you use to tell what an essay is about? (*theme*) Why are there three different terms for three similar things? Is it possible that young writers suffer more from confusion than lack of instruction?
3. When you write, do you think of which transitional device you will use when you get to the end of your paragraphs?
4. How can you make paragraphs natural and understandable for seven and eight year olds so eleventh-grade teachers won't have to teach paragraphs again?

Mechanical Control

The **meaning markers** in writing, often called *mechanics*, represent an important part of the writer's craft. When we see the word *mark*, for instance, we construct meaning, either a noun or a verb, depending on the context. When we see the word written as *Mark*, we construct one of the previous meanings in a new context (first word in a sentence) or we construct a new meaning altogether (someone's name). The size and construction of the first letter in the word can dictate its meaning. Capital letters are not merely for penmanship exercises; capital letters are meaning markers. They matter.

Read this word: *hes*. How do you pronounce that word? It's a consonant-vowel-consonant (CVC) pattern, and what we know about CVC patterns is a short vowel sound (*sat, bet, pit, not, nut*). *Hes* must rhyme with *bet* and *pet*, right? Wrong. It's missing its punctuation. The word is *he's*. The vowel is long. The apostrophe changes the word from nonsense to meaning, from a nonword to a contraction, from one pronunciation pattern to another. Punctuation matters.

In balanced writing instruction, mechanical control means capitalization and punctuation. The matter of **usage** appears in our discussion of sentences, and although all of capitalization and punctuation occurs only in sentences (save for indention in paragraphs, which Nystrand [1986] refers to as punctuation), they're isolated here (and in Chapter 5) for emphasis. In addition, spelling is usually included in discussions of mechanical control, but the writing-spelling interaction appears in detail in Chapter 14.

Systematically teaching young writers the conventional use of capital letters and punctuation marks contributes dramatically to their ability to write well. There is no evidence that young writers learn to use capital letters and punctuation marks properly if they write a lot. To the contrary, it appears from national writing sample assessments (NAEP, 1998) that each generation of young writers is writing more than ever before but no better. Of course, *no better* isn't defined precisely in capitalization and punctuation terms, but mechanical control does appear as a factor on national assessment rubrics, and there's no question that if quantity is the variable, by now it should have led to an increase in writing quality.

Some theorists hold that capitalization and punctuation don't matter so much in the draft because writers go back and make corrections when they revise and edit. That's an appealing thought, but it doesn't work that way. Mechanical matters that are highly practiced in writing context tend to appear in drafts; those that aren't tend not to appear in drafts, and they're not likely to be corrected in revision either because they're not well known.

Suppose you want to put two little sentence ideas together into one large sentence that connects the two with the word *and*, but because you don't know about commas in compound sentences (and a distressing number of postsecondary students don't), you don't use one. What do you think is the probability that you will insert the requisite comma in the compound sentence when you edit your draft? Right. None. You didn't know the convention when you drafted. You won't know it when you edit either.

We teach the meaning markers of capitalization and punctuation directly in balanced writing instruction so young writers will know them. This means that we do not teach the mechanics in occasional tiny lessons, as the children need them. Rather, we plan for and teach capitalization and punctuation on three explicit bases.

First, we plan for and teach high-frequency and high-utility capitalization and punctuation **conventions** (Fearn & Farnan, 1998b). A cursory peek into a comprehensive secretary's manual reveals that there are up to one hundred conventions for capitalizing and punctuating English, with over one hundred variations and exceptions. Almost no one knows them all. Clearly, there are some meaning markers that are of higher utility than others.

Second, we teach meaning markers as young writers need them to write the sentences they write spontaneously, as well as the sentences they write because we teach them. There is no reliable scope and sequence for capitalization and punctuation conventions, save for the implications of what we know from what young writers write. That's the foundation for the scope and sequence chart in Figure 3.1.

The first sentences that children write will require an end mark (period or question mark; first sentences tend not to be imperatives that require exclamation marks) and a capital letter. That's when to teach end marks and capital letters that begin sentences. Second graders tend to write compound sentences. When these sentences start to appear, it's time to teach the comma in compound sentences. Third graders are able to write complex sentences, so we teach complex sentences in the third grade and include the comma convention. Very few writers under the age of about eight easily understand the vicissitudes of singular and plural possessives, so apostrophes should be limited to contractions until possessives appear in third graders' writing. For second graders who write with possessives, we teach the apostrophe. Then in the third grade, we begin teaching sentences that use possessives, and we teach the spelling patterns and the proper placement of the apostrophe, knowing that relative mastery will occur over a two- to three-year period.

Third, we teach meaning markers in the context of young writers' writing. Consider a lesson that introduces the comma in complex sentences. The first activity in that lesson—before any teacher commentary, before any statement of objective or purpose—is a sentence writing cue that virtually guarantees a complex sentence from at least half of the third graders: *Think of a sentence in which the first word is* although. (Chapter 4 explores this lesson in detail.) The lesson uses student-written sentences as the material for teaching the rest of the class to write complex sentences and place the comma. In balanced writing instruction, there are no practice sheets that contain sentences written by someone else, into which young writers insert apostrophes and commas.

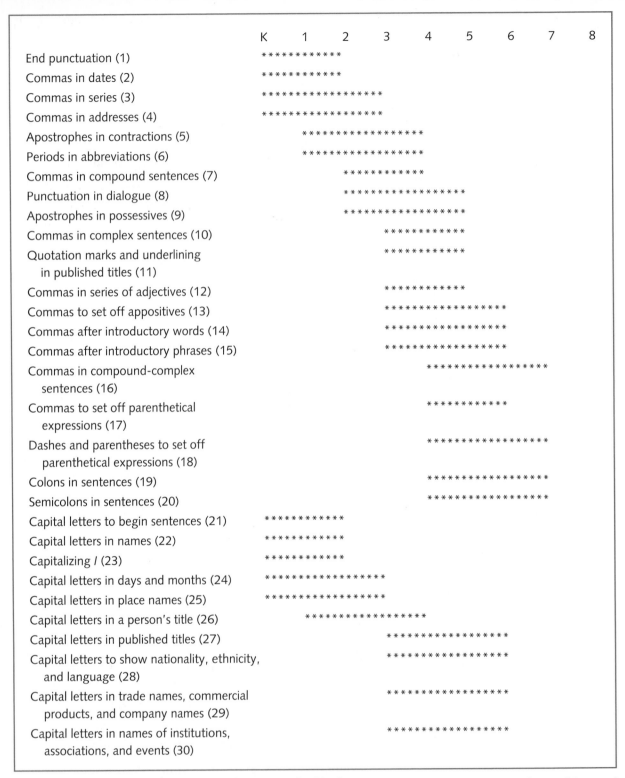

FIGURE 3.1 Instructional Time Line: Awareness to Mastery. Source: Reprinted with permission from Leif Fearn and Nancy Farnan, *Writing Effectively: Helping Children Master the Conventions of Writing*, 1998.

Writing instruction means that young writers must write. Writing is not the same as editing what someone else has written by inserting capital letters and punctuation marks.

Instruction in mechanical control is primarily about writing and only secondarily about editing. It focuses on high-utility and high-frequency capitalization and punctuation, and it follows young writers' development.

REVIEW AND REFLECTION

1. In balanced writing instruction, we teach the conventions that young writers are likely to use. What are those conventions, and when will they be critical?
2. We teach the conventions as young writers need them. How can we know when they need certain conventions?
3. We use young writers' writing as the instructional context. Give an example of what that means.
4. We teach capitalization and punctuation as writing, not as editing. When students understand capitalization and punctuation as writing, they will know enough to use them in their editing. How can we know that?

Four Modes of Discourse

The modes of discourse—description, analysis, compare and contrast, and criticize and persuade—represent constructive attributes in writing and reading. These constructive attributes help readers construct meaning from print because the print is crafted in certain ways.

The modes of discourse represent ways that writers can use language to make an impact on readers. They are ways of crafting the language. They can be used throughout the genres and appear in writings as large as whole books or as small as single sentences. Young writers can deepen the impact of their writing by using the modes of discourse well.

Description

The descriptive mode of discourse encompasses certain specific attributes that help the writer paint an image or idea in words—for example:

- size *(On his belt buckle was a motorcycle a small man could ride.)*
- motion *(He leaned back slowly so every creak in the ancient chair was audible)*
- position *(and stopped precariously short of tipping over backward.)*
- shape *(His belly bore testimony to years of trying to drink Canada dry.)*
- color *(Rage rose from under his collar,)*
- texture *(facial muscles rippled, even under his ample jowls,)*
- atmosphere *(and moist heat, oppressive even for Waco,)*

- mood *(made his words stick in his throat.)*
- order or disorder *(This was the scene after months of strained peace between them.)*

Description should cause readers to experience the action played out before them or the ideas illuminated, so they can fully understand. There is lightning action in readers' minds. To achieve clarity for readers, writers must slow the action into frames that readers can see, feel, and hear.

There are nine sensory images in the Texas scene above, each one carefully focused on parts of the whole. Readers can see the whole from the descriptive parts.

Description is a mode of discourse that occurs in every genre (fiction, autobiography, report of information, and so forth). It reveals elements of story grammar in short fiction. Description captures the research process and findings in reports of information, and it characterizes the writer's rationale in persuasive writing. It makes the biographical subject live and the autobiographical incident real.

Sometimes ideas or images are so complex, and so seemingly chaotic, that the writing itself is an "incomparable way to think better" (Van Doren, 1991, p. 126). A third grader describes, for example, exactly how she manipulated the lighting conditions to measure the effect of light on the germination of lima beans. She knows what she did, but she can't merely write that she tried as many lighting conditions as she could. Instead, she takes each condition in turn and describes what it is, what it means, and how she used and controlled it. That is descriptive.

Analysis

Analysis makes the assumption that wholes are made up of parts, and the whole can be known and understood through the parts. Analytic writing organizes the parts, arranges them in an order, and shows the relationship between cause and effect. It is different from description in that it begins with the whole and breaks down the whole so readers can use the parts to reconstruct the whole. Description provides carefully painted parts that readers use to construct their own whole. There is only one whole in the analytic mode of discourse, and the writer begins the writing by telling readers what it is.

Analysis is used for the purpose of making complex things clearer. It's the mode of discourse that Isaac Asimov used in his collection of essays titled *Of Matters Great and Small* (1975), each designed to help readers understand enormous ideas such as the highest number, astronomical distances, and the inevitability of life. In his analysis of the highest number, he showed how to write 1 followed by 10 decillion zeroes, which would cover "all the surfaces of all the objects in the known Universe, even with each zero the size of a hydrogen atom" (p. 284). Having begun with an utterly incomprehensible representation (1 followed by 10 decillion zeros), he leads readers to a comprehensible representation that featured his own exponential notation (10/10/10/34). The quantity remains

incomprehensible to almost everyone, but the representation no longer covers all the surfaces in the known Universe with hydrogen-sized zeroes.

It's similar to what a fifth or ninth grader has to do to write directions for drawing a flat pattern that, when folded properly, produces the Platonic solid known as a cube. The writer has to "see" a cube, maybe make one, take it apart so it is flat, and then show readers in stages how to draw the pattern. Writing the stages is analysis of the whole, and the writing is called analytic.

Compare and Contrast

Sometimes ideas and images are well revealed to readers when they are shown alongside something more familiar. Often comparisons and contrasts are expressed in figurative language: metaphors, similes, and analogies. It's impossible to explain the sensation of an airplane's hitting an air pocket to readers who have never flown. But if the readers have ridden a roller coaster, the sensation of the bottom dropping out just past a peak in the ride can be used as an approximation of what the air pocket feels like to airplane passengers.

The compare-and-contrast mode of discourse, like both description and analysis, is used to help readers know and understand the writer's idea or image. Jerry Spinelli had a sense of what Maniac's well-worn sneaker looked like in his book *Maniac Magee* (1990), and he showed readers what he saw when he wrote the sentence about "the soles of both sneakers hanging by their hinges and flopping like dog tongues each time they came up from the pavement" (p. 9). Seeing the comparison gives readers a clearer image than had the writer merely described the worn shoes.

Poets have the reputation of using comparisons and contrasts most often, maybe even most effectively. It might be Robert Frost's comparison of ice and hate that makes his poem "Fire and Ice" stick so tightly in his readers' minds. Certainly when English teachers show the film *West Side Story* as a prelude in a unit on *Romeo and Juliet,* they are trying to capitalize on comparisons between the two. It is also important to discuss how the two stories are different. The comparisons and contrasts clarify Shakespeare's plays for young readers.

Criticize and Persuade

The fourth mode of discourse is nearly the same as the persuasive genre. Writers use criticize and persuade not so much to help readers know and understand an idea or image, but to influence the way in which readers understand an idea or image. Inherent in criticism and persuasion is a writer's sense of what is right and how *right* can and should be achieved. After all, were there no sense of one's own conception of right, there would be no basis on which to criticize another conception of what is right. Having a sense of what is right is fundamental to criticism and persuasion.

Criticism and persuasion can take the form of short editorial commentaries or extended discussions of complex controversies. For example, many texts describe and analyze the effect of Columbus' voyage to what was known as the New World, often relating awful tales about what happened to indigenous peoples. But Alfred Crosby's *The Columbian Exchange* (1972) is a different kind of book; it shows that the demise of indigenous peoples was partly the result of bacteriological migration.

Roger Ebert, with the late Gene Siskel, reviewed films. Their reviews were critical, and their thumbs-up or thumbs-down signature gesture was intended to persuade viewers to go or not to go to the film they were reviewing. The editorial page of every newspaper in the country is about criticism and persuasion. Letters to the editor are often critical of a recent article or opinion in that newspaper.

Fiction writers (Truman Capote comes immediately to mind) often use persuasion to influence how readers think and feel. Writers of reports of information often try to persuade readers to pursue research further. Do you think Robert Frost set out to persuade readers with "Stopping by Woods on a Snowy Evening"?

The modes of discourse represent ways writers can use language to make an impact on readers. They are ways of crafting the language. They can be used throughout the genres. They appear in writings as large as whole books or as small as single sentences. Young writers can enhance the impact of their writing by using the modes of discourse well.

REVIEW AND REFLECTION

1. The modes of discourse represent ways to think about what writing is supposed to accomplish. Think of a piece of published writing you especially appreciate. How did the writer use the modes of discourse?

2. There are descriptive demands in most genres. Think of how description is used in both fiction and nonfiction. Provide examples from your adult reading experience.

3. Some writing is about understanding complex things. There are analytic demands in most genres. Find an example of analytic writing in mathematics and art. How do the two writers use analytic writing to make their writing effective?

4. Some writing can be made clearer if the writer uses readers' prior knowledge for comparison. Many genres can benefit from comparisons and contrasts to help readers make more accurate meanings. Find a poem or song lyric that uses the compare-and-contrast mode of discourse. Share it with a friend, professional peer, or a child, and discuss how the comparison or contrast helped make the poem or lyric clear.

5. Some writing is designed to change readers' belief systems or the way they think about problems and events. The need for criticism and persuasion occurs in all genres. Who is your favorite story writer, essayist, or poet? How does he or she use criticism and persuasion?

Five Kinds of Short Cues

It was Theo Lippman, award-winning editorial writer for the *Baltimore Sun*, in the process roundtable, the celebrated twentieth-century writers' gathering to discuss writing processes (see Chapter 7), who said that he didn't think he could say anything better in 800 words than he could in 350. We make a major point throughout this book of the value of *writing short*. Writing short demands that young writers know and understand their topic and write **precisely.** There is no padding when writers write the most they can in the fewest words.

Short Cues are writing prompts that promote whole pieces of writing in short space and time. In little space, writers can write précis, Word Limiters, and directions. In little time, they can engage in Power Writing and Process Pieces. Short Cues are good for process practice and for both teacher and peer feedback.

Précis

The **précis** (a word of French origin that means a concise written summary of information) is an abstract or prose compilation of important facts and information. In the field of law, it's called a memo. It presents the core or heart of expository or narrative text. (In Chapter 13 we use another term for précis, the *summary*, to talk about writing to learn.)

The précis is short and captures essential points. It demands that young writers

- Determine main ideas and significant facts and distinguish them from supporting examples and details.
- Evaluate meanings in text and construct clear and tight ways to present that meaning.

Précis can be used in a wide array of situations. Consider a précis for Little Red Riding Hood:

> While taking lunch through the forest to grandmother, a little girl is questioned by a wolf who finds out the girl's destination. The wolf arrives at grandmother's before the girl and, dressed in grandmother clothing, awaits the girl's arrival. The girl arrives and remarks about "grandmother's" teeth, eyes, ears. The wolf eventually reveals his identity and attacks the girl. A woodman arrives at the cottage, slays the wolf, and saves the girl.

What's missing in the précis is the elaboration that makes the story a good read. There is no modification, and there is no texture. Only the basic grammar of the story is told.

The writer must know the story. Notice as well that the précis uses no words that aren't near to the story's "bone structure"—its character, setting, problem, and resolution. To write the précis, the writer must write story elements and nothing else.

The précis works at the whole book level too:

> Maniac Magee appeared in town one day and, while only a waif of a boy, he stole people's hearts with his extraordinary physical exploits and admirable soul. He untied Cobble's knot, intercepted the football from Hands Down, faced down Mars Bar, learned the stop ball from Grayson, slept with the deer, tried to tame the kids, and finally moved into a real house, with a number, for the first time in his life.

If you haven't read *Maniac Magee* (Spinelli, 1990), what do you know of the story by reading the précis? The précis tells only about the character. Given that the purpose of the précis is to catch the essence, the bony structure that holds the whole together, what would you say the précis tells you about that essence? Right. It's all about Maniac. There is no story except for Maniac. The précis features the boy because the boy is the story.

A précis can help readers focus on a way to understand a whole piece of nonfiction. A précis for *Cultural Literacy: What Every American Needs to Know* (Hirsch, 1987), for example, might read this way:

> Hirsch questions why, if ability is equally distributed throughout the socioeconomic levels represented in the schools, children perform about equally well in reading, irrespective of social class, only through about the second grade. Thereafter, average and high achievement are more heavily clustered among children of the dominant cultures and middle to upper classes. If the reason could be explained by good and poor teachers or schools, why doesn't the achievement difference appear in the kindergarten? He suggests that the

reason is due to the prior knowledge children bring to school, and the prior knowledge begins to be important in the second grade. Hirsch and his coauthors suggest the schools should ensure that all children have access to the kind of prior knowledge that leads to higher achievement in reading.

The book on which this précis is based has been understood in ways other than the one in the précis. *The précis reveals the way the writer understands the book.*

Given that there is more than one way to understand a story, a book, an article, or an epic poem, there can be more than one précis. Tight and clear writing is certainly one purpose for teaching the précis. However, we also believe that young learners are more likely to understand what they read when there are a variety of perspectives on the reading.

The précis, therefore, is an opportunity for young learners to use writing as a learning strategy through the curriculum, and because the précis is short, children can write many of them. They can also write one, and then exercise the discipline necessary to rewrite it in slightly fewer words. The précis on the Hirsch book above has 129 words. Can you rewrite it in 115 to 120 words? 100 to 105 words? Under 100 words but not fewer than 80? How brief can the rewrite get without compromising the fundamental ideas regarding what the book is about?

Power Writing

The second of the five Short Cues is called **Power Writing** (Fearn, 1980). Most young writers are able to write more than they think they can. Furthermore, most can draft and plan at the same time, thus eliminating most of the procrastination so often associated with planning.

Power Writing is about intensity and writing under pressure. It demands that young writers create their ideas quickly, begin to write, create new and/or continuing ideas even as they draft, and write in the midst of pressure to produce quantity in limited time.

There is merit in what James Thurber said about writing: "Don't get it right; get it written" (Murray, 1990, p. 63). Getting black on white while creating the plan on the run is what the creativity people call fluency. It's pure quantity. The quality increases in direct proportion to the amount of practice young writers have with writing as much as they can and as well as they can. The criterion is always quantity.

The fluency criterion on which Power Writing rests enjoys a long history in creativity research and commentary (Guilford, 1950). Fluency is one of several creative thinking skills that have appeared routinely in the creativity literature. Its purpose is to bring to the surface the myriad ideas we all carry around with us, often unconsciously. In response to the fluency demand, as in the brainstorm, we bring to the surface everything we associate with the task or problem. Once the list of ideas appears in front of us, we can begin the organizational and synergistic processes that so often result in new or at least different ideas. After all, if creativity is the organization and reorganization of knowns, it stands to reason that the more knowns there are, the greater the possibility there is of interesting, maybe even unique, arrangements. Fluency is about producing the list of knowns. Power Writing develops fluency applied to writing.

One more definition is critical here. We refer to the word *draft* over and over in this discussion of fluency, and we also refer to it throughout this book. To *draft* is to put ideas into rough text. The *draft,* then, is that rough text. Rarely included in definitions of *draft* is the assumption that a draft represents a writer's momentarily best effort. Writers do not set out to make their writing rough. Among writers, there are no "sloppy copies." Writers write as well as they can every time they write, knowing that in the draft, the best they can do is an approximation of what their best looks like after their revisions.

Once their fluency has been explored, it's time for the *re vision.* That is when the teacher directs young writers to return to their fluent production and fix it up so it could be hung on the refrigerator door, sent to the newspaper to be published with the young author's name on it, turned in to a teacher for a report card grade, or kept for twenty-five years to show to their own children. Young writers adjust the draft to make it better. In the hundreds of times we have conducted Power Writing, and no matter how many times we have conducted it with the same group of young writers, they always set to work without further prompting, and they always make revisions that make the writing better.

Power Writing offers young writers the opportunity to think of an idea or image about which to write, draft that idea or image, and revise and edit their draft. Because the writing is very short, the whole experience occurs in under ten minutes.

Process Pieces

The third of the five Short Cues is called **Process Pieces** (Fearn, 1985). The Process Pieces activity was developed as a way to help young writers understand how they are approaching and performing their writing. It asks two questions: *What is your writing process today?* and *How did you write that piece?*

Young writers, just like experienced writers, use a variety of processes when they write—even a variety of processes when they all write to the same prompt. Part of learning to write is taking control of writing processes, but before writers can take control, they have to know that a lot of process variety exists, and they need to know how they are using writing processes when they write.

It is also important for young writers to understand what makes writing good. Of course, good writing is mechanically correct, but there is also perfectly dreadful writing in which all the words are spelled conventionally and commas are in all the right places. There is a grand criterion for good writing, and young writers rarely find out what it is if teachers don't teach it. Process Pieces is a place to make sure the grand criterion is featured when we teach writing.

And what is that grand criterion? Read the previous paragraph again. If you think the main idea is that good writing is more than merely mechanically correct and teachers can use Process Pieces to help young writers understand what the "more" is, the writing in the paragraph is "good." It worked. We want our readers to say the main idea is something like what appears in the second sentence in the paragraph above. Good writing is writing that works, and it works if what readers get is at least similar to what the writer had in mind. Process Pieces reveal to young writers what works.

As we show in detail in Chapter 6, Process Pieces writing begins with a teacher cue. The teacher might begin with a word (*dry*) and direct everyone to paint a picture—to see, hear, or otherwise feel what the word suggests to them. That takes about five seconds. The teacher then provides another word (*sandswept*) and directs young writers to reform their image to accommodate the two words (*dry* and *sandswept*). That's another five seconds. The teacher adds a word (*cracked*) and gives the same direction. Now everyone has an image. They write their image in two minutes. They share aloud what they wrote. The teacher solicits what listeners develop as an image as writers read. The teacher asks the writers if what they hear from listeners is what they had in mind when they wrote. If there's a match, the writing is good. If there isn't, the writers speculate on how they can revise to make sure listeners get the image they want them to get.

Word Limiters

The fourth of our Short Cues is called **Word Limiters** (Fearn & Foster, 1979). Whereas Power Writing places a premium on time, Word Limiters place a premium on length. Young writers write three one-minute rounds in Power Writing and one two-minute round in Process Pieces. When they write a Word Limiter, they get a precise word count target (*Describe the appearance of a rose in sixteen words*) or range (*Using not fewer than ten words or more than fourteen, describe the appearance of a rose*).

Young writers face two kinds of demands in this Short Cue. First, they must plan carefully. However, the planning rarely occurs before the writing begins. Most of the time, young writers begin to write, count what they have, scratch out some words, and begin again, this time paying greater attention to word selection. Word Limiters make young writers plan and draft precisely.

It's apparent that young writers predict the number of words in sentences as they write because we see them counting the words on their fingers. They have a target number or range, and it becomes immediately apparent to them that they don't have room for imprecision.

Word Limiters confront young writers with light frustration. They have eleven words to work with, and they have to capture what is important about a book, what is memorable about a flower, what a landfill smells like, or what a sunburn feels like. They get it written and have eighteen words in two sentences. They have to drop seven words, but which ones? They must refigure the writing itself. That's revising. But they think the words they wrote were the right ones, or they wouldn't have written them, so they're reluctant to make the kinds of fundamental changes that include throwing away the original draft. That's what is often frustrating about writing. That is what young writers face when they craft a Word Limiter.

Directions

Finally, there is the Short Cue we all know as *directions*. Most of us have written directions in language arts class. It usually happened around a holiday and involved cooking. The most famous one is *Write directions for roasting a turkey*. Seven year olds don't know much about how to roast a turkey, so they write things that are funny. It's all great fun, and there's good reason to have fun in our classrooms, especially as we learn to write. So go ahead and write more directions for roasting turkeys and making peanut butter and jelly sandwiches.

But we suggest reserving time for some important things to learn about writing well from writing directions. None of these important things is learned, at least not very well, when the activity is conducted mainly for the laugh.

We suggest that young writers write serious directions for accomplishing simple tasks, give the directions to a reader who doesn't know what the directions are written to accomplish, and see if the writing is sufficiently precise to make the reader do exactly what the writer intended. If the writing isn't precise, the writer revises until it is.

For example, can you write directions for drawing a simple geometric shape in four sentences that do not include the name of the geometric shape? (See Chapter 6 for a more complete discussion of this task.) Now give the written directions to someone who, with no oral guidance from you at all, follows the directions as you have written them. When your partner finishes the reading and drawing, is there the shape you intended? If not, which direction threw off the reader? What could you do to revise that sentence so it is more precise?

Aside from the discipline of writing precisely, there is something else going on in this Short Cue. Suppose the cue were to write directions for subtracting 27 from 42? If the first direction reads, "Borrow 1 from the 4," not only is that arithmetically imprecise, it's inaccurate. We don't borrow 1 from 4; we borrow one ten from four tens. The difference is enormous. *Direction writing presupposes that the writer knows the subject very well.* Put another way, the quality of the directions is a window into writers' writing skills, but it also an assessment of the extent to which writers understand what they are writing about.

REVIEW AND REFLECTION

1. Short Cues provide young writers with an opportunity to write whole pieces with an emphasis on fluency and precision. What is a way to use Short Cues to help young writers understand their own writing processes?
2. Several of the Short Cues feature feedback on the basis of which young writers can determine how well they write. What is the difference between criticism and feedback in writing?
3. We described an example of how the direction writing Short Cue can be an assessment of arithmetic knowledge (42 minus 27). What is another example of how a Short Cue can be an assessment tool?

Craft and Interactive Language Arts

The sentence is a basic and essential element in writing and the larger language arts. Over half of the "rules of style" in Strunk and White's *The Elements of Style* (1979) relate specifically to the sentence. The sentence is so fundamental, so essential, in fact, that if people can think in and write good ones, they can write; if they cannot think in and write good sentences, they cannot write.

It's the third day of the second week of the kindergarten. The teacher has the twenty-two children in the class in a semicircle on the rug, their bottoms firmly planted on their own carpet squares, the teacher sitting on a low-slung rocker. There's a Big Book about a squirrel, and the teacher is showing the illustrations, directing children to raise their hand to talk about what they see and to listen as she reads the text on each page. On the third page, the text reads,

"Grey Squirrel sees his nest high in the tree."

The teacher tells the children to close their eyes: "As I read, I want you to try to see what the words tell you. Paint a picture in your head of what the words tell you." Then she reads the passage and closes the book.

"What do you see?" the teacher asks. Everyone has constructed an image, and they all want to share:

Children share their images. © Elizabeth Crews, Stock Boston

> "The nest is made out of sticks."
>
> "There are three squirrels in the nest."
>
> "One is a baby."
>
> The kindergartners had an opportunity to concentrate on, to pay attention to, the message in the sentence and construct an image in their mind. As they share their images, they also discover that there are many possibilities for imaging from the sentence, and their tolerance for multiple perspectives is enhanced.
>
> Their teacher then opens the book and asks, "What do you see?" It turns out that what they said they saw from the words is very much like the illustration on the page. "You are just like the illustrator. You both made pictures from the words."
>
> The conversation about the illustration finished, the teacher returns to the print. Only four children in this classroom can read (it's the second week of school), but that doesn't keep the teacher from using print just as she used the illustration. "Listen as I read from the page: 'Grey Squirrel sees his nest high in the tree.' What did I just read?" the teacher asks. One child says, "Words." Another says, "Sounds."
>
> "Yes, I read the words, and the words have sounds. Look at this." As she reads again, she sweeps her hand over the print, left to right, in time with her read-aloud. "What is this called, this piece of language I just read? What is that called?"
>
> In most kindergartens, even in the second week of school, there will be a student who will say gleefully, "It's a sentence." If there is no such child with the prior knowledge, likely accumulated from hours on someone's lap watching and questioning during read-aloud, the teacher supplies the term: "It's a sentence, boys and girls. It's a sentence. We will work very hard on sentences this year."

That little vignette isn't very dramatic and isn't at all unique. Just about every kindergarten teacher everywhere conducts such a vignette sometime during the year. Kindergarten teachers have that little conversation, and they enhance it throughout the year, because it's the right and natural conversation to have with kindergarten children about language, reading, books, and print.

The conversation doesn't appear to be about writing, not in the second week of the kindergarten when only four children in the room can read. But in fact it is precisely about writing because we can't talk about sentences without talking about writing, and it's the sentence to which the teacher refers in that Big Book early in the year. It's also about the main idea in the sentence. The interaction between reading print and writing it is natural and automatic.

As the teacher initiates a formal sense of what a sentence looks like, sounds like, and does, she is establishing a foundation for writing that will be used sometime during the year and will be elaborated on for the rest of every child's life. That's what the interaction between writing and the larger language arts means. It's also what intentional instruction in writing looks and sounds like during the second (or sixth, ninth, or sixteenth) week of the kindergarten.

Some kindergarten teachers take the conversation further very soon. "What does the sentence make you see?" a teacher will ask, and he'll make the point that sentences can do that—make you see something. "Sentences help us paint pictures or think of ideas," the teacher reminds the children.

The conversation about sentences is about what sentences do, and there will be a lot of such talk over the school year. There will also be conversation about what sentences look like: "There's a dot at the end of the sentence, and that dot is called a period. It tells readers when the sentence is finished. We need those periods. They are like signs on the roads outside. If we didn't have signs, we'd never know where to stop. If we don't have periods, we don't know where the sentence stops." That's intentional instruction. Every time there is reference to the period, it's an instance of practice. Every time the teacher writes something and calls attention to the period, it's another instance of practice.

As soon as the first child writes a sentence on purpose, the teacher reminds that child about the end mark. The deliberate focus, or attention, is on the image or idea, and with practice, the automatic attention includes the period.

Just as the youngsters create their ideas and images and automatically attend to periods, they also learn to pay automatic attention to spelling every word as well as they can. They are only five years old, so they don't spell very many words correctly, but the teacher knows that if they pay attention every time they write, they will practice moving toward conventional spelling. It isn't so much lists of accurately spelled words that make a good young writer; it's daily and progressive movement toward conventional spelling because they know it is important.

These kindergarten children don't "fail" their work for lack of end marks and conventional spelling, and spelling and periods certainly don't dominate the interactive language arts. Instead, the children write as much as they can, as well as they can, every day. Throughout the year there are daily references to and reminders of the craft of writing in the print they read, the print the teacher reads aloud, the print the teacher writes on the board, and the print the children write on newsprint as they sprawl on the floor, markers in hand.

The Role of Craft in Balanced Writing Instruction

In 1851 Léon Foucault used a pendulum to demonstrate Earth's rotation. He didn't invent the pendulum. It isn't clear, in fact, that the pendulum resulted from anyone's invention, but in 1554, while studying the hanging lamps in the cathedral of Pisa, Galileo concluded that the time of the swing was independent of the swing's width. He wasn't strictly correct, but his studies did direct attention toward the pendulum and accurate clocks. That's probably more than you needed to know about the pendulum, but it leads to a point, and who knows when the pendulum information might come in handy if you have to dazzle your friends at a party.

The point has to do with craft in balanced writing instruction. One of the annoying characteristics of some observers of education, both inside the profession and out, is their apparent inability to comprehend complexities because they see the world in simplicities. We refer specifically to swings of the pendulum. If it isn't this "method," it must be that one. We have what are referred to as "reading wars"—controversies that pop up every several decades over whether we do or do not teach phonics. In mathematics, the pendulum swings to arithmetic operations at one end or problem solving at the other. In history, it's tradition at one end or revisionism at the other. They force the whole curricular world into those kinds of narrowly defined pendulum swings.

So it is in writing instruction. There was a time when English curriculum was divided into three components: literature, language, and composition. Literature meant reading from the classic-laden canon and then writing reports. Language meant **"grammar,"** a euphemism for diagramming sentences, seeking adjectives in lists of sentences on worksheets (or worse, in naked lists of words), and putting apostrophes into singular and plural possessives that appear in sentences. Then there was composition, which meant a piece of writing turned in to the teacher every Friday and returned on Monday with comments and a grade.

In the 1970s, we began to look at writing in terms of how people do the act itself. A different conception of writing was called by the name *process,* which we describe in detail in Chapters 7 and 8. With the advent of what began to be known as "process writing," there were some, both in and out of the profession, who so dichotomized the field that if a teacher talked about the need to teach sentence parts (adjectives, pronouns, and predicates, for example), that teacher had violated the process. On the other hand, detractors have said that a process emphasis means there is no discipline in language instruction, so it is no wonder the children aren't writing so well any more.

Craft has a critical role in balanced writing instruction, just as balanced writing instruction has a critical role in interactive language arts. The ability to craft written language is fundamental to writing well. Crafting written language might be akin to shooting a jump shot in basketball; certainly a jump shot is critical to playing basketball, but it isn't playing basketball. Writing good sentences and spelling the words conventionally are critical to writing, but they aren't all there is to writing.

A Summary: Craft

Craft in balanced writing instruction focuses on sentences, how sentences cohere, paragraphs, how paragraphs cohere, and the meaning markers known as capitalization and punctuation. Craft is always taught as writing and uses young writers' own writing for instruction. It is systematic and direct, with the system and direction dictated largely by the needs of the young writers we are teaching. Of course, we "seed" those needs along the way in order to ensure that the balance we seek in learning to write occurs. But if we are absolutely effective in teaching craft, and craft alone, we remain far short of satisfying the objectives of balanced writing instruction.

REVIEW AND REFLECTION

1. If we teach about sentences in the kindergarten as described in the Grey Squirrel vignette, the assumption is that we're establishing a craft foundation for writing. What might be another kindergarten vignette that adds to the foundation?

2. How do you think teachers should use what they write on the board when only a small fraction of the children can read?

3. Do you think children's creativity or spontaneity is compromised by systematically teaching aspects of craft when you teach writing? If so, how would that be apparent in their writing?

4. Have you ever seen a Foucault pendulum? Write a sentence about how Galileo was right and another about how he was wrong regarding time and distance. Reduce the length of your sentence by 20 percent of the words. Is that using craft instruction across the curriculum? How is the writing creative?

4 Teaching Craft: Sentences

BEFORE YOU READ

- Learning demands attention. How do we make craft instruction sufficiently compelling that young writers concentrate on the lessons?
- Learning occurs when learners understand lessons on their own terms. How do we ensure that young writers think and write their own creations of the craft?
- How can direct instruction promote the kind of practice that will make young writers accomplished with the craft of writing, while at the same time supporting the creative discipline in writing?
- How much instructional time in a balanced writing program should be committed to the craft?
- What is the nature of the interaction between craft instruction and oral language development and use?

Getting Ready to Teach the Writer's Craft

We saw in Chapter 3 that craft in writing involves how language is constructed. Craft by itself is not writing, any more than scales are music or the jump shot is basketball. Craft is building blocks. Craft mastery is absolutely necessary for writing well, but it isn't sufficient, just as mastery of the craft of carpentry is not sufficient for making furniture, but the ability to use tools properly in the working of wood is absolutely necessary.

The ability to use sentences, relationships between and among sentences, paragraphs, relationships between and among paragraphs, and basic mechanical conventions is necessary to write well. Young writers learn to craft the language by paying attention to and practicing accurate approximations of what good writers do when they write well. This chapter features classroom operations that focus on the craft dimension of balanced writing instruction. The craft lessons in this chapter represent approximations of how good writers think and write.

These are daily lessons for intentional instruction that represent approximations of how writers think and write. They lead young writers to a literacy goal over time. Even the most accomplished writers do not admit to having mastered the sentence, for example, for no one ever expects to be able to write the very best sentence possible, one after another. Everyone continues to experiment and learn so they can write as many of the best sentences possible. Young writers should experiment and learn every day throughout their formal school experience.

Remember that balanced writing instruction is not hierarchical. That we begin with craft does not mean that we teach craft until young writers learn it, then teach process, and then write stories or reports. Balanced writing instruction features craft, processes, and genres all at once, and while some of the chapters in this book categorize elements of balanced writing instruction for explanation, even here it is impossible to accomplish isolation. Writing processes underlie all writing instruction, even at the level of simple sentences in this chapter. When young writers get beyond one sentence, what they write begins to take on **form,** or attributes of genre. We recognize those "splash-overs" into processes and genres as we describe instruction in the craft of writing.

Oral Language

We begin by emphasizing to young writers that writing is something that goes on in the mind. We can push it out of our mouths or out of our pencils, but it goes on in the mind.

Formal craft lessons can begin within a week or two at the beginning of the kindergarten and at virtually any other point in the English-language acquisition process, because the writing that goes on in the mind can be displayed or revealed just as well orally as scribally. (Scribal writing is a hard copy record.)

Writing occurs mentally. We think progressively automatically in the sentences we write as we become increasingly accomplished. Then we display the result of the thinking, the construction of the mind, orally. In fact, the whole process is oral and aural (listening) because the mental monitoring is hearing. We hear the language being developed in our minds, even as it is being developed.

ESL The value of deliberate mental language for students whose native language is not English is obvious. In their earliest deliberate writing sessions, in English or in their primary language, writing is explicitly oral and aural. Those are the sensory domains in which language is acquired in the first place. ■

Not only is writing an oral and aural experience in its construction, it's oral and aural in display. When Rachel raises her hand and talks her sentence, the sentence sound goes out into the room's ether for everyone to hear. If the teacher repeats Rachel's sentence, the sound is heard twice in the room. If the teacher asks Rachel to say her sentence again, it is heard three times, and then the teacher repeats Rachel's repeat, and the sound of the sentence permeates the room four times. Rachel constructs her sentence once and writes it orally twice. She hears her sentence repeated by the teacher twice. There are six children who volunteer their sentences today. That's 24 sounds of children's sentences. There are five days in the week, and if what we did on Monday were repeated each of those days, the children would have direct experience with 120 sentence sounds. Shall we spend five minutes every day through the year with such oral writing activities? That would put 4,320 sounds of sentences into children's aural spaces. If that is not enough English sentence sounds for language learners to acquire a sense of the pitch, juncture, and intonation patterns in English sentences, it's certainly a robust start.

Oral practice also promotes fluency in writing. In the earliest years and the earliest stages of learning to write, scribal writing is slowed dramatically because young learners' concentration is on the details of getting it down rather than the communication. That is inevitable. No matter how temporary the details are, the youngsters have to concentrate on them because the skills aren't yet automatic. In the time they spend thinking about a detail (spelling), they cannot think about the big picture (sentence). With the oral display of sentences they have written in their minds (oral writing), all of the concentration on details is eliminated. They construct the sentence and write it orally, completely circumventing the surface details that can so confound the earliest writers.

It is important to notice in the craft material throughout this chapter, and especially in the earliest stages of sentence learning, that young writers work at the oral level first. Then they display their sentences on paper. And when they go to paper, they have already rehearsed their sentence mentally to such an extent that they can concentrate on some of the surface details without compromising the larger sentence objective.

Scope and Sequence

Scope and *sequence* are curricular terms that refer to *what* will be taught, *to whom*, and *when*. Scope and sequence in this chapter are arranged in four parallel strands. Because craft learning is important at all levels of the instructional program, there are applications through the grades. However, because craft instruction and learning occur differentially from student to student at all levels of the instructional program, each instructional application of the craft has to be applied according to the students for whom it is intended.

In K–12 schooling, there are thirteen grades for which differential applications have to be made, but it isn't necessary to make thirteen explicitly different applications of a given activity. In this chapter, there are five levels:

1. The *K–1 level,* for early primary children, initial learners, or even older ones who need the earliest sort of instruction in the craft of writing.

2. The *2–3 level,* for later primary learners, children who already know how to think about and use basic attributes of craft, or even older learners who need instruction or refresher work on more basic craft understandings.

3. The *4–5 level,* for upper elementary learners who are ready to handle some of the more sophisticated attributes of the craft. These may even be middle-level or secondary students who need to think about and practice some attributes of craft necessary to work effectively in middle-level or secondary classrooms.

4. The *6–8 level,* for middle-level students who have a good foundation from earlier years on which to build the insights and the practice necessary to be effective mature writers. If middle-level students lack that foundation, we go back and establish it.

5. The *secondary level,* for mature writers who have the foundation necessary to write relatively accurate extended discourse automatically and can benefit from direct instruction in some of the more complex applications of what they already know.

Those are the five parallel levels of application on which this chapter is based. With each activity, the five applications are not of equal length. Some craft activities are more foundational, and while there are weeks of application at the K–1 level, there may only be ten minutes worth at the 6–8 level.

When we think about what to teach and when, we grapple with curricular scope and sequence. Scope and sequence in this chapter refer also to how instruction is applied to three kinds of teaching and learning:

Awareness instruction, that is, calling attention to something about writing so young writers can learn to notice it and begin to work with it. Awareness can occur in ten minutes or ten months, depending on the learners, what they bring to the learning task, and their special needs.

Concentrated practice through direct, or intentional, and systematic instruction. Direct, or intentional, and systematic instruction is intended to establish a skill or a way of thinking about writing. This can occur over a period of years, depending entirely on the individual attributes of the learners.

Teaching for mastery, or practice. This teaching occurs over very long periods of time—in the case of the very best writers, over a lifetime. It aims at eventual automatic use of a skill.

It is necessary for young writers to write in the craft every day. We begin with sentence thinking and writing. With the very first instance of instruction, young writers begin the sentence-a-day. Later it will be a paragraph-a-day, a whole process-a-day, a genre-a-day. Beginning in kindergarten, young writers write well at least one time every day.

Becky's oral sentence: These are my fingers.

Sentences

The **sentence** is where writing begins. People who can write a sentence can write; people who cannot write a sentence cannot write. We have made three propositions clear:

- Writing a sentence is not an act of faith.
- The sentence is a thoughtful, deliberate, planful piece of writing that becomes increasingly automatic in thinking and writing the more it is practiced.
- The sentence is a whole piece of language, not an arrangement of parts.

We begin thinking about instruction with those three propositions in mind.

Sentences from Observations

Language Arts Standard

Students listen to oral messages and respond in clear and coherent sentences.

Young writers need to be aware that they can commit everything they see and hear to sentences, they can share their sentences with an audience, and the audience can make meaning from sentences. The children become increasingly aware of the sound and use of sentences by thinking about them, sharing them, and listening to them.

Sentences from Observations is one of the earliest craft awareness activities. It can begin within a week or two of the opening of the kindergarten year.

 INSTRUCTIONAL SCENARIO

In the Classroom with Sentences from Observation

Teacher: Boys and girls, we are going to write this morning. Yes, I know, you don't know how to make all your letters yet, but that won't matter because we are going to write in our heads. Always remember, writing is something that goes on in your head. Then you can push it out of your pencil, or you can push it out of your mouth. This morning, we will write in our heads, and we will push it out of our mouths. Everyone, I want you to look around the room and find something you might like to write about. Just look around until you see something.

Justin, do you have something? Good. It's a book. Good. Everyone. Find something and hold it in your head.

Now think of a sentence that contains what you found. Think of one sentence. Your sentence will have the thing you found in it. Shantel?

Shantel: A book?

Teacher: You found a book, Shantel?

Shantel: Yes.

Teacher: Tell me in a sentence, Shantel. [If Shantel does, you're on your way. If she doesn't understand, model the sentence.] Your sentence might sound like this: *I found a book.* You tell me your sentence, Shantel.

Shantel: *I found a book.*

Teacher: Good, Shantel. That is a sentence. Let us hear your sentence again. [Shantel reads her sentence from her mind. Write Shantel's sentence on the board, and read it aloud.] Shantel, read your sentence. [Shantel reads.] You read that very well. Who else has a sentence to share with us?

COMMENTARY

The teacher did several instructional things in the scenario:

- She reflected to Shantel that she can write.
- She established that writing is thinking.
- She provided a source for thinking about something to write.

- She solicited student writing and used a model for corrective feedback.
- She asked for the correct piece of writing from the young writer.
- She reinforced the correct writing by calling attention to the fact that Shantel did it, and she named what Shantel did.
- She wrote Shantel's sentence on the board and ensured that Shantel could read her own sentence.
- She provided another example of what she sought: the sentence.

The teacher focused on Shantel's sentence, not the book, because the lesson is about the sentence. In the scenario, the kindergarten students heard the sound of a good sentence three times.

E S L Notice that the teacher reads (repeats) young writers' sentences as each child shares. That puts the sound of the teacher's voice into the room. One of the most powerful influences in language learning is modeling. As a general principle, the greater the representation there is of ESL learners in the classroom, the greater is the need for the sound of the teacher's model. In this case, the sound isolates the English sentence. ■

The scenario features thinking, oral language, listening, and reading, all in the context of writing one directed sentence. Thus, the whole of the language arts interact to accomplish a single and whole writing achievement.

VARIATIONS

Sentences from Observations can be used in a wide variety of situations:

1. "Close your eyes and listen for sounds. Think of a sentence that contains the name of a sound you hear."
2. "Think about what you see when you walk home from school. Think of a sentence that contains the name of something you see when you walk home from school."
3. "Remember what the kitchen in your home looks like. Think of something you have in your kitchen. Think of a sentence that contains something you have in your kitchen."
4. "When you are outside at night, what might you see? Think of a sentence that contains the name of something you might see when you are outside at night."

E S L Capitalize on the children's experiences in Sentences from Observations. The sentences come from the *children's* experiences, some of which can be quite specific to the world that the children in a diverse classroom inhabit. Honor those experiences, and promote them as appropriate. Give young writers the opportunity to think and write in the experiences they bring to school. That is what is authentic about their early writing. ■

Sentences from Observations Through the Grades

Levels 2–3:   Second and third graders can respond to cues and tasks very much like those in the instructional scenario for K–1 learners, and they can do so both orally and on paper. Whenever they think and write, the basic mechanical conventions are important on an age-appropriate basis. When they ask how to spell a word, we tell them to spell it as well as they can. We use the sentences they read aloud as object lessons for capitalization and punctuation, but we remember that the focus is on sentence thinking and writing.

A simple fluency activity can provide a wide array of ideas for sentence thinking and writing. For example, solicit a list of red things children see around the room, or green, yellow, flat, fluffy, or long things they see around the room, on their way to school, at home, or on the playground. Write the children's suggestions on the board, so each idea can be the basis for a sentence thinking and writing cue—for example:

"Write a sentence that contains the name of something that is red."

"Write a sentence that contains the names of two things that are yellow."

In the second and third grades, young writers can look around the room and think of things that come in twos, then think in and write sentences that contain the numbers and the names of the things:

"Write a sentence that contains the name of something that comes in threes."

Second and third graders will be writing their sentences on paper and reading them aloud. Spelling as conventionally as possible (see Chapter 14) is always important. Seven and eight year olds understand that words have a certain appearance that they have begun to recognize from their reading, specifically, and from exposure to print, generally.

Second and third graders wrote the following responses to sentences from observation:

The flag represents our country.

The Fraction Quilt is full of colors.

On the wall I see pitchers.

The disk in the cmputer.

Grades 2–3

Language Arts Standard

Students will write clear and coherent sentences that elaborate on a central impression.

Sentences from Observations can be a craft warm-up, a prerecess organizer, a postrecess settler, or a homework assignment that takes three to five minutes. By the end of the third grade, this activity will be used in social studies, science, the aesthetics, and other content areas.

Language Arts Standard

Students will select a focus for paragraph-length writing and create paragraphs that present and explain the central focus.

Levels 4–5:   During a field trip to the local police station, the children carry a pad of paper and take informal notes in single words and phrases. When they return to the classroom, they think in and write three single sentences, each of which contains one item from their list.

We conduct increasingly complex fluency activities in the fourth and fifth grades—for example:

"Make a list of things that come in fours, fives, or sevens, and think in and write sentences that contain those items."

"Write two single sentences, each of which contains one agricultural export from Costa Rica. Put the export in the first half of one sentence, and put the export in the second half of the other sentence."

Language Arts Standard

Students will develop a topic sentence.

A topic sentence activity can be used for other senses—for example:

"What is the one-sentence description for musical passages that will help readers know which music is being played?"

"Is it one soft drink, or is it another?"

"How can the tastes of soft drinks or wedges of fresh fruit be written in single sentences so readers know which one is being described?"

Sentences from Observations also can be used for homework and various organizational activities—for example:

"Notice what company made your refrigerator. Write a sentence that contains the name of that company."

"Find where the box of salt is kept in your kitchen, and write a sentence that contains the name of that location."

The following sentences are characteristic of how fourth and fifth graders handle Sentences from Observation.

My Poster about David Livingstone caught my eye when I was looking around because I used bright colors and attracting things

The sweater is very, very warm and cozy.

Mancala is a very fun game to play, especially me.

Grades 4–5

Levels 6–8: After about the fifth grade, Sentences from Observations can be used with four or five ideas or variations on the four or five suggestions. It is useful to emphasize writing in subject matter areas—for example:

"Make a list of what you know about a triangle. Write a sentence that includes one item from your list. Write a sentence for each item on your list. Arrange your sentences into a paragraph about triangles."

Given Word Sentences

The Given Word Sentence—a sentence that contains a given or dictated word—is a *deliberate* opportunity for young writers to think *deliberately* at the sentence level. Writers often think *deliberately* when they write, but first, and even eighth, graders, don't know what that means. Most confuse it with being quiet and looking as if they're paying attention. If we want them to think *deliberately* when they write, we have to use writing activities that make them think *deliberately* when they write. Notice the italicized word throughout this paragraph. The Given Word Sentence helps young writers learn to plan deliberately when they write sentences.

INSTRUCTIONAL SCENARIO

In the Classroom with Given Word Sentences, a Sentence That Contains a Given Word

Teacher: Boys and girls, think of a sentence that contains the word *rain*. I want one sentence, and one word in that sentence has to be *rain*. Write the sentence in your mind. We will push it out of our mouths this morning. Anton?

Anton: *It will rain today.*

Teacher: *It will rain today.* Yes, Anton, that is a sentence. Someone give me another one. [Solicit up to five or six sentences. Reinforce each one by calling it a sentence. Write two or three of the offerings on the board. Call on a child whose sentence is on the board to read it. If it's early in the kindergarten year, read the sentence first to put the sound of it in the child's head. Then ask the child to read it.]

COMMENTARY

The Given Word Sentence takes three forms, graduated in demand for concentration. A sentence that contains a given word is one form. The next form dictates the given word and the sentence length, and the third form also dictates the position of the given word in the sentence. The more concentration there is, the more thoughtful planning the children engage in. The sentence thinking may not be an exploration of a writer's own purpose, but it does provide young writers with a genuine opportunity to recognize what sentence planning is and feels like.

E S L Young English-language learners exert enormous concentration on their English-language lessons. This is an opportunity to capitalize on their deliberate attention by focusing it on learning that will pay explicit rewards. If the youngsters concentrate on the language development in this kind of activity, they will learn to think in and write sentences that work. ▪

A classroom Word Wall.
© 1994 Jean-Claude
LeJeune, Stock Boston

In this first of three variations of the sentence thinking and writing activity, young writers think in sentence form and include a word given to them. It can be a spelling word, a vocabulary word, one of the words-of-the-day that appears on the Word Wall, or a miscellaneous word the teacher thinks everyone will know.

The teacher listens to young writers' sentences and repeats them aloud. In direct and deliberate writing instruction, especially in the earliest grades, there is a specific purpose for the repetitions. Early in the learning process, children must begin to hear what sentences are supposed to sound like. They need an automatic and auditory sense of the difference between sentences and non-sentences.

Literate writers **subaudibly** "hear" their sentences being played out as they emerge on the screen or flow from their pen. Young writers can learn to access the same kinds of sentence cues that experienced writers use. That is why teachers repeat young writers' sentences.

The first instructional scenario above focused on a given word in a sentence. That is one level of deliberate attention in the Given Word Sentence activity. The next scenario increases the magnitude of deliberate attention by focusing young writers' concentration on both a given word and sentence length.

Something very different occurs in this variation on the Given Word Sentence. In the first variation, where the children are given a word to include in the sentence, the children clearly concentrate, but their concentration is on trying to find a way to get the given word into a sentence. In the second variation, almost

INSTRUCTIONAL SCENARIO

In the Classroom with Given Word Sentences, a Sentence of Specified Length

Kristina [in response to the teacher's cue to think of a sentence that contains the word *rain*]: *Rain is good for plants.*

Teacher: *Rain is good for plants.* Yes, Kristina, that is a sentence. Listen to Kristina's sentence, boys and girls. Kristina, read your sentence again. [Kristina reads.] Boys and girls, how many words are there in Kristina's sentence? Read again, Kristina. [Kristina reads.] Larry? Yes, there are five words in Kristina's sentence. Everyone, I want you to think of a sentence that contains the word *rain,* but this time I want your sentence to contain exactly five words. Think of a five-word sentence in which one of the words is *rain.*

Larry: *The rain fell down.*

COMMENTARY

Language Arts Standard

Students will write clear and coherent sentences.

Clearly the children have to be more sophisticated than most are during the second week of the kindergarten to handle this variation on the Given Word Sentence. We have conducted this variation successfully in many first grades and throughout the grades thereafter.

everyone in the room begins to count. (When we conduct the activity with adults, everyone counts too.) Although counting is not writing, experienced writers do pay attention to the construction of their sentences, and that is what young writers are doing, primitively perhaps, when they count.

Watch as it unfolds in a second-grade classroom. There's Jorge in the front row. He's counting the words on his fingers. He stopped and started again with his first finger. Oops, he stopped again and returned to his first finger. He is deliberately attending to the construction of his sentence and realizing halfway through that he has too many (or too few) words. He stops and begins again. He is not only counting; he is paying deliberate attention to how he is forming his sentence. He is listening to it being played out. He hears the end coming, and he realizes that the end he hears, but hasn't achieved yet, is more than five words away. So he stops and starts another sentence.

Experienced writers listen to how their sentences are being played out, and they reconstruct as they go to make sure they are writing sentences, not nonsentences. They listen for the sentence sound. Young writers can learn to listen for the sentence sound as well. Second graders wrote in response to the following Given Word Sentence prompts:

Second-grade Given Word Sentence response.

"Think of a three-word sentence that contains the word *rain*."

"Think of a four-word sentence that contains the word *rain*."

"Think of a five-word sentence that contains the word *rain*."

"Think of a five-word sentence that contains the word *snow* [or another weather word]."

"Think of a four-word sentence that contains the word *animal* [or another spelling word]."

"Think of a five-word sentence that contains the word *city* [or another social studies word]."

Given Word Sentences Through the Grades

Language Arts Standard

Students will write clear and coherent sentences that elaborate on a central impression.

Levels 2–3:   If second or third graders have worked with the Given Word Sentence in earlier grades, this is the time to extend sentence length. If they haven't experienced Given Word Sentences, begin with a K–1 scenario. Second graders are able to think in and write these kinds of deliberate sentences up to eight or ten words long. Third graders can extend to a dozen words.

We do not assume that long sentences are better sentences. On the contrary, throughout this book, we advocate writing short rather than long. Young writers need to know that they can make their writing accomplish whatever they want it to accomplish. That includes the ability to write longer sentences that incorporate a variety of details.

Longer sentences aren't merely short sentences with more words. Longer sentences demand a longer attention span, the ability to think in longer passages that include greater detail, and the ability to keep the word flow going through an extended idea. All of that is learned.

INSTRUCTIONAL SCENARIO

In the Classroom with Given Word Sentences, the Position of the Given Word Is Specified

Teacher: We have been thinking in and writing three- and four- and five-word sentences for two weeks now. We also wrote two stories in the past two weeks, and everyone wrote four autobiographical incidents. The social studies group wrote two collaborative biographies on famous musicians, and the mathematics research group is still working on its reports about the geoboards. Kristina, I think you were the one who gave us that first five-word sentence. Do you remember it?

Kristina: *Rain is good for plants.*

Teacher: Yes, that was it. Everyone, listen to Kristina's sentence again, and let me know where our word is. In which of the five positions in Kristina's sentence is the word *rain*? Yes, it is the first word. Kristina wrote a five-word sentence with *rain* in the first position. Everyone, think of a five-word sentence with *rain* in the first position.

COMMENTARY

Kristina and her friends are in the second grade. Watch the intense concentration this time. The children will recite very patterned-sounding sentences. Kristina's sentence had *rain good for plants.* The next four will have *rain good for all manner of things.* "Good!" the teacher will say, and she'll read back every sentence. This is about the sounds of sentences in the room, and deliberate attention applied to the construction of sentences.

Here are some more prompts:

"Think of a five-word sentence in which the word *rain* is in the second position."

"Think of a five-word sentence in which the word *rain* is in the third position."

"Think of a five-word sentence in which the word *rain* is in the fourth position."

"Think of a five-word sentence in which the word *rain* is in the fifth position."

This is what four second graders wrote in response to those Given Word Sentence prompts:

The rain will come down.

It is hard rain today.

The strom mad cold rain.

Today There is rain outsid.

Second-grade Given Word Sentence responses.

Now the teacher says, "Boys and girls, look what you just did. You wrote four sentences that contained the word *rain* in four different positions. You can make your sentences do anything you want them to do. You can think them one way or think them another. We will practice this sort of sentence thinking all year." When you use Given Word Sentences, notice the positive effects of the youngsters' growing feeling of competence.

Also in the second grade, but more likely the third, this activity is an excellent opportunity to initiate the writing-spelling interaction. Rather than mere dictation, for example, which demands only that test takers remember the dictated sentence and copy it from memory, the first word on the test could be stated as follows:

"Number One: *door*. Write a five-word sentence in which *door* is in the third position."

Now the test takers have to spell the word correctly in their own thoughtful sentence. Third graders are thinking and writing in the spelling test. Of course, teachers determine whether students must spell all of the words in each sentence correctly.

The red door is open.

Our screen door broke yesterday.

The wooden door burned up.

Third-grade spelling test with Given Word Sentences.

Levels 4–5: Use the Given Word Sentence as a warm-up exercise for sentence lessons, as a quick think-and-write just before or after recess, or as independent sentence practice for five to ten minutes of homework. Some teachers have placed a box of writing cues (Given Word Sentence Q-cards) just inside the classroom door. As students enter in the morning, they take a Q-card and write to the cue during any independent time. Their writing is their "ticket to recess." On the way to morning recess, they give their paper to the teacher and drop the Q-card in the box. Coming in from recess, they pick up a new Q-card, and the sentence becomes their ticket to lunch. They do it again for afternoon recess. That strategy ensures three deliberate sentences every day. The teacher spot-reads the sentences and may share some orally with the class. Then the teacher puts the sentence papers in the "pick-up" box for students who want to get theirs back. At the end of every week, those left in the "pick-up" box are discarded. Remember, this is practice at deliberate thinking and writing in sentences.

Language Arts Standard

Students will apply knowledge of language structure and language conventions in their writing.

Nine and ten year olds can continue their practice with longer sentences, and teachers can use Given Word Sentences in spelling activities. When there is a priority on language structure, for example, and if the spelling word were *door,* there could be several sentence thinking and writing activities such as those that follow:

"Write a five-word sentence in which *door* appears in the fourth position."

"Write a six-word sentence in which *door* appears in the fourth position."

"Write a six-word sentence in which *door* appears in an odd-numbered position."

"Write a seven-word sentence in which *door* is used as a noun in the third position."

"Write a seven-word sentence in which *door* is preceded by an adjective in the third position."

In prompts such as 4 and 5, we assume that fourth and fifth graders have already worked with definitions and the traditional "underline the nouns" activities. Now they pay deliberate attention to sentence parts applied to their own writing.

E S L That vocabulary is learned in sentence context is virtually self-evident. However, merely writing a sentence that contains the new word has very little to do with knowing the new word. Because native English speakers have a deep and detailed sense of their language, they are able to sense an adjective-sounding word on a vocabulary list and put it in an adjective position in their vocabulary sentence (*ferocious—It was a ferocious tiger*). English-language learners do not have that deep sense of how English works, so their concentration on word meanings and their attention to how words are used will help them get more out of traditional word study. ■

Fourth and fifth graders work heavily on the writing-vocabulary interaction (see Chapter 15), an excellent activity for writing with new words or writing with words in new ways. Here is an example:

"Think of a sentence that contains the word *cell.* Now, think of a six-word sentence in which *cell* is used in the fourth position."

The second instruction makes greater thinking and writing demands. It becomes increasingly necessary for the young writers to know what a word means and how it can be used when the position of the word in a sentence is dictated.

There are many cells in blood.

Oxygen is made by photosynthesis.

The sun makes photosynthesis possible.

Fifth-grade writing-vocabulary interactions with Given Word Sentences.

Levels 6–8:   The Given Word Sentence continues to be a thinking and writing activity that emphasizes concentration and deliberate planning. It is enough of an intellectual puzzle that middle-level learners will find it interesting.

If sentence parts receive attention, here is a good place to make applications—for example:

"Write a sentence that contains an adverb."

"Write an eight-word sentence in which an adverb appears in an odd-numbered position in the second half of the sentence."

The point in such instruction is not terminology; the point is the function of various sentence parts *in sentences that young writers write.* It isn't enough for the young learners to know that a word is an adjective, and it isn't even enough to know an adjective is a descriptive word. Students must know that adjectives have an impact on nouns in their own sentences. The following sentences show that young writers can write sentences that contain modifiers, not merely define modifiers. The prompt is at the left.

| Adverb, odd-numbered position | The herd of young antelopes leaped *high* enough.—Kelley, seventh grade |

| Adverb, odd-numbered position | Marcie asked *quietly* about the hymn.
—Stephanie, seventh grade |
| Adjective, odd-numbered position | No one ever knew about the *crippled* man.
—Paul, seventh grade |

Middle-level students also use the Given Word Sentence for the spelling and vocabulary interactions explained for grades 4 and 5. In addition, consider the frustrations that upper-elementary and middle-level teachers often experience when students do well on tests but don't use the forms properly when they write. A group of seventh graders successfully completed a test on singular and plural possessives, but when they were asked to write a sentence that contained a singular possessive, they were confused. It was interesting to see several of them, after they wrote Given Word Sentences, look up suddenly with that, *Oh, now I get it!* surprise. Young writers don't necessarily understand or use possessives merely because they can insert apostrophes in sentences. They understand and can use apostrophes when they can write with possessives.

Secondary Level: It is not uncommon to hear high school teachers lament that students "can't even write a sentence." Of course, they *can* write a sentence, but they might not be doing it with the deliberateness that produces graceful or even merely thoughtful extended discourse. The Given Word Sentence activity helps develop the deliberateness.

Sentence Sessions

The Sentence Sessions are among the more powerful writers' craft development activities. They generalize to just about any writing instruction purpose or any need young writers can have in learning to write. It is probably safe to say that Sentence Sessions, properly used in all of their variations, could be the craft foundation of balanced writing instruction.

There are now three ideas to arrange and two possible rearrangements. This can be a very revealing activity for young writers, for it is clear to them after a while that they have enormous power with a pencil in their hand. They can put ideas in just about any order in a sentence, and they hear a wide variety of variations on how the same three ideas can make images in sentences.

But when they begin rearranging three ideas, they *have to change* the form of one or two of them. If they begin with an old man driving a car in the rain, then have to put the old man at the end of the sentence, they might write that it was raining on the car when the old man drove to the store. Now it isn't *rain* as a noun; it's *raining* as a verb. They don't necessarily know how to describe it, but they can do it, and the teacher calls attention to it: "Look, Romel, you changed the word from *rain* to *raining*. Boys and girls, what are some other ways we can write words that have *rain* in them?" Among the possibilities are *rain, raining, rained,* and *rainy.* In later grades, someone always says *reign.*

INSTRUCTIONAL SCENARIO

In the Classroom with a Single Sentence Session

Teacher (second grade): I am going to write an idea on the board, and I want you to think of a sentence that contains the idea. We are working with an idea this time, not a word. You don't have to use the word or the words I write on the board. All I want in your sentences is the idea. For example, how could I put an old man in a sentence without using those words—without writing the words *old man*? Corliss?

Corliss: You could say *grandfather*.

Teacher: Yes, that would work because grandfathers are usually older men. Chloe?

Chloe: *Old codger*?

Teacher: That would work too. Good. You don't have to use *old man,* but you may. You may also use any other word or words that will put the idea of old man in your sentence. Now think of a sentence that contains the idea of old man, and write it in your mind. Jesse?

Jesse: *My grandpa likes to read to me.*

Teacher: *My grandpa likes to read to me.* That's a sentence. Good, Jesse. Ruthie?

Ruthie: *When my granddad comes to my house, he always brings me some presents.*

Teacher: *When my granddad comes to my house, he always brings me some presents.* Yes, Ruthie, that is a sentence. [After five sentences, each with a reference to a grandfather, the teacher changes the task.] Those are all sentences. Now I want you to think of a sentence that contains the idea of old man, but the old man can't be your grandfather. Think of another way to get an old man into your sentence. Yes, Pietro, you had something right away.

Pietro: It's the one I had before. *There was an old man in the store when I went to get my new shoes.*

COMMENTARY

Language Arts Standard

Students will apply knowledge of language structure and conventions to create a point.

It is important for young writers to begin managing ideas as quickly as possible in balanced writing instruction.

A Single Sentence Session begins the sentence thinking and writing process formally without making it mysterious. The teacher states the idea that will be included in the sentence; young writers decide what words they will use to fulfill the given idea, and they construct their own sentence to accommodate the idea.

This is, in fact, what experienced writers do when they write. Experienced writers construct sentences (and larger pieces of writing) explicitly to explore and arrange ideas.

The Single Sentence Session is about thinking in and writing one sentence—a whole piece of language that accommodates a whole idea and makes an image or idea. Go back to Pietro's sentence. Imagine it being read in a second-grade (or a fourth-, sixth-, or ninth-grade) classroom. Pose a follow-up question: Ask the students what they see or hear when they picture Pietro's sentence. What makes Pietro's sentence work is that it paints an image.

Language Arts Standard

Students will write clear and coherent sentences that contain a focus.

Children's first teachers could begin with Single Sentence Sessions or Sentences from Observations on that day early in the year when intentional writing instruction begins. As soon as the students can count the words, they can use Given Word Sentences. By the end of the first grade, they can be using at least two of the three sentence thinking and writing activities posed so far.

Two first graders' Single Sentence Sessions with *old man* appear below:

> *My grandad is a old man.*—Ruben, first grade
> *He had fls teth.*—Alma, first grade

BACK TO THE CLASSROOM WITH SINGLE SENTENCE SESSIONS

Teacher: Boys and girls, we have been thinking in and writing old man sentences since last Monday, and you're all very good at it. This time I want you to think of a sentence that contains the idea of old man, but I also want something about the weather in your sentence. What do you think I mean when I say an idea about weather? Dion?

Dion: Something like the snow?

Teacher: Dion, think of a sentence that has snow in it.

Dion: *It's snowing outside.*

Teacher: That certainly is a sentence. Now, everyone, think of one sentence that contains the ideas of both old man and weather.

Martha: *An old man was walking in the rain.*

Teacher: Good, Martha. Everyone, listen to Martha's sentence again. Martha, read your sentence again, and in a big voice so everyone can hear. [Martha reads.] Now everyone, what do you see? Dion?

Dion: It's raining real hard, and there's this old man who is lost in the storm.

Teacher: Yes. Ramon, you had your hand up.

Ramon: I don't think he's lost. I think he's just out for a walk, and it started to rain, and because he's old, he don't care.

Teacher: [After listening to about three or four sentences:] Everyone, write your sentence on your paper. [After the minute it takes them to put their sentence on paper:] Now I need some readers.

Language Arts Standard

Students will write clear and coherent sentences in which they group related ideas and maintain a consistent focus.

COMMENTARY

The young writers have two ideas to accommodate. They have to arrange the two ideas, and almost always they write sentences that have the old man early in the sentence and weather late. If the children are up to it, it is time for this activity to begin fulfilling its more sophisticated promise.

BACK TO THE CLASSROOM WITH SINGLE SENTENCE SESSIONS

Teacher: This time I want the same two ideas of old man and weather, but I want you to write your sentence so weather is the first of the two ideas in your sentence, and then put in old man. No, Eloise, you don't have to make *weather* the first word, just the first of the two ideas. Okay, Eloise, what do you have?

Eloise: *It was raining when the old man walked to the store.*

Teacher: Yes, Eloise, that one works. Good for you. Everyone, write your sentence on your paper.

 When children begin working with syntactic structures (that is, sentences and sentence bits) at twelve to eighteen months of age, they experiment with how the structures work. That experimentation is their own, but older people in the environment give them feedback in the form of more accurate models. For example, Eric asks, "Who's going to babysitter me?" The older child nearby says, "Cindy is going to be your babysitter." Eric's experiment worked because he got an answer, and the answer is in the form of another sentence that uses the key word more accurately. The experimentation is critical in language development. Single Sentence Sessions give English-language learners an opportunity to experiment with how sentences can be made to work. The teacher provides feedback in the form of models that are variations *on the student's own sentences.* ■

COMMENTARY

The next step in the activity is one sentence that contains three ideas: old man, weather, and vehicle. When the teacher asks, "Who can tell me what a vehicle is?" several children will offer cars, buses, and motorcycles. Reinforce the offerings, and summarize by telling them that a vehicle is anything we can ride in to take us somewhere. That is sufficient for the moment.

INSTRUCTIONAL SCENARIO

In the Classroom with Double Sentence Sessions

Teacher: I'm pleased with the sentences you are writing in our sentence thinking and writing activities, but I'm even more pleased with your reports. Romel told his group he was writing his sentences by trying to think of ideas he had to include. Your writing is getting better and better. That is why we practice.

For today I want us to keep working with those three ideas we started with: old man, weather, and vehicle. This time we will write more. You're so good with one sentence, I want you to think of a way to arrange those three ideas through two sentences. Write two sentences in your mind, and make them paint a bigger picture with the three ideas. You may put two ideas in one sentence and one idea in the other, or you may put all three in one sentence and write what you think might be the second of the two sentences. Now Felicia, let's hear what you have.

Felicia [a second or third grader]: *The grouchy old man had to sit in his car for a whole hour. It just kept raining so he couldn't get out.*

Teacher: Oh, Felicia! Do that again. Read your sentences again very clearly and with a nice big voice so we all can hear. [Felicia reads.] Read just your first sentence. [Felicia reads.] What do you see, boys and girls? Desiree?

Desiree: I see an old man sitting in his car, and he's really mad and talking to himself.

Teacher: What does the first sentence tell us about why the man is sitting in his car? Felicia, read just your first sentence again. [Felicia reads.] Ken?

Ken: It doesn't say why he's there.

Teacher: Read your second sentence, Felicia. [Felicia reads.] Why is he sitting in his car?

Charles: It's because it's raining outside.

Teacher: We need that second sentence for that information, don't we? What about that second sentence all by itself? Who is "he" in that second sentence? Felicia?

Felicia: It's the old man.

Teacher: But we don't know that from the second sentence. We have to have that first sentence. The two sentences work together, don't they? Everyone, write your double sentences, your two sentences, on your paper.

COMMENTARY

When the children write two sentences, they are building bigger main ideas, often using pronouns as transitions in their second sentence, and extending their attention beyond a single sentence. They are looking deliberately at a bigger picture now.

The teacher can call attention to any one or a combination of factors in the development of their writing abilities—for example:

"What is a pronoun, and what is it used for?" Then, "This time, boys and girls, I want you to use a pronoun in your second sentence."

"What do we mean by transitions?" Then, "This time, boys and girls, I want you to use a pronoun as a **transition** between the first and second sentences."

"What is the big idea in the first sentence? Notice that the one sentence gives us a big idea. What is the big idea in the two sentences? Notice how the main idea gets bigger as there are more sentences. Writing is about making main ideas in sentences and making them bigger with each additional sentence. If we put all three ideas in one sentence, there's one main idea. If we put the three ideas in two sentences, there is still one main idea; it just takes two sentences to tell it." (Yes, the teacher did slip in the term *main idea* there.)

"We can arrange any number of ideas in any number of sentences."

INSTRUCTIONAL SCENARIO

In the Classroom with Triple Sentence Sessions

Teacher: Same three ideas, boys and girls. Yes, Eduardo, you know where we were going with this. Right. Same ideas, three **related sentences.** You may make any arrangement you want to make, but the three sentences will work together to make one idea. Think all the way through three sentences, and when you have the piece written in your mind, notice what the big idea is. See if you can hear or see what it's about. Now everyone think. [Pause fifteen seconds for thinking. Fifteen seconds, when the children are working in their heads, is a very long time, especially if they've been working toward this for several days or weeks.]

Does everyone have a triple? Write your triple on your paper. Remember, we always spell the words as well as we can because spelling always counts. And remember that there are three sentences this time, so pay attention to capital letters and punctuation marks. Get everything as right as you can. You have two minutes.

Vernon: *There was rain all day. The old man couldn't mow his grass because it was too wet for his tractor. It made him mad because it would grow so tall before he could mow it.*

Fifth graders wrote the following triple sentence combinations:

> *The old fisherman was tired at the end of the day of fishing. It was stormy in the af-ternoon. He had a hard time keeping water out of his boat.*—Jason, fifth grade
>
> *Do you want to hear about the old man? Good because I'm going to tell you. He drove his car in the rain.*—Edward, fifth grade
>
> *His wiskers were dripping wet from the strom. He had on a hat that was all wet too. His car was broken down on the road.*—Carly, fifth grade

COMMENTARY

Now the young writers have not only written sentences from which a peer and teacher audience can make meaning, but they have written main ideas that they can discern and that an audience can discern. Instruction now has taken young writers through re-lated sentences and to the verge of the paragraph.

VARIATIONS

Sentence Session variations include combinations of ideas that young writers use to con-struct single and multiple sentences. Just about any combination will serve the purpose. It is not necessary to arrange ideas that seem to make logical sense (character, setting, action). The logical sense in Sentence Sessions comes from young writers' deliberate thinking and meaning construction. The following examples come from incorporating the ideas of book, color, and music—the first one with a double sentence structure and the other with a triple sentence structure:

> *My mom likes to go to the bookstore to read. She likes the pretty colors there and the music they play.*—Grace, fifth grade
>
> *I can never read when my brother is playing his music. I'd rather paint. At least I can think when I paint and his music is playing.*—Nicole, fourth grade

Here are ideas for Single Sentence, Double Sentence, and Triple Sentence Sessions:

alone, pie, face	wolf, native, numbers
price, gate, lazy	trees, world, fly
spider, cool, harm	jet, lose, heavy, first
tear, gray, early	clothes, heavy, above, close
color, pants, glass	sale, sail, point, friend
flat, fluffy, brown	brave, talk, floor, fresh
grasp, tired, late, build	heat, tear, badge, food

Sentence Sessions Through the Grades

Levels K–1:   Sentence Sessions in the kindergarten are mainly oral early on and become scribal as the year progresses. A language arts standard in oral language might read: *Students will write and speak in coherent sentences.* Sentence Sessions promote speaking and writing in coherent sentences that contain discernible main ideas.

Levels 2–3:   Second and third graders can move from single sentences to doubles; many of the children will be able to do triples. All of the children will be able to adjust the order of appearance of ideas in single sentences. Second, and certainly third, graders are ready to think in main ideas and how several sentences work together to establish and enhance main ideas. Direct young writers to use ideas from social studies (transportation, highways, air traffic controller) or science (circuit, filament, wire) for Sentence Sessions.

Levels 4–5:   Fourth and fifth graders have two years to become virtually automatic at sentence thinking and writing, constructing and adjusting main ideas, and elaborating on main ideas. The value of beginning the thinking and writing in the kindergarten cannot be overstated because young writers are ready by the fourth and fifth grades to manipulate ideas and sentences in every possible way and become so practiced that they can write coherent sentences and combinations of sentences with virtual automatic attention, just as experienced writers do.

To ensure such a level of expertise, even as fourth and fifth graders are writing through the genres, the teacher can establish a separate activity, called "A-Sentence-a-Day." Early in the fourth-grade year, the teacher makes available a file of Q-cards for Given Word Sentences, Observation Sentences, and Sentence Sessions and makes the assignment that every student in the room is to write at least one sentence every day in response to a sentence Q-card.

Levels 6–8:   Many middle school students do not write paragraph-length pieces easily because the building blocks of writing have not become automatic literacy behavior.

Sentence Sessions are excellent activities for middle-level students who need practice in sentence thinking and writing. They are developmentally able to handle Single, Double, and Triple Sentence Sessions. Those activities remain challenging even in the middle school because they demand creative thinking.

 For students at any level who are learning English as a second language, Sentence Sessions are an especially important activity. During the variations on a Sentence Session activity, second-language learners benefit from the sentence sounds that are constantly in the air and in their ears during oral sharing of sentences. They also benefit when Sentence Sessions incorporate the specialized vocabulary of content areas. When students are learning English as well as content-area material, the more practice they have using the ideas and concepts embedded in the vocabulary and the more examples of vocabulary use they are exposed to, the better their learning will be supported. ▪

In addition, Sentence Sessions continue to be useful as a writing context for content-area terminology and concepts. An example from social studies would be: "Arrange the following ideas in three related sentences: compromise, ratify, protection."

Secondary Level: Applications at the secondary levels are similar to those in the middle school. There is always value in practice, for no one, not even the most experienced writer, ever claims to have mastered sentence thinking and writing.

Word Pyramid Sentences

Language Arts Standard
Students will spell high-frequency words correctly.

Word Pyramid Sentences (Fearn & Foster, 1979) is an activity in which young writers can engage weekly, several times per month, or only periodically for practice or as an intellectual game. There are several layers in the activity, each with its own objective.

Word Pyramid Sentences Through the Grades

Levels K–1:   Relatively late in the K–1 years, it is likely that the sort of deliberate word thinking and spelling characterized by pyramid building is feasible for many children.

Levels 2–3:   This is just the right age range for early implementation of Word Pyramids and Word Pyramid Sentences. Many second graders are beginning to accumulate a store of words with which they are sufficiently familiar to practice spelling. They can begin in response to the direction, "Make a list of words you know that begin with the letter B." They won't know how to spell all of the words they can think of, but those are precisely the words they have to learn how to spell because they think of the words.

INSTRUCTIONAL SCENARIO

In the Classroom to Build Word Pyramids

Teacher: Write your last name. Look at the first letter in your last name. My last name is Clark, so when I look at my name, I see the letter C first. I'll write my letter on the overhead. You write your letter on your paper. [Pause] Everyone, now watch what I'm doing. I'm going to write a three-letter word that begins with my letter right under my letter. See, I wrote the word *can* under my letter. My word begins with my letter, and my word has three letters in it. You think of a three-letter word that begins with your letter, and write it under your letter just as I did. Peter?

Peter: So I can write *pet*?

Teacher: You have it just right. Good for you, Peter. From now on in the next few minutes, I want you to trust what you think without asking me if you're right.

Now everyone, think of a four-letter word that begins with your letter, and write it under your three-letter word, so it looks as if you are building a word pyramid.

Then think of a five-letter word that begins with your letter to write under the four-letter word, then a six-letter word, a seven-letter word, and so forth. Keep thinking of words and writing them. In two minutes, we'll see how big you have made your pyramid.

COMMENTARY

Two things have happened at this stage of the Word Pyramid Sentences activity (which can be used all by itself, weekly, throughout the year).

First, spelling in writing context means spelling the words a writer thinks of (see Chapter 14). Critical to spelling, therefore, is young writers' thinking of words. The scenario causes students to think of words that begin with a certain letter and write them in a word pyramid.

Second, what young writers are also doing when they build their word pyramid is deliberate spelling practice. Go ahead, readers, think of the first letter of your last name, and then think of an eight-letter word that begins with your letter. (Yes, do it.) Now, what did you notice? Right. You were counting letters as you spelled the words. That's deliberate attention to how words are spelled. People learn to spell words by paying deliberate attention to the appearance of the letter patterns in hundreds of words. For purposes of spelling, making word pyramids could be a weekly activity throughout the school year.

And there is more. Spelling by itself is not writing, and although it's useful to think deliberately about how words are spelled, the activity has no merit beyond the confines of spelling. Spelling should *always* interact with writing.

BACK TO THE CLASSROOM FOR WORD PYRAMID SENTENCES

Teacher: Who made it to five words? Six? Seven? Eight? Anyone more than eight? Peter? Good for you. Now, boys and girls, I have something else I want you to do.

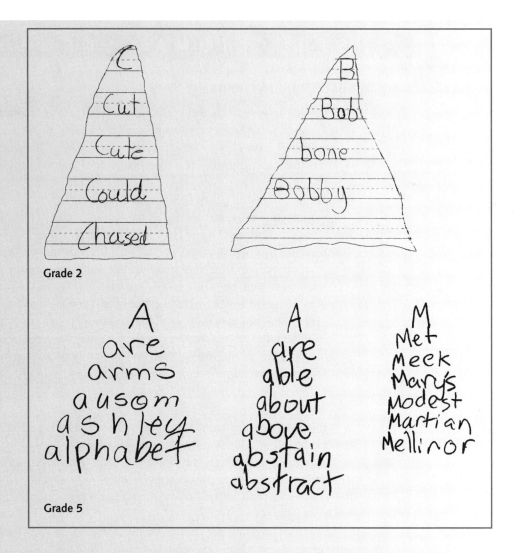

Grade 2

Grade 5

Look at my four-letter word on the screen. It has four letters, right? Good. I'll call it my fourth pyramid word. If it has five letters, what will I call it? Jason?

Jason: The fifth pyramid word?

Teacher: Yes. Very good. The sixth pyramid word will be the word with six letters. If I ask you to think of a sentence that contains your third pyramid word, José, what word will you use?

José: *Jam?*

Teacher: Yes. Good. Everyone, think of a sentence that contains your fourth pyramid word. Evangeline?

Evangeline: *Each of the girls came to my party.*

Teacher: What was your pyramid word, Evangeline?

Evangeline: It was *each.*

Teacher: Terrific. Bret? Nick? Sandee?

COMMENTARY

This layer of the activity can be patterned precisely after the Given Word Sentences. The students first write sentences that contain pyramid words (*Think of a sentence that contains your fifth pyramid word*), and then they write sentences of specified length that contain pyramid words (*Think of a seven-word sentence that contains your fifth pyramid word*), and finally, they write sentences of specified length in which pyramid words appear in specified positions (*Think of a seven-word sentence in which your fifth pyramid word appears in the third position*).

We occasionally hear that the children will not be able to comprehend all of those directions at once. The key to making sure children can comprehend complex directions is to give them the directions in successive stages while making sure they know what to do and how to do it. The first test of many of the activities in this chapter, specifically the Given Word Sentences, was in a special day class for children with learning disabilities (Fearn, 1981) where the children worked effectively with the task and understood the directions very well because of the attentional demand.

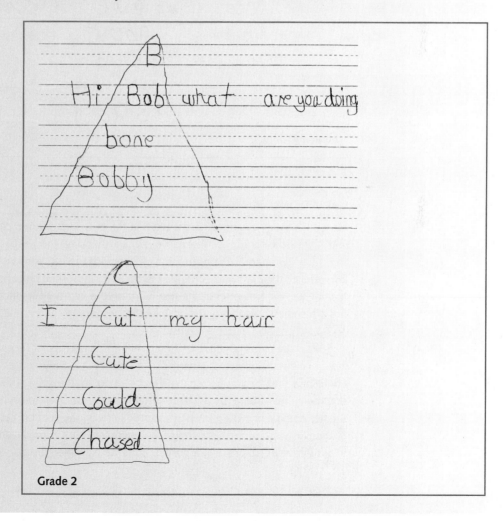

Grade 2

Mary and I Met Ellenot Barnes
Mary's Meek Modest Martian Mellinor.
Mary's
Modest
Martian
Mellinor

A
are
are you able to read?
about
above
abstain
abstract

Grade 5

VARIATIONS

Vary the activity by changing the word in the cue. The children can start their pyramid with the first letter in their last name. On another day, they begin with the first letter from their first name. Over time, they begin with the last letter in their first name, the last letter in their last name, the first letter in their mother's first name, the consonants, the vowels, the last letter in the first word on the Word Wall, and so forth. The possibilities are endless. Also, vary the activity with respect to sentence length, word selection, and word position in the sentence.

So far, the pyramids have been theme free. Suppose in a recent reader response to literature discussion activity many of the readers said they noticed in *Stone Fox* (Gardner, 1980) that "if you try real hard you can do anything." Today's word pyramid could emphasize that theme by asking, "What is a five-letter word on that theme?" The themes could come from science (nature, animals, the sea) or social studies (World War II, the westward movement, indigenous peoples). Once the children have built themed Word Pyramids, they are in a position to write extended discourse from the pyramid.

Language Arts Standard
Students will use correct
word order in written
sentences.

In the second and third grades, the children can also write Given Word Sentences as described in the Instructional Scenario above, which promotes word order thinking.

Levels 4–5: At these levels, the spelling activity just described for second and third graders can be conducted weekly and nearly independently. Each morning, or two or three times each week, as the children come into the room, there is a direction on the right corner of the board: "Make a Word Pyramid in which each word ends with G. Write sentences for the odd-numbered pyramid words in which the words appear in even-numbered positions." Everyone knows that the Word Pyramid with sentences is their ticket to morning recess.

Levels 6–8: In these middle-level grades, the spelling portion of the activity can be a regular feature at least weekly, and maybe twice weekly, in class, with peer help, then dictionary help, to achieve accuracy. Paragraphs or more, based on themed Word Pyramids, are helpful if only to maintain a high level of distributive practice (continuous practice over time). Writing the Given Word Sentences at least weekly also maintains the youngsters' focus on deliberate crafting of sentences.

Secondary Level: By the time students are in the ninth grade, they should have achieved a large degree of automaticity in the craft of writing. Of course, because even the most experienced writers practice, it is never a waste of anyone's time to stretch their ability to spell words they know but don't routinely write and to craft sentences deliberately that demand their concentration (*Write an eleven-word sentence that contains three nouns, two modified by adjectives, and one two-syllable verb modified by a prepositional phrase*). That assumes, of course, that they have already received the sort of deliberate craft instruction we have described in this chapter.

If secondary students aren't at the point of automaticity, this activity is right for such practice. If they come to the tenth grade unable to maintain attention to their purpose for writing while crafting the sentences and spelling the words automatically, they have to learn it in the tenth grade, or they won't be able to do it in the eleventh. And until they can write that way, they cannot write well.

Sentence Combining

Strong (1993) provided teachers with a powerful tool for helping young writers think deliberately about the construction and management of sentences. Called *sentence combining,* the activity enjoys considerable research support (Hillocks & Mavrogenes, 1986). Used as the only sentence instruction strategy, however, sentence combining does not enjoy such positive support (Hillocks & Smith, 1986).

In balanced writing instruction, sentence combining is *one* craft activity among many, buttressed by a host of additional instruction in the processes and genres, all interacting with the rest of the language arts to constitute instructional balance; therefore, sentence combining alone does not support all of learning to write. Sentence combining should be *an* instructional tool.

Traditionally, sentence combining has been aimed at moving young writers toward the ability to write increasingly sophisticated syntax that includes not only compound and complex sentences, but longer and better-constructed simple sentences as well.

Language Arts Standard

Students will use simple and compound sentences in writing.

In the activity, young writers are provided two simple sentences with the direction to make one sentence from the two. That basic standard can be expanded to make one sentence out of three simple sentences, two out of three, two out of four, one out of four, and so forth. The earliest solution to the problem of combining two simple sentences is one compound sentence. Thus, *The car is black. The car is fast.* becomes *The car is black, and the car is fast.* A more sophisticated solution would be *The car is black and fast,* or *The black car is fast.*

INSTRUCTIONAL SCENARIO

In the Classroom with Sentence Combining

Teacher: You see two sentences on the board. Lisa, read them for us.

Lisa: *Watch the black cat. The black cat is running fast.*

Teacher: Yes, thank you, Lisa. What is the big idea in those two sentences? What are they about? Lisa?

Lisa: The black cat is running.

Teacher: Who can think of a single sentence that contains the ideas from both of the sentences on the board? Remember, I want only one sentence, but the sentence has to have all of the ideas.

Germaine: *Look at the black cat running fast.*

Teacher: Listen to Germaine's sentence, everyone. Read it again. [Germaine reads.] Does it have all of the ideas from both sentences? Who else has one sentence that contains all of the ideas? Vivi?

Vivi: *I can see the black cat that is running fast.*

COMMENTARY

There are two levels of thinking in the sentence combining that Lisa and Germaine did. They had to recognize the ideas presented in the two sentences, and they had to arrange those ideas into one sentence. The sentence thinking is exactly like that in Single Sentence Sessions. Now, however, young writers, not the teacher, identify the ideas they arrange into one sentence.

VARIATIONS

One variation is to adjust the order of ideas. In the two sentences, there is a black cat, there is running fast, and there is an assumption of an observer. Both Lisa and Germaine put all three ideas into their single sentence. Now change the prompt by directing the children in the class to think of another sentence that contains all three ideas, but the ideas have to appear in this order: running fast, observer, black cat. Yes, the children do exactly what you are doing. They also begin to see if the pieces will fit to complete the word puzzle. Perhaps your sentence reads something like mine: *Running down the street, I saw a black cat.* Now, was that the black cat running, or was it you? That's a new problem to solve. It's what makes these kinds of writing tasks thoughtful and authentic. Experienced writers have to read and think about what they have written from a reader's point of view, and if it can be ambiguous, they must rewrite to clarify.

BACK TO THE CLASSROOM FOR SENTENCE COMBINING

Teacher: We have been combining two short sentences into one sentence for several days now. What if I wrote three sentences on the board? Who thinks he or she will be able to combine the three sentences into one sentence? Remember, this isn't just two sentences into one; it's *three* sentences into one. Let's see what you can do. [The teacher writes, *Sandra has a ball. The ball is made of rubber. She bounces the ball on the sidewalk.*] Remember, think of what the ideas are, and then think of the sentence. Damian, so fast? You go ahead and think some more just to make sure you have just the sentence you want. I will call on you first. [Pause five more seconds.] Damian?

Damian: *Sandra has a rubber ball, and she bounces it on the sidewalk.*

Teacher: Yes, that is one sentence, but does it contain all of the ideas? Tendra, what do you think? Did Damian's sentence have all of the ideas? Damian, read your sentence again. [Damian reads.] Tendra, I want you to think of a way to rewrite the sentence so it doesn't begin with the girl's name.

Tendra: *The girl bounces her rubber ball on the sidewalk, and her name is Sandra.*

COMMENTARY

Notice that the sentence combining can be made into a rearranging activity when the teacher applies extra directions: "Don't put the girl's name in the beginning." "Use a word other than *sidewalk*." "Put the rubber ball at the beginning of the sentence" (and so forth). Can *you* combine the sentences into a simple sentence?

VARIATIONS

Sentence combining can feature any number of frames, or arrangements of sentences. It begins with what appears to be the simplest frame of two short sentences combined into one longer and most likely simple sentence. If the two-into-one frame involves longer or even complex or compound sentences, the task is more complex. Notice the complexity of combining the following two sentences into one sentence.

- While the goats were grazing on the hillside, two hawks hovered above.
- The hawks hovered for ten minutes before one suddenly dove toward an outcropping near the goats and came away with a field mouse.

Although that is a two-into-one sentence frame, it is much more complex than is the one about the black cat. It is important to notice that the complexity of the writing task can vary considerably within a single frame.

BACK TO THE CLASSROOM FOR SENTENCE COMBINING

Teacher: Someone read the sentence I have on the board. Maribel?

Maribel: *Although the seven dwarfs worked very hard in the mine, we never do get to know what their work was, and Snow White didn't seem curious enough to ask them.*

Teacher: Boys and girls, I have a different sentence thinking and writing problem for you today. I wrote only one sentence on the board. I want you to think of a way to rewrite the one sentence into two sentences.

Nunzio: *No one knows what the seven dwarfs did when they went to work in the mine. Snow White didn't want to know, so she didn't ask them.*

Sentence Combining Through the Grades

Levels K–1: One of the twelve standards for the English language arts (NCTE/IRA, 1996) is about applying knowledge of language structure and conventions. Application presumes prior knowledge. Sentence combining and arranging serves as a way to establish conscious knowledge of formal language structure as well as conventions such as appropriate word order and the use of modification. Simple oral sentence combining with two-into-one and three-into-one frames has an important role to play in laying the foundations for conscious knowledge of language structure.

Levels 2–3: Notice the elements in the second- and third-grade writing standard paraphrased from one state's list of standards.

The second and third grades are the right time to use sentence combining as a fundamental element in balanced writing instruction. Sentence combining features applied reading comprehension because young writers identify the ideas they have to accommodate in the sentences they write. It also features thinking and writing in one or more sentences, depending on the assigned frame.

> **Language Arts Standard**
>
> Students will distinguish between sentences and nonsentences, use correct word order, and demonstrate the use of various kinds of sentences.

Second graders

The car is fast. My brother has a fast car. It is red.
It is red. My brother's car is red. It is fast.
It is my brother's car. My brother's fast car is red.

Fourth graders

I have a computer at home. I like to work and play games on my computer at home. Sometimes I surf the Internet.
I like to work on the computer. On my computer at home I like to play games and surf the Internet. I also work on it.
I play games and surf the Internet.

Levels 4–5: The paraphrased fourth- and fifth-grade standard is addressed by sentence combining. The standard speaks directly to sentence combining; however, there is something very important about what sentence combining can do to satisfy the standard in the fourth and fifth grades. Such a standard demands prepositional phrases, parenthetical constructions, and appositives, for example. Isolated instruction, no matter how expert, rarely translates to application in everyday writing, but in sentence combining activities, an appositive, for example, has a distinctive role to play. If fourth graders don't know the appositive, sentence combining is a context in which it can be taught directly and in context, then practiced, also in context, to increase the probability they'll use it in everyday writing. Sentence combining is an example of craft-writing activities that offer a writing context for grammatical abstractions.

A sentence combining task can also cue certain kinds of sentences. If we have taught the compound construction (see Chapter 5), the sentence combining cue can read: "Combine the following two simple sentences into one compound sentence." After teaching complex sentences in the third grade (see Chapter 5), the sentence combining cue can read: "Combine the following simple sentences into a complex sentence" or "a sentence that begins with the word *while*."

Levels 6–8:   Although we urge sentence combining instruction and regular practice through the fourth and fifth grades, language arts standards for the middle school years also target what sentence combining can deliver. Notice the paraphrased standard.

Although several of the sentence thinking and writing activities in this chapter focus on single sentences, sentence combining represents a good context for working on the standard.

Secondary Level: High school students, we assume, have already mastered the series of sentence thinking and writing standards listed throughout this chapter, but there remain some who have not. Basic activities such as those used in the fourth through the seventh grades can help to remediate high school students for whom sentence thinking and writing continue to be a challenge.

Secondary students, and middle-level students as well, can be challenged by more complex sentence combining activities. Think of a way to combine the following sentences into one five-sentence paragraph:

> It was late in the afternoon. Only the best skiers remained on the slopes. The sky was of a blue that he had never seen before. The last rays of the sun made shadows of trees reach across the whole of the mountainside. He could see the fireplace smoke coming out of the lodge chimney and meandering through the fast-approaching night. There was a wet chill in the air as he skied his way down the mountain toward the lodge. With a heavy dusk settled all about, and his eyes slit as protection from the cold, he didn't see the rock outcropping from the last mogul.

Here is a tenth grader's completion of this activity:

> It was late in the afternoon when the sky was dark blue. The last rays of sunlight made shadows on the mountainside as only the best skiers remained on the slopes. The skier could see fireplace smoke coming out of the chimney at the lodge. There

Language Arts Standard

Students will use both simple and compound sentences to combine short and related sentences that use various kinds of modification.

Language Arts Standard

Students will use simple, compound, and compound complex structures, properly placed modifiers, and parallel structure in all written discourse.

> was a wet chill in the air as he skied his way down the mountain toward the lodge. With the heavy dusk all around, he didn't see the rock outcropping from the last mogul.—Tenth grader

Although teachers often write their own sentence combining activities, Strong (1986) provides scores of excellent activities.

Sentence Problems

This is not an activity in its strict sense. It is the capstone for our focus on intentional sentence instruction through the grades. Our discussion throughout has been directed at teaching sentence thinking and writing. We have emphasized planful, systematic, and accurate sentence thinking and writing from the very first encounter with writing in school. Properly conducted, intentional sentence teaching prevents writing problems at the sentence level.

Nevertheless, there are young writers, and some writers who aren't so young, who write **nonsentences.** Over the years, some of those sentences have been called "incomplete" sentences as distinct from "complete" sentences. We haven't referred to "complete" and "incomplete" sentences so far in this book. Nor have we referred to that entanglement of coordinating conjunctions and comma splices known as the **"run-on sentence."** Incomplete sentences and run-on sentences can be prevented, and if not prevented, eliminated. These final few paragraphs in this chapter are about eliminating sentence writing problems. But first, we have to clarify terminology.

Sentence is defined as "a grammatical unit that is syntactically independent and has a subject that is expressed or understood and a predicate that contains a finite verb" (American Heritage Dictionary, 1993; see also Harris & Hodges, 1995; Francis, 1958).

What, then, is an "incomplete" sentence? The term is *sentence. Sentence* labels what the language string is. A *sentence*, by definition, cannot be "incomplete." The term "incomplete sentence" is a linguistic impossibility, a logical absurdity. A string of language either is or is not a sentence.

Given the definition of *sentence*, the term "complete sentence" makes no sense either. If the language string is a sentence, it is complete. To modify the perfectly good term *sentence* with the word *complete* is redundant.

If you think we make much ado about not very much, consider that the language we teachers use has everything to do with how well young writers learn to write. If writing teachers use terminology that doesn't make sense, even to linguists who study the field, the term cannot possibly make sense to the young writers in the most desperate need of terms they can understand and use.

When we tell young writers they have to write "complete" sentences, we also tell them what a "complete" sentence is: A "complete" sentence expresses a "complete" thought. Now think like a seven year old, which is the age of the young writer who has to make sense of that term. Little Shane writes, "Because she couldn't find the ball under the table." His teacher says that isn't a "complete" sentence because it doesn't express a "complete" thought. It is reasonable for Shane to be confused because he thinks that not being able to find the ball under the table is quite complete. Of course, we don't just leave him hanging there on the "incomplete" thought; we ask him, "Who?" And he says, it was Judy, and he points to the pronoun. Now what do we do? We tell him it's still "incomplete" because we don't begin sentences with *because*.

We get deeper and deeper as we go, adding to Shane's confusion by giving him one kind of information that doesn't make sense to a seven year old and other information that is flatly wrong. Shane will never understand how not being able to find the ball under the table isn't a "complete" thought because the fact is that thoughts don't occur incomplete. Thoughts are complete in the moment when they surface. Furthermore, all kinds of wonderfully literate sentences begin with *because*.

There are two reasons that young writers, and writers who aren't so young, write nonsentences. One, especially among young writers, is that they don't hear sentence boundaries. Good writers hear the language they are writing as they are writing it, and because they know what sentences are supposed to sound like, they write sentences, as opposed to nonsentences, even in their roughest drafts. Neither good writers nor poor ones think of subjects and predicates when they craft their sentences or finish a sentence and then ponder whether they have a complete thought. Good writers have a sense of sentence that they have developed over their years of writing practice. They listen to language around them and read good writing, which they use to monitor their own writing.

The second reason that young writers, and not so young writers, write nonsentences is that they don't know how to write a sentence. They don't know what a sentence is. They need to know what a sentence is in terms that a five year old, a seven year old, or an eleven year old can understand and use to write sentences immediately. They need information they can use to do it right the very next time they try to write.

Fixing Sentence Problems

There are two kinds of sentence problems: young writers don't hear sentence boundaries and/or they don't know what a sentence is. This chapter emphasizes the sounds of sentences. The teacher models sentences so the sounds of sentences permeate the room. All of the sentence work in this chapter is explicitly thoughtful and expressed orally at first, repeated by the teacher, and repeated again by the children.

What is a sentence? A sentence is a piece of language that sounds like what Geraldo just read and what the teacher repeated. If we listen to sentences every day throughout kindergarten and first, second, third, and fourth grades, the sentence will become an automatic sound, as it is for experienced writers. Young writers begin to think purposely of sentences that contain subjects and predicates, modifiers, and phrases. The foundation of sentence learning is thinking in sentences, writing sentences, and reading thoughtful sentences aloud for everyone to hear every day.

We'll avoid any definition that can confuse young writers (*a verb shows state of being*) or is in any part inaccurate (*adverbs end in -ly*). We'll avoid the assumption that people use their knowledge of parts of speech as a guide when they write. Instead, we'll think in and write hundreds of sentences and hear thousands of sentences. In that way, the children will come to know what a sentence is and what a sentence sounds like.

INSTRUCTIONAL SCENARIO

In the Classroom to Fix "Fragments"

Erin has written, "Large hands that had worked many afternoons on the playgrounds of the city." The teacher then asks the rest of the class, "Think of a sentence that contains Erin's ideas." And Hermie comes up with this: "He had large hands that worked many afternoons on the playgrounds of the city."

Teacher: Erin, listen to how Hermie rewrote your sentence. [Hermie reads.] Listen to the sentence again. [Teacher reads.] Can you hear the sentence?

Erin: Yes.

Teacher: Read the sentence you wrote. [Erin reads silently.] Now listen to Hermie's rewrite. [Teacher reads.] Can you hear the difference?

Erin: Yes.

Teacher: Good. Rewrite what you wrote so it is a sentence.

COMMENTARY

We've heard more than once that what the teacher in the instructional scenario did can make Erin feel bad and not want to write any more. In fact, the scenario reflects what we've done hundreds of times in classrooms. It never makes Erin feel bad, and it isn't what makes her not want to write any more. What makes Erin feel bad is doing it wrong. What makes her frustrated is not being shown how to do it right in terms she can understand and use. What makes Erin not want to write is day after day of doing it wrong and not being shown how to do it right. When Erin knows how to do it right, she feels terrific.

We've also heard that we can't use what we did in the instructional scenario if Erin is a teenager because she'll think it's silly. Erin is fifteen. So is Hermie. Most teenagers think things are silly because they are. Learning to do something right isn't silly.

Finally, we've heard we can't do what we did in the Erin and Hermie scenario if the young writers are learning English as a second language because they'll feel their attempts at English are being criticized, and they'll be resentful and stop trying. We worked with fifty-seven middle-level students, all of whom were learning English as a second language (Fearn & Farnan, 1993). We taught precisely what we describe in this chapter in precisely the way we describe it. Analytic assessment showed significant improvement in thirteen weeks, the students' status in statewide testing improved from the lowest quartile among demographically similar students to the middle third of all students, and at the end-of-year family literacy fair, we detected no resentment or avoidance as the students glowed over their portfolios.

Sentences: Looking into a Fourth Grade

The plan book page in Figure 4.1 is from Kathleen's fourth-grade January schedule. By the middle of the year, she had already taught a lot of the activities she learned in the summer writing institute.

Kathleen had this to say about the schedule:

Most of my fourth graders could keep up with the schedule, but I just had to move ahead because when I tried to plan so everyone could finish every day, I didn't get as much done as most of my children needed. So I work individually with some of them to help them move along.

I do the Sentence-a-Day by having sentence-writing cards in the Writing Center, and everyone has to pick up one card every morning and write the sentence by morning recess. I don't actually have the ticket-to-recess plan in place, but most of them have it done by recess anyway. The rest I remind to have it done by lunch or afternoon recess or before they go home. I often have one or two taking it home to finish, but most of the children write that sentence just about every day.

I rarely set aside more than twenty minutes a day for these sentence activities. That leaves time to do the bigger writing activities, and some of those I do in social studies, literature, and science anyway. The Word Pyramids don't take instructional time because those are also done during independent time. The kids love them, and some are doing them all the time just to compete with each other for the longest pyramid.

I have found that by writing sentences every day throughout the year, their writing gets much better. I don't have to spend any time at all with incomplete sentences or run-ons after about January or February, and when I get one or two on someone's paper, all I have to do is tell them to listen to their sentences. They make the corrections every time.

I still teach the grammar my district requires, but I don't do it in writing periods. The testing at the end of the year asks the students about parts of speech, and they know them really well because I have them write sentences with parts of speech.

Monday	Tuesday	Wednesday	Thursday	Friday
• Sentences from Observation, Oral (6)	• Sentences from Observation, Oral (6) • Sentence Combining (10)	• Sentences from Observation, Written (10)	• Sentences from Observation, Written (10) • A-Sentence-a-Day	• Word Pyramid (6) • A-Sentence-a-Day
• Single Sentence Session (10) • A-Sentence-a-Day	• Single Sentence Session (10) • Sentence Combining (1) • A-Sentence-a-Day	• Double Sentence Session (10) • Word Pyramid (5) • A-Sentence-a-Day	• Double Sentence Session (10) • A-Sentence-a-Day	• Given Word Sentence (10) • Word Pyramid (5) • A-Sentence-a-Day
• Single Sentence Session (10) • A-Sentence-a-Day	• Double Sentence Session (10) • Sentence Combining (10) • A-Sentence-a-Day	• Given Word Sentence (10) • Word Pyramid Sentences (10) • A-Sentence-a-Day	• Double Sentence Session (10) • A-Sentence-a-Day	• Triple Sentence Session (10) • Word Pyramid Sentences (10) • A-Sentence-a-Day
• Triple Sentence Session (10) • A-Sentence-a-Day	• Sentence Combining (10) • A-Sentence-a-Day	• Triple Sentence Session (10) • Word Pyramid Sentences (10) • A-Sentence-a-Day	• A-Sentence-a-Day	• Word Pyramid Sentences (10) • A-Sentence-a-Day

FIGURE 4.1   Fourth-Grade Plan Book Page

REVIEW AND REFLECTION

1. Early in this chapter we stated clearly that people who cannot write sentences cannot write. Do you think that is a true statement, or do you think there are exceptions? If there are exceptions, explain them.
2. There are several references to ESL in this chapter. With a partner from your class, plan a three-day series of lessons designed to teach sentence thinking and writing to second graders whose native language is not English.
3. We described the subject or theme of a sentence as its main idea. Usually main idea is associated with paragraphs. Why do you think we use the term *main idea* when talking about sentences?

4. Having read this chapter, how would you define the concept of sentence to a six year old? How about a fourteen year old?
5. If you have a daily language arts period of twenty-five minutes in your schedule, how many minutes per week do you think you might commit to sentences in the second grade?

A Summary: Sentences

We teach sentence thinking and writing intentionally with the objective that thinking and writing in sentences will become automatic. Young writers can concentrate their deliberate attention on constructing larger ideas and images even as they automatically think in and write sentences. This chapter recommends several kinds of deliberate sentence thinking and writing activities that accommodate the abilities of young writers through the grades. The best instructional procedure is to avoid sentence problems by teaching intentionally from the beginning. However, should sentence problems appear, they can be "fixed" by teaching sentence thinking and writing, not by avoiding the problem, assuming it will take care of itself if they write enough, or by pretending the writer's craft at the sentence level just isn't important.

5 Teaching Craft: Mechanical Control

BEFORE YOU READ

- What do you think of when you hear the word *mechanics* in the context of writing?
- To what extent do you think the mechanics are important in the whole picture of writing well?
- With a partner, make a list of what you think are the most commonly used capitalization and punctuation conventions. At what grade levels, if any, would you teach each convention?
- At what grade level do you think young writers should have the most common capitalization and punctuation conventions mastered?
- What do you think is the place of sentence parts instruction (parts of speech) in writing instruction? For what purposes would you teach the labels, the definitions, and/or the concepts?

What Are the Mechanics in Writing?

The **"mechanics"** of writing typically are capitalization, punctuation, parts of speech, usage, syntactic structures (sentence construction), and spelling. The preponderance of this chapter focuses on capitalization and punctuation.

Many writers, young and old, and even quite experienced and successful students, have enormous difficulty with the mechanics of writing because they assume that mechanics occur in revision, and correctness will emerge through occasional tiny lessons and lots of unfettered writing.

That assumption is thoroughly flawed.

First, if it's silly to propose that young writers write badly on purpose unless they're told to (and who would tell them to write badly?), it's reasonable to say that they write about as well as they can whenever they write. If they make significant punctuation errors in their drafts, it seems reasonable to say that they made at least some of those errors because they didn't know how to punctuate correctly. And if they write as well as they can when they draft and make significant punctuation errors, what makes anyone think young writers will know how to get it right when they revise?

We begin, then, with a rule of thumb: *Mechanics matter*. Mechanics matter all the time; in all writing; in all its forms and purposes; and in all the drafts, including the first one, because capital letters and punctuation marks are meaning markers. Meaning markers convey meaning.

Read the following two sentences:

1. Meet me in the living room for coffee.
2. Meet me in the Living Room for coffee.

The sentences are identical save for two capital letters in sentence 2 that do not appear in sentence 1. What is the living room in sentence 1? What is the Living Room in sentence 2? If you answered that it's a room in the house in sentence 1 and the name of a coffee house in sentence 2, you read the meaning differences conveyed by lower and upper case letters. Capital letters are meaning markers. They always matter.

Now read these two sentences:

1. The bird's feathers were ruffled by a strong breeze.
2. The birds' feathers were ruffled by a strong breeze.

Yes, you are ahead of us. You already know. There is one bird in sentence 1 and more than one bird in sentence 2. You knew because the placement of the apostrophe changed a significant portion of the image conveyed by the sentence. Punctuation marks are meaning markers. They always matter.

Intentional instruction in and performance expectations for mechanics must always be age- and ability-appropriate. Also, all writers of all ages and abilities should feel responsible for using meaning markers as correctly (conventionally) as they are able in the preparation of any piece of writing. It is reasonable to expect first graders to use capital letters to begin their sentences and end marks to signal the end of their sentences. It is reasonable to expect fifth but not first graders to use commas properly in complex sentences. We base the sense of responsibility on reasonable developmental expectations.

Remember the rule of thumb: *Mechanics matter*. We make the rule of thumb work by doing four things:

1. We teach so *young writers know what the mechanical elements are* that make their writing work. Young writers have to know what makes their writing work.

2. We teach so that *young writers know how to use the mechanical elements* that make their writing work. Young writers have to know how to do what works.

3. We teach so that *young writers use the mechanical elements* as well as they can throughout the preparation of every piece of writing, not merely when they revise. Young writers have to practice doing it right all the time.

4. We teach so that *young writers want to use the mechanical elements* that make their writing work. Young writers want to do what they know and understand and find they can do well.

All instruction therefore must be in the context of their own writing and must be directed at making young writers' writing work. All instruction must emphasize the application of age- and ability-appropriate mechanical accuracy all the time. And all instruction must be directed at making young writers competent, for it's the experience of their own competence that makes them want to do it right.

Conventions: The Meaning Markers

If young writers are to know what the mechanical elements are, the mechanical elements must be clear and unambiguous. In the *Random House Dictionary* (1996), there are exactly one hundred conventions for punctuating (eighty-three) and capitalizing (seventeen) your writing. There are seven for colon use, eighteen for using quotation marks, and sixteen for commas, with four variations on the one for commas in series.

Second graders routinely write sentences that contain items in series. But it isn't necessary for them to know everything about using commas to separate items in series. Second graders who write sentences that contain items in series need only know that the sentence doesn't work if they don't use marks to let readers know how many items there are. So we tell second graders that when they write sentences with items in series, they have to let readers in on *how many*, and they do it with commas. Then we spend a day or two, or maybe a week or so, teaching them how to write those sentences with the commas, and thereafter we hold them responsible for writing those kinds of sentences properly.

If we aren't going to teach all one hundred of the capitalization and punctuation conventions, with variations, on what basis do we select those we are going to teach? The basis is young writers' need. Because second graders tend to write sentences with items in series, second grade is the time to teach that comma convention. Second graders also tend to write several sentences connected with coordinating conjunctions. So that is a good time to teach compound sentences and the comma that makes compound sentences work. On the other hand, it's the rare fourth grader who writes well enough to need a semicolon, so except for that rare student, there is no reason whatsoever to teach the semicolon in the fourth grade.

The list of thirty high-frequency and high-utility capitalization and punctuation conventions set out in Figure 3.1 was developed on the basis of young writers' need. Included on the list are colons, semicolons, dashes, and parentheses for more accomplished writers. Remove those from the list, and there are twenty-six conventions for most young writers, all unambiguously stated, and 252 weeks between the first day of the kindergarten and the last day of the sixth grade. If they are distributed equally through the seven years (which they aren't), that would be one convention every forty-eight school days. Given that content load, is there any reason that ninth-grade English teachers should have to teach the comma in a compound sentence to any young writer who has been in school since the kindergarten?

The answer is yes, for several reasons. First, if the convention were not taught, there isn't any reason that ninth graders should have mastered it. Second, the convention may have been taught ambiguously and the students were left confused. ("You don't need a comma if the independent clauses are short." We didn't make that up.) Third, some young writers have been told not to worry because they'll eventually get the conventions right if they write enough. (We didn't make that one up, either.) Fourth, if young writers put a comma into the extra space in other people's sentences, they won't know much of anything about the comma in compound sentences. Finally, even if they did master the comma for editing purposes, they still may not know much about using it in writing.

The rest of this discussion of conventions is committed to eliminating the five reasons.

Teaching Punctuation Conventions

The evidence shows that a functional approach to teaching the mechanics of writing is more effective than practice exercises (Calkins, 1980). Characteristically, *functional approach* means concentrating on editing, while the practice-exercises approach means isolated or noncontextual worksheets. Happily, the possibilities for teaching the mechanics of writing do not divide neatly into two extreme categories.

Craft instruction, properly conceived and conducted, doesn't burden young writers with worksheets that have no writing context, it doesn't leave mechanical control for revision, and it doesn't delude young writers with the ridiculous platitude that if they write a lot, mechanical correctness will eventually work itself out.

Teaching the craft of writing means using the conventions to help young writers master the sentences that contain them; the instruction is focused not on rules or editing but on writing. Craft instruction means emphasizing to young writers that what they know about the conventions matters *whenever* they write. Finally, craft instruction means including attention to conventional writing in assessing writing samples and when conferencing with young writers.

INSTRUCTIONAL SCENARIO

In the Classroom for Commas in Series

Teacher: I talked with Brandi, girls and boys, and she agreed that I may use one of her sentences to teach a lesson. Everyone, read Brandi's sentence: *We played games and had dinner and ate birthday cake.* How many things did the children do at the party? Sandy?

Sandy: Three: played games, had dinner, and ate birthday cake.

Teacher: Yes, they did. They did three things. I want to make a small change in Brandi's sentence. There's a word Brandi used two times that she had to use just once. Bob?

Bob: It's *and,* and she can take it out and put a comma in.

Teacher: Come up here and show us. [Bob takes out the first appearance of *and* and replaces it with a comma.] Boys and girls, Bob is right, but I have another question. What about the other *and*?

Manny: You have to have that. It would be *had dinner ate birthday cake* if you took it out.

Teacher: Yes, it would. So what about a comma there?

Manny: Do you have to put a comma there?

Teacher: Listen to this sentence: *I had eggs, bacon, toast, and juice for breakfast.* How many things did I have for breakfast?

Victor: Four things: bacon, eggs, toast, and juice. It's four.

Teacher: Well, then, listen to this one: *I had eggs, bacon, toast and jam.* How many things?

Victor: Three: eggs, bacon, and toast and jam.

Teacher: How do you know?

Several at once: Because that's how it is. You have jam on your toast.

Teacher: But what if you didn't already know how it is? What if you had to read the first sentence and the second sentence and learn how breakfast is? How do you know from the sentences?

Victor: It's because you don't put a comma in the second one.

COMMENTARY

Language Arts Standard

Second graders will cor-
rectly use commas to separate words in a series.

Victor got it: if the last two items in the series are different, we use a comma between them; if they aren't, we don't. We don't say that, of course. These are second graders.

Second graders eventually will use distinctions based on whether the last two items are discrete, but that isn't the purpose in the second grade. Rather, the purpose is to get them to replace *and* with commas to tell readers how many things there are in the series. If they do that with some consistency during the second and third grades, we can tell them about the distinction in the eighth or ninth grade or even when they're college juniors. If they use a comma between the last two items in the series all the time, they'll rarely be wrong because most of the time the last two items in the series will be discrete.

Having explained the convention, do they know it? No. Will they be able to use it when they edit their own work? Maybe a few will. They've had a lesson and now practice to make it automatic.

During writing instruction the next day, the teacher says, "Girls and boys, do you remember what we said about the comma in sentences when we have several things in a row? We call that a series. Good, I see lots of hands. Today we're going to write some sentences. Everyone, think of a sentence that contains the names of three of your friends, one right after the other. No, don't put it on paper. Write it in your mind. Good. I want to hear one. Heather." Heather says, "I went to the party with Grace, Paula, and Carla." "Good, Heather," replies her teacher. "Now I want you to read your sentence again, and this time, every time you come to a comma, say it out loud." And Heather reads, "I went to the party with Grace comma Paula comma and Carla."

The teacher listens to several more sentences and then directs the young writers to write their sentence on paper. They read their sentences aloud. The teacher stands behind readers to make sure the commas are placed properly. When they are not, the teacher leans over the child and shows how. The teacher listens to several sentences read aloud, some with the commas voiced, or read aloud.

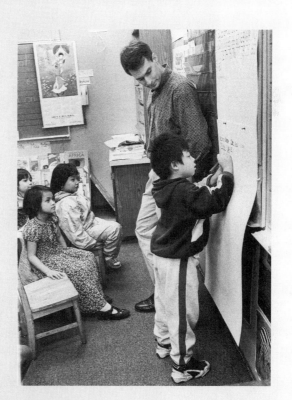

Writing at the board.
© Elizabeth Crews

Then the teacher cues another: "Think of a sentence that contains the names of three of your best toys." Follow with sharing aloud, writing on paper, and reading aloud. "That's enough for today."

VARIATIONS

The following day, the teacher directs two more sentences with items in series. Then he makes the day's writing assignment, an autobiographical incident (a sort of journal entry that tells of an experience) (see Chapter 10), and tells the students that they are to put into their autobiographical incident at least one sentence that contains items in series. They make the transfer from formal instruction on a punctuation convention to using that convention in their own writing.

There is a box under the sign that reads WRITING TABLE. Point to the box and tell everyone that there are writing Q-cards in the box: "Starting tomorrow, each of you must pick out a Q-card when you come into the room first thing in the morning and write the sentence as a ticket to recess."

There will be Q-cards that direct sentences with items in series to be used as tickets to recess for a week or two. There will be several larger writing experiences in which the second graders use a sentence or two with items in series. Thereafter, the teacher will expect, and hold everyone responsible for, using commas in series properly.

Four months into the third grade, the class moves on to a more difficult punctuation convention: using a comma to separate the introductory dependent clause from the independent clause in a complex sentence.

 INSTRUCTIONAL SCENARIO

In the Classroom with Complex Sentences

Teacher: Girls and boys, do you remember when we wrote those sentences that had a certain word in a certain position in a sentence, and I told you how long the sentence could be? Good. We're going to do it again, but this time I have a different reason, so you have to think very carefully. I want you to think of a sentence that has at least six words and the first word is *although*. Yes, a sentence of at least six words and the first word is *although*. Write the sentence in your head. [Pause.] Edgar?

Edgar: *Although I was hungry, I didn't get any dinner.*

Teacher: Ah, everyone. Listen to Edgar's sentence. Read it again, Edgar. [Edgar reads.] Listen to that sentence. [The teacher dramatically leans to the left.] *Although I was hungry* [the teacher dramatically leans to the right], *I didn't get any dinner.* [The leaning dramatizes that there are two parts in Edgar's sentence.] Listen again. [She leans one way and reads the first clause and leans the other and reads the second clause.] There are two parts in Edgar's sentence, boys and girls. Look at the sentence in your head, and make sure you can hear two parts. The two parts are important in this kind of sentence. Linda?

Linda: *Although my mother didn't want to, she had to get up.*

Teacher: Linda, read just the first part. [Linda reads.] Read the second part. [Linda reads the second part.] Now read the whole sentence. [Linda reads. Then the class listens to several more.] Now, boys and girls, I want you to think of another sentence in which the first word is *although,* but this time I want something in the sentence about a mealtime or having something to eat. Think, now, and write the sentence in your mind. [She pauses until those inevitable several hands shoot up.] Good. Now everyone write the sentence on your paper. [She roams the room to see how many young writers are finished or nearly so in approximately one minute. When it appears that most are finished, it is time for oral sharing. She tells those who are not finished to keep writing until they have their sentence on paper. During the roaming, she responds to the inevitable question about how to spell with, "Spell it as well as you can." And when it's time for oral sharing, she makes sure that the first writer called on has it right.] Clarissa, you had your hand up. Read your sentence.

Clarissa: *Although it was time for dinner, my brother wasn't home.*

Teacher: Good, Clarissa. Read it again, and when you get to a comma, call it out loud.

Clarissa: *Although it was time for dinner comma my brother wasn't home.*

Teacher: Ah yes, Clarissa. That is very nice. Everyone, listen to Clarissa read her sentence, and listen for the comma. [Clarissa reads again.] Now everyone, read your own sentence, and put the comma in there between the two pieces of the sentence just as Clarissa did. [Pause.] Scott, you read. [Scott reads.] Again, Scott, this time so we can hear the comma. [Scott reads.] Boys and girls, what do you notice about where we are putting the comma? Justin?

Justin: Between the two parts of the sentence.

Teacher: Yes, and we will write a lot of those sentences during the next week or so because I want you to be able to write them in your stories and autobiographies.

COMMENTARY

The teacher used young writers' own thoughtful sentence writing as the context in which to highlight the convention for using a comma in a complex sentence. First, everyone had to think in and write a complex sentence. We have found that third graders can think in and write such sentences, and the cue in the scenario works for the preponderance of them after about the third month of the third grade.

Second, everyone had to hear what the sentence sounds like so their own notions could be confirmed. That is why, in these earliest intentional teaching sessions, the teacher always calls on someone who has it right. The teacher wants a correct model *from the students.* The teacher calls on a correct model for the sentence and another for the comma.

Third, the teacher emphasized the sounds of both the sentence and the comma in the sentence. There is no sense in labeling the clauses. Third graders don't understand teacher terms, and even if they did understand "introductory adverbial clause" and "independent clause," they would never use that terminology as a guide when they write. People write their thoughts and images. Fiction writers listen to their characters talk, and editorial writers listen to their sentences in the ears of their readers. Third graders write complex sentences not because they know they're complex, but because they can hear them.

The terminology isn't relevant to these children's ability to write the sentence properly, and writing the sentence properly is the point of the lesson. Writing the sentence properly includes using the comma. They have to know the comma to write the sentence correctly. Of course, if they don't know the comma convention, they can't use it when they edit, either.

E S L The value of the oral emphasis cannot be overstated, especially for young writers working in a new language. Not only must they develop an auditory sense of how sentences work, they must also have an auditory sense of how the mechanical conventions work. In spelling, young writers become proficient partly because they come to know what words are supposed to look like. In punctuation, they become proficient *partly* because they hear commas in sentences. ▪

VARIATIONS

The purpose of the intentional instruction of complex sentences is to ensure that everyone can write complex sentences properly and automatically. Young writers are competent with complex sentences when they write them correctly without thinking deliberately about it. Of course, we also want young writers to be able to edit the complex sentences they draft and revise by combining simple sentences in their draft into complex sentences. But they have to be able to write them to do all of that. To that end, there are several variations that must occur:

1. They think in and write sentences that begin with *although*. They use those kinds of sentences in their everyday writing, on purpose at first, more easily with practice.

2. They think in and write sentences that begin with *because*. They use those kinds of sentences, and sentences that begin with *although*, in their everyday writing, progressively more easily over a period of several weeks.

3. They think in and write sentences that begin with *since, while, though, when,* and so forth over several months of guided practice. They include complex sentences in their everyday writing, deliberately at first and then automatically by the end of the fifth grade. We may even give an extra point when such sentences add to the quality of everyday writing.

4. We recognize that in every third grade there are young writers who, for a multitude of reasons, don't get the idea and never use complex sentences properly and automatically. We don't beat their heads on the desks. It is possible to write beautifully in the third and tenth grades without ever using a complex sentence.

These are complex sentences that third and fifth graders wrote in response to the kind of prompt we've described.

> *Although it isn't raining, I have my raincoat any way.*—Kristina, third grade
>
> *While the boys went to the store, my mom and I got the rice redy.*—Angela, third grade
>
> *Becauze of the dogs, none ov us evr went to that house.*—Andy, third grade
>
> *Since the last time we played, we practiced, and we got a lot better.*—Luther, fifth grade
>
> *Although we cheered as hard as we could, our team still lost.*—Angel, fifth grade
>
> *When it was all over, the dogs stopped howling.*—Chris, fifth grade

Commas in Complex Sentences Through the Grades

Levels K–1: Neither of us has ever taught this kind of lesson successfully prior to the third grade.

Levels 2–3: The previous instructional scenario is written for third graders about three months into the school year.

Levels 4–5: It now becomes critical for most young learners to be able to write complex sentences confidently. Complex sentences and compound-complex sentences are language strings designed to handle the sophisticated ideation that begins to appear when young writers are nine to eleven years old. If the youngsters don't come into the fourth grade with an initial sense of their ability to write complex sentences properly and automatically, they must acquire that sense immediately. The third grade is the appropriate one in which to introduce intentional instruction on the complex sentence; the fourth and fifth grades are the years during which young writers must practice under guidance and independently.

Levels 6–8: Begin the sixth grade with a direction to write a sentence that begins with *although* or *because.* When students say that sentences aren't supposed to begin with *because,* simply inform them that *because* is a perfectly good word to use when starting a *certain kind* of sentence, and it will take about ten minutes to teach them to do it properly. Then use the previous instructional scenario for using commas in complex sentences. By about midyear, if it's important to the curriculum committee in the school, the committee writing standards, the testing agency, the parents, or the children, teach them the terminology. Each of the two parts of the sentence is called a *clause*—"a group of words with a subject and a predicate used to form either a part of or a whole sentence" (Harris & Hodges, 1995). The second clause stands alone as a sentence, so it is independent; the first clause will not and is dependent on the second clause. Thus the complex sentence in this lesson begins with a dependent clause, ends with an independent clause, and uses a comma to separate the two clauses. Then direct more sentences by using the terminology—for example, "Write a complex sentence in which the dependent clause begins with *as.*" Practice complex sentence writing in response to cues and in everyday writing until they appear regularly in the students' writing. Encourage revision by using complex sentences in sentence-combining activities.

Secondary Level: Young writers need complex sentences to handle the complexity of their own ideas. If they cannot handle that level of sophistication when they arrive in the tenth grade, that is a good place to begin. The previous instructional scenario has been used with third graders and adults.

Capitalization and Punctuation Conventions: What They Mean and How They're Presented in the Standards

Rather than explain each of the thirty capitalization and punctuation conventions in the detail we have used with commas in complex sentences and commas in sentences with items in series, we provide a list (see pages 130–131) with each convention from the chart in Chapter 3 (column 1), an example of its use in a sentence (column 2), our suggestion for the range of time when it should be taught based upon what young writers write (column 3), and when instruction is recommended in a comprehensive set of language arts standards (column 4).

Instruction for each of the thirty conventions in capitalization and punctuation can be patterned after that already detailed for commas in series and commas in complex sentences. The stem for the writing cue for each convention is the same: "Think of [and/or write] a sentence that contains . . ." For convention 26 (capital letters in a person's title), a stem would read, "Write a sentence that includes the name of your doctor [dentist, mayor, president, etc.] and his or her title." If it isn't clear, write a model on the board: *I was surprised to find Mayor Sands at my school.*

You will notice from the chart that there are thirty conventions taught in ranges of two, three, and four years to accommodate intentional instruction, guided practice in isolation and in writing and editing context, and independent practice in writing and editing context. That's three years to teach compound sentences and the proper use of a comma to separate the independent clauses and four years to teach possessives and the proper use of apostrophes in singular and plural forms of possessives. We can accomplish this teaching and learning load for the preponderance of young writers if six conditions are met:

1. Teachers know the conventions.
2. Teachers intend to teach the conventions.
3. Teachers' intentional instruction is applied to what young writers write.
4. Intentional instruction is followed by guided practice and then independent practice in both writing and editing contexts.

5. Young writers know that capitalization and punctuation are important meaning markers in writing, used whenever they write.

6. Teachers value the accurate use of meaning markers sufficiently that young writers are held accountable for proper use. Teachers never say, "Capitalization and punctuation don't count as long as you get your ideas out."

Parts of "Speech": What They Mean and How They're Taught in Writing

Words are identified on the basis of the positions they fill and the roles they play in language structures. There are two ways to know these words we call **"parts of speech."** One way is to look at the position they fill in a language structure. In the sentence *The old man meandered absentmindedly down the street,* the third and eighth words fill positions that are always filled by words we call *nouns,* and if the first were not *man,* it could be *woman* or *giraffe.* If the eighth were not *street,* it could also be *woman* or *giraffe* (although those would make an odd image). The fifth position is filled with a word we call an *adverb.* The fifth position could be filled with *slowly, painfully,* or even *home,* and each of those words in that sentence would be an adverb by virtue of the fact that it occupies a position in the sentence occupied by words we call adverbs.

One designation for parts of speech, then, is the position the word fills in a sentence or sentence part. The other way to know the words we call parts of speech is to look at the roles they play in a sentence or sentence part. In the sentence about the meandering man, the second word tells something about the word that follows it, and the word that follows it is a noun. Words that tell something about nouns are called adjectives. So we know the second word is an adjective because it tells about a noun, and it occupies a position reserved for adjectives.

Before we elaborate on the two ways to identify parts of speech, it is important that we clarify the title of this portion of Chapter 5. We call it parts of "speech" only because that is the term English and language arts teachers use. In fact, however, we are not talking about speech; we are talking about parts of written sentences. Almost no one in the fifth or tenth grades ever conducts a grammatical analysis of speech as we know it or identifies the indirect objects when someone talks. It's in writing, and at the sentence level, that this discussion occurs.

Now we will go back to what an adjective is. In the context of English and language arts books, Weaver's definition (1996, p. 244) is characteristic: "An adjective is a word used to describe or 'modify' a noun." This definition satisfies the second of the two ways of identifying the nature of a word in a sentence. Notice, however, that the definition is not the one that appears in so many classrooms: "An adjective is a describing word." The reason that "describing word" is not a useful definition for an adjective is that a describing word can also be an adverb

Convention	Example in a Sentence
1. End punctuation	Billy went to the party. Did Pat go? No, she did not!
2. Commas in dates	Nancy was born on October 13, 1947.
3. Commas in series	Her favorite foods are pizza, pickles, and mud pie.
4. Commas in addresses	It happened at 1931 Peach Street, Kilgore, Texas.
5. Apostrophes in contractions	That giraffe won't ever climb an oak tree.
6. Periods in abbreviations	Our dentist is Dr. Sands.
7. Commas in compound sentences	The dentist is Dr. Sands, and his assistant is Dr. Carty.
8. Punctuation in dialogue	"Don't come in here," she said, yanking at the paper.
9. Apostrophes in possessives	The bird's nest fell into the tigers' wading pool.
10. Commas in complex sentences	While we all waited, he slept soundly.
11. Quotation marks and under-lining in published titles	"The Final Form of the Butterfly" by Lark Burkhart appeared in the May 1986 issue of <u>Crazyquilt Quarterly</u>.
12. Commas in series of adjectives	The large, green cucumber won the prize.
13. Commas to set off appositives	James Crawford, our coach, was a special man.
14. Commas after introductory words	Below, the river ran through the gorge.
15. Commas after introductory phrases	After the party, the boys headed home.
16. Commas in compound-complex sentences	When there are four of us, we order together, and we don't worry about who will pay.
17. Commas to set off parenthetical expressions	When there are only three of us, such as on Tuesdays, we are careful to divide the check exactly.
18. Dashes and parentheses to set off parenthetical expressions	Then when there are two of us (sometimes it happens on Mondays) we order separately—often ordering the same things.
19. Colons in sentences	It was cold that day: brittle, raw, wet, and piercing.
20. Semicolons in sentences	I'd like to see it rain more; the plants need it here.
21. Capital letters to begin sentences	"Don't leave me here!"
22. Capital letters in names	Kristina left her shoes at Don's house.
23. Capitalizing *I*	Go see if I left the shoes at Don's house.
24. Capital letters in days and months	There are four Mondays in March.
25. Capital letters in place names	We met in Phoenix, Arizona, and drove to Casa Grande. Before, we had gone to Oklahoma in the Midwest.
26. Capital letters in a person's title	We were thrilled to meet Senator McCarthy and Mayor Bradley on the same stage.
27. Capital letters in published titles	Everyone had to read *Green Pencils and No. 2 Lead*.
28. Capital letters in nationality, ethnicity, and language	Most Mexican people, including indigenous Indians, speak Spanish.
29. Capital letters in trade names, commercial products, and company names	Neither Xerox nor Coke can be used to name anything not made by Xerox Corporation and Coca-Cola.
30. Capital letters in names of institutions, associations, and events	Villanova University is a member of the National Collegiate Athletic Association and regularly competes at the Penn Relays on the University of Pennsylvania's Franklin Field.

We Suggest Teaching in These Grades	Standards Typically Specify Competence in These Grades
K, 1, 2	1
K, 1, 2	2
K, 1, 2, 3	2
K, 1, 2, 3	4
1, 2, 3, 4	4
1, 2, 3, 4	Not indicated
2, 3, 4	6
2, 3, 4, 5	2
2, 3, 4, 5	4
3, 4, 5	5
3, 4, 5	4
3, 4, 5	4
3, 4, 5, 6	5
3, 4, 5, 6	Not indicated
3, 4, 5, 6	Not indicated
4, 5, 6, 7	6
4, 5, 6	Appositive in grade 5
4, 5, 6, 7	Parentheses in grade 4; dash in grade 7
4, 5, 6, 7	5
4, 5, 6, 7	6
K, 1	1
K, 1	1
K, 1	1
K, 1, 2	2
K, 1, 2	3
1, 2, 3	2
3, 4, 5	4
3, 4, 5	Not indicated
3, 4, 5	4
3, 4, 5	3

(which describes how the man walked), a verb (which describes what the man did), an article (which describes the number of men), or even a noun (which describes who the sentence is about). A word is an adjective because it's in an adjective position in a sentence *and* it tells something about a noun.

One example makes the point about position and role. The word *run*, by the "action" definition of verb, is a verb, except in a sentence like this one: *The dog's run was planted in new grass.* There, the second word, by definition a noun, is an adjective because of the position it occupies and the role it plays, and the word *run*, a verb by definition, is a noun by role and position.

Parts of Sentences in Writing Instruction

Most teachers don't like to teach parts of sentences because they know it's a concession to high-stakes testing and will have little or no influence on the writing, reading, or oral language abilities of any student. The students don't like it either. They know they won't understand much better when it's over, and the grammar test will be factored into their overall English grade. Some parents do like it because they suspect there's something educationally worthy about it, even though they don't know what it is.

Our discussion here is intended to validate parents who believe there might be something educationally worthy about it, to ensure that the students understand something when it's finished, and to give teachers reason to believe they haven't wasted their students' time:

- People who understand parts of sentences have a common language for talking about writing.
- Some people who understand parts of sentences have a way to know how to make their writing work better.
- Teachers who understand parts of sentences can use what they understand to frame intentional writing instruction that makes young writers think.
- Young writers who understand parts of sentences know it and acquire a sense of competence because of it.

Teaching Parts of Sentences

Sentence parts occur at the sentence level, so teaching parts of sentences must occur in the sentences that young writers write. If work with parts of sentences occurs with sentences that other people wrote (e.g., peers' writing), it should be deferred until *after* students learn sentence parts in the context of their own writing.

Noun

Nouns can be identified by any of five criteria:

1. Nouns are preceded by noun determiners (*a, an, the*).
2. Nouns have two inflections (plural and possessive).
3. Many nouns may be identified by various noun-marking derivational suffixes (*-ion, -ity*).
4. Nouns fill certain characteristic positions in sentences relative to other sentence parts.
5. Certain patterns of stress distinguish nouns from other identical words (im´print : im print´).

Language Arts Standard

Learners will identify and correctly use nouns and verbs.

Remember that we are talking to second and third graders. Of these five criteria, they are most likely to learn and be able to use criterion 4. Seven year olds don't know words like *imprint* and *noun determiner*. They're three years from understanding *possessive*.

Recall the Given Word Sentence in Chapter 4: *Write a six-word sentence in which* rain *appears in the fourth position.* Go ahead, write it in your mind now. (We need something with which to work, and it has to be yours, not ours.) Now look at the sentence in your mind. *Rain* appears in the fourth position in a six-word sentence. What is the designation or label for *rain* in your sentence? Is it a noun (*It was hard rain that fell*)? Is it a verb (*Will it likely rain this Thursday*)? Is it an adjective (*We had a rainy day today*)? If you were in the fourth grade, we'd have you read your sentence aloud, and on the basis of information we've brought from the second or third grades, we'd all speculate on what kind of word *rain* is in your sentence and in the sentences of your classmates.

Then we'd notice where *rain* appears when it is a noun. Look at the *rain*-as-noun sentence from the paragraph above: *It was hard rain that fell.* What other words could we put in the position occupied by *rain*? Some possibilities are *snow, hail, sleet, words, music, wood, sunbeams, ice,* and *emotion.* Those are all nouns because they occupy a position in the sentence occupied by nouns. In fact, any word you put in that position would be a noun. Some words wouldn't make much sense (*elephants, pianos, noses*). What doesn't fit in the position is a word such as *pretty.* We can have a hard elephant fall, but we can't have a hard pretty fall. The language just doesn't work that way.

Here is a way for you to introduce this subject:

> Boys and girls, think of a six-word sentence in which *snow* [or something similar] is in the fourth position. What did we call those words, boys and girls? Nouns? Good. New sentence. This time I want you to think of a six-word sentence in which there is a noun in the fourth position.

That is a very important thinking and writing cue because it does two things that rarely occur in sentence parts teaching. First, everyone must concentrate on a noun. They are concentrating on what a noun does in their sentence. If they do that enough, they will learn about nouns. Second, they are thinking about nouns when they write. If we ever expect noun learning to have something to do with writing, the noun learning has to be in writing. Noun lessons almost always occur as finding and underlining. No wonder it rarely has anything to do with how well students write. It's rarely, if ever, about writing.

It's important to make sure young writers don't get the wrong idea about nouns. So the following day, we ask the children to think of a seven-word sentence in which a noun appears in the third position. We don't want ten year olds to generalize that nouns always appear in the fourth position of a six-word sentence.

And then we make the sentences progressively longer. Notice the first time a young writer shares a sentence that contains several nouns—*Soft music came from her stereo on the desk*—and call attention to the second noun. Then ask, "What else could go in that space?" Some possibilities are *closet, television set, voice,* and *mind.* Next, ask, "How about the third noun? What else could go in that position?" *Floor, window sill,* and *couch* are possibilities; they are all nouns. The next cue can be, "Think of a sentence that has a noun in the third and sixth positions."

We aren't saying that teachers ought not tell young writers that nouns name persons, places, and things. Instead, we're suggesting that what we know about how people learn dictates that young learners must focus or concentrate on what we want them to learn in the context to which we want it to generalize, or work. We want them to learn about nouns, and we want their knowledge of nouns to affect their writing. So the goal is to teach nouns in a way that ensures the learners concentrate on nouns, and do it in writing. It's okay to define nouns; it just won't affect anyone's writing.

Now, let us look at the parts of sentences most characteristically taught and tested and see how the discussion on nouns relates to other sentence parts.

Verb

Does anyone not agree that a verb is a word that shows action or state of being? We teach verbs for the first time in the second or third grades. Does anyone know a second or third grader who knows what "state of being" means? Can anyone pose a reason for telling a seven or eight year old that a verb shows state of being? If not, how do seven and eight year olds come to understand how the word *was* in the sentence *He was short* shows action?

There are five verb-marking criteria, just as there are five noun-marking criteria: four inflections (*s, ed[t], ed [d],* and *ing*); past tense changes with vowel change (*freeze-froze, drink-drank*); add /t/ and change the base (*sleep-slept, buy-bought*); add /d/ and change base (*sell-sold, do-did*); and /t/ after voiced consonant (*build-built, bend-bent*). You can teach those verb markers to seven year olds so they *know* verbs, but if you want to be realistic, you'll help them understand the role and position of verbs in sentences. They can understand that. (So can the rest of us who couldn't name the verb-marking criteria to save our lives, even though we're adults and just read them.)

Here are some ways to accomplish the goal:

- "Think of a sentence that contains the word *falling*. Write the sentence in your mind." Then listen to several, and redirect the sentence thinking and writing cue: "Think of a sentence in which the word *falling* appears in the third position. In the fourth position. In the second position. Now think of a five-word sentence that has *falling* in the second position. In the first position."
- "In the sentence *Mark and James carried their bicycles home,* what other word can be put in the fourth position?" Make a list on the board as the children volunteer words. Let's say the first volunteered word is *pushed,* so ask the young learners to think of a sentence in which the word *pushed* appears in the second position and then the third position. Then ask them to think of sentences that contain the various verbs on the list.
- Ask the youngsters to think of a sentence that contains a verb, and call on the young writer you know has it right. His sentence is *He pushed me down on the playground.* So now, you say, "Everyone, think of a sentence that contains the word *pushed.*" Then listen to several sentences that contain verbs.
- The next day, listen to several more sentences that contain verbs. The new cue is, "Think of a sentence that contains a verb and also contains a noun." Continue to, "Think of a sentence that contains two nouns and a verb," "Think of a sentence in which a noun appears in the third position and a verb in the fourth," and "When you write your autobiographical incident today, I want you to use at least six verbs."

Before we go to another sentence part, does anyone think young writers' knowledge of sentence parts will make them write better? The evidence indicates that it does not (Hillocks, 1986). Do you think that learning nouns and verbs as described above will help young writers write better? There is no evidence that it will, and there is no evidence that it won't, but the absence of evidence is not evidence of absence. Test it in your classroom. See if there's any change in the ability of young writers to write sentences as the result of these kinds of sentence writing activities. If you're interested, see if they understand nouns and verbs any better too.

Adjectives

"The primary defining or identifying quality of adjectives is their exclusive ability to fit into both the environments left blank in a structure such as: the _____ man seems very _____" (Francis, 1958, p. 268). Thus, adjectives appear between noun determiner and noun and immediately following a qualifier (*very*). We like the Francis definition, but we don't like to use it as a definition. We'd rather say to third graders, "Think of a sentence in which *man* is in the third position and *the* is in the first. What words could we put in the second position?" Write their suggestions on a list on the board (*old, scraggly, crippled, little*). Then,

Language Arts Standard

Learners will identify and correctly use adjectives and adverbs.

"Think of a sentence that uses the first word on the list. Think of a sentence in which the second word, *scraggly,* is in the third position."

As with nouns and verbs, make adjective sentence thinking and writing Q-cards to put in a box in the Writing Center. Each four- by six-inch card contains a writing cue such as, "Write a six-word sentence that contains an adjective in the second position." Make forty cards for the box. Inform everyone that during independent time each morning, they have to select a card and write the sentence on a scrap of paper. The sentence is their ticket to recess. After two months of the third-grade year, there will be four boxes in the Writing Center, each labeled with a sentence part: noun, verb, adjective, and adverb. Young writers make a selection from each box at least twice each week. That ensures that everyone writes at least one sentence focused on four sentence parts twice a week.

Adverbs

The adverb is a complicated sentence part marked by three criteria: position in a sentence, construction, and spelling. Its position tends to follow a noun, as in *The man worked on his job* _____, and a verb, as in *The man ran* _____. Adverbs are often compound words (*lengthwise, backwards,* and *someplace*). The spelling pattern often is /ly/ added to certain kinds of words. Those are the characteristic adverb markers.

It's dangerous to tell young writers about /ly/ because, being young, they overgeneralize and think that adverbs have to end in /ly/. Then they miss all the ones that do not. And the complications involved in the compound word construction make it not very useful for young writers because there are all sorts of compound words that are not adverbs (a few are *cowboy, statehood,* and *newspaper*). The sentence part indicator of greatest use for young writers is the role the word plays in the sentence and the position it occupies.

Here are some ways the lesson might go:

Language Arts Standard

Students will identify and correctly use coordinating conjunctions (grade 4); nominative, objective, and possessive pronouns (grade 5); indefinite pronouns and present perfect, past perfect, and future perfect tenses (grade 6); and infinitives and participles (grade 7).

- "Look at my sentence on the board: *The man walked slowly down the street.* What other words could we put in the fourth position?" List the words on the board. Then write sentences that contain the words on the board, followed by sentences that contain the words on the board in the adverb position.
- "Write a sentence in which the word *fast* comes right after a verb."
- "Write a six-word sentence in which a verb is in the fifth position and a word that tells about the verb is in the sixth position."

Other Sentence Parts

There are pronouns, prepositions, prepositional phrases, direct and indirect objects, objects of prepositions, and coordinating conjunctions. The intentional teaching strategies are variations on the prototypes above.

If young writers are going to satisfy the Language Arts Standard, they also need to know how the sentence parts are related to each other. When they know possessive pronouns and can write with possessive pronouns according to the cue, they need to understand and write with the possessive pronoun to satisfy their own writing needs. The cues could be as follows:

- "Think of a sentence that contains a possessive pronoun in the sixth position in a six-word sentence."
- "Write a sentence in which a noun appears in the second position and a possessive pronoun appears in the sixth."

When the young writers know verb and adverb, they need to write sentences for which they have to think in the relationship between verbs and adverbs—for example:

- "Think of a sentence in which an adverb tells something about the verb."
- "Think of a sentence in which a verb appears in the fifth position, and an adverb tells about speed or distance, destination, or direction."
- "Think of a sentence in which a prepositional phrase describes something about a noun or verb."
- "Think of a two-sentence piece that names a dog in the first sentence and uses a pronoun to name the sex of the dog in the second sentence."
- "Think of a compound sentence in which the coordinating conjunction appears in the seventh position."

Mechanical Control: Looking into a Second Grade

Ms. Jackson is an experienced second-grade teacher in a small midwestern school district. Her one-month plan book page, in Figure 5.1, reveals how a teacher can teach mechanical control very explicitly without committing inordinate time while making sure that everyone in the room understands what the conventions are and how they work in authentic writing. Here is Ms. Jackson's explanation for this one-month plan:

First, understand that the plan is only for my work in mechanics for only one month. I also teach a lot of genres, and, of course, I work on sentences and paragraphs every day. The numbers in parentheses show numbers of minutes for each instructional activity. One of the things that makes my room different from most of the other primary rooms in my district is that I have fifteen minutes every day on creative thinking and creative problem solving. I can't prove it, but I'm convinced that's one reason that my children write so well by the end of the year.

Early in the year, I like to start the children off knowing that they are responsible for making their writing correct. I review what I think they should have learned in the first grade. I usually have three or four children end up in a small group where I teach those capitalization and punctuation lessons.

Monday	Tuesday	Wednesday	Thursday	Friday
• Review End Marks • Review Commas in Dates • Reinforce Comma in Series	• Review Capital Letter to Begin Sentence • Commas in Series (10)	• Review Capital Letter in Names • Reinforce Apostrophe in Contrac-tions (10)	• Review Capital Letter in Pronoun • Commas in Series (6) • Apostrophe in Contractions (10)	• Apostrophe in Contractions (6)
• Reinforce Comma in Address • Capital Letters in Place Names (10)	• Comma in Series (Independent) • Capital Letters in Days of the Week and Months of the Year (10)	• Commas in Addresses (Independent) • Capital Letters in Place Names (6)	• Apostrophe in Contractions (Independent) • Capital Letters in Days and Months (6)	• Introduce Comma in Compound Sentence (10) • Capital Letters in Place Names (Independent)
• Review Period in Abbreviation • Comma in Compound Sentence (10)	• Comma in Address (Independent) • Period in Abbreviation (Independent)	• Comma in Series (Independent) • Comma in Compound Sentence (10)	• Apostrophe in Contraction (Independent) • Comma in Com-pound Sentence (Independent)	• Period in Abbreviation (Independent) • Capital Letters in Days and Months (Independent)
• Comma in Compound Sentence (Independent)	• Apostrophe in Contraction (Independent) • Capital Letters in Days and Months (Independent)	• Commas in Addresses (Independent) • Capital Letters in Place Names (Independent)	• Commas in Series (Inde-pendent)	• Comma in Compound Sentence (Independent)

FIGURE 5.1   Second-Grade Plan Book Page

There are always some things that need to be reinforced, so I spend a couple of sessions on those and then give them lots of independent practice. I like to do the independent practice in packets that they work on during independent time, mainly in the morning, or for homework.

Then there are new things to teach in the second grade. In the plan book page, those are commas in series and in compound sentences. I give the whole month to those early in the year because the children write compound sentences, and they write with items in series. I teach those by having them write compound sentences and sentences that have items in series. Then I include prompts for writing compound sentences and sentences with items in series in their independent writing packets. Sometimes they write compound sentences that have items in series. They're very clever.

I do some work on mechanics every day because having their writing correct is one of the reasons that their writing is good. It makes them careful and attentive. Sometimes I don't get it all in, but it's a priority, so I come pretty close most months. I hold my students responsible for doing what I teach, and they write correctly in their papers the rest of the year. Most of them do most of the time. I have to remind some of them, but by the end of the year in my room, I don't have anyone who doesn't write in sentences that are correct, and my students write a lot.

Some of this I teach in other curricular areas. Apostrophes in contractions and capital letters in the days and months, for example, I teach in spelling. Addresses and place names come in social studies, and there are a lot of abbreviations in social studies. It doesn't matter where it comes as long as they get it.

REVIEW AND REFLECTION

1. We have used the term *intentional* throughout this chapter as a modifier for the word *instruction*. What does *intentional instruction* mean for everyday lessons about mechanical control?
2. How would you describe the role of capital letters and punctuation marks in sentences?
3. How would you describe the role of adjectives and adverbs in sentences?
4. What is the role of practice in learning the mechanical conventions listed in this chapter?
5. With a partner in your class, write a three-day plan for teaching the use of the apostrophe in singular and plural possessives for fifth graders.
6. How would you explain the relationship between sentence writing and punctuation at a parent meeting?
7. With a partner, write a rationale for teaching parts of "speech" appropriate for presentation at a curriculum meeting at which you plan to persuade committee members to reconsider eliminating parts of "speech" from standards consideration.

A Summary: Mechanical Control

What we traditionally refer to as the mechanics includes, for the most part, capitalization and punctuation. They make an enormous difference in whether a writer's idea or image is communicated effectively.

The range of capitalization and punctuation conventions is enormous, and few, if any, young writers can ever learn it all, even if it's taught consistently and well. Happily, it's necessary to learn only the most frequently used conventions. Those represent most of the meaning markers that most literate people will need to write most of the time.

What is most critical about teaching mechanical control for writing is to teach it *in* writing. The ability to put marks into sentences that other people have written badly doesn't generalize to the ability to write. Good writers may not be good editors, and good editors may not be good writers. We teach the capitalization and punctuation conventions by directing young writers to think in and write sentences that demand them. As they write with the conventions, they begin to habituate their use in writing.

6 Teaching Craft: Paragraphs, Modes of Discourse, and Short Cues

BEFORE YOU READ

- What is the relationship between sentence thinking and writing and paragraph thinking and writing?
- What does it mean to refer to the paragraph as an organizational device?
- As you read this chapter, think about the similarities and differences between how you define a paragraph and how we define the paragraph in this chapter.
- Notice what "writing short" means in this chapter.
- Recall the last formal piece of writing you worked on for your university studies. Which modes of discourse did you use in that piece of writing?
- With which of the Short Cues have you had direct experience? Compare your own experience(s) with how short cues are described in this chapter.

Beyond the Sentence

The sentence is the fundamental building block of all writing in English, but it isn't the reason for writing. A sentence isn't what is called "extended discourse," nor does it tend to develop an idea. It can establish an idea or image, but exploring that idea or image often requires more than one sentence. The level of discourse that tends to explore an idea, or image, is the paragraph, or more. We write not to make sentences but to use sentences to explore larger ideas or images.

Usually writing instruction moves from single sentences to **paragraphs** in one leap. Along about the second or third grade, there is a sentence unit or series of lessons, and then children turn the page of the language arts book and find the shaded box. Inside the shaded box are several sentences, the first of which, they're told, doesn't start at the left margin. They're also told that all the sentences in the shaded box are about the same thing, and they can find out what that thing is by reading the first sentence. There are names for everything. The first sentence is called the "topic sentence" and the "indented sentence."

Also along about the second or third grade, the teacher asks the children to write short pieces about what they read or about their social studies lesson from yesterday. Sometimes the teacher calls the short pieces *paragraphs*. Later in the grades they may be called *summaries*.

The teacher also asks the children to *describe* their pet or the kitchen in their house. In some fourth grades, teachers ask children to describe their best idea in a way that others will think it's a good idea.

These writings all require more than one sentence to tell a bigger story or describe a bigger image. It is enormously demanding of writing skill and very important for becoming a competent writer.

This chapter is about taking the basic ideas young writers learn about sentence thinking and writing, and extending those ideas to longer pieces. However, the writings are longer only in the sense that they contain more than one sentence. The purpose of writing beyond the sentence is to help young writers master the ability to think in and write unified ideas. In this chapter, that means mastering the paragraph and relationships between and among paragraphs. It means handling ideas and images in modes of discourse and Short Cues.

Paragraphs

Harris and Hodges (1995) have no entry for *paragraph* in *The Literacy Dictionary,* but they do for *paragraph meaning,* which they define as "the content or significance of a paragraph" (p. 178). The *American Heritage Dictionary of the English Language* (1996) defines *paragraph* as "a distinct division of written or printed matter that begins on a new, usually indented line, consists of one or more sentences, and typically deals with a single thought or topic or quotes one speaker's continuous words." Savage (1998) defines *paragraph* as "groups of related sentences" (p. 215).

It is instructive that in every definition, the focus is on a unified idea—a main idea. A paragraph is about something, and the "something"—the main idea—

defines the paragraph. All of the intentional paragraph instruction in this chapter therefore is about main idea. Equally important is what this chapter is *not* about:

- There is no reference to any number of sentences that should appear in a paragraph because any number is arbitrary and unrelated to how a paragraph is defined.
- There is no reference to the kinds of sentences that should appear in a paragraph because the idea of kinds of sentences is arbitrary and unrelated to how a paragraph is defined.
- In the definitions, there is no reference to a topic sentence. Topic sentence has nothing to do with what makes a paragraph a paragraph.
- There is no reference to designs in intentional instruction activities. Paragraphs do not look like triangles, diamonds, or hamburgers. They look like paragraphs.

In other words, the entire focus in paragraph instruction is on main idea because that is what a paragraph is.

Paragraphs come into being from two directions. Sometimes writers write paragraphs, in the sense that they think, *Okay; I've finished that paragraph and now will begin another.* Perhaps more often, writers *find* paragraphs, or arrange what they've written into paragraphs, in the sense that they think, *Okay; I've written quite a bit here; I'll read it and see how I can organize it.* It's because writers so often find their paragraphs—that is, arrange what they have written into paragraphs—that what young writers read in their literature anthologies and social studies books only occasionally look like the paragraphs they are sometimes directed to write according to a formula in language arts class.

The activities that follow emphasize both writing paragraphs and finding them. We begin with a writing activity.

Paragraph Completion

Language Arts Standard

Students will create paragraphs that establish and support a central idea.

When learners of any age face a complex learning task, the teacher tries to arrange the task so that during the earliest stages, learners don't have to do everything simultaneously. Good instruction builds bridges between what the learner can do and is trying to learn how to do. In the language of learning psychology, those bridges are called *successive approximations.* Thus, in paragraph writing, the earliest attempts don't have to demand all at once from young writers the main idea in a whole paragraph and all the sentences. Perhaps it is sufficient for the earliest paragraph writer to think of only the main idea (Fearn & Farnan, 1999a).

INSTRUCTIONAL SCENARIO

In the Classroom for Paragraph Completion

Teacher: Boys and girls, look at what I have written on the board. Read it to yourself, and think of what it is about:

Brian searched and searched. Then he looked down . . . That is when he saw . . . He was happy to see . . .

Teacher: What do you think it is about? Selma?

Selma: It's about Brian, and he is looking for his dog and he found him.

Teacher: What do some of the rest of you think? What is it about? Barney?

Barney: He could be looking for his shoes and he looked down the laundry chute and found them.

Teacher: That's true. Everyone, do you agree that it's about Brian looking for something? All right. Now read it again, and this time think about how the sentences could be finished. The first one is already finished, but there are three more. Think of how you can finish the sentences so the paragraph would be about Brian looking for something and finding it. [Pause about fifteen to twenty seconds to think.] Now, on your paper, I want you to write the paragraph by completing the sentences. Everyone, write the paragraph.

COMMENTARY

This is a bridging activity. The main idea is inferred, the first sentence is written, and the other three sentences are started. The children are in the second grade, and this is their first attempt at something so complex as a paragraph. If we wait until next year, it isn't any easier for them because they're still working on their first several attempts at paragraph thinking and writing. In fact, if we wait until they are eleven years old to begin, they'll still benefit from the bridge, from the *successive approximations,* to get them started.

> Brian searched and searched. Then he looked down ondr his bed. That is when he saw his shos. He was happy to see his shos bekz no he cod go to scol.—Gilbert, second grade

Gilbert's paragraph has all of the necessary attributes of a paragraph according to definitions in a comprehensive dictionary of reading and language arts terms published jointly by the International Reading Association and the National Council of Teachers of English, a reading and language arts textbook, and the Language Arts Standard. If you are able to notice a main idea, if you have an idea or an image, that idea or image is the main idea of Gilbert's paragraph. Although it is very important to spell words correctly, the temporarily spelled words do not change the fact that Gilbert's paragraph has a main idea. It's Gilbert's first attempt at writing a paragraph, and he not only did it, he did it right. The teacher can say, with conviction and without any hedge to protect Gilbert's feelings, "Gilbert, you wrote a paragraph. Good for you!"

E S L Paragraph Completion responds directly to the need for comprehensible input. If a writing requirement is complex for native English speakers, imagine its complexity for children who have to comprehend the complexity of the writing demand in a second language. Paragraphing is made comprehensible for speakers of native languages other than English with Paragraph Completion. They begin with a main idea of their own invention and sentence stems that help them focus on that main idea. With Paragraph Completion, we increase the probability that children whose native language is not English understand what they are learning, and we decrease the number of obstacles between them and the learning objective. ■

VARIATIONS

Approximations, if they are going to take young writers to paragraph mastery, have to be successive or demonstrated over time. Gilbert and his second-grade friends write to Paragraph Completion frames similar to the one in the instructional scenario until they can do it easily and well, but along the way the bridge has to get smaller, and they have to do more of the work.

In Paragraph Completion, there is one way to make young writers do successively more of the work: Give them less and less. In the Paragraph Completion frame that follows, they get the first sentence and significant portions of the next three sentences. After several weeks of such frames, perhaps three times each week, each time with a different main idea, there can be a slight change:

Mary and Jane skipped along the path. The pretty little kitten . . . It was . . . Mary petted . . . Then Jane . . .

This time there is an additional sentence. Also, there is slightly less information in the second, third, fourth, and fifth sentences. What do you think is the main idea in the paragraph? As you quickly write the paragraph in your mind, what do you see Jane doing? What does *it* refer to in the third sentence? Where is the path? How do you know all that? Do you think this paragraphing activity mobilizes curiosity (wondering or pondering)? When writers use information that reflects their curiosity in the paragraph, that is creative. When they add or embellish, that is creative as well.

Language Arts Standard
Students will create multi-paragraph texts.

Perhaps the jump from the first frame to the second is too great. If it is, don't change the second one so much. Nevertheless, there has to be some change, because the learning progression has to be successive. The change has to be forward moving. Eventually young writers won't use any frame at all. Paragraph Completion is simply a way to get them from where they start to where they are independent, and not to confuse them or frustrate them along the way. Paragraph thinking and writing *can* be hard, but it doesn't have to be hard. And there is no reason, given a year's worth of Paragraph Completion, that most second graders, and certainly all third graders, can't be well on their way to independence with writing paragraphs that work.

There is one additional variation on the Paragraph Completion activity. Go back to Gilbert's paragraph about Brian's finding his shoes. Now assume that Gilbert is a third grader who has become quite good at this activity. He can look at a frame, see the main idea, and write the paragraph, all within maybe six to eight minutes. One day the teacher asks a very important question after Gilbert reads his paragraph aloud: "Gilbert, what do you think is the main idea of the next paragraph?" Now Gilbert has to think not only in one paragraph but in the transition to the next paragraph.

The variations on the "next paragraph" theme are numerous—for example:

- "What do you think is the first sentence in the next paragraph?"
- "What do you think is the last sentence in the paragraph that comes just before the one you just wrote?"
- "What do you think is the main idea in the paragraph just before the one you just wrote?"
- "What do you think might be the first sentence in the next paragraph and the main idea in the paragraph after that?"

It's at this point, when young writers are thinking in two- and three-paragraph clusters, that they are working on coherence because they are thinking in big pictures—images that are bigger than the sentence, even the paragraph. Now they are thinking like experienced writers.

Paragraph Completion Through the Grades

Levels K–1: There is plenty for children at those two grades to do in writing before they're confronted with writing extended discourse in paragraphs. That does not mean they don't see, think about, talk about, and read paragraphs.

Levels 2–3: These are the proper grades for introduction of the paragraph as a writing device. Later, we treat the paragraph as an organizational device.

Of course, Paragraph Completion, with all of its variations, can be used through the grades with young writers who need to understand paragraph writing or eliminate confusions regarding paragraph writing. But if young writers leave the second grade with a sense of what a paragraph is, they can leave the third grade able to write paragraphs fluently.

Levels 4–5: Many fourth graders do not think in and write paragraphs fluently. (Many fifth graders, and sixth and ninth graders, don't either.) Paragraph Completion is an appropriate way to establish the foundations for paragraph writing and eliminate the confusions the young writers have picked up along the way. If a teacher can conduct a ten-minute paragraph thinking and writing lesson for fifth graders who then write a good paragraph every time, and understand how they did it so they can be confident that they can do it again, that teacher will be a vivid memory for those youngsters forever.

Language Arts Standard

Young writers will group related ideas and maintain a consistent focus.

Language Arts Standard

Students will create paragraphs that establish and support a central idea, include supporting sentences that supply simple facts and details, and include a concluding sentence that summarizes the main idea.

The problem with the Language Arts Standard for Levels 4–5 is the assumption that every paragraph concludes with a summarizing sentence. In fact, the only paragraphs that end with conclusions or summaries are those that do not make a transition to another paragraph. The rest end with a sentence that takes readers to the next paragraph. If a transition sentence is viewed as a summary or conclusion sentence, however, we can satisfy the standard with the Paragraph Completion activity.

The one adjustment you have to make as young writers get older is in the content of the paragraph completion frames: The following frame offers a more complex main idea and a demand for greater inventiveness with the sentences.

> Today it stormed. Cold rain . . . The strong wind . . .
> My face . . . In late afternoon . . .

It may also be useful to develop the frames from content-area textbooks. For example, once the students have read and discussed a section in social studies on indigenous peoples, take one of the paragraphs from the text and make a frame out of it:

> When the settlers moved west, they came in contact with Indian people of many tribes. One of the tribes . . . They were . . . They lived in . . . The Sioux people hunted . . .

> When the settlers moved west, they came in contact with Indian people of many tribes. One of the tribes was the Sioux. The Sioux people were nomadic because they moved around and carried their houses which were teepees of poles and skins sewed together around with them. They lived in the Dakotas. The Sioux people hunted buffalo and other animals that roamed the prairie.—Fifth grade

These grades are excellent for moving young writers into the transitional thinking that occurs when we ask, "What do you think is the main idea of the next paragraph?" When fourth and fifth graders can write their single paragraphs from a variety of frames, ask the transition question and practice it several times. Then announce that from now on when they write one paragraph, they will always write something about the next one or the previous one.

Levels 6–8: Paragraph Completion can be used through the grades, though, we hope, with an ever smaller number of young writers in need. The explanations we have already provided apply through the middle school years and secondary school.

Sentence Sessions

Intentional instruction in sentence thinking and writing in Chapter 4 includes a series of instructional scenarios for Sentence Sessions. Recall that there are Single Sentence Sessions, then Double Sentence Sessions, and finally Triple Sentence Sessions. The cue or prompt is to arrange one or more ideas (*bounce, old man, color*) in one, two, or three related sentences. When young writers arrange several ideas into two or three related sentences, they are approximating paragraph thinking.

INSTRUCTIONAL SCENARIO

In the Classroom with Paragraph Building from Sentence Sessions

Teacher: Think of a way to arrange the following ideas into three related sentences: bicycle, box, a color, a character, and a time of day.

Enid: *My brother got a bicycle for his birthday. It came in a box, and when he opened it, it was mostly blue. We had a party for him that night, and all his friends were there.*

Teacher: Good for you, Enid. What's the main idea of your triple sentence piece?

Enid: My brother's birthday.

Teacher: Do you think it is finished? Do you think the main idea is as complete as you want it to be, or can you hear another sentence or so?

Enid: I think it's just one more sentence about how we have birthday parties in our family and that my brother's was a really good one because of the new bike.

COMMENTARY

The Sentence Sessions have multiple purposes because when young writers write that second and third related sentence, they have a paragraph going, and sometimes it is even finished. When the teacher questions them, as in the scenario with Enid's sentences above, they think about the main idea and whether or not it is finished. If it isn't finished, they can add a sentence or two to finish it. This is another activity that almost always produces a paragraph for every young writer in the room.

Working with both Paragraph Completion and Sentence Sessions, there is an opportunity for young writers to write at least a paragraph a day. The teacher can have a paragraph thinking and writing cue on the board every morning, and the paragraph can be the ticket to morning recess. There can be another paragraph for a ticket to afternoon recess and maybe even another for homework. That plan would have third and fourth graders writing two or three thoughtful paragraphs every day for maybe four days a week. That's 12 paragraphs a week, 48 per month, and, if they can keep it up through the year, over 400 thoughtful paragraphs by the end of the third or the fourth grade. Of course, it would never be 400 such paragraphs in a year because at some point along the way between 1 and 400, most of the young writers in the room will master the idea and won't need that sort of practice any more.

This is the time when one of the biggest problems that writing teachers face rises up and makes itself known: Who is going to read all of those paragraphs? There is a very important rule of thumb in serious writing instruction. You might want to post it on the classroom wall and distribute it to parents:

> If young writers write enough to learn to write well, no teacher can read it all; if a teacher can read it all, young writers cannot be writing enough to learn to write well.

The right answer to the question about who reads all of the paragraphs is, Not the teacher! Consider two parallels: Piano teachers don't listen to their students' every practice session, and basketball coaches don't watch all the jump shots in all the driveways in town. Nor do writing teachers read all the writing in the room. Young writers have a right to feedback from their teacher at least once every week. If they write every day and receive feedback only once, there's four days' worth of writing on which they don't get teacher feedback.

The work has to be checked so the teacher knows it has been done. A good policy is to spot-read every assignment to keep up on progress and collect information on which to plan instruction. It is also appropriate to read at least one piece of writing from every young writer in the room every week and have a conference with every young writer about what you read that week. The basic idea for the following conference questions came from a demonstration conducted by Donald Graves, noted writer and writing teacher, two decades ago in San Diego.

1. What are you [what were you] trying to do in this piece of writing?
2. What have you accomplished so far?
3. What do you have to do yet?
4. What can you do to make this piece better?
5. What do you have to do on this piece that I can help you understand better?

Those kinds of conferences are as short as one minute and rarely longer than about three minutes, so if the average is two minutes and there are thirty-five young writers in the room, the conference time is seventy minutes a week, or about fifteen minutes a day. Teachers can handle that, and young writers can benefit from it.

ESL One of the problems with early paragraph writing is that there are too many elements to control. English-language learners need clarity. Without it, they'll do the work, but the probability of confusion is multiplied by the fact that they're working in a second language. The specificity of the Sentence Session approach to early paragraph writing, and the single focus on the main idea, increases the comprehensibility of this enormous leap from sentence to paragraph. ■

Sentence Sessions Through the Grades

Levels K–1: The earliest writers think in and write single sentences and, well into the first grade, doubles. They will write in their minds, and some will write on paper. The interactions between teacher and young writers can focus on ideas in one sentence and two related sentences. Even in the first grade, teachers can refer to *main idea* when there is conversation about two related sentences.

Levels 2–3: These are the grade levels when the foundations of paragraph thinking and writing can be laid down most clearly. Second graders don't know that paragraphs are hard; they're ready merely to make their main ideas larger. It is certainly not beyond the capacity of young writers to experience one session per week in which they write single, double, and triple sentences, perhaps writing even a fourth sentence to achieve closure on a main idea. Many of those paragraphs, if not all of them, should go home with the children on Friday as refrigerator door decorations.

Levels 4–5: Paragraph instruction is routine in these grades. Some fourth and fifth graders already have experience with the enormity of the leap from sentence writing, which they may do reasonably well, to paragraphs, which they may not understand. Much of what they do not understand is the artificial formula work: the hamburger with bun on top and bottom and meat in the middle. They know hamburgers. They just don't know sentences as meat and buns, and it gets more complicated with references to tomato and onion. The Sentence Sessions go directly to the authentic paragraphing point: When we write paragraphs, we explore a main idea.

Levels 6–8: A third to a half of the students in middle and secondary school have a good handle on paragraph writing and can write good paragraphs just about whenever they want to. Another third can write reasonably good paragraphs much of the time. Up to a third remain confused.

We're not suggesting that the literacy problems of the world will disappear if seventh-grade teachers use Sentence Sessions. We are suggesting that if the hamburger analogy or the five-sentence formula left a third of the fifth graders confused and frustrated, they probably will again. The Sentence Sessions focus students' attention on main ideas, not fast food and sentence counts. That's what paragraphs are about. Middle and secondary students might understand that better.

Organizing Paragraph Sentences

Paragraph sentences are single sentences that can be arranged into main idea clusters, or paragraphs. The paragraph is more an organizational device than it is a purely writing device. Writers are just as likely to use paragraphs as a way to organize their writing as they are to write paragraphs when they draft. They are far less likely to set out with the purpose of writing a paragraph, then another one, then another, and so forth. And they are explicitly unlikely to write paragraphs according to a formulaic template that includes a certain number of certain kinds of sentences in a certain sequence.

Happily, there is less formulaic paragraph instruction in schools today than there was even a decade ago. Although a variety of paragraph writing formulas

Language Arts Standard

Students will create paragraphs that establish and support a central idea.

persist, most teachers aren't comfortable using them and do so only for lack of an alternative.

But most of us still don't teach paragraph thinking in a specifically organizational sense either. We teach young writers to write paragraphs, and we urge them to use paragraphs when they think about revision, but there is insufficient intentional instruction, especially in the early grades, directed at helping young writers understand how paragraphs help them organize their thinking and writing, how paragraphs clarify, or even reveal the meanings they have drafted. Organizing Paragraph Sentences represents intentional instruction for revealing, clarifying, and organizing meanings.

INSTRUCTIONAL SCENARIO

In the Classroom Organizing Paragraph Sentences in the Fourth Grade

Teacher: Read the sentences on the screen very carefully to yourself for practice because I want someone to read them aloud. [Pause] I see some hands. Kasandra?

Kasandra: *Each day, the sun came up hot and bright. June was a very hot month. At night, the sun went down in a blaze of red fire. It shone all day, burning the grass and making the dogs pant. It was very hot last June. Many people sat in the pool every day.*

Teacher: Thank you, Kasandra. You read very well. What is that about, girls and boys? What is the main idea of those sentences? James?

James: I think it's about how it was so hot, but it isn't right.

Teacher: It isn't? They are my sentences. What did I do that troubles you?

James: They aren't right, like they don't come right.

Kasandra: They're mixed up.

Teacher: Really? Who has a better sequence? I saw Shirlee's hand first.

Shirlee: The first sentence should be "June was a very hot month"; then, "Each day the sun came up hot and bright"; then, "It shone all day burning the grass and making the dogs pant"; then, "Many people sat in the pool every day"; then, "At night the sun went down in a blaze of red fire"; and then "It was very hot last June."

Teacher: Very nice, Shirlee. Larry, you had your hand up as soon as Shirlee began to read.

Larry: I think the first sentence should be, "It was very hot last June," and the last one should be, "June was a very hot month." The rest of the sentences should be like Shirlee did it.

Teacher: Jerry? Do you have an idea?

Jerry: I think you could make the first sentence, "Each day the sun came up hot and bright," and then say, "It was very hot last June." [There is a chorus of "Nooos" in response to Jerry's suggestion.]

Teacher: Wait. If we did it the way Jerry suggested, would it work? [Everyone agrees that it would work, but Larry's and Shirlee's were better.] Good. Everyone, write the sentences in the order that you think is the most interesting and will make the main idea most clear. Remember, if it's on the screen, there is no reason not to spell every word correctly.

COMMENTARY

There are two learning opportunities in the instructional scenario that begin to lay a foundation for fourth graders' understanding of critical abstractions in writing. First, the activity makes clear that there is more than one plausible way to organize writing. Second, the only way to know what is plausible is to see if it works.

Shirlee's arrangement worked. Larry changed Shirlee's to another that also worked. James had still another arrangement, and the teacher told everyone to write what they thought might work, so there may be several more arrangements. Finding plausible patterns is important in paragraph thinking and revision.

It is also very important for young writers to use the test as early as possible in their learning-to-write experience by asking, "Does the organization work?" It is the test they will use forever in their writing because it is the test readers, editors, and employers use for determining whether writing is good.

Language Arts Standard

Learners will create multi-paragraph texts that feature a clear organizing structure.

BACK TO THE CLASSROOM TO ORGANIZE PARAGRAPH SENTENCES

Teacher: [Having arranged the class in pairs of young writers] I am distributing packs of sentence cards. Each card has one sentence on it, and there are twelve sentence cards in each pack. Lay the sentences out on your desk so the two of you can see all of them at once. Everyone, let's read the sentences out loud.

- Well, who does that goat think he is, coming across your bridge and only saying that another is coming?
- "Someone should write a story about the unfairness so little children will know about what happened here," you think.
- "Who is that tramping across my bridge?" you ask.
- But the third one is a big goat, and he butts you through the air, hurting you badly.
- But this second goat tells you that he is only a little goat and you should wait for the third goat.
- You feel that you have the right to protect your bridge, so you come out to see the third goat.
- The goat tells you not to worry because there will be another along any minute.
- "Hey! Who is that tramping across my bridge?" you ask a second time.
- And sure enough, someone did.
- That was a very unfair thing that happened, you think, as you nurse your painful bruises.
- Think of it: this is your bridge and someone comes across without even asking.
- And in time, along comes another goat.

First, I want each pair to agree on a sequence for the twelve sentences. Move them around so they are in an order that works. [This takes about three to five minutes.] Now look over your sequence and see where the main ideas change. Find the main ideas, and separate the sentence cards into clusters. There may be only one, maybe two or three, or maybe even four or five. Separate the sentences into main ideas. [This takes about three or four minutes.] If you found yourselves with a sentence or two that you don't think you can use, set that sentence or those sentences aside. And if you find you need another sentence or two or three, write those sentences on a piece of paper. [This takes about two or three minutes.]

Now this is the last part of this activity. Between the two of you in each pair, rewrite the story as you want it to appear. You may use the sentences you have, or you may write some new ones. [This takes about ten minutes.]

Now let's hear some of your stories read aloud. [Hester and Lester read.] How many paragraphs do you have?

Hester: Five.

"Who is that tramping across my bridge," you ask.

Think of it; this is your bridge and someone, in this case a goat, crosses it without even asking.

Well, who does that goat think he is, coming across your bridge and only saying that another is coming?

"Hey! Who is that tramping across my bridge?" you ask a second time.

The goat informs you not to worry because there will be another along any minute.

And in time, along comes another goat!

But this second goat only tells you that it is him, a little goat, and, "Don't worry because a third goat is coming."

Now you feel that you have the right to protect your bridge, so you come out from under it to see this third goat.

But the third one is a big goat and he butts you through the air, hurting you badly.

"That was a terribly unfair thing that happened," you say to yourself as you nurse your painful bruises.

"Someone should write a story about the unfair event so that little children will know about what happened here," you say to yourself.

And sure enough, someone did.

Teacher: Someone else read. [Anne and Marie read. They have six paragraphs.]

COMMENTARY

These fourth or fifth, or maybe even third, graders read to figure out what the writing is about. Then they find an arrangement that works best to clarify what the writing is about. Having found an arrangement, they identify the main ideas and then rewrite the whole piece according to their thinking and arranging. Finally, they publish their work by sharing it with an audience and receive feedback from that audience about how well the writing worked. That is what writing and revision looks like when practiced by experienced writers who make their living at it.

VARIATIONS

The only limit on what you can use for Organizing Paragraph Sentences is the reading ability and prior knowledge of the young writers. Most children know "Three Billy Goats Gruff," and for those who don't, it is easy enough to read the story aloud for several days before using it.

Another source of material for Organizing Paragraph Sentences is the content areas. Organizing Paragraph Sentences can be used to review prior knowledge and establish directions for learning (Ogle, 1986). Prior to a unit on Southwest Indian people, for example, consider using the following twelve sentences:

- *Pueblo people live in villages built mostly of stone and adobe.*
- *There are over 200 Indian tribes in the United States that include about a third of a million Indian people.*
- *The Hopi Reservation in Arizona is surrounded on all sides by Navajo land.*
- *The largest reservation that contains the largest tribe is the Navajo.*
- *Of the four main Apache tribes, two are located in New Mexico.*
- *The only real apartment house pueblo is at Taos, New Mexico.*
- *Pueblo people seem to have come to Arizona and New Mexico from an area in what we now know as southwest Colorado.*
- *The Acoma Pueblo was very old when Europeans came to what we know as the American Southwest.*
- *The Navajo Reservation is in three states—Arizona, New Mexico, and Utah—and is about the size of West Virginia.*
- *In central New Mexico, the Mescalero Apache people have a horse racing track and a ski resort.*
- *Hopi people live much as the Pueblo people in New Mexico live.*
- *San Carlos and White Mountain are the two Arizona Apache tribes.*

> There are over 200 Indian tribes in the United States that include about a third of a million Indian people. The largest reservation that contains the largest tribe is the Navajo. The Navajo Reservation is in three states—Arizona, New Mexico, and Utah—and is about the size of West Virginia.
>
> The Hopi Reservation in Arizona is surrounded on all sides by Navajo land. Hopi people live much as the Pueblo people in New Mexico live. Pueblo people seem to have come to Arizona and New Mexico from an area in what we now know as southwest Colorado. Pueblo people live in villages built mostly of stone and adobe. The Acoma Pueblo was very old when Europeans came to what we know as the American Southwest. The only real apartment house pueblo is at Taos, New Mexico.
>
> Of the four main Apache tribes, two are located in New Mexico. In central New Mexico, the Mescalero Apache people have a horse racing track and a ski resort. San Carlos and White Mountain are the two Arizona Apache tribes.—Two fifth graders

Another variation that has been very useful, especially in earlier grades, is the use of simple directions that can be written in four sentences:

- *Begin at the left end of that line and make a straight line down one inch long.*
- *Make a straight line from left to right one inch long.*
- *Connect the ends of the two lines with another straight line.*
- *You are going to make a shape.*

The easiest way to make sentence cards is to copy them from books. The following four-sentence collection came from a social studies book:

- *It took 1,700 years to build.*
- *The wall has enough stone to make an eight-foot wall around the world.*
- *The Great Wall of China is 2,500 miles long.*
- *It is the longest continuous building project in the world.*

E S L
One of the language learning attributes of students whose native language is not English is that they very likely read the second language before they write it. Organizing Paragraph Sentences capitalizes on the reading and thinking abilities of English-language learners. The sentences that they organize can be from the material they are learning to read. Even better, the sentences can be from their own self-reports of their weekend experiences, their vacations, their interests, and so forth. If there is an experiential difference between students who do and do not speak English as their primary language, using students' own experiences will eliminate the differential. The point is organizing. What they organize is irrelevant. ■

Organizing Paragraph Sentences Through the Grades

Levels K–1: There are a variety of sequencing activities appropriate for children in the kindergarten that will establish the idea of sequences necessary to eventually work with paragraph sentences.

Levels 2–3: The organizational focus should begin in second grade. Sequencing is important not only when young writers revise, but when they draft as well.

The third-grade standard has young writers moving into the kinds of formal paragraphing behaviors found in many language arts textbooks. To the extent that good paragraphs feature topic and other sentences that support the topic sentence, there is merit in focusing on such kinds of sentences. When the classroom activity is Organizing Paragraph Sentences, the focus is on main idea and organizational thinking. In the Great Wall of China collection of sentences above, one of them is clearly a topic sentence. The third-grade standard can be satisfied with Organizing Paragraph Sentences.

Levels 4–5: In the fourth and fifth grades, paragraph thinking and organization can be a weekly feature, often supported by Organizing Paragraph Sentences. It would be useful for fourth and fifth graders to discuss the paragraphs they "find." For example, on the indigenous peoples collection of sentences, a pair of fifth

Language Arts Standard

Second graders will group related ideas and maintain consistent focus.

Language Arts Standard

Third graders will develop a topic sentence and supporting sentences.

graders has organized the twelve sentences into four main ideas. The first of them reads as follows: *There are over 200 Indian tribes in the United States that include about a third of a million people. The largest reservation that contains the largest tribe is the Navajo. The Navajo Reservation is in three states—Arizona, New Mexico, and Utah—and is about the size of West Virginia.* These are the discussion questions:

- What is the central or main idea?
- What is the topic sentence?
- What are the supporting sentences?
- How do the supporting sentences support the topic sentence?
- What is the concluding sentence?
- Is the concluding sentence one that concludes the main idea, or is it just the last sentence in the paragraph?
- If the last sentence does not conclude the main idea, is the cluster of sentences still a paragraph?
- What defines your paragraph?
- What makes it a paragraph?

Language Arts Standard

Learners will create an organizing structure that balances all aspects of the piece and makes effective transitions that unify key ideas.

Levels 6–8: The activity in Organizing Paragraph Sentences is fundamentally organizational. A seventh-grade language arts standard highlights this larger organizational purpose.

Once young writers understand relationships between and among sentences and the organizational nature of paragraphs, they must apply what they understand to larger pieces of writing. No matter how much time is committed to sentences and paragraphs in language arts and English classes, the purpose of writing remains at the level of larger messages.

The twelve-sentence activity we described in the second instructional scenario and the content-area variation (indigenous peoples) concentrate on the seventh-grade standard. It would be useful to participate in an organizational activity several times a month. Young writers should work with partners sometimes and alone sometimes. And they should always rewrite the organized piece, in class or for homework, sometimes collaboratively and sometimes individually.

Secondary Level: High school applications of Organizing Paragraph Sentences are just like those for the middle grades.

Paragraph Analysis

Many language arts and English textbooks, workbooks, and worksheets typically contain several paragraphing sheets, at the top of which is a paragraph, usually in a shaded box. Then there are four questions for young writers to answer after reading the paragraph:

1. What is the main idea of the paragraph in the box?
2. Write the sentence that best expresses the main idea of the paragraph.

3. Write the sentence that explains the main idea of the paragraph in the box.

4. Write the sentence that summarizes the main idea or draws a conclusion from the paragraph in the box.

Young writers read someone else's paragraph, write one phrase, and copy three sentences. When they are finished, they turn in the paper as homework or in-class seatwork. When we use such an activity in paragraph writing lessons, not one student in the class writes a paragraph. It's as though there were an activity devoted to playing tennis, and everyone learned to identify the parts of a tennis racket. The ability to identify the sentences in a paragraph has nothing at all to do with the ability to write a paragraph.

Just because the boxed-paragraph activity doesn't require young writers to write a paragraph doesn't mean we ought not use it. But the activity needs this question: "What might be the main idea of the next paragraph?" And when it has this question, this might be the best paragraph writing assignment young writers will ever see. They have studied the existing paragraph carefully enough to know its main idea and to have selected three of its sentences to copy. Because the last sentence they copied was very likely the last one in the paragraph, they have a good start on a transition into the next paragraph. All they have to do is keep going.

Of course, there can also be a direction that follows: "Write the next paragraph." Now the paragraph worksheet includes writing whole paragraphs. The tennis lesson is no longer only about the parts of a tennis racket. Now they're stroking a simple forehand.

Modes of Discourse: The Paragraph and Beyond

There are several more examples of extended discourse in this chapter. These are not as long as genres; they tend not to be whole stories, essays, or reports. But they are important nevertheless. This section examines four **modes of discourse: description, analysis, compare and contrast,** and **criticize and persuade.** Those modes can be used in larger **genres.** Writers describe their characters in short fiction, they analyze a complex process in technical writing, they compare and contrast attributes of, say, wolves and coyotes in reports of information, and they criticize and persuade in their editorial commentaries.

The modes of discourse also work in combination. For example, George Will, a nationally syndicated columnist, often analyzes a political issue, describes alternative possibilities, and attempts to persuade readers, all in a single 750-word column. The modes of discourse are important for writing well. They can be shorter than whole genres but longer than one or two sentences. They occur beyond the sentence.

Writers influence readers by causing knowledge or commitment. That influence is often carried in the modes of discourse.

Descriptive Writing

The idea of description is to put images before readers. It's not always visual, of course. It's idea and image. It's what we hear and see, taste and think, feel and do. There are important aspects of characterization embedded in how a woman drinks her coffee during a managers' meeting, how a child jumps rope, how a man walks across the deck of a rolling ship. Descriptive writing puts the image in readers' minds and souls.

Description is systematic, sequential, and sensory. It features a variety of attributes to facilitate image or idea. Following are some examples of sentences that use some of the attributes:

Attribute	Example Sentence
Size	*He calculated an inch, the distance between the first and second knuckles on his right index finger.*
Motion	*The tension in the stadium was electric as the high jumper rocked back and forth, from the ball of her foot to the heel, back and forth, waiting for the right instant to begin her approach.*
Position	*Darryl and Jim ran side by side, purposely together, carefully calibrating their strides to make sure they crossed at the same time, even as the enraged crowd screamed for a winner.*
Shape	*Beans stood taller than everyone else on campus, straight, angular, extra thin.*
Color	*When he opened his hand and began to peel his orange that cold and snowy afternoon, someone far away could have imagined a fire in his hand* (Soto, 1990).
Texture	*Smoke hung heavy in what they called a hogan when Kristina bit into the fry bread on her plate. It was surprisingly sweet, puffy inside with crispy crust, and warm.*
Significance	*Nothing the wolf ever heard exhilarated her like the sound of clicking hooves and antlers, the smell of fresh manure, and the heat from so many bodies. But it was their terror that excited her most. The caribous' eyes bulged into huge globes.*
Atmosphere	*Ramona sat ramrod straight in her wicker chair opposite Park. She was too terrified to move. Every eye in the restaurant was fixed on the color of her skin.*
Mood	*They could smell each other's fear. The slightest sound outside brought hair on their backs to a prickly stand.*

Writers often experience the image or idea they want to describe for readers literally played out in front of them in three dimensions, completely finished and in full color. The action is literally in the writer's mind. To bring the action to readers, the writer must slow each frame of the action and make it into language that readers can use to construct the action again. Description is the mode of discourse writers use to make language from each frame of action.

Each objective for writers is followed by several writing activities. That pattern runs throughout this section on modes of discourse.

Objective 1 for Descriptive Writing

The writer forms a mental image and describes that image for readers:

1. "Without using the word *square* or *box,* write directions for drawing one. Your description may be no more than four sentences in length."
2. "Describe the shape of a football for someone who has never seen one."
3. "Select an object you are likely to find in the cafeteria: a cup, a milk carton, a fork, a food tray. Study it carefully, and draw it in your mind. Then write directions for drawing the object."
4. "Describe your shoes. Be sure to include the inside and outside, the tops and bottoms."

Objective 2 for Descriptive Writing

The writer forms an imaginary mental image and describes that image for readers:

1. "Think about the trunk of a tree. Imagine that you are nonsighted. How could you know the trunk of that tree only by its feel? In not more than four sentences, describe how a reader could recognize your tree only on the basis of how the trunk feels."
2. "Imagine a lemon's stem is its north pole. Imagine cutting the lemon in half at the equator. Using only color and texture, write about what the inside of the lemon looks and feels like. Now examine a real lemon, and write again."
3. "I have given each of you an ordinary pebble. Write a description of it so that someone who reads your description can identify your pebble from among four others. No one may mark the pebbles in any way."
4. "Describe the swimming movements of a tropical fish in the classroom tank."
5. "Imagine a playmate whom you could have at your house whenever you want. Describe what kind of person the playmate would be."

Descriptive writing applies through the genres. As the fiction writer views a stormy street scene in which a character is trapped with no shelter from the rain and wind, the image is complete, wet, cold, blustering, and lonely, perhaps even terrifying. Readers must feel the terror and cold rain, see the automobiles cruising by without noticing, and hear the cracking of a tree limb as it comes loose from the trunk and crashes to the ground. Readers must see the autobiographical scene and feel the pain at the Thanksgiving dinner, loving family all about, but father far away in a cold prison cell. They must understand the argument a writer makes against tearing down the old building so a parking structure can be built. Descriptive writing crosses all the genres.

Analytic Writing

Analysis is organization. It is finding and explaining order. It is the expression of problem solving and the methods of science. Analysis is systematic, and because systems are arrangements of internally related parts (number systems, alphabetic systems, musical notation systems), it is important in analytic writing to present the related parts in the larger context. Analytic writing therefore tends to pose the context early.

Analytic pieces of writing tend to begin with a statement that tells readers what the piece is about. That sort of introductory language provides readers with a hook on which to hang the details or parts that follow.

Having established the organizational scheme, the writer proceeds to detail the elements that make up the scheme. Analysis tends to follow a cause-and-effect process. It tends to tell readers that B results from A and C from B, and if the reader can understand that much, it soon becomes clear that the next point is D. That makes all sorts of sense to readers because everyone knows the system.

But if you don't know the system and you are presented with ABCD, you might never figure it out if the reader doesn't establish the scheme first. Suppose the scheme were a four-word sentence in which the first word is a two-letter verb, the second word is a four-syllable adverb, the third word has two syllables followed by a comma, and the fourth word is a proper noun. Now, aren't you thinking about that sentence? We're working on word order in a sentence. That is what analytic writing does. It begins with the scheme, the system, and it follows with the details.

The reporting form for scientific writing is analytic. It begins with the question or problem. Then it presents the details of procedures, findings, conclusions, and implications.

Given what we know of analytic writing, it is clear that's what we should call the five-paragraph formula (or the three- or seven-paragraph formula). There is a thesis statement in the beginning (the scheme or system), followed by the details in order. So instead of referring to a formulaic "essay," we should be talking about *formulaic analyses.*

The analytic mode of discourse is logical when it moves from point A to B to C, and it is chronological when it moves from first to second to third. In both cases, there are parts in an order that helps readers understand the whole.

Both description and analysis depend heavily on parts to reveal the whole, but description leads readers to the whole by presenting the parts, while analysis tells readers what the whole is and then explains how the whole is formed by presenting the parts.

Objective 1 for Analytic Writing

The writer begins with the whole and explains the meaning by elaborating on the parts:

1. "Begin a paragraph with the following sentence: *Long division is a complex mechanical process for finding equal parts.* Finish the paragraph by explaining the steps in solving 329 divided by 72."

2. "Explain how the character Maniac Magee in Jerry Spinelli's book by the same name is an example of fairness."

3. "Visualize a red rose—a big one in full bloom. Pretend a new friend has never seen a rose. Explain a rose to your friend, beginning with the big image and then using the big image to detail what a rose is, what it looks like, and how it smells."

Objective 2 for Analytic Writing

The writer explains a complex idea or image that is formed from a prompt:

1. "Write what you think that the First Amendment to the U.S. Constitution means."

2. "Read *Elbert's Bad Word* [Wood & Wood, 1988]. Explain how the story represents higher-class society."

3. "Copy the Pledge of Allegiance. Now write an explanation for what the Pledge of Allegiance means."

A short story about making counterfeit currency can require analytic writing. The writer would have to reveal to the reader how the character made printing plates, acquired the special paper from the Crane Paper Mill, and got the special ink. It is a very complex process that would require analytic writing.

The procedures section in a research report is analytic. A report on how Carl Sandburg highlighted the self-fulfilling prophesy in social interactions when he wrote "Who Was That Early Sodbuster in Kansas?" would require analytic writing. The influence of our writing increases as we use analysis appropriately.

Compare-and-Contrast Writing

Comparison features similarities, and contrast features differences. The clarity of writing increases with the use of comparison and contrast to reveal ideas and images.

Often comparisons and contrasts are expressed in figurative language—metaphors, similes, and analogies. We write that the half-miler floated around the track, that she ran with the grace of a dancer, that her performance was to track what Martha Graham's was to dance. But none of those comparisons will work if readers don't already know about floating, dancing, and Martha Graham. It is critical in any attempt at comparison and contrast to capitalize on what readers know. This is one place in writing where writers must know their readers very well.

Comparing and contrasting can be likened to a precise application of context. Writers are saying to readers: "I can help you understand what I am writing by showing you examples [comparison] and nonexamples [contrast]." The writer shows readers what the image is like and what it isn't like—for example, *A North Pacific storm is cacophonous, not merely loud; rhythmic, not random; penetrating, sopping wet; pure like new snow; a pristine experience every time, never just another rainy day.* That sentence contains one comparison and three contrasts.

When comparing and contrasting equal treatment and equality, a writer may contrast the idea by suggesting that when we see a doctor for a throat irritation, the doctor doesn't prescribe enough medicine for everyone because everyone doesn't have the same irritation: *Equality* [writes the author] *means having access to the doctor; equal treatment means making sure that everyone has the same medicine. It was Thomas Jefferson who said, "There is nothing so unequal as the equal treatment of unequals."* That example about equality and equal treatment contains an analogy and a contrast plus three more contrasts in a play on words.

The sentence about a North Pacific storm is intended to help readers who have never been there understand, if not indirectly sense, that such a storm is an event played out on the skin and in the ears, an experience of memorable purity that leaves a sweet taste. The ideas of equality and equal treatment are highlighted with the analogy and the contrasts. The pieces are certainly descriptive, but the descriptions themselves capitalize on the contexts of readers' prior knowledge.

Objective 1 for Compare-and-Contrast Writing

A writer compares images or ideas by focusing on similarities between and among the images or ideas:

1. "Choose two pieces of writing by one of your favorite authors. Show how the two pieces of writing are similar."
2. "Pretend you are writing for readers who know little or nothing about hockey, soccer, and lacrosse. Write a piece of at least 150 words that shows how the three games are similar."
3. "Alabama and Pennsylvania are referred to as geographic sister states. Compare the two states so that readers will know how they are similar enough to be called geographic sisters."
4. "Write a four-sentence piece in which you compare addition and multiplication by explaining their similarities."

Objective 2 for Compare-and-Contrast Writing

The writer compares images and ideas by focusing on differences between and among the ideas and images:

1. "Think about the possibility of dividing one of the following three states into two separate states: Texas, New York, or Minnesota. Describe in what way the state you select would be separated, and explain why the two new states would be different from one another."

2. "Study your left thumb for 30 seconds. Then study your right thumb for 30 seconds. Now place the two thumbs side by side and study them together for 30 seconds. Write about how your thumbs are sufficiently different for someone to be able to tell them apart."

3. "Having read Jean Little's *Hey World, Here I Am* [1986], write about how Kate and Emily are different. Include at least five ways to tell Kate and Emily apart."

4. "Think about at least three ways in which multiplication and division are different. Explain those differences between multiplication and division in a piece of at least five sentences."

Objective 3 for Compare-and-Contrast Writing

The writer uses both similarities and differences to write about ideas and images:

1. "Select two characters from two different short stories, and write a piece of at least 150 words that shows how the two characters are both similar and different."

2. "W. E. B. Du Bois is widely recognized as one of the greatest intellectuals of the twentieth century. Martin Luther King, Jr., is widely recognized as one of the greatest civil rights leaders of the twentieth century. Compare the two men by explaining their similarities and differences."

3. "As part of your study of the Constitution, clarify the difference between ratification and adoption. Describe the two terms by explaining similarities and differences."

4. "Write a piece between 65 and 80 words long that describes both similarities and differences when comparing the feet of gorillas and humans."

The compare-and-contrast mode of discourse is difficult to separate from descriptive writing. Even the prompts we have given often use the word *describe*. While it is common for descriptive writing to compare and contrast in order to highlight attributes, the compare-and-contrast mode of discourse explicitly targets similarities and differences, usually in the same context, and often figuratively.

The use of comparisons and contrasts in writing promotes a kind of thinking that strengthens writing. When young writers think about comparisons and contrasts, they have to invent contexts that are broader than their target idea or image.

All of the genres benefit from comparisons and contrasts. It is important in short fiction, for example, to distinguish characters in the story and make distinctions within a character over time. We enhance persuasive writing by comparing and contrasting our argument with the arguments of others. Often we give life to a biography when we make it clear how the subject is both similar to and different from another biographical figure studied earlier. Our letter to our aunt is especially clear to her when we compare the book she sent with several others we have read recently.

Criticism and Persuasive Writing

Criticism and persuasion is the mode of discourse directed toward influencing the way in which readers know and understand image and idea. This mode of discourse is extremely complex for the youngest writers. We have found that most children under the age of about ten can use their time more productively with other kinds of writing.

The difference between criticism and persuasion and the other modes of discourse is that criticism and persuasion does not leave it to readers to construct meaning; a persuasive piece tells readers the meaning they should construct.

Criticism and persuasion is not limited to relatively short pieces that have come to be called essays. Farley Mowat, the Canadian writer whose *Never Cry Wolf* (1963) has become known throughout the world, based his book on criticism of his government's treatment of wolves. The effect of his book was to persuade people to think of protecting wolves. Mowat's *A Whale for the Killing, Sea of Slaughter,* and *People of the Deer* all criticize human destruction of the human and animal ecology. The entire books are persuasive.

However, most young writers construct their critical and persuasive pieces in short pieces—usually a page or two. The mode of discourse is the point, the purpose, of the writing. If there is a dictated formula, it is merely the form. Adherence to a form rarely serves the persuasive purpose.

Critical and persuasive writing are important parts of how we write in the genres. They enhance reports of information, for example. In a report on Alexander Hamilton's role in the ratification of the Constitution, for example, a writer has to persuade readers that Hamilton's participation in the writing of the Federalist Papers was a significant contribution. The report of information is supposed to be an objective piece of writing, but it has to be persuasive too.

Many pieces of short fiction are intended to tell readers how writers think about problems and controversies as well as influence how readers think and feel. In "King Midas," a persuasive component is apparent. Aesop's Fables and many fairy tales have a persuasive component, as did early school reading books and as have, according to many observers, today's social studies books.

Objective 1 for Criticism and Persuasive Writing

A writer takes a position on a topic and explains the opinion. The writing focuses primarily on the opinion and only peripherally on persuasion of the reader:

1. "Write a review of a story you have read recently. Describe what you noticed in the story and what the story reminded you of. Write something of the character and the plot line. Include a critical reaction to the story."

2. "What is your reaction to the idea of increasing the length of the school day and the school year for the purpose of more effectively competing with the achievement test scores of children and youth around the world?"

3. "Write what you think of the idea that students should have to wear uniforms to school."

Objective 2 for Criticism and Persuasive Writing

The writer takes a position on a topic and explains that position in a way that is intended to influence how readers think about the topic:

1. "Think of a characteristic of yourself of which you are especially proud and that is important to you. Write an introduction of yourself to an employer."

2. "Pretend you are the parent of a ten year old, and you have received a letter from the school that says your son or daughter will have to begin wearing a school uniform next year. Write what you will say to your son or daughter to persuade him or her that the uniform idea is a good one."

3. "Write an argument of at least 75 words in favor of requiring restitution to the victim as part of all sentencing procedures."

E S L Readers should notice throughout the modes of discourse as well as Short Cues that all of the writing has a direct communication purpose that readers can explicitly understand. Although we don't like the inferred dichotomy, these writings are more "authentic" than those that came before. In early paragraph writing, the emphasis is on the paragraph; in the following writings, the emphasis is on the message.

All of the commentary on the efficacy of instruction for English-language learners focuses on achieving as much authenticity in the language as possible. Young English-language learners have specific messages to send in the modes of discourse and Short Cues. It might make better sense to them as they grapple with writing that extends beyond the sentence. ■

The Modes of Discourse Through the Grades

Levels K-1: Description—most of it oral—is a staple of young writers' earliest writings. Certainly in the first grade, they can begin writing single-sentence descriptions of their drawings and the trip to the bakery, for example. The teacher's task is to help young writers insert aspects of description into their sentences—for example, by asking, "What did it look like? What did it feel like? What sounds do you hear? What does it feel like?"

We can introduce similarities and differences this early in the process as well. Young writers can discuss how oranges and lemons are alike and different, how cucumbers and bananas are alike and different, or how two books they have just listened to are alike and different.

Levels 2–3: The second- and third-grade applications of descriptive writing can occur in the morning's first meeting. Children can be assigned the task of orally sharing something they have with them, with the focus on the quality of the description. Typically the descriptions emphasize the senses. Dolly, for example, described what her mother's piano looks like. Cory shared what cookies feel like in her mouth when they've just cooled after baking. When the sharing session is over, everyone returns to their tables and writes what they shared.

Direction writing is fundamentally analytic writing. Third graders can write directions for drawing a square, but to do so, they have to "see" a square as a whole, break down the whole into its component parts, and then write each part in order. That is analytic thinking and writing.

Levels 4–5: Write a direction on the board each Thursday morning. When the children come into the room, they know they are to use some of their independent time during the morning to write in response to the description prompt. They write on 5 1/2- by 8 1/2-inch sheets of paper prepared by cutting regulation-size lined paper in half (so the writing task doesn't seem so formidable). The descriptive prompts always begin by directing the children to describe— for example, "Describe what a rose looks like when it's open," "Describe what the kitchen looks like right after dinner," or "Describe a boy who is afraid."

Analytic writing occurs in the fourth and fifth grades. It may be that fourth- and fifth-grade persuasive writing (see the genres in Chapter 10) is the best context for analysis, as well as the criticism and persuasion mode of discourse. Faced with a controversial topic such as whether skateboarding on public sidewalks should be allowed, young writers have to think about the complexities of the topic and its alternatives. Persuasive writing is not merely having an opinion and writing it. It requires that we know the possibilities and the logical conclusions of each possibility (Fearn & Farnan, 1999b). That is analysis within the persuasive mode of discourse.

Levels 6–8 and Secondary Level: Some of the example prompts in this section are specifically appropriate to middle and secondary students. Notice how young writers can write about a single piece of literature in all four modes of discourse.

Short Cues

The specific purpose of **Short Cues** is to ensure that young writers have whole writing experiences virtually every day so they can have the experience of seeing a whole piece of writing come from their minds regularly. Short Cues don't represent a writing program, but they can be an important part of a writing program that emphasizes whole pieces of writing.

Précis Writing

A **précis** is a summary or an abridgment that captures the essence in as few words as possible. It is quick, short, and tight. The writer of a précis sees or understands the idea or image, breaks it down to its barest bones, and writes only the bones that represent the original idea or image. A précis likely takes more time to think and write than it appears it should from its length because it requires just the right words to make its point. Such disciplined thinking is why a précis can be short.

For very young writers, we ask, "Think of the story we read aloud yesterday. Think of a way to tell the story in one sentence." First graders will tell the plot. "All right, I will give you two sentences this time, but I want you to include the main character when you tell the story." The teacher writes several two-sentence versions on the board and asks, "Now, who can change Carson's two sentences into one sentence and not forget the story and the character?"

Fifth graders can write a précis for *Too Many Tamales* (Soto, 1993) or *Alexander and the Terrible, Horrible, No Good, Very Bad Day* (Viorst, 1980). In social studies, they write a précis for *Mojave* (Siebert, 1988).

 Notice the role of précis writing in reading comprehension. Because it focuses on getting the central ideas out of a piece of writing and making them belong to the reader, it can focus the reader's deliberate attention on mentally constructing meaning while reading. That is a more realistic kind of reading, for it actively engages the reader's mind. It clarifies what is meant by reading comprehension. Young English-language learners benefit greatly when they know what to do and what it means. ■

Here are some other possibilities for a social studies class:

"What, in fact, does it mean when we read 'no taxation without representation'?"

"Rewrite in your own words, and in not more than two sentences, what you think Abraham Lincoln meant when he said, 'Four score and seven years ago, our forefathers brought . . . all men are created equal.'"

And if a class has been reading about famous artists, the teacher can say, "Write a précis for *When Pigasso Met Mootisse* [Laden, 1998]."

Power Writing

Power Writing is a short piece designed first for fluency and then for revision, but also for writing process awareness. (See Chapter 8 for an exploration of the revision application of Power Writing.) The premium established by the teacher is time. There is never more than one minute available for a round of Power Writing, and our experience tells us that there need to be about three rounds each time Power Writing is conducted. The first objective of Power Writing is to help young writers understand their capacity to produce far more writing than they ever dreamed they could in a short period. The second objective is to help them understand what revision means because Power Writing produces authentic drafts on the basis of which young writers can in fact revise. The third objective is process awareness. These objectives are explored in greater detail in Chapter 8.

The instructional procedure for Power Writing is simple. After directing young writers to prepare for writing, put two cue words on the board—for example, *pony-mountain, running-stalking,* two spelling words, or two vocabulary words from science—and direct young writers to select one as their topic. Immediately tell them to write as much as they can as well as they can on their topic, and that they have one minute to do so. At one minute, call time, and tell them to count their words. Record their word count on a chart on the board arranged on ranges of words as follows:

	Round 1	Round 2	Round 3
16–20 words	_____	_____	_____
11–15 words	_____	_____	_____
6–10 words	_____	_____	_____
0–5 words	_____	_____	_____

Run the totals as high as necessary to accommodate the fluency scores of students in the room. With young writers in the second grade or lower, make the increments on the chart two or three words rather than five. Conduct Round 2 with two different words and Round 3 with still two more.

Readers may be sensitive to the pressure that Power Writing places on young writers. Of course, everyone needs time to process their thoughts and get them on paper, and Power Writing doesn't ignore that; the activity helps young writers learn how to process more efficiently.

As young writers realize that the criterion for the chart is quantity, they begin to write fast. Then ask that they select their second round, or their third, and rewrite it as though they were going to turn it in for a grade, or post it on the refrigerator, or send it to their grandparents to show how well they write. Give them two to four minutes to revise. Debrief the revision by asking them to share and explain what they did to their draft. What they share are the applicable revision skills for those pieces of writing. Interestingly, each piece of writing demands its own collection of revision skills. One of the most critical parts of revision that young writers have to learn is that what writers do when they revise depends on what they write.

When we ask, "How did you do it?" we open the discussion for process self-reports, and everyone has an opportunity to observe the variability of writing processes and learn what the variability means (see Chapter 8).

Overall, however, Power Writing is about writing short. There is no form demand whatsoever. It is all about function, and the **function** is fluency under time pressure.

Process Pieces

Process Pieces are also timed, but the cue or prompt leads young writers to their own formation of ideas or images and then directs them to write their idea or image—in two minutes. The primary objective is writing process awareness. The writing tends to appear in one, two, or three sentences. It is rarely longer. It also tends to be very descriptive and often metaphoric.

The process awareness question is similar to Power Writing: "How did you do that?" The discussion that follows each young writer's reading leads to several writing processes, each written on the board so young writers can fully comprehend the variability. As a follow-up during the year, we can direct everyone to do today's process piece according to the process that one young writer revealed in the awareness discussion. There is merit in helping young writers come to know and use a variety of ways to approach and perform their writing.

When young writers read their process piece aloud, we can provide direct feedback on the quality of their writing by responding to the question, "What do you see or hear or otherwise sense from listening to Lindy's writing?" (See Chapter 8 for a more comprehensive description of the discussion.) If the process piece is about an idea, the question becomes, "What idea(s) has Lindy's writing given you?"

 The value of Process Pieces for young writers who bring possibly different perspectives to school from cultures and ethnic experiences different from the school's mainstream is that they write about and share how they view what we're asking them to do in school. The central question in process pieces is, "How did you do that?" ▪

Word Limiter Writing

Word Limiters tighten the demand for precision in ways otherwise very difficult to accomplish in the classroom. Word Limiters have their origin in Samuel Coleridge's epigram regarding the difference between prose and poetry. To paraphrase, Coleridge said that prose is the right words for the right reasons, and poetry is the right words for the right reasons in the right positions. The objective of Word Limiters is to give young writers direct experience with right words, right reasons, and right positions.

The Word Limiter cue or prompt specifies a topic and the number of words allowed. Thus, we might say to a group of fourth or seventh graders, "Think of how you could describe a violet for someone who has never seen one. Write your description in thirteen words." Of course, it seems terribly artificial to specify a number of words that way. Under authentic circumstances, one writer may be able to accomplish the task in nine words while another needs thirty-seven. Remember the objective: Word Limiters is about the development of a skill for brevity and precision and about word selection and word placement. Writing Word Limiters is to authentic writing as completing addition facts is to mathematics. Adding columns of figures isn't authentic mathematics, and Word Limiters isn't authentic writing. As long as no one confuses this or any other Short Cue with a writing program and therefore uses it for anything other than a specific skill development objective, Word Limiters won't compromise young writers' ability or inclination to write authentically.

Word Limiter writing emphasizes precision perhaps best in the line by the character Death in Somerset Maugham's play *Sheppy*. Death's line, known to some as "Appointment in Sumarra," begins, "There was a merchant in Baghdad who sent his servant to market to buy provisions." In an impact analysis of the line, Fearn (1983) showed how just those right words written just that way mobilized the prior knowledge of the play's readers to virtually construct the story themselves on the basis of nothing other than Maugham's written cues. Precision means using exactly the right words, and none more, to accomplish the writer's task.

Direction Writing

Direction writing is exactly what the words say it is: about writing directions. Direction writing is especially useful for young writers because the effectiveness of the writing can be checked objectively and immediately. If a young writer writes directions for drawing a square, and a reader who is following the written directions draws a triangle, the directions didn't work; therefore, the writing didn't work.

Teachers have been using direction writing for years, often for its humor, for when we get a bunch of young children talking and writing about how to cook a turkey, their ideas are often very funny. But direction writing as a Short Cue doesn't go for the laugh. This is a serious writing effort committed to offering specific cues or prompts for direction that can be written short and relatively quickly and that give writers immediate feedback about how well their writing works.

The objective of direction writing is to promote the clearest, tightest, most precise writing possible. Because the cues or prompts are usually relatively simple, the writing tends to be short, and occasionally very short. This is also a kind of writing that is enhanced by creative thinking. For example, in a sixth grade, in response to the prompt, "Write directions for drawing a square," one young man drew a square, wrote a sentence that read "Draw this," and drew an arrow from the sentence to the square. The boy's directions didn't fit what the teacher had in mind, but in fact, what he did was a classic demonstration of flexible (creative) thinking.

The square drawing cue has been the most common in getting young writers started writing directions. The square is well known and easy to visualize, and it can be committed to directions in exactly four tight sentences. So that first attempt at direction writing produces what the objective intends: clarity and precision. However, the result is usually not so pleasing. The primary problem is imprecise vocabulary—for example, *Make the line go the other way,* or *Draw the line up,* or *Make a line to close the ends.* Often the children write on the basis of what they know, not what the reader must know. Most of the written directions fail when they are read by readers who are directed to do exactly what the directions say.

Then readers and writers meet together to share what they experienced as confusions in the directions, and writers get their papers back to revise. Following massive revisions directed at making the writing work better for the reading audience, it is amazing how much tighter, less ambiguous, and often shorter the directions are.

Young writers can write directions for drawing all of the geometric shapes as well as the forms for making certain geometric solids that arrange flat geometric shapes (cube, tetrahedron, and so forth). They write directions for completing certain common tasks such as sharpening a pencil in a crank pencil sharpener and starting the computer. There are also directions for movements around the room—for example, "Walk from the teacher's desk to the lunch cubbies and then to Craig's chair at Table Three" written for readers who don't know about lunch cubbies, the teacher's desk, and Craig's chair.

Every written direction should be put to the test. Directions should be read and followed, readers should give writers feedback, and writers should revise on the basis of the reader feedback.

Short Cues Through the Grades

Levels K–1: Oral language continues to be paramount among the earliest writers. They can give and follow directions and can capture the main idea of stories read aloud. In the first grade, many can write single- and double-sentence précis and directions for accomplishing simple tasks.

Levels 2–3: The précis becomes a basic writing task now. Certainly in the third grade, young writers can capture the essence of the literature they read and listen to. Power Writing has enormous appeal for third graders, and in the second grade they begin to understand how Power Writing makes them write more than they thought they could. Second and third graders love to write directions, and at these ages, they can share their directions in dyads in order to learn the extent to which their own directions work for other readers. We suggest at least one Short Cue experience every week in these grades, in addition to at least one paragraph writing activity and one mode of discourse writing activity. That will be three whole pieces of writing each week through the second and third grades.

Levels 4–5: Fourth and fifth graders should deposit into their writing portfolios at least three, and preferably five, pieces from this chapter, perhaps two paragraphs, and two additional pieces from the modes of discourse and Short Cues. All three kinds of writings should focus on content areas in order to help young writers understand the power of writing in their content area learning. Reader response cues can be used in both fiction and nonfiction—for example:

> "In not fewer than 15 or more than 25 words, what did you notice from reading the biography of Sojourner Truth?"
>
> "Write directions for planting a lima bean in an experiment to test the effect of natural sunlight on germination and growth."
>
> "Describe what you think were the feelings of the Indian Stone Fox when he arrived just short of the finish line and saw Little Willy with Searchlight."

Those kinds of short writings provide practice in writing the modes of discourse while using writing as a learning device. These are also the grades in which both Power Writing and Process Pieces should occur with some regularity. In the case of Power Writing, the emphasis should be on revision as well as drafting. In Process Pieces, the emphasis should be on revision in response to feedback from the peer audience.

Levels 6–8: Young writers in the middle school should be using these shorter writings several times each week—once for teacher review and at least twice more through the content areas. More important, however, is the influence of prior years of working with the modes of discourse on larger pieces of writing. Young writers' descriptions, their ability to compare and contrast, and their ability to make (not have) an argument should be increasingly apparent when they write persuasively, craft short fiction, and report on what they have learned about, say, the impact of the westward movement on indigenous peoples west of the Mississippi River.

Secondary Level: Much of what secondary students write is in the genres, and their genre writing should now reflect expertise with paragraphs and relationships between and among paragraphs and the use of the modes of discourse throughout their genres. But it's clear that if tenth and eleventh graders, and even twelfth graders, have not come to grips with, for example, paragraphs, the material in this chapter continues to be a useful alternative to the writing experiences that have come in previous years.

Beyond the Sentence: Looking into a Third Grade

Mr. Rodriguez is a third-grade teacher in a large, urban school district. His first year of teaching convinced him that writing could be the pathway to better reading, so he enrolled in a special graduate degree program that focused on what we define in this book as balanced writing instruction. The format in Figure 6.1 is

Monday	Tuesday	Wednesday	Thursday	Friday
• Writing Sample Assessment (5) • Paragraph Completion (8)	• Paragraph Completion (8) • Power Writing (5)	• Power Writing (5) • Organizing Paragraph Sentences (10)	• Paragraph Completion (8) • Organizing Paragraph Sentences (10)	• Power Writing (5) • Organizing Paragraph Sentences (10)
• Single-Double Sentences (10) • Descriptive Writing (10)	• Power Writing (5) • Single-Double Sentences (10)	• Single-Double Sentences (10) • Descriptive Writing (10)	• Power Writing (5) • Organizing Paragraph Sentences (10)	• Single-Double Sentences (10) • Descriptive Writing (10)
• Paragraph Completion (8) • Compare-and-Contrast (10)	• Single-Double-Triple Sentences (10) • Word Limiters (7)	• Power Writing (5) • Compare-and-Contrast (10)	• Single-Double-Triple Sentences (10) • Word Limiters (7)	• Compare-and-Contrast (10) • Organizing Paragraph Sentences (10)
• Word Limiters (7) • Single-Double-Triple Sentences (10)	• Power Writing (5) • Process Pieces (10)	• Word Limiters (7) • Single-Double-Triple Sentences (10)	• Organizing Paragraph Sentences (10) • Process Pieces (10)	• Writing Sample Assessment (5) • Process Pieces (10)

FIGURE 6.1   Third-Grade Plan Book Page

from his first month of paragraph, modes of discourse, and Short Cues instruction. Here is Mr. Rodriguez's explanation of his plan book page:

> The plan book page shows part of the first month plan in writing for my third graders. Actually it's about half of the plan. I scheduled 30 minutes each day to teach writing. The plan book page shows almost 17 minutes daily [the numbers in parentheses]. I try to give the children experience every day with every level of writing, but I never allow any direct teaching activity to take more than ten minutes. Their concentration wanders after that.
>
> The assessment on the first and last days of the first month is for communication with the children, parents, and principal. I give the children a prompt and get the average number of words they write in five minutes, the average sentence length, the average number of clauses per sentence, and the average number of mechanical errors per sentence. All that takes about two minutes per paper. I can show the children what they have learned in a month, and that's the best motivator for them. It also shows parents and the principal one of the ways the children's writing is developing. After the first month, I do various assessments only three more times in the year.

Although I schedule thirty minutes every day for teaching writing, I don't do all thirty minutes at the same time. It's distributed throughout the day. Most of the longer writing is in social studies, literature, and science. I also found that when the children write descriptions and directions in math, they understand the math better.

Where it shows compare-and-contrast writing in the plan book, I call that "similarities" and "differences" for the children, and we talk and write about how things in the content areas are alike and different. For example, they read a lot of biographies, and I read a lot of biographies to them. Then they write about how two people are alike and different.

I do the Organizing Paragraph Sentences from the social studies book. I make sentence cards from chapters they haven't read yet, so when they get to those chapters, they have prior knowledge about the content and how the chapter is written.

And finally, I use the Process Pieces writings for revision. They read aloud in small groups, and everyone has to tell the readers what they noticed in the reading. Then they go back to their desks and revise what they wrote so it makes their audience notice what they want to be noticed.

I have taught this way for two years now. I can't imagine not teaching this way ever again. It takes the children a month or so to figure out how to keep up with the load, but they do, and then they love it because they know they're reading and writing better every day.

REVIEW AND REFLECTION

1. Write a description of what a paragraph is. Compare your description with a partner's. Discuss the similarities and differences between the descriptions and what you remember about how paragraphs were described when you were in the elementary and middle school.
2. Write a précis for this chapter. Compare your précis with those of others in your class.
3. Paint a word picture (Process Pieces) of the kitchen on the morning after a party. Be sure to put references to texture into your word picture.
4. Select a grade level, and design a plan for using the modes of discourse and Short Cues during one month of a nine-month school year. Given your plan, calculate the amount of writing the average young writer is likely to do during the month for which you planned.

A Summary: Teaching Craft

The main idea in writing is the main idea. Although most people don't call the point of a sentence its "main idea," what a sentence is about is its main idea. Most sentences also have supporting details, framed in single-word modifiers as well as phrases and clauses that enhance the main idea. When we write two related sentences in a Double Sentence Session, there remains one main idea that is just a little larger now. A Triple Sentence Session produces a main idea that is larger still.

In this chapter, we explore the main idea into still larger territory. The paragraph has a main idea, and two paragraphs in a row also have one main idea that is now large enough to need two paragraphs to tell it. Each mode of discourse has a main idea, as does each response to a Short Cue. It is always the main idea, in a descriptive or analytic piece and in a paragraph and a sentence.

Young writers need a lot of experience exploring main ideas. By offering many kinds of such experiences, this chapter extends young writers' sense of main idea beyond the sentence.

7 Thinking About Processes in Writing

BEFORE YOU READ

- What do writers do when they write? How do writers write?
- What are the differences between experienced and novice writers' writing processes?
- When do writers plan their writing?
- When do writers revise their writing?
- Write a description of your writing process(es).

Process in Balanced Writing Instruction

Writing process is about how writers approach and perform writing. To approach writing is to plan, to identify principal ideas, to build the big picture for the writing. To perform writing is to draft, rethink principal ideas, research, revise, and edit. Writing **process** covers the entire procedural world associated with writing.

Process is another word for *mental procedures*. The anchor question is: What do writers do when they write? The only source of information about what writers do when they write is, of course, writers themselves. So to know what's going on during writing, we ask writers.

If the writers agreed to a roundtable discussion, the transcription of the audiotape might appear as shown below. The words are the writers' own, taken from interviews with them and from autobiographies. On the initial appearance of each writer in the roundtable, the genre specialization appears in parentheses. The interviews and commentaries from which the writers' words have been taken are contained in Asimov (1979, 1980), Cowley (1958), Lloyd (1987), Murray (1990), Plimpton (1989), and Steinbeck (1969). We ask that you play along for a few moments as the writers, assembled around a large table, respond to a teacher's questions about how they write.

Teacher: My students are always saying that they don't know what to write about. How do you come up with ideas for your writing?

Ernest Hemingway (Fiction): Whatever success I've had has been through writing what I know about.

E. L. Doctorow (Fiction): Writing teachers invariably tell their students to write what you know. That's, of course, what you have to do, but on the other hand, how do you know what you know until you've written it? Writing is knowing. That kind of advice is foolish because it presumes that you have to go to war to do war.

Lloyd Alexander (Fantasy): I do a lot of research before I start to write the first draft.

Seymour Simon (Nonfiction): I keep an ideas file. I get my book ideas from anything that interests me. I don't decide to write a book and then look around for a subject to write on.

Rosemond Lehmann (Nonfiction): Everything is stored up and one never knows what comes up to the surface at any given moment. A period of gestation is certainly necessary. A writer works from the material she has.

Françoise Sagan (Fiction): You have to write to start to have ideas.

James Baldwin (Fiction and Nonfiction): You're trying to find out something that you don't know.

Teacher: I think I understand. I'll have to mull it over a while to figure out how to make those comments fit in my classroom, but it seems as though there are lots of different ways to come up with ideas for writing. Now I have a second question. I ask you to remember that my students are young and novices at writing. What can you share about how I can help them get started and keep moving? How do I help them plan so they know what they're doing?

Doctorow: Trust the act of writing. With the beginnings of a work, you really don't know what's going to happen.

Tom Archdeacon (Journalist): I get a long legal pad. I write Intro at the top. I figure out my lead anecdote. Then I try to think what the main line of the story is. My outline is pretty detailed, even the transitions.

Doctorow: Tell them it's like driving a car at night. You never see further than your headlights, but you can make the whole trip that way.

Frank O'Connor (Fiction): Get black on white. I write any sort of rubbish which will cover the main outlines of the story; then I begin to see it.

Sinclair Lewis (Fiction): Writing is just work—there's no secret.

Isaac Asimov (Fiction and Nonfiction): The piece evolves as it rolls out of the typewriter and moves in its own direction, quite outside my control.

Madeleine L'Engle (Fiction): Inspiration usually comes during work, rather than before it.

Robert Parker (Fiction): There is no right way. But there is a wrong way. The wrong way is to finish your writing day with no more words on paper than when you began. Writers write.

Teacher: That wouldn't help much if I were looking for a system. Mr. Archdeacon, you plan so carefully that you have your story worked out before you start.

Asimov and Doctorow just let the writing roll along to see what happens, and there are all kinds of variations in between. It's clear from what you say, though, that there is no secret—that it's just hard work, and my young writers have to write, write some more, and keep writing. I can work with that in my classroom. I know that several of you said there are only thirty minutes you can spend here, so let me ask another question quickly. None of my students likes revision very much, but writers have to do it. Have you any suggestions?

Kathryn Lance (Fiction and Nonfiction): I used to hope that as I got better I would have to revise less, but the opposite seems to be happening: as I gain more experience I become more self-critical and spend even more time on rewriting and polishing.

Robert Cormier (Fiction): Listen, a brain surgeon has to get it right the first time, but a writer can always rewrite and fix and tinker and get the better word. You can always seek a better way of saying something.

William Styron (Fiction): I seem to have some neurotic need to perfect each paragraph—each sentence—as I go along.

Elizabeth Hardwick (Nonfiction): One of the things writing students don't understand is that when they write their first draft, they have merely begun, and that they may be merely beginning even in the second or third draft.

John Updike (Fiction): Writing well involves two gifts—the art of adding and the art of taking away. Of the two, the first is more important, since without it the second could not exist.

Roald Dahl (Fiction): Good writing is essentially rewriting.

Joan Didion (Fiction): My writing is a process of rewriting, of going back and changing and filling in.

Thornton Wilder (Playwright): There are passages in every piece whose first writing is pretty much the last. But it's the joint and cement, between those spontaneous passages, that take a great deal of rewriting.

Teacher: That doesn't give me a teacher system either, but what you say will validate my young writers. They certainly experience revision as hard work. Maybe because Mr. Wilder spoke last, I remember what he said most clearly. That does help me a lot. I keep telling my students to just get it down, but some of them work hard at each sentence. Some of you do that too. I guess some of you write just as some of my young writers write. We keep coming back to the same theme. There doesn't seem to be one way. Finally, what would you tell my students if you had a chance to give them your best advice?

François Mauriac (Fiction): Every writer ought to invent his own technique.

Asimov: There is nothing marvelous or artistic about it. I just think and think and think until I have something.

Theo Lippman, Jr. (Journalism and Commentary): Teach them to write short. It forces you to rewrite, and there isn't any padding.

Wilder: There are totally different requirements for ordering mind and language. Reporting is poles apart from shaping concepts into imagined actions. It is proverbial that every newspaper reporter has a half-finished novel in his bureau drawer.

Doctorow: Writing is immensely difficult.

Doris Lessing (Fiction): You should write, first of all, to please yourself.

Susan Sontag (Fiction and Nonfiction): I don't believe you should think about audience. I believe you should think about the writing.

Asimov: I never try to give literary advice myself, for the simple reason that every writer has a different technique and that what works for one may not work for another.

Teacher: This has been interesting. Even though Dr. Asimov doesn't give advice, I think I got some. It seems you all agree that writing is not fun and games, that it's hard work, and I have to support my students' hard work. In their writing, it isn't the length of the writing that's so important as the number of the writings. Also, writing processes vary from writer to writer, from genre to genre, and even within genres. You all seem to emphasize that writing is about thinking. But most of all, what I've learned about writing process I've learned from writers talking about their own processes. I think if I want to know about writing processes in my classroom, I have to ask my students to do what you just did. I have to ask them to self-report their own writing processes. Thank you all very much for that insight most of all.

What Do Writers' Self-Reports Tell Us About Writing Processes?

There are three questions that have to be asked, and answered, when the words of the experts are used in a discussion about teaching children to write.

First, *do the self-reported processes of experienced writers generalize to teaching boys and girls to write well?* The answer is yes. The reason is simple. Everyone who writes experiences the same kinds of problems, although not in precisely the same way. For example, every writer, no matter his or her age or experience, faces the problem of finding ideas to write about. The difference between experienced and novice writers is that many experienced writers know and understand the problem and have worked out ways to deal with it. For instance, some writers say it's always important to finish a writing session in the middle of a good flow of ideas in order to begin the following session with percolating ideas. Some writers keep an idea book, or pay attention to people around them, or listen to people talk, or read this or that favorite or especially well-written book over and over again.

Nearly all writers find that good writing comes mostly from rewriting. Some say it directly that way, as Roald Dahl did in the roundtable, but everyone self-reports about rewriting. Everyone also self-reports about drafting. Some say their drafts are quite careful and clean, while others just get down anything so they can get to the rewriting, which is what they define as their real writing, anyway.

Both novice writers and experienced writers struggle to stay on task. Steinbeck often found himself not writing: "I lost two days. This is why I give myself the leeway of time. I do not know what happened. I just went completely to pieces. I suppose it can and does happen to everyone" (Steinbeck, 1969, p. 71). He promised himself that he would get to the writing that day; then the day progressed, and he hadn't written anything. He remarked about the amazing number of pretty girls passing his window. He gave himself twenty more minutes before "lashing" into the writing. He thought more about the little box he was building (cabinetmaker that he was). He remarked about how he had changed the surface of his writing table. "And now," he finally wrote, "my lazy time is over—really over I think—and my allotted time for dawdling is over too" (p. 72).

Finding ideas, writing drafts, rewriting drafts, and being persistent are problems that all writers face, no matter how experienced they are. Both experienced and novice writers learn to solve those problems.

The second question we have to pose in response to the writers' self-reports in the roundtable is, *To what extent is it possible to have a single writing process that is useful for instruction?* Is it possible to nurture a writing process that is not stage-bound, even one that leaves room for looping back in a recursive manner?

Imagine a second grader in his first writing lesson early in the year. The teacher tells the class that they are going to write about yesterday's trip to the dairy. The teacher tells them they have to think of a list of ideas they remember from their trip. Our second grader, upon hearing the writing task, begins to hear his first sentence playing in his mind. But then he hears the teacher say they need a list of ideas. Now imagine that this second grader has been writing for three years, at first on the walls in his room at home and then on large pieces of newsprint his mother began to tape on those walls. He never made a list before when he wrote, but this is school, and there's always something new here. So he participates in the list-making activity, knowing that he'll get to write pretty soon.

But he doesn't get to write his story pretty soon. When the list is on the board, the teacher announces that they have to organize the list into categories so they'll know what to write about. Does the boy think he already knows what he's going to write about? Probably not. His attention has been diverted from writing to making and organizing the teacher's list. It almost certainly doesn't occur to him that, given his own literacy history, there is something wrong here: either his experience as a writer has been wrong all along, or the teacher is teaching him something that violates his experience. It's most likely that he begins to compartmentalize writing into two categories: what he does when he writes for the teacher in school and what he does when he writes for real. You might say that's okay for this second grader, but what about children who don't write at home and have little or no literacy history on which to draw? They have nothing with which to compare the teacher's directions, so they come to believe that when they write, they first make a list.

Even that would be okay if it were accurate. But recall the writers' roundtable. How many of the writers self-reported that they begin their writing with list making? Only one reported especially detailed "front-loading" of ideas and structures. The rest, both fiction and nonfiction writers, reported mainly that they have to write to reveal the ideas and structures.

Shouldn't we be helping young writers understand what the writers understand—that there is no process formula or frame of reference for writing; that the processes change with the genre, the day, and the mood; and that writing process belongs to the writer? Shouldn't we help them enter and experience the world of writing just as experienced writers experience it, with its frustrations, problems, sense of adventure and exuberance?

There is a third question from the writers' roundtable: *What do the writers' statements about their processes mean for teaching boys and girls to write?* Essentially what those self-reports mean is that what writers do when they write is the result of their own experiences as writers. They do what works, and it appears from their self-reports that they have to work out writing processes on their own, "teaching themselves from their own mistakes," as Faulkner said (Cowley, 1958, p. 129). "There is no mechanical way to get the writing done," he said. "The young writer would be a fool to follow a theory" (p. 129). Notice that Faulkner didn't say that there are no theories or that young writers shouldn't create theories of their own. He said that young writers would be fools to follow *a* theory.

The writers' roundtable tells us that intentional writing instruction has to emphasize creation of theories about writing processes. Chapter 8 is about teaching writing so young writers come to know and use writing processes that fit their own writing needs.

What Do We Know About Writing Processes?

All writing reflects complex mental and psychomotor processes. The term *process writing* should never be interpreted as a conceptual alternative to a sort of *non-process writing*, for process is the nature of all writing (Tobin, 1994). If young writers are not using complex processes, they are not writing. People who merely say again what someone else said are typing, not writing.

Why, then, do we use the term *process writing*? Why does it connote something that seems to describe a writing program? The answer probably rests in the context of how it was first used.

A Brief History of Writing Processes

For what seems like forever in educational terms, teachers made weekly writing assignments, and students wrote to the teacher's assignment in a way that they knew would satisfy the teacher's grading system. Then the students turned in their papers toward the end of the week and received them back toward the beginning of the next week, with the teacher's comments in the margins and a grade. In some classes, the grade may have been split between content and mechanics. Students then immediately got another assignment from the teacher to be turned in on Friday again. And so it went throughout the year, or at least for the portion of the year designated as *composition*. It was a system in which writing instruction, such that it was, worked only for those who learned from the teacher's comments. It was also a system that paid little attention to what young writers thought, valued, or did when they wrote.

In the early 1970s, a revolution of sorts changed forever the product-centered writing experiences of young writers. One of the earliest researchers responsible for the revolution is Janet Emig, whose investigation of eight twelfth graders (Emig, 1971) used a four-stage description of a creative process she found in Wallas (1926). That process listed, in sequential order, four *stages* of creative thinking: preparation, incubation, illumination, and verification.

The process Emig used connected Wallas's four stages of creative thinking and creative problem solving to Cowley's (1958) four stages in the composition of a story: germination of the story, conscious meditation, draft, and revision. From those, Emig theorized a four-stage description of writing process that served "as the center of the delineation of the writing process in [her] study" (p. 28).

Notice that Emig developed a theory about writing process *before* she began observing her research subjects. It turned out that Emig's twelfth-grade subjects did not compose in the linear (stage-bound, uninterrupted) fashion implied by the four-stage process she took into the study. There were all sort of hesitations and reformulations as they wrote. She called the hesitations and reformulations "recursive" (to go back) and suggested that there are also what she called "anticipatory features" (to think forward) occurring during the writing (Emig, 1971, p. 84).

Implications of the Research

Clearly Emig's twelfth graders participated in their writing much as the writers at the roundtable participated in theirs—on their own terms, in their own ways, and according to what their thinking and writing demanded in the midst of the writing.

Emig's research helped to promote the change in the field of writing instruction that began in the early 1970s. Writing instruction before the change was *product writing*; what followed was called *process writing* (Marshall, 1994). The change represented a different way to think about writing instruction. Before, the thinking was about *what* people wrote; after, the thinking was about *how* people wrote.

In our attention to writing process, we have learned a great deal about what writing processes are, how both novice and experienced writers use them, and what various processes can mean for instruction. So what do we know?

Writing processes do not work in any sort of linear or stage-bound fashion. Emig (1971) was very specific about that three decades ago. Although the creative thinking and creative problem solving and fiction writing processes that she took into her study suggested stages and linearity, she noted that her research subjects did not display anything like stages or what she called "left-to-right, solid, uninterrupted activity with an even pace" (p. 84).

What, then, do young writers do when they write, and what does that mean for instruction? The evidence indicates that a great deal of their prewriting occurs not before writing but during writing (Hayes & Flower, 1980).

That being the case, the typical implementation of teacher-directed prewriting *before* young writers begin composing likely preempts young writers' attempts to activate and organize their own memories and connections relevant to the topic. If instruction does for young writers what young writers should be doing for themselves, the instruction can interfere with the development of young writers' ability to think for themselves as they write (Bereiter & Scardamalia, 1987). They merely copy their *prewriting* ideas into sentences.

One of the reasons that writing process is impossible to codify in any systematic or predictable manner is its very nature. Murray (1985) tells us that writers do not think up their meaning and then write it down. "The act of writing," Murray says, "is the act of thought" (p. 3). Murray's sense of writing processes adheres to what Bereiter and Scardamalia (1987) say about the attentional demands of writing. The complexity of writing is not due so much to the number of factors that demand writers' attention (spelling, capitalization, sentence structure, focus, and so forth) as it is to the fact that all of the demands compete for attention *at the same time.*

The complexity of writing processes, and the futility of trying to teach as though there were *a* process, is highlighted by the relationship between process and circumstance (Murray, 1985). The pressure of time, for example, often changes the way a writer performs the act of writing. A young writer may write an autobiographical incident one way if there are two days before it is due and in another way if it is due in an hour. In addition, the process changes depending on who is likely to read the writing. Young writers write one way for peers and another for teachers.

The evidence seems to suggest more than one kind of composing or drafting process. There seems to be a difference between less and more mature writers, and the difference is not necessarily tied to chronological age. Moffett (1994) refers to the difference as *writing to show* versus *writing to know.* Writing to show is called *knowledge telling* in which young writers use linguistic capabilities shared by everyone (oral language ability, for example) to write ideas that reveal information alone. Knowledge redirects "oral language abilities into producing written text" (Bereiter & Scardamalia, 1987, p. 4). Less mature writers tend to *tell what is in their minds* and declare themselves finished when they run out of thoughts or ideas.

Writing to know is more like *knowledge transforming*, that is, constructing ideas and images through writing. Knowledge transforming is more a way of using writing for the construction of knowledge.

A knowledge-telling report on wheat farming in North Dakota, for example, would feature the information a young writer accumulated and organized about North Dakota wheat farming. The same topic in a knowledge transforming report could contain information similar to the former report, but it might move the writer to speculate about shortened growing seasons and why wheat, and not corn, is North Dakota's main grain crop. When the knowledge is told in the first report, the report is finished. In the second report, the information promotes curiosity or speculation, and the writer uses the information and the curiosity to construct knowledge not originally accumulated.

Consider the possibility that if teachers introduce every writing experience with a relatively systematic kind of prewriting and young writers begin to habituate the teacher's prewriting strategies, young writers may never move from telling writing to transforming writing that can occur only on the basis of the thinking that is activated because of the writing itself.

There seem to be differences between how novice and experienced writers use writing processes. One difference is in knowledge telling and knowledge transforming. Another is that novices are writer based, and experienced writers are more reader based (Flower, 1979). Writer-based text production is based on how knowledge is represented in the writer's mind, and reader-based text production is shaped more by what writers think *readers* need. More mature writers monitor their writing with an eye and an ear to how the meanings come across.

Flower and Hayes (1980) found that novice and expert writers can be distinguished from one another by their use of planning time and procedures. Although Bereiter and Scardamalia (1987) suggest that not all writing need be planned, it is clear that good writers know how to mobilize effective planning procedures.

Bereiter and Scardamalia (1987) describe writers' increasing ability to differentiate planning from text production. Planning here means action aimed at achieving a goal (Hayes-Roth & Hayes-Roth, 1979). At the earliest stages of writing development, writers' thought processes are so closely tied to their text production that it is impossible for an observer to notice separation between planning and composing. With experience, however, there appears a greater difference between thinking of what to write and the writing itself.

Hayes and Flower (1980) point out that planning by experts is a distinct mental activity that occurs mainly in the early portions of composing, an important point. Bereiter and Scardamalia (1987) found that novices tend to plan only once when they write, rather than think through the entire piece of writing. Experienced writers, on the other hand, often have a global sense of the direction and overall content of a writing task. They have a sense of purpose that they monitor throughout the writing. However (and this is important), both Emig (1971) and Gould (1980) found, as reflected in the roundtable, that even experienced writers routinely tend not to plan their work very extensively *before* they begin to write. As Hayes and Flower (1980) point out, experienced writers' planning often occurs even in the midst of the draft. Every piece of writing need not be planned in detail before drafting, but good writers do plan the big picture.

The discussion of what we know about writing processes so far has focused on the fluid nature of these processes and how novice and experienced writers' processes differ. Another focus of the research on writing processes is at the level of reflection and revision.

Flower (1979) suggests that *one reason that young writers have difficulty revisiting or revising their own writing is that their writing is egocentric or writer based.* It is constructed from what the young writer knows or remembers. Given that what they write is a reflection of their view, they are most likely unable to take a reader's point of view of their own writing. They know what their text means, and they are unable to see how anyone could fail to understand. To revise is to "de-center," as Piaget calls it—to see something from two perspectives at once.

Only if the writing is other-centered can the writer see the perspective of the writer and the reader at once, and that is what revision requires. Merely to reserve a day or a stage for revision has almost nothing to do with causing revision to occur.

Frank (1992) found that fifth graders could think about the two audience groups (third graders and adults) at once when they revised an advertisement to fit them both. Kroll (1985) faced writers in grades 5, 7, 9, 11, and college with a linguistically complex story that they had to rewrite for third-grade readers. Kroll found that fifth graders revised on a word-for-word basis, replacing hard words with easier ones, while older writers essentially rewrote the piece, protecting its meaning and structure. Kroll's findings line up with those of Flower (1979), who found that the revisions of novice writers are mostly cosmetic improvements that do not represent interactions between the text and its intended meaning.

Given that writing processes are neither stage bound nor linear, it is likely that processes such as revision occur in the midst of the draft, probably affecting even the planning process. Writing process research on experienced writers is filled with evidence of reflective activity (revising) that includes goal changing, problem solving, and predicting what is to come (Flower & Hayes, 1980, 1981). That might seem to be explained with an assumption that writers reflect in a sort of internal or subaudible dialogue way about the writing, even as the writing occurs. However, there is nothing in the research literature, or even the self-reports of experienced writers, and certainly not in the early investigation by Emig (1971), to document the existence of any internal dialogue. Experienced writers ask themselves where they are and where they are going, but there is no evidence to document any ongoing internal, subaudible reflection by either novice or experienced writers.

REVIEW AND REFLECTION

1. Now that you have read the writers' roundtable, what can you say about writing and writing processes?
2. The research most responsible for moving the profession's attention toward *how* students write (writing processes) was conducted by Janet Emig. What did Emig find in her research?
3. How would you generally describe your writing processes? Write a self-report that is between a half-page and a page in length to share with one or more peers or colleagues.
4. Describe in what ways *what* you write affects your writing processes.
5. Describe at least two ways that novice and experienced writers might use writing processes differently.

An Iterative Model of Interactive Writing Process

An iterative model for the interactive writing process accounts for interactions between writing process elements over and over again. The model shows repeated *interactions*—not recursive applications of process elements, but repeated application of the interactions between process elements. Figure 7.1 shows an iterative model for interactive writing process.

There are three interactions in the iterative model for interactive writing process (*a*, *b*, and *c* in the figure). The interaction labeled *a* is between prewriting and drafting. This interaction shows that the drafting itself has a planning function. Writers in the roundtable, to say nothing of what we all self-report about our own writing, routinely report something akin to E. L. Doctorow's statement that when you drive, you can see only as far as the headlights on the car illuminate, but you can get to your destination that way. Writers, to stay with the metaphor, might plan only into the next sentence or paragraph, but they continue planning based on what they just wrote. Writers can write their draft that way.

The exploration of one idea reveals the next one. We have all had the experience of writing on one idea and having an idea that will occur several paragraphs later germinate in our mind. Clearly, even as we draft, we plan, and we thereby experience the interaction between two elements of writing process.

Notice, however, that the interaction is not recursive; we do not go back and forth between drafting and planning. The planning and drafting are occurring *at the same time*, not alternately. They are interactive, not recursive. The process is iterative because writers repeat the interaction.

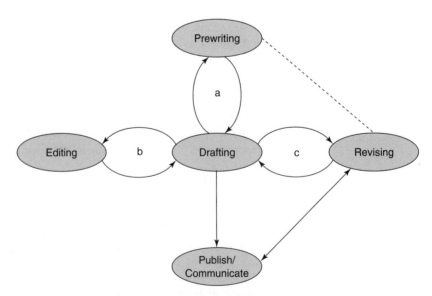

FIGURE 7.1   Model of Interactive Writing Processes

At point *b* in Figure 7.1, there is another interaction, this one between drafting and editing. William Styron said in the roundtable that he has a need to perfect each paragraph, even each sentence, as he goes. When you write, do you ever find yourself stopping in midsentence to select a different word from the one you just wrote, to change a comma to a semicolon, to start the sentence differently, to re-spell a word? That interaction between drafting and editing shows how experienced writers can pay attention to several things simultaneously, as in the example above, to idea development and flow and a simultaneous concern for surface correctness.

The ability to pay attention to idea development and flow, as well as surface correctness, demands that surface correctness is automatic, which means well practiced. If young writers have to attend deliberately to every punctuation mark, they will be unable to use a drafting and editing interaction fully.

If writers are able to draft, make surface corrections, and choose alternative words without compromising the flow of the draft, then the drafting and editing functions of writing process are working simultaneously and iteratively.

Writers not only make surface corrections in the midst of their concentration on the draft; they often make substantive adjustments in what they have written to fit what they intend to write. The interaction labeled *c* in Figure 7.1 shows this drafting and revision interaction. That is what Roald Dahl was referring to in the roundtable when he said that good writing is essentially rewriting.

Although vast amounts of fundamental rewriting occur when a draft appears finished, or after what we might call the "first draft," a surprising amount occurs in the midst of that first draft. It is routine for writers to rewrite a portion of a draft to accommodate a new thought that has arisen in the drafting and planning interaction. When that happens, there's a drafting and revising interaction.

Think about your own writing experiences. Haven't you found yourself in the midst of a writing project, formally planned or being planned as the draft rolls out of your mind, and suddenly you realize that there's a terrific spur on the main idea you hadn't thought of before? And what happened? If you decided to use it, you went back several paragraphs and made room for the new idea, rewriting one or more paragraphs so the new idea would move right into a place originally designed for a different idea. That was revision. It happened during the draft, and it didn't compromise the draft. It shows the drafting and revision interaction, not a switch from drafting to revision, but both drafting and revision occurring at the same time, feeding on each other.

The iterative model of interactive writing process shows what writers of all ages talk about when they self-report their own writing processes. They rarely self-report anything that functions in stages, anything that is linear, or anything that alternates back and forth from one process function or element to another. Most characteristic, writers of all ages self-report that they have lots of things going on at the same time, and it's hard to keep track of them all or to know when one begins and another ends.

Writing processes are difficult to explain because basic aspects of writing process don't begin and end. Writing process is fluid. The draft occurs throughout. In fact, every portion of every piece of writing is a draft, as Emig (1971) suggested when she pointed out that writers deal with larger genre and smaller sentence segments of discourse in the same way. It's only when writers stop working on a piece (good writers never think a piece is *finished*) that they have a *final draft*. Everything before that is a numbered draft: first, second, third draft, and so forth. It's all drafting, and in the course of the drafting, writers are adjusting the plan, revising, and making surface corrections as the need becomes apparent. It's all repetitiously interactive, from beginning to stop. Writers stop because a clear sense of an end, or being finished, is so very elusive.

REVIEW AND REFLECTION

1. How are *recursive* and *iterative* explanations of writing process different?
2. Reflect on your experience as a writer. Think about whether you ever revise in the midst of drafting. Recall when you found that the drafting itself revealed new or different plans.
3. How would you describe the process differences between knowledge telling and knowledge transforming?

INSTRUCTIONAL SCENARIO

In the Classroom Using Power Writing to Highlight Iterative Writing Process

Recently a teacher in a fifth grade directed young writers to select one idea from the two she was about to write on the board and use that idea as the topic around which they would write as much as they could as well as they could—in one minute. There were the inevitable questions: "Do I have to write in sentences?" That's how writing works best. "Does spelling count?" Spelling always counts, but don't stop writing just because you can't spell a word you want to use. Just write as well as you can. "How will we know it's a minute?" I have a stopwatch. Good. Here we go. The teacher wrote on the board: *pony* and *mountain*. "Pick one. Go."

Most of the children wrote for the entire minute. Two stopped along the way and said they were finished. The teacher didn't tell them to continue. One little guy furiously wrote a list of words as they came to his mind. At one minute, the teacher told them all to stop and count their words. Someone asked if "the" counts; the teacher said it did. "Put the number at the top of your paper," she told them. Pause. "Count them again, and if you get a different number, write the smaller of the two at the top of your paper."

It took only about fifteen seconds to get the counting done. "Now I'm going to write two more ideas on the board," she continued. "You will pick one and use it as your topic. You will write for one minute—as much as you can and as well as you can." She wrote *running* and *mosquito*. "Pick one. Go."

The list maker now wrote in sentences. Neither of the two who stopped before stopped again. In one minute, the teacher told them to stop and count their words twice and write the smaller of their counts at the top of their paper. When they finished the count, the teacher asked, "How many people wrote more this time than you did the last?" Twenty-seven of the twenty-nine children in the room raised their hand.

YOUNG WRITERS' SELF-REPORTS

The teacher told the class that they would come back to the writing at another time, but, "For right now," she said, "I want you to put a circle around the second piece you wrote. How many wrote about running?" Several raised their hand. "How many wrote about mosquito?" Most of them raised their hand.

"I have something for you to think about," the teacher said. "I want to know how you did that. How did you do the writing." Several of the children raised their hand. "No, not yet. I want you to think for a moment. I put two words on the board and told you to pick one. Everyone made a selection, and in only a second or two, I said to begin writing, and everyone did. You just started writing. How did you do that? Not one person in the room couldn't think of anything to write. No one had any planning time. How did you do that?"

She paused a moment. Four hands waved in the air. She motioned them down and asked again, "How many of you knew what you were going to write before you began to write?" Two boys and one girl raised their hand. "Kristina, you knew exactly what you were going to write before you began?" Kristina said she did—that she just saw the whole thing about the mosquito at the picnic and the woman jumping up and spilling the potato salad. Jorge said he knew what he was going to write too, because he remembered the mosquitoes in his bedroom when he lived in Florida.

The teacher directed her comments at the three children who had their plans prepared before they began to write: "You were able to do all of your idea planning in a second or two. Did you make a list?" No one had made a list. "Did you think of an idea cluster?" No, they didn't see an idea cluster. "It all just came to you?" That's the way the three children described it.

The teacher went to the others in the room. "The rest of you didn't have it worked out before you began?" No. "But you started to write anyway?" Sharmaine said she didn't know what her writing would be about, but she had a sentence to start with. "Would you read that first sentence you wrote?" the teacher asked. Sharmaine read: *A mosquito is an annoying insect.*

"When you started the first sentence, did you know what the second sentence would be?" Sharmaine said she didn't think that far. "When did you know what you would write in the second sentence?" Sharmaine was sure and direct. She said that when she thought of calling the mosquito annoying, she knew the next idea would be about what made the mosquito annoying. "Well, then," her teacher probed, "did you think about the annoying part of the mosquito when you started the first sentence?" No, Sharmaine said, that just came to her. "And the rest of your piece? What is it about?" "It's about the annoying insect and all the places it can be annoying," said Sharmaine, but she added that she didn't get to all of her ideas because she had to stop writing in one minute. "So you had more ideas than you could write? Where did those come from?" Sharmaine said that they just came to her as she was writing.

A REVISION LESSON

The teacher directed the children to work on the second piece they wrote—the one about either *mosquito* or *running*. She told them to "fix up their one-minute piece so you could hang it on the refrigerator door." The teacher told them to make it as good as it could possibly be, and they would have twice as much time as they spent drafting it: two minutes. Go!

Most of the fifth graders worked revising their papers most of the two minutes. When the time was up, the teacher asked what they had just done. Megan said they were revising. The teacher acknowledged that revising was probably what it is called, but what specifically did they do? One young writer started it off tentatively by saying, as though it were a question, that he moved a sentence from the end to the beginning. The teacher wrote that on the board. Hands shot up across the room, and the teacher wrote on the board as fast as the children called out their revision and editing behaviors. When there were nine revision and editing behaviors, the teacher turned back to the class and said, "Boys and girls, that is what I mean by revision and editing. When I tell someone that a paper needs to be revised, those are what you do. We're going to practice doing those things to our papers most of next month."

The revision and editing behaviors on the teacher's chart the following day read as follows:

> I put a sentence from the end to the beginning.
> I put periods in.
> I wrote more at the beginning so people would know what it's about.
> I changed some words to make it more clear.
> I wrote an ending.
> Mine was so bad no one could read it so I wrote it better.
> I changed some spelling words, but I fixed a sentence first.
> I didn't make mine all in sentences the first time, so I fixed them.
> I put in more descriptive words.

PLANNING FOR ITERATIVE WRITING PROCESS INSTRUCTION

The teacher listened to several of the children read what they had written and asked them to describe the process they remembered from their writing. As they self-reported their processes, the teacher wrote notes on the board:

> I think of ideas as I write.
> I change some ideas I had when I started.
> I think of me in the topic.
> I write what I thought of when I got the topic.
> I just keep writing what comes to me.
> I made a list in my head.

The teacher said that she could see at least two ways to think about how we write and maybe we should all see if we can write both ways. She told them that it appears some of them were planning and drafting all at once, and some others were planning and then drafting. She set up a plan for the following week from which everyone in the room would try to use both kinds of processes and see which one seemed to fit better. (See Chapter 6 for Short Cue directions.)

Tuesday	Wednesday	Thursday	Friday
Short Cue, no preplanning time	Short Cue, 10 sec. planning time	Short Cue, no preplanning time	Short Cue, 20 sec. planning time

When this schedule was repeated in the second week, the fifth-grade teacher found that many students were also revising as they drafted. She pointed that out to them. In the schedule for the third week, the teacher used a metal cricket every fifteen seconds to signal everyone to read what they had written and make changes if they wished. On other days, she directed them to write with no review and no revision during the draft. After several weeks, many of the young writers were beginning to reflect on how their processes changed as they tried various kinds of writing.

Throughout the year, the teacher's writing program had everyone in the room writing at least three pieces simultaneously all the time. One young writer might be working on short fiction, a collaborative social studies report, and an autobiographical incident during writing time, at home, and during independent time at school. As one project was finished and shared in Writers' Workshop for peer feedback, the student would start a new project or go into his working portfolio where there were dozens of "starts" cued by the teacher and cut off before anyone could get more than a page written. The students began accumulating the starts on the first day of school when the teacher assigned the first one. There followed another teacher cue every day. And the students also selected topics for their writing projects.

In addition to the requirement that every young writer submit for teacher review at least one finished piece every week, every third piece submitted had to contain at least one page with a **Process Reflection,** or self-report of process. These process self-reports became the catalyst for a monthly **Writers' Roundtable** in the classroom, a forty-five-minute conversation among the young writers about how they write, how various processes seem to fit certain kinds of writing, and what they are learning about themselves as writers.

What Is the Role of Writing Process in Balanced Writing Instruction?

"The problem," Tobin (1994) writes, "is that the writing process has become an entity, even an industry, with a life of its own, certainly a life apart from its first theorists. Donald Graves often tells the story of his shock and dismay when he first overheard two teachers discussing the differences between what they described as 'the three-step and the four-step Graves writing process'" (p. 8).

Our objective in balanced writing instruction is to remove process from its exalted position. Elbow (1981) describes a more proper interaction among process, craft, and genre (our terms, not his) when he notes that we can tell, as readers, when content works better than form, or vice versa. He later tells us that we make wording changes precisely because we know that the change affects the larger content. In other words, these literacy elements do not work in isolation; they work symbiotically. Elbow notes that word changes influence content. Content and wording work together.

In exactly the same sense, the choices that writers make about how they will approach (find ideas, plan, organize) a writing task and how they will perform the task (draft, adjust plans, reorganize, revise) affect the content of the piece. The balance is in the symbiotic, even synergistic, relationship.

In balanced writing instruction, how young writers craft their writing is a critical part of how they use writing process. Part of writing process affects, and is affected by, the ability to craft the language. In addition, the process for telling a story may be different from that for writing a laboratory report in science class. Writing process affects, and is affected by, the ability to select the right form to communicate the intended content.

When we deemphasize or even remove any one of the three elements of the balance, the whole is wounded, sometimes mortally. Balance protects the whole, and the whole is the reason for the writing.

A Summary: Writing Processes

The instructional focus on writing process that characterized the 1970s rested on what Yagelski (1994) calls "a way of describing and understanding what writers *do* when they write" (p. 206). Two decades of research on what writers do when they write have revealed essentially what experienced writers self-report about their writing: writing process is idiosyncratic to the writer and the circumstances of the writing, and the accumulated evidence about writing process, including the self-reports of experienced writers, reveals nothing linear or stage-bound about the processes of novice and experienced writers.

If, as Yagelski (1994) writes, "process-oriented pedagogies grow out of that understanding," then writing instruction should promote young writers' experimentation with writing processes and their self-reports about their writing processes.

Such experimentation and shared self-reporting will engage the community of writers in active and authentic analysis of what writing is, what it feels like, and how it's done. As young writers think about writing processes in that way, they can develop a sense of control over how to approach and perform writing. Control increases confidence, and as young writers become more confident, they can focus on the point of their writing, not on whether they are doing it right and definitely not on whether they can do it at all.

REVIEW AND REFLECTION

1. What do you think are at least two very important things we know about writing processes?
2. This chapter urges teachers to engage young writers in examining their own writing processes. What might you say to explain to a teacher what you know about the necessity of having young writers self-reflect about their own writing processes?
3. Write a self-report about your own writing process based on what you remember from writing informal letters to your close relatives. How do you write those communications, whether in letter or e-mail form?
4. How do you write a formal piece as a report of information or a technical report? How is that process different from the one(s) you use when you write something informal?

8 Teaching and Learning Writing Processes

- What do we want young writers to understand about their writing processes?
- Are there differences between the writing processes that young writers use when they are in school and when they are not in school?
- Is there a writing process that all young writers should master?
- What are some ways to help young writers learn about their writing processes?
- What are some values that might accrue if young writers read their writing to one another and revise on the basis of their peers' feedback?

A Rationale for Teaching Writing Processes

In Chapter 7 we described writing processes from the perspective of the research literature and the self-reports of practicing or experienced writers. It is clear that there is no such thing as "the" writing process, no single formula for describing how writing happens. There is also nothing stage-bound about writing processes. Writers, novice and experienced, do not follow a procedural scheme through *stages* in order to get from the first ideas to last draft.

We also found in Chapter 7 that writing is one among the host of complex mental processes that characterize human behavior and that all complex mental processes can be at least self-described, if not explicitly observed. Individual writers self-report their writing processes differently, depending on the genre on which they are working.

What we did not find in Chapter 7 is evidence that the ability to describe one's own writing processes improves the quality of one's writing. This book is based on our belief that the more writers control what they do when they write, the more confidence they have when they write. A related assumption is that confidence is a powerful contributor to writing ability.

One instructional dimension in this chapter, therefore, is designed to help young writers understand what they do when they write. Also, because we expect to help young writers become specifically skilled *and* generally confident, another instructional dimension in the chapter is designed to help young writers learn to use their writing processes in ways appropriate to a wide variety of writing purposes.

Helping Young Writers Understand Their Own Writing Processes

How do we know what we do when we write? We self-report, just as professional writers self-reported in Chapter 7. That is, we think about what we do when we write, and we tell about it, either orally or in writing. So we help young writers, in any grade, understand their writing processes through their self-reports.

Power Writing for Understanding Writing Processes

The writing activity that follows appears in detail in Chapter 6 as a Short Cue; here we explain it in the context of writing process awareness. Power Writing (Fearn, 1980) is designed to promote fluency. The teacher makes sure everyone has paper and something with which to write, and tells everyone they will write as much as they can as well as they can in only one minute. The teacher then writes two cue words on the board (let's say *pony—mountain*), announces "Go," and calls time after sixty seconds. That is Round 1. There are three rounds, and word counts for each round are charted on the board. Let's take a look at Power Writing in a teaching scenario.

We emphasize the chart heavily because it is the internal reinforcer for students engaged in the activity. We describe various purposes for Power Writing in this book. When we study writing processes, the purpose for Power Writing is *awareness*. Notice in the teaching scenario that the directions move along. Yes, there is some frustration, but only in the initial use of Power Writing. Most young writers come to the activity having been given all the time they need to write. In Power Writing, they find out that *what* they wrote isn't as important as is *how much* they wrote. That is not a good choice in writing, and to value quantity over quality is not as appropriate to writing as it is to, say, bowling. But there is a writing process purpose in Power Writing that makes quantity transcend quality *just this once*. Because it focuses attention on quantity, the chart on the board is important in Power Writing.

INSTRUCTIONAL SCENARIO

In the Classroom with Power Writing

Teacher: You are to write as much as you can as well as you can. Write for the whole minute. Don't stop. I will write two words on the board. You pick one. Use the word you pick as the idea you will write about. Here are the words: *pony* and *mountain*. Now, when I say "Go," you begin to write, and write for the whole one minute. Go.

COMMENTARY

While the young writers are writing, the teacher draws the following chart on the board.

	Round 1	Round 2	Round 3
46–50	_____	_____	_____
41–45	_____	_____	_____
36–40	_____	_____	_____
31–35	_____	_____	_____
26–30	_____	_____	_____
21–25	_____	_____	_____
16–20	_____	_____	_____
11–15	_____	_____	_____
6–10	_____	_____	_____
0–5	_____	_____	_____

After one minute, the teacher calls "Stop."

RETURN TO THE CLASSROOM WITH POWER WRITING

Teacher: Put your pencils down. Count your words. [Pauses for them to count.] Put the number right above what you just wrote. I want to see the hands of those whose number is between 0 and 5. [Writes the number of people who raised their hand in the space under Round 1 and just to the right of 0–5.] Now raise your hand if your number is between 6 and 10. [Puts the number of hands under Round 1 and to the right of 6–10. Continues until there are no more hands raised.] Very good. Girls and boys, here are two new words for Round 2. [Writes *running* and *yellow* on the board.] You pick one and use it as your topic on which to write as much as you can as well as you can. You have one minute. Go. [After one minute, calls time again, directs the children to count their words, and counts raised hands for each level of quantity, putting the number under Round 2. Finally, in Round 3, the words are *taxi* and *horse*. After one minute, the teacher calls time. The children count their words, and the teacher records the number of hands on the chart under Round 3.]

COMMENTARY

There is little or no interaction in Power Writing except for questions. Someone *always* asks if spelling counts. Here is the answer: "Spelling always counts; always spell as well as you can." Someone will ask what to do if she can't think of anything to write: "Always try to write something," is the answer. And usually someone asks if it has to be in sentences. The response is, "The language only works in sentences."

The source of the idea words is unimportant: past spelling words, terms from social studies, or words that just pop into mind. Nonetheless, the words should be ones that young writers know something about.

"How do you know," some teachers ask, "if the number they raise their hand for is really what they wrote?" We don't, and neither will you. It doesn't matter. We asked the children to raise their hand. We didn't tell them they'd have to swear by the accuracy of their count. We're not going to ask them *what* they did; we're going to ask *how* they did it. Let's look at that scenario.

INSTRUCTIONAL SCENARIO

In the Classroom Using Power Writing for Writing Process Awareness

Teacher: Well, girls and boys, you may relax now. Look at how the numbers on the chart go up in each round. It looks as though you are able to write a lot in only one minute. Yes, Leo?

Leo: But it isn't very good. Mine got worse each time.

Teacher: I should guess so! You were trying to write as much as you could.

Leo: Sure, but I didn't try to make it so anyone could read it.

Teacher: I didn't ask you to write so someone could read it. I asked you to write as much as you can as well as you can. Did you do that?

Leo: But I could write it better.

Teacher: Could you write as much as you did and write it better too?

Leo: No. I had to go so fast I couldn't write it any better.

Teacher: That's what I asked you to do. Leo, now that we're talking about how you wrote, tell me, how did you do it? Think about that last round. How did you do that?

COMMENTARY

Students get anxious when they think they haven't done it right, whatever "it" is, and Leo saw his numbers go up but his legibility go down. He's confused. The worst thing we can do when we teach young writers to write is leave them confused. Let's look at how the teacher resolved Leo's uncertainty.

BACK TO THE CLASSROOM

Leo: What do you mean?

Teacher: Well, you selected an idea, and you began to write. You didn't have any planning time. You just started. Did you know what you were going to write before you started?

Leo: No. I just started.

Teacher: But how? You can't write if you don't have a thought. We've been saying all year that writing starts as a thought, and then we write what we think. What was your thought?

Leo: Oh, I wrote about a horse, and as soon as I thought about a horse, I could see this horse I saw once on television, so I wrote about that.

Teacher: When you thought about the horse, did you have the plan worked out?

Leo: No. I just started to write about the horse, and the ideas just came out.

COMMENTARY

Everyone in the room is hearing Leo say he didn't plan his writing before he started, and they're seeing the teacher just listen and continue asking questions. There's more to this writing process than merely starting with a big letter and hoping something happens before you get to the end of the line. Hearing that there is an alternative to a clustered list, an outline, or a **scaffold** is helpful as a beginning.

BACK TO THE CLASSROOM

Teacher: Read your first sentence, Leo.

Leo: It says, *I saw this horse on television.*

Teacher: Do you remember writing that sentence?

Leo: Uh-huh.

Teacher: Do you remember when you got the idea for the next sentence?

Leo: It was when I was writing the first sentence. I got a picture of the horse, so I wrote about it being almost red and having this great saddle.

Teacher: You didn't know about that when you first started? You didn't think about that when you started writing your first sentence?

Leo: No. It just came out.

Teacher: Boys and girls, we have to learn more about the writing process Leo just described. Kristina?

Kristina: I did it that way too.

Carley: I didn't. I knew about the taxi because my mother and I were in a taxi last Saturday.

COMMENTARY

The teacher used the children's experiences to begin to uncover their unfettered writing processes. There are always responses like Leo's and Kristina's, and there are always others like Carley's. There is always variety in how writers write, their processes, and it is important for young writers to notice the variety. But in that first Power Writing session, the experiences of Leo, Kristina, and Carley are very important.

It is very important to notice that the teacher asked the young writers how they wrote, not how they *should* write. Faced with a writing task under pressure, the young writers wrote something. We can use our question and their responses to validate young writers' own experiences and broaden the ways they can approach writing tasks. Writers like Leo and Kristina are about to practice processes more like that of

Carley, and Carley is about to practice processes similar to what Leo and Kristina reported.

Process validation is very important. When young children come to school, they have been writing for as many as two or three years, primitively to be sure, but writing nevertheless. They know what writing is and how they do it. If a teacher tells them that writing has to occur according to a system that is foreign to them, they have to wonder whether their own direct experience is wrong, or if the teacher is wrong. It is much better to validate their own experience and use the range of experiences of their peers as additional possibilities they can learn to use. It isn't that writing instruction defers to children's experiences; rather, good instruction honors their experiences and teaches additional possibilities.

Power Writing reveals additional possibilities. Recall the writers' roundtable in Chapter 7 and how the writers described their writing processes. Some of these writers depended on carefully "front-loaded" plans; others suggested that the writing itself reveals the plan. You heard both of those processes, respectively, in what Leo and Carley described. There are all sorts of variations that young writers can experience to broaden their range and control.

INSTRUCTIONAL SCENARIO

In the Classroom Planning and Then Using Power Writing

Teacher: You all remember Power Writing. We're going to do it again, but just a little differently. There will be two idea words on the board, from which you'll pick one, just as we did the last time. But this time, when you have selected a word, I am going to give everyone time to think of a plan for the writing. Esther?

Esther: Will we do lists before we write?

Teacher: Only if you want to make your own. Or you may make lists in your head, if you like. Perhaps you will just think about the idea word and some experiences you have had. Think of how you might write about the idea. Here are your words [writes *ship—jumping* on the board]. Pick one. Now think of what you might write. You don't have to write anything on your paper unless you want to. Just think about a plan for writing. I will tell you when to begin writing. [Pauses fifteen seconds.] Begin. [Calls time in one minute.] Count the words, and complete the chart. [Conducts Rounds 2 and 3, each time with fifteen seconds to think, counting words and recording on the chart.]

COMMENTARY

This writing allows for some thinking and planning time. It is only fifteen seconds, but that is plenty to affect the experience of some planning rather than the extemporaneous writing in the original Power Writing activity. Remember that Carley indicated that she did some planning in that first activity, and she had only a second or two between her idea selection and the teacher's "Go!" So fifteen seconds is a fair amount of thinking and planning time for this purpose.

Now the teacher solicits **self-reports** again. Everyone has thought and planned at least a little. Students share their experiences. Our work with children suggests that you might hear some of the following kinds of statements:

- Because they had some time, they had what they wanted to say worked out before they began to write, and they wrote pretty much what they had worked out.
- They had ideas, but what they were thinking was all a jumble until they started to write, even though they had planning time. They will say that they couldn't think of anything good until they started to write.
- They had some good ideas, but when they started to write, the ideas changed, so they wrote the ideas that popped into their head when they were writing.
- They never did get good ideas, so they just wrote anything so they would have lots of words, but they didn't like the idea words this time.

To highlight the importance of process, and to remind everyone that there are many possibilities, it's time to begin making a writing processes wall chart on butcher paper with the following bulleted points on them:

- "I have it figured out before I start, and then I write it down."
- "I have some plans before I start to write, but then I begin to follow some of the ideas that pop into my head as I write."
- "Sometimes the ideas don't ever come, so I have to write as much as I can, and if there aren't any more ideas, I stop and put that paper into my portfolio for another time."
- "Sometimes I don't know what I am going to write until I start writing, and then I have to write and think at the same time, but that works sometimes."

Remember that these classroom scenarios are about awareness of writing processes. The question is, How do your writing processes work? The wall charts remind young writers of the various ways to think about using processes.

Power Writing is appropriate through the grades. We have found no one after the age of about seven who does not find it interesting and challenging and who cannot self-report his or her writing processes. Once students learn how to self-report writing processes using Power Writing, it becomes helpful to make writing process self-reports an integral part of the larger writing program (see Chapter 10). We recommend that young writers self-report their writing processes at least monthly and in various genres.

Part of the students' awareness is coming to understand that their processes for short fiction do not necessarily generalize to reports of information, where they might use a different process. It is enlightening to hear fifth graders, for example, share the processes they used to write a report of information. There are always many students who report that they began by planning the report, did the research, and wrote to the plan. And there are always some who report that they didn't know what research they would need until they started to write, so they did their research as they went. Sometimes students need a little organizational help; it's hard for ten year olds to think, write, plan, conduct research, and organize all at the same time. However, they don't get better at writing reports of information by being forced into a form. The way that they improve is by learning how to organize what they've done. (Chapters 9 and 10 explore organization and Power Writing in more depth. Chapter 4 also looks at organization.)

Process Pieces for Understanding Writing Processes

Process Pieces are short writings explicitly about the quality of the writing rather than the quantity. Sometimes the best writing is the shortest, so we don't compromise quality when we direct students to write short pieces.

In Power Writing, young writers wrote for one minute with little or no planning time in response to a cue word. In Process Pieces, they write for twice the time in response to an image they construct before they begin to put pencil to paper.

The teacher sets up the writing with a descriptive cue—for example:

> There is a hawk soaring high above the ground, floating on rising warm air currents, peering below as it floats one way, turns, and floats the other way. I want you to see that hawk. Feel the air. Hear the sounds. The hawk is just floating on the rising warm air. What does it look like? It almost never moves its wings. It just banks one way, floats down the valley, then banks the other way, and floats back up the valley again. Make an image. Paint the image in your mind. [Pauses.] I want you to write your image. You have two minutes. Write the image you have in your mind. [After two minutes:] Finish writing the sentence you are writing now, and stop. [Waits about fifteen more seconds.] I want a reader.

E S L Young English-language learners need to experience the least amount of interference possible between their own language and experiences and the new school tasks. In Process Pieces they are writing about their own images, based on their own experiences. The teacher articulates the cue, but the teacher is careful to use the children's own experiences while not specifying the image. The teacher is very clear: Paint your own image. ■

INSTRUCTIONAL SCENARIO

In the Classroom with Process Pieces

Teacher: I want a reader. Tess? Good. Read with a big voice.

Tess: *It is hot outside. The hawk is looking for a mouse to eat. On the ground it is hot and dry. The brush and leaves are all brown. It is cooler where the hawk is. His claws and beak are sharp and waiting for something to grab and eat.*

Teacher: Good, Tess. Read again. Everyone listen very carefully as Tess reads. [Tess reads again.] Now, Tess, read one more time. Big voice. Everyone, image along as Tess reads. Everyone, use Tess' words to help you build an image. [Tess reads again.] All right, Tess. Thank you. I need some volunteers now. What is your image from Tess' reading? Aaron?

Aaron: I could see a red-tailed hawk in the afternoon. He was looking down all the time.

Teacher: Someone else. What did you see or hear? What did you sense from Tess' reading? Sharilyn?

Sharilyn: It was like a desert. I saw some cactus. And maybe a dead animal the hawk was looking at.

Ellsworth: There is a mountain because the air is going up. The hawk is near a mountain.

COMMENTARY

Tess is getting a good bit of feedback on what her audience gets from her writing—*not* criticism, that is, no "good" comments or "bad" comments but only the images her audience got from her writing.

BACK TO THE CLASSROOM

Teacher: Tess, are those images that you had in mind when you wrote? Did Aaron, Sharilyn, and Ellsworth have it right?

Tess: Except for the desert. Everything else was really good.

Teacher: Are you happy with what your readers got from your writing?

Tess: Uh-huh.

Teacher: What about the desert. You didn't have a desert, but Sharilyn saw one. Is that okay?

Tess: It doesn't matter. The desert is okay.

COMMENTARY

Now Tess gets to judge the impact of the feedback on what she thinks is her purpose. The writer always gets to judge in an authentic writing environment. If the writer doesn't judge the influence of the writing, the writer turns to the teacher as the judge. The teacher is a legitimate judge, the writer is another one, and the audience is still another judge.

BACK TO THE CLASSROOM

Teacher: What if it weren't okay? What could you do with what you wrote to make sure no one got the image of a desert?

Tess: I could maybe write that there were some trees and grass. That wouldn't be the desert.

Teacher: Yes, I agree. But you say it's okay for someone to see a desert. That doesn't change your image.

Tess: Yes.

Teacher: Then you wrote it well. We know writing is good when it makes ideas or images for readers that are the same as or close to those the writer had in mind.

COMMENTARY

The teacher finishes this brief interaction with Tess by turning the inquiry to revision possibilities. Tess is still in charge, as she must be in an authentic situation. As the writer, she makes the decision about whether to revise in response to audience feedback, and if so, how. The teacher also repeated, as the teacher will throughout the year, the authentic criterion for good writing: *It's good if it works.*

The teacher will ask for three or four more readers and solicit feedback from three or four peers in response to each reading. This entire exercise will take about five to seven minutes to get feedback in response to the three or four readers.

There are two repeated readings each time. The first reading begins to get everyone attuned to the reader's tone and image. They listen to the second reading, and then they image in response to the third. Three readings of a piece this short do not take much time, and the two extra readings give the reader more stage time and the others more time to listen and construct their images.

The feedback has three purposes:

1. In the course of a week, everyone gets to hear other people talk about their writing.
2. Feedback is the basis on which revision can occur. When the writers read their writing aloud and hear what others see in it, they have some information about how well they wrote.
3. Young writers find out what quality means. Often they think that "good writing" is long, or spelled right, or has "complete" thoughts in the sentences. They need to learn that writing is good when it *works*, and their task in writing is to make sure their writing works. There is no way for them to know if it works or to know how it works without feedback.

When the peer audience provides feedback, it isn't necessary to have a formula that instructs them how to deliver it—for example, "Give two positives for every negative," or "If you don't have something nice to say, don't say anything," or

"Don't criticize because our friends won't want to write the next time." We teach young writers feedback, *not* criticism. In the peer response to Tess' writing, there was no criticism at all, but Tess did get a good bit of information about her writing. We will come back to feedback later in this chapter.

INSTRUCTIONAL SCENARIO

In the Classroom Where Process Pieces Reveal Writing Processes

Teacher: Tess, how did you write that? Did you see your whole image before you started to write?

Tess: No, but I saw the hawk.

Teacher: What about the leaves and brush and the change in temperature between where the mouse is and where the hawk is?

Tess: I didn't see that right away.

Teacher: When did you start thinking about the heat, brush, and leaves?

Tess: Oh, I was writing, and then it came to me.

Teacher: You began to get the ideas as you were writing? You were drafting and planning both at once?

Tess: Uh-huh. [Pauses.] Oh. Sure.

COMMENTARY

Self-reports from Tess and her friends will range all the way from her sudden awareness that she's planning and drafting at the same time to Larry, who says he had it all worked out in his mind before he started. The teacher will ask Larry how long it took to get it worked out, and Larry will say it was just there, that it didn't take much time— maybe a second. On another day, Larry will take more time to plan, or he will plan and draft simultaneously. As young writers self-report and share their own writing processes, they begin to understand what writers do when they write. In addition, they learn what everyone else in the room is doing when they write, and they begin to see that although the processes change with the genre, each student tends to develop habits that work for him or her. So Larry tends to be a planner before the fact, and Shirlee tends to trust that her writing will reveal where she wants to go. That's what writing process awareness is, and Process Pieces represent a short, image-based piece of writing that reveals writing processes clearly and quickly.

Now back to Tess. If she hears something from her peers that doesn't fit her image, there is another scenario.

BACK TO THE CLASSROOM: IF TESS DECIDES TO REVISE

Teacher: What do you think, Tess? Did you hear feedback that lined up with the image you had in mind when you wrote?

Tess: No. I didn't have it in a desert. I didn't see the hawk near a mountain. He was looking for a mouse or something, but not a dead animal.

Teacher: What do you want your readers to see when they read your piece?

Tess: The hawk floating and looking for a mouse or something. And it's nice and green with blue sky and maybe a stream. But no mountain.

Teacher: How could you make sure that's what your readers see when they read your piece?

Tess: Maybe write about the grass and bushes. I could write that there is a mouse trying to get in its hole, and maybe that it's hilly because of the warm air rising. If I said it's hilly, no one would see a mountain.

Teacher: Do you think that would do what you want?

Tess: Maybe. I could see.

Teacher: You go ahead and revise your piece for a few minutes while we listen to some more readers. When you have it the way you like it, raise your hand, and we'll listen again.

COMMENTARY

In that classroom scenario, Tess indicated that the feedback she heard didn't reflect what she wanted her writing to accomplish. The teacher helped her see how she might revise her piece, share it again, and listen to audience feedback again.

An important part of Process Pieces writing, and an equally important part of writing processes generally, is how young writers think about what they are writing. Self-reflection and listening to audience feedback produce an awareness of revision and editing need. There always comes a point when young writers write (and when anyone else writes, for that matter) that they ask, "Will they like what I wrote? Will they understand?" Many classrooms have an author's chair—a place where a young writer gets to sit, share writing, and receive feedback from peers. Process Pieces offers the opportunity for peer feedback, and subsequent revising and editing as necessary. A classroom (at any grade level) could have the author's chair opportunity for anyone who wants to volunteer, as well as Process Pieces twice a week or so, engaging as many as four to six young writers each time, a dozen a week, so everyone gets peer feedback through Process Pieces at least twice a month.

In the case of Tess (and any other young writer for whom feedback doesn't fit their intended image or idea), there is no need to remind her that revision is part of the mix, so she must find something to change. The reason that Tess handles revision in a surface manner (spelling, punctuation, legibility) most of the time is that she doesn't in fact have anything to revise. She wrote as well as she could. Her need doesn't come from a wall chart; she revises because she knows, based on feedback, that her draft wasn't right.

Young Writers Learn More About Writing Processes

Experienced writers tell us that writing is hard work that is tedious and unpredictable. Dorothy Parker said the only reward for writing is in having done it. William Styron says it's like walking on your knees from Vladivostok to Madrid. (For anyone not immediately familiar with the trip from Western Europe to the edge of Siberia, going the long way around, it's a long way, especially on your knees.) And it doesn't get easier when you are good at it. Elizabeth Lehmann says that writing got harder as she began to understand it. Writers sit at dinner and, like James Thurber, struggle over the wording of a troublesome sentence. If it's so hard for the best writers, what makes young writers who aren't very good at it want to write? That is an important question.

In Chapter 7, we listened as several of the most celebrated writers of the twentieth century joined together in a roundtable conversation about their writing processes. They were questioned by a teacher who asked about how their processes work in order to get some insight into how the best writers write. We learned from that conversation that there are all sorts of ways to go about writing, that there is no single pattern, and that the best writers talk most about the hard work. So if there were a wall chart, it would read

WHEN YOU WRITE, WORK HARD.

Motivation Based on Understanding What Writers Do

The hard work might look like this description of the process that Argentine writer and language stylist Jorge Borges uses:

> The first lengthy effort would go into molding the opening sentence of the story in question, ceasing work on it only after it had taken on precisely the shape he desired. Then he slaved over the paragraph itself, reading it many times over until it seemed absolutely satisfactory. Only at that point would he venture on to the following paragraph; this process repeated itself again and again up to the final line of the story. (Bell-Villada, 1981, pp. 37–38)

That certainly appears hard. But it's also hard to do it the way E. L. Doctorow described it in the roundtable: "Trust the act of writing; in the beginning, you really don't know what's going to happen." Anyone who has written that way knows how hard it is.

It's important to acknowledge that writing is hard work because so much of the discussion about writing is focused on how to "motivate" young writers to write. We talk almost endlessly about getting young writers to write, and successful writing instruction is often judged by young writers' enthusiasm for writing. This motivation is sometimes more about how happy young writers are to write than how well they write and more about getting them to write enthusiastically than about getting them to write well. Clearly, what we can learn from accomplished writers and national writing sample analyses is that writing with enthusiasm and writing well do not enjoy a cause-and-effect relationship.

Writers tend to say that writing is what they do between occasional flashes of inspiration. It's hard to persevere, but that's the only way to find out there's something to like about writing. What's hard about writing is not knowing—not knowing it's all right to think it's hard, not knowing that the very best writers run into walls and can't think of anything else to write, and not knowing that problems in writing are almost always solved by working on them.

What's hardest for young writers, as opposed to experienced writers, can be that they don't know that it's all right to struggle. Suppose you are in your first distance footrace and while you know how long it is, you've never run this one before, so you don't have a sense of what that distance feels like. You start to run, but no one will tell you when it will be over. So you run, and just like everyone else in the race, you get tired. But unlike everyone else, you don't know that it's okay to be tired, and you don't know how to pace yourself. You don't know how tired you're supposed to get, and you don't know what to do about it. This is the hardest thing you've ever done. It's hard for experienced runners in the race, too, but they know it's only two laps around the park. They know how to conserve their energy and how tired they're supposed to be at every point along the race course. The race isn't any less hard for them than it is for the novice, but they understand it. It's way past time to let young writers in on the courses they're running, the processes they're using, the experiences they're having.

Motivation for writing comes from having control of how we write, how we think about writing, and how we feel when we write. *The motivation is in the control.* That is the key element in motivation, for novice writers and experienced writers alike.

The Emig Paradigm Revisited

Recall from Chapter 7 that Janet Emig (1971) identified a scientific procedure for handling complex processes. She reported that the eight high school students she studied seemed to use complex processes similar to the ones she found reported by people in science. Unfortunately, Emig's report became institutionalized into a label ("the" writing process) and "the" procedure (linear stages or steps), charts on the walls of classrooms, impassioned professional rhetoric, countless articles and chapters about recursive stages, and a mountain of anecdotal reports that far exceed the scope of what Emig was able to observe among eight students.

Young writers can learn a great deal about themselves and their writing by thinking about their writing processes. Over the years, it has become clear that young writers can learn how to frame writing topics, trust the act of writing, and work with their own writing.

Teaching About Writing Processes

Having an idea isn't hard; it's *framing* or designing a writing topic that's difficult. The problem young writers experience most often is expressed when they raise their hand and say, "I can't think of anything to write." The usual response is, "Write what you know." The reason that response so rarely helps is revealed in the writers' roundtable in Chapter 7. E. L. Doctorow told the teacher that the advice about writing what you know is logical—and wrong. As Irving Wallace wrote, "Da Vinci did not have to attend the Last Supper to paint it" (Brohaugh, 1987). We don't write what we know. *We write what we care about, and we come to know what we write* (Fearn, 1983).

How can we find out what the young writers in our classrooms care about?

INSTRUCTIONAL SCENARIO

In the Classroom Identifying What Young Writers Care About

Teacher: Girls and boys, I want you to make some lists. You need paper and something with which to write.

READER ACTIVITY

We'd like you to make these lists, as well, so you'll need a piece of paper and a sweep second hand for timing yourself.

BACK TO THE CLASSROOM

Teacher: These are one-minute lists. I will give you something to make a list about, and you will have only one minute to list as many things as you can. Get as many items on your list as you can. Here is the first list. Make a list of things that make you giggle. One minute. List as many as you can. [Waits one minute exactly.]

Draw a line under that list and begin another. This time make a list about things that make you cry. [One minute.]

Draw a line under that list. Make a list of things you love. [One minute.]

Draw a line. Make a list of things that are warm. [One minute.]

Make a list of things that make you afraid. [One minute.]

Make a list of things that make you angry. [One minute.]

Make one more list. Make a list of your passions, all of the things you care about. [One minute.]

COMMENTARY

On those seven lists are just about as many ideas as there is time to write about in a lifetime. Of course, an idea isn't necessarily something you know a lot about; instead, it is something that pops up on a list of things you care about. They're only ideas. They have to be framed into writing topics, and then they have to be framed into writing.

Framing a Topic

Gene Wentz, a retired SEAL (Sea and Air Land Special Forces), walked into Betty Abell Jurus' (owner, Writers' Bookstore and Haven, and convener of the Writers' Haven Writers) life several years ago and said, "I have a story, and I need someone to write it." Betty is an experienced writer, but she'd never been to Vietnam, had never held a firearm larger than a .22 pistol, and didn't know a hootch from a hutch, but the topic seemed interesting. It was something she cared about and could learn enough to write about.

Gene taught her to creep into some strangers' campsite at night, close enough to execute a silent kill, and leave without their knowing she was there. She wrote from Gene's notes. She wrote about firepower she never heard or smelled, geography she never saw, people she never met. Gene taught the vocabulary of the men, and Betty wrote it. She wrote the moments of terror surrounded by hours of boredom. When *Men in Green Faces* (1992) was finished, Betty could talk about the life of a SEAL in the jungles of Vietnam as though she had fought beside them. She wrote the book not because she knew its content but because the idea intrigued her. She framed the intrigue into a writing topic, and the writing topic into a book, because she became an expert through the writing. She came to know because she wrote, and she wrote because she cared.

The trouble with lists of ideas is that they don't contain any writing topics. Josh, a fifth grader, writes an item under "Afraid": rabid animals. By itself, that doesn't mean much. So merely making lists of passions doesn't help young writers, or older ones, for that matter, enter into a world of fluent writing. It isn't that "rabid animals" isn't an idea; it's that it isn't framed.

A writer wrote of riding a New York ferry boat one afternoon and seeing a young girl sitting alone. With no special intent, he made a mental note about the girl. Then later he wondered: Who could she be? Where could she be going? Why was she dressed in those clothes? He began to frame the idea. As he thought more about her and framed the idea, his story began to take shape.

What about Josh's "rabid animals"? How does a fifth grader frame that idea so it is useful for writing? Fear of rabid animals is the start. Imagine a nine-year-old girl being told by her grandfather about rabid foxes on their farm. That's something to write about. Begin with some questions. Where is that farm? What kind of farm is it? Who is that little girl? Does she go to school? Does she live with her grandfather? Is there a grandmother? Might the little girl be visiting from the city? Is the state where the girl lives important to her character? Is the state where the farm is located important to the story? If the little girl learns about rabid foxes early in the story, when will she confront one of those rabid foxes? What are the circumstances of the confrontation? What will happen in the confrontation? Did the little girl do something wrong that put her out in the field all alone to face that rabid fox? Now we're getting into the business of *framing* a writing topic.

Writing topics come not from lists but from questions. Creative thinking skills are in operation when we search for writing topics. One of those skills is *fluency*. Ideas are fleshed out, framed, and made into something to write about by *elaborating* on them. But fluency and elaboration merely produce more ideas. Now what?

Look at the questions. Which of them about the little girl and rabid foxes has to do with characters? Which ones are about the little girl? Which ones are about other characters? Once those general questions about characters are organized, we have to decide which of the characters is the main character: the little girl or the grandfather? Or, once we begin organizing, is there a third character emerging? What more do we learn about the prospective story by thinking about the characters, or the setting, or the problem? This organizational process is called, in creative thinking skills terminology, *organizing chaos.*

All of that thinking is what has been referred to as "prewriting." But that kind of prewriting doesn't produce a plan for writing. It produces a plan for starting. *Starting* means beginning to draft. It is at the point at which they start to draft that writers begin to frame their topic. That is the distinction between having ideas and framing a topic. Many young writers have plenty of ideas, but until they make them into something to write about, they don't have anything other than lists.

Because what Emig found was a connection between processes in science and the writing processes of eight twelfth-grade writers, and because scientific processes are best characterized as creative problem solving, what we have to learn most from Emig's research is the role of creativity in writing.

 ## INSTRUCTIONAL SCENARIO

In the Classroom to Frame Writing Topics

Teacher: Make a list, boys and girls, of your very best characteristics. What do you think good friends would say are the best things about you? Think of people who know you best and what they would say. Think about your mother or father, or maybe a brother or sister. What would people who know you and like you say are the very best things about you? I'll give you one minute to make a list. Put as many things on the list as you can.

READER ACTIVITY

We want you to make this list as well. Think of husbands and wives, best friends, partners, perhaps your children. What would those people say are your best qualities?

BACK TO THE CLASSROOM

Teacher: [After one minute.] Stop. Yes, Andrea?

Andrea: Can I read mine?

Teacher: No, we're not going to read them right now. We're going to organize them. First, divide the items on your list into three groups. You may label the groups 1, 2, and 3, or you may make three new lists, if you like, but you have only one minute for this. Make three lists, and if you think of any new items, you may use those too.

[After one minute.] Now I want you to label or name the categories or groups. If you found three groups for your list, name each group. If you found two, name those. If you couldn't find more than one, name that one. Give each group a name. Yes, Dexter?

Dexter: I had to make four groups, but I only have one thing in the fourth one.

Teacher: Then you need names for all four groups. [Pauses while they name their groups.] Now look at your groups and decide which one best describes you. Choose the one group that you think has the best name for describing you and the best items under it. Put a circle around that category. [Pauses while they make their selection.] Yes, Kenneth?

Kenneth: Is it okay if I put one thing from another group in my group?

Teacher: Of course. They're your lists. [It really doesn't matter. These are their items, their categories, their selections. The teacher is only setting them up.]

COMMENTARY

The young writers have made their list, and they have organized it into categories that reflect best attributes or characteristics. They have a good start on the road to framing a writing topic. A similar process, called list-group-label, where students make lists of terms, divide them into categories, and label the categories (Taba, 1967), has been used to reveal relationships among social studies terms.

BACK TO THE CLASSROOM

Teacher: Now, girls and boys, here is the hard part, maybe. You're going to build onto your lists. Pretend the category you chose isn't about you. Instead, it's about another child your age, but the child doesn't live here in this state. Your character lives at least 500 miles from here. You will have to go to a map and decide where your character might live.

Tomorrow I want you to be able to tell who your character is, where your character lives, and how the problem of your story comes from something you know about where your character lives. For example, if I had my character living in Kilgore, Texas, I could have her trapped overnight in the oil museum. I happen to know there is an oil museum in Kilgore, Texas, and I also happen to know that Kilgore is over 500 miles from here.

COMMENTARY

The teacher has taken the children into their imagination, yet another creative behavior. For homework, the young writers have to name their setting and invent a problem for their character that has something to do with the place. By the following day, most of the children will have invented their own way to begin their story, complete with character, setting, and problem. This strategy works for most children beginning in about the third grade.

Notice in the next-to-last sentence of the previous paragraph the word *most* in reference to the children in the class. Occasionally good lessons engage all of the children, but if teachers assume that good lessons will always engage everyone, there will be massive disappointment in our professional lives, especially with respect to writing. Writing, as opposed to copying or completing worksheets, is a personal thing. In the classroom, we're making it a general thing. Good writing lessons are likely to be effective even though they are general. They will engage most young writers, and those who are not engaged will often go along. But it's the rare writing lesson that engages everyone, every time.

INSTRUCTIONAL SCENARIO

In a Tenth-Grade Classroom to Write Nonfiction

Teacher: We've just spent several weeks reading and studying about Latinos who have made a difference in the history and culture of the United States. Remember that for our purposes, *Latino* means people of mixed Indian and Spanish ancestry. You've worked on two different themes, politics and culture, and in last Friday's culminating whole group conversation, we discussed twenty-seven especially significant people who lived during the past fifty years. Later in the year, we'll do the same sort of writing with Indian people whose lives have had a major impact on the United States. But for now, it's Latino, so each study pair in the class will select one of the names that came up last Friday. Do some thinking about your selection before class tomorrow, and come to class with a name ready. Also, before class, read the four-page biography on that person from your book.

COMMENTARY

In a high school literature class, the teacher has decided it is impossible to appreciate the range of literature available if readers don't have a sense of the movers and shakers within that range. In the context of literature, therefore, the teacher weaves culture and history threads. The most recent two weeks focused on people whose ancestry is mixed Indian and Spanish.

BACK TO THE CLASSROOM

Teacher: [The following day] Now, folks, in your partnerships, make a list of items that tell who your subject is or was. Name other people who lived at the same time, people and events who were changed because of your subject's life and contribution, and what your subject is known to have said or written. Make as long a list as you can. Yes, Hector?

Hector: Luis and I are going to do Linda Chavez, and we have some things about her from the four-page biography. The entry is in *The Hispanic 100* [Novas, 1995]. But there aren't any books about her, so how do we get more information?

Teacher: What do you know about her?

Luis: She was a teacher, and she was in the teachers' union.

Teacher: What do you know about her teachers' union? What did she do in the teachers' union? What are some questions you could ask about who she is? You and Hector make a list of questions. Everyone, look over your list of what you know about your subject, and then make a new list, this time of questions about your subject. Then arrange your questions into three groups. Name the groups. What sources are likely to contain information about those categories? Who might know?

COMMENTARY

The teacher is engaging tenth graders in brainstorming, elaborating, and arranging the elaborations. It isn't the list of ideas that is most important here; it's the act of making the list, working on elaborations, arranging the elaborations, and framing the arrangements into manageable pieces so they can be used as sources of information. The teacher turned Luis and Hector onto the World Wide Web, where there was sufficient information about Linda Chavez' life, so they could work to complete the research and writing task.

BACK TO THE CLASSROOM TO BEGIN THE DRAFT

Teacher: How many of you are ready to begin your draft? That's almost everyone. Yes, Julie?

Julie: We—Bill's my partner—have a lot of stuff, but we don't know where to start.

Teacher: Others? How many haven't found a good way to begin the draft? [Six hands go up.] The rest of you begin, and write as much as you can as well as you can. I'm going over to the table with several folks. Don't disturb us for a few minutes. [At the table] Think of two words that could be used to describe your subject. Luis, you and Hector are working on Linda Chavez. Give me two words about her.

Luis: *Teacher* and *union leader*.

Teacher: What do you know about her as a union leader?

Luis: Lots of stuff.

Teacher: You and Hector begin writing as much as you can as well as you can about Linda Chavez, the union leader. Try this. Both of you write as much as you can as well as you can for two minutes. Then compare your papers and settle on only two ideas on which to write.

COMMENTARY

The start is similar to the Power Writing exercise earlier in this chapter. The draft is "as much as you can as well as you can." Because the teacher has done some framing of the writing topic in this tenth-grade classroom, there is a real advantage now because writers have information at the ready. If they don't begin, go back to Power Writing, and when three rounds are completed, tell them, "Look, folks, I just watched you write an average of twenty-seven words per minute with no chance to think about where or how to start. Now you know where to start, and you have the writing topic framed. If you want me to sit here with a stopwatch while you do it one minute at a time, it's okay. If you'd prefer to work at your own pace, that's okay too. It's time."

Within about ten minutes, somewhere in just about any classroom a hand will go up, and the following exchange will ensue:

Teacher: Yes, Jane?

Jane: Do we have to follow the planning we did?

Teacher: Why do you ask, Jane?

Jane: We don't have anything about where he went to college. We have to find that out.

Teacher: When did you discover you needed that?

Jane: When we were writing.

Teacher: Everyone, listen to what happened to Jane and Richard. Jane, describe the problem. [Jane describes the problem.] Everyone, very often we don't know what we need to plan for in writing until we start to write, so while you are writing, don't hesitate to do something that isn't in your plan.

E S L Allowing students to work in pairs or small groups for these activities provides support for children learning English as a second language. The students become a part of the idea generation and organization procedures, but they don't have to carry the whole load by themselves. They can contribute ideas by using vocabulary with which they are familiar, and they can get support from their peers, who can help by supplying vocabulary for ideas and categories. If possible, it's useful to pair the student whose native language is not English with another who is bilingual in both English and the native language of the partner. ■

Clarifying What It Means to Help Young Writers Learn About Writing Processes

Helping young writers learn more about writing processes isn't the same as promoting a formula, or "doing" a process over and over. It is helping them learn how to think in ways likely to identify ideas, to give texture to ideas and turn them into writing topics, and then pursue those topics through to fruition.

That last part—*pursuing topics through to fruition*—is missing from virtually all educational conceptions of writing processes. It is where the iterative process described in Chapter 7 becomes clear. Once writers are started, there occurs an interaction between the drafting and the planning, so writers plan and draft simultaneously.

Writers draft and revise simultaneously more and more intensely and relentlessly as they become better writers. Dorothy Parker said that it takes her months to write a story; she thinks it out and then writes it, "sentence by sentence—no first draft. I can't write five words but that I change seven" (Cowley, 1958, p. 79). Her rewriting and polishing isn't mere revision in the recursive sense that while you draft, you sometimes make changes that seem like revision. For Parker and for countless other writers (to name another, Jorge Borges mentioned earlier in this chapter), the rewriting, the revising, and the polishing are part of the drafting.

As this book is being written, a member of our local writing community is struggling with the iterative drafting-revising interaction. She has a good novel going, with well-crafted characters, a believable plot line, and a setting that serves the characters and plot. But several of her characters are becoming somewhat sympathetic when her plot line demands that they be villainous. The writer has to figure a way out of the thicket she's creating for her characters. She works at it every day. She drafts again, and then again. She reads each draft and revises again.

This writer's problem is not with ideas or frames for writing topics. It isn't with writing. (She's a professional, and she writes superbly.) She chose her writing topic, so the writing is authentic. She isn't blocked. No one is standing over her with a stopwatch or threat of a grade. She doesn't have to fit her writing to an artificial rubric. Rather, she is faced with that last and hardest part: *pursuing her writing through to fruition.* She is struggling with the iterative interaction between drafting and revising. Right now, she thinks her story doesn't work. It isn't plausible, and she thinks her readers won't believe it. She's struggling with what she thinks doesn't work.

The drafting-revising interaction that the writer is experiencing isn't one of repeated applications of drafting and revising. It isn't *recursive* at all. It's *symbiotic* (more than one portion of a process working to the mutual advantage of each other). Drafting and revising don't work in an alternating series; they're interactive.

The question isn't *whether* there is an iterative interaction between drafting and revising. The question is *how* the iterative interaction between drafting and revising becomes part of the way young writers experience their writing. The question is *why* some young writers begin to understand the iterative interaction between drafting and revising, while others either experience revising as a stage that follows drafting or refuse to revise at all. It's because in all of their experience, they have written as well as they can. They have never written a draft, so there has never been any need for revision.

Now they're in school. In school, they learn new things. One of the new things is to rethink, to re-vision, their writing. They have to learn how to do that and when, and to learn that they need a draft with which to work and feedback on the basis of which to rethink.

Pursuing writing through to fruition requires perseverance. One major difference between young writers and experienced writers is that experienced writers have learned to concentrate on making their writing work, knowing that the only measure of whether writing works is feedback from their audience. As they write, experienced writers listen as they expect an audience would listen. Listening and writing are part of writing processes.

The Process of Making the Writing Work: Writers' Workshop

Young writers can come to understand how they approach and perform their own writing. They can learn about, or become aware of, their own writing processes. They can learn the extent to which, if any, their processes change depending on the genre in which they are working or the purpose of the task or audience for their writing. They can also learn more about writing processes than they know from their own experience. Their own experience is valuable, but we send children to school with the expectation that they will take out of the school door something more than they brought in.

A sixth grader spoke of the ring of an audience in her ears: "When I am writing my papers, I find myself thinking about the feedback I was getting, and the feedback I was giving. It gave me another way to think about my writing." She's listening to her own writing as though she were a reader, just as the experienced writer of the revenge story was doing when she found herself with sympathetic characters. The sixth grader is talking about how her writing is affected by what her audience would say, and what she would say, about it. That sense of audience gave her a way to think about her writing. How did this sixth grader get to the point where she could hear her audience as she wrote? Where did the ring of an audience come from? It came from the Writers' Workshop, a place where writers bring their writing and read to receive feedback.

The Writer's Workshop we refer to stems from that conducted by San Diego's Writers' Haven Writers and by Jerry Hannah in the Pirate Workshops at the Santa Barbara Writers' Conference. It is not the same as the small group organizational meeting by the same name (Tompkins & Hoskisson, 1991) or the *writing workshop* (Atwell, 1987), designed for minilessons, organization, topic selection, and writing time. The Writers' Workshop to which we refer in this chapter is exclusively for the purpose of oral sharing of writing and audience feedback.

The Writers' Workshop has its roots in the college literary societies, one of the earliest at Harvard in 1719 (Gere, 1987, p. 10), and has been a major part of writers' processes ever since. It is a safe place, always bound by procedures of some sort that the participants agree on. The writers' purpose for participating in Writers' Workshops is to acquire the greatest amount of useful feedback in the most efficient manner. The procedures vary widely. The ones we have used tend to feature certain patterns (Farnan & Fearn, 1993):

1. *Groups are limited to five to seven participants.* With fewer people, there isn't enough feedback for writers; more, and the session takes too long, and people's attention fades.

2. *Manuscript pages are not distributed to participants.* Feedback is based solely on oral readings. Participants have to pay careful attention and take notes.

3. *Writers read their work without introduction or explanation.* Each writing must work without explanation. Writers aren't allowed to set up the audience.

4. *Everyone in the group is responsible for delivering feedback on each piece of shared writing.* No one may pass or say, "I don't have anything to say."

5. *All feedback must be delivered to the writer.* There are no side conversations about anyone's writing.

6. *All feedback must be worded in a way that the writer can use it for revision,* if the writer chooses to revise. It isn't useful to say, "I liked [or didn't like] the piece."

7. *Feedback is typically worded as declaratives because the writer is a listener in Writers' Workshops.* If the writer is asked questions, the writer begins to talk.

8. After there has been feedback all around the group, the writer may ask questions for clarification, but *writers may not defend their writing.*

9. *No participant in a Writers' Workshop is required to revise on the basis of audience feedback.* We have found that young writers, like experienced writers, can't wait to get alone so they can revise.

10. When everyone in the group has had a chance to read aloud and receive feedback, then the Writers' Workshop is over.

Writers' Workshop in a Sixth Grade

We introduced Writers' Workshop and the concept of feedback in a sixth grade through one session of Process Pieces. Having provided two minutes for young writers to write an image of a soaring hawk, a student read aloud once, twice, then three times, and we asked the rest of the students what they saw, heard, and generally sensed. After several offerings from peers, we told the class that what they said about the reading is called *feedback.*

Writers' Workshop in session. Elizabeth Crews/Stock Boston

"Feedback," we told them, "is similar to what happens when you look in a mirror. The reflection is an image of what you put in. In Writers' Workshop, the feedback is a reflection of the impact of the writing." Then we told the students that we would begin the first Writers' Workshop group the following Wednesday, one week later, and everyone in the room must have fresh material ready. They would be writing short vignettes about sports figures.

Before leaving, we asked the teacher to prepare a list of four or five students who could be counted on to learn the process in one session and function independently thereafter. When we arrived at the classroom a week later, the teacher had the list of four students ready for us. We began with some of the more independent students, *not the better writers.* The plan was to begin a new group each week in this class of thirty-four, so early groups had to be able to work with little guidance as we worked with later groups. We set it up to succeed.

We called the four preselected students to a small circle in the front of the room. We told the rest of the class to watch and listen, to be tape recorders, because we were going to ask for their reflections when we finished. Then Leif took his seat in the small circle, reviewed the procedures, and began. The scenario that follows is a transcription of the videotape we prepared from that first session.

INSTRUCTIONAL SCENARIO

In the Classroom for an Actual Writers' Workshop Script

Leif: Nicole, you're up.

Nicole: *Joe DiMaggio was the star of the drama that took place on the big league baseball field. He was exciting to watch with his graceful stance, his loose and easy style as he chased fly balls that seemed far out of reach, and his rifle arm that cut down many runners at home. In 14 seasons with the Yankees, he made a lifetime batting average of .325, hit 361 home runs, and batted in 1537 runs. He played in 10 World Series and 11 All-Star games, was voted American League MVP 3 times, and was elected to the Hall of Fame in 1955. Joe DiMaggio was truly an important player during his baseball career.*

James: I'd say that there's a lot of detail about the RBIs he hit, how he gunned down people at the bases, and how he was a fabulous baseball player.

MaryAlice: I liked how you said he looked graceful when he caught fly balls because I never thought of baseball players as graceful.

Anna: I like how you used so much detail because if you didn't use it, I would be lost.

Leif: I agree with what the folks have said so far. The details are terrific. And the vocabulary you used—*graceful stance, loose easy style, rifle arm*—those are picture words, and the piece comes through very clearly. Nice piece.

[James read his piece, received feedback, then MaryAlice was up, and so forth around the workshop circle.]

When the demonstration workshop ended, the rest of the class told what they observed, heard, and thought about it. The following week, the demonstration students conducted their own workshop, and an adult leader started a new one. Each group's first workshop experience included an adult leader who briefly reviewed the workshop rules and modeled feedback when it was his or her turn. In five weeks, everyone in the room was in an independent workshop group, and the teacher roamed the room, keeping an eye on what was happening so that when the sessions were over (in about twenty minutes), she could conduct a debriefing of the whole class.

Results of the Sixth-Grade Writers' Workshop Experience

The eight months of weekly Writers' Workshops were videotaped for careful analysis of what went on in the sessions and the preparation of a master demonstration tape, which we use in our summer Writing Institute for Teachers. An analysis of the feedback over the eight months showed that it clustered in five categories.

Sixth Graders' Feedback in Writers' Workshops	
Categories and Descriptions	**Percentage of All Feedback Instances**
Feedback about craft (e.g., word choice, style, sentence design) "You used *cuckoo* too much." "I never thought about baseball being graceful." "Your descriptions were good, but you used *and* too many times."	28.4%
Feedback about clarity "I didn't understand what *ERA* means, and I didn't understand *RBI* either." "I know you wrote about how he dressed, but what's his personality? What does he think?"	27.6%
Feedback about detail "Tell a little more about how he looked." "I liked how you went into detail about how old he was and why the teacher chose him."	22.4%
Feedback that was negative "I never did find out what your story is about."	16.4%
Feedback that was positive "That's wonderful." "Gosh, I wish I could write like that."	5.2%

Clearly the young writers learned to deliver feedback, and their feedback was primarily focused on what we most appreciate about young writers' work and most often find troubling when it's absent: craft, clarity, and detail.

Many people tend to avoid read-and-critique processes in writing because they are afraid to expose something so personal as their own writing to public view. But that fear is far more characteristic of adults than it is of children, so it is adults who tend to make rules such as, "Give two positives for every negative." After participating in weekly Writers' Workshops for eight months, the students said they preferred what we called "corrective" feedback (they called it "negative") to positive feedback because they felt negative feedback showed them how to get better.

There is also a prevailing view, especially in the education profession, that corrective feedback, defined or interpreted as negative, has a harmful effect on young writers' inclination to write. Many teachers fret that peer and teacher feedback that is not positive will interfere with young writers' enthusiasm just when they need their enthusiasm the most. In spite of anecdotal reports of the devastating consequences of teacher and peer criticism, Groff (1975) found no harmful effect of criticism on young writers' inclination to write. Groff's review is now twenty-five years old, and we are aware of no *evidence* in dispute of what Groff found.

Of course, we aren't talking about criticism here anyway. This is feedback. It is a reflection on how the writing works. To ensure that workshop participants learn what feedback is and how to deliver it, it is critical to model feedback stems with young writers in their Writers' Workshops. We have found the following feedback stems and models to be especially effective:

Feedback for Fiction

1. Your character talked to me.
2. I like the words you put in the character's mouth. They worked.
3. I like the way you described . . .
4. The first paragraph made me want to hear the rest of the story because . . .
5. I could smell the grass. I could feel the rain. I could hear the sea.
6. I'm not sure I can hear the character you described using those words.
7. The problem you gave the character didn't seem as though it were something that character would have worried about.
8. The story was terrific until the last page. Then it was over so fast, and I'm not so sure that character could have solved the problem that quickly.
9. There was a lot of information about the main character, but I don't feel I know him very well because the information was all about how tall he was.
10. You wrote that the day was cloudy. Can you write it so we know it's cloudy without telling us? Something like damp haze hanging in the air, or something like that?
11. You gave a lot of information that helped me understand the difference between the two characters. I think I could pick them out of a crowd.

Feedback for Nonfiction

1. I'm not clear about the question you tried to answer in your report.
2. I was confused about your main point.
3. I noticed that every paragraph in your piece is designed with exactly the same three parts in exactly the same order.

4. Your opinion is very clear in the first paragraph, but I wasn't persuaded by the argument. It seemed the second argument was weak.
5. The way you wrote the first paragraph, with that question at the end, made me want to read the rest.
6. At the end, you wrote a summary, but it seemed that the last part should be a conclusion.
7. I'd like to know more about the information that leads to the conclusion you wrote at the end.
8. I like the way you reminded the readers of your main points at the end of the writing.
9. I feel that the information in the fourth paragraph might work better earlier. If I remember correctly, it might fit in the second paragraph.
10. I'd like to hear you read it with your last paragraph coming first.
11. What exactly did you do in your experiment? I know what you found, but I'm not sure what you did.

You Asked?

There are a variety of questions teachers and parents ask about Writers' Workshops. Here are answers to nine of the most frequently asked questions:

1. The length of written pieces students bring to Writers' Workshop varies, but we suggest that young writers hold their reading time to about two minutes, and never more than three minutes. If students' writings are lengthy, they can choose to read and get feedback on a one- to two-minute portion.
2. Group stability is vastly overrated. By changing workshop membership every couple of weeks, everyone has a chance to experience the whole range of feedback quality.
3. Teachers can manage multiple groups simultaneously by roving about the room and checking in on each workshop. Today's multiple-group classrooms demand management, mobility, and monitoring not just for Writers' Workshops but for the whole day. If you can manage rotation stations and independent interest centers, you can manage Writers' Workshops.
4. Much of elementary school student feedback falls into two categories: need for more clarity and need for more detail. Elementary students also comment on word selection and sentence design. The least frequent kinds of feedback we've found in classrooms where feedback is explained and demonstrated are praise ("Your story is wonderful") and nullification ("I think you got your story from TV").
5. Interestingly, elementary students' feedback tends to reflect what their teachers value. The most frequent feedback focuses on the need for more detail and more clarity. Students are at least as discriminating about the quality of writing as are teachers. Our experience has shown that a peer audience is neither more nor less severe than is a teacher audience.

6. Early on, there tends to be some minor reluctance on the part of a few students regarding reading their work aloud. Because the Writers' Workshop is a safe place and because feedback is by definition helpful, any early reluctance melts away within a session or two.

7. It is a rare workshop group in which all members are equally good at delivering feedback. Even among experienced writers, some are better than others at feedback. We found some students who were as good as any experienced writer we knew, and there were others who just went through the motions. It's that way in mathematics class too.

8. We have never encountered a problem with "negative" criticism. We never talk of negative criticism because neither positive nor negative comments are relevant to feedback. But students talk about positive and negative, and many much prefer what they refer to as negative feedback. One student said she already knew she could write, so she didn't benefit from praise; she wanted to know what she could do to improve.

9. Of course, Writers' Workshop will work with primary children. There are primary applications of Writers' Workshops yet to come in this chapter.

They Commented: It's Always Good to Hear from the Students

In interviews at the end of the year, the young writers voiced a variety of very encouraging comments. Following are some of them:

"Teachers' feedback is important, but kids' feedback is more valuable because kids know what other kids are trying to say in their writing."

"We didn't know anything about feedback in October, but we learned about it through our talks and by using it in Writers' Workshops."

"When I am writing my papers, I find myself thinking about the feedback I was getting and the feedback I was giving. It gave me another way to think about my writing."

"I need negative feedback more than I need positive feedback. I already know I can write; I don't need to be told over and over that I'm good at it. I need to know what I'm not doing well."

"I learned more about writing this year in Writers' Workshop than I learned in my other years of school. I got to hear so many other people's writings and learned new techniques, and I also wrote more for the workshops."

"The teacher reads writing to grade it; kids read and listen to see if it works."

"I never felt bad by anyone's criticism of my writing."

"Some people weren't always prepared, and it showed. Sometimes I didn't get very useful feedback."

One result of Writers' Workshop in a sixth grade is confirmation of what we all know. Everyone in the room isn't equally good at the task, but students can learn about direct and functional feedback; students honor their teacher's effort but recognize the limitations of teacher feedback; they can learn what is emphasized; and they tend to feel they learn to write better as a result of participating in Writers' Workshops.

But this was the sixth grade. Beginning in the fourth or fifth grade, the Writers' Workshop as described sounds perfectly feasible, with minor adjustments to accommodate individual and group differences. However, what about third graders, or even first graders?

Writers' Workshop in the First Grade

Ms. Phaneuf teaches first grade and has used a Writers' Workshop format with her first graders for several years. After a few weeks of school, when the students are able to write at least one sentence, she formally introduces the feedback sessions in which the students will be involved. She reads Marc Brown's *Arthur Writes a Story* aloud. The book describes how the main character, Arthur, struggles to write a story that will be interesting to others.

Arthur Writes a Story serves as the catalyst for a discussion in which students come to understand that writers, which includes them, do not complete the final version of their writing the first time they write it. Ms. Phaneuf points out to her first graders that it is often very helpful to get feedback on a piece of writing from people who might be reading the writing. As an example, she reads aloud a piece of her own writing in which several bits of crucial information are left out. She then asks the students if they have any questions about what she wrote. When the students ask questions, she demonstrates how she could change her piece so it would be clearer and they could get a better picture in their minds.

At that point, Ms. Phaneuf tells her students about the feedback and revision program they will implement. Every Monday, each child will sign up for a day during the week when she or he will read a piece of writing aloud to the class from the author's chair. Four or five students will sign up for each day. Students will choose to read a piece from their journals or a story they have in progress.

At the author's chair, each child reads a piece of writing, and the other students share something they like about the writing. Then the writer-reader is allowed to call on three students who ask questions about the writing. Ms. Phaneuf writes these questions and keeps them until the next day, when the student revises. Revision addresses the questions the student-listeners asked, as well as any suggestions that the teacher chooses to make. Students receive feedback and revise their writing based on that feedback once each week for approximately four consecutive weeks. After that, the feedback sessions move to every other week in order to provide more time for direct or intentional instruction of lessons in writing.

Ms. Phaneuf gives her students instruction on how to ask questions of authors. She wants them to do this in a way that best alerts the authors' attention without needlessly hurting their feelings. For example, instead of saying, "Why didn't you tell us what color the shirt is?" Ms. Phaneuf encourages students to say, "What

Author's chair in session. Elizabeth Crews

color is the new shirt?" In other words, they ask for the information that was omitted without passing judgment. The class practices their questions with her twice before officially starting the program and once in a while throughout the course of the program, whenever the teacher feels the students need a reminder.

The children who read for feedback work with Ms. Phaneuf at the revising table the day after the author's chair. She sits at the inside of the U-shaped revising table with the students seated around the outside facing her. They work on the pieces they read the day before. Ms. Phaneuf reads to each child the feedback from the day before and helps each young writer think about the feedback and what it means for changing the writing to make it clearer. She also provides instruction for each student depending on the rewriting needs. This direct instruction includes such things as the appropriate place in the writing to answer a question, turning two sentences into one sentence, and using phonics skills to spell words.

Once each child finishes revising, she or he reads the revised piece to the class. The class notices how the questions were answered, whether the piece is now longer or more detailed, and how the picture from the writing is better now than before. Ms. Phaneuf compliments each writer, and everyone receives a round of applause once they read their revised piece.

Revision instruction continues in this way until about mid-February, or the sixth month of the school year, at which time Ms. Phaneuf begins to teach the children how to give constructive comments to their peers about their writing. She models proper language so students can communicate that they are confused about something the author wrote, or have a suggestion to make it better, without hurting each other's feelings. She teaches such phrases as, "I did not understand . . . , I was interested in . . . , I wish you could have told us more, I was not clear why . . ." The children are also encouraged to continue letting authors know which parts they liked about the writing and why.

Beginning about mid-March, the class moves from a whole class feedback design to one where students work in groups of four students (what are called *table groups*). Each first-grade student receives peer feedback on a weekly basis again, but only two days of the week are used, which leaves the other three for direct instruction. Five fifth-grade students help Ms. Phaneuf make the transition to table groups. She conducts a fifth-grader staff development program in which the fifth-grade leaders observe feedback sessions for two days and notice how Ms. Phaneuf records student feedback.

Once trained, each fifth-grade student works at a table group of first-graders. Fifth graders help the younger ones run their feedback session. On Mondays, after writing and editing a piece of writing, each first grader takes a turn reading a piece to the others in the group. Students give constructive comments and ask questions of each other, just as they had done in the whole class setting. Fifth-grade student leaders assist by recording comments and questions for each of the first graders. Usually Ms. Phaneuf circulates from group to group, assisting where necessary. Sometimes she pulls a small group of students aside to reteach a skill they are struggling with in their writing.

On Tuesdays, the first graders revise their writing based on the feedback they receive on Mondays. The fifth graders assist each table group of first graders, revising as Ms. Phaneuf had before. Again she circulates, helping students as needed and taking the opportunity to pull a group of students aside and give them additional personal instruction.

Having older students (fifth graders in this case) or trained adult volunteers assist in Writers' Workshop is helpful because the teacher is then free to provide individualized small group instruction. However, sometimes when only three six year olds give feedback to a peer, there is not enough quality feedback on the basis of which young writers can revise well. Ms. Phaneuf suggests that instructors of very young writers who use Writers' Workshop in their classrooms monitor how the feedback system is working and make adjustments to fit each situation.

In all variations, it is critical to remember that feedback is a useful message to writers, not a mere judgment about whether the writing is good or not good. Additionally, feedback must be followed by revision. It is important for young writers to use feedback as they think about revision. There is no rule that they must follow the feedback, but they must think about it. Feedback that speaks directly to the writer and includes suggestions for how to make the writing clearer helps young writers think about revision.

REVIEW AND REFLECTION

1. Look back at the material on Power Writing in this chapter. Remember that people tend to learn what they do. What are young learners doing in the Power Writing activity? What can you assume they are learning?
2. Using the same principle that people tend to learn what they do, what can you assume young writers learn when they engage in Process Pieces?
3. What do you think young writers are doing in Writers' Workshop? What do you assume they are learning from their Writers' Workshop experiences?
4. What is the difference between a topic and an idea? What does it mean to frame an idea for writing?
5. What do you think is the benefit of spending time in a writing instruction program on helping young writers understand their own writing processes?
6. What is there about your own writing processes that you think would be helpful for young writers in your classroom to learn?

A Summary: Teaching and Learning Writing Processes

That writing is a complex process is self-evident. The nature of that process has been under scrutiny for several decades. The conclusions that can be drawn at this point are that everyone who writes does so by mobilizing some sort of process and that process is idiosyncratic to the task. Thus, we speak of writing processes, not "the" writing process. In this book, we speak of interactions among the kinds of things writers do when they write—interactions between drafting and planning and between revising and planning, for example, and interactions between those two interactions and drafting. We know about the interactions from the enormous amount of self-reported information from practicing writers.

Balanced writing instruction includes attention to writing processes that is focused in two directions: (1) helping young writers understand what they do when they write and (2) helping young writers learn more about writing processes so they are able to mobilize an array of ways to accomplish it. To help young writers understand their own processes, they need to self-report on their own writing. To help them learn more, they need to know and practice what other young writers do when they write. Balanced writing instruction becomes a social experience for young writers when there is as much writing and discussion as those two objectives entail.

We strengthen the social aspect of writing even further when we engage young writers in listening to each other's work and providing feedback from the perspective of a peer reader. That feedback also offers information on the basis of which young writers can think deliberately and insightfully about revision.

9 Thinking About Genres in Writing

BEFORE YOU READ

- How do readers know when writing is good?
- What does the word *genre* mean in the context of writing?
- Is a research report or a technical explanation more or less creative than short fiction?
- Given a similar topic, what kinds of demands does a short piece of writing make on a writer that a longer piece of writing does not make?
- What are the attributes of quality for the various genres?

What Do We Mean by "Genres"?

Genres are categories or kinds of writing, with distinctive features or rhetorical elements that speak to their purpose. Fiction is a genre. Among its distinctive features are characters, settings, problems, and resolutions. Additional features characteristically found in fiction are foreshadowing and plot. Fiction's purpose is emotion, values, and beliefs. It capitalizes on the writer's passion for the story (Gardner, 1983). Some of the features of fiction generalize to other genres. Passion and detail, for example, are fundamental to all writing, but it is in fiction that the character is a (though not always the) primary feature. *Hamlet* isn't called *Hamlet* for want of another title, and while *Much Ado About Nothing* has a non-character title, it's about Beatrice and Benedick, Claudio and Hero, Leonardo, maybe even Dogberry. *Moby Dick* is about Captain Ahab.

There are various ways to categorize writing. One way is fiction and nonfiction. Fiction includes stories, poetry, and drama because all three are about what Gardner (1983) calls "the fictional dream," that state in which the reader is *in* the story. Nonfiction includes everything else, mainly reports, biographies and autobiographies, and persuasion.

Another two-category system divides writing into narrative or story-like and argumentative or persuasive functions, both of which can be used throughout the various genres (Andrews, 1995). For example, Farley Mowat's widely translated book *Never Cry Wolf* (1963) is written as a narrative, but it serves as a powerful argument against persecution of wolves. Fables and parables, both classified as narratives, are usually moral arguments.

Still another two-category system divides writing into narration and exposition. Narratives include stories, autobiographical incidents, biographies, and poetry. Expositions explain, so the category includes reports of information and persuasive essays.

There are two categories of essay. One is the essay as exploration, which the Frenchman de Montaigne invented in 1580 (1958) as a form to explore what he thought about a variety of topics so he could leave a philosophical legacy. The other is the schoolized formula that tends to be assigned in odd numbers of paragraphs and usually adheres to a scheme that is sometimes detailed down to the sequence of kinds of sentences.

The lines between genres often blur, especially when genre designations are defined for purposes of simplicity (exposition and narration, fiction and nonfiction). And although academic discussions about how to treat this or that genre are interesting, those kinds of conversations, as well as conversations about where the category lines should be drawn, usually don't respond clearly to instructional needs in the formative years of literacy development.

Genres are critical in balanced writing instruction because the purpose of writing is carried out in both form *and* function, both form *and* content, both product *and* procedure or process.

Writing well is not a contest between what we write and how we write. Rather, it is an *interaction* between what we write and how we write. When we refer to craft and process, we're referring to how we write. What we write is the domain of genres.

The genre is the product. It is what we write, and why we write. We write to make meaning in a product so we can preserve our own meanings for our own use at a later time.

The purpose of genre study is to promote form as one important part of learning to write (Fearn, 1983). The product is the aim, the object of writing. The product counts; "the quality of the product does matter" (Tobin & Newkirk, 1994, p. 12).

REVIEW AND REFLECTION

1. *The end result of writing counts.* Why do you suppose it is important to make that statement?
2. *The end result of writing is an interaction between craft and process, on one hand, and genre on the other.* Explain how you think that statement exemplifies the concept of balance in writing instruction.

Genres in Balanced Writing Instruction

We have identified seven labels that are often used to name school-relevant genres. Six of them are commonly taught. We think the seventh, technical writing, deserves a spot in the genre scheme in balanced instruction.

Genres Commonly Written in School

Short fiction, including drama	Autobiography
Report of information	Biography
Persuasion	Technical writing
Poetry	

Variations on the Genres

Within the seven genres, there can be embedded other kinds of writing in school—for example, the evaluation essay, which is traditional in school language arts programs. The primary purpose of the evaluation essay is to make a judgment about something and set out the reasons for the judgment. We subsume evaluation under persuasion because persuasion is about taking a position and offering a rationale. Problem-solution writing is a hybrid of the report of information and persuasive writing. One portion of problem-solution writing is providing information about a problem and one or more solutions. Another portion involves persuading readers that the problem is serious and the solutions reasonable.

Modes of Discourse

Also important as extended discourse are what are sometimes called the *modes of discourse,* which are forms of text with a purpose. They include description, analysis, compare and contrast, and criticize and persuade. (We described them in Chapter 3 and discussed instructional applications in Chapter 5.) Description is important partly as an end of its own (as a way of crafting language), but also in the skill of the storyteller in revealing a character, an essayist in showing a rationale, or a scientist in explaining a procedure.

The Genre Scheme

The genre component of balanced writing instruction, then, contains seven specific genres that interface with several additional kinds of extended discourse.

Genres	Modes of Discourse	Short Cues
Short fiction	Description	Précis
Report of information	Analysis	Power Writing
Persuasion	Compare and contrast	Process Pieces
Poetry	Criticize and persuade	Word Limiters
Autobiography		Directions
Biography		
Technical writing		

Short Fiction

We call it "short" because that's what most young writers write. Short fiction runs between 197 and 9,999 words. The 197 is the word count of what has become known as "Appointment in Sumarra," the line by the character Death in Somerset Maugham's play *Sheppy*. Death's line contains all of the classic attributes of fiction as well as all of what we associate with story grammar, and it's only 197 words long. At the other end of the short fiction range is the novella's 10,000 words. It's doubtful that very many young writers are writing novellas. It's the rare young writer who could make fiction work in under 197 words, and it's a rare young writer who will write fiction at the novella level.

We call it "fiction," not "story," because in the classroom, particularly in the lower grades, almost everything is called a story. First graders are urged to write a story about the picture they just painted, about their last birthday, about the trip to the zoo. Those aren't fiction; they're descriptive captions, autobiographical incidents, and perhaps reports of information.

Why Write Fiction?

There are two reasons. First, fiction makes enormous demands on writers' mental discipline. Anton Chekhov said, "The art of writing is the art of abbreviating" (Boles, 1984, p. 7). Consider the complexity of peeling back everything except the barest cues, which readers then use to reconstruct the texture of the scene. Death's line in Somerset Maugham's *Sheppy* begins, "There was a merchant in Baghdad who sent his servant to the marketplace to buy provisions." In only sixteen words, Maugham introduces two characters and a setting within a setting. What have you constructed about the merchant? The servant? The marketplace? What cues did Maugham offer in the first part of his sentence that took you to the images you constructed from reading it?

Good fiction entails the ability of writers to understand readers' prior knowledge and write the cues that capitalize on that prior knowledge. In the quotation, how did Maugham capitalize on what his readers already know?

Boles (1984) calls capitalizing on readers' prior knowledge "clarification of the complex" (p. 7). The reader doesn't need extensive explanation and can see clearly with a few clear-cut hints. The extraordinary demands of short fiction on the writer include knowing the images the writer wants the reader to construct and selecting just the right words to make those images just as the writer intends them to be made. The key to short fiction is precision in the writer's mind.

Some people would say that abbreviation and precision are most critical in fiction. That's one reason why we should include short fiction in balanced writing instruction. The second reason for emphasizing short fiction in balanced writing instruction is the larger curricular payoff. Fiction could become a routine way for teachers across content areas to help their students explore, understand, and reconstruct subject matter. Fiction could be the direct experience, the prior knowledge, on which students understand their literary heritage.

Follow the role of short fiction through the curriculum. What is the story behind the war between the North and South in the middle of the nineteenth century? What is the story grammar, the organizational scheme on which the war would rest were it written as a story? Who were the characters? What did they look like? How did they walk and talk? Where did they come from? How did they come to their involvement in the conflict? What did they say? If they were arranged at a roundtable today, what would be their conversation? How much about the nineteenth-century war between the states would fifth and ninth graders learn if they learned the characters in the conflict sufficiently well to make them talk among one another at a twenty-first-century roundtable (similar to the writers' roundtable in Chapter 5)?

Put Robert E. Lee at the table where the topic is military missions and political motives. Put Frederick Douglass there. Also at the table are W. E. B. Du Bois (because he was born just after the war and lived through Reconstruction), Jefferson Davis, a foot soldier from the North and one from the South whose diaries inform their talk, and someone's mother or brother whose diaries are primary sources. A sixth-grade class will find out who the principals are and learn enough about them to make them talk as characters in the very story that brings them to that table. Some people believe that there would be no history without characters. Study the characters to learn the history.

Or study the characters to learn the physics. Start with Copernicus and Galileo. Include Isaac Newton, Enrico Fermi, Niels Bohr, and Marie Curie. They aren't any harder to know than Red Cloud, Chief Joseph, and Sequoya. When we know the scientists, we'll know something about the science.

If Mark Twain were the main character in your story, what would be the main problem, the conflict, in the story? Fiction is about something. What would be the plot line in a story in which Dwight D. Eisenhower were the main character? What if George Gallup were the main character? To write fiction demands that we know characters, settings, and plot lines. To write fiction in which Rachel Carson is the main character would demand knowing Rachel Carson and the intellectual and passionate world in which she lived.

Writing the Elements of Fiction

Third graders can write fiction well (though not all of them equally well). That doesn't mean cleverly as much as it means properly, and *properly* means that all of the elements of fiction are woven into a whole that leaves readers with ideas and images, pictures into a new world, and an appreciation for a new character. Third graders can craft the stories from character biographies, accurate conceptions of settings, plausible problems, and believable solutions. As they learn how it's done, they appreciate those who have done it especially well. That is how they can understand their literary heritage, at least to the extent that the heritage is in fiction.

But their heritage isn't only fiction. It's also great speeches that move people to action, essays that live in readers' souls, poems that tell of love and death, and lyrics of such power and beauty that we sigh at their hearing. Those can all be stories too. The lyrics of "The Star Spangled Banner" represent characters, setting, problem, and resolution. There can be a story in the Pledge of Allegiance, the preamble to the United States Constitution, the Declaration of Independence, and Abraham Lincoln's Second Inaugural Address. Emily Dickinson is a story. Lincoln and Douglas are a story. The whole of literature study could be told and understood in story grammar context.

All of that—the brevity of short fiction, the clarification of the complex, the precision, the cross-content learning, and the influence on literary heritage—can be addressed through careful instruction in short fiction, which means two things (Gardner, 1983):

1. Understanding and using story grammar
2. Striving for the fictional dream

At the earliest age, young writers have to learn how to understand the characters they are creating. They do that by observing these characters and inventing short biographies for them. Faulkner said that the writer "is trying to create believable people" (Cowley, 1958, p. 133). Young writers need to think about what makes a character believable. When they all read *Elbert's Bad Word* (Wood, 1988), they have to spend some of their time thinking and talking about why they think it's possible for a little boy to have one or more of Elbert's experiences and what it is about Elbert that they think works.

Young writers have to show their readers the places their characters go. Readers have to be able to feel the rain, smell the flowers, and hear the train whistle. If the teacher doesn't show young writers how to think about showing versus telling, the images are unlikely to appear in anyone's writing except for the most talented few. We run schools for everyone, and everyone can show the rain and the rose if there is sufficient instruction, modeling, and practice.

The second part of Faulkner's comment about creating believable people is "in credible moving situations" (Cowley, 1958, p. 133). He is talking about the plot, what is happening, the problem, and the resolution. Those have to be credible or plausible. Even in science fiction, the science has to be accurate.

Young writers have to notice how even fantasy takes them on trips they can understand if they are willing to suspend disbelief for the fictional moment. It's this suspension of disbelief that ushers in Gardner's fictional dream (1984).

Watch the eyes of five and six year olds as the teacher reads a good story. The children enter the world of the story, come to know the characters, feel the problems, and sigh with relief when the character finds a way out. Young children are good at suspending disbelief. They enter the fictional dream easily.

The fictional dream is that place we enter when a story grabs us and won't let go. For adults, it's what keeps us turning the pages well into the night, tired but not sleepy, frightened when the character faces danger, elated when the character achieves, saddened when the character's beloved dog finally succumbs to old age. And when the story ends, we return from the dream, sigh, and have the effect of the story forever implanted in our own literary landscape. It works because it's believable.

What Makes a Good Story?

- The writer uses characters to tell the story.
- The settings of the story are relevant to the problem and fit the life of the characters.
- Something happens.
- Readers become part of the story.

Part of what young writers experience in a balanced writing program is the fictional dream. It's emphasized when they read and when they write. Always, they are writing to what could happen under the circumstances of the story they are building.

REVIEW AND REFLECTION

1. A good story engages readers in the plot line, characters, or both, but most fiction writers tend to favor either character or plot. Are you a character reader and writer, or a plot reader and writer?
2. Stories are about something (problem and resolution) or someone (character). They start by setting up the problem, and they end with resolution. What is your favorite story about? Who is it about?
3. *The shorter the story is, possibly the more stories young writers can write; and the more good ones they write, the better they become at writing short fiction.* Do you agree or disagree with that statement? Explain why.
4. Short fiction writers strive to achieve in readers a sort of dream state that brings readers into the story. What are some stories that took you into a fictional dream?

Report of Information

This is the report we've all done in school. There are two kinds. One is the paper we did on Missouri or some other state in the fifth grade. The other is the laboratory report we did in the second grade when the teacher brought in the chicks, and we wrote our observations as they grew. The report of information requires elements of craft that are similar to all kinds of writing because all writing occurs in sentences and organizational patterns and meaning markers. But the form is different, so the way we use the craft is different.

Traditional Reports of Information

Students traditionally prepare a report of information in the fall and another in the spring. At least one of them each year tends to be in social studies. A characteristic fourth-grade unit is "native" Americans. The social studies book contains sections on Indian people in the Northeast, Southeast, Northwest, Southwest, and prairie states and describes specific tribes for each section of the country. The children hear about the Sioux, Cherokee, and Navajo, and rarely, if ever, Muckle-shoots, Makahs, or Quileutes. All teachers know exactly how to set up the plan for the report:

- Require sufficient length to show that the children learned from the activity.
- Require at least three references to provide some experience with library research and bibliographic form.
- Offer topic choices so the children will feel their work is relevant to them.

Typically the teacher organizes the class in dyads to ensure collaborative work and states the task in this way: "Write a report that shows what you learned about your topic. You must use at least three references. Only one reference may be an encyclopedia and only one may be from the Internet. Your report must be at least six pages long."

Most of the reports turned in are literate, occasionally even interesting. The children write about what the Sioux ate, how the Cherokees learned to read, and how the Navajos weave rugs. Most of the information is widely known and trivial. Only one report tells of more than one Sioux reservation. None mention what *dineh* means. One group mentions Sequoyah, but spells it wrong. Two children choose Cherokees because they claim to have Cherokee blood.

In the spring the report is in science. In the second grade, the children plant lima beans in paper cups and write reports about growth under various conditions of light, liquid, and soil. They work collaboratively. Their reports all have four parts: (1) What did we do? (2) How did we do it? (3) What did we find? (4) What does it mean? Everyone writes that lima beans need water and light to grow.

Reports of information are traditionally directed at satisfying one or both of two objectives: (1) encourage learners to explore and write about their explorations, and (2) assess what learners know. Both are legitimate objectives.

Reconsidering Reports of Information

Consider the most valuable commodity in school: time. The fifth-grade class writes Indian reports of six pages, not counting references, and there are fourteen pairs of fifth graders. That makes the teacher's reading load 84 pages. If the students are in a middle-level seventh grade and the teacher has three periods of social studies, each period with fourteen pairs, the teacher's reading load is 252 pages.

Now consider what the possibility is that fifth or seventh graders can show what they learned in five pages just as well as they can in six. If collecting information and writing it in report form is the objective, can they satisfy the objective in four pages? Is it possible that what they collected is only worth three well-written pages, and they pad to get the other three pages? (Is there any reader of this paragraph who has never wondered how to get another two pages out of a term paper idea?)

If the information can be written in four pages, why write five? Why read a page you don't have to read? Can you teach from a five-page paper better than you can from one four pages long? Could it be written in three pages? Writing short makes enormous demands on knowledge and writing skill. It was Theo Lippman who said, "It takes 375–400 words. . . . I think if I had 800 or 1000 words I would not say any more and I would not say it as well" (Clark, 1982, p. 106).

We don't mean to forsake long pieces for young writers' experiences, and we're not suggesting that longer writing ought never be an instructional purpose. We're merely suggesting that young writers, faced with a four-page assignment, could write what they know in three, and maybe in two, pages. If they could write what they know in two pages, the fifth-grade teacher would have a paper load of 28 pages rather than 84.

If children can learn some social studies content and something about writing in an expository genre by writing reports, why not assign two reports of three pages in the fall instead of one of six pages? If we believe that practice is associated with getting better, it stands to reason that writing two good reports is better than writing one good report.

If the process is repeated in the spring, the fifth graders will write four reports of information that year, twice as many as is typical. The more times they write well, the more practice they get at using writing processes productively. One basic principle in all writing, and especially in writing reports of information, is that writing short increases the amount of information young writers study, the number of times they write, and the demand for quality.

Remember that when we recommend that reports of information be assigned with a premium on quality rather than quantity, we are not suggesting that young learners never write longer pieces. But what evidence do we have that writing longer papers teaches young writers to write longer papers well? None. What we know is that if young writers do not have experience writing something, they won't become better at it merely by doing it again. We're suggesting that young writers write more reports of information well, and thereby become increasingly able to write in the genre.

> ### What Makes a Good Report of Information?
>
> - The writer knows enough about the subject to write with an authoritative voice.
> - The writer uses terms accurately and writes in a clear and relatively formal manner.
> - All information is specific and accurately defined.
> - Where appropriate, sequences are clear and replicable (e.g., in science reports).
> - The writer makes the focus of the report clear and remains with that focus throughout.
> - Where appropriate, the writer takes the reader to a conclusion based on the writer's research.

Research for Reports of Information

Fundamentally, reports of information focus on what writers have learned through research—not only through newspapers, books, magazines, and the Internet but also interviews and surveys. They are accumulating and using knowledge they didn't have or use before.

Because research requires a substantial investment in time, what's most important is whether the topics satisfy the people who are investing the time. Fulwiler (1985) writes that young writers should search for answers to their own questions. That is certainly what experienced writers do. Virtually every reference to research from the 119 writers interviewed for C-SPAN's interviews with writers, "Booknotes" (Lamb, 1997), talked about their questions, their interests, their passions, and the writers also talked about how the research occurred throughout the report-writing process, not before it began. In the classroom, discussion of research is part of the discussion of report thinking and writing itself.

Those Sioux did live on the prairie; they built tepees; and they lived off buffalo, antelope, sheep, and various small animals. Crazy Horse, Sitting Bull, and Black Elk were Sioux. Where do the Sioux live today? How many Sioux people are there? How many Sioux reservations are there? Why did reservations begin? What does assimilation mean for Indian people? What does *Lakota* mean? Where is Standing Rock? Who is Vine Deloria? What do Sioux people do to earn a living today?

Yes, Connie, there are lots of Sioux people today. Sure it's on the Internet. What would you like to know? How many? Okay. What else? Where they are? Where do they go to school, where do they work, and do they have computers? Those are good questions. See what you can find.

Of course you can get information about other Indian tribes, Calvin. You want to find out about Apaches? Which group? There are two in Arizona and two in New Mexico alone.

You heard about the United States Public Health Service, Rosa? How do you think you might be able to learn about an Indian hospital and Indian doctors? Well, why not walk to the office, and ask Ms. Kelly how you might dial our telephone to get information for Gallup, New Mexico.

These aren't just Indian reports. This is gathering information about topics the children can learn to care about. Certainly the teacher seeded the questions. We can't assume that children have enough information to ask questions that interest them. Teachers help children seek and clarify.

We also adjust the routine. Instead of the traditional state report, maybe we assign industry reports or region reports. Those would be about iron mining, coal mining, and steel production—where they are, how they are related, and what they have to do with automobile production. Agriculture reports could be about potatoes, or corn, or the ingredients in a fast food favorite. Where does all that stuff come from, and how does it get to the bag you carry out of the restaurant? A region report might be about the Upper Midwest: what states comprise it, what do farmers grow there, what do manufacturers make there, what do average people do there, and what is the role of the Mississippi River.

Part of what we do with reports of information, then, is plan for as many young writers as possible to conduct their research on topics they care about, even to the extent of expanding their horizons so they have some idea about what there is to care about.

We adjust the form of the research assignment so the questions relate to something in the children's lives. Research isn't about fast food necessarily; it's about agriculture, but fast food is the prior knowledge connection to the agriculture question. It isn't about the Mississippi River, but that the river has something to do with a report on the Minnesota Twins.

We move the focus of laboratory research toward developing information and away from mere demonstration. We boil some water, collect the condensation on the lid, and write about how heating the water changes it into vapor and cooling it changes it back to water again. That's basic science information, and young learners have to know those properties of matter and how the changes occur. A demonstration can clarify science information, but the emphasis in writing is on what the information means. Will rubbing alcohol behave the way water behaves? Why doesn't spaghetti sauce collect on the lid of the pan when you simmer spaghetti?

The question in science is, What are the questions? We don't write reports about topics or even questions. We write science reports about what happens when we try to answer questions. The report is about where the question came from, what we did in our attempt to find answers, and what we might do next in finding answers. Science is about questions and how we pursue answers. The report is about the quest and the information.

Research reports in science, then, need be only as long as it takes to inform readers about the context and the quest. In the second grade, that can be five sentences in four sections:

Section 1. My question was, How important is sunlight in growing lima beans?

Section 2. I had three Dixie cups and planted a lima bean in each one. Then I put one in the closet, one in a room with a light bulb, and one on the window sill.

Section 3. The one on the window sill grew best, the one under the light bulb grew next best, and the one in the closet didn't grow much at all.

Section 4. I think lima beans have to have sunlight to grow right.

Fifth graders can conduct the same study, but they will measure germination in intervals of time, the power of the two light sources, the watering procedures, and so forth; and they will take steps to see if the dynamic they learned about lima beans and light applies to string beans, corn, and tomatoes. Then they might explore next steps to discover something about what sunlight means to plants, how plants use sunlight, and the effect of plants on the quality of the atmosphere. And they'll write each question, each procedure, each result, each conclusion, each next step, and additional questions. They learn about thinking in and reporting science.

REVIEW AND REFLECTION

1. Reports of information provide young writers with a forum for displaying what they have learned about questions they care about. What science or social studies report have you done that focused on a question you cared about?
2. Is the outline of a research report the scientific method, or is it a sort of shorthand way to share the final design and results of a scientific procedure?
3. Should the writing be just as important as the information in a report?
4. In 100 words, write what you know for sure about a state in the Midwest. Can you capture the same information in 75 words?

Persuasion

Persuasive writing is based on argument, that is, logical reasoning, discussion, debate, and a connected series of statements or reasons intended to establish a position (Andrews, 1995). Argument in persuasive writing is a way to think about ideas and audience. In the report of information, writers present ideas to a presumably dispassionate audience as objectively as they can. In persuasive writing, on the other hand, writers write to influence the audience to think the way the writer thinks. Writers write arguments in persuasive writing. They don't *have* arguments; they *make* arguments.

That definition of persuasive writing is very important because until young writers understand what persuasion means, they are reduced to trying to write using a formula in a textbook or one dictated by the teacher. There is nothing especially wrong with a format as long as it is a vehicle for expressing persuasion.

But if what young writers learn is a format or formula, they can easily satisfy that without ever establishing an argument.

Persuasive writing, then, is a series of statements or reasons designed to establish a position or make an argument. Andrews (1995) suggests that argument implies a response to another position. Thus, persuasive writing is reasoned discussion in the form of statements designed to establish a position, perhaps in response to another position. Let's look at each of the elements in the definition of persuasion.

First, there is *reasoned discussion*. Every definition of reason refers to logic—a process of drawing a conclusion on the basis of facts or assumptions (hypotheses). For example, given that an 80-pound adult wolf eats about a fourth of its body weight in raw meat about once a week and there are three adults in the local group, and two 1,000-pound steers have disappeared in the last month, it is impossible for the wolves to have been responsible. Persuasive writing presents and follows the facts and offers a conclusion.

A second element of persuasion is the *presentation of statements in a way that is designed to establish a position or point of view.* Clearly, persuasive writing is about the writer's position. In *The Twentieth Century: A People's History* (Zinn, 1998), the author writes, "My focus is not on the achievements of the heroes of traditional history, but on all those people who were victims of those achievements, who suffered silently or fought back magnificently" (p. x). At the end of his Preface, he writes, "That . . . is my approach to the history of the United States. The reader may as well know that before going on" (p. xii).

Statements a writer makes may be enough to fill a book (in Zinn's case, 443 pages) that lead to the writer's conclusion (Zinn's Chapter 13). It is the statements that establish a writer's position or point of view and are themselves part of the conclusion.

A third element in persuasive writing is an *assumption that another position, and perhaps other positions, can exist.* Of course, if one's own position has been reached through reason, we may assume that other positions came into existence through reason as well. The persuasive writer therefore states and arranges the argument to influence readers to believe one argument is superior to all others.

Farley Mowat is best known around the world for his *Never Cry Wolf* (1963). There are three points of view in this book—the Canadian government's, the writer's, and the indigenous peoples'—and although Mowat informs readers of each one, it is clear which of the three he grows to distrust.

Persuasive writing skills include the ability to use facts and examples, reasons, comparisons, and analogies. All of those are used to make the writer's point and persuade readers to accept it.

The question is how to craft arguments with sufficient power to persuade readers. There are four writing skills invariably found in writings that persuade:

- *Facts and examples.* Persuasive writers illustrate their position. Faced with the accusation that wolves' appetite for meat has decimated the caribou herd, a wolf biologist might use the example of adult wolves' weekly meat consumption capacity, the number of wolves in an area, the number of caribou in the area, the body weight of the average caribou, and healthy wolves' instinct to kill only to feed themselves. Then he would conclude, "The arithmetic doesn't work. Wolves can't eat that much meat."

Persuasive writers must know a good bit about the subject. If columnist George Will is writing to persuade readers regarding voter turnout, he has to know the trends, the demographics, and the possibilities.

- *Reasons.* Charles Osgood (1991) tells us that the reason children misunderstand the Pledge of Allegiance is that the pledge has no connection to their everyday lives. Education critics in the United States tell us every several decades or so that the reason Johnny can't read is insufficient phonics instruction.

- *Comparisons.* Persuasive writers compare one condition with another. Molly Ivins (1993), in reference to the size of government, compared government to a tool and made the point that the tool is about as good or bad as what you use it for and how you use it.

- *Analogy.* The argument that if something fits in one circumstance, it probably fits in another is an analogy. Of course, there are all sorts of false analogies, but the fact that commentators' analogies are often false doesn't limit their use. One clever analogy came from a column by Charles Osgood (1991) about people getting into trouble by talking before thinking. He wrote that talking without thinking is like swallowing without chewing. Is it accurate to compare talking and thinking with swallowing and chewing?

The Essay

De Montaigne (1958) invented the essay for the purpose of testing his responses to various subjects and situations. He called this literary form *essai,* which means "trials."

What is very important to understand about de Montaigne's invention is the experimentation in it—the tentativeness of his responses to various subjects and situations. He explored the topics of child rearing, lying, books, and so forth. To its inventor, the essay was an exploration that leads to a point. Put another way, the essay cannot have a thesis statement in its lead because the writing is about the writer's attempt to find a thesis. If there is a thesis statement at all in the classical essay, it would appear toward the end. In his essay titled "On Books," de Montaigne (1958) writes four paragraphs, totaling nearly 700 words, before he mentions the topic at all. It appears the essay is about books he likes, for there are several examples throughout, but there is no concluding, or thesis, statement anywhere.

That essay is very different from what typically occurs in school. We are suggesting that young writers need the opportunity to use writing as an exploration for them to figure out what they think. It is also clear that persuasive writing does have a point to make, and its readers need to know what that point is.

What Makes Good Persuasive Writing?

- The writer reveals the nature of the question or controversy in the beginning of the writing.
- The writer's position is clearly apparent in the writing.
- The writer offers reasons for the position on the question or controversy.
- The writer accounts for the possibility of other opinions on the question or controversy.
- Writers select facts as fairly as possible and use them as honestly as they can.

We suggest that teachers make persuasion an important part of balanced writing instruction. We recommend both exploratory and formulaic writing because formulaic writing is part of the schoolized culture. However, young writers also deserve the opportunity to use writing as an intellectual exploration. They might craft an essay that contains the issue and their clearly stated position on the issue at the very beginning. Or they might write an essay on a topic of some controversy, and use the writing to clarify what they think and feel, and perhaps end with a position statement.

REVIEW AND REFLECTION

1. Persuasive writing establishes and explores a position. Imagine using the persuasive essay in its classical sense to arrive at an informed or confident position as the result of the thinking and writing, without knowing your conclusion before you begin. What might that persuasive essay be about?
2. The position is arrived at through reasoned discussion that includes accommodation of an alternative position. What does "reasoned discussion" mean in the midst of argument?
3. Persuasive writing features examples, reasons, comparisons, and analogies. Use any two of those devices to build a conclusion about the effect of the fashion industry on women in general or young women in particular.
4. Reconstruct or reorganize what you wrote for item 3 above so the thesis appears for the very first time in the conclusion.

Poetry

Poetry is an ancient literary form that has been central to the world of literature and, as Aristotle described it, "an art of imitation . . . to speak metaphorically, a speaking picture, with this end, to teach and delight" (Anderson, Buckler, & Veeder, 1979). Sounds of verse filled the palaces of medieval kings. Poems have been written to capture religious beliefs, life's philosophies, and love's ups and downs. Shakespeare's sonnets are famous for their reflections on love and loving, and well known today. His eighteenth sonnet begins with lines that will be familiar to many of you:

Shall I compare thee to a summer's day?
Thou are more lovely and more temperate:

Robert Pinsky, poet laureate and consultant in poetry of the United States, whose book of poetry was nominated for a Pulitzer Prize in 1996, refers to poetry as a "silent treasure" to be handed down to our grandchildren and great-grandchildren. His concern is that poetry not be silent, but that it become a vital part of the curriculum in schools and colleges, something that currently is missing. In his role as poet laureate, he began the "Favorite Poetry Project," in which he invited people from all over the United States to send in their favorite poem and reflect on why the poem had special meaning for them. Thousands of people responded with poems by authors ranging from Chaucer to Gwendolyn Brooks. Those responding connected their poems to childhood memories, lost loves, times of sorrow, and moments of joy. They sent poems they enjoyed and wanted to share, that they read again and again, often memorizing. The individuals who participated in the project were of all ages, religions, and professions; what they had in common was a love for poetry and, in particular, for their special poems.

Along with his coeditor, Maggie Dietz, Pinsky compiled these poems in an anthology called *Americans' Favorite Poems: The Favorite Poem Project Anthology* (1999). He was committed to capturing the beloved poems of Americans and creating a place where they can be enjoyed as part of the American cultural landscape.

At a web site called the Online NewsHour: Poems (http://www.pbs.org/newshour/bb/poems/poems.html), you can hear Pinsky read some of his favorite poems by other poets. At each reading, he offers a brief commentary on the poem or the poet. For example, at his reading of Shel Silverstein's poem, he mentions Silverstein's predecessor, Edward Lear, master of the limerick and nonsense poem, and we hear Pinsky read Silverstein's poem about Mr. Lear.

Poetry is a unique genre in which the poet uses the length of the line as a literary device to create meaning. It is a quintessential form of literature, especially when viewed through Cullinan's definition of literature as "all instances in which language is used imaginatively" (1989, p. 8). (We'll have more to say about this definition in Chapter 13, on the writing-reading interaction.) Jane Yolen, writer of over two hundred books for children and adults, describes poetry as "the soul of literature" (Hopkins, 1998, p. 168).

Before they can write poetry, children must experience it—thoroughly, deeply, over time, and as a source of enjoyment and joy. Without the experiences, there will be little or no understanding or appreciation of this genre.

To teach young writers to write poetry, we must allow them to experience firsthand the personal satisfaction of the genre. It is the experience that should be paramount as writers of poetry. In fact, we would go so far as to say that we do not believe that, in any literal sense, teachers can actually *teach* poetry. What we can do, however, is ensure that our students experience it.

What do we mean when we say that poetry should be personally satisfying? What would this mean, for example, in a first-grade classroom? Children love the rhythms and rhyming sounds of nursery rhymes, and they quickly learn to chant along with the teacher: Little Miss Muffet / Sat on a tuffet / Eating her curds and whey. / Along came a spider / That sat down beside her, / And frightened Miss Muffet away.

Poems by Jack Prelutsky, Shel Silverstein, and David McCord are full of fun, surprise, and laughter and are favorites with children. Hopkins (1998) reminds us that Silverstein's poetry is also popular with adults. In 1981, *A Light in the Attic* was number 1 on the *New York Times*' Best Seller List, and it remained on the list for three years. Hopkins' *Pass the Poetry, Please!* is in its third edition (the first edition printed almost thirty years ago). He describes interviews with well-known children's poets who are also popular with adults. In Hopkins' interview with Prelutsky, Prelutsky relates that his goal was to make poetry delightful and be about what children care about. He says that "good poetry for children is simple, universal, accessible, and direct. It does what children do—tells you something, then stops; there's no wandering. It catches your heart or your mind. I like to tell children that a good poem is delicious—as delicious as a chocolate-chip cookie!" (Hopkins, 1998, p. 146).

We agree. Good writing, poetry and prose, is delicious, and that's what we want children to experience, because things that are delicious also tend to be personally satisfying.

What Makes a Good Poem?

- The poet controls line length in a way that enhances the feeling, sound, and meaning of the poem.
- The words are carefully chosen to create a feeling, sound, or picture. (We don't know who said this, but it's been attributed to Samuel Taylor Coleridge, so we'll give him credit: The poet chooses the right word for the right reason in the right position.)
- The verse goes straight to the heart and mind of the reader, engaging the senses, the imagination, and the emotions.

After about third grade, curriculum guides begin to add generous doses of the literary elements when discussing poetry. The question, "What did the author mean?" is often used to monitor whether readers have understood what they've read. But maybe there are better questions that can focus students on the experience of the poem, allowing them to inhabit it rather than dissect it—for example:

"What did you notice [interesting, surprising, confusing, etc.] in the poem?"

"How does the poem make you feel?"

"What does the poem remind you of or make you think about?"

"What is your favorite part of the poem?" (Farnan & Romero, 1989; Kelly & Farnan, 1994).

Robert Frost, master poet and former poet laureate of the United States, gave voice to the value of personal satisfaction when reading poetry. He knew that his poem "Stopping by Woods on a Snowy Evening" was sometimes interpreted as a "death poem," based particularly on the last repeated lines, "and miles to go before I sleep." His response to this was, "I never intended that, but I did have the feeling that it was loaded with ulteriority" (Latham, 1966, p. 188). Frost, in other words, felt the poem was loaded with meaning, but he had no specific intended meaning when writing it. In fact, he remarked that he liked the way the last lines sounded. He also made the point that "every poem is a voyage of discovery" (Latham, 1966, p. 188).

The danger in ignoring the importance of the reader's connection to a poem—in not making the child's and adolescent's interest and delight paramount in the reading and writing of poetry—is captured in the last line of Jean Little's poem, "After English Class" (Little, 1990, p. 28). She begins her poem with the line "I used to like 'Stopping by Woods on a Snowy Evening,'" but because the teacher tells what everything stands for, makes an academic exercise out of the "hidden meanings," her poem ends with the sad commentary, "Next time I drive by, / I don't think I'll bother to stop."

Children and adolescents deserve the opportunity to have consistent and regular exposure to poetry in its various forms, many of which we'll describe in the next chapter when we discuss ways to help access the genre of poetry through their own writing. They deserve the opportunity to hear poetry; to practice and read poetry; to experience its rhymes, rhythms, and playfulness; to inhabit the lines, the words, and their meanings; and to exercise the poet's craft by writing their own poems.

We recommend a Web site because of all that it has to offer teachers in the worlds of poetry, language arts, and use of technology for collaboration and learning: Mrs. Silverman's Second Grade Class: Online Autumn (http://comsewogue .k12.ny.us/~ssilverman/autumn/index.html). At this award-winning site (six awards to date) you'll find poetry written by second-grade students from across the United States and Canada. Mrs. Silverman's objectives in creating this site included (1) helping children develop early literacy skills, (2) promoting poetry and literature appreciation, (3) giving children an opportunity to be "producers as well as consumers of information on the World Wide Web" and giving them experience using the Internet for online collaboration, (4) providing integrated learning experiences, and (5) creating a resource for second graders to read. Classroom teachers, with their students, posted students' work on the site, along with lesson objectives, lesson plans, and activity descriptions, all centering on the theme of autumn. The site is visually appealing; each classroom's contribution contains lovely pictures, graphics, and music. Students' reflections are also included, and they write about how much they enjoyed writing poetry; learning new concepts (for example, about falling leaves) and new words in the process; reading poetry by children from other parts of the United States and Canada; and visiting the site to see their own work. Donald Leu, professor of education at Syracuse University and expert in educational technology, wrote in the site's Visitor's Comments, "You do all of us a wonderful service by making our instructional worlds on the Internet a more beautiful place." We agree and encourage you to visit the site.

REVIEW AND REFLECTION

1. What poem would you contribute if your school were conducting a Favorite Poetry Project similar to Robert Pinsky's, and why would you contribute that particular one?
2. Think of five to ten ways that you could bring a poem a day into the classroom.
3. What makes poetry different from the other genres?
4. Why do you think it is important to make poetry a central part of children's and adolescents' experience with literature?

Biography

Everybody likes a good story, and biography, about real people and the real events they created or influenced, is a good story. Our late friend and colleague Robert E. McCabe remarked once that history is stories about movers and shakers—the discoverers, he called them, the people who changed the world in large and even small ways. A biography is a good and accurate story about real people and how they lived and made a difference.

Hart (1978) wrote a collection of over one hundred short biographies of the most influential people in history, ranked in order from the most to the least of the one hundred. Those one hundred represent people who changed the world in very large ways. Hart's book was followed by Salley's (1993) collection of short biographies of the one hundred most influential African Americans, Salley's in turn by Novas' (1995) series of short biographies of the one hundred most influential Latino contributors to American thought and culture, and Novas' by Felder's (1996) short biographies of the one hundred most influential women of all time. In those four volumes is information on over four hundred people (plus several minibiographies of those who didn't make the main list) who have had a role in shaping the world. They're all stories about real people who have left a sufficient legacy to be remembered as influential. We know them through biographies—the stories people have written about them.

Biography might be the highest form of knowing. Yeats said that there is no existence save for the trail of souls, that we know nothing other than the stories of people's lives (Kridel, 1998). Emerson echoed Yeats when he said, "There is properly no history; only biography" (Kridel, 1998, p. 7).

What a wonderful way to study in the content areas. If Bob McCabe was right about history being about the movers and shakers, if Yeats and Emerson were right about the place of biography in human history, then clearly a major way to study the content areas is through reading and writing biography. Study in literature becomes, in part at least, the biographies of Hawthorne, Faulkner, and Dostoevsky. Part of physics is Newton, Einstein, and Fermi. Music is the lives and achievements, and the disappointments as well, of Mozart, Haydn, and Prokofiev. And in physical education, it's the stories of Bob Mathias, Milt Campbell, and Vasily Kuznetsov.

Because biography is a record of a life (Garraty, 1957), the biographer must both care and be careful. The young biographer must know a great deal about the biographical subject, which means there will be careful research invested in the project. The youthful biographer must also care about who the individual is or was, his or her contribution, family life, and what was important to the individual.

It's a waste of young biographers' time to have to write a biography (a report) on someone from history, literature, science, or the arts whom they don't know, about whose work they don't much care, and whose life they find uninteresting. But that ought not limit their writing to rock stars and ball players. Teachers can inspire interest where it didn't exist. We inspire by sharing the relationship between C. K. Yang and Rafer Johnson, close friends and competitors from different nations. We generate interest in the aristocratic Frédéric Chopin by reading aloud about the Polish artist, called "the truest artist I have ever seen" by Eugène Delacroix whose charcoal of Chopin hangs in the Louvre. The story of Johann Kepler's failing to track the path of Mars accurately because his assumption of a circular orbit was wrong is both compelling and a near-perfect description of what science means.

Ronald Clark's biography (1971) of Albert Einstein makes the point that biography is a whole story. Clark gives attention to Einstein the boy and adolescent, the physicist, the pacifist, the Zionist, the musician, the husband, and the father. The biographical subject is a whole person.

The wholeness of the story, however, should not eliminate the possibility of snapshot biographical writing. Benjamin Franklin may be one of the most versatile geniuses in all of history. Perhaps it is most efficient to write biographies in slices or, in tomographic (x-ray of a certain plane of the body) terms, BioScans. (See Chapter 10 for further discussion of BioScans in the classroom.) One slice might be Franklin the businessman. Another might be Franklin the scientist. There might also be Franklin the politician, or Franklin the writer. Perhaps a whole class could work on Franklin and come together with various slices, which they meld into a whole picture.

There are several ways to approach biographical writing (Oates, 1991). The scholarly approach depends on facts, and facts alone, and seeks the purely objective presentation of the biographical subject. The critical approach is an examination of the facts rather than the purely detached presentation of the facts in the scholarly biography. The biographer's judgment is part of the critical biography. And the narrative approach is a warmer, more personal, though still factual and critical, presentation of the biographical subject.

The narrative biographer is mainly telling a story. The critical biographer is analyzing the facts and telling the story as an analysis. The scholarly biographer is writing the story as close to purely objectively as possible.

What Makes a Good Biography?

- The writer lets the reader know the significance of the person selected for biographical writing.
- There are sufficient details in the biography to enable readers to understand the subject or focus of the biography.
- The writer attempts to bring the subject alive by giving the subject voice and action.
- There is a focus in the biography, a foundation on which the whole is built.

It is useful to know the three approaches because while young writers certainly read more narrative biography, they can learn how to make judgments and weave the story around an examination of evidence. Using all three forms on the same subject can paint the subject more clearly than can any of the three alone.

One example of how young writers can use the differences among the forms of biography to understand their subject would be a group project on George Washington. If two or three children were to study and write from a scholarly perspective, two or three more from a critical perspective, and two or three from a narrative perspective, it's likely the three biographies would be different, in detail if not in substance. For example, the coin-throwing and cherry tree stories often appear in narrative biographies to build larger-than-life heroism, but neither appears in any scholarly biography. They may appear in the critical biography, but critical biographers call attention to the width of the Potomac River and the implausibility of anyone throwing anything across it.

If there are twenty-seven children in a fifth grade, there could be three biographical studies going on at the same time, each from three perspectives. There could be a study of Thomas Jefferson, John Adams, and George Washington, all at once, each from three perspectives, and the project could culminate with a "Founders Faire," attended by parents and a reporter from the local newspaper, during which the children, in roundtable form, discuss three of the most well-known people we typically identify as among the nation's founders.

Given the resources, the children could participate in a similar project with Harriet Tubman, Sojourner Truth, and Phillis Wheatley. At another time in the year, they could focus on Geronimo, Tecumseh, and Sequoyah. The more times they read, write, and discuss biographical subjects, the more practiced they become at collecting information and writing it in one of the three forms: scholarly, critical, or narrative.

REVIEW AND REFLECTION

1. If you have not read at least three biographies, at least one of which is comprehensive, you probably should before you assign biographical reading and writing in a classroom.
2. Make a list of six biographical subjects about whom you care sufficiently to research and write their story. Compare the lists of six around your class and notice the variety.
3. Biographies can be written in a scholarly, a critical, or a narrative form.
4. What are some biographies that third, fifth, or seventh graders could research and write in language arts class to enhance learning in other content areas?

Autobiography

In the introduction to what he called his "monstrously long" autobiography, Isaac Asimov (1979) said he didn't begin it at age twenty-nine because nothing of any importance had ever happened to him. He began the autobiography some years later because, he said, although it remained true that nothing of importance had ever happened to him, he had written over two hundred books and figured some people might be curious about how he did it.

An autobiography is the story of a person's life, written by the person (*auto* means "self"), which stands as a kind of legacy or a record. Autobiography comes in a variety of forms. Asimov's comes close to being his lifelong daytimer with a story for many of the days. De Montaigne's *Essays* (1958) is a record of what he thought. W. E. B. Du Bois wrote three autobiographies. The first appeared in 1921 when he was fifty, the second in 1940 when he was seventy, and the third in 1964 at the age of ninety. Why three? He found it necessary to redefine himself several times.

People tend to write autobiographies because they are well known or influential. Certainly seven and twelve year olds may be well known in the neighborhood, influential in the family, and popular in the classroom, but their lives tend not to be of the sort that produce very much autobiographical enthusiasm. Nevertheless, everyone's life is a collection of incidents that are important to the people who live them. There are many references in this book aimed at encouraging people to write the stories of their lives.

Autobiography is different from all the other genres because all the others have a certain detachment. The writer is always writing about someone else, something else, or somewhere else. Only in the autobiography does the writer set out to be intimate, self-centered, and personally reflective. Short fiction might have a character who is a variation on what its third-grade writer remembers from her life, but she can always hide herself behind the fiction. In the autobiography, she says forthrightly, "This is me as I see me, and if I'm honest, there is not much of me hidden from view."

Autobiography is different from the other genres in balanced writing instruction on still another basis. If the writers are, say, in the second grade, they haven't been paying very careful attention to their lives during the tender ages between birth and seven. That is not to say that momentous events have not occurred in their young lives. It's just that for most children, most momentous events (the dog knocks over the food dish, older sister knocks younger brother in the head, father burns the Saturday morning eggs) aren't very memorable after a day or two or to a wider audience. There are, nevertheless, momentous events that last a lifetime (a pet's death, a dramatic deprivation, a special holiday celebration, summer camp, little brother sticks a fork in an electric outlet). Mostly, however, we live lives that we don't find sufficiently extraordinary to record because we suspect, and we're usually right, that other people won't find our lives fascinating.

In balanced writing instruction, we don't write autobiographies. We write snippets of autobiographies, or autobiographical vignettes, often called *autobiographical incidents*. They record our feelings about this day, our memory of that rainstorm, what we can remember about the last birthday, what we want to remember about the discussion we had with our best friend. We write autobiographical incidents often, we have a place to keep them, and we keep them there—all of them, forever.

What Makes a Good Autobiographical Incident?

- The writer tells readers what they need to know to understand the incident.
- The writer lets readers know, explicitly or implicitly, why the incident is sufficiently important to write about.
- The writing is coherent and moves toward the central point of the piece.
- The writer names people associated with the incident and provides sufficient detail to give readers appropriate sensory connections to the incident.
- The writer dramatizes the incident with surprise, suspense, and/or dialogue.

The plan for childhood and adolescent autobiographical incident writing is to write at least two every week throughout the school year beginning in the second grade. Given a second-grade year of 36 weeks, that would be about 70 autobiographical incidents in the second grade. The process continues in the third grade for 70 more, and the fourth for 70 more, the fifth for 70 more, and the sixth for

70 more. By the end of sixth grade, everyone will have about 300 to 350 autobiographical incidents in their autobiography folder. That's very close to being an autobiography of the elementary school years of one's life.

There is some likelihood that some of the children will have habituated that sort of life recording, and they'll continue after the sixth grade, even if their teachers don't make the assignment. But if everyone were to stop right there at the end of the sixth grade with 300 to 350 pieces and did nothing but wrap the file in a box and save it for thirty years, its value would be impossible to calculate. Wouldn't you like to find that box of 300 autobiographical incidents written when you were seven, nine, and eleven years old? Also, wouldn't students' autobiographical incidents be an interesting addition to the classroom library? Twice a year, students could select one or two of their autobiographical incidents to be bound into a classroom volume, available for everyone to read.

This sort of weekly writing won't happen unless it's cued, and teachers everywhere know very well that it doesn't do to tell young writers to "write something about your life." It also doesn't do to count on birthdays and vacations as subjects. There aren't enough birthdays and vacations to sustain autobiographical incident writing through the year.

The incidents that last through the years are those that focus on what we can do, what we've learned, whom we have known, what makes us laugh and cry, what we've read, what we've written, and what makes us afraid. Young writers are likely to be compelled by, "I had to try very hard, and I finally learned how to do it."

Autobiographical incidents are not graded or scored. They are read by the teacher on the writer's invitation. Teachers may respond to autobiographical incidents, but only on a separate piece of paper, preferably a 2- by 3-inch sticky note. A sticky note doesn't offer much room to comment. Ron Allen, late dear friend, Native American poet in residence at Oxford University, theater critic, and playwright, returned Leif's fiction manuscript in a stout box. Inside was the manuscript and a note the size of a postage stamp. In tiny print, he had written, "Good work can be acknowledged in a small space." Then in even smaller print he wrote, "Character works, setting vivid, problem works, solution doesn't."

All comments on the sticky note should be feedback, not criticism or praise. Feedback is reflective. The feedback stem reads: "When I read your incident, I saw, I felt, I noticed, I thought." Those comments may, of course, be followed by a suggestion or two: "You might consider expanding this into another one," or "On your next autobiographical incident, consider writing something about why the event is so important to you."

The autobiographical incident in balanced writing instruction ensures that everyone in the room has at least one piece of extended discourse in process at all times. It ensures that children have a regular opportunity to write about what they know best, that they get to write on their own terms on a regular basis, and that all young writers have a chance to use their writing skills to make a record that they can value over time.

REVIEW AND REFLECTION

1. The autobiography is written by a person about his or her own life. Why not start yours right now?
2. How could you ensure that what the children begin in the primary grades continues through the grades and can be delivered as an elementary school autobiography to parents at sixth- or eighth-grade graduation?
3. What is the difference between feedback and criticism, or feedback and correction, or feedback and grades?

Technical Writing

Technical writing is a fundamental genre for communicating information. It takes many forms: business letters, Web pages, desktop publishing, e-mail, summaries, lab reports, project proposals, technical reports, and project notebooks that record procedures, progress, and important details related to a project. Given that the fundamental objective of business and technical writers is to inform, instruct, describe, explain, and document, we discuss technical writing in both business and industry together.

In technical writing, the audience always comes first. Writers must remember that the writing is successful only if it ensures unambiguous communication to readers. We ensure unambiguous communication by controlling sentence length and eliminating unnecessary words. Simple sentences without a lot of elaboration get to the point and serve readers' understanding.

Effective technical writing occurs in active rather than passive voice, and with active rather than passive verbs. The subject should always be explicit, not implied. The sentence structure is a clear subject-predicate-object construction.

Technical writing requires thinking and preparation, like all other kinds of writing. Most technical writing requires a writer to think through the following procedures:

- Decide the purpose for the writing. What is the objective?
- Identify the readers. What do the readers need to know? What do they already know? What language will they understand?
- Decide how detailed the writing should be. How much detail does the reader need?
- Accumulate information. Conduct research as necessary.
- Organize the information. The organization can take several forms, which include going from a general statement to the details (general to specific), going from specifics to a general statement (details leading to a general statement), going from cause to effect, providing a sequence, and comparing and contrasting.
- Write a draft.

- Revise, perhaps soliciting feedback from another reader.
- Write a final draft.

Applied to a business letter, technical writing emphasizes purpose and audience. If students were writing a letter to explain to the school principal why the school should have snack time in the morning, they have to make the request, but they would also consider the principal's reaction to the request.

Every business letter is a sales letter, whether selling an idea, point of view, or product. In the letter to the principal, the students are recommending something they think will make the school a better place. Therefore, they need to consider how to be persuasive. They might want to emphasize the benefits to the reader and the school. What would the principal consider important to the school and its students? How could these ideas be presented in a way that persuades?

Related to the letter's persuasive influence is the letter's tone. What would the reader find important or compelling? It is important to show the reader a genuine willingness to honor his or her point of view and needs. In the business world, this is called a *service perspective*.

Another form of technical writing is the technical manual. Students could write technical manuals that include operations (how to make a tetrahedron kite or how to clean the room). They can write user functions (how to use the computer or the school library) or a maintenance manual (how to take care of the class pet or the science center). They could write technical proposals that include a cover letter, an abstract, the proposed project, background of the submitting students, budget (including a time line), and appendixes (e.g., materials needed, letters of support, letters of commitment). An example of a technical proposal in the classroom would be a proposal to describe what students plan to do for a group project. (See Chapter 10 for teaching technical writing.)

What Makes Good Technical Writing?

- Technical writing features an active voice.
- The sentence structure in technical writing is simple and tight.
- Paragraphs in technical writing are organized from main idea statement through elaborations on the main idea.
- Writers carefully select words that specifically fit the purpose and audience.

Technical writing emphasizes basic principles associated with many kinds of writing that we may not specifically call technical writing. The more complex the ideas are to present, the more important is the need for clear and concise writing. The purpose of technical writing is to aid the communication of complex ideas.

The dangers of unclear technical writing are enormous. A mechanic who does not understand the technical manual's directions for replacing main bearings on an automobile can ruin the engine. Medical personnel who do not understand a technical report can misdiagnose under emergency circumstances. There are scores of examples that highlight the importance of technical writing. If a purpose of education is to prepare students for their future, technical writing should be an integral part of balanced writing instruction.

REVIEW AND REFLECTION

1. Rewrite a character description in a short story as though it were a technical explanation. We should always write what we expect our students to write.
2. Write a letter of inquiry to a major business in your community, and craft the letter as technical writing.
3. Discuss the relationship between technical writing and both research reports and reports of information.

A Summary: Thinking About Genres in Writing

The genres are categories or kinds of writing. For the purposes of balance in writing instruction, we've discussed seven genres: short fiction, poetry, report of information, biography, autobiography, persuasion, and technical writing.

The reason for teaching genres specifically is to recognize readers' prior knowledge (expectations) with regard to how text is organized. Readers come to fiction, for instance, expecting to find a story. They come to reports of information expecting a question and an answer. Readers come to like reading biography because they like participating in the lives of significant people. If a reader picks up what looks like a biography and finds it doesn't show someone's life, the reader's expectation is violated. If writing well is in any way communication with an audience, one of the primary commitments of a writer is to not violate readers' expectations.

None of this is about avoiding writings that trouble readers or fail to lead the audience into new territory. A study of genres in balanced writing instruction means thinking about the focused interactions between forms and functions to serve the needs and expectations of an audience best.

Although the genres tend to be distinct, they also overlap. A portion of a story about the care and feeding of human clones would include technical writing about nutrition and physical culture. A narrative biography appears very like a story, and a scholarly biography might look more like a report of information. A critical biography is often intended to be persuasive, and many informative texts are explicitly persuasive. The form feeds the function, and the function dictates the form.

Only when we understand the specific aspects of form and function are we able to offer young writers balanced instruction that they can understand and practice. Through the grades, we can help them develop control over both form and function in writing. Young writers don't learn to write so they can show their sentence competence any more than young readers learn to read so they can show their phonics skills. They read to construct meaning from print and grow in the process. They write so they can make messages and communicate with their audiences. The genres are about the purposes of the messages and how to construct them so they are as effective as they can be.

10 Teaching and Learning the Genres

BEFORE YOU READ

- Does prompting or directing young writers' writing preempt the authenticity of their writing?
- How is creativity apparent in writing through the genres?
- Can persuasive writing be creative?
- What are form and function? How can intentional instruction balance the relationship between form and function?
- How do we balance seven genres, plus craft and iterative writing processes, in a language arts program often limited to twenty-five to fifty minutes per day in the elementary grades and fifty minutes per day in the secondary school?

The Problem, a Solution, and a Plan

The Problem

Picture a llama, that beast of burden from South America. The story goes that a llama will carry just so much weight, and each llama knows the limit precisely. Load on the cargo right up to and including the llama's limit, and the animal will rise and carry the load up the road or across the Andes. But one stick over the llama's internally known weight limit, and the animal will refuse to rise until that stick is removed. In fact, the llama is apparently so sure of its limit, and so set on refusing to carry beyond its limit, that if the driver were to overencourage an overloaded llama, the animal will mobilize its considerable salivary facility and spit on the driver. The llama's load tolerance is finite.

In an average elementary school day of approximately 300 minutes, with 40 minutes for lunch and 30 minutes for two recesses, there are about 230 instructional minutes available. Subtract 45 to 90 clock minutes typically reserved for reading, and there are 140 to 185 instructional minutes left. Cox (1999) shows 75 minutes for language arts, while Templeton (1997) schedules 70 minutes. If we assume only 60 minutes for language arts, we're left with 80 to 125 minutes for mathematics, social studies, science, the aesthetics, physical education, the inevitable assembly, the equally inevitable mandates from the board of education, and the periodic art scramble in preparation for open house.

Available clock minutes for instruction represent the llama's load limit. The language arts, reading, history, civics, geography, art, music, physical education, science, and the importance of flossing represent the load. Somehow the curricular load has to be carried by our clock-controlled llama. Fortunately, the clock-controlled llama doesn't spit; it just runs out. Every good teacher laments at the end of so many days that time ran out before instructional need ran out. You're beginning to see the problem.

Add to the magnitude of the problem the fact that there are seven broadly defined genre categories. We have 60 minutes for an interactive language arts program that includes comprehensive instruction in the craft of writing and the processes. And we're suggesting only 60 minutes for language arts. How is that time-controlled llama going to carry the curricular load?

The Solution

Happily for us all, some of the very best llama drivers in the world are teachers, and they figure out ways to get education done in the face of seemingly impossible circumstances. The llama will carry the load because, as all cargo loaders know, balance is the key to loading all carriers. In a 300-minute day, the curriculum has to be properly distributed.

This chapter is about teaching the genres, which means writing widely in all seven of them. That's the load, and the key to distribution is authenticity. The purpose of writing a genre is not to show the ability to write it, but to send a message or to record an idea or image. Sentence instruction is about sentences. Persuasive writing instruction is about persuasion. While sentence instruction is about the writing, genre instruction is about something in addition to the writing. The distinction is very important to teachers who face the time-controlled llama with an enormous curricular load.

On one side of the llama, the teacher loads some American history. The history load includes a biography of James Madison, a persuasive piece about Federalist Number 10, and a report on how the Constitution moved from adoption to ratification. The load represents no significant language arts time past teaching the three genres. The writing is part of history instruction. With intentional genre instruction, the writing is better, and the history is better too. The writing is loaded on the history side, and the llama doesn't know the difference.

That's the solution to the time problem. It isn't that the genres are merely integrated into the larger curriculum. The genres interact with the larger curriculum to make the larger curriculum more effective and give the genres a raison d'etre.

The Plan

In this chapter, we introduce each genre with a brief definition and writer's objective, followed by one or more procedures for intentional instruction, usually framed as instructional scenarios.

Short Fiction

Short fiction tells a story in the shortest possible space. A story is good when characters tell it, something happens, and readers become part of the fictional landscape.

Morphological Approach to Story Plotting

A rough definition of a morpheme is a combination of phonemes that has meaning. A morpheme is most characteristically equated with a root word or an affix. In a morphological approach to story plotting (MASP), we are making lists of words (and sometimes phrases) that can be combined and from which stories can be plotted. (We don't know whether it's true, but if Fran Strikker, writer of the Lone Ranger series during the golden age of radio drama, used this story plotting strategy, we're pleased to give him full credit.)

 INSTRUCTIONAL SCENARIO

In the Classroom to Set Up MASP

Teacher: I want you to make a list of characters for stories. Think of names, like Gloria, or descriptions, of a new puppy, that could serve as characters in a story. Rachel?

Rachel: *Grumpy grandfather.*

Teacher: That's the first one. More. I need about ten.

COMMENTARY

The teacher writes students' ideas on the board as students volunteer them. The eventual list includes the following terms: *grumpy grandfather, little girl, puppy, computer specialist, farmer, girl at the prom, car mechanic, Dopey, teacher, racer.*

READER ACTIVITY

We want you to make these lists as well. Make a list of characters and then one of story settings. Keep up with the children as they go.

BACK TO THE CLASSROOM

Teacher: Good. Now we need another list. Think of places where stories could happen. These are story settings. Chloe?

Chloe: *Forest*?

Teacher: That's one. More. [The eventual list includes: *forest, kitchen, Germany, Montana, swamp, city, apartment building, movie theater, school bus*.] That's two lists. I need another one. Think of problems that characters have in stories. In the story we just read aloud, Elbert had to get rid of the bad word. What are some story problems? Roger?

Roger: Somebody's really poor.

Teacher: Poverty. How about some more? I'll write them on the list right here beside the story settings. [The eventual list includes: *poverty, grandfather is sick, the car won't start, the car is stolen, the car is carjacked, the car starts on fire on the freeway, someone is trying to get a job, someone is arrested and didn't do it, a girl is lonely in school*.]

COMMENTARY

The young writers have generated several story ideas or story grammar ideas. That is the basis on which they can design their own story starts.

BACK TO THE CLASSROOM

Teacher: Good, boys and girls. There is one more list, but we'll do it later. Right now I want everyone to pick one item from each of the three lists. I want you to write the one you choose from each list on your paper. I think I might choose *farmer, swamp,* and *someone is arrested and didn't do it*. Everyone, choose one from each list, and write your selections on your paper. Now I want everyone to think of how your character, your setting, and your problem can be made into a story. Write the story in your mind. Don't put anything on paper. I'm only giving you one-half minute to see if you can invent a story. Go. [Monitors the thirty seconds.] Who can tell a story? Marvin.

Marvin: *A car mechanic lived in the city, and he had all kind of cars that wouldn't run right, so that was his business where he went every day, and one day a teacher came in with her car that wouldn't start, and they started to know each other. Then they . . .*

Teacher: Stop. Don't go any further, Marvin. You have a story with two characters. They each have a job, and one of the characters can help the other. Do you know what is going to happen?

Marvin: Sure. They're going to . . .

Teacher: No, don't tell us. It's your story, so you get to write what happens. But remember, we have to be able to believe it. You have to write those characters so we will know them, and whatever you do with them has to work. Go ahead, Marvin. It's your story. See where it goes. Yes, Inez; you're next.

COMMENTARY

These fourth graders have an opportunity to craft the skeleton of a story. In fact, what Marvin did aloud is construct a story start. Each young writer must now flesh out the story starter to make a plausible whole. In this fourth grade, the longest story was sixteen pages and took four days to write. The shortest one was one page and took three days. Four children didn't write at story time.

Nine of the twenty-six children in the fourth grade wanted to read their story in Writers' Workshop, so the teacher formed two workshop groups for them. Two wanted to read their story aloud in front of the whole class. Right after lunch on Friday of that week, there was a story hour for their read-aloud. Ten children said they weren't ready to share by the end of the week, so they put their stories into their portfolios for more work. One fourth grader wrote her story but didn't like it. She reluctantly agreed to put her story in her portfolio instead of throwing it away.

Stories You Might Start (SYMS)

Young writers need to experience a miracle once in a while. William Faulkner said that stories happen when we invent a character and follow him (or her or it) around for a few days. He meant that characters talk when we get to know them well enough and they tell you about a story you might start (SYMS). So go ahead and invent one and wait for the character to reveal the story.

INSTRUCTIONAL SCENARIO

In the Classroom to Set Up SYMS

Teacher: Girls and boys, think of a character's name and write it at the top of your paper. I will write my character's name on the board: *Theresa.* Now I want you to give your character an age. Write the age under the character's name. I will write Theresa's age: *thirteen.* Next, give your character a place to live. Write the name of a city or town under the age. I write *Gallup, New Mexico* under Theresa's age on the board. Now you have a character's name and age, and you have a place for the character to live. Now write a time of day. You may write a clock time. I'm going to write *morning* under Gallup, New Mexico, on my list on the board.

COMMENTARY

In this setup of the SYMS story frame, the teacher writes on the board as the young writers are writing. Therefore, the teacher puts four ideas on the board, and when the writing begins, the teacher follows the writing directions.

BACK TO THE CLASSROOM

Teacher: Good. Now, I want you to write the first sentence in your story. In your first sentence, you will include the name of your character and the time of day. That's all in the first sentence. Don't worry about what your story is about. Just write one sentence that contains the name of your character and the time of day. [The teacher writes: *It was early in the morning when Theresa heard her mother's call from the kitchen.*]

COMMENTARY

Often when you turn from the board, a child is sitting with hand raised. When you get to the child's desk, he hasn't written anything because he's been sitting there with his writing hand in the air. Direct him again: "Write a sentence that contains the name of your character [Willie] and the time of day [lunchtime]." He may say that he can't think of anything to write. Ask him to remember when he wrote Single Sentence Sessions (see Chapter 4) with two ideas. This is just like a Single Sentence Session. The two ideas are the character's name and the time of day.

BACK TO THE CLASSROOM

Teacher: [In a quiet voice intended not to disturb.] When you're finished with the first sentence, write the next sentence, and make it contain either your character's age or the place where your character lives. [The teacher writes: *When she opened her eyes, she could feel the cold snow of the New Mexico winter in the air outside.* Then she turns from the board and continues in a quiet voice so as not to disturb those who are beginning to fall into their story.] Write the next sentence, and put in your character's age. [The teacher writes: *Theresa knew she had to get up for her first day in the new junior high school, but she snuggled down into her covers anyway.* Once again she turns to the children and makes one more direction in a quiet voice.] Write the next sentence, and the next, and keep writing for five minutes just following one sentence, one image, one idea, after another and see how far you can go.

[Then the teacher turns back to the board and writes more of the story about Theresa, the Navajo girl who is going to a new junior high school that is under the control of the Nation and is designed especially to emphasize Navajo culture and language. She doesn't want to go because she doesn't want to leave her friends in her old school, but she will find the language and culture school a good place to learn.]

COMMENTARY

Write your own story on the board. Theresa is your authors' character, and her problem is one we know about. Every teacher has to write his or her own story on the board.

This is a story start under the writer's control. All the teacher does is promote four ideas. Young writers use those ideas as a way to frame and move their story along. Interestingly, few of the children spend much time watching the teacher write, but those who do get an image of what the writing looks like. The teacher should write for several minutes, or as long as it takes to get the equivalent of a paragraph or so on the board. There are about a half-dozen students who will fall into their story. The teacher's commentary won't disturb them at all.

BACK TO THE CLASSROOM

Teacher: [In a quiet voice.] Many writers start with a character and allow the character to tell the story. It works for many of us, but not all the time. There are several people in our room who have fallen into their stories, and they're not paying any attention at all to me. Keep working on your stories for another five minutes. Let your character tell you what to write. Write what you see and what your character is likely to say. Then you can put this story start into your writing portfolio and come back to it at another time, or not at all if you don't like it.

At this point, if you are using this secenario, continue with your own story, returning to the group to answer a question or provide some guidance as needed. It's most necessary for everyone to see you doing what they were directed to do.

After the second five minutes, call time, even for those who have "fallen through the hole in the paper" (to use Stephen King's line from his book *Misery*). Two days later, direct them to write the name of another character, another town, another time, and another age. Follow the instructional scenario. When they have had ten minutes, tell them that next Monday and Wednesday during story time, they may return to one of their story starts, or begin still another. Remind them that they must have at least two pages of a story start ready for Writers' Workshop next Friday. (See Chapter 8 for Writers' Workshops.)

The young writers are now working on two different ways to begin and pursue stories. If you are willing to allow young writers to finish stories on their own terms and in their own time, continue with story starts. The act of writing will eventually produce some finished stories. If, however, you want a more systematic schedule for finishing stories, tell them that you want a finished story at the end of September, October, January, February, March, April, and May, so they must concentrate on finishing a story quite soon because September is almost over.

The key to learning how to write short fiction is to invent and write a lot of it. Much of what young writers have to learn about writing short fiction is the invention, and both MASP and SYMS provide opportunities to invent short fiction.

Common Story

Fiction is extremely difficult to write. Stories are difficult because they have characters, settings, problems, and resolutions running through them, all related to one another in plausible ways. In addition, characters talk, and the talk has to fit the characterizations. Stories also make all of the same literacy demands all other writing makes. Because stories seem so very difficult, it is useful to help young writers get through a story or two, so they see that they can. In Chapter 6, we explained a bridging procedure for thinking and organizing in paragraphs. The *Common Story* does the same thing. It is a bridging activity for short fiction.

Essentially, this is a common, or a well-known, story told from a perspective or point of view different from the one used in the original story. In the early 1970s, the D. C. Heath literature series contained "Three Billy Goats Gruff" told from the point of view of the troll. One of us wrote "The Maligned Wolf" (Fearn, 1975), the wolf's view of "Little Red Riding Hood," and followed that with *The Fear* (Fearn, 1983), a year in the lives of Farley Mowat's five wolves (*Never Cry Wolf*, 1963) from a perspective inside the den. The advantage of the Common Story for young fiction writers is that the writer already knows the story grammar and needs only switch focus and concentrate on plausibility and literacy.

INSTRUCTIONAL SCENARIO

In the Classroom to Set Up the Common Story

Teacher: I have a story, boys and girls:

A painter painted the benches in the park and put signs on each bench that read: FRESH PAINT. There was one park bench right under a big tree, and in that tree lived many park creatures. There were ants, squirrels, birds, and one spider named Martha. It just so happened that on the day the painter painted and put the sign on the bench, Martha was making a silken thread from a branch high in the tree down to the ground. As she made her silken thread, the breeze kicked up, but her thread was strong, so she just held on until the wind died down. Down she went toward the ground. Then out of the corner of her eye she saw that the sign had blown away, and out of the corner of her other eye she saw a little girl skipping down the path carrying a bowl of breakfast, which looked a lot like cheese and yogurt. The girl stopped and eyed the bench. Martha, thinking the girl might sit on the bench and ruin her dress, spun faster so she could warn the girl. Just as the girl was getting ready to sit, Martha dropped down on some more silken thread in front of the girl. Well, the girl screamed and dropped her breakfast right there on the path, and she ran away. Martha felt so bad about scaring her, but at least she was pleased to have saved the girl's dress.

READER ACTIVITY

A teacher who intends to use the Common Story idea for short fiction writing must write several Common Stories to get the idea and to produce some authentic, noncommercial, examples. So start now with writing a Common Story.

BACK TO THE CLASSROOM

Teacher: What do you think of my story? Suzanne?

Suzanne: That's "Little Miss Muffet." It's a spider and a little girl, and she has curds and whey, but that isn't the right story.

Teacher: No? What's wrong with my story?

Marie: It's supposed to just scare the girl.

Teacher: Maybe my story is the way it's supposed to be. My story is the one the spiders tell. [Lots of laughter.] You don't think spiders can tell the story?

Everyone: No!

Teacher: Well, who told the story you know? It certainly wasn't the girl, or else it would say, "I sat on my tuffet," not "Little Miss Muffet sat on her tuffet." Who told that story?

COMMENTARY

This is point of view. It isn't necessary to have a formal lesson about point of view in fiction or any other genre. It has already been highlighted in the teacher's opening story. The students know what it is by now.

BACK TO THE CLASSROOM

Teacher: What do you think? Who told the story about Miss Muffet and the tuffet?

Hanh: It was probably just a story writer.

Teacher: And the story writer decided to tell the story the way the girl would want it told?

Hanh: But that's the way the story is.

Teacher: Not my story. Mine is from the spider's point of view.

Ben: I just read a story about "Little Red Riding Hood" as if the wolf wrote it.

Teacher: Yes. I have that book. What about the "Three Little Pigs"? Whose point of view is in that story?

Chloe: The pigs'. But it would be different if the wolf told it.

Teacher: How would it be different?

Chloe: Well maybe the wolf wasn't trying to knock down the pigs' houses.

Teacher: Maybe. I know a house where there are three sisters and one mother, and one of the sisters makes the other two sisters feel bad because they aren't as pretty. Barbara?

Barbara: Cinderella!

Teacher: What if one of the stepsisters told the story? Everyone, think of a story you know all about. Then think about how it would be different if it were told from another character's point of view. I'll give you ten minutes to think and write.

COMMENTARY

In our experience, it does little good to explain point of view or perspective. It's best to *show* the students what a change of point of view will do to a story and then, if it's important, explain the abstraction in a context.

Notice that when Chloe started to talk about the "Three Little Pigs," she already had a sense that the story would be different if told from another point of view. This second grader caught on right away. Most of the rest of the class will too.

This teacher will take aside those for whom the scenario didn't click and explain it in greater detail. Any well-known story can be used for the activity. Sometimes newcomers who aren't familiar with the growing-up stories of children born in the United States need to think about stories they brought with them or stories their elders tell at home. In our experience, it doesn't take any longer in the United States to pick up Common Stories than it takes to pick them up in other countries.

It may be necessary in the earlier grades to do this orally a few times. It may be useful to write a Common Story or two on a flip chart as a group. If the children are very young, their first Common Stories might be told as language experiences, transcribed by the teacher or adult helper in the room.

When the young writers are older, just about everyone in the room will write at least one Common Story, and many will crank out such stories just to see how much they can make each other laugh.

One of the reasons that these stories work so well for young writers is that much of the complexity of writing short fiction is eliminated. All they have to do is adjust perspective.

Just as they have several MASP story starts and several SYMS story starts in their writing portfolio, the students should have several Common Story starts as well. After three weeks or so of school, most young writers will have a half-dozen or more stories in various stages of progress, and they will begin one or more new ones each week. Their portfolios are beginning to look like those of experienced writers. Remember that experienced writers have to finish stories or they don't get paid. In the third grade, the children have to finish stories too. Six to nine a year is a reasonable expectation.

MASP, SYMS, and Common Story represent three instructional procedures that cause young writers to design their own short fiction starts. MASP features story grammar. SYMS takes young writers on a ride through their own story. And Common Story ensures that they write a whole story without having to invent each part.

However, actual writers do have to invent each part, and the inventions often promote the rest of the story. All of the following activities begin as Short Cues. Short Cues make the greatest possible impact with the least possible number of words. We use Short Cues so young writers can write whole pieces that do not cost whole days of writing time. (Short Cues are described in detail in Chapter 6.)

Characterization Short Cues

When teachers direct young writers to describe a character or write a characterization, young writers usually go for physical attributes, and if they do it right, they include a lot of details. Let's use the following characterization as an example:

> Gloria was eleven years old and lived in the country. She had yellow-blond hair that fell onto her shoulders and blew in the breeze. She wasn't very tall. She worked hard on her chores, so she got lots of exercise, which made her very healthy. She played sports in school because she was strong from working on her chores. She was a good student in school. She paid good attention in class and learned her lessons well.

Using this as a base, the teacher can take off in a number of ways—for example:

> "Let's characterize Gloria again. In not fewer than twenty or more than twenty-five words, describe Gloria's hands so an observer who does not know her will know that she lives in the country and does chores every day.
> "Pretend Gloria is in a school assembly. She is one of four hundred children in the room. Put a picture of Gloria in your mind as she sits in the room. In no more than four sentences, write directions for a stranger to find Gloria. You may use only what Gloria looks like."

Now we know what Gloria looks like, and we can characterize how she lives by describing her hands. More characterizations will flesh out Gloria:

> "Write a description of how Gloria turns in her chair when someone behind her calls her name in class."
> "What does Gloria's voice sound like on the telephone?"
> "Gloria ran into a barbed wire fence when she was three years old; where are the scars, and what do they look like?"
> "What happens to Gloria's face when she is happy?"
> "What happens to her face when she learns that her favorite pet died? No, she didn't cry. What does her face look like?"

Much writing works best when it shows readers rather than tells them. Short Cue characterizations of Gloria show how to know Gloria. Characterization is about showing characters' appearances, behaviors, emotions, thoughts, and interactions with others.

Another way to provide Short Cues for the children is to tell them to be people watchers:

> "Describe a stranger on the basis of the way she walks."
> "Describe a chimpanzee on the basis of how it walks."
> "Describe the hands of a police officer."
> "Describe what a police officer looks like when her face appears at the driver's window of a car she just pulled over."
> "Go to a shopping mall, sit on a bench, and wait until someone who looks interesting passes by. Follow that person a safe distance behind for about ten yards. Pay attention to how the person walks. Then sit on a bench again and

write a description of the person on the basis of how she or he walks. Speculate about who the person is. Who are the person's parents? Why is the person at the mall? Who is the person's best friend? Write all of that in no more than 100 words."

Then the next instruction is, "If any of the characterizations you wrote suggests a story to you, continue with the writing and see how far the story goes."

Setting Short Cues

The key in setting descriptions is also showing readers rather than telling them. Here are some setting Short Cues:

"A supermarket will be the setting for your story. In not fewer than fifty or more than sixty-five words, make a word picture of what the inside of a supermarket looks like just as you walk through the electronic doors."

"Select either the dairy section or canned goods in the supermarket. Write as much as you can as well as you can about that section in not more than one minute. Make your readers know they are in either the dairy or the canned goods section of the supermarket. How do we know the dairy section or the canned goods section aside from what it looks like?"

"Write a word picture for a ballpark during an exciting game."

"Write a word picture for the kitchen of someone who is a wonderful cook. You may write only about the aromas."

Again, the next instruction is, "If any of the setting descriptions you wrote above suggests a story to you, continue with the writing and see how far the story goes."

There are no plot cues in this chapter. Plot cues (Pretend it's raining very hard and a little boy is lost) are story starters, and story starters deprive young writers of the joys and frustrations of invention. A kind of plot cue that does not preempt invention is the single-line cue—for example:

"Baby chicks might be cute right after they hatch, but just wait."

"Burned in my memory is the sound of those footsteps behind me."

"'You're a good man,' he said as the cold rain poured down."

Another plot cue is story titles on the basis of which young writers develop a story—for example:

Down Scope

Crosshairs

Sandwiches Galore

REVIEW AND REFLECTION

1. Short stories contain characters, settings, problems, and solutions. When we read stories, we expect to find those elements. It isn't nice to fool readers by violating their expectations.
2. Young writers can invent their own stories. Invention is a way to create. What else do you think might be creative about writing short fiction?
3. Do you think practicing story parts will or will not compromise creativity in story writing?
4. Young writers don't have to finish every story they start, but they do have to finish a certain number of stories, just so they get the idea of what finishing is like. No one knows how many stories they have to finish to get the idea.
5. Why is it valuable for young writers to experience story starts that don't go anywhere?
6. The better short fiction writers in the class will discover what it feels like to have their own writing make them cry. As Robert Frost said about writing, "No tears for the writer, no tears for the reader." What emotions have you experienced from reading your own writing?

Report of Information

The report of information is a presentation of the best factual information the writer can accumulate, with the writer's interpretations and understandings. In a rough sense, there are two kinds of reports of information. One is the subject report in social studies, language arts, or elsewhere through the curriculum. It is the report on Catherine the Great, the Quileute tribe of Indian people, potatoes in Idaho, or gold mining in South Africa. The other report of information is the presentation of research young writers conduct through the curriculum, from growing lima beans in paper cups in the second grade to dissecting earthworms in tenth-grade biology and isolating the five hearts. For want of better terms, we will call the first one the *subject report* and the second one the *research report*.

Subject Report

The subject report is an independent learning device that gives each student an opportunity to define and pursue a learning concentration or direction. For example, social studies units in the fourth grade are often built around the state in which the students live. In a subject report, all of the fourth graders may focus on something of their own interest regarding their own state. When all of the reports are finished, they become text for everyone in the class to read.

Think about a fourth grade in Pennsylvania and the opening conversation about reports of information.

INSTRUCTIONAL SCENARIO

In the Classroom to Talk About the Function of a Subject Report

Teacher: We're going to write reports now about our state. The question for report writers is, What do you want to know? Reports are about what you want to know. We share with others what you learned. I'm going to do a report too. I want to know more about the first statewide superhighway in the United States. Christine?

Christine: The Turnpike?

Teacher: You're right, Christine. What is the full name of the Turnpike?

Fred: The Pennsylvania Turnpike.

Teacher: That's right. There is a half-page of information about the Pennsylvania Turnpike in our social studies book, but if I wanted to know more, what might I look for?

Billy: When it was made?

Teacher: Yes. That is very important, but I can find that in our social studies book. Let's look on page 137 and read the section on the Turnpike.

Richard: Maybe you want to know how they made the tunnels.

Teacher: Yes; that isn't in the social studies book.

Ralma: Who decided where it would go? Who said what the route would be?

Janie: Why are the rest stops where they are? Who said where they are supposed to be?

GeorgeAnn: Why was the first one in Pennsylvania?

Teacher: I'll think about those questions for my research. What do I mean by "research"?

Richard: You want to find out. You're going to go to books and get the answers.

Teacher: Yes, research is about finding out. Is research only about books? Suzanne?

Suzanne: No. You can get answers on the Internet.

Jeannie: The phone. You can call someone.

Teacher: Good. I'll take all that under advisement. Now what about you? What do you want to know?

COMMENTARY

Subject reports are about collecting information in response to what the writer wants to know. The opening scenario is about inquiry. What are the questions? What do we want to know?

READER ACTIVITY

In your class, with a partner or alone, make a list of topics associated with the state in which you live. Part of framing a report topic is finding associations between and among individual topics to form more meaningful report questions.

BACK TO THE CLASSROOM

Teacher: Now, boys and girls, what do you want to know about Pennsylvania? [The following topics reflect the thirty-four items that resulted from this brainstorm:

Delaware Indians, Bucks County, Lancaster County, Lake Erie, Philadelphia, New Bloomfield, William Penn, first oil well, Bowman's Tower, New Hope, steel mills, Pennsylvania Dutch, Benjamin Franklin, Carlisle Indian School, Jim Thorpe, and Jerry Spinelli.]

Now I want you to decide on a topic that you want to know more about. Maybe it's something not on the board. Maybe it's something that ideas on the board make you think about. You decide on a topic. Then you have to decide what you want to know. I want you to write at least three questions about your topic.

Now it's selection time and question time. There will be no research until there are questions. The initial questions represent where the research process starts, not necessarily where it goes, because almost inevitably research into initial questions opens new questions.

When the students have come up with topics in which they are interested, the teacher gathers them for an orientation to the reporting form. They need to know the function of the report of information (what it's about and why we do it) in order for the process to have sufficient authenticity to make it useful. But they also need to know the form. They need to know what the audience will be expecting from their subject report and how to form their report so the audience will be satisfied.

INSTRUCTIONAL SCENARIO

In the Classroom to Talk About the Form of a Subject Report

Teacher: I want to make sure you know what your report will look like. When you read each other's reports, what will you want to know?

Janie: What they learned. The topic. The subject. What they read about.

Teacher: And what is that?

Ben: It's their questions.

Teacher: Their questions. Yes. In the report, we have to tell readers what the questions are. If you read a report that says the Delaware River is the longest river in the world, what would you think?

Ben: It's wrong. The Nile is the longest.

Teacher: Yes, but it's in the report.

Christine: Where did it come from? It's wrong.

Teacher: You want to know where the writer's information came from?

Christine: Sure.

Teacher: So do I. After the questions, report writers write about how they answered their questions. They tell whom they talked to, what they read, whom they called, where they looked on the Internet. The report starts with the questions and then tells readers how the research was done. Now what do you want to know from the report?

Ben: We put what we found out.

Teacher: After you tell readers about the questions and how you found some answers, you write what you found. The findings are the answers to your questions. Then what?

Ralma: The end?

Teacher: Ralma, you decided to research the history of your parents' restaurant. When you're finished and you write the history in your report, I want to know something about what you think. I'd like to know your conclusion, maybe a general paragraph about the history of the restaurant. Boys and girls, the report will be written in these four parts:

- Questions
- Procedures
- Findings
- Conclusions

It's like what we have learned about stories. There are certain things we expect to find in stories. There are certain things we expect to find in reports too.

COMMENTARY

That is a brief look at how the teacher presents the form and function of a report. There will have to be lessons on the procedures, the findings, and the conclusion. That is why the teacher conducts research and writes a report. When it's time to learn about writing the procedures, the teacher will write his or her procedures on the board to provide a model. The teacher may do the same thing with findings and conclusions. Each time, the teacher's own report of information can be a model.

Here is an example of what a fourth-grade teacher wrote to show his students each part of the research process:

Question: Who is William Penn, and why is he an important figure in the history of Pennsylvania?

Procedures: Encyclopedia Britannica on the Internet Search on the name William Penn. I also interviewed the librarian at the college. Finally, I read the entry on William Penn in the Larousse *Biographical Dictionary* (1994, p. 1142).

Findings: William Penn was an English Quaker and colonialist who is given credit for founding and naming the state of Pennsylvania. The story is that the name of the state includes his name (*Penn*) and the word for woods (*sylvan*), so it is actually Penn's Woods, or Pennsylvania. The Larousse *Biographical Dictionary*, however, says that in 1681, the British crown gave William Penn claim to some territory named "Pensilvania" in honor of an old British admiral with the same name. The land was on the Delaware River in North America. Together with his Quaker friends, he sailed for the Delaware River in 1682 to establish a place where he and his friends could practice their religion freely. He was on friendly terms with native peoples in the area and planned the city of Philadelphia.

Conclusion: Although William Penn may not have named Pennsylvania, he was one of the people responsible for starting the state. He began colonization of what would become Pennsylvania and planned the city that would become Philadelphia. We do not know the immediate effects of William Penn's colonization on native peoples, but that would also make a good report. William Penn is an important figure in the history of Pennsylvania because he is one of the first Europeans to settle there.

The first subject report may be a rough go as the children get used to it, and it could take as long as two weeks from generating topics to being ready to submit the whole report. Often each part has to be modeled, discussed, and explained. Many of the children need individual conferences. But the second report, which should be set up within a week or two of the completion of the first report, will be much easier and take less time. By midyear, after the children have written three or four subject reports, they will be quite familiar with the process, the form, and the function and getting quite good at it.

They should write subject reports across the curriculum: several biographical reports of information, more in geography, a couple in mathematics, certainly one or two in physical science. It is feasible for elementary school students, certainly by the third grade and through middle school, to write a subject report each month during the school year. Even five each year would equal about two dozen subject reports, all properly formatted and conducted to satisfy their intended purpose, by the end of the middle school.

There are two more questions that have to be answered, especially with respect to writing as many as five or six subject reports each year. One question is, Do I have to read them all? The second question helps answer the first question: How long should the reports of information be?

In balanced writing instruction, no young writer will ever hear a teacher say, "The report has to be at least six pages long and have at least three references." Authentic subject reports are about learning and reporting in four parts, never about numbers of pages or numbers of references. Oh, and teachers have to read enough to inform feedback and subsequent instruction.

Research Report

The research report is the form people in science use to share their research with an audience who expects that format. It's a reporting form for sharing science. While the research report is very orderly, science is messy. Science is unpredictable while the research report is very predictable. The research report is not the method of science. Its function is to report science, not to define it. The form is what readers of science expect.

INSTRUCTIONAL SCENARIO

In the Classroom to Introduce the Idea of Basic Research

Teacher: What would you say if I told you that sixth-grade girls can do more push-ups than sixth-grade boys can do?

Boys: No! Impossible! Boys are stronger then girls!

Mark: I bet anything that Raul can do more push-ups than any girl. He can do fifty. I saw it in football practice.

Teacher: So if I find a girl who can do sixty push-ups, that means girls can do more than boys?

Mark: No. Maybe you can find one, but that doesn't mean anything.

Teacher: How can we know if I'm right?

Scott: Let's just do it. All the girls and all the boys do push-ups and see who does more.

Teacher: Okay, there are fourteen girls and eleven boys in this room.

Billy: No, only eleven girls can do them.

Teacher: Which eleven girls?

Theresa: Let's have all the girls do push-ups, and the best eleven girls will do it against the boys.

Billy: That's not fair. You can't just use the best.

COMMENTARY

The teacher has introduced the basic question about research in less than a half-minute. Mark and Billy saw immediately the complexities of sampling in experimental research. They're only eleven years old, but they already know one of the problems they'll face in this investigation.

BACK TO THE CLASSROOM

Teacher: Which girls, then? Incidentally, what is a push-up? Do we count everything, or do we only count the ones done correctly? Should boys and girls all do their push-ups at the same time of day? Richard is the biggest boy, and Jeanne is the littlest girl. Is it fair for them to be in the same contest? How about Monroe? He walks with crutches. Should he be in it?

Monroe: I can do it. I can do more push-ups than anybody!

Teacher: Boys and girls, we have a problem here. If we are ever going to know if I'm right about my hypothesis, we're going to have to make it fair. Frankly, right now I'm only interested in the hypothesis and the variables. We can get to the push-ups later.

COMMENTARY

There is a specialized vocabulary in research, and researchers need to understand it in order to conduct the research properly and write the report. The classroom scenario established the context for two research terms: *hypothesis* and *variable*. Those are complex ideas for sixth graders because they are new to them and they are abstract. The push-up scenario set the stage for making the abstractions understandable.

The teacher is going to use the opening prediction as the example of hypothesis. At this stage in the research process, *hypothesis* means "prediction." Later in the year, the teacher may expand the definition with terms such as *supposition* or *conjecture*, but for now, the statement to the effect that girls can do more push-ups than boys works as a hypothesis.

The teacher will define the questions about which students, the time of day, what is a push-up, and so forth as variables, and fairness in this investigation means making the variables even, or controlling their influence. As the year progresses and the children become comfortable with the idea of variables and fairness, the teacher will use the term *control* for the idea of fairness, so it is important to control the variables to make the investigation fair. Of course, fair is what makes the results trustworthy, and the results are trustworthy if they are likely to occur again and again under similar circumstances. That is called *reliability*. Our experience tells us that we can establish the ideas of hypothesis, control of variables, and trustworthiness in the sixth grade.

We've also found that it is useful to display the terminology of research and the form in which research is reached or shared. We put sentence strips (large strips of oak tag that contain single sentences) with terms and definitions in the research center:

research	Any study designed to test a hypothesis.
hypothesis	A prediction that the research is designed to test.
variable	Anything that can affect how the research will come out.
data	The facts that come from the research. Usually the data have to be organized and interpreted.

There is also a chart in the classroom that shows the form in which research is reported. The report form is different from the "method of science" chart. The chart highlights these differences:

Form for Reporting Research	The Method of Science
Question	What do you want to know?
Hypothesis	What do you already know?
Procedures	What do other people know?
Findings or results	What is your question or problem?
Conclusions	Clarify what you want to know.
Recommendations	Form a hypothesis.
	Establish and follow procedures and collect data.
	Organize and interpret the data.
	Draw conclusions.
	Answer your question on the basis of what you have learned.
	Rethink what you want to know now that you have learned some things you didn't know before.

Over several days, the sixth graders agreed to select every other boy and girl from alphabetized lists of sixth graders in three schools in the district. They agreed not to use the five biggest boys and the five biggest girls on the two lists of boys and girls. They agree that a push-up would require a straight back, hands shoulder-width apart, and a dip that brings the nose within two inches of the ground. They agreed that a boy and a girl should judge each participant and that the whole experiment would take place during morning recess at each school. When the data were available, there were whoops and cheers among the girls and disbelief among the boys.

INSTRUCTIONAL SCENARIO

In the Classroom to Discover the Form for Writing Research

Teacher: All right, boys and girls. There are some data we have to report. Everyone, look at the chart in the research center. We're going to write this report together right here on the board. What is the first part of the research report? Charles?

Charles: Question.

Teacher: And what is our question?

Linh: Can girls do more push-ups than boys?

Teacher: Yes. That is the question. I'm going to write it as the first sentence of the report. Notice how I write the sentence: *Our research question was, Can girls do more push-ups than boys under controlled conditions?* What does that sentence mean? Andrea?

Andrea: It's the question, and it means we control the variables to make it fair.

Teacher: Yes, Andrea. That is exactly right. Everyone, is that the question that guided our research?

All: Yes.

Teacher: Good. That is how we begin. Our readers have to know what we attempted to find out. That's all we need as the start for our report. What comes next?

Eugene: The hypothesis.

Teacher: That is correct, Eugene. Everyone, say the word *hypothesis*. What do you remember about the hypothesis?

Byron: It's what you think will happen. You predict it.

Teacher: What should I write for the report? I need a sentence or two. I'll begin: *We hypothesize that . . .*

Byron: *We hypothesize that girls will be able to do more push-ups than boys.*

Teacher: All girls? All boys? Any kind of push-ups?

Saldavar: No; we make it fair.

Minh: We control the variables.

Teacher: In the hypothesis, we can say it this way: *We hypothesize that girls will be able to do more push-ups than boys under controlled conditions.* What do we mean when we write "controlled conditions?"

Minh: We control the variables. Who does the push-ups, and what is a push-up?

COMMENTARY

The scenario continues through the write-up of the report on boys and girls doing push-ups. The teacher writes on the board as they dictate and models as necessary. There is no elaboration. The question and hypothesis were one sentence long. They wrote the procedures in two sentences, the finding in one sentence, and the conclusion in one sentence. The conclusion, incidentally, read: *Under the conditions we used, sixth-grade girls did slightly more push-ups than sixth-grade boys did.*

A lively discussion occurred on the matter of recommendations. They ventured into the science of it all and decided it would be interesting to see if girls' and boys' push-up performance could be improved if they both practiced.

The teacher invited the sixth-grade class next door (which did not participate in the research) to come into the room right after lunch. With the report covered by a wall map, the teacher said, "When the report is uncovered, take a couple of minutes to read it silently. Then I have some questions to ask you."

After some "Yeas!" and "No ways!" the teacher asked several questions, all of them answered correctly:

1. What was the research about?
2. How did my sixth graders conduct the research?
3. What did they find?

Then the teacher asked, "If your sixth grade doesn't believe what my sixth graders found, maybe your sixth grade should do the research again." They thought that was a terrific idea. "But," the teacher warned, "if you want to test the study these sixth graders did, you have to do it in exactly the same way." Several of the other sixth graders protested and said it was done wrong.

"Then do your own study," Minh said. "But if you're going to test our study, you have to do it our way." Minh's classmates, having exchanged their gender braggadocio for a defense of their own science, agreed.

The other sixth grade did do it again, but with different sixth graders, and they found that the boys' average number of push-ups was seven more than the girls' average. By then, however, the original sixth graders had lost interest in the study and had begun planning an investigation of levers. By the end of the year, that class of sixth graders had written eleven research reports; the later studies were conducted and reported in cooperative groups, and no report was longer than a single page.

1. How do the purposes differ for the two kinds of reports of information (subject report and research report)?
2. Why is a report of information an important kind of writing?
3. In your own words, describe the relationship between form and function in reports of information and in another genre of your choice.

Persuasion

We do not use the term *essay* because persuasion is the dominant function or purpose. Young writers are going to write persuasion, and we don't want the myriad meanings of the word *essay* to confuse the instruction. There are whole books that have a persuasive influence. *Desperate People* (Mowat, 1959) and the Bible come immediately to mind.

In Chapter 9, we learned that the function of persuasion in writing is making an argument. By definition, persuasive writing is reasoned discussion designed to establish a position, perhaps in response to another position. A reasoned discussion uses facts or assumptions to construct a conclusion.

Readers of persuasion expect the writing to be clear about the topic or issue on which the writing is based. They expect to know the elements in the topic or issue, the facts and assumptions the writer has used, and the conclusion the writer reached by following the facts and assumptions. Writers of persuasion have to construct their writing so readers' expectations are satisfied. That is what makes the writing work.

INSTRUCTIONAL SCENARIO

In the Classroom to Introduce the Idea of Persuasion

Teacher: We have been together five months so far this year in the fifth grade. I assign homework pretty regularly, and occasionally you have to work maybe an hour on it. Right?

All: Yes.

Teacher: Well, I think it's time to up the workload just a little because you're going to have lots of homework in the sixth grade. I'm going to assign homework four nights each week.

Camille: That's too much! We have other things to do, you know.

Teacher: I know that, Camille, and I don't want to overburden you, but if you have homework on Monday through Thursday, you'll have three nights without homework, and if I limit it to one hour each night, you'll only have four hours a week.

Julia: We don't want any more homework.

COMMENTARY

Everything the teacher did to this point in the classroom scenario is directed at promoting Julia's comment, which is the basis for the first persuasive writing activity.

BACK TO THE CLASSROOM

Teacher: Wait. This isn't about what you *want*. It's about what you *need*. Now I happen to know that one of the things you will have to do in the sixth grade is think clearly and carefully. So if you can think carefully and clearly about this homework topic and persuade me that you are clear and careful thinkers, I'm willing to revisit my notions about homework. Is that fair?

COMMENTARY

Persuasive writing is about clear and careful thinking. It is not about a form. It's about how well writers think.

BACK TO THE CLASSROOM

Ben: What do we have to do?

Teacher: Well, let's begin with Camille. You said homework four nights a week is too much. How much is just enough? When does "too much" start? I have to know what "too much" is.

Camille: It's just that I have flute one night and gymnastics two nights, and on Wednesdays I have computer club.

Teacher: Does that mean you can't do homework on the nights you have gymnastics, computer club, and flute?

Camille: Well, no. I just mean the homework will be something else I have to do.

COMMENTARY

This interaction with Camille, and the rest of the interaction with the class, is directed at getting the young writers to take their arguments apart and consider what they mean. Camille said that four nights is too much. What is "just enough"? What does "too much" mean? If there is computer club on Wednesdays, is that all the student can do? The lesson asks questions that cause Camille to study her opinions and notice what her rationales mean.

BACK TO THE CLASSROOM

Teacher: Maybe you can talk to your flute teacher about having flute on Saturdays, and that will give you an open night for homework.

Camille: Monday's the only time she can give me my flute lesson.

Teacher: Well, boys and girls, here's the problem you have to think about carefully and clearly. Most of us have lots to do in our lives, just as Camille does, so having a flute lesson, or basketball practice, or computer club is the same for all of us. If you are going to persuade me that I have to revisit my plans for homework, you're going to have to think of different reasons. Lucretia?

Lucretia: What about if there really is more homework in sixth grade?

COMMENTARY

The teacher engaged the young writers in enough conversation to arrive at the point where it could be said, "You're going to have to do better than tell me how busy you are." Lucretia went for it and asked the right question—the one about the teacher's premise.

BACK TO THE CLASSROOM

Lucretia: If there isn't more homework in sixth grade, then do we still have to do more now?

Teacher: That's a very good question. Part of thinking clearly and carefully is asking good questions. What are some other good questions on the homework topic?

Huyan: I don't think homework is bad. But some homework isn't very good. Last year the teacher just copied out of a book and handed us a packet for the whole week.

Teacher: So what's your question, Huyan?

Huyan: Should we have to do extra homework just because somebody wants us to? Shouldn't we learn something?

Teacher: That's another good question. What are some more questions you can ask about homework?

It is very important for young writers to understand the role of deliberation when they think about their persuasive writing. Persuasion, remember, is only as effective as the argument the writer makes about a topic or issue. That argument is made of questions about the topic or issue, and the questions focus on opinions and assumptions on which the issue rests. The teacher said that fifth graders have to prepare for the sixth-grade homework load. One question must be directed at the teacher's assumption that fifth graders have to prepare for a heavier homework load in the sixth grade.

It isn't sufficient to write, "I don't think there should be more homework because I don't have time to do more, and besides, when school is over for the day, I want to relax at least a little." Even if the teacher is able to guide young writers through a process of expanding on that sentence to make several paragraphs, we're still left with a so-what piece of writing.

There are three or four sentences on Huyan's question and others about homework quality. What makes good homework? The teacher leads the conversation so the students flesh out the question about homework quality.

The teaching scenarios concentrate on the function of persuasive writing. Genre writing is always about function, so function, or purpose, is always clarified first. Then comes a discusion of the form that best communicates the function or purpose.

There will be no discussion about the number of paragraphs that go into persuasive writing except that there should be a paragraph for each main idea plus

INSTRUCTIONAL SCENARIO

In the Classroom to Think of the Questions for Persuasive Writing

Teacher: What was your question, Lucretia?

Lucretia: Is there really more homework in the sixth grade? We could ask sixth graders how much homework they have.

Teacher: You could, but for what I want you to write, you don't have to. Suppose there is more homework in the sixth grade? Then what?

Lucretia: Then maybe we should do more.

Teacher: What about Huyan's question? What was your question, Huyan?

Huyan: Shouldn't we learn from the homework?

Teacher: What if there is more in the sixth grade, but it's busywork?

Elmer: Then we shouldn't have to do more just for that.

Teacher: Suppose you were going to write something to me about my homework plan. Lucretia, what is the question? [Lucretia says her question again. The teacher writes it on the board or overhead.] Now what? Lucretia, you said if there is . . .

Lucretia: I know. What if the next sentence was this: *If there really is more homework in the sixth grade, maybe we should get ready when we are in the fifth grade.*

Elmer: But we shouldn't have to do more homework if it's just to give us something to do.

Teacher: Let's put Elmer's sentence in the next paragraph.

COMMENTARY

Questions clarify writers' thoughts. The teacher is guiding the questions. Persuasive writing doesn't necessarily include the questions themselves, but it does contain possible answers to the questions. Lucretia's sentence was like that. She wrote, "If there really is more homework in the sixth grade, maybe we should get ready in the fifth grade." The next step for Lucretia and the rest of the class is to determine how to flesh out the opening sentence in the paragraph. Is there any merit in an increasing amount of homework as students get older? If there isn't more homework in the sixth grade, shouldn't there be? There are probably three or four more sentences for the paragraph about Lucretia's question.

one to open and one to close. Nor will there be discussion about the number of sentences that go into paragraphs except to emphasize that readers must understand the main idea.

These sixth graders will read several persuasive pieces from the newspaper, although the writing might be past the reading level of many students in the room. Columnists George Will and William Raspberry work very well in being read

INSTRUCTIONAL SCENARIO

In the Classroom to Think About Form That Serves the Persuasive Function

Teacher: I need an opening sentence. Sean?

Sean: *One day Mrs. Liddle said she was going to give more homework.*

Teacher: Let's make that the first sentence for now. What exactly did I say? That can be the second sentence. The third sentence could be my reason. Then what happened?

Sean: We said we didn't like your idea.

Teacher: All right. Now we need to inform and persuade readers about your position on the issue. Do I understand correctly that you think it's a bad idea?

All: Yes!

Teacher: Good. Then what is one of your arguments?

Lucretia: It's the one about if there really is more homework in the sixth grade.

Teacher: And we have some of that already written. What's next?

Elmer: Mine.

Teacher: We have some of that too. Then what?

Patricia: I think we should write something good about homework. We aren't saying that homework is bad.

Teacher: Good point. Where would you put that?

Patricia: Right after the first paragraph.

Teacher: [After more conversation about ideas and details.] We need a final paragraph that tells readers what you can conclude from your thinking. You have written about what homework is, whether more in the fifth grade is necessary to get ready for the sixth grade, and what good homework should look like. What do you conclude?

Lucretia: That if there isn't more homework in the sixth grade and your plans for homework aren't about really good homework, you should forget it.

COMMENTARY

The teacher will lead them through that final paragraph, and they will read it aloud from the board, noticing how it is constructed and what it does. There will be discussion about questions, about trying to think as readers would think when they read the piece, and about how the piece ends.

aloud, and their pieces feature what these scenarios can establish: they're clear and not formulaic.

Chapter 9 contains a very specific point about the exploratory essay—the written piece that doesn't appear to have a point at the beginning but thinks its way to a conclusion, or thesis, at the end. That sort of writing certainly has to occur, but in the early stages of persuasive writing, young writers need some structure on which to hang their ideas. The final instructional scenario above provides just enough of that sort of structure.

Persuasive writing is difficult for young writers because they are more oriented to having than making arguments. They aren't oriented to deliberation. They're far more familiar with taking a stand and merely standing on it because that's the model to which they have been exposed. They are exposed to having and protecting positions. They don't see very much deliberation in the media and government, and don't see people making arguments. So they do what they know when faced with the persuasive task. The teacher's task is to slow them down, cause them to think critically, and get them to concentrate on the questions and conclusions.

REVIEW AND REFLECTION

1. Describe the difference between making an argument and having an argument.
2. Explain why it would be useful to conduct a lesson on such critical thinking skills as evaluating, justifying, comparing, contrasting, and interpreting.
3. Why is it important in persuasive writing to hear the argument from the reader's point of view?
4. As part of the persuasive writing portion of balanced writing instruction, it will be helpful to bring newspapers into the classroom and concentrate on the editorial section. How might this experience support students' understanding of persuasive writing?

Poetry

Bill Moyers, by vocation a journalist, wrote a book about poets because he loves poetry and talking to poets helped make their work more accessible to him. The conversations helped him understand the passions and the experiences that made them poets. He attended the 1998 Geraldine R. Dodge Poetry Festival, called the "Woodstock of poetry," and recorded the poets' conversations and poems. Out of that came a PBS documentary and his book, *Fooling with Words: A Celebration of Poets and Their Craft* (1999).

Moyers was in high school when his teacher announced that the class would be doing something different from their usual study of literature, vocabulary, and parts of speech. She read poetry aloud, and they listened, without questions or analysis. She "insisted that poetry requires attention before it welcomes analysis" (p. xvi).

Today Robert Pinsky, poet laureate of the United States, would give that same advice. When Moyers asked Pinsky what the listener or reader of poetry is supposed to do, Pinsky responded, "Just three words. Read it aloud. Read it aloud. And don't worry about interpreting it. . . . Just read it aloud to relish the consonants and vowels and the way the verbs and adjectives and nouns do their job"

(p. 205). He makes the point that first it's important to fall in love. Then, "you'll want to analyze it, know the history of it, and know what intelligent people think about it" (p. 204). Our interest must be piqued. The interest and desire to know more will follow, not the other way around.

You'll remember that we emphasized this idea in Chapter 9 when we introduced the genre of poetry. Our task as teachers is to help students experience the poem delightfully, inhabit it personally, and fall in love with the genre. Only then can we productively guide students to explore the poet's craft, hear what other people have to say, think about the poet's intentions, and consider the ideas (themes) carried through the lines.

The only way for children and adolescents to experience poetry is to hear it read aloud, fluently and with feeling, and to read it every day. What is unknown is never accessible to us and can be intimidating and even frightening. At the very least, the unknown may be perceived as uninteresting. Teachers have an opportunity to make poetry known by making it a part of their students' lives, thus making it familiar and accessible to them.

Along with experiencing poetry, it's important for children to write and share their own poetry. In this section of the chapter, we'll look inside a classroom and discuss some activities that can make poetry accessible to students and part of their lives.

Central to the poet's craft is that poets, unlike writers of prose, use line length to create meaning and effect. Of course, we can illustrate that to students by reading poetry and pointing that fact out to them. One way to help children and adolescents experience line length firsthand is through *found poems*. Begin with three or four sentences from any text appropriate for the young writers in your room. Let's look in on a fifth-grade class.

INSTRUCTIONAL SCENARIO

In the Classroom for Found Poems

Teacher: Boys and girls, we've been reading poetry for quite a while now. Do you remember at the beginning of the year when we all went to the library and brought about twenty poetry books back to the classroom? Julio, do you have a question?

Julio: I just wanted to say that I liked reading my favorite poem, "New Kid on the Block."

Teacher: Yes, I liked each one of the poems you all read. I remember that Alicia read a poem from Gwendolyn Brooks's collection of poems called *Bronzeville Boys and Girls*, about boys and girls living in an inner city. You read poems by Myra Cohen Livingston, David McCord, Shel Silverstein, and Gary Soto. "Oranges" by Gary Soto is one of my favorites. I liked hearing all the poems we read. Remember that I said one of the things poets do is control the length of each line in order to say exactly what they want to say in just the right way. We're going to do something called a found poem. We're going to experience for ourselves just what poets do with line length.

READER ACTIVITY

Look again at what the teacher did to begin her children's odyssey with poetry. She collected numerous poems and poetry collections and gave her students reading time. They had a chance to read widely, and they chose favorite poems to share with the entire class. They also read poems aloud, quietly, and to one another. They practiced the poem they would eventually share with the class. They were immersed in a world of poetry. An immersion activity makes the world of poetry real and inviting.

With three or four of your colleagues, have your own immersion experience as the teacher did in her classroom. Then debrief the experience together.

COMMENTARY

The teacher chose an excerpt from one of her favorite writers, Diane Ackerman, and her book *The Moon by Whale Light.* Ackerman writes about bats, alligators, whales, and penguins. These are not typical reports of information. Ackerman's reverence for her subjects shines through her prose. Because the students had been studying about mammals, the teacher chose an excerpt about bats. Some of the students had written a report on North American bats and described to the class the phenomenon of echolocation. The teacher knew her students would understand an Ackerman excerpt. On an overhead transparency, she wrote,

> Bats listen for sounds to return to them, and if the echoes start coming faster or louder, the bat knows the insect it is stalking has flown nearer. Judging the time between the echoes, a bat can tell how fast its prey is moving and in which direction, and some bats are sensitive enough to hear a beetle walking on sand. [Ackerman, 1991, p. 30]

She then clustered her students into groups of four and gave each group a transparency and an erasable transparency pen.

BACK TO THE CLASSROOM

Teacher: All right, your task with your group is to rewrite Diane Ackerman's words as a poem. You cannot change any words or punctuation marks. As poets, you decide where to end each line. When you are finished with your poem, copy it onto the transparency, and I'll ask a representative from each group to come up to the overhead projector, share your poem, and read it aloud to the class. Janice?

Janice: Does that mean we make a poem out of what you have on the transparency, but that we can't change *any* of the words?

Teacher: Yes, Janice, that's exactly right.

COMMENTARY

The teacher circulates to make certain students are on task and they understand exactly what to do. In about eight minutes, each group begins the draft of its poem. The teacher announces that she'll soon begin asking each group's reporter to share what they have done.

BACK TO THE CLASSROOM

Teacher: It looks as though each group is finishing its transparency. We'll begin our readings in five minutes.

Max: Here's our poem. [Max places the transparency on the overhead projector and reads, pausing slightly at the end of each line before going to the next and modulating his voice to match the text.]

> Bats listen
> for sounds to return to them,
> and if the echoes start coming faster
> OR LOUDER,
> the bat knows the insect it is stalking has flown nearer.
> Judging the time between the echoes,
> a bat can tell how fast
> its prey
> is moving
> and in which direction,
> and some bats are sensitive enough
> to hear a beetle walking on sand.

Teacher: That's a very nice poem, Max. As poets, you've done some interesting things with line length. [Shawna jumps up, holding her group's transparency.] Shawna, your group can go next. [Shawna's voice too pauses to emphasize the effect of line breaks.)

> Bats listen for sounds to return to them,
> and if the echoes start coming faster
> or louder,
> the bat knows
> the insect
> it is stalking
> has flown nearer.
> Judging the time between the echoes,
> a bat can tell how fast its prey is moving
> and in which direction,
> and some bats are sensitive enough to hear a beetle
> walking on sand.

COMMENTARY

Students learn quickly that controlling line length is a powerful skill in the hands of a poet. They understand that line breaks are used to create meaning and effect. When Shawna read lines 4–7 in her group's poem, her voice slowed, pausing at the end of each short line, drawing out the sounds as if her voice were painting a picture of the bat purposefully stalking its prey. Each group invents its own poem, using Ackerman's words, to create a picture of a bat's use of echolocation.

Monitoring the Poem-a-Day Project

The Poem-a-Day Project is a good way to bring the experience of poetry into students' lives. Children's and adolescents' experiences with poetry should not be less than their experiences with stories, novels, or essays. Poetry should not be contained in a two-, three- or five-week unit—to be read, studied, and quickly forgotten after students create the obligatory book of "My Poems."

How to Begin   Start the poem-a-day project with poems you love and you think your students will enjoy. Like all other read-alouds, it's important to practice each reading so that your voice rises and falls with the rhythms and highlights the rhymes. It will pause at just the right moments, speed up or slow down, depending on the tone and the message. Don't hesitate to show the emotions you feel every time you inhabit a poem. Laugh when a poem strikes you funny, and let your students know that sometimes the word power in a poem can make you cry.

Draw attention to the poet's words by posing questions: Why do poets choose one word over another? Why do some words energize, while others are flat and dull? Call attention to the sights, sounds, and images. How does the writer create word pictures? In Soto's poem "Oranges," the young boy walks with his girlfriend "down the street, across / A used car lot and a line / Of newly planted trees, / Until we were breathing before a drugstore." He didn't just write "we walked to the drugstore." They walked until they were "breathing before a drugstore." Engage youngsters in a conversation about the difference between the two images. In Soto's poem, we can also draw attention to the story, the characters, the setting (where and when did it take place?), and the story itself. What is it about? What are the mood, the feeling, and the tone? What does the writer do that creates the tone, and how are readers affected by it?

These are all part of the experience you can offer to students. Once you make the commitment to make poetry accessible to your students, you can design the rest of your observation.

What's the Question?   In the poem-a-day project, the objective is to make poetry part of children's lives, to make it accessible and encourage children to be readers and writers of poetry. The question for observation, then, is, What impact does the poem-a-day project have on children's interest in and inclination to read, write, and share poetry?

How to Design the Project   You'll need a teacher's log in order to document the impact of sharing on students. Select a focus or two, and keep records in the log for perhaps a month—for example:

- Do the children begin choosing poetry to read on their own?
- Do they write poetry on their own during writing time?
- Do they share their poetry during sharing time or from the author's chair?
- Do they check out poetry books from the school or classroom library?
- What changes can you define regarding their reactions to poetry and poets and about words?

It's difficult to report the effect of what we do in classrooms unless we collect evidence that can answer some of our questions and inform our instruction. In such an informal monitoring project, you can see firsthand the impact of your work with children and adolescents.

Continuing to Make Poetry Accessible Through Writing

No discussion on making poetry accessible through writing is complete without mention of Kenneth Koch, whose classic books on poetry writing, *Wishes, Lies, and Dreams* (1970) and *Rose, Where Did You Get That Red?* (1973), have for years provided wonderful ideas for making poetry accessible to children. Based on his work with children in New York and in Africa, in *Rose, Where Did You Get That Red?* Koch describes how he brought into their lives adult poets (e.g., Blake, Whitman, Shakespeare, Herrick, William Carlos Williams) and made them accessible through the children's own writings. For example, children read William Blake's "The Tyger," which begins "Tyger! Tyger! burning bright / In the forests of the night / What immortal hand or eye / Could frame thy fearful symmetry?"

They discussed the idea of symmetry and found out that their bodies too were symmetrical. They discussed various lines and phrases until everyone had a sense that the poem's narrator was talking to the animal and, in the case of Blake's poem, asking about how it could have been so marvelously created. Koch posed a writing idea to students: "Write a poem in which you are talking to a beautiful and mysterious creature and you can ask it anything you want" (1973, p. 37).

One student's poem was entitled "Dog." It began, "Dog, where did you get your bark? / Dog, where did you come from? / Dog, why are you here?" (p. 41). Students asked if the creature could answer back, and Koch said it certainly could. As a result, some poems included two voices, a narrator's and a respondent's: "Rabbit, where did you get those long long ears? / They grew like stalks upon my head" (p. 50). A ninth-grade student in Swaziland began his poem with "O, Majesty Lion, saluted I. / Who made you to be the king of animals?" (1973, p. 58).

E S L Poetry is a reflection of the poet's thoughts. It is the voice of the poet that shines through. Therefore, poetry is one of the most accessible genres for all children. Once they understand the nature of poetry, they are able to let their voices come forth in their writing. Poetry offers one way for the voices of all children, regardless of language background, to bring their ideas and experiences, their cultures and beliefs, to the fore. ■

In *Wishes, Lies, and Dreams*, Koch asked children to write a poem in which every line begins with "I wish." Marion, a third grader, began his poem: "I wish I had a home of my own. / I wish I had a baby brother. / I wish I had a dog" (p. 71). Annie, a fourth grader, begins her poem with a clever wish: "Oh! If I had a wish I'd want, I'd say, I'd like to have all my wishes come true. / I'd wish I had a mink coat" (p. 76).

Koch and the teachers with whom he worked experimented with color poems (describe a color), used to . . . but now poems (patterned poem with couplets that read, "I used to, but now . . ."), comparison poems (poems that show how two things are alike and different), noise poems (poems about noise), quiet poems (poems about silence or quiet), and poems written while listening to music. Koch found that "it wasn't copying that was going on but something more like the usual artistic process of learning through influence and imitation" (1970, p. 35). He found that children learned poetry techniques from the great poets, but also from reading and sharing their second- or third- or sixth-grade poems with one another.

For older children, a structured form of poetry called acrostics is interesting. It's fun and easy to learn. Here are a couple of examples:

Lively	So warm.
Exceptional	Upward in the sky,
Interesting	Not to be touched.
Fun	—Anonymous
—written by Nancy	

Another form of poetry that is highly accessible for older children and adolescents is haiku, a short poetic form consisting of three lines of five, seven, and five syllables each. Poets often take literary license with the exact syllable count, but the general number of syllables guides haiku, which is Japanese in origin and probably the shortest poetic form in the world. The poet must choose words carefully because brevity is at the heart of haiku writing. Also, haiku is about nature, and it often mentions a season. Here is a sample of haiku written by Basho, a Japanese haiku master. His poems can be found on-line at http://members.aol .com/markabird/basho.html. Notice that he does not adhere exactly to the five-seven-five count, although it's obvious that it guides his writing:

It has rained enough
to turn the stubble on the field
black.

The sea darkens;
the voices of the wild ducks
are faintly white.

The leeks
newly washed white,—
how cold it is!

A good source for children's haiku poetry is at http://www.tecnet.or.jp/~haiku/. At this site, you'll find children's haiku from around the world, and each one is illustrated by the poet. A sample of the poems you'll find at this site is accompanied by a bright red ladybug on a leaf:

Mysterious bug,
In scarlet cape with black dots,
Creeps upon a leaf.

As in all other forms of poetry, the poet is always searching for the right word in the right position for the right reason.

REVIEW AND REFLECTION

1. How would you define poetry?
2. How could you make an interactive relationship between poetry and social studies programs, or mathematics?
3. Describe one way you could introduce poetry writing to your students.
4. What is the role of reading aloud in the study of poetry?

Autobiography

Edward Hallett Carr, a noted historian, wrote that as a graduate student with a specialization in Greece during the period of the Persian Wars, he believed he owned the complete printed history of the period in the volumes he had on his shelves (Carr, 1961). But he was wrong because history is made of people's stories, and no accumulation of volumes contains everyone's story. If there is a story left out, the record is incomplete.

Carr eventually realized that his collection of volumes represented an accident of attrition, or a selection, that included only some stories. He realized that in his lifetime as a practitioner of history, he could not know the whole story because he couldn't know all the stories.

Anne Frank: A Young Girl's Story. Culver Pictures.

Although it is popular to claim that history is written by winners and conquerors, in fact, history is written by people who write. Think about everything you know about Central Europe between about 1932 and 1945. Think about the history books, lectures, memorials, commercial and documentary films, wall posters, and photographs from those dozen years. What do most people know perhaps best about that time? A young girl's story. The diary of a teenager has told a more dramatic tale of the time to more people than most of us have read in any other source.

Autobiographical writing, which is about people's stories, gives young writers throughout the grades an opportunity to focus on the ideas and images they know best: their own.

 INSTRUCTIONAL SCENARIO

In the Classroom to Think About Autobiography

Teacher: In a few words, write a phrase about something you have done or that has happened to you that stands out in your mind. Yes, Jessica?

Jessica: Like a birthday or a vacation or something?

Teacher: Yes, or something else that stands out for you. Number 1, write a phrase that tells what it is. Number 2, tell where it happened. Number 3, make a list of who was there. Number 4, write feeling words that tell how you felt when this event happened.

COMMENTARY

That is a lot of direction. Nevertheless, we think writing teachers should guide young writers as they write autobiographically early in the learning process.

READER ACTIVITY

Write responses to the four questions, and follow along with the teacher in the scenario. Writing teachers have to write what they prompt their students to write in their classrooms. Otherwise, they won't know what the students experience when they follow the directions, and they won't know how to answer young writers' questions or guide young writers under individualized circumstances.

BACK TO THE CLASSROOM

Teacher: We are going to write what are called autobiographical incidents. Would anyone want to try to define what autobiographical writing is?

Sandra: It's like biographies but it's about us.

Teacher: Yes, Sandra, it's writing about ourselves. That is why I want you to write something that happened, where it happened, and who was there. And I have some more questions. Number 5, write a sentence about what happened just before the event you wrote in Number 1. Write that sentence. Then for Number 6, write a sentence that tells what happened right after the event. Number 7, write the name of a person, or a very short description of a person, who could have had your same experience. There is one more. Number 8, write a sentence or two about why you remember that event.

COMMENTARY

Questions 5 through 8 may be for young writers who have been writing to the first four questions and have gotten quite good at it.

Writing responses to all eight items shouldn't take more than about six to eight minutes for young writers at and after the fifth or sixth grade. The questions encourage them to think about their incident in a variety of ways. Question 8 is one of the most critical items in almost every autobiographical incident evaluation rubric. It is important for readers to know why the incidents selected are important enough to write about.

BACK TO THE CLASSROOM

Teacher: Now, boys and girls, I have something I want you to do with your list. You have eight items. I want you to organize them in order. Look through the eight items and decide which one is most important to you. Yes, Seth?

Seth: Do you mean the first one?

Teacher: Pretend you were going to tell someone about what happened to you. Which one of your eight items do you think is the most important? Then which one do you think is the next most important, and which one you think are the third and fourth and fifth most important ones? Put numbers beside each item to show which one should be first, second, third, and so forth.

COMMENTARY

The eight items encourage young writers to think about the event on which they will focus in their autobiographical incident. Many young writers organize their writing according to the eight items and respond to each one. The items help young writers think about the incident.

With especially young writers, it is helpful to limit the number of items to two or three and expand the number over time. With second graders, for example, begin with the name of the event or incident, where it happened, and how they felt about it. That will provide an autobiographical incident of at least three sentences. As soon as possible, include Item 8, about what made the incident stand out in their mind.

At this point, young writers have thought through the incident, generated a number of ideas around it, and organized those details in something of a rank order.

For those who have not yet begun, it is time to begin the draft. Most young writers draft to their rank order, but some deviate quickly from it. There is no single writing process here; there are only some directions, some suggestions, some instruction, and some time.

I N S T R U C T I O N A L   S C E N A R I O

In the Classroom to Get the Early Autobiographical Incident Draft Started

Teacher: Before recess, you named an autobiographical incident topic, you made a list of details to include when you write about the incident, and you put the details in a sequence. Now I want you to write the first sentence of your autobiographical incident. You may look at your list to find what you want to write in your first sentence, or you may just write the first sentence without looking at your list. Now write the first sentence. [Pauses sixty to ninety seconds for sentence writing.]

COMMENTARY

Some teachers shy away from time limits in a writing lesson because they feel it compromises young writers' spontaneity or creativity. We have two comments regarding the time limits. First, this lesson is about following some directions that ensure autobiographical writing. Second, some creativity is spontaneous, and some spontaneous activity eventuates in creative production, and both are sufficiently powerful that teacher direction can rarely compromise them among third and seventh graders who are just learning autobiographical incident writing.

BACK TO THE CLASSROOM

Teacher: I need someone to read aloud the sentence you have written. Michael?
Michael: *I got a new computer game for my eighth birthday.*
Teacher: That's a sentence that can begin an autobiographical incident. Let us hear another sentence. Edgar?
Edgar: *My brothers and sister and my mother were at the zoo with me when we went last weekend.*
Teacher: Now, everyone, write your next sentence. And write the next one too, and the next and the next. I won't interrupt for five minutes.

COMMENTARY

About half the class will write for much or all of the allotted time. Some will write another sentence or two and stop, raise a hand, and say that they can't think of anything else to write. Direct them to their list and tell them to use another of their own ideas to write more about their incident.

This activity is intentional and teacher directed, certainly at first. It is the first autobiographical incident the young writers have done, and you want as many as possible to do it right the first time.

The activity is both creative and authentic. It's also sufficiently directive to ensure that many will write something in which they can take pride. Many others will get a start that they can put into their writing portfolio and work on again later. Some won't have made much progress, but there's always tomorrow. Experienced writers know about tomorrow.

Among the many autobiographical incidents we have received over the years in response to the eight-item protocol, the following by an eighth grader is characteristic of the authenticity. We've reproduced it precisely as it was submitted in longhand. Following the incident are her responses to the eight questions which she wrote and then rank ordered.

That evening everyone was bustling around making last minute arrangements for our Thanksgiving dinner. The long cherrywood table was set with a red table cloth and the flower centerpiece was replaced with a bowl of fresh hot sweet yams with marshmallows and pinnaples. The mashed potatoes were placed on the table along with the hot buns and the nice. The turkey was the last to be placed on the table. Every one gathered around the table looking for available seats. My uncle and aunt were at the head of the table and my grandparents at the end of the table. My five cousins and my older sister and older brother were on the side. Every one was there but my dad who was spending his Thanksgiving in a dim, small jail cell all alone.

Even with being surrounded by my family I felt alone and sad. When the plates were crammed with steaming food we all clasped our hands together and took our turns saying grace. When it was my turn, Different thoughts jumbled in my head. My dad not being there, my mom who knows where. But my grandparents were there and my aunt and uncle were there healthy so I knew I did have something to have grace about.

1. Thanksgiving without my dad.
2. Aunt Donia's house.
5. Brother, five cousins, aunt and uncle, grandparents, sister, and I
3. Happy, thankful, sad, lonely, envious
8. I had spent the night at my aunt's house.
6. I spent the night at my aunt's house.
4. Because it was a time to be thankful and in my mind I didn't have much to be thankful for.
7. No only my brothers and sisters.

There are thinking and writing cues on the basis of which young writers can invent autobiographical incidents. We recommend they focus on what young writers think, feel, and do in their young lives. For example, students of all ages can think about and write on the topic, "Something I Know How to Do." It wouldn't be an incident in the sense of a single event, but it certainly is autobiographical. It also doesn't require extraordinary expertise. The cue doesn't say "something I do better than anyone else." It is merely about things we know how to do.

There are a variety of cues to keep the process moving:

- Things we can do well
- Things we do that make us feel proud

- Things we have taught to someone else
- Things we do to get attention
- Things we have learned
- A decision we had to make
- Things we like to do
- Things we can do all by ourselves
- A choice we had to make
- A time when we had to be leader
- A time we had to share
- A time we didn't want to ask for help
- Things we are trying to learn and struggling with
- A time we did the right thing when others were not
- Things we are getting better at because someone is helping us

We are social creatures. Much of who we are, what we think, how we feel, and what we value are the result of our social interactions. Here are some cues that draw on these areas:

- Times when I did something that made someone else feel good
- Times when I have helped
- Times when I tried hard to meet someone
- Times when I tried hard to make a friend
- Times when I disappointed someone
- Times when someone disappointed me
- Times when I kept my word
- Times when I made someone else feel included
- Times when I made someone feel listened to

We have times when we feel proud of ourselves, disappointed in ourselves, and brave. We also feel fearful sometimes and effective at other times.

There are also a host of people we know and have known, and every one of those people has left a mark on us. Some of the people have influenced who we are or what we think. Young writers can make a cumulative list of people they know and have known. They can keep the list on a disk, upgrade it regularly, and keep the last names in alphabetical order. Then once each week, young writers can recollect events and situations that involved one of those people. That will be content for one autobiographical incident. Here is an entry from one of our own lists.

> Miss Cornell: I never knew her first name. She was my third- and fourth-grade teacher, the last real teacher, until high school when I met Coach Crawford, I felt safe around. She lived over a general store and post office down rural County Line Road past Upper State and Lower State Roads in Eureka, Pennsylvania, just where County Line split onto Limekiln Pike. She was a spinster, probably a normal school

graduate. She cared about her students, and not once that I remember did she hurt anyone or say anything bad about anyone. While my mother and father tell me I was a pretty good student in her two grades, I don't remember much from those two years. I recall having a crush on a girl named Nan, and I recall that Bobby Myers had his appendix out. Bobby Myers knew math, which I remember because when we had division, I had no idea what was going on and he did. Miss Cornell was maybe forty then. She was a good person. I hope she lived her life in quiet peace and satisfaction for having done a good job doing good work.

Think of how many people you know and have known in your life, and the ones you haven't come to know yet. Each one is a little story, and each little story adds detail and range to your autobiographical writing.

It is important for young writers to save their autobiographical incident writing. There should be a second-grade book, then a third-grade book, a fourth-, fifth-, and sixth-grade book. That would make five books of autobiographical incidents through elementary school.

Also, don't forget to ask for student volunteers to share their autobiographical incidents aloud. Over time, young writers will come to know about each other, which can weave threads of community in the classroom.

REVIEW AND REFLECTION

1. Have you begun your own autobiography? If not, begin now.
2. Should autobiographical incident topics be selected by young writers and not cued by the teacher? If not, why not?
3. Explain how a cued or prompted autobiographical incident can be creative and authentic.

Biography

The curricular framework for history and social science in our state of California refers to "People Who Make a Difference" as the focus in the second grade and "Continuity and Change" in the third. In the second and third grades, significant attention goes to biography in the state curriculum framework (History—Social Science, 1988) and in a wonderful little aligned publication titled *Literature for History—Social Science* (California, 1991). In the literature companion to the framework are listed the widely recognized biographical subjects at the second-grade level:

Martin Luther King, Jr.	Sally Ride	George Washington Carver
Galileo	Beatrix Potter	Louis Braille
Noah Webster	Paul Revere	Sir Francis Drake
Rosa Parks	Louis Pasteur	Clara Barton
Corazon Aquino	Peter Stuyvesant	George Gershwin

Scott Joplin	Theodore Roosevelt	Louis Bleriot
Henry Ford	Henry Cisneros	Marie Curie
Peter the Great	Charles Drew	Benjamin Franklin
Thomas Jefferson	Thomas Edison	William Penn
Benjamin Banneker	Jackie Robinson	Elizabeth Blackwell
Jim Thorpe		

At the third-grade level, there are eighteen more names, some of them overlapping the second grade contingent:

Thomas Jefferson	George Washington	Squanto
Daniel Boone	Columbus	Benjamin Franklin
Martin Luther King, Jr.	Harriet Tubman	Sojourner Truth
John Hancock	Abraham Lincoln	Mary McLeod Bethune
George Washington Carver	Peter Stuyvesant	Frederick Douglass
Paul Revere	Robert Fulton	James Watt

Several dozen biographical subjects are represented in the recommended reading matter for second and third graders, an enormous biographical load in these two grades. Teachers have several choices regarding how to teach the material:

- Select several subjects whom second and third graders can come to know well.
- Select several subjects who best exemplify major patterns of study.
- Select the several subjects for whom the teacher already has reading resources.
- Select those subjects with whom the teacher is most familiar or who best exemplify what the teacher decides are the most crucial patterns of study.
- Select those subjects who fit bulletin board themes.

Recall from Chapter 9 three approaches to biographical writing and study: scholarly (facts and facts, alone), critical (examination of facts), and narrative (personal story). Both scholarly and narrative approaches are feasible in the elementary school. The critical approach is probably better suited for somewhat older learners who are already familiar with the focus of a given biographical subject. Older learners would more likely be in a position to make judgments:

- What makes sense? Does it make sense that a military man would stand up in a small boat in rough water on a stormy night?
- What is possible? Can anyone throw anything as far as the width of the Potomac River?
- What is plausible? Do you believe that a seven year old would say, "Father, I cannot tell a lie. I chopped down the cherry tree"?

The first task for biography learners is to grapple with the question of what kinds of people have biographies written about them. What is a "mover and shaker," a discoverer, an explorer? What makes a person important and interesting? What makes the people on the second- and third-grade lists significant? A critical thinking question might be why those people are on the list. A scholarly question might relate to facts that put those people on the list. The narrative approach follows answers to the scholarly question.

INSTRUCTIONAL SCENARIO

In the Classroom for Biographical Orientation

Teacher: Boys and girls, we are going to study biographies of Sally Ride, Beatrix Potter, and Rosa Parks. First, we have to be sure we know what a biography is. Bonnie?

Bonnie: It's about somebody. It's who a person is.

Teacher: Yes, that's good. A biography is a story about a person's life. We read and study a biography so we can discover and appreciate who a person is. We are going to read about the people on the list here on the board: Sally Ride, Beatrix Potter, and Rosa Parks. Does anyone in this second grade know any of those people?

Randy: Is the first one a motorcycle rider?

Teacher: I appreciate your idea, but no, that's not who Sally Ride is. Boys and girls, there must be a reason that those people are on the list. I want you to find out why their names are on our list. What could you do to find out who those people are and why we should read and write about them? Clara?

Clara: We could read about them.

Teacher: Yes, we are going to read about them, but why those people? How can we find out what makes them important enough to read about?

Eleanor: We can ask you.

Teacher: You can. I will tell you who Sally Ride is. Sally Ride is the first woman astronaut to go into space on the space shuttle. She is on the list because she is an astronaut. Now you have to find out why Rosa Parks and Beatrix Potter are on the list.

Donald: I can ask my brother. He will know because he knows everything.

Teacher: Good. Tomorrow we will meet on the rug again and share what we found about who these people are. Then we can start to read about them.

COMMENTARY

The instructional scenario takes the first step in accumulating prior knowledge. The next time the class meets, there will be some information about Rosa Parks and Beatrix Potter and some more about Sally Ride. Not everyone in the second grade will have remembered to ask family members, but several will, and their contributions will establish a foundation of general information about the three people.

In this second grade, the plan is to work with one biography each week: Rosa Parks, Sally Ride, and Beatrix Potter. The children will hear presentations and watch videos about these women, and the teacher will share information. The purpose of this first month of biographical study is orientation to the idea of biography, reading about people's lives, and beginning to write biographical pieces. The students will read and study just enough about each of the individuals to be able to write several sentences.

After collecting information, the teacher will conduct a short interactive writing session (see Chapter 13) during which the children, with teacher guidance, dictate sentences that are posted under the name and picture of the biographical subject. In a week, the class will accumulate a dozen sentences. After three weeks, there will be a dozen for each of the three persons selected for study.

The teacher begins the biography writing process by emphasizing several critical points that are germane to both reading and writing biographies:

1. We collect information and make notes about what we learn.
2. We select from our collected information what we will write.
3. We are as true as we can be to the information we collected.
4. We write in our own words, to the extent that it is possible.

As the year moves forward, the biographies increasingly will reflect the children's own words. In the beginning, the specific lessons about information selection, collection, and truth are more important. The children's own words will follow.

This month's biography program will finish with each young writer selecting a person about whom to write. Of course, the children may write with any information they are able to accumulate, but the teacher and the children will have sufficient information on the board with which to write a second-grade biography. Their biographies will be displayed in the writing center after each young writer reads his or hers aloud to the rest of the class.

Two objectives will be accomplished during this first month of second grade. Every second grader will know who Beatrix Potter, Sally Ride, and Rosa Parks are. That is slightly more than a tenth of the second-grade list above, and there are eight more months in the second grade. The second objective is that everyone will have written a biography based on information accumulated together.

And there is a third objective satisfied in the biography writing activity. Each second grader has accumulated sufficient prior knowledge to read books about the three biographical subjects independently.

Later, when the young writers are fifth or eighth graders, a teacher will introduce a biographical unit called "Founding Fathers." The teacher will list John Jay, Alexander Hamilton, and James Madison on the board and tell the students that these are the men who wrote the Federalist Papers. And then the teacher will tell them, "Before reading from the Federalist Papers, we're going to learn about who the writers were, and we're going to do some biographical writing for each one of them."

The seven work groups will spend several days collecting information on their slice of a James Madison biography. On the fourth day, each group will write its

INSTRUCTIONAL SCENARIO

In the Classroom to Think and Write in BioScans

Teacher: We're going to look at biography in slices, just as we look at slices of bread, and each of us will be working with a different slice. This project is called BioScan. We're going to work on James Madison first, then John Jay, and then Alexander Hamilton. We will work with each person for about a week. The class together will write all three biographies, but each one of us will work on only one slice. Let's begin, and we'll see how it works as we go.

  What would you expect to find in a biography of James Madison?

Eloise: When he was born and died. What he did. Where he lived.

Fatima: Why he is important. I remember in third grade we learned that biographies have to be written about important people. Why is James Marvin important?

Teacher: James Madison.

Fatima: James Madison.

Glen: Was he the president or something?

Teacher: I have written your ideas on the board. We have *Federalist Papers, Founding Fathers, born and died, why he is important, offices he held.* I would like to add one of my own questions about James Madison: What is he most famous for?

  That makes six slices of a biography on James Madison, and we have twenty-seven fifth graders in this room. If we divide into work groups, we will have about five people in each group.

COMMENTARY

The James Madison BioScan may not produce very much because its beginning is relatively simplistic. However, once students do one, they'll have a better sense of what a biography can reveal, so when they plan for the BioScan on Alexander Hamilton, they'll have better idea slices, more information, and a better biography.

slice collaboratively. On Friday, there will be a "Bio Faire" during which each of the seven groups shares its BioScan on James Madison. The conversation on Friday will reveal a good bit about James Madison—perhaps more than any one of the children is likely to accumulate by reading any single elementary school–level biographical entry on the man.

And there is more. Over time, young writers learn what goes into biographical writing. They learn about biographical slices, write their slices, and eventually collaborate as a class to put the slices into a chapter book about the subject of the biography.

About midyear in a fifth or sixth grade, the teacher will introduce a look at biographical study and writing.

INSTRUCTIONAL SCENARIO

In the Classroom to Write the Critical Biography

Teacher: We have been reading and writing about George Washington for a week now. This time we are going to think about some of the things we have found. Gloria, what did you ask me about yesterday? About the river?

Gloria: Where is the Potomac River?

Teacher: Look at the map. Why did you ask about the Potomac River?

Gloria: It said that George Washington threw a dollar across the Potomac.

Teacher: *It said he threw a silver dollar across the Potomac.* So what is your question?

Gloria: Can he do that? I mean, how far is it?

COMMENTARY

Here comes the critical part of biographical reading and thinking. When Gloria asked if he could do that, she was asking about feasibility: Can it be done? is a fair question.

BACK TO THE CLASSROOM

Teacher: Look in the almanac. How wide is the Potomac River?

Gloria: It says it's 383 miles long, but it doesn't say how wide it is.

Teacher: You need to find out how wide the river is where Washington is supposed to have thrown the silver dollar.

Gloria: If it's like the Brasos River in Texas, where my brother goes to college at Baylor, he couldn't throw a silver dollar that far.

Teacher: Boys and girls, is that a lie about him throwing the silver dollar?

Sonja: Maybe it's that thing we talked about in reading last week—about the figure words.

Teacher: Figurative language?

Sonja: Yes, that's it. Maybe it's like figurative language. Maybe it's an exaggeration.

Teacher: But why? Why exaggerate about George Washington?

Sonja: Because he's the father of our country, and we have to respect him because he's like the most important president ever.

Teacher: Should we include the exaggeration in our biography?

Ted: Not if our biography is about the facts.

Teacher: The biography that Gloria's group read isn't about the facts?

Gloria: Is it okay to make a biography with exaggerations in it?

Teacher: There are several kinds of biographies.

COMMENTARY

The children are beginning to understand that in the world of biographies, we have to read several to begin to know the biographical subject. That is what makes the children perceptive readers.

This is where the teacher introduces scholarly, critical, and narrative biographies. It is where the children get some of the background they need to read biographies insightfully. Now is the time when there can be a BioScan based on three different slices: narrative, scholarly, and critical biography. George Washington is an excellent figure on whom to begin such a study. There are warm and personal biographies on him, critical analyses, and scholarly biographies. The critical analyses can be relatively sophisticated, and teachers have to use their judgment in determining what critical information is appropriate to share with ten year olds. Is it appropriate to share with fifth graders that Washington owned slaves? Is it appropriate to expect ten or eleven year olds to understand the context under which Thomas Jefferson might have fathered children with a slave? Was Columbus an explorer, or was he an invader? Could he have been both, depending on the points of view of two biographers? If so, this is an excellent time to begin helping young readers and writers—young historians—in fact, understand that when they read two different versions, one of them is not necessarily a lie.

Certainly the more biographical reading that young readers do, the more familiar they will become with the nature of biographical text and the various kinds of biographies, to say nothing of the variety of people represented in biographical study. Young writers need to read several kinds of biographies, and they need to write biographies, both individually and collaboratively.

REVIEW AND REFLECTION

1. What do you think would be your choice in teaching biographical studies: many significant people each year, or a few who fit the social studies units?
2. How would you be inclined to feature scholarly, critical, and narrative biographical approaches in your writing program?
3. On what basis would you select biographical studies? What would be your selection criteria for deciding what biographical subjects to emphasize?
4. Children in elementary school almost always write about George Washington, Thomas Jefferson, and Martin Luther King, Jr. Why don't they just as regularly write about John Adams, Alexander Hamilton, and W. E. B. Du Bois?

Technical Writing

Technical writing has several purposes that include to inform, to instruct, to describe, to explain, and to document. All of those purposes focus on readers, the audience in technical writing. We have referred before in this book to the "Does it work?" criterion for what makes good writing. Nowhere else is this criterion so clear as it is in technical writing.

It is important to include technical writing in balanced writing instruction because of the discipline it requires of young writers. They have to write short and in simple and clear sentences, which requires enormous attention on their part. Try to write one page on anything, and write in simple sentences, but don't make it sound like a second-grade reading book. It is hard because we think in complex and compound sentences.

Technical writers have to know the main ideas they want to convey, and they need a good sense of how to organize their main ideas. Technical writing crosses other genres, but its purpose is always the same: to avoid any miscommunication by being direct and clear.

If the objective is to write simple sentences that contain no more words than necessary to convey the point, here are some exercises for the children:

"Revise the following sentence into not more than ten words that ensure the direction's specificity: *Draw a line of approximately four inches in length across your paper at about the midpoint.*"

"Revise the following sentence into the active voice: *It is the outside nut that locks the inside nut onto the bolt.*"

"Revise the following sentence into the active voice in not more than ten words: *Holding your other hand on the board so the knuckle on your thumb can serve as a guide for the first thrust of the saw will help make a clean first cut.*"

"Write a sentence that tells a reader how to change the date on a wristwatch."

If the objective is to compose directions for perceiving and/or completing a task, here are some activities:

"Write directions on how to get from your house to school. Use only the active voice and no more than three simple sentences."

"Write directions for drawing a rectangle. Use no more than three simple sentences."

"Write an explanation for how to use commas in a sentence that contains items in series."

"Think about how to change the battery in a flashlight, and pretend you are writing directions for someone who has never seen a flashlight, has no idea what a flashlight is for, and knows nothing of the terminology (*bulb, cap,* and so forth)."

Technical writing cuts across the genres. In those portions of business communication where clear meaning is critical, good business writers will use technical writing strategies. Much of what we know as research reporting features technical writing. Editorialists often write technically. For example, when George Will or Robert Novak writes about big government, he explains in the technical prose of the regulation he is criticizing. One of us wrote a short story several years ago in which the main character counterfeited U.S. currency. A section of the story had to be written in technical prose to show readers how the character got the paper, mixed the ink, and printed the bills.

1. Count the words in the paragraph above and rewrite the paragraph in 25 percent fewer words without compromising the meaning and details.
2. How would you describe the technical writing you have read?
3. In what other genre can you see technical writing skills being used?

Planning Calendars for Genre Instruction

Although there certainly is no hierarchical scheme for intentional instruction in the genres, it appears that young writers prior to about the third or fourth grade have special difficulty with opinion and persuasion writing. But with that one exception, there do not appear to be genres in which the youngest writers cannot engage effectively, if only orally. The question, then, is how to arrange the genres through a school year.

The middle elementary grade annual calendar and the one-month break-out in Figures 10.1 and 10.2 show how much writing the middle elementary students can

September	February
BioScans Autobiographical Incident (Weekly)	BioScans Cooperative Research and Writing Fiction, Ongoing
October	**March**
BioScans Cooperative Research and Writing Fiction, Ongoing	BioScans Autobiographical Incident (Weekly) Persuasive Writing Fiction, Ongoing
November	**April**
BioScans Autobiographical Incident (Weekly) Fiction, Ongoing	BioScans Cooperative Research and Writing Fiction, Ongoing
December	**May**
BioScans Cooperative Research and Writing	BioScans Autobiographical Incident (Weekly) Persuasive Writing Fiction Closure
January	**June**
BioScans Autobiographical Incident (Weekly) Opinion Writing Fiction, Ongoing	Final organization and preparation of writing portfolios for end-of- year Community Literacy Faire

FIGURE 10.1 Prototype Annual Genre Calendar, Grades 4–6

Monday	Tuesday	Wednesday	Thursday	Friday
• Reading Biographies • Short Fiction	• Reading Biographies	• Planning Biographical Reports • Short Fiction	• Writing Biographical Reports	• Complete Biographical Report Writing • Sharing Biographical Reports
• Reading Biographies • Short Fiction	• Reading Biographies • Set Up Cooperative Research	• Planning Biographical Reports • Conducting Research	• Writing Biographical Reports • Short Fiction • Conducting Research	• Complete Biographical Report Writing • Sharing Biographical Reports
• Reading Biographies • Short Fiction	• Reading Biographies • Writing Research Reports	• Planning Biographical Reports • Writing Research Reports	• Writing Biographical Reports • Writing Research Reports	• Complete Biographical Report Writing • Sharing Biographical Reports
• Reading Biographies • Short Fiction	• Reading Biographies • Sharing Research Reports	• Planning Biographical Reports • Sharing Research Reports	• Writing Biographical Reports • Short Fiction	• Complete Biographical Report Writing • Sharing Biographical Reports or • Sharing Short Fiction

FIGURE 10.2   Prototype Second-Month (October) Genre Calendar: Middle Elementary Grades

do under instructional direction. The one-month breakout could be from October on the annual calendar. On Monday of the second week of the month, they read biographies and work on their fiction. On Tuesday, they read more biographical material, and the teacher sets up a cooperative research project. They plan their biographical report on Wednesday and conduct their research. On Thursday, they write their biographical report of information and continue working on their research. On Friday, they complete and make public their biographical reports of information. They begin writing their report of the week's research three days the following week and report to the class the last Tuesday and Wednesday of the month.

These young writers would be busy if they were only writing in the genres, but intentional instruction in the craft and processes of writing occurs in addition to the genre plans in the calendars below. Notice that research writing is in science and social studies, and the biographies are in literature and social studies. Both K. M. Foster and E. Lamping, now retired teachers, whose collaboration with the authors over the years helped guide our expectations, made them work.

If the teacher were to adhere to the calendar in the figures, young writers in the second month of fifth grade would be actively engaged in reading and writing activities on the following schedule of frequency:

Activities	Allotted Number of Times	Probable Number of Writings
Reading biographies	8	
Planning biographical writing	4	
Writing short fiction	7	2
Writing biographies	4	4
Conducting and writing research	4	1
Sharing in public (publishing)	4	

The young writers would plan and write seven pieces in the second month of school. They would have an opportunity to publish every Friday. They would write alone and collaboratively. Their writing would occur in three genres. And in the following month, they would remain with biographies and fiction, while adding autobiographies.

It's a rich plan, and all fifth graders may not be able to keep up. Assume for a moment that a fifth-grade class could be half as productive. That would mean young writers would write three to four pieces in the month, publish, write alone and collaboratively, and work in two or three genres. In a year, that could mean they write thirty to thirty-five pieces across the genres, alone and collaboratively, and publish regularly. Between the second and sixth grades, such young writers could write 150 to 175 pieces through the genres, work alone and collaboratively, and publish. And if they worked according to the biographical commitment embedded in these plans, they would also know probably 150 to 180 of the primary movers and shakers in social studies, science, the arts, and literature.

REVIEW AND REFLECTION

1. How do you think the authors discriminate, if at all, between "creative" and "noncreative" writing?
2. How does your distinction between form and function agree or disagree with the distinctions made in this chapter?
3. You have 100 minutes a week to teach writing. How many minutes would you reserve for intentional instruction in the genres? How many would you use for writing processes? The craft? What is your rationale for committing time as you have?
4. Among the genres, what is your strength? Why do you think that is?
5. How do the modes of discourse enhance intentional genre instruction?

A Summary: Teaching and Learning the Genres

The seven genres represent a considerable teaching and learning load in balanced writing instruction, but the load is feasible because the genres occur in the context of the rest of the comprehensive curriculum. We use technical writing principles and skills in everything we write that requires any measure of precision. Biographical writing is the core of social studies and certainly a major backdrop for the arts, sciences, and literature. Short fiction is a context for both science and social studies. Autobiography is the generation of primary sources on the basis of which future historians write history. Genre writing supports elements in the comprehensive curriculum, and when the genres are used carefully, they can enhance the learning in which students engage throughout the curriculum.

Genre writing also enhances the essential discipline on which writing rests because it is about the relationship between form and function. Young writers must learn the sentence, how sentences can be organized to make paragraph structures, and how to use meaning markers (capitalization and punctuation) effectively, but none of those is the reason for learning to write. We write to make the meaning most characteristically carried in extended discourse, and that meaning is most often organized in the genres. Young writers write best when they think carefully about their purpose(s) and organize their writing to best serve their purpose. Genre study is about the discipline of using form to serve function, as well as how to use writing to serve the comprehensive curriculum.

It is very important in genre studies to notice that there is no formula, mastery of which guarantees a well-written genre. Short fiction is "good" when it creates something of a fictional dream for readers, regardless of its form. Reports of information respond to questions or problems, and persuasion makes arguments that influence readers. Whether or not the report appears in six paragraphs and the persuasion in five is irrelevant. Both must contain the elements that characterize the form, whether in six sentences, ten paragraphs, or twelve pages.

The basic assumption on which genre instruction rests is that young writers master the genres as they write in the genres, often and well. Writing short is fundamental in genre instruction. Young writers will understand and write effective persuasion as they write many persuasive pieces that persuade, many reports that inform, and many poems that move their readers. The axiom that only perfect practice makes perfect is as fundamental in genre study as it is in spelling and sentence writing.

11 Technology and Writing

- Think of the many ways that technology has influenced the way you live, work, and learn over the past decade.
- How does technology influence the way you write, and perhaps even what you write?
- What does research tell us about writing and technology?
- What ways can you think of to integrate technology with writing and language arts?

The National Center for Educational Statistics (NCES, on-line at http://nces.ed .gov/pubs2000/2000086.pdf) tracks how well schools are progressing toward the goal of having every school and classroom connected to the Internet by 2000. The statistics, currently available through 1999, show that approximately 96 percent of public schools were connected to the Internet. That's in contrast to 35 percent in 1994. Nationwide, by fall 1999, 63 percent of instructional rooms were connected to the Internet, compared to only 3 percent in 1994. Another way to view the data is to look at the ratio of students to computers. On the average, in 1998 there were six students per instructional computer in the nation's public schools. The goal is to have one computer for every four to five students.

These numbers, however, do not reveal that large urban schools tend to have access to fewer computers and are less likely to be linked to the Internet than are smaller suburban schools. In addition, schools with 50 percent or more minority students enrolled, 71 percent or more students eligible for free or reduced-price school lunch, and schools in the Northeast had a lower proportion of rooms connected to the Internet as of 1999.

Those statistics give a snapshot of the widespread and quickly increasing, although not necessarily equitable, use of technology for instruction. But even if we didn't have access to the statistics, it's obvious that technology is becoming a force in our daily living and learning.

Consider how technology has already changed our lives—for example:

- We rarely send letters with stamps and envelopes to colleagues, friends, and family. We even receive birthday and New Year's wishes in electronic greeting cards.
- We communicate with anywhere from twenty (a university course) to five hundred or more people (a professional organization) all at once using listservs.
- We create documents with word processing software. We edit and revise; create tables, charts, and graphs; add pictures; and, if we wish, attach a document to an e-mail message.
- We send and receive photographs over the Internet. We recently viewed on-line the first pictures of a friend's newborn son.
- We shop on-line.
- We teach classes, or portions of them, electronically, using e-mail and the World Wide Web.
- We go on-line to the university library, from home or the campus office. We also visit libraries at various other places around the country—on-line, of course.
- We take virtual trips to museums in the United States and around the world.

We could go on, but you get the point. Technology has drastically changed the way we interact with others, work, and live. In this chapter, the focus is on how technology has influenced what we write and how we write. Let's begin by looking at what research tells us about writing and technology.

Influence of Technology on How We Write

When computers initially appeared in classrooms for instructional use, they were used primarily for drill and practice activities (clicking on the correct multiple-choice item in response to a question) and for word processing (using the computer as a sophisticated typewriter). There's no question that word processing "has become the writing technology of choice in school and workplace settings" (Hawisher & Selfe, 1999, p. 34). And increasingly, **hypertext** and **hypermedia**, presentation software such as **PowerPoint,** the Internet, and **discourse networks** such as e-mail are becoming central to classroom computer use.

The first questions asked about computers and writing related to how much easier it was to compose on the computer, as opposed to using paper and pencil.

It was assumed that the writing itself didn't change. In their review of research on writing and technology, Dahl and Farnan (1998) noted that not until the 1980s did research begin to examine the complex relationship between writing and technology; then they reported on that research.

It's important to look at some questions that have been asked—Does the technology change how we write? Does it make writing easier? More difficult? Does it help young writers write more effectively?—and what we've learned from the research.

Does Technology Affect Writing and the Way We Write?

Computer-assisted composition (CAC) software includes menus and screens that help writers by prompting brainstorming of additional ideas, encouraging rereading of what has been written, and posing questions about sections in a writing piece, such as the introduction and the conclusion (LeBlanc, 1993). In addition, spelling and grammar checkers focus writers' attention on the craft aspects of writing. By encouraging certain processes and activities, software can certainly affect "how writers think about their writing" (Dahl & Farnan, 1998, p. 94). Because of this, some teachers advocate turning off these functions so as not to interfere with young writers' composing processes. They worry that spell checkers will co-opt children's desire to learn to spell. But perhaps the opposite happens: maybe these checkers focus young writers' attention and make them increasingly better spellers. This is an important area for future research. We also can't forget that spell checkers don't do everything for a writer. For example, if we write a sentence such as *Than, Bobby threw the ball across the field*, the spell checker will overlook the fact that the word *than* doesn't fit in that sentence. But then, you might say, that's where grammar check comes in handy. What does the grammar check do with that sentence? Does it draw your attention to the introductory word?

What Is the Difference Between Writing with Pen or Pencil and Writing with a Computer?

Haas (1990) found that the kinds of notes writers made were different when they composed on a computer as opposed to writing with pencil or pen and paper. For example, when writers used pencil and paper, they tended to make more elaborate notes that contained arrows and other graphics that helped them think about the structure and organization of their writing. When they used a computer, their notes tended to be more textlike and to be focused almost exclusively on content, not on content and organization. Haas concluded that perhaps the best situation would be to combine the use of pencil and paper with the use of the computer when composing, or that computer software should contain features aimed directly at helping writers plan and organize their ideas. Hawisher (1986) suggested that the problem might be that global planning and large-scale revisions require a sense of the larger text. If writers have access to rereading only what's directly on the screen, they may have difficulty seeing the big picture of their text. For that reason, it might be useful for writers occasionally to print out their draft in order to reread the entire text, or to use both pencil and paper and the computer when planning their writing.

Cochran-Smith, Paris, and Kahn (1991) found in their research that many variables affected the relationship between computers and writing. These included writers' keyboarding skills, teachers' instructional goals and their attitudes toward computers, and classroom organization. In this complex milieu, the researchers concluded, students who used computers for writing tended to revise more, write longer compositions, and produce text that was freer of surface errors related to the conventions of writing (spelling, punctuation, and capitalization), compared to youngsters who used pencil and paper.

In a review of thirty-two studies, Bangert-Downs (1993) found similar results. Students using computers for writing tended to write longer compositions that were also judged to be of higher quality than were compositions written with pencil and paper. But he also reported that word processing itself does not necessarily result in better compositions; the teacher's learning goals, the type of instruction, and opportunities for practice all affected outcomes of writing.

Another interesting effect, found in studies by Dickinson (1986) and Bruce, Michaels, and Watson-Gegeo (1985), is that children tended to be more collaborative, that is, they worked with one another on their writings, when using the computer. They planned together, conversed about what to write, discussed spelling, and responded to one another's content. According to the researchers, these things may have happened more when students were working with computers because of the public display of their work on the screen. As students walked around the room and talked to one another, their work was on public display for others to see and talk about.

When Jones and Pellegrini (1996) looked at the effect of word processing on first graders' writing, they found that students' narratives were more cohesive; students paid more attention to word choice and putting ideas together. The researchers were not surprised, because students did not have to worry as much about the mechanical aspects of writing—the formation of letters, handwriting, and placement of words on a line. Finding similar results with another study, Cochran-Smith et al. (1990) concluded that with the technology, children were freer to think about writing as "verbal composition" (p. 240)—about words and ideas.

What does research tell us about computers and adolescent writers? Generally it appears that students' writing is judged to be of higher quality when written with word processing, as opposed to using pen and paper. In a study of students' expository writing, Owston, Murphy, and Wideman (1992) found that the essays were of higher quality, though not significantly longer, than when using paper or pen. In an attempt to find out what made the writings better, they looked at spelling differences between word processed and handwritten papers. They found no significant spelling differences. They did, however, discover that students revised throughout their writing when using word processing. Furthermore, students tended to do the most revising during the initial drafting of a writing, before their texts were considered finished. The changes they made tended to be small ones within sentences and paragraphs rather than large structural changes and reorganization.

When Daiute (1986) looked at middle school students' revisions when they used word processing, she found that they corrected more errors than when using pen and paper. Their revisions were also noticeably different. Students tended to add to their writing more often with word processing, especially at the end of a writing. She found that initial drafts tended to be shorter with word processing than with pen or pencil, but that final papers tended to be longer. Also, students' revisions tended to be at the microlevel rather than major organizational changes. However, when the word processing software prompted students to reflect on their thinking and writing, the revisions were more likely to include significant changes in organization. Again, it appears that the software itself directly affects the writing.

How Does Technology Affect the Writing of Students with Special Needs?

Word processing seems to be a valuable tool for children with learning disabilities. When the software contains aids for thinking and writing, such as prompts to support reflection, instructions on procedures for writing, and spelling and grammar checkers, students were better able to work with their texts and add and delete ideas (Morocco, 1987; Morocco, Dalton, & Tivnan, 1992). In addition, teachers' explicit instruction to aid the writing, such as giving strategy lessons on brainstorming and concept mapping, had positive effects on students' writing (Storeyard, Simmons, Stumpf, & Pavloglou, 1993).

One year-long study (Lewis, Ashton, & Kieley, 1996) looked at whether the keyboard itself represents an obstacle for students with special needs. When compared with students writing by hand, they found that using word processing lowered students' fluency in writing (rate of text entry) by about 50 percent. However, different technologies seemed to have different effects. The researchers looked at five groups of students. One group, without instruction in its use, used the standard QWERTY keyboard. Another received instruction in keyboarding. A third used an alternate keyboard with keys arranged alphabetically. The fourth group used a word prediction program, Co:Writer, to enter text; and the fifth group used this same word prediction program with the speech synthesis feature activated. Co:Writer, developed by Don Johnston, Inc. (http://www.donjohnston .com), works with other programs, such as word processing software, to reduce the amount of typing students must do. Students activate Co:Writer by pressing the "=" key. A window pops up and the student begins writing. When the first letter of a word is typed, Co:Writer attempts to predict the word the student wants to enter in the document. For example, when a student types an "m," the program predicts "most," "main," "mall," "man," and "men." The student can hear any of these words read aloud and, if one is correct, select it by clicking on it or typing its number. If the list of suggested words does not contain the word the student wants, he or she types a second letter and another set of words is predicted. In classrooms with students in grades 4 through 12, the researchers found that the fourth group had the highest rate of text entry and also showed improvement in writing quality. The next most effective strategy was using the QWERTY keyboard along with keyboarding instruction; here students showed the greatest improvement in writing.

REVIEW AND REFLECTION

1. In what ways can technology support students' development as writers?
2. In what ways might technology be an obstacle for students' writing, and how might a teacher work with problems that might arise?
3. How has the use of technology in teaching and learning changed over the past decade?
4. How would you respond to the following statement: *Young writers write better when using word processing than they do when using pen or pencil and paper.*
5. What did you find most interesting regarding research results in the area of writing and technology?

Influence of Technology on What We Write

Certainly what we write is influenced by the medium in which we choose to write. For example, what we write on the Internet is disseminated widely, so our purposes for writing and what we write are influenced by the medium itself. Currently 98 percent of information on the Internet is in the form of print (Moore, 1999). However, Moore broadly defines Internet texts as "any text containing word, sound, or image, whether singly or in combination, which is produced using, or held on, any form of IT" (p. 50).

Let's look briefly at the Internet itself.

What Is the Internet?

The Internet, a system of computer networks, didn't exist until the 1960s, "when individuals at the Rand Corporation, under the leadership of Paul Baran, created an innovative communications network designed to ensure that military communications would not be interrupted even in the midst of battle" (Dahl & Farnan, 1998). Although the military did not make use of this network, four universities in the United States were influenced by this work and became connected by a computer network. Eventually this network grew into the information superhighway that covers the globe. (For more information on the history of the Internet, see http://www.pbs.org/internet/ for the site titled *Life on the Internet.*)

The Internet is accessed through an Internet service provider (ISP), a company (e.g., MCI, AT&T, or the numerous other companies that supply this service), or an organization (e.g., a university) whose computer systems connect individuals directly to the Internet. The World Wide Web (WWW), part of the Internet, is most commonly accessed through a Web browser, software that provides a way to navigate through the Web pages. (A comprehensive glossary of Internet terms can be found at www.netdictionary.com, which contains over four hundred definitions of terms used in relation to the Internet.)

The Web is a hypertext medium (more about this later), that is, basically "a series of screens containing words or images" (Moore, 1999, p. 50). Screens link to other screens through words or images, and the Web links can be accessed through ISPs all over the world. Moore (1999) reminds us that there are some things to consider when using the Internet:

- It is continually changing. It began as a word-based system but now includes audio and video, experienced in real time. What will it be like in three more years? Or five or ten? No one knows, and we wouldn't presume to speculate.

- Anyone with access to a *server,* a computer linked to the Internet, can publish on the Internet. There are no censors or gatekeepers. Therefore, it's wise to be a critical and discriminating consumer of the information that is there.

- There is software available that automatically blocks access to sites selected by the user. Schools and libraries often use it to block access to material considered undesirable for children and adolescents.

- Internet addresses are not permanent since texts on the Internet are dependent on individual servers. That's also true for sites described in this book, although we've tried to ensure that they are all current as of the book's printing.

- The Internet encourages collaboration and sharing. Many of the sites in this book reflect the collaborations and sharing. As examples, check back to the poetry sites described in Chapter 10.

What Is Networked Discourse?

The Internet has changed how we communicate with one another. E-mail, discussion groups, chat rooms, and listservs are proliferating. Although these means of communication involve typing a message onto a computer screen, they are often called *talk* or *chatting.* It is not, however, face-to-face communication, and interactional cues such as tone of voice, facial expressions, voice, and gestures are missing. Writers may lose their sense of audience, and language can sometimes become emotional, even hurtful. There's a term for that: *flaming.* Some researchers have found that if there is a clearly defined goal for the discourse, with purposes and participants' roles clearly defined, flaming is not as likely to occur (Hartman et al., 1991).

In e-conversations (*e* for *electronic*), some new conventions have arisen: a smiley face, made with a colon, dash, and close end of the parentheses [:-)] and a wink, made with a semicolon, dash, and close end of parentheses [;-)]. E-conversations take place in a number of ways:

- *Chat rooms*—real-time discussions in which the emphasis is on a conversation among participants. It is the most interactive of the e-communication processes and is often referred to as a *threaded discussion*. Real-time discussions are said to be in a *synchronous format,* meaning that chatting and posting among participants occur simultaneously, like oral communication, or chatting.

- *Listservs*—a collection of individual e-mail addresses all linked to one common e-mail address. When one person posts a message and sends it to the listserv address, it is sent to all of the linked addresses. Individuals subscribe to a listserv by providing their e-mail address to the moderator, or "keeper" of the list. Listservs are referred to as an *asynchronous format,* meaning that messages are read after they have been written, not as they are written.

- *Newsgroups*—special interest groups that occur in an asynchronous format. Newsgroups are defined by the topic of discussion and, in joining, individuals can read what others have said and then add their own thoughts.

Another term for networked discourse is *computer-mediated communication* (CMC). Beach and Lundell (1998) conducted a study with twelve seventh graders who participated in CMC for three months. They used Macintosh Aspects, a networking software program that connected their computers in the classroom. Students communicated together in groups of four, each sitting at separate computers. In these synchronous exchanges, students wrote and received immediate responses from their peers. They reported that they enjoyed the CMC because they could post their ideas without being interrupted, unlike in typical classroom conversations. One student commented, "If you have something important to say, then you don't get interrupted" (p. 96).

Beach and Lundell saw greater equity among students in their participation when compared to typical classroom discussions. Shy students who were somewhat intimidated by face-to-face interactions felt more secure. As they shared their responses to stories they were reading, they posed questions for each other and often offered provocative ideas designed specifically to elicit responses. In fact, students felt rather left out if they posed an idea that the other group members ignored in subsequent interchanges. The focus in their interchanges was always on the evolving message, their agreements and disagreements, and not on a finished product. The researchers concluded that in this classroom, CMC involved clear purposes for communications: establishing social relationships, sharing reactions to a text, debating an issue, brainstorming ideas, collaborating on a project, and feedback for one another on their writing.

As a result of their research, Beach and Lundell offered several recommendations for using CMC in the classroom:

- Provide time for students to play and experiment with the technology so the novelty will wear off quickly, allowing them to concentrate on their communications.
- Keep CMC groups small (usually fewer than six participants), because then the conversations are more manageable. When groups are too large, students tend to have trouble keeping track of the conversations.
- Model the various response modes for students. For example, show students how to begin by restating a message they're responding to ("You said you thought Elbert's mother was mean to wash his mouth out with soap . . .") and how to disagree while being sensitive to others' perspectives ("I understand that you think Elbert's mother was being mean to him, but I have another opinion").
- Use printouts of chat transcripts to help students reflect on their conversations. It will help them recall ideas shared; evaluate the appropriateness of social roles and their participation, ensuring that conversations are always considerate of audience and never involve flaming; and generate questions based on the conversations.

Beach and Lundell found that "through participation in CMC exchanges, students are being transformed as readers and writers. They can evaluate those transformations as part of a portfolio self-reflection by reviewing transcripts from the beginning, middle, and end of a course" (p. 108). In other words, students can reflect on how their exchanges change over time and how their insights develop and change.

Grabe and Grabe (2000) describe an exciting form of networked discourse called the Learning Circles Project. Sponsored by the International Education and Resource Network (I*EARN), the project creates virtual communities of eight to ten networked classes in which students collaborate to investigate a theme together. Students in these classrooms "open the circle" by getting acquainted, and then they "engage in a number of interrelated projects that focus on the common theme. Each participating class takes primary responsibility for planning a project that involves participants from the other classrooms in a small way" (p. 75). (For more information on the Learning Circles project, visit http://www.iearn.org/iearn/circles/lc-home.html. The site contains Learning Circles projects on themes of caring for our world, people and perspectives, and others.)

Because computer technology is a relative newcomer to the world of teaching and learning, it's important to look at what we're learning about its effectiveness. So far in this chapter, we've discussed what we have learned from research in classrooms where children are using the technology. Much of that research has centered on word processing and its effect on what and how youngsters write. Some of it has focused on computer-mediated writing and how it has influenced adolescents as they think and interact. However, there are other applications involving writing and technology. Let's look at a few of them.

REVIEW AND REFLECTION

1. Networked discourse is becoming increasingly prevalent, but there are sometimes problems associated with it. What are some of the problems, and how might they be alleviated?
2. What is the value of networked discourse in classrooms among students?
3. What are some important points to keep in mind regarding using the Internet?

Ideas for Infusing Technology into Teaching and Learning

In this section, we describe several ways that teachers are using technology in curriculum (*what* they teach) and instruction (*how* they teach). We'll visit Web sites and discuss how writing and the other language arts interact as children create meaningful texts for public sharing. We'll look at WebQuests, an Internet research process, and visit a high school classroom where students are using hypertext to support their reading and meaning making with poetry.

A Second-Grade Classroom Newspaper on the Web

Imagine that your classroom has only one computer. Imagine that you have a class of twenty-four second graders who say newspapers are boring. Imagine further that this is an ethnically diverse class of students who range in ability from being designated gifted to being in special education; moreover, over 30 percent of these children do not have computers at home, and 40 percent do not know where keys are located on the keyboard.

The class task is to create a student-written multimedia classroom newspaper using Hyperstudio and to create a hard-copy version using word processing. This newspaper will be available to parents, the school administration, other students, and interested community members. In fact, this is not an imaginary scenario. Let's look into Mrs. Sanderson's second-grade classroom to find out what occurred, resulting in *Mrs. Sanderson's Second Grade Times* (Lund & Sanderson, 1999).

Based on her students' negative response to reading about newspapers—they found them boring and difficult to understand—Mrs. Sanderson looked for a compelling and engaging way to help students understand the newspaper and the kinds of writings found there. She had only one computer in her diverse class of twenty-four second graders. Nevertheless, she was interested in developing students' ability to use the computer, in addition to increasing their reading and writing skills.

They used Hyperstudio, hypertext software that allows the user to incorporate various media, such as sound, video, and graphics, into a hypertext program. Reinking (1997) defines hypertext as "nonlinear electronic text that provides readers with options to explore links between individual segments of text." They also used the Student Writing Center (SWC), word processing software that includes a newspaper template. They created the newspaper using SWC and, after revising, editing, and organizing the writing, cut and pasted everything into the Hyperstudio cards. But that's getting ahead of ourselves. Let's go back to the beginning.

At the beginning of the project, which ran from October to June, when the newspaper was published, students read and studied newspapers that were brought into their classroom. (Check with the newspaper in your area. Many newspapers across the country have excellent Newspaper in Education programs and, upon request, will supply newspapers to classrooms.) Mrs. Sanderson, together with her student teacher, taught basic aspects of the newspaper, such as its structure (e.g., headings and bylines) and how the content differed among the various sections.

The class decided that the audience for their newspaper would be parents, other students, teachers, administrators, and other interested persons. All students assumed specific responsibilities as members of the newspaper staff: writers, photographers, and artists. For example, two students were coeditors of the paper, and two students wrote an advice column. During the school year, students wrote articles, columns, jokes, and riddles; interviewed parents and other individuals and wrote articles based on the interviews; and carefully revised and edited each piece several times until they were certain that each one was ready for publication.

Students decided that the hard-copy paper would be produced in a two-column, 8.5- by 11-inch format, using a template similar to the one in the SWC software. In the multimedia version that included a video clip in a social studies article, graphics, and sound, every article was put on its own card or "page." The paper was truly a "multimedia event" (Lund & Sanderson, 1999). Although they produced a hard copy of the newspaper, students were most excited about the Web version and the CD they produced of the multimedia version. The CD contained all of that year's Hyperstudio projects in the school, and parents and others purchased over four hundred copies of the CD.

Lund and Sanderson (1999) reflected on the obstacles they encountered, as well as the benefits, and what they learned through the project. It's not surprising that the teacher and students were somewhat frustrated by having only one computer in the class. Students were enthusiastic about the project and "clamored for their turn when the computer was used." They learned to collaborate as several of them worked together on a particular task at the computer. The teacher and students also had to learn to use the hardware and software. For several children without computer experience, using the keyboard and manipulating the mouse proved to be challenging tasks.

Overall, the teacher found the work thoroughly enjoyable and highly motivating for the students, who became immersed in the world of newspaper writing and production as they created one for an authentic audience. Students learned about collaboration, new tools of technology, and a great deal about newspapers.

Mrs. Sanderson noted that parents and other adults who participated in the project were critical to its success, as everyone learned about the technology and how to create and produce a newspaper (see Figure 11.1).

Mrs. Sanderson wanted to promote students' reading and writing skills with this project and help them learn about newspapers and technology. Although it was difficult to evaluate precisely the effect of this project on students' reading and writing skills, all students were extensively engaged in reading and writing processes and the project's interactive language arts format. The demands for reading and writing were high as students worked to create a finished product for

Mrs. Sanderson's 2nd Grade Times

Volume 1, Number 2   Standard Edition   © June 5, 1998

Our Beach Party

By Diana Smith

At the end of the year party, our class will have a beach party. We will play with the beach ball, have a water balloon fight, and maybe a water sprinkler. We also will have food and drinks. It will be fun.

The 2nd Grade Super Field Trip

By Tina Young

On May 22, we went on a field trip to Pensacola. We went on a bus that looked like a train. We were out of uniforms, but boy was it HOT! We saw lots of animals because we went to the Gulf Breeze Zoo and the Naval Museum and ate lunch close to there. We had lots of fun. My favorite animal was the monkeys. They were funny. We got back at 4:15. The time schedule wasn't perfect, but it was great. Being with mom was the best part. I'm glad we got to go.

Question: What does a pumpkin pirate wear?

Answer: A pumpkin patch.

Question: What do you get when you put a cat in the refrigerator?

Answer: A cool cat.

Our P.E. Teacher: Miss Swan

By Mary Jones & Sarah Turner

Miss Swan has been the P.E. teacher at Austin for a long time. We interviewed her so we could get to know her better.

Mary & Sarah: What is your favorite color?

Miss Swan: Green.

Mary & Sarah: What is your favorite subject?

Miss Swan: P.E. [physical education]

2nd graders: Where is your favorite place to go?

Miss Swan: Target [a department store].

2nd graders: What is your favorite book?

Miss Swan: Any Danielle Steele book.

2nd graders: What is your favorite thing to do?

Miss Swan: Buy Beanie Babies [plush toys].

2nd graders: What is your favorite food?

Miss Swan: Spaghetti.

2nd graders: What is your favorite pet?

Miss Swan: My dog Annie and my cat Bubba.

FIGURE 11.1   A Page from the Web Showing a Newspaper Page. Reprinted with permission of the International Reading Association and David M. Lund and Deborah A. Sanderson "From Printed Page to Multimedia: Evolution of a Second-Grade Class Newspaper."

authentic public consumption. The task demands of the project required that students hone their oral language and listening skills for conducting interviews and for planning and collaborating on the newspaper's development. Mrs. Sanderson was aware that students were learning content, as well as developing their language arts skills. She noted that students "learned about newspapers and how they are constructed and had come to appreciate them as an important medium for mass communication." Students read for information as they researched their articles, and they learned to read critically what they and their peers wrote for publication. They wrote, revised, and edited carefully, wanting to ensure their work was in the appropriate form for the intended audiences. One young girl summed up the students' feelings: "I felt good about seeing the paper on the computer screen and part of it was mine."

A Trip Through the Underground Railroad

At http://www2.lhric.org/pocantico/tubman/tubman.html a class of second graders takes us on a trip through the Underground Railroad. During the course of the school year, the class read and studied biographies of important figures in American history, the focus of the history curriculum. During Black History Month and Women's History Month, they especially focused their readings on Black Americans and women. As a culminating activity, students decided to create a Web site dedicated to the person they would choose as the most important person they'd read about in American history.

They established a set of criteria and used a process of critical analysis to determine who the individual would be. The criteria were that the person (1) is well known, (2) helped people who were in need, (3) overcame obstacles in order to accomplish something, and (4) had accomplishments that influenced our nation's history. After much discussion and debate, the children chose three finalists: Martin Luther King, Jr., Thomas Edison, and Harriet Tubman. They then created a chart that listed each of the criteria down one side and the three names across the top.

Through further discussions and evaluation, they rated each person on a scale of 1–3 on each criterion (with 3 being "possesses the trait totally") and chose Harriet Tubman to be the focus of their Web site.

	Martin Luther King, Jr.	Harriet Tubman	Thomas Edison
The person was well known.			
The person helped people who were in need.			
The person overcame obstacles.			
The person did things that affected our lives.			

Not only was the creation of this site a truly exciting project for students, it illustrates an effective integration of curriculum, instruction, and technology. On one "page" of the site, the teacher provides notes on lessons that led up to development of the site: the American history curriculum; her emphasis on critical thinking skills (especially analysis and evaluation), classroom discussion, and collaborative decision making; the classroom simulation of the slaves' flight through the Underground Railroad; and how the class, with the help of the teacher, created the Web site, for example, using Puzzlemaker on the Web to create crossword puzzles for the site.

The children write on the site that the teachers

helped us write this web site to share with other children. We created a *time-line*, we wrote a *QUIZ*, we wrote some *character sketches*, we wrote *poems* about Harriet and we even made some *crossword puzzles* about Harriet Tubman for you to work on. We hope you enjoy it.

The words that we have italicized in that quotation are colored blue on the Web page, to indicate that clicking on them will link a reader to the items mentioned. The time line is especially interesting. It reads like a story of Tubman's life, complete with illustrations that students drew using KidPix software. Other links from various pages on the site lead to informational references for teachers and related classroom activities.

This award-winning site (eleven awards to date, including the Highlights Teacher Net Classroom Site Award and the Pacific Bell Knowledge Network Blue Web'N Site Award) illustrates well the interaction between technology, writing (for publication), reading (for information), oral language (discussion), and listening (required in discussion-based critical thinking). We echo what the children said: We hope you enjoy it!

Internet Research with WebQuests

In 1995, Bernie Dodge, professor of technology at San Diego State University, described on the Web a new idea for using the Web for research. In collaboration with Tom March, a colleague at the university, they called the idea WebQuest. Since then, word has spread, and teachers at all levels have been using WebQuests. As described at http://edweb.sdsu.edu/webquest/webquest.html, WebQuest is

an inquiry-oriented activity in which most or all of the information used by learners is drawn from the Web. WebQuests are designed to use learners' time well, to focus on using information rather than looking for it, and to support learners' thinking at the levels of analysis, synthesis and evaluation.

Linked to the WebQuest site is another useful award-winning site, also developed by Bernie Dodge: Seven Steps Toward Better Searching (http://edweb.sdsu.edu/webquest/searching/sevensteps.html). This site offers step-by-step clues to becoming a "master searcher" on the Web, including how to use bookmarks and narrow a search, when to use upper- and lowercase letters in writing a topic to search, and how to search the Web in languages other than English. One of the goals of WebQuest is to help learners use their time well when engaged in inquiry on the Web.

The page that gives a template for developing WebQuests (http://edweb.sdsu .edu/people/bdodge/webquest/buildingblocks.html) begins, "Putting a Web-Quest together is not much different from creating any kind of lesson." This page also contains a description of the six basic elements of a WebQuest:

1. The Introduction, which orients learners to the lesson with some background information that will prepare them for what they are doing and spark their interest.

2. The Task, which tells what the learner will have accomplished. For example, if the Harriet Tubman site had been created as a WebQuest, the task might be written as follows: *To create a Web site that shows the life of Harriet Tubman and why she was an important figure in American history.*

3. The Process, which describes succinctly and clearly exactly what learners will do to accomplish the task: the activities students will be doing, the skills they will need, and the procedures they will use.

4. Resources, which is a list of Web sites where students can begin. Students can also use non-Web resources—for example, interviews, text sources, original documents, video, and audio—and the teacher can direct students to them.

5. Evaluation, with an evaluation rubric that teachers can use to assess students' thinking processes in their completion of the WebQuest. One of the WebQuest objectives is to support students' critical thinking, especially analysis, synthesis, and evaluation.

6. Conclusion, where students are encouraged to do some or all of the following: summarize their work, reflect on what they've found, extend by asking questions, and generalize from their findings.

At the WebQuest site, Dodge provides a link to a matrix of WebQuests that teachers have developed and used. The WebQuests are categorized by the grade level at which they were used: grades K–3, 4–5, middle school, high school, and adult/college. We encourage you to go to this page and look at specific examples through the grades of fully developed WebQuests. WebQuest itself is a process that masterfully promotes interactions among technology, curriculum, and instruction, and highlights the reading-writing interaction through inquiry and research.

Hypertext in a Middle School English Classroom

Although Nancy Patterson did not use WebQuest in her eighth-grade classroom, she designed a classroom project that involved student inquiry and the Web. It centered on using the Web to help students extend their understandings of poetry

(Patterson, 1999). She wanted her students to go beyond searching the Web, to be able to find information they could use to create hypertext webs that would help them develop an in-depth understanding of a poem they had read. In addition to using Web-based resources, students were free to use other resources.

In this classroom, students read collections of modern American Indian poetry, and then, in teams, they chose one poem to explore in depth. After selecting a poem, they noted words and phrases they wanted to know more about or have clarified. Patterson found that students needed time to learn to use the hypertext program in the context of their task. They used Storyspace, a hypertext writing program published by Eastgate Systems that allows students to create different documents that they can link to one another.

Students began by typing the poem in the first frame of the hypertext web. One group underlined the phrase "evil Spaniards" and set about researching the Spanish conquest. As they researched, they kept notes of their findings. After they were confident that they had sufficient information on a particular topic, they categorized their findings, recorded them by topic area on separate hypertext pages, and created links between them and the poem. In addition, students learned about organization by color-coding their hypertext pages as they clustered around certain topics or ideas. For example, all pages dealing with American Indian legends might be coded light blue.

Through this process, students found relationships among ideas and pieces of information. Students read dozens of articles on the Web and in the library. Each team's Web contained approximately twenty pages. Patterson concluded that using hypertext software, unlike traditional report writing, allowed students to do the following:

- See texts from a new perspective, "as a network of links" (p. 72).
- See more than one way to connect ideas.
- See text as not always linear.
- Use a writing format that gave them experience with emerging technology.

Patterson reported that her students thoroughly enjoyed this process. They were motivated and engaged, often staying in her classroom after school to move their work along. During the nine weeks of the project, students were immersed in the interactions among technology, reading, writing, and the other language arts processes.

REVIEW AND REFLECTION

1. Discuss the language arts skills that are enhanced through activities such as those described in the previous section of the chapter.
2. How can technology be used to promote critical thinking and learning?
3. Discuss with a partner or small group an idea for a WebQuest, using the Internet for inquiry-based work.

Obstacles to Using Technology in Teaching and Learning

Up until now in this chapter, our goal has been to convey the idea that technology interactions with language arts teaching and learning are natural and complementary. However, this should not be confused with simplicity. In fact, there are many potential problems with designing instruction around the interactions (some of them implied in the scenarios described in this chapter)—for example, teachers and students may not be familiar with the intricacies of using hardware and software, and resources may not be sufficient, either in technology or in training resources.

Snyder (1999) lists three areas that present obstacles to the technology-writing interaction:

- Equipment that poses problems for the users
- Lack of technical support
- Little or no curricular planning for bringing computers into teaching and learning

In her research in grades 6 and 7, Snyder found that teachers had positive attitudes toward using technology in their classrooms. They were more interested in using technology within their classes than in going to an isolated computer lab for an hour a week, time they felt was not productive. Although over a two-year period she did not find that technology transformed the teachers' classrooms, she did find that teachers were interested in being "brought up to speed" in the use of technology in their English classrooms. But they were stymied by lack of support for using the hardware and software. And more than that, they were unsure how to use technology specifically for instruction and student learning.

Lack of resources, often of time, knowledge, and experience, seems to be at the heart of the problems associated with technology and writing. Knowing this, we can, as a profession, begin to target some of the difficulties in order to facilitate for all teachers the technology interactions with teaching and learning.

A Summary: What We Know About Technology in Writing and Language Arts

We know that technology is rapidly changing the way we live, work, and learn. There is danger, however, in viewing educational technology as the only, or even primary, avenue to increasing student achievement. Research tells us, however, that it can, in some ways, be *an* avenue. The task of educators is to use technology thoughtfully. That means being informed about the research and also conducting additional research to answer the critical questions: Does technology add value to my teaching and students' learning? In what ways does it support students' learning and achievement?

This chapter has presented an overview of the accumulated research to date. However, inquiry around the use of technology must be an ongoing process. We explored some ways that technology can support the development of students' critical thinking and their writing and language arts skills. For example, we looked at the skills and abilities that students used in order to complete learning activities using the Internet. As you consider using Internet activities, think about what skills students need to complete the tasks and how you can use the activities to promote students' achievement in writing, reading, collaboration, critical thinking, and researching. Make the technology work for you and your students, and monitor your students' achievement and attitudes. Only on the basis of teachers' experiences and students' performance can we discern the value of technology in teaching and learning.

12 Assessment in Balanced Writing Instruction

BEFORE YOU READ

- What is the difference between assessment and grading?
- What does "assessment to inform instruction" mean?
- If assessment does not inform instruction, whom or what does it inform?
- What should an assessment system value? Posed another way, what attributes of writing should an assessment system measure?
- Is it possible to quantify writing (make assessment objective), or is writing such an art that assessment can at best be only subjective?
- To what extent should the writer be the assessor in a writing program? Should writing be mostly self-assessed, partly self-assessed, or not self-assessed at all?

Assessment: What Are We Talking About?

At around the turn of the century, the people in charge of education in Paris decided their educational efforts would be more efficient if they knew before the first year of school which little ones were likely to be successful in school and which ones were likely not to be successful. So they contracted a fellow whose specialization was children and how they develop and learn. He figured a way to

323

assess school suitability for the children (all boys) in Paris. French boys who scored well on his test tended to perform well in their Parisian schools, and those who did not score well tended not to perform so well.

Some years after the test was developed, an American university professor came across the test and the test maker, translated the test from French to English, did some simple arithmetic with the test score and each test taker's chronological age, and administered the test to about fifteen hundred boys and girls in his university town—Palo Alto, California, home of Stanford University. The professor's name was Lewis Terman, and these subjects became the first generation for the mammoth longitudinal investigation that came to be known as the Genetic Studies of Genius (1925). (The Frenchman who wrote the initial cut of the test, incidentally, was named Alfred Binet.) The resulting score was a ratio between test score (mental age) and chronological age multiplied by 100, which became known as intelligence quotient (IQ).

Now let's put aside the fact that the test always has had far more to do with what the test taker knows than with whatever intelligence is (and at the time that was mostly speculation), and put aside as well the fact that what the test taker knows is useful only to the extent that it is very similar to what the test maker valued as worthy to know. Put aside that whatever Terman found when he tested his fifteen hundred boys and girls was heavily skewed by the fact that those children lived in Palo Alto, California, and grew up, to a large extent, with their Stanford University professor mothers and fathers. And, finally, put aside for the purposes of this discussion the fact that the sociological, political, psychological, and educational questions that plague the test have made its use problematic.

It's okay to put all of those questions, problems, and facts aside because this chapter isn't about IQ testing. It's about what an assessment instrument, an assessment system, is good for. The test Binet wrote and Terman introduced in the United States was good for predicting school success. It wasn't much good for assessing intelligence. If the assessment instrument is good (i.e., *valid*) for one thing but isn't good (or *valid*) for what we want it to accomplish, why waste the time?

What Is Assessment Good For?

An assessment instrument, or assessment system, is good for telling us what exists, and/or how far we have to go to get where we want to be.

Suppose you decided that good writing included quality sentences in reasonable variety (short, long, simple, compound, complex), mechanical control, a recognizable organization, and a focus on the assigned topic. Suppose you got so good at *seeing* those attributes of student writing that your ability to score them was almost always exactly like other teachers' ability to see them, and if you scored a paper a 4 on a scale of 1 to 6, other teachers would score that paper a 4 as well. Now suppose you are a fourth-grade teacher who asked everyone in your room to write in response to the same prompt. Then you sent their papers to a group of teachers who were very good at reading and scoring student papers, and you got the scores back after a week. The average score in your room turns out to be 4.3. The best scores in your room were 6, and the lowest scores were 2. From these scores, you know that the average writer in your room performs better than the projected average (3.5 would be average on a 1–6 scale), and you have some students who write very well (at 6) and some who don't (at 2). Those scores reflect the ability to write organized prose on the assigned topic in mechanically accurate sentences. Your average student can do that.

You get those scores in November. Now what do you teach? What kind of instruction does each student in your room need to become a better writer? How much writing instruction is necessary in your class? What ideas, concepts, principles, and skills do you need to teach, to which students, for how long? What characteristics of good writing are you teaching, and were those characteristics scored in the pre-November assessment process? How will you know if your instruction has made your students better writers? We'll address those questions, and others, in this chapter.

REVIEW AND REFLECTION

1. Assessment tells what *is*—the state of affairs as they are when the assessment is conducted.
2. The state of affairs is a basis on which we can plan for what follows, or on which we can make plans for making something follow.
3. In writing, we assess to learn how well young writers write and to plan for the instruction that follows. What do we know about the students in the scenario above? What do we not know?

Assessment in Writing: Three Requirements

Remember that an assessment tells us what is and what has to happen to get to where we want to be. Clearly, in writing we have to make professional decisions about what we value in our students' writing, we have to be able to measure or otherwise identify in students' writing what we value, and the assessment data (the information) have to tell us what to teach and to whom.

What Do We Value in Students' Writing?

Before we develop an assessment tool or program, we have to determine what we're looking for. In the case of writing assessment, what is good writing? What attributes of writing are we assessing to determine if the writing is good? That seems a relatively easy task, but in fact not everyone agrees that attributes of good writing are found in the written product itself.

Assumptions About Assessment Conditions

Gray (1995), criticizing the assessment process of the National Assessment of Educational Progress (NAEP), revealed a professional decision about what to value in students' writing. He discussed three flaws in large-scale writing assessment, in which young writers write for a specified period of time in response to a cue or prompt they haven't seen before:

- Students don't necessarily write their best because writing assessment isn't tied to the motive to get good grades.
- Students don't select the topics on which they write.
- Students write under *intense* (Gray's italics) pressure.

Gray's (1995) professional decision about what to value begins with ensuring students' motivation, student selection of topic, and reduction of pressure. His criticism of the NAEP assessment protocol is an example of professional disagreements about what we value.

Agreements by Practicing Writers

Fearn (1999) suggested that student writing should reflect practicing writers' values about writing. Practicing writers' self-reports let us in on what they think are attributes of good writing, but most collections of writers' interviews and epigrams (short, pithy sayings) do not address the question of good writing directly. Therefore, we went to the Writers' Haven Writers, a group of screenwriters, novelists, short story writers, and nonfiction writers. Most have a healthy publication list, and several make their living as writers. We asked the direct question: *What is good writing?* (e.g., *What makes writing good?*) The writers' answers clustered into five response patterns:

- *A form* that is logical and that readers can follow. Good writing has a beginning, a middle, and an end. There is an internal structure that readers recognize and can follow.
- *Sentences that are clear and precise.* Writers value the quality of sentences. It's instructive that when they gather each Tuesday to share what they're writing and reading, one of the most often heard exclamations is, "Here, read this sentence." Then they marvel about its precision. They talk about word choice and word order. They do not use terms such as *subordinate clause*, and there is never any commentary about subjects and predicates, completeness and incompleteness.
- *Good writing has a voice.* Readers know good writers' perspectives and passion from reading their work. The writing has sensory appeal. One of the writers talks endlessly about this and the idea that good writing has texture. Good writing affects readers.
- *Good writing is clear.* The writers were not at all vague about what clear means. It means precise—that is, just the right words for just the right

reasons. It means that a sentence of sixteen words can always be rewritten in fourteen, and a piece of eight hundred words can always be rewritten in not more than six hundred.

- *Good writing features a good idea well told.* Good writing is about something, and it compels readers. Good writing makes readers care.

- *Writing is good if readers like it.* Most writers are pretty pragmatic about what they do, and they know that what they do doesn't matter much if no one reads it. So the notion that writing is good if readers like it isn't uncommon in the larger writers' community. Another way to say what one writer here said is that good writing has to work. Good writing does what it was intended to do; and if it does, it will be read.

Agreements by Teachers

Spandel and Stiggins (1997) developed a widely accepted and widely applied list of "the six key qualities most often cited by teachers as significant" (p. 34):

- *Ideas that are clear, detailed, and relevant to the topic and reflect original thinking.* (The last idea would be better labeled *creative* or *critical* thinking. *Original* connotes thinking that, by definition, won't appear in more than one or two papers at a time.)

- *Organization that is recognizable, logical to the reader, internally consistent, and goes somewhere.* The last idea is very important, for a lot of student writing, and adult writing for that matter, is full of ideas that don't go anywhere. In writing, we call that *motion* without *movement*.

- *Voice, the personal flavor* that makes a reader exclaim, "Oh, Kristina wrote that!" It's how we know a Eudora Welty story from a William Faulkner story; each author has a voice when writing, and we recognize the voice when we read their writing. It's the appearance of a writer's connection with the topic, sense of audience, and, as Spandel and Stiggins write, "the capacity to elicit strong response from the reader" (p. 45). These authors also define *voice* as "liveliness, passion, and energy."

- *Word choice that reflects the right word for the right reason.* Writers call it "falling in love with the word." A rich vocabulary does not make a good writer, but there is no good writer without the right words to release their ideas.

- *Sentence fluency,* which Spandel and Stiggins describe as "rhythm, grace, smooth sentence structure, readability, variety, and logical sentence construction" (1997, p. 45). While readability, variety, and logical construction are relatively clear, rhythm, grace, and smoothness, while recognizable, are difficult to explain. We tend to say such writing is very good, but when someone asks what that means, we might respond with something such as, "I can't describe it; it just flows so nicely."

- *Conventions,* that is, matters of correctness, "an editorial touch" (Spandel & Stiggins, 1997, p. 45). Conventions include seemingly surface attributes such as capitalization and punctuation, as well as spelling and the surface marker of paragraphing.

Writing Requirements of School

There are also professional decisions about what makes good student writing as it is tied explicitly to school needs. Writing in school is not necessarily the same as writing in the larger world, where mass media writing occurs and is read. There, very few people do the writing that everyone else in the literate community reads. There are many more people who read the magazines on drugstore shelves than there are writers published in those magazines.

In school, on the other hand, everyone is a writer. Everyone is expected to write often and well, and no one is allowed to be only a reader. Under that condition, what are the attributes of good writing? Consider what young writers in school have to do.

- Young writers in school have to be able to write on demand, often what the teacher assigns, and complete the writing in the time frame dictated by a teacher, who is in turn constrained by the fifty-minute hour or the twenty-five-minute language arts period. To be successful in school writing, young writers have to be *fluent*.
- Young writers' performance has to appear *increasingly mature* as they progress through the grades. Good writing in the second grade isn't good writing in the fourth. By the fourth grade, they have to show that they can write longer and more sophisticated sentences and organize their sentences in clusters that reveal main ideas. As they get older, they have to demonstrate command of various genres and begin using writing to construct their own knowledge.
- Young writers have to demonstrate *command of an increasing number of mechanical conventions* as they get older, and they have to show that their mechanical control is increasingly automatic. We expect first and third graders to make many temporary spellings because they haven't seen enough words often enough to know what all the words they try to write are supposed to look like. But soon after about the third grade, we expect that young writers will know when their spellings are temporary and that they will spell them correctly before they consider their writing finished. In school, we expect mechanical correctness.

Those three attributes, or expectations, of school writing are so ingrained and so predictable that virtually all sixth or seventh graders will do quite well in writing class if they can write on cue, write in sentences that work, arrange their sentences in logically sequenced main ideas, and make their writing mechanically correct. In fact, that kind of writing will serve writing performance needs through school and even into the university.

What Do We Value in Student Writing?

The first of three requirements in assessing writing is to make professional decisions about what we value in student writing. Following are several attributes already discussed in this chapter:

Gray, Regarding Conditions for Writing	Practicing Writers' Perspectives	Spandel and Stiggins, Regarding Teachers	Requirements of School
• Motivation • Topic selection • Reduction of pressure	• Clear and precise sentences • Clarity, brevity, precision • Voice • Logical form • Being about something that compels readers	• Clear ideas • Recognizable organization • Voice • Effective word choice • Sentence fluency • Effective use of conventions	• Writing on demand • Sentence maturity • Genre awareness • Mechanical control

The items aren't the same across the sources, but there are patterns of similarity on which we can build a practical assessment system. The ability to write correctly appears in Spandel and Stiggins' list, as well as the list of school requirements; the same is true of ideas and fluency. The writers, the school, and Spandel and Stiggins all value sentence writing, and the writers and Spandel and Stiggins emphasize organization or form that works. Writers and schools both value the relationship between form and function (genre awareness). And Gray's assessment conditions certainly would enhance the other attributes.

Based on these agreements regarding what we value in student writing, we can say that good student writing can be identified by seven attributes:

Attributes of Good Writing

- Features sentences that are clear, precise, and mature
- Has a recognizable organizational pattern
- Is mechanically conventional
- Involves choosing the right word for the right reason
- Features the best form for the intended function
- Reveals writers' voice, passions, and perspectives
- Occurs when writers can generate ideas as needed and explore them fluently

Every reader may not agree with every item on the list. Every experienced teacher certainly doesn't. But it would be difficult to make the reverse argument: that good student writing need not feature well-formed sentences, need not be organized in a recognizable manner, or need not show attention to the relationship between form and function.

There are also other possible attributes of good student writing, perhaps about as many as there are teachers to suggest them. None of the lists, for example, includes creativity, although Spandel and Stiggins' description of voice might dance around its edges, even though a fair amount of the writing promoted in the nation's classrooms is called creative writing. None of the lists calls for any specific organizational system in student writing, although a good deal of school writing is explicitly form based (thesis statement up front, papers in three to five paragraphs, paragraphs having a specified number of specified kinds of sentences, and so forth).

You should keep in mind that very few lists associated with writing will accommodate every teacher's or writer's needs, so the fact that something you value isn't on a list doesn't mean you can't use it in an assessment program. Lists are about patterns, and what we've described is a pattern based on conversations with teachers and writers. That is a place to begin.

REVIEW AND REFLECTION

1. The attributes of good writing come from a variety of sources: the literature about teaching writing, the judgments of experienced writers, and the nature of school itself.
2. The attributes of good writing fall into patterns that contain clusters of attributes. It is more important that teachers agree on the patterns than on the individual attributes.
3. We use the patterns of good writing as the foundation of assessment systems.

How Do We Identify and Measure What We Value in Student Writing?

We've established that it's critical that we know enough about what we value in students' writing to be able to identify it and measure it. There's an old adage associated with testing, the origin long forgotten, that says something like, "If you can operationally define it, you can test it." So the question here is, What do the characteristics of good writing look like when they appear? We've deliberately omitted the concept of voice for this discussion because it is a sophisticated attribute of writing that is difficult to define operationally for young readers and writers. Therefore, we focus on the six questions implied by the other attributes of effective writing:

- What is a clear and mature sentence?
- What makes an organizational pattern recognizable?

- What does "mechanically conventional" mean?
- What is the right word for the right reason?
- What does writing look like when form is appropriate to function?
- How do we know that students can generate ideas and explore them fluently?

Those are the questions that have to be answered when we move toward construction of an assessment instrument or system. We have to know not only what we are looking for, but how we recognize it when it occurs.

What Is a Clear and Mature Sentence?

Defining a sentence is like trying to nail a hunk of Jello to a tree. Bryson (1990) noted the nailing task when he wrote, "Some of the most basic concepts in English are naggingly difficult to define. What, for instance, is a sentence?" (p. 134). Bryson never does get around to defining what a sentence is, and although he does refer to "full thought" and subject and predicate, he ridicules the subject-predicate portion of a definition as hopelessly convoluted.

Weaver (1996) defines a sentence as "something punctuated as a sentence" (p. 257). This definition accommodates Bryson's criticism of the subject-predicate definition, for it allows the one-word-sentence response to the question, "Did you take out the trash?" The Harris and Hodges *Literacy Dictionary* (1995) defines a sentence as having one or more words, a grammatical unit, punctuated by pauses, typically expressing an independent statement or thought. Finally, when Spandel and Stiggins (1997) expand on their reference to "sentence fluency," they refer to variety in sentence construction, eliminating the immaturity of endless connectives, and accurate application of mechanical conventions.

Spandel and Stiggins move the discussion from mere definitions to a concern for clarity and maturity. We have a general sense of what a sentence is, and we know one when we see it, although the arguments about what is and is not grammatical or elegant have persisted for centuries. As teachers, we know a sentence as one or more words that convey an image or idea bounded by hard pauses (end marks). Let's move on to the idea of clarity and maturity in sentences.

Consider the matter of clarity. A colleague wrote recently, in response to a call for possible meeting times, "Ten to twelve every day but Friday is not good." Our friend missed on the basic sentence criterion of completeness, but let's think instead about the matter of clarity. What do you think he is saying about his schedule? When can he meet? We thought he could meet every day between ten and twelve, except Friday. He later clarified what he meant: "Ten to twelve Monday through Thursday is not good, but it's okay on Friday." He knew precisely what he wanted to convey and was dumbfounded that we missed it, but as we study it over and over, it is as though we are seeing either a vase or two faces; it's there, but then it slips away. Even had he "completed" his sentence, it still wouldn't have worked the way he intended. The sentence is not clear.

Clarity is what happens when a reader's understanding is what a writer intended. If a reader has to read a sentence several times to figure it out, the sentence is not clear. To notice sentence clarity doesn't require a degree in English grammar or, for that matter, even the ability to diagram a sentence. It requires only the ability to notice whether sentences that we read work. If what we read makes images or ideas easily and freely, without repeated readings for the purpose of encoding meaning, it's clear. If we have to figure it out, it isn't clear. When we read young writers' papers, we can determine the extent to which their sentences are clear.

Variety, elimination of endless connectives, and accurate mechanical conventions. Variety in sentence construction simply means that all the sentences are not designed the same way. Some sentences begin with a prepositional phrase (*During the ride, we saw four elk*). Others begin with an article, an adjective, and a noun (*The little girl . . .*). An occasional sentence begins with a dependent clause (*Because she was just beginning to learn the piano, she was nervous before her performance*). There are compound sentences, and while they are few, there are also compound-complex sentences. (Reread that sentence for an example of a compound-complex sentence.)

What Makes an Organizational Pattern Recognizable?

To a large extent, the answer to this question is related to our experience as readers. The experience of reading provides models of what good writing looks like, or how it *reads*. Part of how writing reads is its form, and from the very first of our reading experiences, we develop notions about writing. We learn, for example, that a story has characters; that characters have problems; that the problems get solved; and that all of that is played out somewhere, the setting. We aren't taught story grammar, but we learn it, and we expect to see it when we read a story. If it's supposed to be a story and it doesn't have characters or obstacles, it doesn't have an organizational pattern we recognize.

To recognize organization, we have to have experience with it. The word is *recognize* (*re cognize*)—to cognize again. We have cognized, perceived, known, become aware of, before, and now we will do it again. An organizational pattern is recognizable if it is similar to what we remember and can apply again. Good writing therefore shows attention to what readers know about how a piece of writing is to be formed. In an essay, writers have to be sure there is a focus, or a thesis—something the essay is about. It has to appear explicitly or be implied. The reader can be led to it, or it can be stated early and then explained, but there has to be something in the writing that tells readers the point of the piece. Readers expect it; if they don't recognize it, they're disappointed or confused, and they don't think the writing is very good.

Part of what makes organization recognizable, then, is that it satisfies readers' expectations. One recognizable organizational pattern is very general: a beginning, a middle, and an end. Readers expect that what they read will set them up for what is to come, give them background, a beginning, a start. Readers expect that the writing will follow through on the set-up. Then they expect the writing to end, not merely stop. Sometimes young writers' stories just stop. They have a beginning and lots of middle during which some compelling action occurs. Then the writers get tired or bored or both, and they write a sentence such as, "And then he woke up." It could happen, of course, and while readers know the story is over, they don't recognize the organizational pattern as legitimate.

We must not forget that there is a basic recognizable organizational pattern. Good writing, in that general way, has a beginning, a middle, and an end.

What Does "Mechanically Conventional" Mean?

In a phrase, the term *mechanically conventional* includes a class of attributes that are critical for novice writers to learn and understand so they're able to control meaning in their own writing. This learning is part of the path that leads from novice to experienced writing.

Mechnically conventional writing is arranged in sentences. It is also capitalized and punctuated properly.

In mechanically conventional writing, words are spelled accurately. Items in series are parallel. Paragraphs have identifiable main ideas. And in longhand, the writing is legible.

What Does Appropriate Word Choice Look Like?

As is the case with all of these assessment criteria, a young writer's age is a very important part of this attribute of good writing. It isn't reasonable to expect a word such as *stride* in most second graders' sentences about how the proud girl walked to the piano. Second graders don't talk that way. *Stride* isn't part of their routine talking and writing vocabulary, although some are likely to know what it means when they hear it in context. *Meander* is another such word. So are *saunter*, *strut*, and *swagger*. They're all about how a little girl can get from one side of the stage to the other. But second graders are likely to write *walk*, or *walk fast*, or *run*, or *walk like she's trying not to run*. Those words make the picture in writing by seven year olds. They would be recognized as appropriate word choices on a second grade assessment. But it is reasonable to expect more precise word choices from fifth graders. On fifth-grade papers, second graders' reasonable word selections would earn middle to low scores.

This is not a call for artificial words. The writing doesn't get better just because the ratio of syllables to words increases or because there are more words from the "infrequently used" list. *Run* is a perfectly good word, and the right one when a fifth or ninth grader is writing about the portion of the fenced yard reserved for the dog, or the track meet when everyone was surprised to see how fast Rick Cuthbert had gotten during the summer.

But mice usually don't *run*; they *scamper*. Huge running backs *plow* and *slash*; little ones tend to *scamper* and *dart*. The sun *shines* on most second graders; it *blazes* and *blisters* when fifth and seventh graders are around. Most outfielders *run* to catch fly balls; Joe DiMaggio *floated gracefully* under them. The words make a difference. The meaning might be about the same, but there's no way the word *run* tells about DiMaggio. *Float* is the right word for the right reason.

As young writers become increasingly experienced and automatic with the characteristics of basic literacy, they can think more about just the right word for just the right reason. When they do, readers will notice, and assessments can quantify it.

What Does Writing Look Like When Form Is Appropriate to Function?

Research papers are supposed to tell readers the problem or question, the procedures, the results, and the conclusion. Autobiographical incidents are supposed to reveal the incident, details about the incident, and some indication of why the incident is important enough to write about. Those are organizational patterns that connect form to function.

Function refers to the purpose of a piece of writing—what it is designed to accomplish. Sometimes its purpose or function is to record information so the contents won't be forgotten. That's the purpose of a short note that hangs on the refrigerator door or is inserted into the daytimer at just the right day. The form is brief, often arranged in phrases and single words rather than sentences, and usually in a list. For the function, that form works well.

Grantland Rice, one of the great sports writers, opened a newspaper article in 1948 with a line that perfectly fit the purpose of the column (Halberstam, 1999): "The greatest figure the world of sports has ever known has passed from the field. Game called on account of darkness. Babe Ruth is dead" (p. 140).

The article is a solemn bit of writing, one anecdote after another that captured Babe Ruth for the ribald, warm-hearted, hard-living sports icon that he was. It closed with, "No game will ever see his like, his equal again. He was one in many, many lifetimes. One all alone" (p. 143). In between are the verbal images. The function of the piece was to ensure that readers could know the size of the man and the size of his death. Rice showed the relationship between form and function, and he did that often.

When we read young writers' work for assessment purposes, we are looking for a form that works—that is, the purpose of the piece is clear in the way it is presented.

What Does Writing Look Like If a Writer Has Generated Necessary Ideas and Explored Them Fluently?

In a study of Writers' Workshops in a middle school classroom (Farnan & Fearn, 1993), one of the more common kinds of feedback that sixth graders delivered to their peers was lack of detail. These sixth graders routinely were able to come up with a central idea about which to write, but they had difficulty with the idea flow necessary to enhance their central idea with details that would flesh it out. The feedback that sixth graders gave each other indicated that they knew immediately the difference between writing that did and did not feature sufficient details to fully explain ideas and images.

Teachers identify the difference as well, for a common teacher comment on student papers is, "You need to give your readers more details." Teachers and young writers know when a piece of writing fails to give readers the full range of ideas associated with the main topic or focus. It isn't that the writer didn't provide all of the necessary ideas; it's that she put them down and didn't write enough about them. When writers talk about revision, they sometimes use the term "mining deeper" as a way to take ideas further.

Good writing fills the reader. It provides the ideas and details necessary to fill out the focus, the thesis, the main idea. This is an enormously important part of an assessment system. This is an attribute that discriminates between young writers who can do the basic literacy things well (the sentences, the paragraphs, the mechanical control) and those whose writing is approaching maturity. The former writing is good, and appropriate through much of the elementary school; the latter is what writers begin to do after they have begun to master the basics of literacy.

How Do Assessment Data Inform Us About Teaching Writing?

Assessment data must inform parents, the larger public, teachers, and young writers. The requirements of assessment systems vary, depending on which audience it is intended to inform.

Informing Parents Locally

The information we accumulate from assessments of writing has value that is dependent on the reasons for the assessment. If we're assessing young writers' writing performances to satisfy parents' desire for information about progress, the data we collect must reflect writing performance according to how the parents understand writing in school, and in terms parents are likely to understand. Most parents want to know how well their children are doing in school, but often the turgid jargon of the profession and obscure definitions of young writers' performance fail to inform. For example, the following quotation appeared in a district's explanation to parents about portfolio assessment:

> The portfolio assessment allows the children and teachers to negotiate the children's best work through the genres over the year and determine their ability to address various audiences in ways appropriate to their self-selected purposes. The assessment system, of course, does not compare any child with any other child in order to protect the creative origins of each piece of writing.

Parents reading this wonder, "Does that mean they can write, or what?"

We can answer parents' questions far more simply by determining clear objectives for the assessment, explaining those objectives clearly, and showing how well young writers write when their work is judged against those standards. It's much more informative to tell parents something like this:

> We looked at four writing samples this year, one every two months, and judged them on the basis of four criteria: focus on the assigned topic, proper use of sentences and paragraphs, logical organization, and mechanical control. Eighty percent of the children wrote much better at the end of the year than they did at the beginning. I will be pleased to discuss your own child's writing in a private conference.

Now parents think, "I know about the room in general. So now I'll have a conference to find out how my child did."

Informing the Public Officially

Large-scale assessments, or what have become known as high-stakes assessments, are for the public at large and use enormous numbers of student samples. Statewide assessments at selected grade levels and the NAEP are such assessment efforts. The results tend to be reported in a single score determined from a *rubric*, a set of guidelines or criteria.

When large-scale assessment results are reported, often in the newspaper and in news conferences, they're shown as comparisons from year to year, from district to district, from school to school, and often among economic and ethnic groups. The public's reaction to these reports can be satisfaction or despair: "They're doing better, and that's very encouraging" or "Why do the schools in my district always come in last?"

Large-scale assessment data that inform the public tend not to inform teachers about what they should do differently or more of. For example, they often show writing performance as a number on a four- to six-point scale. Now even if you know that the criteria on the scale include focus, effective sentences, well-organized paragraphs, overall organization, and effective mechanics, what plans do you make about what to teach when the score comes back and shows the average in your room at 4 on a scale of 1 to 6? Is 4 good? It's above the average of possible scores, of course, but is the average writer in your room good at focus but not so good at mechanics, pretty good at sentences but not so good at focus and organization? What does a score of 4 mean?

It is unlikely that a single assessment system is equally useful for informing all interested populations. Each population has its own reason for wanting assessment information. Writing teachers are not disinterested in what parents and the general public value, but their primary need is for information about what to teach, to whom, and when.

Writing assessment data can provide teacher-useful information, that is, specific information about students' performance against various criteria. And if teachers can translate assessment criteria into instructional implications, the assessment process can have a specific and rewarding effect on achievement. This depends on two factors: **validity** and **reliability.**

The Assessment Criteria Must Be Valid

That assessment criteria must be valid—that is, reflect, or predict, good writing—doesn't seem very complex. Why in the world would there be a writing assessment that didn't reflect or predict good writing? This is not a case we're interested in making in the negative, so we'll use only two examples of possible assessment criteria that focus on a typical schoolized perspective on writing but aren't, in the way they are defined and used, associated with good writing.

In one case, there are assessment rubrics that call for a thesis or purpose statement in the first paragraph. If the thesis statement does not appear in the opening paragraph, the student writer's score drops from 6 to 5. Although good writing is well organized and a thesis statement in the written piece is an example of organization, it is not true that a thesis statement must appear in the opener.

A second example of assessment not focusing on good writing occurs when an assessment rubric penalizes young writers for starting sentences with words such as *and* or *because.* Clearly the appearance of *and* over and over as the first word in sentences is at least a sign of immaturity, but avoiding it altogether has nothing at all to do with writing well. To start sentences with *because* is unrelated to writing well or poorly. The exception is when students write only an introductory clause (*Because I'm sleepy*), in which case the problem is the nonsentence, not the first word.

Assessment data reflect or predict good writing when they are directly related to or lead to good writing. For example, one of the seven attributes of good student writing on which nearly everyone agrees is a recognizable organizational pattern. If there were a 6-point scale on which organization were judged in Ms. Leach's fifth grade, and fourteen of the thirty-two students scored below 3 in October, it is clear that Ms. Leach needs to teach organization to at least fourteen students in her fifth grade. And if she does teach organization, and what she teaches is, in fact, organizational thinking, some among the fourteen students who scored 3 or less in October will score better than 3 in March. The assessment informed instruction, and the result is that some of the fifth graders write better in March than they did in October.

Take this back to the negative examples. If fourteen of Ms. Leach's fifth graders score 3 or less in October, and she teaches those students to put a thesis statement in their first paragraph (and they do it), the scores will go up in March. But that will mean only that they're putting thesis statements in their first paragraph, *not that they write better.* On the other hand, if Ms. Leach's fifth graders score 3 or less against a criterion such as "mature sentences," and she teaches them how to use *because, although,* and *while* in complex sentences (and they do it in March), the scores will go up, and properly so, because complex sentences show sentence maturity and sentence maturity is associated with good writing.

A *predictor* of good writing is somewhat less clear, but useful to think about and implement nevertheless. This time, let's look at the writing development of Mr. Ortega's second graders. The writing sample is taken in October, and six of the second graders write five words or fewer. If they are writing five words or fewer in a twenty-minute **free-write** in October of the second grade and they continue that way through January, what is the probability their writing will improve in that period? Little, and maybe none. The second graders' fluency, that is, their ability to put black on white, is not necessarily a signal of good or poor writing, but it might be a predictor of whether their writing becomes better this year.

Mr. Ortega notices the inability of six of his students to get black on white, and he uses what he noticed in the assessment process for subsequent instruction. Twice each week through January, Mr. Ortega conducts Short Cue sessions (see Chapters 6 and 8) with those six second graders and anyone else in the room who wants to participate. In February he conducts another assessment. After nine weeks of writing for fluency, all of the six second graders who had written five words or fewer in October write fifteen words or more in February. Just getting black on white increases their opportunity to eventually write better. Fluency is a predictor.

The Assessment Process Must Be Reliable

Reliability—that is, predictability—means that scorers understand the criteria and apply them evenly to all papers. If scorers are meeting as a group to read and score five hundred student papers, their judgments have to be the same, or very similar, from scorer to scorer. If one scorer, or rater, reads a paper and scores it a 5, other raters have to rate it a 5 or at least within one point of 5 as well.

But we are talking about one teacher in one classroom reading thirty papers for assessment purposes. If Mr. Ortega reads Kristina's paper and rates it 5 on a scale of 1 to 6, he has to use exactly the same criteria when he reads Donald's paper. He can't think, "Well, Donald tries so much harder than Kristina does, and she has so many extra advantages. I just feel I have to give Donald the benefit of the doubt."

For writing assessment purposes, there is no benefit of the doubt. If Donald doesn't write as well as Kristina does, the benefit of the doubt won't make him write better. What Donald needs most is clear instructional direction based on an analysis of his writing performance, then further assessments to monitor his progress. He needs the instruction, and he needs to experience his progress directly. Instruction based on performance gives him a chance to improve, and the assessment data give him the opportunity to see his improvement.

The key here is how well each teacher scorer or rater understands the criteria in the scoring guidelines, or rubric. One way to ensure that we apply the criteria consistently through the class is to make the criteria as objective as possible. We know that writing is an art, but even art can be exposed to judgment, and the judgments can be objectified. In drawing, for example, we achieve a sense of depth by using overlap. We can assess the quality of a second grader's drawing by counting the instances of overlap in a given picture intended to achieve a sense of depth.

But, you might say, suppose the young artist, for art's sake, made the trees one-dimensional lollipops on purpose? Good for her, and shame on us if we didn't tell her before she began the drawing assessment that the trees are to look as much like real trees as she can make them. She wanted ambiguous shadowing? Good for her, but not during assessment of her ability to use objectified drawing skills.

We can also objectify writing assessment. We can count words. We can count sentences and divide the number of words by the number of sentences to find sentence maturity. We can count clause structures and divide by the number of sentences to find sentence maturity. We can count mechanical miscues. We can score the writing with a 4 if the organizational system is clear, unambiguous, and logical and a 1 if it is not.

It's no less possible for, say, beginning fifth graders to write in a basically literate manner than it is for them to know how to divide. We assess the arithmetic understandings and behaviors associated with division, and we teach them. If we assess the literacy understandings and behaviors associated with basic literacy, and teach them, we'll get the basic literacy.

And then there is the art. We want voice, and voice has certain characteristics that can be counted. Count the number of times you sense passion and the extent to which the writing reveals the writer. Or at least notice such attributes of voice and give the paper a 6 if they're present and clear, a 2 if they're only murky, and a 1 if they're nonexistent.

Good writing is creative. We know what creativity is and what it looks like. When young writers use metaphor, they're thinking flexibly. Count the metaphors. When they ponder in their writing, when they speculate about what can or ought to be, they're thinking curiously. Count the musings or speculations. Their details indicate elaboration; count the elaborations.

Alma writes of her wonderful Thanksgiving dinner—the people, terrific food, and feelings. She writes of her holiday celebration just as her classmates write theirs. But Alma ends her piece with a caution because she knows of a man on the corner, a man she sees every day, who won't eat a warm meal this evening because he doesn't eat a warm meal on any evening. Alma is the only writer in the room whose writing includes such a caution. Her paper is unique in the room in that regard. Uniqueness is called originality. Originality is a creative thinking skill. Alma gets an originality point.

If we know what creativity looks like, we can assess its appearance. If we confuse creativity with wizards and blue smoke, it can't be part of an assessment system. We think creativity should be part of an assessment system. We know it can be defined, assessed, and influenced by instruction.

If assessment processes are to be effective, they have to be sufficiently clear so that scorers or raters know the criteria. Their judgments regarding the criteria must be applied evenly, even objectively, from writer to writer. Then the only question left to answer is what the assessment process can look like in our classrooms.

REVIEW AND REFLECTION

1. An assessment system in writing must contain the clearest definitions possible of the patterns of good writing.
2. The patterns of good writing must be sufficiently reflective of good writing that if young writers' performance features those patterns, they will be scored as good writers. In other words, the indicators must be valid attributes of good writing.
3. The patterns of good writing in the assessment system must not only predict good writing performance, but the assessment system itself must also be predictable. By that is meant that the system works the same way every time. It must be reliable.

Five Writing Assessment Systems

There are a variety of purposes and audiences for writing assessment, and writing assessment systems for each of them. Parents want to know how their children are doing, but what teachers need to know, parents probably won't use. What the general public wants to know is not sufficiently specific to satisfy parents, and it has almost nothing to do with instructional guidance. If we satisfied teachers, parents, and the general public, we'd still ignore young writers themselves. There are many assessment purposes and audiences. Here we look at five writing assessment systems that satisfy the various purposes and respond to various audiences.

Analytic Assessment

An analytic writing assessment system rests on "the underlying premise that if we are to teach students to write, we must define the components of good writing" (Spandel & Stiggins, 1997, p. 33).

Earlier in this chapter we discussed seven attributes of good student writing on which several sources of information seem generally to agree:

1. Clear, precise, and mature sentences
2. Recognizable organizational pattern
3. Conventional use of mechanics
4. Fluent idea generation
5. Precise word selection characterized by the right word for the right reason
6. Form that reflects function
7. Presence of a writer's voice and passions

Using these attributes, we can begin to construct an analytic assessment system.

Remember that looking at the seven attributes for assessment purposes does not suggest ignoring whole student writing. Analytic assessment rests on Spandel and Stiggins's premise that if the whole is to improve, the components of the whole have to be identified, measured, and taught. We explored that premise in the discussion of how assessment criteria must reflect good writing (valid criteria) and how the assessment process must be predictable (reliable use of criteria).

An analytic assessment system is best suited for teachers' assessment and instructional needs. That is not to say that the general public wouldn't understand analytic information or that parents wouldn't value it.

Let's say that a second-grade teacher wants to increase the children's ability to write compound sentences (because the teacher knows that students will need these more complex structures to express their increasingly mature thinking), reduce the gap between temporary and conventional spelling, and get as much black on white as possible (develop fluency). It is appropriate, then, for analytic assessment in that second grade to begin with three criteria measured three times during the year.

During the first month of school, the second graders wrote a teacher-cued writing sample on which they worked for ten minutes just before recess. First, they drew and painted a picture of their house. Then for the ten minutes allotted, the teacher asked them to "write as much as you can as well as you can" about their picture. They had no help as they wrote their sample.

The student record for this first month lists each student's name. Jean heads the list:

	Student Record Sheet		
Name	**Number of Words**	**Number of Compound Sentences**	**Percent Words Spelled Correctly**
Jean	19	0	58

Jean wrote 19 words (about 2 words per minute) during the ten-minute writing. She wrote only simple sentences, and she spelled 11 of the 19 words correctly (11 ÷ 19 = 58% correct). Jean's performance looked a lot like that of nine other second graders in the class.

The teacher works with Jean's group, teaching compound sentence thinking and writing, and fluency. He also works especially hard with Jean's group on words they think of when they write (see Chapter 14 for more about that spelling principle), spelling them in their compound sentences, and including them on the special Word Wall in the classroom writing center.

At the end of the third month of school, the teacher assesses his students' writing again. This time he includes the use of end marks in sentences because it has been a problem and he has been emphasizing it heavily. Therefore he adds end punctuation errors to his chart:

Student Record Sheet

Name	Number of Words	Number of Compound Sentences	Percent Words Spelled Correctly	Number of End Punctuation Errors
Jean	27	1	78	2

Jean wrote more words in the same allotted time (ten minutes) than she did on the previous assessment. One of her sentences was a compound structure. She spelled 21 of the 27 words correctly (78 percent), and of her four sentences, she failed to use an end mark twice. She made good progress in fluency, compound sentences, and spelling. There will be more instruction in those areas in the next two months, along with an emphasis on end marks. Part of the teacher's instructional time in writing will include increased attention to generating ideas and getting them written down. It's clear that the teacher had specific expectations for his students' writing performance, and he built his analytic assessment around those expectations.

The point of explaining a prototype analytic assessment and instructional plan in a second grade is not to dictate what second-grade teachers should emphasize. It is to show the relationship between analytic assessment and instruction. *The key is to select attributes of good writing that you want to establish this year, assess to see how well your students use them, organize writing instruction time to increase students' expertise with those criteria of good writing that you value, and assess again to document their progress as young writers (and yours as their teacher).*

In an eighth grade, analytic assessment might well have different emphases. Ms. Atkinson's fourth-period middle school English class prepares a writing sample on Thursday of the first week of school. She tells her students they are to write as much as they can as well as they can about something complex they have learned during the past six months. She allots ten of the forty-seven minutes in the period for them to write their sample.

Ms. Atkinson's objective this year is not only to increase fluency, sentence maturity, and mechanical control, all at the level of early drafts, but also to connect form with function when form is not dictated. That is the reason for using the cue as she did. Her students are free to format however they please, as long as they explore something they have learned.

Most of these eighth graders write 8 to 10 words per minute (185 divided by 10 minutes), with sentences ranging from 9 to 12 words (number of words divided by number of sentences). They tend to write simple sentences of reasonable length, but they do write multiclause sentences—about one in five to one in three (number of clauses divided by number of sentences). When Ms. Atkinson counts clauses, a simple sentence counts as 1, a complex sentence as 2, and a compound sentence as 2. The mechanical error rate is very high for her eighth graders: nearly two per sentence (number of errors divided by number of sentences).

Finally, these students aren't very good at making form serve function. Hector, who is fairly typical in this class, wrote a simple description of how he learned to ride a skateboard down a railing. His description was relatively clear and direct. It read the way all of his other schoolized writing reads: beginning, middle, and end, each section implicitly labeled, the writing entirely devoid of its purpose: to show that Hector is an expert at this complex skill. When assessing form and function (F/F on the following record sheet), Ms. Atkinson uses a 1–4 point scale, with 4 being highest. Here's Hector's line on the Student Record Sheet:

Student Record Sheet

Name	Number of Words	Words/ Sentence	Clause/ Sentence	Error/ Sentence	F/F (1-4)
Hector	185	10.6	1.3	1.9	2

Ms. Atkinson reserves two hours a week for writing instruction. In the next several weeks, she focuses on basic mechanical conventions for the sixteen students who need a brush-up, and compound and complex sentences for everyone whose ratio was under 1:3 (fewer than one multiclause sentence out of every three they write). But she will commit most of her instructional time to how they can use various genres to communicate their ideas and experiences. They will write about something they have learned in the past six months, and they will write it in five different forms: short fiction, autobiographical incident, poetry, report of information, and technical report. They will also write an actual historical event in story grammar format and a report of information as an informal letter to a close relative. Then she will assess again.

The value of analytic assessment systems is that they provide information about how young writers write, as measured and judged against criteria associated with teacher-selected standards of good writing. And that information about each student's writing has direct implications for subsequent instruction, the influence of which can be assessed later. Analytic assessment results can be recorded through the year, organized at the end of the year, and presented to parents on an individual student basis. These results can also be aggregated for reporting to a whole class, site administrators, district personnel, members of the board of education, and the local media. When we assess with valid standards of good student writing and teach to the needs revealed by the assessment results, students progress in the direction of better writing. We have a responsibility to report progress to parents about their own children and to the general public regarding larger groups of students.

Primary Trait Assessment

Primary trait assessment systems focus on attributes of effectiveness regarding impact on an audience. Spandel and Stiggins (1997) describe primary trait scoring on the basis that "writing is done for an audience and successful writing will have the desired effect upon the audience, mainly due to the impact of the primary, or most important, trait within the piece of writing" (p. 31). For example, writers write biographies to reveal something about an individual. They choose to write about a particular person for a specific reason. The primary trait of a biography is that it provides information about an individual in a way that shows why he or she is interesting or important, that by some measure the person's life is significant.

Primary traits are therefore specific to the purpose of a given piece of writing. The general purpose of all writing intended for an audience other than the writer is to influence that audience. Remember that the reading audience brings its prior knowledge to the print and constructs meaning (comprehends) through an interaction between the text and the prior knowledge, which includes what readers know about the nature of text itself. Thus, when readers read short fiction, they know that it will be organized according to their sense of story grammar. They expect to find character, setting, problem, and resolution. If the short fiction is to work, it has to satisfy readers' expectations with respect to story grammar.

Each genre has a purpose, each purpose accommodates readers' expectations, and the extent to which readers' expectations are satisfied is directly related to writing having the writer's desired effect on an audience. Reports of information are very different from short fiction, for example, and maturing readers know the difference. It is the adroit implementation of the primary trait of a piece of writing that ensures impact on its audience. Primary trait assessment, then, is directed at young writers' implementation of primary traits.

Primary trait assessment is better suited for use with other assessment systems rather than alone. If Mr. Vizcarra is teaching reports of information, it is certainly important for him to assess his students' ability to organize their writing to reveal and explain the question, the information, and the conclusion or summary. *The primary trait of reports of information is effective organization and presentation of information in response to the key question.* But his students may be able to organize and present the information reasonably well, perhaps at 4 on a 1 to 6 scale, but their basic literacy may be 2 on a 1 to 6 scale, and their voice 1 on a 1 to 6 scale. Assessment of the primary trait in reports of information doesn't necessarily give a sufficient image of student writing.

The fact that primary trait assessment may not provide a sufficiently large picture of student writing does not compromise its usefulness. Consider a third-grade teacher using primary trait assessment.

Ms. Young teaches third graders, and one of her missions in writing instruction is to ensure that when her eight year olds leave her room, they will have written enough reports of information (six in all) to write them properly and not fear them when they are assigned in later grades.

She begins early in the year with a writing project in social studies. Each third grader selects one of forty U.S. presidents for whom she has accumulated biographical information that third graders can read. She asks the students to think of some things that might be interesting to know about the president they selected. She distributes the basic social studies writing activity sheet that they will use throughout the year. The sheet shows five items:

Report of Information

1. What is your question? What information did you decide might be interesting to find?

2. Where did you look for your information? What did you do to get what you found?

3. What did you find out about your question(s)?

4. What else did you find out about your topic?

5. What can you conclude from your study?

A response to each item on the writing activity sheet can be written in one or two sentences. When the children are finished writing their project, they have a report of information that features the genre's primary trait: an organized way to present information on a topic.

The next report of information begins two weeks later. The students read about animals they learned about from the book *Animals Nobody Loves* (Rood,

1971), and they complete the writing activity sheet to record what they learned in response to the questions they formed.

In the middle of the third month of school, they begin their third report of information, but this time they do not use the writing activity sheet. The writing activity sheet is now displayed as a chart on the wall in the Writing Center, and Ms. Young directs them to write their report according to the chart, but in their own words and on their own papers.

During the year, they also complete two biographical reports of information, a report on geography, one on endangered species, one on a question that centers in some way on the more than two hundred Indian reservations in the United States, and one on community helpers.

Ms. Young begins her primary trait assessment with the third report of information. She gives 3 possible points each for items 1, 2, 3, and 5 (3 × 4 = 12), plus 2 possible points for item 4; and 2 possible points for general impression (16 possible points). Students who score below 10 receive small group direct instruction on how to think in each of the items on the chart and individual coaching as they write the next report. It is a rare third grader in Ms. Young's classroom who does not master the organizational structure and writing style, the primary trait, of reports of information.

The task is to identify the primary traits of the various kinds of writing in which young writers engage in school. This is a judgment, but most of us know what we want when we assign a piece of writing. We know the critical attribute that is central to a piece of writing. In Chapter 10, there are descriptions of what makes effective writing in each genre. Those descriptions are useful in identifying primary traits.

Holistic Assessment

Holistic assessment systems view "writing based on a general impression, usually represented by a single score" (Dahl & Farnan, 1998, p. 113). The underlying assumption is that whole pieces of writing reflect the interactions among the various aspects of a written piece, so scoring takes the whole into account. Holistic assessment takes two different forms, as Spandel and Stiggins explain (1997).

Focused Holistic Scoring

Usually holistic assessment is based on a rubric. When each criterion (mechanical control, for example) is broken out on a scale of 4, 5, or 6 points, the term is *focused holistic scoring*.

A focused holistic scoring rubric might be based on the seven attributes of good student writing that opened this chapter or selections from among the seven.

If mechanical accuracy were one criterion in a holistic assessment rubric of five criteria (selected from among the seven above) and the rubric were based on a 4-point scale, the mechanical accuracy portion of the assessment might read as follows:

> **Mechanical Accuracy**
>
> 4 points: Free of distracting mechanical errors
>
> 3 points: Few mechanical errors, and those that appear are typical of what good writers may commit, even after editing
>
> 2 points: Frequent mechanical errors, some of which are sufficiently distracting that the reader must read several times to achieve the writer's meaning
>
> 1 point: Many mechanical errors of such distracting quality that portions of the writing are difficult to understand

Raters would consider the mechanical accuracy of the writing as one part, along with four other criteria (perhaps numbers 1, 2, 5, and 7), each broken out as mechanical accuracy is shown above. The assessment provides separate scores that reflect each of five criteria. For example, let's say a third grader wrote a report of information and scored a 3 on mechanical accuracy, 3 on organization, 2 on word selection, 3 on clear and mature sentences, and 2 on form and function. We know this students' overall score is 2.6 (13 ÷ 5)—just under a 3 on a 4-point rubric. We also know that she needs work especially in areas of word selection and on the form of her writing serving the purpose or function.

General Impression or Holistic Scoring

The following rubric is similar to those widely used in statewide writing assessments. Statewide writing assessment rubrics typically range in point values from 4 to 6. This 4-point rubric is designed for middle-level assessment:

> **General Impression Holistic Rubric**
>
> 4 points: The writing is clear, focused, and interesting. The organization of the writing helps move the reader through the piece in an orderly manner. There is a sense of writer voice in the writing that comes through in word selection and varied sentence structures. There are no, or very few, errors in conventional writing.
>
> 3 points: The writing is clear and focused, but it may not be very interesting. There is an apparent organizational structure, but it is either artificial or weighted down with some irrelevant detail. Word selection is ordinary, and sentence structures lack variety, so the writer's own voice is hard to detect. There may be several surface errors, but they do not interfere with the reader's ability to understand the writer's message.
>
> 2 points: The writing includes basic detail without development. There may be an apparent attempt at organization, but the ideas lack a sense of wholeness. Vocabulary is limited and/or inappropriate to the task, and the sentence structure is simple. Mechanical errors may make understanding difficult.

> 1 point: The writing lacks a focus or purpose. Organization is not apparent at all. The vocabulary is limited, and sentences are choppy or rambling. There are non-sentences, and numerous mechanical errors severely compromise readers' ability to understand the piece.

Typically raters are extensively trained to use a rubric using sample, or *anchor*, papers. Raters compare the paper they are rating with other papers that have already been scored, called *exemplars*. In scoring fifth graders' papers on a 4-point scale, for instance, there would be four papers: one an example of a 4, one an example of a 3, one an example of a 2, and so forth. Raters are trained using papers that other raters have already scored. Raters score sample papers, compare their ratings with the exemplars, and discuss how they arrived at their scores. The objective is that, over several ratings, raters will begin to score papers very similarly. After the training, two raters score each paper, and in cases where there is a disparity greater than one, a third rater scores the paper. In that case, the final score can be figured on either of two bases: the average of the three raters or the score that occurred more than once.

Holistic scoring is used heavily in large-scale, high-stakes writing assessments at the state and national levels. The single score is easy for everyone to understand, and the process is efficient and relatively inexpensive. It is not uncommon, for example, for experienced raters to score papers in one minute or less and to need a third rater with fewer than 10 percent of their ratings.

When holistic scores are posted, their value has a certain understandable internal logic. That is, there's a sense that a score of 4 on a 6-point rating system (6 is high) is a shade better than average even without seeing the scoring rubric. A score of 5 would be better, and a score of 6 as a class average would be very good, but some people would suspect that it probably reflects raters who were too easy in their judgments. If the class average were 2, there might be concern, especially if this were the only class in the district that averaged under 3.

But what of the teacher? Let's say the average score in a classroom is 4 on a 6-point scale. The printout sent to the teacher shows that the class average is 4, five students scored 6, and eight scored 2 or less. The teacher does not need to be reminded that 2 is not good, 4 is okay, and an average of 5 would be better. Moreover, what does the teacher know from the scores for each student and the average about what to teach, and to whom, when, and how?

The teacher knows he needs to increase the scores in the room, especially those of the eight students who scored under 2. He knows who those eight students are. What does he do for them between now and the end of the school year? What does he do for the several who scored at 4 to move them to the next level? Does he know what he did to get those who scored 6 to where they are on the scale?

The lack of specific instructional implications is a shortcoming of holistic scoring. Holistic scores, even while looking at the rubric or exemplars on which the scores are based, do little to inform teachers about what to teach, to whom, and when. Even with the rubric right there, the teacher has only a general score that lumps criteria together in the rubric. He doesn't know if one child's score of 4 is high because she focused on the prompt effectively or because her paper is organized clearly. Nor does he know if the student didn't get a 5 or 6 because raters didn't understand her organization or found her errors distracting.

Focused holistic scoring tells a bit more because the criteria for good writing are separated, and each one is given a score. That gives the teacher a more specific look at students' strengths and areas of need.

Every scoring device, every rating system, and every measuring instrument has its proper use. Calibrated glass tubes are good for determining body temperature, but they don't work well for measuring linear distance. Tape measures are better for determining linear distance but useless at determining how well a person can hear. IQ tests can make predictions of school success, but they don't explain intellectual prowess. Reading achievement tests provide a sense of how well large numbers of students read, not whether they do. And holistic assessment of writing is good for getting a sense of where large numbers of young writers fall along a short scale, but they don't explicitly inform teachers about what to do next.

Portfolio Assessment

The problem with any assessment procedure in writing is that it is applied to only one piece of writing, and any writer, both novice and experienced, can, on any particular day on any particular writing task, write less well than she is able. Virtually everyone agrees that one snapshot is not an accurate image of anyone, whether it is one picture on one driver's license or one writing performance in response to one prompt.

A better way to determine the quality of young writers' work is from collections of their work. A writing portfolio is a purposeful, integrated collection of student writing that demonstrates achievement, or progress, and effort (Paulsen & Paulsen, 1994) and makes teachers and students partners in assessment. Portfolios can bring assessment in line with instruction and allow teachers to monitor young writers' progress over time on the basis of many indexes of writing rather than one or even several. They also allow teachers to engage young writers more directly in conferences about progress and effort and provide regular feedback throughout the instructional year.

Portfolios take a variety of forms. Standardized portfolios contain specifically determined pieces of writing collected at predetermined intervals or writing samples selected by teachers and students for assessment. The formal assessment of writings in a portfolio is usually conducted by the teacher on the basis of a rubric, perhaps a 4- or 6-point rubric similar to others we've discussed in this chapter. Portfolios so judged are prepared specifically for the purpose of assessment.

There are as well portfolios that contain, just as formal portfolios do, collections of student work and self-assessment inventories, but these portfolios are more closely aimed at being catalysts for teacher-student interactions. They provide a basis for discussions about what young writers were trying to accomplish with each piece, what the young writer thinks about the piece, what the student thinks she or he could do to improve the piece, and what kinds of plans or goals the student has for improvement before the next assessment conference.

Portfolios can represent a place for young writers to keep their writing. At the end of the month, young writers organize their portfolio, provide a contents page, and rewrite their best pieces so they're legible. Then everyone fills out a self-evaluation form and puts it in the front of the folder. The teacher reads through the portfolio, makes comments, and suggests ways to strengthen it in preparation for open house.

Portfolios are for authentic assessment. The authenticity comes from young writers' having a choice in selecting what is included for writing assessment, selecting what they will write about, having as much time as they need for the writing, and making their own judgments about how well they've written to the prompts they have selected for the audience they have identified.

When portfolios are used for in-classroom assessment, their value for teacher and students is easy to discern. If portfolios are used for assessments across classrooms, or if portfolio assessment were to be used to show the writing abilities of fifth graders throughout a district or state, it would be critical for the assessment system to satisfy questions about validity and reliability.

Reliability of Portfolio Assessment

Herman and Winters (1994) reported on eighty-nine studies associated with portfolios between the mid-1980s and mid-1990s. They found only seven reports in which portfolio assessment was both reliable and valid. Their review led them to describe four factors that can ensure high reliability:

1. Specific and clear criteria associated with development and evaluation of the portfolio. In other words, it must be clear what selections are to be part of the portfolio, how they are selected, and under what conditions the selections were prepared or written.
2. Sufficient time set aside to train teachers for portfolio development and scoring.
3. Assessment guidelines or rubrics that everyone understands and values.
4. Raters who have an expert understanding of student writing performance. This is very important because scoring from one paper to the next cannot be reliable if scored by an untrained eye. Without training, the scoring is subjective and useless for assessment purposes.

Validity of Portfolio Assessment

The other question is whether portfolio assessment measures or evaluates the attributes of writing that we think it is measuring or evaluating. To establish the validity of portfolio assessment, scores from portfolio assessment are compared with scores on the writing samples from other assessments. Herman and Winters (1994) reported on a Vermont study that found a weak to moderate correlation between two sources of writing scores for the same students. Gearhart, Herman, Baker, and Whittaker (1992) found almost no relationship between portfolio ratings and scores on more standardized measures of writing ability.

The data regarding the validity and the reliability of portfolio assessment are at best weak. Thus, this assessment, from a measurement perspective, does not enjoy much credibility, especially as it may be used to compare students' performance or progress across classrooms. Inside the classroom, as long as the teacher is consistent from student to student, the authenticity that characterizes portfolio assessment makes it useful as *an* element in a teacher's larger assessment system.

Teachers' experiences with portfolio assessment and research on it leave us with several recommendations regarding planning for and using portfolios for writing assessment:

- Structure the content of writing portfolios to match the objectives of the assessment. If the assessment is designed to compare all fifth graders in a school, for instance, the portfolios in all the fifth grades would have to contain examples of the same kind of writing, submitted on the same schedule, and written under the same conditions.

- Ensure that portfolio raters have access to the conditions under which portfolio entries were assigned and written. If some students had help with their writing and others did not, that difference affects raters and ratings. If some teachers' expectations for writing performance are dramatically different from others', or if some teachers allot more time than others for the writing, the difference can affect ratings.

- Make the goals and performance criteria clear to both students and teachers. Everyone must understand the procedures and purposes and how those will be judged.

- Be sure that teachers and students collaborate on what pieces will be selected for assessment. Teachers can help students make selections that are representative of students' ability and fit the standards for the assessment.

Portfolio assessment shows great promise because of its value in bringing teachers and young writers together in a collaborative effort that includes both instruction and feedback. The portfolio assessment process makes young writers partners in the assessment of more authentically written pieces. Student attitude toward assessment is enhanced when they are a part of the process (Johnson, 1995).

Before portfolio assessment results can be used for comparative purposes outside the confines of single classrooms, the process must be carefully evaluated for reliability and validity.

Self-Assessment

The only way for young writers to be engaged fully in their writing is for them to have a hand in every procedure, every decision, and every portion of their learning and performance. Their connection with their literacy development can be strengthened when they participate in selecting what they write, when, and for what audiences. We value students' ownership of their writing when we identify and encourage their own writing processes. And we encourage young writers' responsibility for excellence when we make them part of the assessment process.

Writer self-assessment occurs in formal inventories, through rubric development, and in informal conferences. One day years ago we observed Donald Graves, one of the prime movers in the writing instruction field in the last two decades, in a simulation of a student conference. He sidled up to a participant and asked, "What are you trying to do here in your writing?" (*Think about your purpose, your agenda, your own sense of what the writing is to be about.*) Then he asked, "Where are you now?" (*Okay, young writer, you know what it's about and why you're doing it. So how is it working? It's your writing; how's it going?*) Finally, he asked, "What do you think you have to do now?" (*So what's the immediate agenda within what you've already told me is your long-range purpose?*)

Within the conference, the teacher has a chance to help young writers clarify purposes, audiences, and immediate objectives. The teacher can also suggest ways to satisfy those purposes and objectives and answer questions that come up only because young writers are thinking directly about *their* writing on *their* terms. In general, however, the power of the conference is self-assessment because young writers look more carefully, or perhaps for the first time, at what they are trying to accomplish, what their progress looks like, and what they have to do to get to where they want to get. The teacher is guide and counsel for young writers who are doing the self-examination.

Boyle's (1996) self-assessment investigation was at the opposite end of a continuum from Graves' informal conference. Boyle hypothesized that if her fourth graders better understood the assessment criteria, they would write better. She targeted persuasive writing for her investigation, in which her students were directly responsible for collaborating with her on rubric development and for using the rubrics to score their own and their peers' papers. She also looked at the relationship between teacher evaluations and student evaluations when both used the same assessment rubric.

In Boyle's classroom action research, two fourth-grade classes wrote five persuasive pieces, the first and fifth as pre- and postsamples used for comparison within and between groups. In the treatment class, young writers collaborated with their teacher on the development and use of holistic assessment rubrics designed for persuasive writing. The children used those rubrics as they wrote, assessed, and rewrote their persuasive pieces. In the control class, young writers wrote, received teacher feedback, both oral and written, and participated in conferences with the teacher. They also rewrote their pieces on the basis of teacher feedback. They did not participate in rubric development, nor did they use the rubrics to assess their own writing.

Boyle's findings revealed significant differences between the treatment and control groups. The treatment students' postwriting scores were significantly higher than those of the control students. Clearly students who participated in developing scoring rubrics and learned to use them in self-assessment wrote better persuasive pieces. Another of Boyle's findings is instructive regarding young writers' ability to self-assess: when students in the treatment class and other teachers in the school scored a set of writing samples, students and teachers agreed on 83 percent of their scores. Obviously students had learned to be astute in their assessment of persuasive writing.

Boyle's students' development and use of rubric assessment was highly structured and systematic, in contrast to Graves' relatively informal self-assessment conferences. What they have in common is that both engaged young writers in taking responsibility for the quality of their own writing performance and processes. Graves did it with informal inquiry and guidance. Boyle did it with formal rubric development applied to students' writing. In both cases, young writers had a stake in judgments about their own writing. That is an essential part of young writers' development that self-assessment can promote. *The instructional value of assessment is in feedback for teachers and young writers. Teachers need the feedback to inform planning and teaching. Young writers need it as a guidance system.*

Boyle's investigation and its instructional implications point to the value of making young writers part of the process of planning and conducting assessment. The fact of participating seems to influence young writers' performance. The same dynamic occurred in a study of writers' workshops (Farnan & Fearn, 1993), where the investigators found that the feedback young writers received in workshop sessions began to influence their thinking when they were alone writing new pieces. Clearly feedback functions as a self-monitoring device.

Self-Assessment Inventories

Self-assessment can take on still a different appearance. The following self-assessment inventory, designed as a catalyst for conversation between teacher and student about writing, gives the student an opportunity to think about the writing first so the conference can be fully productive (Fearn & Foster, 1979). This inventory was completed by sixth-grader Bridget, whose responses are shown in italics:

Self-Assessment Inventory

Give yourself approximately 30 minutes to complete this inventory. Think carefully about each item. Read your paper several times, and concentrate on what you think works well and what does not work as well as you would like. Remember, self-assessment is for your benefit. Your teacher may use your self-assessment inventory as a guide for a writing conference with you, or you may just put the self-assessment in your writing portfolio and compare it with another you may do at a later time. The purpose of this self-assessment is to make sure you are part of the assessment process in writing.

1. What is the title of the paper you are assessing? _The Chrysanthemums_

2. Did you write as well on this paper as you are able to write? Did you spend enough time to write as well as you can? _I don't think this critique of the story is the best, and I didn't take enough time to make it as good as I could. I only did a rough draft with not very much revision._

3. What is the strongest characteristic of your writing in this paper? _I think I saw what Steinbeck wanted his readers to see. His message came through easily for me. I think I wrote his message clearly._

4. What is the weakest part of your writing on this paper? _The grammar. I didn't do this paper carefully enough to make it correct, but I think my meaning came through anyway. But maybe some readers would have to read some of it more than once because I didn't make it correct._

   If you have any questions about the strengths and weaknesses of this paper, write them for discussion in a conference. _I'm never sure where the paragraphs are supposed to stop and start. I'd like to know if I did it right on this paper, and if I did, why. If I could understand where the paragraphs are supposed to be, I could do it right all the time. I just make them where I think they are, and I can never remember how many sentences they're supposed to have. But I know about main ideas._

5. In one sentence of not more than 20 words, write the main idea of this piece of writing. Write in one sentence what it's about. _I tried to write John Steinbeck's message in a way that my readers would understand it._

6. Show on the scale how well you think you accomplished the purpose you wrote in number 5 above.

Totally Successful	(Mostly Successful)	Not Sure	Mostly Unsuccessful	Totally Unsuccessful

Write a sentence about what you think you might do to make the writing better. *I'm not sure. I could make it more correct, but I can't know if I really did write Steinbeck's message so readers would understand it until someone reads it and tells me. But I think the reader should know that I understand the symbolism in the story.*

7. Would you like to have a conference with your teacher about this piece of writing? *Yes* Would you like to use this self-assessment in the conference? *Sure* Do you ever talk with anyone else about what you are writing?

Whenever I write, I talk it over with my father.

Such a self-assessment inventory is useful because it makes young writers part of the assessment process, and that by itself is valuable. In addition, the inventory can be used in conjunction with other assessments in writing. For example, at the same time you conduct an analytic assessment, young writers could do a self-assessment, and then the two assessments could be used together in a conference. That way, young writers can compare their perceptions of their writing with assessment data, and any disagreements could be a topic of discussion in the conference. Furthermore, as Boyle (1996) found in her study, as young writers work with their teachers in the assessment process, both partners' assessments tend to become increasingly similar. Assuming that teachers are on the right page, it's good to have teachers and students on the same page.

REVIEW AND REFLECTION

1. All assessment systems are designed to inform.
2. Assessment systems in writing must inform teachers regarding instruction. Assessment in writing must inform teachers about what to teach, to whom, and, perhaps, how.
3. All assessment systems feature specific criteria for quantifying or judging writing performance. Both kinds of assessment systems are useful.
4. The criteria in writing assessment systems can be as objective as tallies and ratios or as subjective as rubrics that ask for judgments.
5. We select assessment systems to satisfy the need for information and the audience for whom the information is needed.

Grading and Assessment

Many teachers have to make judgments about their students' writing, perhaps every week, and report those judgments on a periodic schedule. The process begins early in students' school careers, so young writers sometimes become so accustomed to teacher judgments that these judgments become confused with teacher permission. Many students are unable to write until they have their teacher's response to the question, "Is this okay?" The question means, "Is this what you are looking for?" Their writing is no longer, if it ever was, for their own communication in writing. The purpose for writing becomes satisfaction of the teacher's wishes.

Writing to satisfy the teacher's wishes doesn't occur because teachers assess young writers' writing performance and offer feedback and guidance during conferences. It occurs because a system of teacher judgment and reporting dominates writing in school. It isn't the *writing* on which young writers focus. It's the *grade*.

The grade is the scheme teachers use to tell young writers how well they have satisfied the teacher's expectations for the student's performance on the teacher's writing task.

Teachers' Concerns About Grading

Many teachers are troubled by the requirement that they assign grades to student writing. Their concerns are reflected in their questions. Over a period of several years, we collected teachers' questions about grading. There were thirty-four questions that we determined were sufficiently different one from the others to qualify as *separate* questions. After thirty-four, every question was mostly like ones we already had.

The thirty-four questions clustered into eight categories, shown here in order of the frequency of questions in each category. The number of questions in each category is noted in parentheses. (The frequencies do not add to thirty-four because several questions fit more than one category.) We've provided two questions that best exemplify each category:

1. Grading Variables (11)
   - What is the most important part of a writing to grade?
   - Is it better to give two grades for writing: content and mechanics?
2. Grading Standards (8)
   - Should grades be a subjective evaluation based on a student's current ability, or should grades reflect a standard based on the expectations of what students should be able to do ?
   - What can I expect from second [third, fifth, ninth] graders?
3. Grading Process (6)
   - Should I inform students of the prompt and the grading criteria before they write?
   - How can I be consistent in my grading of student writing?
4. Grades as Motivators (4)
   - What do we tell parents about "effort" grades when the parent doesn't see any significant progress in the child's writing? [This question could also be placed in an eighth category called "Communicating with Parents."]

- Should we ever boost grades for borderline students?
5. Grading the Products (4)
    - Should we grade rough drafts or only final products?
    - How do we decide which of the many writing projects are worthy of grading?
6. Grading Criteria (2)
    - If poor mechanics are not necessarily an indicator of poor writing, at what point is a student held accountable for mechanical correctness?
    - In the third grade, should I be concerned with content, mechanics, and neatness on a piece of writing? If all three are important, how do I distribute the points for each one to come up with a grade?
7. Portfolios (1)
    - How do I give a grade when portfolios are the only measure of progress?

The frequency of questions in each of the categories reveals that teachers have three major concerns about grading: what to grade, standards for grading, and grading processes.

Clearly teachers are concerned about what variables to include when they grade, and that concern focuses primarily on the relationship between content and mechanics. Teachers suspect there is something very important about a young writer's grade that transcends mechanical control, but teachers also know, perhaps intuitively, that how young writers handle meaning markers, sentence structures, and spelling is important as a grading variable. Teachers are very concerned about how to handle that relationship.

Many teachers feel they have resolved the ambiguity and are quite passionate about their resolutions. A review of the NCTE Talk e-mail listserv archives (http://www.ncte.org/lists/ncte-talk/archives.html) shows teachers' questions, other teachers' answers, and many teachers' passions regarding how the grading conundrum should be solved.

Teachers are also focused on standards for grading. They know that not all young writers are equally able. At the same time, they appreciate a measure of consistency of standards, if not uniformity, when they're faced with evaluations of student performance. It's a dilemma that concerns teachers greatly.

The third most frequently asked questions about grading from our investigation concern how the grading process is conducted. Many teachers think procedurally. It's an artifact of the professional life.

Grading Versus Assessment

There is an intuitive relationship between grading and assessment. It seems reasonable that good writing will receive a high score in just about any assessment process and will also earn a high grade. And it therefore seems to follow that poor writing will be shown to be poor in a good assessment system and will receive a poor grade. The trouble with intuition is that it often suggests inappropriately simple relationships between complex things, and the inappropriate simplicity makes the relationships wrong.

That's the way it is with the relationship between grading and assessment. In fact, grading and assessment are very different in purpose and audience. They're similar, at best, only because grading *can* be a subset of assessment. *If* young writers know the process and the criteria ahead of time, and *if* they have a role in how the process and criteria were determined, and *if* they have a role in how the assessment data are used in the grading process, *then* assessment data can be useful as a source of information for grading purposes.

Let's assume these conditions are met for a third grader. Analytic assessment data that show a young writer's sentence and mechanical performance well below reasonable expectation *for that child* could be *part* of the calculations and judgments the teacher makes about that child's grade on a report card. Assessment data therefore *can* feed into the mix on the basis of which the teacher assigns a grade. But to figure some sort of scale that equates writing sample assessment data to a grading scheme both trivializes the assessment and equates the two when they're clearly designed for different purposes and audiences.

Consider the audiences first. Assessment information is primarily for teachers. It tells teachers the instructional needs in the class: which students need what kinds of instruction. That sort of information is of little value to parents and the larger public. When assessment information is aggregated to show achievement trends throughout a district or state, or even the nation, it is useful to parents and the larger public but not at all useful for grading purposes. Of course, sometimes aggregated assessment data are used to "grade" schools, districts, and states, but that sort of grading isn't what parents look for when they open a report card and expect to see how their fifth grader is doing in writing. The audiences are different, and their needs are different, so the two processes, assessment and grading, rarely serve both audiences.

Now look at the reasons for assessment and grading. We assess student performance in writing programs not only to inform teachers about instruction, but to communicate with the public about how well students write. The public has a right to follow the achievement development of students in its schools. Assessment determines how well students are doing, and when those data are presented properly, they keep the public informed.

Grading, on the other hand, has nothing at all to do with the larger public. In fact, it's none of the larger public's business how well a certain student writes. Furthermore, were we to share assessment information in this book, we could do so to our heart's content as long as we shared generic data; but if we wanted to single out one boy named Kenneth, we'd have to have his parents' agreement on file. What Kenneth does is private and the business of Kenneth and his parents alone. We communicate with Kenneth and his parents through a grading system.

We communicate with the larger public with generic assessment data. Kenneth's parents may find those data useful as well. They might want to know how their son's grade is related to the trends. They have a right to visit Kenneth's teacher to pose the question, and Kenneth's teacher should be able to show Kenneth's performance in the context of his peers. But that conversation is for Kenneth's parents, not the local newspaper.

Grading and assessment are not the same. They exist to satisfy different purposes and inform different audiences in different ways. Grades tend to be situation-specific judgments based on classroom-level criteria. Assessment is more objective, and it often speaks to unnamed audiences far beyond the boundaries of one classroom. It also provides information that informs instruction and gives teachers and students feedback about performance. Assessment information could be used in a grading scheme, but typically, the relationship between grades and assessment data has to be determined one young writer at a time.

Principles of Grading in Balanced Writing Instruction

It is impossible to make a list of prescriptions for grading young writers' writing. All teachers have a plan that they invented in order to answer the kinds of questions in the categories that began this section on assessment and grading. Because grading schemes are unique to individual teachers, no list of prescriptions can accommodate individual needs. Nevertheless, we can make suggestions for what to include in your thinking when you develop your own grading scheme:

A grading scheme identifies what will and will not be graded. What will be graded: Journals? Short fiction? Weekly reports of information? Autobiographical incidents? Perhaps your young writers will be working out of a portfolio that contains many unfinished pieces, and after the first month of school, you have a rule that one finished piece must be turned in for a grade every Thursday, so the students get to choose what will be graded. Part of the grading scheme is a system for *what* will be graded.

A grading scheme reflects a value system about what constitutes good writing and is ability-appropriate. Values for third graders' writing aren't the same, or shouldn't be the same, as those for tenth graders. In developing a grading scheme, it will be useful to return to the performance criteria early in this chapter to see how representatives from those seven criteria can be calibrated to serve the grading needs at a particular grade level.

There need to be performance criteria within that value system. If the grading scheme values organization, it must identify what the organization looks like. That may be as general as a high grade when short fiction includes each of four attributes of story grammar believably tied together and resulting in a plausible ending. It may be as specific as a book review in a certain number of paragraphs, each paragraph having a dictated number of sentences and each sentence fulfilling a specified role in the paragraph. If organization is a value in the scheme, the scheme has to include what organization means.

The grading scheme should accommodate teachers' capacities, as well as their expectations. Teachers can make their own determination of what will be graded. Suppose a teacher decides that everything she assigns should be graded. If the students are writing under teacher direction as much as they must if they're to learn to write well, every week they're working on as many as four or five pieces of writing and finishing as many as two or three. This teacher needs to do some simple arithmetic (average number of pages per piece of writing, number of pieces turned in each week, and time needed to read the average piece) to determine the work load of reading these pieces.

With respect to expectations, remember that we're more likely to get what we inspect than what we expect, so the grading scheme should *inspect* what we *expect* from our students. If, for example, we expect students to revise their work, we should grade (inspect) each successive draft. If we expect mechanical correctness, include mechanical correctness in the criteria. In the primary years, we don't want fluency compromised by students' inability to spell the words. In that case, grade for fluency and the quality of their temporary spellings, and as young writers become increasingly skilled, narrow the range of acceptability in their temporary spellings while continuing to pay off for fluency. If it's in the grading scheme, it's more likely to appear in the writing. Each appearance in the writing is an instance of practice, and practice makes permanent.

Consideration of teachers' capacities should also include what students learn from the grading and, given that, how many grades they need for full benefit. A formal reading and grading scheme can ensure that young writers have their teacher's attention on regular occasions. The attention, of course, is on their writing, and it also occurs in conferences. If young writers deserve at least one of those events each week, they need to prepare one piece of writing for teacher reading and feedback each week. We know of no evidence that shows greater achievement in writing when students receive two grades per week rather than one, or three rather than two.

A grading scheme should include plans for engaging both parents and young writers in the development of grading criteria and performance standards, thus informing both about how the grading plan will work. Young writers need to know the grading criteria and performance standards for which they're striving. And when parents know the grading criteria and performance standards, they're in a better position to work with the teacher in advancing young writers' literacy.

In short, a grading plan includes the following components:

- The kinds of products that will be graded
- The grading criteria and performance standards
- The teacher's realistic capacity to read and grade, which limits the number of grades that are feasible per week
- Ways to engage young writers and their parents in the development and operation of the grading scheme

REVIEW AND REFLECTION

1. What are some ways to make certain an assessment system will guide instructional planning?
2. How can an assessment system inform a grading system?
3. With a partner, make a list of at least three attributes of what you agree constitute good writing at a selected grade level. Then identify a way to assess student performance on those attributes so that the assessment information is useful to the students' teacher for instructional planning.
4. If writing were a fundamentally creative activity, what attributes of creativity do you think apply to writing, and how could they be assessed?
5. Make an argument for teachers being the major source of criteria for good writing. Make an argument for experienced writers being the major source of criteria for good writing. How could you use both sources at a grade level of your selection?

A Summary: Grading in Balanced Writing Instruction

Assessment of writing performance has to satisfy several audiences. One of those audiences is teachers; their needs can be satisfied only by information that is relevant to the classroom. Writing assessment information, or data, therefore must be teacher-useful. Assessment must produce information that teachers can understand and use for instructional planning.

Writing assessment is based on criteria for what constitutes good writing. A variety of sources of information can be useful in determining those criteria. In this chapter, we used practicing writers, the literature on writing and writing assessment, and the realities that teachers and students face in school. From those sources, we identified seven criteria of good writing.

No one form of assessment can satisfy all audiences. Analytic assessment seems the best design to satisfy a teacher's needs because it yields data that can be immediately translated into instructional implications at the level of individual students and whole groups. Broader, rubric-based assessment systems that produce less complex scores are better suited for large-scale assessments that monitor generally how well students write at certain grade levels. There are clear procedures for designing all kinds of writing assessment systems.

The matter of grading invariably comes up when anyone discusses assessment in writing. It is important to emphasize that assessment and grading serve different audiences. Grading speaks to students and their parents. Assessment speaks to teachers and the larger public. Grading and assessment have different purposes as well. Grades serve to show students how their performance compares with others on a range from unacceptable to excellent; assessment shows how young writers' performance compares with criteria of excellence. Sometimes assessment information can be useful as one item among many in a grading scheme. But teachers must remember that the two systems are different in important ways.

No one should mistake an assessment system for a writing program, but no one interested in constructing an instructional program in writing should ignore the place of assessment in the plan. It is no less important to have a serious assessment component in a writing program than it is to assess students' performance in a reading program.

PART III

Interactions: Teaching Writing and the Language Arts

13 Writing-Reading Interactions

BEFORE YOU READ

- What is meant by the term *literacy set,* and how is it related to a child's early literacy development?
- How does writing influence reading, and, conversely, how does reading influence writing?
- What is the value of the writing-reading interaction in Book Clubs?
- What kinds of writing-reading interactions best support students' learning across the curriculum?

This chapter takes a look at writing-reading interactions and examines how they support and promote children's development as literate citizens. Entire books have been written on reading-writing connections (e.g., Heller, 1995; Nelson & Calfee, 1998), and it would be impossible to explore the subject fully in one chapter. The purpose of this chapter is to provide an overview where, as in the rest of the book, the focus is on the concept of *interactions*—specifically on how writing-reading interactions promote students' literacy development. Notice that speaking and listening are woven throughout as we highlight their purposeful interactions with reading and writing. The emphasis here is on the word *purposeful.* Becoming a fully literate human being requires development of listening and speaking skills, as well as the more high-profile skills of reading and writing. In this chapter we describe how writing and reading interact and in that interaction support young learners' development of skill and expertise in all the communication arts and in learning across the curriculum.

Developing a Literacy Set

Throughout the crucial years of early literacy learning, children develop what Holdaway labeled a *literacy set* (1979, p. 49). Although he coined that term over twenty years ago, it's a powerful concept that still applies. His concept of a *literacy set* refers to being psychologically set, meaning that an individual has "an ability to tune in with appropriate action" (p. 49). In the case of literacy development, this means that children have the enthusiasm, confidence, and skills to make use of print and incorporate it into their lives in a variety of ways. This is not the same concept as what in the past was called *reading readiness*, a phrase that implied there was a time of "unreadiness" that preceded "readiness."

The concept of literacy set does not mean that at one moment children are not ready for literacy, but at another time they will be. On the contrary, a literacy set develops over time, through a child's accumulation of experience with and knowledge of language and its uses.

A Closer Look at Elements Associated with a Literacy Set

This section of the chapter describes the four components of a literacy set: *language factors, print factors, discourse strategies,* and *imaginative operations.* Language factors refer to understanding the sounds and structures of language and the central role language plays in our lives. Print factors relate to learning about letters, words, and text, and includes learning how print differs from speech. Discourse strategies involve understanding structures of texts, such as fiction (i.e., story grammar) and expository text, and communicating through these structures in oral and written language. Finally, imaginative operations refer to a reader's active application of the imagination as a critical part of meaning-making.

Language Factors

By approximately six months of age, children replace their babbling and cooing sounds with the sounds of the native language in which they are immersed. Before that, they can distinguish and produce speech sounds from all spoken languages (Kuhl, 1993). However, as the months pass, their range of sounds begins to narrow to those in their native language. That sound system is called the *phonology* of language; the smallest significant units of sound are called *phonemes,* sounds represented by vowels and consonants.

Children also learn about the order and structure of their language. Every language has a structure for conveying meaning. In English, meaning units occur in *morphemes. Cat* is a *lexical* (word) *morpheme,* a meaning-bearing unit of language. *Bound morphemes* are units of sound that must be attached to other meaning units—for example, the prefixes *re-, un-,* and *pre-* (e.g., *replace, undo, preliterate).* Inflectional endings are also morphemic elements of language, small units of language that carry meaning (e.g., -*es* and -*ed).* When morphemes are put together to form larger units of meaning, they form words and sentences.

There are also syntactic structures that represent the word order of English sentences. Consider these four words:

puppies   four   dalmatian   rambunctious

Order them in a way that you think makes sense. Then decide why you created that particular word order. You might want to share your order with a partner to see if the two of you agree. Chances are, if that person is operating according to syntactic structures in English, you will.

Did you say "four rambunctious dalmatian puppies"? Most people do. Why? The answer is that those of us for whom English is our native language learned about word order in English before we were actually conscious of language learning. Did you come up with why you put the words in that order? Did you use a particular rule? If your answer is no, you're again with the majority of people, because there are no rules that specifically address this particular order. Generally in English, adjectives are placed before what is described, so it makes syntactic sense in English for *puppies* to be placed last. But why *rambunctious* before *dalmatian*, and why place *four* before *rambunctious*? The answer is that that's the way we use the English language. It follows the tacit rules of word order in English. We can describe the word order, but that doesn't mean we have a rule by which we learned to sequence the words. The example highlights the fact that we don't learn all there is to know about language use through rules. Much of it we learned at a very early age, auditorily, through immersion in language.

The study of *linguistics,* defined as the science of language, encompasses many elements of language study. Phonology and syntax are two. There is also *semantics*, which relates to the meanings we attach to language, including understanding subtle variations and shades of meaning. For example, knowledge of semantics allows us to understand the difference between a mansion and a bungalow. Both words denote a place to live, but they are very different places.

Another area of language study is *pragmatics*, the use of language in real-life situations to communicate a speaker's meaning. It involves speech as well as body language, and the conventions of communication such as turn taking and effective ways to segue to another topic (i.e., change the subject).

The objective here is not to provide a course on basic linguistics, but to make the point that there are many facets of language that children learn early in their lives, given that they are born into and exist in a world of language.

Print Factors

While children are immersed in a world of speech from birth, the world of print is quite different. Imagine you were seeing a book for the first time. Think of all the things you would *not* know: how to hold the book, what the marks on the page mean, and where to look first in order to begin making sense of what you see. Children learn a great deal through their early experiences with print—for example:

- There are letters.
- Letters come together to form words.
- There are spaces to mark boundaries between words.
- Some marks are not letters but are, instead, meaning-bearing conventions of print, such as commas and periods.
- Letters come in different sizes (capitals and small letters), and that difference has meaning.
- Letters map to sounds (the phonetic principle) in ways that are often predictable.

In their literacy set, children develop a complex repertoire of expectations for patterns in print with its various conventions (e.g., capitalization, punctuation, spelling) and how it differs from the language of speech. Many of these expectations are the result of children's early writing experiences (more on this later in the chapter).

REVIEW AND REFLECTION

1. What is the difference between the concept of reading readiness and the concept of a child's emerging literacy set?
2. Choose one of the language factors, and explain its role in a child's developing literacy set.
3. What would you expect to see in a classroom that supported children's developing knowledge about language and print factors associated with a developing literacy set?

Discourse Strategies

Discourse strategies are also related to a child's developing literacy set. *Discourse* is defined as oral and written communication larger than a sentence (Harris & Hodges, 1995). When we talk about discourse strategies, we're talking about how to make meaning in conversations and from running text. This includes how to make meaning from context and how to make inferences or fill in the gaps with meaning as we read.

Stories and Story Grammar.   In the case of stories, readers must understand the story grammar, which includes the sequencing of events and ideas that make up the plot, as well as the concepts of setting, problem, resolution, and characterization. Most children come to school with some concept of story, based on their early experiences with storytelling, listening to stories being read, and even watching story lines unfold on television.

We cannot, however, assume that all children understand the grammar of stories. Story grammar activities can help children actively reflect on story elements and therefore make explicit that which might not be so clear for some children.

INSTRUCTIONAL SCENARIO

In the Classroom with Story Grammar

Mr. Calloway has just finished a read-aloud of *Alexander and the Terrible, Horrible, No Good, Very Bad Day* (Viorst, 1980) to his third-grade class. He has a deep and dramatic voice, and the students love to hear him read. He has read this story many times over the years, and his voice modulates perfectly to capture Alexander's exasperation and upset over this "no good, very bad day."

Teacher: Before we begin reading, boys and girls, I have a question for you. How many of you have ever had a bad day? [Almost all the children raise their hands.] All right, I'd like you to get a picture in your mind of what made the day bad. [After a couple of seconds, he continues.] I'm going to give you two minutes to write two sentences that tell what made it bad. [Mr. Calloway's students are used to writing in the class, and when he says, "Begin!" they all begin writing. He walks around the class and peers over students' shoulders. He sees that James has written, *My friends and I were playing ball in the street. I threw the ball and it went through my next door neighbor's window.*] James, in a minute will you please share what you've written?

James: Sure.

Teacher: Just a few more seconds. Finish the idea you're writing, and I'd like to hear from some of you about what you've written. [He calls on James first because he knows that James has a good model of two sentences telling about his bad day. James reads.] Okay! James has read two sentences that tell about his bad day. Who will read next? [Elisa raises her hand.] Elisa, read about your bad day.

Elisa: *I fell off my bike and hurt my knee.*

Teacher: That's one sentence that tells us about your bad day, Elisa. What else could you add in a second sentence? [Elisa has that brow-furrowed-I'm-thinking look on her face.]

Elisa: *I hurt my shoulder too.*

Teacher: Oh, that was a bad day! *I hurt my shoulder too* could be your second sentence. Would you read both of your sentences for us?

Elisa: *I fell off my bike and hurt my knee. I hurt my shoulder too.*

COMMENTARY

Mr. Calloway calls on a couple of more students and then asks them to sit back and think, as he reads, about what makes Alexander's day so bad. Mr. Calloway likes to read this book aloud because his students can relate to Alexander's predicaments, and the story's resolution is both positive and realistic. Also, the story line is simple to follow, and the language is clear but sophisticated enough to take readers inside Alexander's head as his day unfolds. Mr. Calloway reads, and then begins his follow-up activity that focuses on the story grammar.

RETURN TO THE CLASSROOM

Teacher: Now I want you to think about the story, about Alexander, and about what finally happens in the end, but instead of all of us discussing the story together, I'm going to put you into groups to talk about it. I'm going to give each group an overhead transparency with a story frame on it. Your job in the group is to talk about the story and complete the sentences so they tell us about it. Each group will choose a recorder to write on the transparency, and every person in the group needs to be ready to come up and share what the group wrote. I'll call on one person in each group to do that. [Mr. Calloway assigns students to heterogeneous groups of three or four students and hands out the transparencies and pens.] All right, boys and girls, I'll give you seven minutes to talk and write.

FOR THE READER

The transparency looks like this:

This story is about _____. It takes place _____.
_____ is a character who _____. The problem in the story is that _____. One thing that happens is that _____. Also, _____. The problem is solved when _____.

RETURN TO THE CLASSROOM

Teacher: I see that most of you are just about finished with your story frames. I'll give you two minutes to finish, and then I'll ask the first person to come up and share what the group has written. [After two minutes, Mr. Calloway calls on Risa.] Risa, would you please bring your group's transparency up to the overhead projector and read for us what your group wrote?

Risa: _This story is about_ Alexander. _It takes place_ in his house and at school. _The problem in the story is that_ Alexander is mad because bad things happen to him. _One thing that happens is_ Alexander gets gum in his hair. _Also,_ he doesn't get dessert for lunch, and his friend does. _The problem is solved when_ Alexander goes to bed, and his mom tells him that people in Australia have bad days, too.

Teacher: Thank you, Risa. Melinda, let's hear from your group next.

Melinda: _This story is about_ Alexander. _It takes place_ at school and at the dentist and at the store. _The problem in the story is that_ Alexander has problems and keeps getting in trouble. _One thing that happens is_ he gets a cavity in his tooth. _Also,_ his mom got mad at him but it wasn't his fault. _The problem is solved when_ his mom tells him that some days are bad, and Alexander goes to sleep.

Teacher: Thank you, Melinda. [To the whole class.] Did Risa's group and Melinda's group say exactly the same things on their story frame?

Students: No.

Teacher: Did they both tell us what the story was about?

Students: Yes!

Teacher: How do you think Alexander feels when his mother tells him that "some days are like that, even in Australia"? [Risa raises her hand.] What do you think, Risa?

Risa: I think it makes him feel better.

Teacher: Why is that, Risa?

Risa: Well, everybody has bad days, and that makes Alexander feel better. One time I had a bad day, and my mother told me that she had a bad day too. She said we'd both feel better if we had some ice cream, and it did make us feel better. She said tomorrow would be better, and it was.

COMMENTARY

Notice that Mr. Calloway's students are adroit at turn taking and that they respond directly to one another during the discussion. From the beginning of the school year, Mr. Calloway has worked to show his students how to function as effective contributors during classroom discussions. He has the following conversation stems posted in his room and encourages his students to practice using them in discussions. He calls this Thoughtful Talk. Mr. Calloway knows how important it is for children to develop their oral language and listening skills, both of which are necessary for Thoughtful Talk.

Thoughtful Talk

I agree with you because _____.

I think it's important to remember that _____.

I disagree with you because _____.

I'd like to add to what _____ said.

I think _____.

I wonder _____.

I noticed that _____.

I think _____ because _____ reminds me of _____.

I like _____ because _____.

I'd like to say something else about _____.

I think _____ is important because _____.

FOR THE READER

When you first try the story frame activity, we recommend that you complete a story grammar activity with the class as a whole. You can have the frame on a transparency and solicit student input to fill it out. This provides a model for when you ask children to do this activity on their own. Then try the activity in pairs or small groups. Here's one you could use with the whole class:

This story is about _____. In the story,
_____ is a character who _____.
This character _____. The problem in the story is that
_____. What happens is that
_____. The problem is solved when
_____. In the end _____.

Story frames can also be designed to address specific story grammar elements. For example, the following frame focuses on setting:

This story took place _____. The author describes
the setting by telling about _____. The author helps me
get an image of the setting by describing _____.

The next frame focuses on characterization:

In this story, _____ is an important character. This
character is important because _____. Two words I
would use to describe this character are _____ and
_____. If I could talk to this character, I would say
_____.

E S L Children enjoy collaborating as they complete the story grammar activities, and the collaborations are particularly effective if there are children in the class who are learning English as a second language. They can participate in the oral discourse of planning answers for the story grammar activity, and they can provide oral input to the process. In this way, they are included in the thinking and talking about a story and its elements, but they are not solely responsible for producing the written response for the activity. ■

MORE COMMENTARY

The children, as they did in Mr. Calloway's class, will have slightly different ways of talking and writing about the story grammar of a particular story. That's all right because, as Mr. Calloway pointed out to his class, there is more than one way to talk and write about the ideas embedded in a story grammar. In the classroom, we can celebrate students' various ways of presenting ideas. This is one of the ways we can honor the individual differences among students' ways of thinking and articulating what they know. If students express ideas that are inaccurate, we can work with them to find out where the misconceptions or misinterpretations came from, and then work with students to discover what might be a more appropriate interpretation, based on what's in the text.

Children also love to take the role of "speaker" or teacher and share their expertise with their teacher and peers. That's why Mr. Calloway's use of the transparency is so effective. Children are focused on the task; they discuss the story elements and how best to articulate them; and they are motivated to complete the story grammar so they will have an effective presentation. While students are working, the teacher walks around the room, clarifying when necessary and collaborating with students as they work to present their ideas.

Working with Expository Texts.   The structure of expository (explanatory) texts is different from the grammar of stories. Expository writings, such as technical manuals, textbooks, and essays, contain patterns that writers use to help them explain their ideas. These informational texts are written in discourse that includes the following common patterns: linear sequencing through enumeration (first, second, third, next), listing, cause and effect, comparison and contrast, and problem and solution.

Here are examples of various expository patterns from the Houghton Mifflin seventh-grade social studies text, *Across the Centuries* (1991):

- Enumeration, from a lesson titled "Mohammed and Islam"

The Sunna were the guiding rules for Islam and were based on the way the prophet Mohammed lived his own life. The most basic of these rules were the Five Pillars of Islam. The ideas behind these five duties came from the Koran, but it was in the Sunna that the leaders of Islam set them down.

The first of these pillars is the profession of faith. (p. 63)

This six-paragraph section of text titled "The Sunna" enumerates and describes the five pillars of faith.

- Listing, from a lesson titled "The Mongols"

There are several reasons for the Mongol successes. They had outstanding leadership, military skill and, most important, horses. On horseback, the Mongols could advance up to 200 miles a day. (p. 162)

- Cause and effect, from a lesson titled "Europe at the End of the Middle Ages"

During the years before the plague, the population of Europe had more than doubled in size. Because the agricultural techniques of the Middle Ages were fairly crude, farmers had trouble growing enough food for the large population. Then disaster struck. Unusually heavy rains fell during the years from

1315 to 1319, causing the farmers' grain to rot in the fields. Thousands of people starved to death. (p. 311)

- Comparison and contrast, from a lesson titled "The Italian Renaissance"

During the late Middle Ages, the government of Italy was different from those of other countries in Europe. In France and England, for example, strong central governments were forming. However, at the beginning of the Italian Renaissance, Italy was made up of about 250 small states. (p. 317)

- Problem and solution, from a lesson titled "A New Order of Ideals"

Parliament wanted the colonists to pay a share of the expense from fighting the Seven Years' War with France. The colonists disagreed. Since they were British citizens, they reasoned, they should not be taxed unless they were represented in Parliament.

Convinced that their rights were being violated, the colonists made a bold decision. In 1776, they decided to reject British rule. (p. 482)

These are just a few examples of the text structures used in expository or explanatory writing. Effective adult readers use text patterns automatically to help themselves comprehend and recall informational material, but children often read informational texts without tuning in to the ideas being presented through the various text structures. These structures are organizational plans for conveying information, and when readers are not aware of the organizational structures or plans, the specific focus of the text can be lost or, at best, can be unclear. In fact, after reading an informational text, children are often unable to recall much of what they have read, and the ideas they do remember may not be very important to the topic (Hidi & Anderson, 1986). Fortunately, teaching students about text structures and, in addition, using writing to support learning (a topic we'll discuss later in this chapter) can result in better comprehension than when children have no such instruction (Taylor, 1992).

Begin with awareness. Draw students' attention to the way in which writers explain ideas through the various text patterns. Discuss with them how these patterns help readers understand the ideas. Students at an early age should become familiar with informational texts. There are many available on a wide range of topics, and children often are more intrigued by informational books than by story books. Five-year-old Kevin's response is not unlike that of many other young children. When asked what books he likes best, he replied without hesitation that he likes books on fish and sharks (he explicitly mentioned both) and dinosaurs. To quote Kevin: "I love dinosaurs!"

If you know children who love dinosaurs, we recommend authors Aliki and Gail Gibbons. Aliki has written several books for primary children: *My Visit to the Dinosaurs, Dinosaurs Are Different*, and *Digging Up Dinosaurs*. Her books take children to excavation sites and museums where workers are assembling dinosaur bones to recreate imposing skeletons. Gail Gibbons' book *Dinosaurs* uses bright colors to highlight these creatures, and children become well versed at tripping the long, complicated dinosaur names off their tongues. (This is not so surprising. These are the same children who learn to say *refrigerator* at a very young age.)

Seymour Simon is a well-known science writer who creates highly accessible texts full of scientific information. He has not only written *The Smallest Dinosaurs* and *The Largest Dinosaurs*, but he has also written over one hundred texts for children on such topics as aerodynamics, icebergs, time, and astronomy. For upper elementary and middle school students, his Einstein Anderson: Science Sleuth series is especially intriguing. Einstein Anderson is a young boy who solves mysteries, some in the classroom and even on the school bus, through the application of scientific principles. The stories are short and make especially effective read-alouds.

It's important to remember that the most powerful predictor of reading comprehension is prior knowledge. Children with absolutely no prior knowledge about a concept will struggle to understand what they read or what is read to them. Given sufficient prior knowledge and the opportunity to become familiar with expository texts, they can become increasingly adept readers of the challenging nonfiction materials they encounter as they move up the grades.

REVIEW AND REFLECTION

1. Why is it important to introduce expository writing to children at an early age?
2. What two to three objectives would you have for a lesson that focused on story grammar?
3. How does being familiar with patterns of expository text help children's comprehension?

Imaginative Operations

Holdaway includes this factor in his concept of a literacy set, and we think it represents an important element in literacy learning. He states that children with a highly developed literacy set "have learned to use imagination in powerful ways." He comments that "knowing how to operate imaginatively is learned behavior, and highly complex learning at that" (1979, p. 55). Language is symbolic. The word *table* is not a place where we sit and have breakfast. Meaning occurs not in the letters and words on a page; it occurs in the mind of the reader. Readers must create images and concepts based on meanings that only they can generate from a reading. Sometimes print does seem to convey very literal and concrete information. If I write, *The sky is blue,* it's difficult to misunderstand the meaning. However, the word *blue* is a color only because the connection is in the reader's mind. Also, depending on our prior knowledge and experiences, we might see a vibrant, bright blue Arizona sky, while someone from Los Angeles might envision a light blue sky seen through a slightly brownish-gray veil of haze.

Rosenblatt (1978) describes readers' meaning-making interactions with text in this way. She calls the text a blueprint for meaning and uses the concept of a transaction to describe the relationship between reader and text. It is in this transaction that reading, meaning reading comprehension, occurs. Readers bring their experiences and prior knowledge to a reading, and the text provides a blueprint on which readers construct meaning.

In her *transactional theory,* Rosenblatt explains that the purpose for reading literature is to have a primarily aesthetic experience. She describes this as having a lived-through experience in the reading—an experience in which a reader "must decipher the images or concepts or assertions the words point to," but at the same time pay attention to "the associations, feelings, attitudes, and ideas that these words and their referents arouse within him" (1978, p. 22).

Rosenblatt uses a continuum to describe two purposes for reading. At one end of the continuum is an *aesthetic reading,* and at the other end an *efferent reading.* The word *efferent* comes from the Latin verb *efferre,* meaning "to carry away." When we read, for example, directions on a medicine bottle or steps for programming the VCR to tape a favorite television show, we are reading for information. If we read the scientific report of information by renowned conservationist John Muir on a little bird found in the Sierra Nevada foothills, the water thrush or ouzel, we are also informed. We carry away information about this bird and its habitat. However, Muir's writing also helps us see this little bird. Muir takes us into the foothills and into the world of the water ouzel (Moffett, 1985) for a lived-through experience that the writer's imaginative language offers. He writes,

> The waterfalls of the Sierra are frequented by only one bird—the ouzel or water thrush. . . . He is a singularly joyous and lovable little fellow, about the size of a robin clad in a plain waterproof suit of bluish gray, with a tinge of chocolate on the head and shoulders. In form, he is about as smoothly plump and compact as a pebble that had been whirled in a pot-hole. (p. 350)

You might wonder how a report of information could be considered an aesthetic reading, a term seemingly reserved for literature. The answer is that Muir's writing is, in fact, a good example of nonfiction literature. Cullinan defines literature as "all instances in which language is used imaginatively" (1989, p. 8). Muir uses descriptive language that includes delightful imagery. He uses personification ("clad in a plain waterproof suit") and figurative language, such as the simile, "he is about as smoothly plump and compact as a pebble that had been whirled in a pot-hole." Muir uses sensory language that allows us to see the ouzel's size, shape, and color. Notice that the power of the language is not in strings of adjectives; it's in the imagery and figurative language. It's as though we're on a bird-watching expedition, peering at the ouzel as it frolics in the streams of the Sierra Nevadas. It's imperative that children learn that reading can be an imaginative journey, a personal journey that is much richer than what anyone else could create for them.

How can we help children develop their imaginative operations? One way might be to ensure they learn how their imaginations can help them "see" what's in a text. Ms. Martin, in her third-grade classroom, shows us what that might look and sound like.

A read-aloud engages students. Elizabeth Crews

INSTRUCTIONAL SCENARIO

In the Classroom with a Read-Aloud

Teacher: The book for our read-aloud today is *Elbert's Bad Word* [Wood, 1988]. I hope you'll like this book as much as I do. I never get tired of reading it! Before we begin, take just one minute to write what you think this book will be about. [Students reach for the Classroom Log that sits on the corner of their desk. It's a personal record of learning situations that is never very far away from them because they use it for writing throughout the school day.] Someone, share what you've written. [Students raise their hands.] Grace, read your sentence.

Grace: *Elbert gets in trouble because he says a bad word.*

Teacher: How many of you wrote something similar to what Grace wrote? [About half the students raise their hand.] Tyler, you wrote something like Grace. What did you say?

Tyler: *Elbert said a bad word and his mother got mad at him.*

Teacher: Those are good predictions. Did anyone have something different from either Grace or Tyler? [Eugenia raises her hand.] What did you write, Eugenia?

Eugenia: *Elbert was afraid to say a bad word because he didn't want to get in trouble.*

Teacher: Yes, that's a little different idea, isn't it? Boys and girls, set your Classroom Logs aside for now, and we'll come back to them later. Right now, I want to tell you that this book is about a party. How many of you have been to a party? [All the children raise their hand. Several enthusiastically wave their hand, wanting to talk about their party.] "Oh, I see lots of you have been to parties. This book is about a different kind of party. It's called a garden party. That means it's outside, kind of like a picnic, but people are dressed up in their best clothes. They are eating deviled eggs and drinking spritzers, a cold drink adults sometimes like to drink, and they are playing a game called croquet, played with a wooden mallet that looks a bit like a large hammer. The objective of the game is to hit wooden balls through little wire arches in the ground. Waiters, called butlers, are serving food to the guests in the garden, and everyone is having a good time eating and listening to a singer and music played on an oboe. [Ms. Martin shows a couple of pictures that depict the guests and the butler serving food.] But then something happens. Let's find out what it is. Oh, yes, boys and girls, this is very important. When I read, I won't be showing very many pictures. I want you to listen and get images in your own mind that let you see what's happening in the story.

COMMENTARY

Ms. Martin reads the story. She's well rehearsed and has to glance only occasionally at the page. As she reads, she pulls her students into the story with her eye contact, voice, and gestures. Occasionally she stops to clarify a word or ask a question. For example, when the text says, "When Aunt Isabella sang opera in soprano," Ms. Martin asks what an opera is. A student queries, "A song?" Ms. Martin responds that an opera is a song that tells a story, like a musical, and it's usually sung in Italian. She continues reading, wanting to clarify ideas that she anticipates might perplex her students, but not wanting to violate the rhythm and flow of the story.

BACK TO THE CLASSROOM

When she finishes the story, she asks a few extension questions, such as, "Why did the bad word go away? How did Elbert feel at the end of the story, and why do you think he felt that way?" She then continues, "Boys and girls, did you see in your mind that bad word, that dark, ugly, hairy word?" The children nod. Yes, they certainly did! "I'd like you to take out your Classroom Logs and draw the bad word. Then we'll all share what our bad words look like."

Children immediately get busy with paper, pencils, and crayons. They can hardly wait to show how ugly that bad word is. Ms. Martin gives them about ten minutes to draw. When their teacher says, "All right, let's see your bad words!" the children are excited to share.

COMMENTARY

Only after the children "ooh" and "ahhhh" over the bad words they're drawn does Ms. Martin show them the pictures in the book, including Audrey and Don Wood's depiction of the bad word. She knows from experience that many of the images the children create will be far hairier and scarier than the ones in the book.

Notice that before Ms. Martin begins reading *Elbert's Bad Word*, she engages her students in predicting what they will read. It's not sufficient for students to have prior knowledge about a text; they must actively tie what they know and have experienced to a reading. Because she knows this, Ms. Martin asks her students to write what they think the story will be about because the writing-reading interaction provides a powerful impetus for cognitive engagement.

She also lets her students know how much she likes the book. She wants to model for students her enthusiasm for books and reading, and one way she does this is to let them know that books are very important to her.

After hearing students' predictions, she orients them to a part of the story that she anticipates may be unfamiliar to them, a garden party, and introduces concepts that might be unfamiliar, such as an oboe and a butler. She has several specific purposes for reading *Elbert's Bad Word* to her students: it has a rich and sophisticated vocabulary; it introduces students to new concepts, such as the "elegant garden party"; and the theme or "big idea"—that Elbert was able to find a better way to display his anger than using the big and ugly bad word—is one Ms. Martin believes is an important topic for classroom discussion. Also, it gives her a perfect opportunity to work with her students on the concept of the power of using their imaginations during a reading. She wants her students to learn that imaginative operations are critical for a full reading and that their imaginations can be filled with exciting and interesting images when reading.

FOR THE READER

Ms. Martin completes a planning guide, which helps her reflect on the read-aloud. She wants to ensure that she will make the most of the experience for her students. Her plan looks like this:

Planning a Read-Aloud

Text: Elbert's Bad Word

Objective(s) for the read-aloud

1. To introduce students to new vocabulary and new concepts
2. To discuss the theme of anger
3. To encourage students to use their imaginations to understand the story

Preparing students for the reading (activating prior knowledge)

1. Ask students to predict in writing what they think the book will be about and ask them to share their predictions.
2. Ask students to share descriptions of parties they've attended. Compare their experiences to the concept of an elegant garden party.
3. Introduce new vocabulary words, such as *oboe, butler, spritzer,* and *croquet.*

Words/phrases/ideas to highlight during the reading (may include questions to ask)

1. What is an opera?
2. Why does Elbert go to see the wizard gardener?
3. What makes the bad word go away?

Follow-up to the read-aloud

Ask students to draw pictures of the bad word and share their pictures. Finally, show the bad word as it's illustrated in the book.

The Influence of Writing on Reading

Writing and reading are not identical literacy processes. In some ways they are similar (e.g., both use language to construct meaning) and in other ways quite different (e.g., one uses existing print; the other requires generation of print). They are, however, complementary language processes, each supporting development in the other.

Research by Marie Clay on the Writing-Reading Interaction

Marie Clay, who coined the term *emergent literacy* (1966), noted the writing-reading interaction when she observed that "writing plays a significant part in the early reading progress" (Clay, 1975, p. 70). Writing involves retrieval of information in order to produce text, and Clay notes that "if a child knows how to scan, how to study a word in order to reproduce it, and how to organize his writing of that word, he has the skills to deal with the detail of print" (p. 71). In their production of print, children develop the following skills and abilities:

- How to attend to print
- How to organize their thinking to explore print forms
- How to tell left from right
- How to analyze letters and sounds visually
- What is important in a word that helps a writer reproduce it
- How to organize one's behaviors to carry out a specific sequence of movements

In other words, Clay noted, "In the child's early contact with written language, writing behaviours seem to play the role of organizers of reading behaviours. . . . [These behaviors] appear to help the child to come to grips with learning to attend to the significant details of written language" (1975, p. 3).

In Chapter 14 we describe the phases of children's early writing development, particularly as they relate to young writers' emerging understandings of sound-letter correspondence and how that is displayed in their spellings. When teachers collect children's writing samples over time, those samples show children's development as they gain control of the conventions of written language.

Two and three year olds "write" for the pure joy of creating shapes and colors. Between the ages of approximately three and five, children become aware that those marks have meanings of their own and that people make them on purpose. Three-year-old Savannah has written what she calls her shark teeth alphabet:

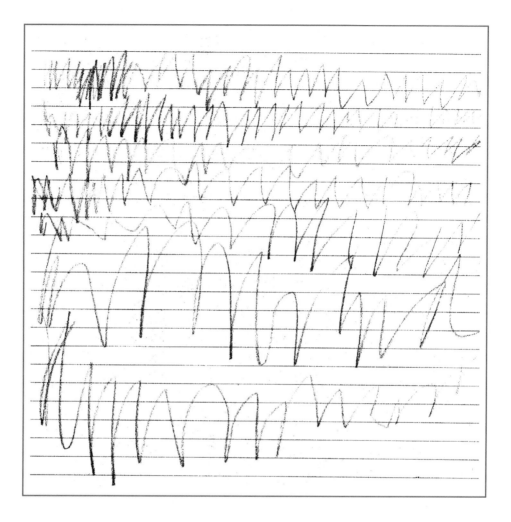

A child's own name is an early sign that he or she is making purposeful meaning. When children begin writing their name, we know several things about their literacy development (Clay, 1991). We know they realize that writing makes messages and that those messages are made of marks placed in a particular order representing a specific pattern of letters. Here's how Gavin, a first grader, writes his name:

At these young ages, children aren't aware that grownups can't read what they've written. Early writing is often a written form of what children speak. However, as they become more aware of the need for their writing to communicate on its own, they begin to pay more attention to the conventions of print that make it generally understandable. Gavin clearly knows some of those conventions. He has learned letter spacing and letter formation, two writing behaviors that place heavy attentional demands on the early writer. As children gain experience in the production of print, certain skills become automatic, which allows them to focus on other areas of development.

Children may try to trace over what a teacher has written under their drawing. While we cannot assume, unless we're observing, that the tracing occurred left to right and that such an activity by itself will teach left-to-right production, it represents an early exploration of letters and their shapes. Children may also try to copy what the teacher has written. In this way they learn to attend to features of letters, discriminate between letters and words, figure out how to space and write on a line, and control shapes (Clay, 1975).

In the following principles of writing, Clay (1975) describes the print factors that emergent writers focus on in their writing development:

Copying principle. By copying words, children are working from the assumption that there are some words they already know.

Flexibility principle. Children experiment with letters and words to show their increasing understanding of print.

Recurring principle. Children often create repetitive sentences to show that they can repeat letters and words when they write.

Directional principle. When children begin to sequence letters one after another on a line, they are beginning to show their understanding of left-to-right directionality, critical to reading and writing. Sometimes children begin at the wrong point on a page, called mirror writing. This may be consistent with their understanding of left-to-right movement, but they simply begin at the wrong place. They begin at the right, then go downward and left.

Space principle. Children's development in both reading and writing reinforces that words are separated by spaces.

Generating principle. Children learn that writing is more than creating delightful marks and shapes. With experience in reading and writing, children learn that those marks, formed in certain ways, make meaning.

Inventory principle. Clay observed that children often pay attention to their own learning in a systematic way. For example, five and seven year olds may systematically make a list of all the words they know or write all the letters they know.

Research by Carol Chomsky on the Writing-Reading Interaction

In the 1970s, about the time Marie Clay was doing her work on early literacy in New Zealand, Carol Chomsky was studying children's early literacy development in the United States. The work of both of these eminent researchers resulted in some similar conclusions about the writing-reading interaction.

Both researchers documented children's emerging writing and noted that it contributed in a variety of ways to their understanding of print. For example, children will engage in writing through the use of temporary spellings, attempting to represent words based on their sounds, before they are actually able to read. Because children learn so much about language through writing, Chomsky even suggested that introduction to the printed word should be through writing (1976). The power in this writing-reading interaction is captured in Chomsky's statement: "The printed word 'belongs' to the spontaneous speller far more directly than to children who have experienced it only ready made" (p. 64).

Chomsky found evidence that children wrote before they were able to read, without formal instruction in either language skill. These children knew some letters of the alphabet and some sounds, but they could not yet read. In their temporary spellings, they tended to represent long sounds by the letter that says the name of the sound—for example:

coat becomes *cot*   *came* becomes *kam*

Short vowels often are represented by the letter name closest to the sound:

bad becomes *bed*   *flipper* becomes *fleper*

L and *R* are used without syllables:

girl becomes *GRL*   *color* becomes *klr*

Can you read what one child whom Chomsky worked with wrote (Chomsky, 1976, p. 58)?

R U D F   *(Are you deaf?)*

What knowledge do these young spellers have, and what do you think encouraged them to write? Chomsky found that they knew some letters and sounds. They were able, for example, to represent *table* by the letters *tabl*. They also could write their name and had a sense of letter sequencing in a word. At home, the adults around them were responsive to the child's interests; they not only accepted what the children wrote, they responded with enthusiasm and joy. The adults reveled in their child's accomplishments.

Interactive writing has its roots in the *language experience approach,* developed almost forty years ago by Ashton-Warner (1963). Educators using the language experience approach would copy the children's words exactly as they dictated. Basically the teacher's role was as a scribe for the children's words. In the 1980s, McKenzie (1985) developed what she called *shared writing,* where teachers and students collaborate on a text, with the teacher serving as the scribe, as in language experience. In the 1990s, *interactive writing* (McCarrier, Pinnell, & Fountas, 1999) was developed to include the students and teacher in a collaborative writing experience, as we saw in Mrs. D's classroom. In interactive writing

INSTRUCTIONAL SCENARIO

In the Classroom with Interactive Writing

Mrs. Dubrowski, better known as Mrs. D, sits on a small chair with an easel beside her. In the tray of the easel are a black marker, correction tape, and a pointer. It's early in the school year, and her twenty first-grade students are seated in a somewhat irregular semicircle in front of her, about three rows deep.

Teacher: Boys and girls, we'll be having open house at our school in a couple of weeks, and we want to have some signs around the room that will tell our visitors about our classroom. Let's make a sign that tells them about our reading corner. What do you think we should write on that sign?

Kaye: The reading corner!

Others: The reading corner!

Teacher: All right, let's write "the reading corner" on our paper. Then I'll laminate the sign, and we'll find a place for it over at the reading corner. How many words will we write? [She repeats the words slowly and holds up a finger for each word: "the reading corner."] Aaron?

Aaron: Three!

Teacher: Yes, you're absolutely right, Aaron. What is the first word we want to write?

Children: *The.*

Teacher: Good! What is the first letter we want to write? What is the first letter in *the*? Elena? [She calls on Elena because she knows that Elena can already write several sight words in conventional spelling.]

Elena: The letter *t.*

Teacher: That's right, Elena. Why don't you come to the easel to write the *t.*

Everyone, because this is a sign for our reading corner and we're giving it a name, The Reading Corner, we need to write a capital *T* to begin the word *the.*

[Elena writes a capital *T.*] Thank you, Elena. Now, boys and girls, what other letters do we need in the word *the*?

Gemma: *T-h-e.*

Teacher: You're right, Gemma; that's how we spell *the.* We already have the letter *t.* So now we need an *h* and an *e.*

Willie, will you come up and write the *h* and the *e* to complete the first word in the sign?

Teacher: Now, listen to the sounds in the word *reading.* [Mrs. D. says the word slowly to highlight the sounds.] We hear the *r* and *e,* but not the next letter, the letter *a.* The *a* is silent and comes after the *e.* The word *read* is spelled *r-e-a-d,* and we want to write the word *reading.* Let's say the word together: *reading.* We add *ing* to the word *read* to make *reading.* Shelia, would you please come to the easel and point to where we want to begin the word *reading*?"

[Shelia goes to the easel and points to a place to the right of the *e* in *the,* leaving a space of about two inches.]

That's right, Shelia. You know a lot about writing. Notice, boys and girls, that Shelia left a space between the word *the* and the next word, *reading*. She knows that we leave a space between words when we write. All right, Shelia, will you write *r* to begin the word *reading*? And remember, because The Reading Corner is the name of a special place in our classroom, we want to begin each word with a capital letter, so we need a capital *r*.

Shelia: Can you show me how to do that?

Teacher: Here, let me put my hand over yours, and we'll make the letter together. [Mrs. D and her students continue writing together until they complete their sign, "The Reading Corner."] There, we have our sign finished. Good work, everyone! We can do signs for our fish tank, the classroom library, the art center, and a couple of other areas in our classroom. I think our visitors will like reading our signs during open house.

the teacher's role varies according to the scaffolding his or her students need to move through the process. Mrs. D provided a high degree of scaffolding for her first-grade students. Later in the year, her interactive writing lessons, which could vary from writings in response to read-alouds to a description of a class field trip, a class letter to a pen-pal, a story extension, a story map, or a brainstormed list of ideas, will have less teacher involvement in the area of sound-letter correspondence and perhaps more involvement and direction in areas such as word choice, punctuation, and sentence structure.

The writing-reading interaction is especially powerful when we realize that when children don't develop strong early literacy skills, including early understandings about print, their problems compound quickly. That phenomenon has been dubbed the *Matthew effect* (Stanovich, 1986; Walberg & Tsai, 1983), after a biblical story that illustrates the concept that the rich get richer and the poor get poorer. Children who do not have clear expectations for print, are confused by what they see on the page, and do not associate print with good feelings and usefulness quickly find themselves left behind as others move forward to work with increasingly complex texts. Those left behind are then faced with print that is too difficult, and as a result, they become less inclined to approach print and instead avoid contact with it. Lack of success and feelings of incompetence lead inexorably to less and less involvement in reading-writing related activities. This is what we were referring to in our discussion of competency theory in Chapter 1.

The Influence of Reading on Writing

When we discussed the research by Clay and Chomsky, we talked about the powerful writing-reading interaction at the level of emergent literacy. This interaction points out how much children learn about print through their manipulation of it—through writing. They experiment as they use temporary spellings, and they use their beginning knowledge of letters and sounds to build their understandings about print. They learn about syntax and meaning making as they generate print. Another powerful aspect of the writing-reading interaction lies in what we learn about print and writing through reading.

Reading Like a Writer

In 1983, Frank Smith wrote an article, "Reading Like a Writer," in which he describes a phenomenon most of us have experienced. It works like this. As we read, we stop now and then to look at a particular word, making a mental note that says, "So that's how the word is spelled." Then there are times we reread to savor the insight a writer captures in a particular sentence, a funny comment that made us laugh out loud, or the way an author crafted the language to create an especially striking image. It's when you stop in the midst of reading and say to the nearest person, "Listen to this!"

Of course, we regularly notice many things as we read. We acquire new vocabulary and learn to spell new words. We find ourselves intrigued by an especially interesting turn of phrase or a particularly vivid image. Most of the time these phenomena don't reach the level of conscious learning, but occasionally something in the writing catches our attention, and we become aware of the text through a writer's eyes. We are acutely aware of how a writer writes—in other words, how a writer spells a word, creates an image, or makes a point by using just the right words.

Smith makes the point that this "noticing" probably happens frequently with experienced readers but that it can be compromised when our attention is overloaded with trying to understand what we are reading, that is, if we are focused on understanding the meanings of words, pronouncing every word correctly, or memorizing every detail.

Let's look at some evidence that shows the effect of reading on writing. Eckhoff (1983) conducted research that looked at the effect that children's reading had on their writing. Her work with two second-grade classes, one class each in two schools, was based on the assumption that reading can have a powerful effect on writing. In one classroom, the teacher used a basal reader in which the text had the style and complexity of what Eckhoff referred to as "literary prose." That meant the sentences tended to be longer, included more complex structures (e.g., "Since they couldn't agree, they built a new city, which they named after our first president" [p. 609]), and did not use controlled vocabulary and repetitive words and phrases. The other classroom's basal reader contained text with a more simplified style and a tendency to include shorter, simple sentences and less sophisticated vocabulary (e.g., "A house was built. The president of the United States would live in this house" [p. 609]).

Eckhoff's results are not surprising, but they are interesting. She found a clear relationship between the basal texts and children's writing. Children who read the basal with a simplified style tended to write sentences with fewer complex structures; tended to write one sentence per line, as did the basal; and frequently used words often found in the simplified text, such as *and* and *too*. In the other classroom, students wrote with more sentence variety and more varied vocabulary.

Dressel (1990) found similar results in a study with fifth graders in which the researcher conducted read-alouds of three short novels to two groups of students. In each group, part of the read-aloud included a discussion of what the author did to create the story and its genre characteristics. Each book was a detective-type story. The primary difference was that the books Dressel read to one group were what had been judged by experts in children's literature to be high-quality stories, while the other group's read-alouds were with books judged to be of lesser quality. As in Eckhoff's study, Dressel found that the children exposed to the higher-quality literature wrote higher-quality stories. At the end of the study, students in both groups wrote detective stories of their own, which were analyzed according to specific literary and genre characteristics. Those who had heard and discussed the higher-quality literature wrote stories that were judged better on the literary elements of plot development, setting, character development, literary style, and mood.

Let's take a look at some implications of Eckhoff's and Dressel's studies for classrooms.

Learning to Read Like a Writer

First of all, we're not certain that someone can be explicitly taught to read like a writer. We suspect, rather, that this is one of those things that is better learned than taught, but that doesn't mean teachers have no role in engaging students to read like writers. One example of doing this is in the read-aloud situation described earlier in Ms. Martin's third-grade class. Ms. Martin plans each read-aloud around certain objectives and experiences for her students. She had several reasons for choosing *Elbert's Bad Word* as one of her read-alouds, one of which centered on the rich and sophisticated language that the children would hear in the story. For example, here's the reader's first encounter with the bad word:

> The word floated by like a small storm cloud. It was ugly and covered with dark, bristly hairs. With a swift flick of his wrist, Elbert snatched the word from the air and stuffed it into his back pocket.

In these three sentences, the vivid verbs *floated, snatched,* and *stuffed* all evoke clear images, and the simile, "like a small storm cloud," adds to the picture that readers are constructing in their minds. During a read-aloud, the teacher can ask questions to focus children's attention on a writer's craft:

Questions That Focus on Reading Like a Writer

- Why did the writer use that word?

- What did the writer do to help you see what happened in the story?

- What did the writer do to create the image of _____ [e.g., the bad word] in your mind?

- Why did the writer say _____ [e.g., *snatched* instead of *got* or *took*]?

- What did the writer [e.g., John Muir] mean when he said _____ [e.g., "the tiny bird was clad in a plain waterproof suit of bluish gray"? Was the bird wearing a suit?]?

In a study of Writers' Workshops, designed for the purpose of providing peer feedback sessions in a middle school classroom (Fearn & Farnan, 1993), we were surprised to hear students comment on how the workshops helped them read like writers (see Chapter 8). Our principal reason for conducting the study was to explore what kinds of feedback middle school students could provide to one another as they participated over the course of the school year in Writers' Workshops. During interviews with a group of these middle school students near the end of the year, we found that they had become more aware than ever before of the various ways that writers, in this case their peers, wrote. They commented that participating in weekly workshops had given them opportunities to hear many different kinds of writings on a variety of topics. One girl stated, "The teacher could never have bored into my head all the different techniques and ways of writing." The teacher realized that these were insights she could not directly teach her students. The Writers' Workshops, which had been carefully structured and monitored throughout the year, had provided an environment in which these things had been learned.

We also know what experienced writers say about the writing-reading interaction. At the Southern California Writers' Conference in 1997, we interviewed a dozen writers, asking them such questions as where they got their ideas for writing, how they would describe their writing processes, and how they learned to be writers. Every one of the writers, all in separate interviews, talked about reading being the most powerful influence on their writing.

Writing-Reading Interactions in Book Clubs

When McMahon and Raphael (1997) began experimenting with Book Clubs over ten years ago, they were interested in developing a reading program that students would find motivating and would involve them in reading and talking about a wide variety of books, many of their own choosing. McMahon and Raphael began with some assumptions, many of which center on interactions among the language arts:

- Oral and written language is a foundation for language acquisition and development.

- Use of authentic reading materials, as well as authentic oral and written activities, is fundamental to language acquisition and development.

- The social aspect of reading must be honored.
- Meaningful literacy activities must allow for learners' active construction of meaning that includes reading, writing, and talking about texts.
- Learning should occur in the context of a community of individuals who learn from their interactions with one another.
- Learning to read should occur through interactions with authentic literature.

Essentially Book Clubs are settings in which readers have opportunities to read literary selections and share their thoughts and ideas with others who have read the same text. Oprah Winfrey made the Book Club a national activity when she selected certain books to read with her talk show audience. These are settings not unlike what happens when any of us reads a book and then finds someone else who has or is reading it. The conversations that result are often punctuated by phrases such as, "What did you think about . . .?" and "I loved the part where . . ." and "I was disappointed when. . . ." These are authentic conversations in which literate individuals share their responses and interpretations from a reading and in which their own thoughts and responses are shaped by what we hear from others.

As McMahon and Raphael, along with other colleagues, developed the Book Club concept, four elements emerged as critical to the process:

1. *Reading*—having a wide range of literary works and opportunities to build reading skills, which is central to the Book Club concept
2. *Writing*—which interacts with the reading by supporting both a reader's thinking about a text and the discussion of it
3. *Book Club*—in which learners meet in small groups of three to five to discuss their common reading of a text, which might be a book, chapter, short story, folk tale, or article
4. *Community share*—opportunities for the students to share ideas that emerge in small group discussions with the larger community or class

The Book Club concept is solidly grounded in Vygotsky's (1978) work on the powerful role that language, oral and written, plays in the development of thought. Also important here is his theory that children are able to learn more when they receive support from more knowledgeable others (e.g., parent, teacher, more knowledgeable peer) than they would learn if they were left on their own. Vygotsky called this the *zone of proximal development*—the difference between what individuals can learn on their own and what they can learn if they are provided informed input and support from others, which he referred to as *scaffolding*.

While the concept of Book Club, or Literature Circles (a variation on the Book Club concept), is important, it is not our purpose here to describe in detail all the variations and possibilities associated with it. Two useful resources for that are McMahon and Raphael's book (1997) and a text by Daniels (1994). What we want to do is take a closer look at the writing-reading interaction in a classroom that uses Book Club regularly.

It's Monday in Ms. Rocha's seventh-grade classroom. Six groups of students, four to five per group, have arranged their chairs in clusters around the classroom and are talking quietly, or as quietly as seventh graders usually talk. They are focused on the conversation inside their groups. During the next thirty to thirty-five minutes, Ms. Rocha sits with one of the groups during their discussion. In each group, students' body language shows their engagement. They lean forward into the group. They gesture to highlight a point. Now and then, one voice rises above the others. A flurry of giggles ripples out from the center of a group. Occasionally students glance down at a sheet of paper in their lap or leaf through the book they have with them.

Obviously this is a classroom where students are familiar with Book Club. It's a little noisy, but it's the good noise that accompanies focused and enthusiastic student engagement with their peers. The process seems to be working like the proverbial well-oiled machine, and it is; and therein lies the story. As with all other experts, Ms. Rocha has a classroom that looks as though it's almost running on some kind of invisible internal energy, automatically and smoothly. No glitches. What we know, however, is that such an image is supported by a tremendous amount of expertise. What to an observer is invisible is supported by a significant degree of preparation, for both herself and her students. We've attempted to make the invisible visible by talking to Ms. Rocha, and we'd like to share some of that conversation.

We had many questions:

How do you start Book Clubs at the beginning of the year?

I begin with the whole class reading a book together and participating in a Book Club, which gives me an opportunity to discuss and model appropriate Book Club procedures.

How are students placed into groups?

I allow self-selection as long as the groups function well as a unit. I ask students to establish a group identity by giving their group a name, something that relates to reading. Two good examples are "The Reading Rainbows" and "Three Books and a Bookmark" (that is, three girls and one boy).

How do you organize the Book Clubs?

I use Daniels' (1994) role sheets the first half of the year to give students tangible functions within the group. These include "Discussion Director," in essence, the group leader; "Connector," who makes connections between the text and experiences outside the text; "Literary Luminary," who highlights important sections or passages and reads them aloud; "Vocabulary Enricher," who brings up especially important, or perhaps confusing, words in a reading; and "Illustrator," who contributes a picture or graphic that represents something in a reading. I find that the need for these well-defined roles is not necessary as students became increasingly skilled and productive members of their Book Clubs.

How do you assess Book Club?

Students receive points for completing their role sheets before the Book Club conversations; for completing their written responses before the conversation; for participating in the conversation itself, which I judge as I observe the Book Clubs and students' interactions; and for keeping their home reading logs up-to-date. I expect that students will do their reading outside class. Typically each Book Club group completes the reading of a novel in approximately two weeks. Also, students self-assess each Book Club meeting. I lead these conversations by asking students what could have been better, what worked in the discussion, and what goals they would like to set to make the next meeting run more smoothly.

How often do Book Clubs meet?

Each group meets every other day for thirty to thirty-five minutes. During that time the group is either participating in a Book Club conversation or is meeting together to prepare for their conversation for the next day.

How do you build your classroom library with sets of books?

All extra classroom monies are spent on books. Bookstores often give teacher discounts, and used bookstores are a good resource. In addition, I ask parents to donate their children's already-read books and donate new books, instead of cupcakes, for a child's birthday or other special occasion. The child then inscribes the book for the class. I try to purchase books that students will enjoy reading. Some popular ones are *Jacob Have I Loved* by Katherine Paterson and *Downriver* by Will Hobbs; and books by Gary Paulsen, Lois Lowry, and Jerry Spinelli are popular.

How would you describe the writing-reading interaction in Book Club?

Let me give a little background. During the first part of the year, students come to their Book Club with the role sheets they've completed. These provide a structured way for students to think about what they've read and have something to share. As the year progresses, they are able to write before their conversations on their own. That's where the one-page writing comes in.

The day before a Book Club convenes, the group meets to plan for their conversation. They have already read a section of the text, and the task now is to decide what questions they want to talk about, what topics they think might be interesting. For example, they question why certain things happen in a story and why characters react the way they do. Topics include how students relate to characters, events, and settings. They also bring up ideas they find important in a reading—topics that relate to the "big ideas" or themes. Students decide on a topic they want to discuss the following day, and either then or later, but before the next day's Book Club meeting, they write one page on which they capture their thoughts about the agreed-on topic.

I have found that if students write prior to their conversations, their responses are higher in categories of interpretation, the meanings they make based on the reading, and evaluation. In other words, they make judgments about the writing, characters, and the story in general rather than simply retelling what they read. When students occasionally forget to write before a Book Club session, they always report that they have a more difficult time contributing and staying on task. My experience is that their conversations are much richer and engaging when they write beforehand. The writing-reading-thinking interaction makes the talking a lot easier, especially for the struggling student.

We thanked Ms. Rocha for her time. These kinds of Book Clubs, and variations that are created across grade levels, are giving young readers opportunities to have an authentic reading experience. Students who are given choice and voice in what they read, with whom they read and talk, and what they write about and discuss are much more likely to have a positive attitude toward reading. Those students bring more of themselves to the reading event, which promotes more reading.

Grattan (1997) explains that with her first graders, she quickly found a starting point for Book Clubs. Her students were eager to begin, but they weren't sure just what the word *discuss* meant. That's where she started. And she began simply, setting some basic guidelines: "Accept and respect what others say; respond by listening, asking questions, or making comments; look at the person who is talking; may interpret, but with courtesy" (p. 273). Helping her students learn about discussions and how to be effective participants in them was challenging for Grattan, but she makes the point that Book Club is not reserved only for older students.

E S L McMahon and Raphael's book contains chapters on using Book Club with students who are learning English as a second language (Brock, 1997) and in first- and second-grade classrooms (Grattan, 1997). Brock found that Book Club provided "a context for guided learning for second-language learners" (p. 145) and "opportunities for guided learning, experimenting with language-in-use, and acquiring a second language" (p. 145). We would add that Book Clubs can highlight the value of cultural diversity when youngsters of diverse backgrounds discuss their interpretations and understandings with one another. In addition, various cultural perspectives can be explored through books such as *Too Many Tamales* (Soto, 1993), about a Mexican-American child who loses her mother's diamond ring as she's making a batch of tamales, and *The Bracelet* (Uchida, 1993), about a child's perspective on being in a Japanese-American internment camp. We highly recommend the Web site http://falcon.jmu.edu/~ramseyil/multipub.htm, The Internet School Library Media Center (ISLMC) Multicultural Page, a meta site, which brings together on one Web site many resources for teachers, librarians, parents, and students. You'll find reviews of books from a variety of cultural categories; extensive bibliographies; and links for K–12 teachers, such as the link to California State University San Marcos' Spanish Books for Children Collection, K–12 lesson plans, and ideas for international projects. ■

Writing-Reading Interactions in Learning Across the Curriculum

Typically when we think about writing in the curriculum, we think about English class or the language arts period. It's also not uncommon to walk into a classroom and see, first thing in the morning or maybe just after lunch or recess, children writing. The teacher may say something like this: "All right, boys and girls, take out your journals, and we'll write for the next ten minutes." Or the cue might sound like this: "It's time to take out your journals. Remember, you must write at least one page. I'll tell you when to stop."

The time allotted for writing may vary from five minutes to fifteen, but usually not more. Then students put their journals back into their desks, and the day continues. Once a week, or maybe even daily, the teacher collects the journals and leafs through the pages to make sure students are taking the writing seriously, which usually means they wrote a sufficient amount to earn credit for the week's journal writing.

What students write in these journals often varies. They might be responding to a quotation or thought-for-the-day written on the board—for example, "Anything worth doing takes hard work." The teacher might direct students this way: "Write about a place you like to visit," or simply, "Write anything that comes into your mind over the next ten minutes."

When teachers talk about their objectives for these journal writing activities, they offer various reasons for the activity. For example, after an especially active time like recess or physical education or even the first thing in the morning, quiet time spent writing can help children get settled and focused on something academic. Some teachers say that the objective is writing fluency. It's true that becoming a fluent writer depends, in part, on a writer's commitment to write. We don't improve, whether at golf, cooking, or being a friend, unless we do it. We want students to write, and the journal is one vehicle for making that happen.

One thing these journal activities have in common is that they are almost completely disassociated from the curriculum—the content or substance we bring into the classroom on any given day to teach and help our students learn. These uses of writing ignore the importance of writing as an integral part of the curriculum. Not only is writing itself a strand of the curriculum (in other words, there is content in teaching children to become effective writers), but writing provides a powerful way to support children's learning across the curriculum; hence the phrase *writing across the curriculum* and the concept of writing-to-learn.

This is not about journaling, although the writing-to-learn process might involve journals. It is not about free-writes, although it might involve free-writes. It is about principles associated with learning and the concept that writing has a powerful role in the writing-reading interaction, especially in its role as a process to support learning.

This is counter to a transmission model of teaching and learning—the idea that we can somehow pass knowledge from one individual (usually a teacher) to another (most often called a student). The purest form of the transmission model is probably the classroom lecture, where lecture is used without many, or any, additional supports to ensure student learning.

The question-answer pattern, which often accompanies it, is alive and well across the curriculum. It's called the IRE pattern (Bellack, Kliebard, Hyman, & Smith, 1966), which stands for initiate-respond-evaluate. The teacher initiates a question (*What color was Little Red Riding Hood's cape?*); a student responds (*red?*), often with an implied question mark after the response; and the teacher evaluates (a smile; a nod of the head; a verbal "good job"; or, if the answer is incorrect, a soothing "not exactly, but good try"). This pattern has been well documented for over thirty years as a common classroom tool to tap into what students are learning. What it taps into, however, is merely their ability to access short-term memory and regurgitate literal information that was just fed (transmitted) to them.

The writing-to-learn process, on the other hand, is based on constructivist principles (Newell, 1998). As a model for teaching and learning, constructivism is based on a deceptively simple concept: the learner actively constructs knowledge. Although the concept may seem simple, processes associated with knowledge construction are not. Eminent constructivist theorists, including Jean Piaget, Lev Vygotsky, and Jerome Bruner, all speak in some way about the learner as an active constructor of meaning and knowledge, of the complex interplay between an individual's prior knowledge and experience and the new input or experiences, an interplay of processes that results in the development of new learnings.

The following are assumptions of constructivist instruction:

- Learning occurs through learners' active construction of knowledge.
- Learners are constantly weighing new information against previous understandings.
- Learners work through discrepancies and confusions on their own and with others, coming to new understandings.
- Learners achieve control of knowledge construction through an interplay between new knowledge and their prior knowledge.

Images of the engaged learner, hands-on instruction, and project-based learning are directly connected to a constructivist view of learning.

James Britton, in his book *Language and Learning* (1970), explored the central role language plays in the way we shape or interpret experiences. He spoke specifically about the role of writing as a way for learners to reflect on and "wrestle with" their thoughts as they work to understand and clarify. Compared to research in other areas of literacy development, such as spelling, emergent reading and writing, oral language development, and use of reading strategies, research on writing-to-learn has been relatively scarce.

Connolly and Vilardi (1989) edited a book about science and mathematics instructors who used writing-to-learn in mathematics and science classrooms. The title of one of the chapters hints at a common view of writing in mathematics: "What's an Assignment Like You Doing in a Course Like This?" (Gopen & Smith, 1989). It probably comes as no surprise that in many math and science classes, little or no writing occurs beyond the writing of mathematics notational language and science lab reports. As Gopen and Smith incorporated writing into a calculus class, several things became clear to them:

- Writing can be incorporated into mathematics classes with a minimum of effort.
- Thinking and the expression of thoughts are so intertwined that one cannot be good unless the other is as well. It became evident to these teachers that if students did not have the language needed to reflect on a concept and could not clearly express ideas associated with it, that was a direct reflection of the quality of their thinking about the concept.
- Writing can help students better understand mathematics.

Short Cues for Writing-to-Learn

The question is, What kind of writing are we talking about? We know that writing can assist learning, but not all writing has the same effect on learning (Langer & Applebee, 1987). For example, when teachers ask students to write short responses to questions, students tend not to do a lot of rethinking or reflecting on content. They simply find information in texts they are reading and copy that information onto study sheets. They do not have to think about relationships among ideas and extend those ideas in any way. (Some of us remember that strategy well.)

In contrast, we can give students writing tasks that will cause them to explore ideas, rethink and reflect on what they're learning, explain, and clarify. These are analytic writing tasks "that require students to compare and contrast, evaluate, explain, and draw conclusions. In other words, students are not asked simply to restate information and ideas, but to think about them" (Dahl & Farnan, 1998).

Short Cues are brief writings in which students think and write in a variety of ways about what they read. Students can do these writings in their learning logs or daily journals, or they can write on half-sheets called *Short Cue Think Sheets*:

Short Cue Think Sheets

Cue:

_____.

My Response:

_____

_____

_____

_____

_____

_____

Teachers can assign these think sheets for homework or as in-class quickwrites. It's a type of worksheet, but what we said about writing applies as well to worksheets: all worksheets are not created equal. In other words, they do not all have an equal impact on learning. Worksheets can foster thinking and learning, or they can consume students' time with nonproductive busywork. It's up to the teacher to assess a worksheet's value, as represented by its potential impact on student thinking and learning.

Short Cues can be written after students read a text and before a discussion, as Ms. Rocha did in her classroom before students participated in their Book Club conversations. The writings serve as catalysts to spur discussion on a topic or text, and when students share these kinds of writings with each other, they are working together to construct their understanding about the text and the content they are studying.

An important instructional component here is to let students read and share their writings with others, either in small groups or with the whole class. The primary reason for sharing is to expose everyone in the room to the variety of ways knowledge can be constructed. Each construction shared adds to the size and complexity of everyone's construction.

Following are Short Cues that teachers have used successfully, putting them in language appropriate to their grade level, in classrooms beginning in first grade.

Short Cues for Writing-to-Learn

- Write one question you have about the ideas or information in the reading. Then tell why you think it is important to have an answer to the question.

- What three [use any number] ideas are most important in this reading? Briefly write about each idea and what you learned about it.

- What do you think was most important in the reading? Explain what is most important in not fewer than twenty-five words or more than thirty-five. [*Variation:* Choose one idea you think is especially important and explain why you chose it.]

- Think about what you read. What ideas or information stand out in your mind? And why do you think you especially noticed the ideas or information?

- Think about what you just read. Write a way to explain it to a ten year old [or any other age]. [*Variation:* Write what you learned as if you were explaining it to someone else.]

- What did you find confusing [interesting, surprising] in the reading? What made it confusing [interesting, surprising]?

- What did the author do in this writing to point out what was most important?

- What did the author do to help you understand what you read?

- Write a sentence [or two or three] that shows the meaning of the word
  _____ .

We know from the research that if writing tasks are going to support learning, they must require students to think about content (Langer & Applebee, 1987). The tasks or cues must require students to use their critical thinking skills to explain and elaborate, evaluate and make judgments, clarify, make connections, and describe relationships. These are thinking skills or patterns that even very young children use. Of course, the students must have sufficient language and experiences to attempt explanations and make judgments, and certainly their critical thinking skills become more sophisticated as they get older. But if they are not asked to begin exercising these skills at an early age, they may never become very good at it. Therefore, we need to begin asking young children to express themselves in ways that require critical thinking. We can ask them to describe, explain, give opinions (evaluate and make judgments), and tell us more about those opinions (elaborate).

It's also important that students have some crucial understandings in relation to writing tasks across the curriculum (Langer & Applebee, 1987). For example, it is important that they know the value of the task and how it supports their learning. We must be explicit with students about:

- Why a task has value and what that value is
- How the task will support student learning
- How what they already know and have experienced will make it possible for them to respond to the task successfully

Furthermore, it's important for teachers to give specific feedback to students about their writing and thinking. When students are sharing their Short Cue responses, we can add clarifying information or make note of content that needs additional explanation, and we can respond immediately to questions that arise from these reflective writings. Students will also respond with thoughts that are insightful and offer important perspectives. This gives us an opportunity to provide genuine praise for students' excellent thinking. When we have opportunities to offer genuine praise to students, we provide them with one of the strongest motivators to continue learning: an earned sense of intellectual power and competence. This experience has physical signs. Children sit straighter and taller in their chairs, their smiles widen, and their body language says, "I'm glad to be here!"

We can also talk directly to students about the critical thinking they're showing in their written reflections. One way we can do this is by developing a Short Cue rubric that might look something like this:

Rubric for Short Cues

2 The writing includes some literal information, but the writer adds to the information by doing one or more of the following: describes an idea or concept in detail, explains it in order to clarify the idea or concept, evaluates and makes judgments (presents an opinion) about why it is important (or interesting, confusing, surprising), and discusses those opinions (elaborates). The writer shows a clear and in-depth understanding of the content.

1   The writing includes mostly literal information, with little explanation, evaluation, or elaboration. The writer doesn't appear to have reflected on or understood the content. There may even be misinformation in the writing, which may represent confusion on the part of the student.

It's important to create rubrics in language that children can understand. The best way to do this is to talk to them about the ideas and incorporate their language into the rubric. Rubrics are not just for teachers; they're for students too.

Using Summary Writing to Learn

Most definitions of a summary list synonyms such as *abstract, synopsis,* and *précis.* Essentially a summary is a compilation of the essential points or ideas from a text or other medium, such as a speech or discussion. For our purposes here, we'll talk about summary writing in relation to text that is read.

Writing a summary requires that readers distinguish important ideas from supporting or descriptive details. Said another way, it requires that students evaluate information in a text and make decisions about what is most important. It then requires that they arrange those ideas in a way that reconstructs the main points clearly and logically. Based on what we've discussed about the role of writing in learning, summary writing is a process that can support students' learning (Rosenshine, Meister, & Chapman, 1996).

It's not sufficient, however, just to ask students to write a summary. They must be taught how to do it. While you're teaching your students to write effective summaries, take the opportunity to conduct some action research in your classroom (see Chapter 1).

Classroom Action Research on Summary Writing

First, model the process with the entire class. Select a passage or section of text and put it on an overhead transparency, or photocopy it so all students will have a copy. A paragraph of five to ten sentences is an ideal place to begin. Read it with your students, and ask them to find the most important sentence (or you can refer to the concept of main idea and ask them to express it in a sentence). After some discussion about which sentence they chose and why, come to a class consensus on which sentence everyone will underline as most important. Next, with input from the students, rewrite the main idea sentence on the board or overhead transparency.

Now go back to the paragraph and ask students to pick out the three or four most important pieces of information that relate to the main idea sentence. You might want to do this activity in small collaborative groups of three or four students, so they have a chance to discuss their choices and explain them to one another. Each small group can reach consensus about these pieces of information and be ready to share them with the class. Then the class as a whole can discuss those choices and come to consensus regarding which ones will be written into the class summary.

Finally, work with the class to write the identified information into two to four sentences. Throughout this part of the process, draw attention to the fact that the sentences should follow one another logically, in a way that makes sense in presenting the information.

After modeling this process once or twice with the entire class, give students opportunities to practice individually and receive feedback on their summaries. As for the action research, you can monitor their work to assess whether they are in fact becoming more effective summary writers. For example, using a rubric for summary writing, it's possible to assess students' accuracy until they have reached a high degree of accuracy on three consecutive passages. In order to have a baseline assessment, before you begin to teach summary writing, ask students to write a summary of a short passage and evaluate it using the rubric. Then, after training over two to three months, evaluate their summaries again to see whether they have improved. Make sure that students have access to and understand the rubric. Also, share the results of the action research with parents, site administrators, and the local newspaper.

Here's a basic rubric for summary writing you can use, or use it as a foundation to develop one with your students:

Rubric for Summary Writing

4 Excellent summary in which the main idea is fully articulated and clearly written as the first sentence in the summary. All important details are present and are written in a logical order. The ideas are linked in a way that makes sense and ties the ideas together.

3 Good summary in which the main idea is written as the first sentence in the summary. Important details are included, although some may be omitted, in an order that seems logical. Ideas are linked in a logical way.

2 Below-average summary in which the main idea may be implied but is not specifically stated as the first sentence. Details are present in subsequent sentences, but some critical information may be missing. The ideas are presented in a way that seems random and unorganized.

1 Ineffective summary in which the main idea is not completely clear. Although the summary contains information from the passage, the ideas are randomly presented in a way that is not cohesive. The point of the passage may be unclear.

A Review of Writing-to-Learn

Let's recap what we know about writing-to-learn:

- Writing can have a powerful effect on reading and learning. It encourages attention and cognitive engagement, without which learning cannot occur.
- Writing works best to support learning when it involves discovery, inquiry, and reflection rather than mere recitation of facts.
- Writing that reviews and consolidates what is learned can help students pull ideas together that tend to be remembered. Reviews and summaries should be written for the purpose of clarifying and rethinking, not for providing material for assessment and evaluation of student learning.
- Writing tasks that ask students to build on information and ideas and to extend their knowledge can assist learning. For example, teachers can use Short Cues such as, "What else would be important to know about the topic?" or "What ideas and/or information do you think (predict) you will find in the next section of the text you read?"

We think Knoblach and Brannon (1983) do a good job of capturing the important role of writing in learning:

> Since writing enables both learning and conversation, manifesting and enlarging the capacity to discover connections, it should be a resource that all teachers in all disciplines can rely on to achieve their purposes. (p. 473)

A Summary: Writing and Reading

Over two decades of research show that writing-reading interactions have a powerful role in the support of emergent and ongoing literacy development, as well as in learning across the curriculum. Crucial to literacy development is the way writing and reading interact to help build a young child's literacy foundation, which Holdaway referred to as the literacy set. Research by Clay and Chomsky in the 1970s illustrated the nature of this interaction in emergent writing and reading. Their research, conducted independently of one another, illustrated that children learn much about language and literacy through their early experimentation with temporary spellings and attempts to create meaning in print. Other researchers documented the writing-reading interaction by noting how the reading of certain texts affects students' writing. Finally, research points to the power of the writing-reading interaction as a tool for learning across the curriculum.

Now it's your turn to be the judge. The previous paragraph is a summary of this chapter, written according to the template for summary writing that we described. Look back to the rubric for summary writing and assess how we did. Did we write a first sentence that captured the essence (main idea) of the chapter? Did we include the most important details that were presented throughout, and, finally, did we tie those ideas together in a way that represented the flow of the chapter in a clear and logical way? In what ways would you say we attempted to tie together the ideas in the summary? You be the judge. What rubric score would you give our summary?

14 Writing-Spelling Interactions

- Why do we teach spelling?
- How do teachers know what words to include in spelling instruction?
- How can spelling instruction ensure both acquisition and retention of words?
- What is *spelling conscience,* and why is it important?

Memories and Questions: A Personal Spelling History

Do you remember the third grade? (Maybe it was the fifth.) It's Thursday evening; dinner is finished, and dishes are washed. You asked the Thursday evening question: "Will someone help me with my words?" That meant a family member would sit with you for five or ten minutes, reading one word after another, as you spelled each one in turn.

During those practice sessions, you ran through each word, maintaining a good pace because the pace helped you spell better. In the third grade, you listened for the sounds in each word, often sounding your way through. In the fifth grade, you remember knowing that the sounds didn't always work, so you focused more on letters and the letter sequences.

The teacher introduced the words on Monday. Tuesday was the day when you focused on the sounds in the words. You wrote a trial test on Wednesday in school. Thursday you practiced roots and affixes. You also wrote the words in blanks left in sentences to show that you knew what the words meant:

fierce   puzzle   quickly

The _____ tiger stalked its prey.

Friday is the test. You numbered from 1 to 10 on half-sheets of lined paper. The teacher called each word, followed with a brief definition, and read a sentence that contained the word. You wrote each word. There may have been three bonus words from the social studies lesson. That was language arts across the curriculum. You turned the test in to the teacher, who scored it at lunch. By 2:00 in the afternoon, you had another 90 or 100 on the spelling excellence chart in the language arts corner.

Maybe it wasn't exactly that way. Maybe your teacher didn't "do" formal spelling. Maybe it was "organic" in your room, or maybe your teacher said, "Boys and girls, our spelling this year will be natural. We'll study the words from our journal writing and science and social studies."

In any case, we remember spelling. We remember being good at it or poor at it. Even today, each of us has a sense of our own spelling ability. Can you remember when you first knew you were a good or poor speller?

- Do you remember being one of the students in your room who always got 90 or 100 on Friday spelling tests? Or maybe you were one of those who nearly always got 50 or 60.
- Do you remember that there were 90- and 100-getters, and there were 40- and 60-getters?
- Do you remember whether the 40- and 50-getters became 90- and 100-getters the next year?
- Do you remember 90- and 100-getters becoming 70- and 60-getters the following year?
- Is it fair to say that third graders who tended to get 40 and 50 in the third grade also tended to get 40 and 50 in the fourth, fifth, and sixth grades?
- Do you think spelling is a sort of talent?
- Do you think some people just seem to know how to spell words correctly almost by instinct?
- Do you think all elementary school children can learn to spell well?
- Do you think it is possible for every child in school to spell well enough to get good scores every Friday, if there are tests every Friday, and at the same time turn in written work that contains only rarely misspelled words?
- Do you think it is important to be able to spell lots of words correctly?
- How well do you think children should be able to spell by the end of the sixth grade? How do we know which words children need to be able to spell? How do we know how well children need to be able to spell words? What is the second-grade correct spelling criterion?

This chapter is about more than the inclusion of spelling into daily journal writing or the integration of spelling and writing. It is about the natural and automatic interaction between spelling and writing. The answers to the questions we just posed are found in the interactions.

Teaching Spelling: Some Early Thoughts

Our discussion of spelling begins with several early questions that have to be answered.

Why Teach Spelling?

There is only one reason for spelling: *We spell so we can write.* People who read have expectations about how words will appear when they see them written down. They notice when words don't appear the way they're supposed to appear. Communication is compromised if the words are not spelled conventionally. Spelling is an important part of the communication process between writer and reader. Teaching spelling is about making effective writers. It is important to remember that we're teaching young writers to spell because, and only because, they are writers.

What Should We Teach?

Teaching presupposes decisions about what to teach. With respect to spelling, what do young writers need to know? Spelling occurs during the act of getting the language of ideas and images on a page. It's in the act of drafting when writers need to be able to spell words. After that, they can look up the words, check them electronically, or ask a friend how to spell. Spelling occurs in the draft.

The next question is, *What words do writers need to know how to spell?* If spelling occurs when writers are thinking of and writing words, the words they need to know how to spell are the words they think of when they write. They certainly don't have to know how to spell the words they don't think of when they write, because they won't think of those.

To recap important points so far, writers spell when they draft, and the words they have to know how to spell are the ones they think of when they are drafting.

When we talk about learning to spell in this chapter, we're always talking about writing. That means we are concentrating on words with utility for writing, not words for the sake of learning to spell words. We'll be talking about teaching high-frequency words and words young writers think of when they write. It is impossible to list words in the latter category, but there are many lists of the former. For example, Cramer and Cipielewski (1995) identified a list of the one hundred most frequently misspelled words through the elementary and middle grades; they are listed in Figure 14.1.

1. too	26. didn't	51. like	76. about
2. a lot	27. people	52. whole	77. first
3. because	28. until	53. another	78. happened
4. there	29. with	54. believe	79. Mom
5. their	30. different	55. I'm	80. especially
6. that's	31. outside	56. thought	81. school
7. they	32. we're	57. let's	82. getting
8. it's	33. through	58. before	83. started
9. when	34. upon	59. beautiful	84. was
10. favorite	35. probably	60. everything	85. which
11. went	36. don't	61. very	86. stopped
12. Christmas	37. sometimes	62. into	87. two
13. were	38. off	63. caught	88. Dad
14. our	39. everybody	64. one	89. took
15. they're	40. heard	65. Easter	90. friend's
16. said	41. always	66. what	91. presents
17. know	42. I	67. there's	92. are
18. you're	43. something	68. little	93. morning
19. friend	44. would	69. doesn't	94. could
20. friends	45. want	70. usually	95. around
21. really	46. and	71. clothes	96. buy
22. finally	47. Halloween	72. scared	97. maybe
23. where	48. house	73. everyone	98. family
24. again	49. once	74. have	99. pretty
25. then	50. to	75. swimming	100. tried

FIGURE 14.1 100 Most Frequently Misspelled Words Across Eight Grade Levels. Source: Cramer, R. L., & Cipielewski, J. F. (1995). Research in action: A study of spelling errors in 18,599 written compositions of children in grades 1–8. In *Spelling research and information: An overview of current research and practices* (pp. 11–52). Copyright © 1995 Scott, Foresman and Company. Reprinted by permission of Addison-Wesley Educational Publishers, Inc.

When Is Accurate Spelling Important?

How well do young writers need to spell words when they draft? (Remember, after writing, they can ask someone about spelling, check electronically, look in the dictionary, and find synonyms they can spell.) Clearly they have to spell words well enough to know what they are so they can read what they have written. That's how well writers have to spell when they compose *writer-based prose* (Flower, 1979), that is, prose written by the writer for the writer's own purpose. Only the writer has to read and understand it. Writers always spell as well as they can.

Remember that spelling has no utility of its own. The only purpose for spelling words correctly is to facilitate communication with the audience, that is, the readers. Therefore, the words have to be spelled accurately when a reader other than the writer will read the writing. That is the *reader-based prose* (Flower, 1979) with which a writer purposefully attempts to communicate with a reader.

As long as the manuscript is on the writer's side of the desk, the writing and the spelling are in the process of progressing toward the highest quality possible for the writer. When the manuscript, that is, the paper, crosses the desk (in other words, becomes available for an audience other than the writer), all of it, including the spelling, has to be *as right as the writer is capable of making it*. Notice the italics. The criterion for correctness should reflect the capacity of the young writer. We'll talk more about the idea of development when we discuss the emergent speller.

REVIEW AND REFLECTION

1. Why do we teach spelling?
2. Explain the statement: *Spelling has no value if the goal is only to become a good speller.*

So far, we have accumulated some basic principles about the writing-spelling interaction:

1. We learn to spell so we can write. Spelling isn't *part* of the writing; spelling *is* the writing, just as punctuation, sentence writing, and the development of a topic are the writing. All serve the purpose of communication.

2. The words that writers must learn how to spell are the words they think of when they write.

3. The spelling that occurs as writers are constructing (drafting) the written language must be sufficiently accurate to allow the writer to read back what she or he wrote.

4. The spelling reflected in the paper when it crosses the desk for eyes other than the writer's must be correct, accurate. Accurate spelling is part of the communication.

5. The responsibility for accurate spelling rests squarely with the writer, no matter the writer's age or apparent ability. There is not a time when the young writer "needn't worry about spelling."

It is *absolutely critical* that these five principles guide the way we teach young writers to write well. It is *absolutely critical* that instruction include the developmental fact that spelling the words as well as they can be spelled operates at various levels of accuracy as children grow. The developmental context is very important in the interaction between spelling and writing.

The Emergent Speller

Spelling is as much a part of children's development as walking, talking, and the acquisition of situationally acceptable behavior. But in the interactions between writing and spelling, the spelling doesn't emerge all at once. Certainly young writers should learn to honor accurate spelling and assume responsibility for it, but spelling correctly takes time; there are developmental demands that children can satisfy mostly because of how old they are and how much language experience they have had. It is important to understand the aspects of spelling development outlined by such researchers in spelling as Gentry and Gillet (1993) and Henderson (1990).

The Preliterate or Precommunicative Phase of Spelling Development

When children are very young, they play with things that seem important to them. Alone in her crib very early in the morning, six-month-old Jordan can be heard babbling, not to anyone in particular. She's just making noises. They aren't just any old noises, though. These are special noises, precommunicative language noises in the sense that they don't mean anything because Jordan doesn't know how to make them mean anything. She doesn't even know that making the noises means something. This is preliterate oral language.

Young writers go through a similar developmental stage in spelling. When Jordan is as young as three and maybe as old as six or seven, her writing is preliterate or precommunicative because it's little more than black on white, or red paint on newsprint, or purple crayon on the bone white wall of the bathroom. There are unintelligible marks as well as letters and icons. Jordan has no concept of word, and she probably doesn't know much about the letters she has written. She may have written from left to right, right to left, top to bottom, or bottom up, or there may be no such directional pattern at all.

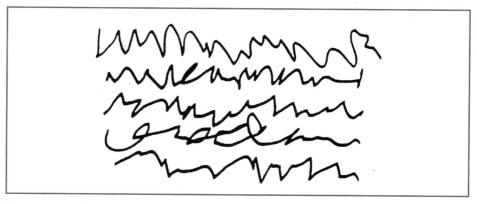

Gentry, J.R., & Gillet, J.W. (1993). *Teaching Kids to Spell.* Portsmouth, NH: Heinemann.

Young writers are imitating writing, and imitation is fundamental to every aspect of language development. The precommunicative writer is tuned in to language. Jordan starts identifying letters, and toward the end of this precommunicative stage, she begins to tell people the story she wrote on the wall.

The Writing-Like Phase of Spelling Development, with Initial Attention to Sound-Letter Correspondence

Eventually Jordan will arrive at a time when what she writes will begin to look like writing. There will be letters, and many of the letters will stand for something, often whole words (*U* for *you*, for example). There will be initial consonants in words, and some initial consonants will be right. Most of Jordan's letters will be consonants, probably because consonants tend to have names that roughly correspond to the sounds they stand for. She is beginning to notice that letters stand for sounds, and the sounds have something to do with words. We begin to label Jordan's spelling as *temporary,* a more linguistically accurate term than *invented.* It is, in fact, a temporary approximation of conventional spelling.

Jordan's spelling is shortened, similar to all early developing language. The second stage of Brown and Bellugi's (1964) oral language development sequence, for

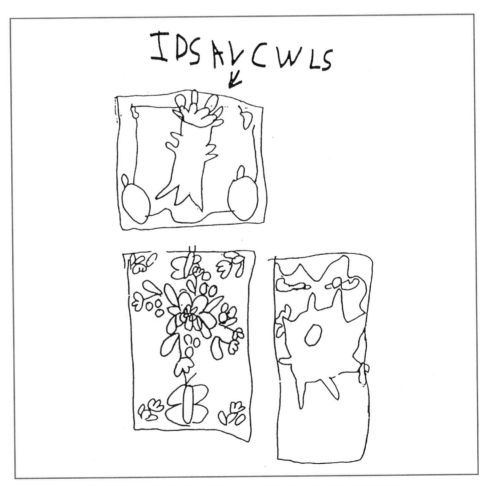

Gentry, J.R., & Gillet, J.W. (1993). *Teaching Kids to Spell.* Portsmouth, NH: Heinemann.

example, is "imitation and reduction," during which the child reduces a five- or six-word sentence to noun and verb—for example, "Jordan is eating her dinner" becomes "Jordan dinner." Spelling by imitation and reduction makes Jordan write *Claus* as *klz*. It's readable. Jordan's spelling eventually moves closer to more reasonable approximations of accurate spelling as she uses more letter names to approximate sounds.

Children now come to understand left to right movement across the page, and they begin to collect sight words and use them accurately more and more often. The stage is set for fluent writing of messages.

The Developing Sound-Letter Correspondence Phase of Spelling Development

Readers can decipher what Jordan writes now. Her spelling isn't conventional, but it is more systematic. She uses letters that represent the sounds she is looking for. She is what is commonly called a "phonetic" speller. Jordan thinks about relationships between sounds and letters, and she has a sense of word boundaries.

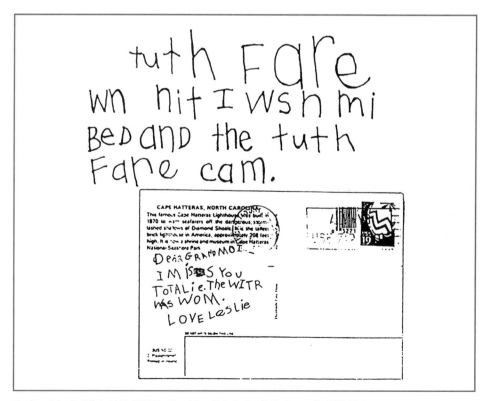

Gentry, J.R., & Gillet, J.W. (1993). *Teaching Kids to Spell.* Portsmouth, NH: Heinemann.

Phonetic spellers adhere to certain spelling patterns. Their endings tend to be spelled as they sound—for example, *walked/wlkt* and *used/uzd*. They have begun to habituate certain sight words they got from reading. Phonetic spellers have seen the words so often and in so many situations (*the, a, and,* and so forth) that they became spelling sight words as well. Sight words are important, for they represent words spelled correctly, and correct words help make writing that an audience can read easily. The ability to write so others can read what you've written is a powerful reinforcer.

The Preconventional Phase of Spelling Development

There comes a time when young writers' spelling begins to look like conventional writing. Prior to this, the focus was on sound alone. Then Jordan begins to notice what words look like. Most of that realization will come from reading, but it also comes from development and from more and more writing.

One of the changes from phonetic to conventional spelling is the use of vowels in syllables. Thus, a phonetic spelling such as *frte* for *forty* will change to include vowels: *forte*.

Good THING to Eat

I like STRALBARES and I like ORRANGE
I like tomato SUPE and I like PECHIS.
I like apples and I like BROCULE (broccoli).
I like COLEFALWORE To, you know.
I like corn and I like green BENES.
I like FRIDE CHEKEN and I like BARBO Q CHEKEN TO.
But most of all I like HO MAED SPOGATE.
THOSS [Those] things are good for you.
That why I put them down.

Gentry, J.R., & Gillet, J.W. (1993). *Teaching Kids to Spell.* Portsmouth, NH: Heinemann.

Preconventional writers also learn what whole words look like. They spell more and more words accurately; some are sight words, but many words they spell accurately because they are beginning to understand how to use their knowledge of how language works. They begin to notice that a sound can be spelled in more than one way. They don't necessarily use their knowledge correctly every time, but they use it enough for readers to recognize their sophisticated knowledge.

The Conventional Phase of Spelling Development

Along about the third grade, young writers' spelling becomes increasingly conventional. While *conventional* does not necessarily mean *accurate* all the time, it does mean predictable, regular, and amenable to formal and direct spelling instruction.

Conventional spellers know what words are supposed to look like, so they tend to know when some of their own are not spelled correctly. They have an increasingly sophisticated knowledge of sound-letter correspondence and how words work. They know about homonyms, for example, and can understand why a big animal with four legs and a saddle is spelled differently from how people sound when they "lose" their voice.

Conventional spellers can learn to use mature patterns that characterize a language that is only 85 percent phonetically regular (*i* before *e* except after *c*, for instance). They are sensitive to appearance and notice when spelling looks right. They're also accumulating a large store of words they know how to spell.

The Concept of Emergent Spelling in Instruction

The concept of the emergent speller is critical for two reasons. First, in its absence, teachers can fail to take advantage of young writers' serious and thoughtful progress in spelling. That does not suggest that the youngest writers ought not be taught conventional spelling. Accurate spellings appear on the Word Wall (Cunningham, 1991), for example. The selection of words for the Word Wall varies. Organizing the words in categories is helpful. The categories can be thematic (ocean words, plant words, community words), or the words can be arranged alphabetically. Adding picture cues for words is helpful for early readers and spellers, especially those who are learning English.

In addition, all students can take charge of developing and maintaining a personal up-to-date word book or writing dictionary. Primary teachers pay daily attention to accumulated sight words from the children's reading. Those words should be on the Word Wall.

The second reason that an understanding of the emergent speller is important in the larger writing program is that it helps teachers understand when and under what circumstances formal spelling instruction should begin. By formal spelling instruction we mean accelerating the accumulation of known words in the spelling-for-writing repertoire. Nearly everything young children do in a literate world adds known words to their writing repertoire almost automatically, but a formal spelling program accelerates the process by making some of the accumulation deliberate and focused.

It's as though teachers are saying, "We have a bunch of words you might need as you write, and many of them fit patterns that will help you with lots of other words, so we're going to study those words and patterns just in case you haven't noticed them from your everyday life in our literate world."

It's legitimate, of course, and almost certainly necessary, to conduct some form of direct instruction in spelling for most young writers. But spelling is itself an artificiality, and spelling a language that is only 80 to 90 percent regular and consistent is an abstraction piled on top of the artificiality. Not many young writers can master an abstraction piled atop an artificiality without help, especially when they're seven years old.

Instructional decisions depend on the phases during which instruction occurs. If there's to be formal and direct spelling instruction during the phase when young writers are thinking mainly of sound-letter correspondence, the direct instruction should focus on arrangements of letters—not so much to make accurate spelling, but to make spelling that is more and more phonetically plausible. Spelling instruction during this phase could center on word families that represent various letter-sound combinations.

Word Families

-at words: *bat, cat, hat, sat, rat*   -ap words: *slap, rap, nap, trap, lap*

-in words: *tin, bin, fin, thin, win*   -it words: *hit, sit, fit, bit, pit, lit*

-op words: *mop, hop, pop, stop, slop*   -og words: *hog, dog, fog, jog, frog*

-et words: *bet, set, get, let, net*   -ell words: *tell, sell, well, bell, fell*

-ug words: *hug, bug, rug, dug, plug*   -ut words: *hut, nut, shut, cut, rut*

By implication, a formal and direct spelling program won't have universal influence on progressively more correct spelling unless it is conducted when young writers are sensitive, or open, to words' appearances as well as their sound and morphemic structure. Furthermore, it is obvious that not all young writers in one second-grade classroom are thinking and writing in the same phase of emergent spelling. Thus, the second-grade teacher who is accommodating emergent spelling is willing to conduct formal and direct spelling instruction so that some children receive one kind of instruction and other children receive other instruction. Henderson (1990) made one of the more insightful and practical statements about general spelling instruction. "No single program," he wrote, "even an individualized one—fits every pupil in every classroom. It is the teacher who must plan, select, and organize time and materials to suit the situation" (p. 98).

Here's what that kind of spelling instruction might look like in a kindergarten class:

Ms. Conner has twenty-two youngsters in November of the kindergarten year. Only seven of those twenty-two are writing, and only two are semiphonetic. Ms. Conner has reserved ten minutes each morning during language period for spelling instruction. She works directly with the two semiphonetic children while most of the rest of the class paints at easels and dictates captions to fifth-grade helpers. Five of the children work with the teacher aide, writing and reading their writing to the adult.

Ms. Conner's work is more systematically spelling-like. Children work with letters and sounds, rhyming patterns, and what words look like, and they put words in sentence context. One of the children's favorite activities is to brainstorm words to Ms. Conner's cue. She asks, "Think of things that are red." As they give her words that name red things, she writes them on her clipboard. When she has ten or so, she tells them the words have to be written on the board; she will do most of the spelling, but she will ask them to think of certain letters and sounds. They're working with their own words—words they thought of—so the necessary prior knowledge is ensured.

She selects one of the red things: fire engine and says, "I'll write it on the board, but you have to help me. How many words do I have to write? Listen— *fire engine.* How many words? How do I begin? Listen as you say the first word. What letter do you hear? What will the first letter be?"

Desiree says *f.* Ms. Conner writes the letter on the board, then proceeds to finish that word and also writes the word *engine.* She goes on down the list, asking for initial sounds and then writing the rest of the word. At this point the focus is on initial letters only. As the year goes on and the children become increasingly confident, Ms. Conner asks them to give her ending letters, medial letters, and vowel letters that correspond with their reading program.

Ms. Conner conducts such lessons nearly every day for the children who begin to show awareness of sounds and letters. Her lessons emphasize children's growing awareness of sounds and letters. She isn't teaching them how to spell, and she certainly isn't teaching them particular lists of words. She is teaching them to pay conscious attention to the sounds, the letters, and the cues to the sounds and letters when they concentrate on their own talk.

The value of the emergent speller concept is in helping teachers take advantage of what young writers are grappling with and learning as they participate in the literate world around them. In addition, the emergent speller concept helps teachers determine when, under what circumstances, and for whom formal and direct spelling instruction should be initiated and conducted. Bear, Templeton, Invernizzi, and Johnston's *Words Their Way* (1996) provides assessments of children's spelling development and describes strategies keyed specifically to children's developmental level. These authors' focus on systematic ways of thinking about spelling instruction would be a complement to any spelling program.

ESL

It's important to remember that the optimal condition is for children to first learn to write, as well as read, in their first language. Then they have a foundation of language knowledge to apply to their learning in the second language. As they transfer their knowledge of first language to a second language, non-standard forms will appear in their writing, just as in oral language. These forms, however, do not point to a lack of literacy development. On the contrary, in writing, "non-English forms, like reading miscues, provide the teacher with information about the student's developing abilities and strategies being used" (Crawford, 1993, p. 232). For example, students may write *es* at the beginning of certain words because that's the form with which they are familiar in their first language (e.g., adding an *e* to *special* because they are applying their knowledge of the Spanish word *especial*). Or they may alter the ending of a word, writing *excel-lente,* using their knowledge of the Spanish word *excelente.* These spellings highlight the power of literacy in the primary language to help children problem-solve as they develop language skills in the second language.

The primary language, then, provides a foundation of language knowledge that supports learning the second language. As children write in the second language, their spellings reveal their pronunciations and knowledge of letter/sound correspondence in the second language (Nathenson-Mejia, 1989). In essence, they are using temporary spellings much like children who might be called emergent readers and writers. One difference is that if children have a solid foundation of literacy in their primary language, they already have a background of literacy development to bring to their language learning in the second language. ■

REVIEW AND REFLECTION

1. Why is it important to understand the emergent speller?
2. What does *temporary spelling* mean, and why is it important to a young child's spelling development?
3. Explain why much of spelling instruction in the early primary grades should be tailored to individual children.

What We Know About Learning to Spell Well

There is a good bit known about learning to spell the language well. These principles of learning reflect over four decades of accumulated evidence.

Evidence Regarding Direct and Systematic Instruction

O'Flahaven and Blassberg (1992) have outlined three attributes of direct and systematic spelling instruction: (1) capitalizing on students' understanding of English orthography (the spelling system), (2) teaching in the context of reading and writing activities, and (3) involving students in decisions about what spelling content is important to learn. If students have a stake in the curriculum, they're far more likely to participate actively on their own terms rather than passively because they have no choice. Further, O'Flahaven and Blassberg make the important point that spelling instruction should occur in the context of how the language works (an understanding of how letters sequence to make words), as well as in writing and reading as spelling contexts.

O'Flahaven and Blassberg's (1992) critical attributes of spelling instruction are also captured in Gill's (1992) description of a literacy program. He emphasizes the importance of "lots of reading in materials that can be read with accuracy and fluency, lots of writing, and direct help with those features appropriate for each child when needed" (p. 452). Spelling instruction, then, occurs in the context of reading and writing and pays specific attention to spelling features that are appropriate for each child.

Spelling instruction that pays attention to English orthography enjoys a research foundation. For example, Tangel and Blachman (1992) showed that children who participate in phoneme awareness activities outperform those who do not, when measured by abilities of phoneme segmentation, letter name and sound recognition, early word recognition, and developmentally superior invented spellings. Yopp (1995) reported substantial evidence that phonemic awareness is powerfully related to spelling acquisition.

References to reading and spelling must be viewed with care because the relationship is not causative. It seems that the connection between spelling and reading is very strong early in the process of literacy development, but the two do not maintain that strong connection as students' knowledge of words and word patterns becomes increasingly sophisticated (Templeton, 1996). The value of fluent reading is that young learners see lots of words every day, and the developmental evidence tells us that young writers begin to approach conventional spelling as they become aware that words have certain appearances as well as phonemic qualities.

References to the importance of time commitment for teaching spelling go back a long way. Over the years, instructional time for spelling has ranged from twelve to fifteen minutes per day, or sixty to seventy-five minutes per week. More recently, the move has been away from formal spelling instruction and specific commitments of daily time for spelling. Assumptions are often made that students will learn to spell simply by reading and writing. Nevertheless, there remain strong recommendations for explicit explorations of how words are spelled, which involves a regular commitment of time (Invernizzi, Abouzeid, & Gill, 1994; Zutell, 1994).

Evidence Regarding Words in Context as Opposed to Words on Lists

Presenting words in context is less efficient than presenting in list form, save for those words for which context is necessary for identifying the word (Templeton & Morris, 1999).

Spelling from lists of words might seem archaic. However, consider what occurs not at the meaning context level but at the level of the single word. When teachers read sentences that contain the spelling word during the spelling test, the sentence cue helps clarify the word, but the sentence is a meaningless cue in the spelling exercise. Students spell words, not sentences.

Discussions about which words are of sufficiently high frequency that young writers should learn to spell them eventuate in lists of words that are compelling by their sheer consistency over the years. Eeds (1985), for example, offers a beginning list of "book words" from children's literature. And a more recent list of words for children's book writers (Mogilner, 1992) reflects words that children are likely to be familiar with.

Mogilner asked reading specialists, university professors in literacy, and panels of children to review the lists. In the end, the lists represented words that educators, publishers, and children themselves agreed should be part of children's store of word knowledge. The following compilation represents the first eight words on four of Mogilner's lists:

Grade 1	Grade 2	Grade 3	Grade 4	Grade 5	Grade 6
across	abroad	able	abandon	abacus	abbey
action	accomplish	absolute	accident	abide	abbot
adult	ace	accept	according	abode	abbreviate
afraid	actor	accompany	accuse	abolish	abdomen
afternoon	advance	account	accustom	abolition	abduct
against	affair	acre	acid	abroad	abhor
age	afire	active	acorn	abrupt	ablaze
ago	aflame	actual	acquaint	absence	abominable

Lists can also be arranged by spelling patterns. For example, the VCV (vowel-consonant-vowel) cluster *bake* can be used in early spelling program lists (*make, cake, lake,* and so forth) along with the VCV cluster in *date* (*fate, gate, late*), providing children the opportunity to spell words according to characteristic patterns, while discriminating between two patterns that can sound very similar and follow similar conventions.

Letter patterns provide readers and writers with predictable cues for spelling. For example, how does a writer know whether the past tense of *hop* is *hopped* or *hoped*? The clue lies in knowing that in many words, when the final consonant is doubled before adding the *ed,* the vowel typically is not a long vowel. So we write, *The bunny hopped.* On the other hand, the long vowel in *hope* remains long when we write the past tense *hoped.* Other words that follow that pattern include *mope* and *mop, slope* and *slop.*

Presenting words in lists also gives children an opportunity to focus on spelling at the word level. It is true that although young writers may spell a half-dozen or a dozen words correctly in list form on Friday but misspell some on Monday when they write, over time they develop a sense of how words are likely to behave, partly from their focus on the words in lists, and also from their larger experience with reading and writing.

The evidence on presenting spelling words in list form does not preclude offering additional words in other contexts. Remember, there is still a Word Wall and each student's own spelling dictionary. Also, everyone in the room is also learning to spell words they use in social studies, mathematics, science, and visual arts.

Evidence Regarding Word Meaning and Spelling

The spelling words taught through the elementary grades tend to be the words children see in reading, the words they use when they talk, and, because they're familiar, the words they think of when they write. Children already tend to know the meanings of these words. This does not mean that knowing what words mean is necessary to knowing how to spell them.

Consider that statement in the context of writing. Even when adults want to write a word but are uncertain about its spelling, chances are they already know what the word means; otherwise, they wouldn't be trying to use it in their writing.

Therefore, teaching word meaning as a major focus in the spelling program does not add to students' ability to become increasingly better spellers.

Spelling and meaning are not entirely unrelated, however. For example, inflectional endings that indicate past tense (-*ed*) tend to be spelled the same way whether they are pronounced /t/ as in *walked,* /d/ as in *played,* or /ed/ as in *hated. Homonyms,* words that sound alike but have different meanings (*bear–bare*) or are spelled alike and have different meanings (*spruce tree–spruce up*), are a good example of the meaning principle in spelling (Henderson, 1990). Words such as *horse* (animal) and *hoarse* (voice) are a part of our language and provide an opportunity for youngsters to realize that spelling includes paying attention to meaning.

Evidence Regarding Games and Other Activities in Spelling Instruction

Spelling games stimulate students to participate in spelling-related activities, but they don't necessarily result in better spelling. Nevertheless, we should make no mistake about the value of gamelike activities in the spelling program. Stimulation of interest is laudatory. Cunningham and Cunningham (1992) point out that it is important for students to develop a sense of when a word "looks right." Games can give young writers many looks at how words appear when they're spelled correctly. The more looks there are, the greater the sense the learners will have of correct appearance.

Thus, although games that seem to compel students' interest seem also to increase spelling performance, the game merely increases the probability of participation in an activity. It doesn't increase the learning.

Word sorts, for example, can be used as gamelike activities that draw children's attention to sounds and spelling patterns. With word sorts, learners classify words by comparing and contrasting the sounds and patterns. As an example, the students might be asked to arrange the following words into four categories, and name the four categories:

definite	intention	osmosis
nation	coordinate	cohabitate
thesis	regurgitate	recognition
accommodate	placate	resuscitate
infinite	kinesis	infinity
regalia	situation	regal

In the arranging, the spellers must look at the words over and over again. For young children, the word sort might look like this:

mat	brace	gate
race	rap	mark
grab	car	fall
shark	ball	bat

Evidence Regarding the Corrected Test

If spelling instruction includes pronunciation activities, various word study activities, and a corrected test, the corrected test contributes 90 to 95 percent of the achievement. In fact, the corrected test alone is often sufficient for mastery or near mastery of a typical spelling list by the upper third of the class. The corrected test appears to be the most important single factor contributing to spelling achievement (Schoephoerster, 1962).

No other activity is as powerful for learning to spell the words as is students' self-correcting a test—that is, corrections by the learners themselves (Henderson, 1990).

There is a good psychological reason for self-correction. Self-correction is about attention. Think back to the discussion in Chapter 2 about attention as a cognitive process critical to learning. People learn because they pay attention. Attention is something of a gating mechanism in learning. If we attend to something, we learn it.

Attention is about concentration or focus. There are two kinds of attention: *deliberate* and *automatic*. Deliberate attention is required when we don't know much about something. When we know something, we still have to attend to it in order to use it, but because we already know it, we attend automatically. For young writers, the task is to become automatic with spelling. To get from needing deliberate attention to using automatic attention requires practice.

The more that young writers attend deliberately to spelling, the more likely they will become automatic spellers, and when they become automatic spellers, they don't have to concentrate on spelling when they write. They can concentrate instead on their message, and for the most part, they'll spell correctly automatically, just as experienced writers do.

Now go back to the corrected test. When young writers write words on a spelling test, they attend to how the words are spelled. If they self-correct, they not only attend to how the correctly spelled words are spelled, but they also attend to the difference between how they spelled some words (incorrectly) and the correct spelling. To self-correct, they have to attend to that difference. That's the power of the *self*-corrected test. Young writers pay better attention to how the words are spelled when they self-correct; thus they learn to spell more words.

Evidence Regarding Writing Words Multiple Times

We all know of children who, when asked to write one or more words ten times, misspell them all ten times, or who write the word—let's say it's *figure*—ten times by writing ten *f*'s in a row down the page, then ten *i*'s, ten *g*'s, and so forth. Henderson (1990) suggests that writing words over and over is "a mild form of torture suitable, perhaps, for the wicked, but not for teaching them to spell" (p. 93).

There is no evidence that writing words over and over increases the ability to spell those words.

Evidence Regarding Focus on Various Modalities for Spelling Instruction

There is considerable controversy associated with all variations on modality-specific instructional intervention. For example, Rosenthal (1974) analyzed the performance of children with language disorders on a series of auditory, visual, and kinesthetic processing tasks and concluded that students' processing difficulties were pervasive across all the modalities. Thus, instruction in an alternative modality had no effect whatever on the children's ability to process language.

Furthermore, it has been known since at least the early 1970s that mildly disabled children perform poorly across the modalities (McGrady & Olsen, 1970). Writing in the air, or auditory, visual, or kinesthetic spelling, certainly interesting as a concept, enjoys no consistent or persuasive evidence regarding students' achievement in spelling.

Evidence Regarding Word-Part Study in Spelling Instruction

"Listen for the syllables," we tell young writers, and it makes sense, because each syllable is a smaller spelling unit and seemingly easier to learn than the entire word. Nevertheless, the evidence doesn't support syllabication as a spelling instruction strategy.

Syllables are sometimes difficult to identify, and linguists have had a difficult time even defining the concept of syllable (Henderson, 1990). Does the word *interest*, for example, have two syllables or three? For most speakers it has two syllables, but spellers tend to rely on three.

Although some syllabic attention can be useful to young spellers—VCCV (vowel-consonant-consonant-vowel) patterns, for example—it is not broadly productive for word study to center on syllable junctures. On the other hand, it is productive to make the memory load smaller. Memory research as far back as 1956 established the active memory capacity of the average person as between approximately five and seven items (Miller, 1956). The implication for spelling a new word is obvious. If the active memory range is five to seven items, how does a child learn to spell *chocolate*, which contains nine items? The answer is, she can't because by the time she gets to the /ol/, the /ch/ is beginning to decay on her.

This is where segmenting information becomes valuable in spelling. Segmentation in spelling isn't necessarily syllabication; it's breaking down the word into units the learner can hold in active memory. A fourth grader can handle the memory load if the word is segmented as *ch oc o late*. (The focus here is primarily on hearing the word spelled, not hearing it pronounced.) Now she has only four items to hold in active memory. We will explore more about the evidence on segmentation later in this chapter.

Evidence Regarding What Is Reinforcing About Accurate Spelling

So what makes young writers want to spell correctly? Clearly, spelling words correctly isn't all that difficult, especially after about the third or fourth grade. That's when the children can read well enough to check their work in a reference book or ask their neighbor how to spell what they think is a difficult word. Most children have entered the conventional phase of spelling development, and they know what correctly spelled words are supposed to look like. They now can sense that a word isn't spelled correctly, or know they have selected a word they aren't sure they can spell correctly and are capable of checking themselves. But many young writers continue to misspell words consistently.

Most young writers are desperately interested in spelling their words correctly. Notice their hands in the air when they want the teacher to spell their words. Their interest in correct spelling isn't at issue. What *is* at issue is whether they develop a sense that they *can* spell the words correctly.

A critical objective of spelling instruction is to ensure that children experience a sense of control over their spelling. The only way to produce that sense of control is to teach spelling in a way that ensures that every young writer experiences directly being a good speller.

We opened this discussion of the writing-spelling interaction by asking that you remember your own spelling experiences in school. Those experiences produce much of young writers' sense of competence with and control over spelling. Most who achieved high spelling test scores acquired a sense of competence and control; most who didn't achieve high scores developed a sense of incompetence and lack of control. If we have spelling instruction that pays attention to what we know about how people learn to spell and we ensure that everyone achieves high scores, we will produce people who have a sense of control.

REVIEW AND REFLECTION

1. Think about spelling programs you've experienced or observed. Does research on spelling support what you've seen or experienced? If so, give examples of how. If not, describe how the programs diverged from what research tells us.

Spelling In and Out of Writing Context

It is clear from evidence presented in this chapter that words in list form are more readily learned than are words in context. Given the essential task associated with spelling, which focuses at the word level, it makes sense, then, to use lists of high-utility words in order to provide young writers with as much confidence as possible in their ability to spell when they write.

However, having established the advantage of lists for word learning, we're still left with the fact that the only reason for learning to spell is to write. The fact that young writers learn to spell words better when the words are studied in lists does not mean that young writers ought not write when they are learning to spell words.

So how do we conduct spelling instruction with words in lists and promote writing at the same time? Every reader of this page can remember such attempts at using writing in spelling in the past, and, in fact, similar activities occur even as you read this page. They look something like the following:

> **Teacher:** *Grandfather.* Write a sentence that contains the word *grandfather.*
> [Young writers write: *My grandfather is old.*]

Many native speakers of English can make that sentence at about twelve to twenty-four months of age. They are, in effect, copying down the grammar in their minds. The activity fails to encourage learners to do anything other than begin with a big letter and hope something happens before they get to the period. If the focus is on the spelling-writing interaction, the writing should be more challenging, more demanding, more thoughtful, planful, and purposeful.

In the *grandfather* task, we want young writers to think in and write sentences that contain the word *grandfather.* And we want them to focus on the sentence that contains the word in such a way that they could not possibly satisfy the writing task without thinking carefully and deliberately about it.

INSTRUCTIONAL SCENARIO

In the Classroom to Write Sentences That Contain Spelling Words

> **Teacher:** I want you to think of a sentence that contains the fifth word on our spelling list. The word is *grandfather.* Natasha?
>
> **Natasha:** *My grandfather is very old.* [There is a smattering of laughter around the room.]
>
> **Teacher:** That works. It's a sentence. How many words are in Natasha's sentence? Yes, there are five. I want you all to think of a five-word sentence that contains the word *grandfather.* René?
>
> **René:** That's from writing. This is spelling time.
>
> **Teacher:** Ah, René, it *is* writing. I'm so glad you remember from several weeks ago when we worked on that sentence-writing activity. Now we're going to use it in spelling. Don't forget, we learn to spell so we can write. I think we'll use that sentence-writing activity a lot during our spelling. I might even use it when I give your spelling test on Friday. Do you have a sentence?
>
> **René:** *My grandfather's face is wrinkled.*
>
> **Lisa:** *My grandfather is very happy.*
>
> **Teacher:** Those are all sentences, and they all contain the word *grandfather.* Now I'm adding a rule. Write another five-word sentence, in which one of the words is *grandfather,* and the first word in your sentence must have at least four letters.

Vicki: *Their old grandfather had breakfast.*

Teacher: Which of the five words in Vicki's sentence is our spelling word? Yes, it's the third word. Everyone, think of a six-word sentence in which *grandfather* appears in the third position. Write it on your paper. Spell all of the words correctly. [The teacher meanders around the room when they read aloud, calling on students she happens to be standing behind. She reads over their shoulder as they read. She directs every reader to correct any spelling errors. If a student isn't sure how to spell a word without help, the teacher writes the word at the top of the student's paper and tells the student to use the word as she wrote it as a model. She then listens to five to six more sentences.]

COMMENTARY

The teacher continues this process by asking her students to write a sentence with the next spelling word. She listens to several and then directs them to write a sentence that contains the next word. She continues through almost half of the fifteen-item spelling list. Then she distributes independent work they can complete during the rest of the day or for homework:

Write the eighth word in the fifth position of a six-word sentence.

_____

Write the ninth word in the third position of a five-word sentence.

_____

Write the tenth word in the fourth position of a six-word sentence.

_____

Write the eleventh word in an odd-numbered position in a six-word sentence.

_____

Write the twelfth word in an even-numbered position of a six-word sentence.

_____

Write the thirteenth word in the first half of an eight-word sentence.

_____

Write the fourteenth word in the second half of an eight-word sentence.

_____

Write the fifteenth word in a six-word sentence right after a word that starts with *t*.

_____

More Spelling Words in Sentences

In another common activity used for spelling, children are asked to write a spelling word in the blank provided, with the three possibilities listed after the sentence: *The old man _____ down the street.* (*walked, scraped, forced*)

Most students select *walked* for the blank. But the selection doesn't mean they know anything about words that end in *ed*, and the completed task has nothing to do with writing. In fact, it would be a more useful task for some second-language speakers if the options included *walk, walked,* and *walking* because then there would be verb selection at least. But still, there would be no writing.

If we want young writers to use the word *walked* in their writing, we direct them to write sentences from the following language activity sheet:

Write one word in each space to make five different sentences:

_____ walked _____ _____ _____ _____

_____ _____ walked _____ _____ _____

_____ _____ _____ walked _____ _____

_____ _____ _____ _____ walked _____

_____ _____ _____ _____ _____ walked

Some may argue that this writing is not authentic, but no one can argue that it is not planful writing, and the point here is to cause young writers to write with their spelling words. The objective is that they *write* with their spelling words, not use obvious word selections to complete sentences someone else wrote.

This discussion is about possible contexts for spelling. So in the previous example, young writers are writing sentences, or creating their own meanings in sentences that contain their spelling words.

Different Spelling Words in Sentences

Now turn to the matter of studying verb forms in the spelling program. Let's say that a spelling lesson features families of words, and one of the families is forms of the verb *walk*. Notice what young writers are doing when they write in these spelling lessons:

Write one word in each space to make sentences:

_____ walk _____ _____ _____ _____

_____ walked _____ _____ _____ _____

_____ _____ walking _____ _____ _____

_____ walks _____ _____ _____ _____

Write sentences using the following directions:
Write a six-word sentence in which *walk* appears in the third position.

_____

Write a six-word sentence in which the word *walked* appears in the fourth position.

_____

Write a six-word sentence in which the word *walks* appears in the third position.

_____

Write a six-word sentence in which the word *walking* appears in the fifth position.

_____

Spelling Words in Paragraphs

A fairly common spelling activity directs students to write a paragraph that uses each of their spelling words. If that activity is focused on the spelling words with limited attention to main idea and coherence, it's seriously deficient for paragraph writing. If there are fifteen or twenty words on the list, one paragraph is not enough to accommodate the list in anything other than a very awkward way, forcing all the words somehow into the several sentences that comprise the paragraph (or what would pass as a paragraph).

Why not divide the task into three parts—and three paragraphs? Direct young writers to write a paragraph in which the main idea is a time when something happened that made them feel good; their paragraph must include any six of the words on the week's spelling list.

When they have that paragraph about figured out, give students the following paragraph cue from Chapter 4: "What do you think is the main idea in your next paragraph?" Once they decide what the next paragraph's idea might be, direct them to write that second paragraph and use six words from the spelling list that they didn't use in the first paragraph. Then ask them: "What is the main idea of the third paragraph?" Finally, ask students to write that third paragraph, using six words from the list that they didn't use in paragraphs one and two. That leaves two words from a twenty-word list. If it feels necessary to account for every word, tell students to use seven words in the first paragraph, six in the second, and seven in the third. The value of this task is that young writers have to think deliberately about main ideas. The main idea is now a context for the spelling-writing interaction.

Remember that we're teaching those kinds of writing tasks (see Chapter 4), so it is quite likely that after several paragraph lessons like those in Chapter 4, students will be able to write such paragraphs as early as the third grade. If the students cannot write such paragraphs, that's a good indication that we need to teach them how to write thoughtful paragraphs on purpose, which they use for purposes of spelling practice.

Fundamental Objectives in Spelling Instruction

Spelling instruction features three objectives, each of which leads young writers to the ability to spell the words they need when they write. While it may seem that the obvious objective is the only important objective in spelling instruction (100s on the weekly test), teachers and parents have bemoaned for years the fact that so many students who turn in a perfect spelling test can't spell the words correctly the following Monday. There is at least an implied second objective when such a complaint is leveled.

Spelling instruction is certainly about the *acquisition* of accurately spelled words, but it is also about remembering what was acquired. That second objective is *retention*. We want young writers to acquire the ability to spell words, but we also want them to retain those spellings so they can use them when the need arises.

The need is writing. When young writers think of a word they need to write, they have to be able to spell it accurately, or know that they haven't spelled it accurately so they can correct it later; and they have to be able to do that without being distracted from the idea or image they're exploring by how a word is spelled. That means they have to be able to apply automatically what they have acquired and retained. *Acquisition*, *retention*, and *automaticity*: those are the word learning objectives in spelling instruction.

Acquisition: Learning How to Spell Words

One of the main reasons that young writers who tend not to spell well continue tending not to spell well is that acquisition of spelling skill demands something most such children often can't give. To acquire the ability to spell a word requires that the learner pay attention to how the word is spelled. Attention is the key. As we mentioned earlier, attention is something of a gating mechanism in learning. Without attention, there is no learning.

Because there is so much stimulation in the environment, young writers have to choose to pay attention to spelling; young writers who don't spell well are precisely the ones who would not select spelling as their focus. So what we have are students with the greatest need for attention and the least inclination to attend.

Not only are those who need it most the least likely to select spelling as their attentional focus, they're also least likely to believe that by disciplining themselves to attend, there's a reward. After all, they have little or no history of spelling effectiveness, so they have little on the basis of which to believe harder work will pay off. On the contrary, they early on convince themselves that they are among those in the world who can never be any good at spelling, and they rationalize that spelling isn't very important anyway.

Now, given that students choose to pay attention to what they do well and on what promises to become something they can do well, the probability is infinitesimal that young writers who don't spell well will attend to how words are spelled when they read and self-correct. As a result, they don't learn to spell much better, and their performance each week proves to them that trying is a waste of their time.

The solution is not to stop teaching spelling in a relatively formal manner. The solution is to ensure sufficient attention to how words are spelled that young writers acquire enough spelling skill to feel that they are competent spellers.

The traditional instructional measure designed to promote attention to how words are spelled is the self-corrected test. Self-correction is very powerful in acquiring the ability to spell words. The problem is how to ensure that as they self-correct their work, students are also paying deliberate attention.

Here's an example of a solution. With age- and ability-appropriate accommodations, this scenario has been conducted for three decades throughout the grades, in both general and special education. It's Monday in Luke's school, and the teacher is getting ready to teach spelling.

 # INSTRUCTIONAL SCENARIO

In the Classroom to Teach Spelling

Teacher: Boys and girls, you need a piece of lined paper and your pencil.

Luke: Isn't it spelling now?

Teacher: Yes, Luke, but we're not going to do it the way we have in the past. Today we're going to start with a test.

Luke: But we haven't studied yet. When do we get to study?

Teacher: We're starting to study now. Number from 1 to 10 down the left side of your paper. I'm going to read the words just as I do when we take spelling tests. You spell the words as well as you can:

1. about	6. could
2. across	7. done
3. became	8. down
4. because	9. even
5. cover	10. ever

[After administering the list, the teacher reads the words again, relatively quickly, ostensibly to make sure the children write them all but mostly to put the sounds of the words into the air again.]

Now I'm going to read the correct spellings, and I want you to score your own papers. If you spelled the word correctly, just leave it alone. If you spelled the word incorrectly, make a mark beside the word because we will be coming back to it. [The teacher proceeds orally.]

Number 1. about. ab out. about.

Number 2. across. ac ro ss. across.

Number 3. became. be ca me. became.

Number 4. because. be cau se. because.

Number 5. cover. co ver. cover.

[The teacher continues to the end of the list of words, segmenting in the same way.]

COMMENTARY

The literature on effective spelling instruction is full of references to self-correction. This is the first of several self-corrections in which the third graders will actively participate today. Self-correction focuses young writers' attention on how the words are spelled.

The words are spelled aloud. That is not to say that young writers ought not use written language as a model, but language is auditory, and learning is enormously complex in the absence of hearing it. The explicit use of hearing the spellings contributes to learning. We want young writers to hear how the words are spelled.

Furthermore, the words are spelled in segments, though not necessarily syllables. The main reason for segmentation is to promote memory. We've discussed the active memory capacity of five to seven items (Miller, 1956). The word in question (*about*) has five items (letters) to remember, but when it is spelled *ab out,* there are only two items (letter clusters) to remember. This is not unlike everyone's telephone number (ten items), which is segmented into area code, prefix, and number (so there are three number clusters to remember, not ten separate numbers).

BACK TO THE CLASSROOM

The teacher has written the spelling chart on the board.

	Test 1	One Letter	Two Letters	Test 2
10				
9				
8				
7				
6				
5				
4				
3				
2				
1				
0				

Teacher: Let me see the hands of everyone who got all ten words correct. [The teacher counts the hands and puts the number under Test 1 to the right of 10.] How many people got nine right? [The teacher puts that number of hands to the right of 9 under Test 1. The teacher continues asking for hands and entering the numbers down the column under Test 1.]

Now I have a question. How many of you marked a word wrong if there was even one letter missing or not in the right place? Ah, everyone. Well then, let's try something a little different this time. I want you to score your test again, but this time you may mark a word right if it is no more than one letter wrong. That means you mark the word correct if there is no more than one letter wrong. There might be an extra letter or one missing, or a letter might be in the wrong place. And if you want to have any word spelled correctly aloud again, just call it out, and I will spell it for you.

There are lots of clarifying questions—for example, "Does it count as one letter if two letters are turned around [reversed]?" The teacher answers all questions as simply as possible because although their questions are very important, the answers are not the point of the lesson. The teacher asks for a show of hands from everyone who got 10 words right [within one letter, of course], and records the number beside the 10 under "One Letter" on the chart, then continues down the numbers. The scores will go up, but the teacher is not finished.

COMMENTARY

The teacher is not suggesting that one letter off makes a word right or is fine spelling. She is not referring to temporary spelling. The teacher is in the midst of a spelling lesson at this stage. The point in a spelling lesson is not necessarily to spell the word correctly the first time, but to *spell it correctly the last time*. Between Test 1 and Test 2, there is intentional spelling instruction. Directing young writers to pay deliberate attention to how words are spelled is an instructional device. If they pay deliberate attention to how the words are spelled, they will learn better how to spell the word. The teacher directs young writers to notice the extent to which a word is spelled incorrectly and asks them to focus on and count the letters, because that makes them pay deliberate attention to how the word is spelled.

The teacher knows she is the best speller in the room, so she spells the words with force and clarity. Also, given that language is learned primarily in the ear, she wants the sounds of words spelled accurately to permeate the room during spelling time. It never matters how often young writers call out the words to be spelled. She spells them again and again, always in segments and always in a clear and strong voice.

There is no need to use the sentences again. The only point here is that young writers pay deliberate attention, that they notice and concentrate on how the words are spelled. Whatever rules the teacher establishes for what constitutes one or two letters are irrelevant. That a child asks the question means that she or he has noticed. That is the objective.

BACK TO THE CLASSROOM

Teacher: Now score your papers again, this time marking as right all the words that are not wrong by more than two letters.

COMMENTARY

Now the third graders pay deliberate attention again to how the words are spelled. In the typical self-corrected spelling test, most students don't pay deliberate attention to how any word is spelled even once.

BACK TO THE CLASSROOM

Teacher: Now let me see the hands of everyone who got all ten words right, with no more than two letters wrong. [The teacher puts the number to the right of 10 under "Two Letters" on the chart, and continues counting hands and recording the numbers down the line.]

Now, boys and girls, turn your paper over and number from one to ten again. Be sure to turn your paper over. [The teacher readministers the test and conducts self-scoring as for Test 1, reading the correct spelling in segmented fashion as she did the first time. Once again, she solicits hands for each level of the scoring chart and records the number of hands at each level under "Test 2."]

A short-term plan book for this scenario is shown in Figure 14.2. Notice in the plan book that after three days of spelling practice, students who have received 80 percent or higher on Test 2 do not have to continue the practice on Thursday or Friday.

The scenario is about spelling by successive approximations (Fearn & Farnan, 1998a; Farnan & Fearn, 1992; Fearn & Rowland, 1983). It is spelling instruction, which is not the same as having a spelling program.

We need to make sure that all young learners believe that conventional spelling is within their capacity—that they can do it and have control over it. We cannot achieve that belief system for anyone whose score every Friday is 20 or 40 or 60. They must earn a high score every week if they are to believe they can spell words correctly. The important word here is *earn*. The learners earn their higher scores by paying attention to how the words are spelled.

We do young writers no favors by eliminating weekly spelling tests. Taking the test away isn't the answer. Making sure all of the children get high scores is the answer. This is all about spelling conventionally when they write. The weekly test is a way (not *the* way or even the major way) to nurture achievement of the eventual objective that the young learners will believe they can learn to spell conventionally.

And remember that in the previous instructional scenario, it's Monday. There have been no worksheets, no word sorts, no phonic analysis, no trial test. It's only Monday, and once everyone knows how it works, the whole activity won't take

Monday	Tuesday	Wednesday	Thursday	Friday
Spelling: Test 1, One Letter, Two Letters, Test 2	Spelling: Test 1, One Letter, Two Letters, Test 2	Spelling: Test 1, One Letter, Two Letters, Test 2	Spelling: Same as Wednesday unless students got an 80% or higher on Test 2	Spelling: Same as Wednesday for anyone not receiving 80% or higher during the week

FIGURE 14.2   Teacher's Plan Book for Third-Grade Spelling Lesson

more than ten minutes. Our experience is that just about everyone in most class-rooms earns 90 or 100 by Thursday. In many classrooms, everyone will have earned 90 or 100. Children who do not earn high scores languish as the 20 to 30 percent of the students who grow up thinking they are poor spellers. Through successive approximation, however, we increase the scores of everyone, and everyone learns to spell more words more conventionally. Remember that people learn to spell words correctly in three ways:

1. They attend to how words are spelled.
2. They chunk the letter patterns to lower the memory load.
3. They focus on the letters and letter patterns in the words.

There are two reasons not to eliminate the weekly spelling tests and the word lists. One is that the evidence tells us that learning words in list form is more effective than learning them in context, and working on spelling directly and systematically is more effective than is working on spelling incidentally, as the need arises. Second, eliminating the lists and the direct instruction also eliminates a systematic opportunity for young writers to study what words look like for writing purposes.

When we're thinking about interactions between spelling and writing, we teach young writers to notice how words are spelled—deliberately, systematically, regularly, and over time. We also teach a wide variety of words for the purpose of increasing every young writer's repertoire of words available for writing.

Another question that has always plagued writing teachers is why young writers can get good spelling test scores on Friday but misspell the same words when they write on Monday. The reason for the discrepancy is that young writers' Friday test performance is more a display of what they memorized on Thursday evening than what they learned about spelling the words. And we know that items merely memorized for short-term retrieval under a specific condition not only deteriorate over extended time, they also disappear when the condition changes. The Thursday evening study session is the time. The test is the condition. Test performance doesn't last until Monday, and the writing condition is different from the test condition.

REVIEW AND REFLECTION

1. What are the three critical objectives in spelling instruction, and why is each one important?
2. Why might young writers avoid the work necessary to become increasingly better spellers?
3. What causes learners to approach a task with effort and perseverance?
4. How can a spelling approach called *spelling by successive approximations* ensure that young learners will approach, rather than avoid, working to become increasingly better spellers?

Retention: Learning How to Retain the Ability to Spell Words

Acquisition of an increasingly large bank of words that young writers can spell accurately is highly important in writing instruction. But young writers also have to remember how to spell the words. How do we teach spelling in a way that will increase the probability that students retain the words?

Learning depends not only on attention, but also on the ability to hold information in active memory long enough for it to be recorded in long-term memory. Recall that Luke's teacher orally modeled the spelling of the words in letter segments. There are five characters in the word *about*, but the teacher read two, not five. Reducing the number of items that learners have to accommodate increases the probability that they will remember the meaningful chunks, not merely the individual characters.

In addition to reducing the number of items, we also have to make sure that the learners remember the information in a way that's directly useful. Luke's teacher recited the spelling model as clusters of letters. If young writers in Luke's class try to remember that the first sound in spelling *about* is the second sound in reading *mother*, and the first sound in reading *under*, they have to translate from sound to letter. But if they remember that the spelling sounds are clusters of *letters*, their memory will contain information they can access without translation.

Also, retention demands more than one generic memory. When we write, we have to be able to reproduce words. We also have to recognize when a word is and is not spelled correctly. Those are two different kinds of memory. That young writers can recall a word when they think of it for writing does not mean they can necessarily recognize if it is spelled correctly.

To retain accurate spelling demands *recall memory*. Recall means accessing from memory the whole form of what is recorded there. When accurate spellings are placed in memory, the whole word, with all of its characters, in segments, and fully formed, is stored. The learning activity in Luke's room promotes recall memory.

Another powerful recall memory spelling activity is word pyramids (Fearn, 1983), which we discussed in Chapter 4. Recall that the children think of words that begin with a certain letter—perhaps the first letter of their last name. The first word contains three letters, the next contains four, the next five, and so forth one letter at a time, until they have a list of nine or ten words (*f - fit - fear - focus - farmer - fitting - famished - fascinate . . .*). Notice that students must think of words and deliberately spell each one until they find one that contains the necessary number of letters. This activity focuses explicitly on recall memory.

If young writers were to pull a word pyramid blank from a box just inside the door two mornings each week, complete it, and turn it in as a ticket to recess, they would think and spell lists of words of their own choosing deliberately twice each week all year. A word pyramid blank, on a 5½- by 8½-inch sheet, looks like this:

b	h	a
_ _ _	_ _ _	_ _ _
_ _ _ _	_ _ _ _	_ _ _ _
_ _ _ _ _	_ _ _ _ _	_ _ _ _ _
_ _ _ _ _ _	_ _ _ _ _ _	_ _ _ _ _ _
_ _ _ _ _ _ _	_ _ _ _ _ _ _	_ _ _ _ _ _ _
_ _ _ _ _ _ _ _	_ _ _ _ _ _ _ _	_ _ _ _ _ _ _ _
_ _ _ _ _ _ _ _ _	_ _ _ _ _ _ _ _ _	_ _ _ _ _ _ _ _ _

Don't confuse word pyramids with a spelling program or with teaching spelling. While it should represent a portion of a spelling program, the word pyramid only causes children to recall and write lots of words. Word sorting promotes seeing lots of words. So do word searches, and free and directed reading. Both seeing lots of words and reproducing lots of words are important in learning to be a good speller. Neither is sufficient; both are necessary.

But recall memory, although important, is the lesser of two kinds of memory modes, at least for spelling. Good young writers know when a word is and is not spelled correctly. They recognize accurate spelling. Good young writers have an enormous number of words they think of when they write that are recorded in their recognition memory. Those are not necessarily words young writers can spell accurately from scratch, but they remember what the words are supposed to look like, so when they read what they've written, they connect their image of the words with what they've written, and recognize similarities and differences.

Words are recorded in recognition memory through attention to (seeing) lots of words. That's why better readers—children who have seen and attended to lots of words—tend to be better recognition test spellers.

The most obvious way to promote recognition memory is to promote lots of reading. But we also need to consider how to do that in the context of spelling instruction, or the spelling portion of writing instruction. There, such activities as word sorts, word searches, and organization of words on lists all cause young writers to look at and pay attention to lots of words.

 INSTRUCTIONAL SCENARIO

In the Classroom to Promote Recognition Memory

Teacher: We're going to make a list on the board. You give me words, and I'll write. I want you to think of nature words. Think of words that could be used to talk or write about nature in general or something about nature. Janie?

Janie: *Water.*

Teacher: That's a nature word. I'll begin here and write your words as I call on you. Charles?

Charles: *Reptile.*

[The fluent thinking activity continues until the space available on the board is filled with column after column of words. It takes about six to eight minutes in a third grade to fill a fair-sized portion of a board or several sheets of butcher paper.]

Teacher: There are a lot of words up here. Look over the list. See if you can figure a way that the words can be arranged in four categories. Just think of the categories. Who has some categories? Pauli?

Pauli: I think there are animals, water things, air things, and maybe science words.

Teacher: Good. Who else has some categories? Anna?

Anna: Geography (like rain forests), animals, plants, and ecology.

Teacher: Those are good categories. Let's try those and then think of some more. I have written Pauli's categories on this side of the board and Anna's on the other side. People on this side of the room try to arrange the words in Pauli's categories, and on this other side, everyone try to arrange in Anna's categories.

COMMENTARY

A short conversation about the categories should follow after about ten to twelve minutes of word writing. Tell the young writers that tomorrow they will categorize the words again according to some new categories. Move the words around through various categories for several days. Remind students to pay attention to how they are spelling the words when they write them in categories on their paper.

Conduct some of the categorizations with young writers in collaborative dyads or triads. When they work together, they have to talk about the words. On Tuesday of the following week, conduct a new fluency activity, this time making a list of words that name things that are green. Categorize on Wednesday and Thursday. Then brainstorm a new list the following Tuesday, this time with words that have two syllables.

This sort of activity is all about looking at words, paying attention to what words look like, and working on ways to think about words. It isn't so much for acquiring words, although that happens; it's more about recognizing what the words look like.

What we're trying to accomplish in the writing-spelling interaction is retention of sufficient spelling to accommodate the needs of young writers when they write. Those needs include acquisition, or learning how to spell an ever-larger variety of words for the purpose of increasing the number of words young writers can use to paint their ideas and images. Their needs also include retention, in two forms. One is recall memory, or retention of words, so that young writers can reproduce those words when they write. The other is recognition memory, or retention of what accurate spelling looks like, so young writers can determine whether words are spelled accurately when they write.

Automaticity: Learning to Spell Words Automatically

While it is necessary to acquire the ability to spell words correctly and to retain the correct spellings we acquire, acquisition and retention alone fail to satisfy the spelling requirement, *for writing*. To acquire the accurate spelling of words, we have to pay deliberate attention to how words are spelled. To retain accurate spellings, we also have to commit deliberate attention to how words are spelled. Acquisition and retention are required when we learn to spell.

When we write, however, our deliberate attention is on the purpose, the audience, the images and ideas that we're constructing as we write. We learned in Chapter 2 that people cannot pay deliberate attention to more than one unpracticed behavior at once. So, if writers pay deliberate attention to how the words are spelled, they cannot pay consistent deliberate attention to their ideas and images. The result is interruption of writing flow as they switch from how to spell words to ideas and images and back to how words are spelled. When writers divert their attention from what they're trying to accomplish in the writing, they lose track, and the writing lurches about with no consistent center or mission. In a phrase, it is necessary to acquire and retain correct spellings of words, but acquisition and retention are not sufficient for the writing purpose.

Knowing that the spelling requirement interrupts writing flow, many teachers tell young writers not to concern themselves with how the words are spelled; instead, spell the words in whatever manner makes sense at the moment, move on, and come back later to correct the spelling. Given that people learn to do what they do, if young writers follow that direction, what they learn is to write without concern for how words are spelled. That sort of writing may help young writers get black on white, but in the process, they practice writing without concern for conventional spelling, even as they're in the developmental stages of spelling when they are able to spell words conventionally.

No, avoiding the anxieties associated with spelling doesn't solve any problems. The solution is in not only acquiring and retaining the ability to spell a burgeoning number of words they think of when they write, but in ensuring enough practice with spelling those words that spelling becomes increasingly automatic. Then, young writers can commit their deliberate attention to ideas and images while they spell more and more words automatically.

The mediator between deliberate and automatic attention is practice. Put another way, when a skill becomes increasingly practiced, it is increasingly automatic. People can pay attention to scores of practiced things all at once. The solution to the spelling interference for young writers is not to avoid it; it is to approach it head-on and ensure enough practice that spelling becomes automatic.

Certainly, most young writers won't accomplish spelling automaticity quickly. They have to practice, daily, looking at what words look like and writing them, mostly in sentences and longer pieces, and in the looking and the writing, they have to pay attention to how words are spelled conventionally. They don't have to write ten spelling words ten times each, but they should write five thoughtful sentences for each of at least five of the words on the weekly list.

Write a sentence that contains the spelling word *jungle*.

Write a sentence in which *jungle* appears in the third position.

Write a seven-word sentence in which *jungle* appears in the fourth position.

Write a sentence that contains the word *jungle*, but make the main idea in your sentence something about a fleeing animal.

Write a double sentence string (Chapter 4) in which the main idea is rainfall in the jungle. Use the word *jungle* at least once in your double sentence string.

To look at words often and become increasingly automatic with what they look like, they should sort lists of words into categories several times each week. Arrange the following list of words into three categories. Arrange them again into two categories. Rearrange them into four categories.

strawberry	tomato	apple	dress
fire engine	bruise	blood	cherry soda
rose	flushed	wagon	hood

In preparation for Friday's Word Faire, read for five minutes in a dictionary and a thesaurus, notice a word and think about what you can teach the rest of us about your word. On Friday, we'll go around the room and listen to everyone's word.

Because it is important to see many words every day in order to become automatic at what they look like when they're spelled conventionally, it is critical to read every day. There should be independent reading, and the teacher should read aloud, guiding young writers through text, noticing how writers use words and how words are spelled.

Finally, automaticity is achieved when young writers value conventional spelling and are held responsible for it. They must know that when their papers cross their desk from themselves as the only audience to others as the audience, both self-respect and respect for their audience require that they make sure the words are spelled correctly.

But the writing-spelling interaction presupposes even more than acquisition and retention, for those operate at the word level alone. Writing is syntactic. It operates at the sentence level where young writers explore and define ideas and images. They need more than a collection of words, however large. They need the intent to spell accurately when they write.

REVIEW AND REFLECTION

1. Distinguish between *recall* and *recognition* memory.
2. Why are both recall and recognition memory critical to being an effective speller?

Spelling Words Accurately in Writing

As we've made clear several times in this book, no one teaches spelling for the goal of spelling. We teach spelling so people can write. The application for spelling is in writing. We want young writers to spell correctly the words they think of when they write.

It's worth emphasizing again what "correctly" means. If the only audience is the writer, the words must be spelled accurately enough for the writer to be able to read the draft. We send that message by saying, "Spell *as well as you can* every time you write." If the writer is to be the only audience forever, the words never need to be spelled any more accurately than the writer needs in order to read them. But when the writer's work will be read by any audience other than the writer, "correct spelling" means that every word is spelled correctly. There is but one criterion for what "correct" means and when "correct" is critical: *the audience.* An audience expects the words to be spelled correctly, and when they aren't, the communication purpose of writing is compromised.

Any message about lack of concern for spelling is confusing. Consider that we teach young writers to spell the words correctly in spelling lessons. We tell them that they study the words so they will be able to spell them when they write. Then when they write, we tell them they shouldn't worry about spelling. This is a confusing message for youngsters.

Young Writers' Commitment to Spelling Conventionally

Sufficient spelling performance in writing depends largely on young writers' *commitment* to spell their words conventionally when they write. Part of the spelling-writing interaction includes establishing in young writers the commitment to spell conventionally the words they use when they write. Commitment is a value system.

Commitment has been discussed in reference to spelling conscience (Cramer, 1998) as a sense of responsibility. In fact, conventional spelling in writing cannot be achieved on the basis of word knowledge alone. There are too many words. It is unlikely that young writers will ever master enough words to be able to spell conventionally everything they think of when they write. The only possibility left for conventional spelling, therefore, is a value system regarding spelling that makes the writer feel responsible for accuracy.

To establish the sense of responsibility, the spelling conscience, we must value spelling. We cannot tell young writers to value spelling, however; we have to put them in a position to assume the responsibility, and then to exercise that responsibility over and over.

- Use Power Writing for spelling awareness (see Chapter 6). The learners draft against a time limit and adjust their draft to ensure accurate spelling.

- Reinforce the post–third-grade rule: *As long as the paper is on your side of the desk, the spelling is your business; when it crosses the desk, the words must be spelled correctly.*
- Never suggest that spelling doesn't count and that content is more important than spelling. Spelling always counts. The meaning of the content is carried in correctly spelled words.
- Value spelling in writing as highly as it is valued on the Friday test.
- Recognize that early spelling is temporary. Value movement toward accuracy. Make spelling a part of every weekly writing conference.
- Encourage awareness of spelling outside school. Reserve a bulletin board for examples of inaccurate spelling the children bring to school from signs, advertisements, and other commercial print.

Only when spelling is valued will it improve in young writers' work. If we're all conscious of good spelling, the spelling gets better.

REVIEW AND REFLECTION

1. Why is it important that writers develop a value system that includes a commitment to accurate spelling?
2. Describe one or two instructional activities that focus on students' commitment to effective spelling.
3. What do effective spellers do to ensure that a word is spelled correctly?

A Summary: Teaching Spelling Versus Having a Program

Just as there is a dramatic difference between *teaching* writing and promoting writing, there is a dramatic difference between teaching spelling and conducting spelling programs. The traditional spelling program tends to introduce a word list on Monday, trial-test it on Wednesday, work on some phonic and structural analysis on Tuesday and Thursday, and test the words on Friday morning. Alternative programs along the way have used words from subject matter textbooks and from students' writing in order to avoid decontextualized word lists. Some districts have their own spelling lists and supply teachers with games and worksheets. With the renewed interest in literacy and writing, and a priority on "authenticity" in all writing, some teachers, and even some schools, have deemphasized spelling on the assumption that if young writers write and read enough, they'll begin to spell better. In some classrooms, word searches have become synonymous with spelling programs. In others, as phonics first comes around again, the assumption is that good spelling will follow. It isn't all that uncommon to hear teachers say they use Word Walls, and that's their spelling program, or they do spelling in minilessons. While there are a variety of umbrellas under which something called "a spelling program" operates, it is important to understand that merely having a spelling program, merely *doing* spelling, isn't the same as *teaching* young writers to spell effectively.

To summarize this chapter on the writing-spelling interaction, recall the three objectives that must be satisfied in any attempt to teach young writers to spell in an increasingly conventional manner as they write.

The first of those objectives is that young writers acquire the ability to spell an ever-increasing number of words and retain those spellings over protracted time. The second is to remember well enough that they spell their words conventionally whenever they write.

Third, teaching spelling well means that everyone develops a sense of spelling competence. Young writers do not avoid writing because they are afraid of spelling. Instead, they write freely, because they know they can spell the words they think of when they write.

Finally, spelling instruction must also provide young writers with the tools necessary for ensuring that the words are spelled correctly. Those tools have to do with knowing when words may not be spelled conventionally, how to make the corrections, or how to select alternative words.

ACTION RESEARCH PROJECT

RESEARCH QUESTION

What's the effect of spelling by successive approximations on students' acquisition of words? On their retention of words?

SAMPLE

Your students

METHODOLOGY

Use spelling by successive approximations with your students' word lists over three weeks. If you don't typically use word lists, choose at least ten words for each of three lists, one list for each of three consecutive weeks. (Review the discussion on how to select words to study for spelling.) Record students' scores for the three weeks. If you have a colleague who would like to participate with you, ask this person to give the same word lists to his or her students, using the more traditional pretest-study-test procedure, and record the students' scores at the end of each of the three weeks. In both classes, add three to five words from the previous week's list to see whether students are retaining what they've learned.

RESULTS

What scores did you record for your students over the three weeks? How did they do on the carryover words from previous weeks? How do your students' scores compare with those of your colleagues' students? On the end-of-the-week test in both classes, are your students' spellings better approximations of conventional spelling?

CONCLUSION

Did the study go well? Were there any problems or limitations? What do your results mean?

15 Writing-Vocabulary Interactions

BEFORE YOU READ

- A primary purpose for vocabulary development is to help writers write better.
- There is a difference between vocabulary development for recognition and vocabulary development for recall.
- It is critical in vocabulary development activities to help young writers understand how words modify and qualify other words.
- It is critical to help young writers understand how the spelling patterns, roots, and affixes affect word meaning and use.
- A body of research literature informs us quite clearly about what is and what is not productive intervention for vocabulary development.

The Main Thing About Vocabulary Development

When Elbert (the lead character in Audrey and Don Wood's *Elbert's Bad Word*) was conked on his great toe by a croquet mallet, he uttered the "bad word" that is central to the book that bears his name. A furry creature, the bad word lurked close by as Elbert got his mouth washed out with soap for his verbal transgression. Elbert, knowing the soap didn't cleanse him of the word, meandered down the path to the wizard's cottage, for he knew, as everyone knows, that mere gardeners don't become wizards unless they can do important stuff, such as solve five year olds' bad word problems. And that is what the wizard did. He baked a tasty little cake for Elbert, into which he mixed some sparkling and crackling words especially appropriate for the moment when a boy's great toe becomes the landing point for a croquet mallet. Wizards are always right and true, so later that afternoon, when Elbert's toe got in the way of the croquet mallet again, he let go with the wonderful words he acquired from the wizard's tasty cake, and the world was right again.

It's a good story. It featured a way for Elbert to solve his problem, which is what stories are supposed to show characters doing. The trouble is that the rest of us don't have wizards. We can't just eat a cake and get the good words we need to make our writing work just right. There are well-advertised audiotapes that promise to make us vocabulary wizards, pages in magazines that list terrific words and their definitions, and special preparation courses for high-stakes vocabulary tests that masquerade as measures of achievement. Certainly the ads are powerful, the pages are appealing, and the courses sometimes increase scores, but rarely does anyone's vocabulary increase demonstrably as the result of any of those direct attempts at vocabulary development. Most people's vocabulary increases the hard way: they work at it.

One major focus in this chapter is what effective vocabulary development work looks like in practice. We know a great deal about that. The other major focus is captured in a comment attributed to Albert Einstein: "The main thing is to make sure the main thing remains the main thing." This book is about writing as the anchor in the language arts program; therefore, the main thing is the role of words in writing.

If we intend for young writers to learn words so they can write better, we have to teach words in writing context. That doesn't mean using writing to teach words someone decided are important to learn. It means discovering the need for words when we write.

Eddie was a fourth grader several years ago, and while working with him and the others in his room, I (Leif) prompted a sentence that was to contain the idea of old man and something the old man was doing. Eddie raised his hand and read the sentence he had written in his mind: *The old man walked slow and crooked down the street.* I asked Eddie to walk across the front of the room the way he described the old man in his sentence. To peals of laughter, Eddie staggered to and fro across the room.

When the laughter died down and Eddie returned to his seat, I asked him if his old man were sick or injured. He said the old man wasn't sick or injured; he was just old. I asked if old people walk the way he demonstrated. Sometimes they did, he replied, but not usually. "But that's what your sentence said," I told Eddie. "The sentence said that the old man walked slowly and crooked. That's what you did in your demonstration."

I explained about the meanings we build in our minds and souls when we read the words authors use when they write. I walked slowly and explained that my walk is what Eddie wrote. Then I asked if anyone had ever seen an old man walk faster. Everyone raised their hand, and many told stories about old men they knew who didn't walk slowly.

I asked Eddie to hang in there: "We aren't criticizing your sentence, Eddie. We're working on a lesson. Your sentence and your superb demonstration are important to the lesson."

This lesson didn't take as long as it seems when it's written here. In fact, everything described so far, and everything that follows in this description up to the point below that reads, "It was time to teach," took slightly over one minute.

I asked Eddie if the man in his demonstration were staggering. Eddie agreed that he probably was. "Were you trying to suggest that he was drunk?" More laughter. (Drunk was funny to those ten year olds.) Eddie said he was acting drunk. I asked if he thought *drunk* was a descriptor of old men. He said it wasn't, but that he did show the crooked part.

"Okay, boys and girls," I said, "Eddie had a good sentence that contained an old man and something an old man did, and Eddie did a pretty good demonstration of the words in his sentence. But the words made Eddie demonstrate things that he said aren't really like old men. The question for this lesson is, What are the right words for Eddie's sentence?"

I addressed Eddie again: "Show us how you want the old man to walk, and we'll try to figure out words for what you do." This time Eddie didn't stagger or feign a drunk or injured man. Eddie walked slowly, not in a straight line, looking around as he walked and seeming contemplative. "What was that?" I asked. Every one of the very few responses modified the verb. Not one of the fourth graders changed the verb. The man walked slowly; he walked wobbly; he walked while looking around; he wasn't in a hurry; he didn't care about the time; he was retired so it didn't matter. "But how did he go from one side of the room to the other?" I asked. "You keep saying he walked. This is what walking looks like." I walked across the room, first fast, then slowly, then several steps, hesitate, and several more steps. I wandered. I meandered. I shuffled. "What are these called?" They called every one by the same verb: *walk*. Then they modified or qualified. It was as though they had two words for human ambulation: *walk* and *run*. To get what they wanted as an image of human ambulation, they added clarifiers or specifiers. It was time to teach.

"Boys and girls, if we're trying to tell how the man moved down the street, what words could we use?" I wrote the words on the board as they called them: *walked, ran, run, running, walking, sprinting, falling, wandering* (Josie said that's what her grandfather with Alzheimer's does), *kicking a rock, feeling his way,* and *walking lost.*

I pulled down a wall map and showed the Sacramento River and asked what word to use to tell what the river is doing. They reverted to *crooked*. "That is a good word," I said, "but it doesn't tell what the river is doing. It tells how the river is doing what it is doing, but what is it doing? I am walking. I am running. I am standing. What is the river doing?

"I have a word for you to think about," I said. "The word is *meander*. To meander is to wind about, to twist, to turn, to stroll. The river is meandering down the valley. Look how it meanders. It moves this way and that, curling around the mountains. It seems to have no purpose." Then I pointed to the Mississippi River between Minneapolis and Dubuque and showed how it runs mostly straight. "The Colorado River runs directly; it rushes down the valley or crashes through the gorge. This Sacramento River seems to get where it is going but is in no hurry to get there. If I meander across the room, it looks like this. It is called meandering across the room. Now, Eddie, give us your sentence again about the old man." Eddie read his sentence: *The old man meandered down the street.*

Learning Words for Writing

Young writers can expand their vocabulary by refining the words they use to describe what they hear, sense, see, and so forth (Moffett & Wagner, 1992). Eddie used a correct word in his new sentence. It wasn't his word. It was mine, and as his teacher, it's my job to give him words. *Meander* is a right word because the image it projects is close to what Eddie had in mind for the old man. The words Eddie chose to modify *old man* at first were imprecise, even inaccurate. He chose two adverbs to modify his verb because he knew his verb was imprecise and didn't convey what he wanted to about how the old man moved down the street. Eddie didn't need more adverbs; he needed a better verb. Writers often say that modifiers are mere excuses for lack of the right nouns and verbs. In school, however, it's common to see an adjective and adverb unit based on the imprecise notion that the more of them that appear in young writers' work, the clearer or more detailed the writing is.

The main thing in vocabulary instruction for writing purposes is not that teachers are wrong to teach modifiers to provide clarity and detail, or that good writers don't modify their nouns and verbs. Rather, it is to provide young writers with as many as possible of the words they can use when they write. Eddie needed better verbs. The vocabulary-writing interaction is about getting more verbs for Eddie—verbs he comes to know well enough that they begin to appear in his writing.

The question is not whether Eddie and his fourth-grade friends need more words in order to write better. They do. Nor is it whether teachers should offer more words in order to help Eddie and his friends to write better. They should. The question is how to ensure that Eddie and his friends have more writing-useful words at the end of the year than they did at the beginning of the year. Part of the answer has to do with getting more writing-useful words to them. The other part is making sure they use them. The accumulated evidence in vocabulary development can shed some light on both parts of the answer.

What Do We Know About Words?

What we know about words is that there are a lot of them. The *Oxford English Dictionary*, published in spring 1989, came in twenty volumes that contain 615,000 entries, 2.4 million supporting quotations, and 60 million words of exposition (Bryson, 1990). We also know that English is a responsive language; that is, its meanings shift and change in response to adjustments in how words are used. *Cool*, for example, is a word that signifies a temperature on the cold side of warm, perhaps closer to but slightly colder than *tepid*. Then it changed. It became a modifier used by young adolescents who said things such as, "Cool," when they listened to music or complimented one another's bell-bottom pants. More recently, the word *like*, traditionally used to designate a comparison of some sort (*Her hair is like silk*) or appreciation of someone (*I like you*), responded to the pressures of youth and became an all-purpose secondary hesitation (*Like her like hair is, you know, like silk, and when she like brushes it, she goes like wow*). The language is adaptable, and its words are capable of taking on just about any roles its users choose to assign.

How Many Words Do We Know?

A host of studies have aimed at determining the number of words people know. The average well-read person, for example, is estimated to recognize about 20,000 words, but even the well-read person uses only about 1,500 to 2,000 of those words in a week's worth of conversation (Bryson, 1990). Bryson reports that the educated person's word bank, or talking vocabulary, is estimated at about 15,000 words.

It is very difficult to do anything other than estimate, though, because "the number of words we use is very much smaller than the number of words we know" (Bryson, 1990, p. 150). That is particularly clear if well-read persons, with an estimated recognition vocabulary as large as 20,000 words, use only 1,500 to 2,000 in a week's worth of conversation. In fact, one estimate of word use showed that a scant 9 words (*and, be, have, it, of, the, to, will, you*) account for up to a quarter of those in common use, and half of the words in common use can be accounted for among 43 words (Bryson, 1990). We used a form of the word *estimate* five times in this and the previous paragraph just to punctuate the point.

One of the problems with estimating vocabulary size on the basis of what writers write is that what we write is not an index of what we know. The words we use when we write merely reflect some of what we know. Consider Shakespeare (Bryson, 1990). The Bard never once used the words *Bible* or *Trinity* in anything we read and attribute to his writing, but their absence from his writing doesn't mean that he didn't know those words.

Accurate measurement of vocabulary size is improbable given the technology and measurement devices available today. We know more than we use in speaking and writing. We invent as we go, often using words for the first and last time just to fit a need. We add affixes we've never associated with certain roots before (e.g., *routinize*), but the construction reveals only the flexibility of the language, not our knowledge of a new word. We come to understand how the language works and how words work in the language, and that understanding, not our explicit word bank, often produces words. One key question, then, is, Where do the words come from?

REVIEW AND REFLECTION

1. What would you say is the most important part of the instruction Leif carried on with the word *meander*?
2. Talk with a partner about whether you think the children are likely to use the word *meander* in their writing after the instruction they received in the lesson above. Would they be more likely to use the word in their writing had they looked it up in the dictionary and written the definition? What do you think is the main difference between the two instructional procedures?
3. If people know so many words, why do so few show up in their writing?
4. Do you think there is a difference between knowing words for reading and knowing words for writing?

How Do We Learn Words?

Vocabulary increases in response to need, and the increase reflects the verbal environment. Vocabulary development responds to experiences and our associations of those experiences with words that name and describe them (Petty, Herold, & Stoll, 1968). Certainly, then, there is little reason to expect much impact when we present words before experiences or words with no experiential context at all.

Rupley, Logan, and Nicols (1998–1999) make the point about experience when they write that vocabulary knowledge closely reflects the breadth of both direct and vicarious experiences. A vocabulary that reflects experiences associated with the zoo does not depend on a day at a zoo; that vocabulary can emerge from vicarious experiences with the zoo as well. A good film will do. So will a half-hour of the Discovery Channel on the Serengeti Plain. The learner needs a motive for paying attention to and learning new words. Experience is something with which to associate new words, a latticework on which to hang new words. Experiences represent the need to have words, for words are what we use to mediate, both mentally and expressively, what we know.

Vocabulary Development in Young Children

Children, especially children, encounter an enormous amount of new experience every day, both direct and vicarious, and they talk about those experiences. Nagy and Anderson (1984) and Nagy and Herman (1987) estimate that a child's vocabulary increases by about 3,000 words per year. Some estimate that children's vocabulary doubles between the ages of three and seven (Jenkins & Dixon, 1983).

Where does that growth come from? We know children are encountering a wide range of new experiences virtually every day. We also know that between ages three and seven, no one is presenting them with weekly lists of new words that they study in dictionaries and report on at the end of the week. In a word, the growth is incidental. It's incidental to their lives, their experiences. They live in environments where things happen, and they acquire words that they need to have in order to label what they're experiencing and to talk about their experiences to others. *Incidental learning* in response to need is the only way to explain children's vocabulary growth. To ignore the role of need in vocabulary development, where need comes from experiences, is to undermine any systematic attempt at vocabulary development.

Children learn more than words in their need-driven vocabulary development. What makes vocabulary authentic, and therefore useful, is what learners come to understand about relationships between and among words—the nuances that make word selection precise. Children need experience with the words too, and they need to categorize meanings, usages, and the roles that words play in sentences.

The experiential and essentially incidental foundations of vocabulary development point to a decidedly indirect perspective on vocabulary development. Nevertheless, this chapter does not eschew direct instruction for vocabulary development. After all, the lesson in Eddie's classroom, where the word *meander* occurred, was direct, experiential, and in response to need. The focus in this chapter—indeed, throughout this book—is on intentional or direct instruction. Intentional instruction applies to vocabulary development as well.

What is not appropriate to vocabulary development is what we do with the isolated, or even contextualized, word lists that some teachers distribute on Monday for Tuesday and Wednesday homework, Thursday review, and a Friday test. There is nothing about any of it that is necessarily inappropriate to vocabulary development. What isn't appropriate to vocabulary development is what the students do with the lists when they do their homework and what they try to reproduce when they take their tests.

It's Tuesday evening when Judy pulls the vocabulary homework from her backpack. There is a list of ten words: *osmosis, mitosis, cell, photosynthesis, investigation, experiment, germination, reproduction, observation,* and *membrane.* Judy's task is to write definitions and sentences that contain the words. So far, so good. Words have meanings, and those meanings should be applied to the experiences children have and the words they use to mediate their experiences. The list includes science vocabulary from the unit under study. Judy's list reflects her experiences.

Judy reaches for her dictionary to begin her homework. This is where the homework begins to go bad. The problem with dictionaries, for the purpose to which Judy is putting hers, is that there is a difference between knowing a definition and knowing a word (Anderson & Nagy, 1993). Dictionary definitions often contain imprecise or incomplete definitions, or definitions that do not precisely fit the context in which the word was used in school or in the textbook. Therefore, many students have difficulty interpreting and applying the definitions. Judy might find multiple definitions of *reproduction* and write her sentence about copy machines or knock-off art. Worse, she might write her sentence about biological reproduction but think of it in the sense of copy machines.

Dictionary definitions usually fail to capture the nuances that make words live and make them useful when children talk and write. Talking and writing are about nuances, not definitions. But the homework and the test are about definitions. Judy looks up the words, writes definitions, and writes sentences. She wrote, for example, *The osmosis penetrated the skin.* Her sentence is grammatically accurate, and there is a connection between her use of the target word and what it means, but she hasn't used the word correctly. In fact, it's unlikely that she will ever use the word in her oral or written language until she abandons the imprecision she learned from the vocabulary lesson. She must understand *osmosis* in a nondictionary fashion. The dictionary is a fine resource for meanings and spellings, but it isn't written to be a vocabulary book.

Most of the plentiful literature associated with the shortcomings of using definitional instruction for vocabulary development is about vocabulary used for reading, and the accumulated evidence shows that definitional instruction is unlikely to result in better comprehension of text (McKeown, Beck, Omanson, & Perfetti, 1983; Pany & Jenkins, 1978; Stahl & Fairbanks, 1986). However, as Stahl (1983) points out, when definitional instruction is combined with context cues (in reading), students are more likely to learn new words than when context cues are used alone. In Stahl's investigation, simply reading a word in context didn't clarify word meaning sufficiently for learners to learn the words, but combined with context, which is vicarious experience, definitions enhance word learning. Out-of-context dictionary definitions do not promote word learning, but dictionary definitions can enhance word meanings acquired from experience.

One final word about the dictionary and vocabulary development lessons is important. Bryson (1990) makes the point about nuances when he writes, "*Rank* and *rancid* mean roughly the same thing, but we would never talk about eating rank butter or wearing rancid socks" (p. 150).

Judy and her friends are about to learn dictionary definitions that often don't fit the way they use words when they talk and write. That's the problem with using dictionary definitions as the learning source. The problem isn't direct vocabulary instruction, it isn't the word list, it isn't homework, and it isn't testing. It's the assumption that because Judy and her friends have written the definitions and the sentences and they have passed the test, they know the words.

Judy's teacher should instead spend Monday and Tuesday talking about biology and using the terminology in the talk, regularly stopping the monologue to check for understanding and question the meanings of target words. Then Judy and her friends will have a frame of reference in which to work when they see the words in the dictionary.

REVIEW AND REFLECTION

1. Recall your vocabulary lessons when you were in school. Were you one of the students who had to write definitions for a list of words each week? How many of those words for which you wrote definitions did you come to use regularly in your writing?
2. Why do you think definitional vocabulary lessons tend not to put words into young writers' writing vocabulary?
3. How would you say teachers should use the dictionary in vocabulary lessons?

Words and Writing

We don't teach words to learners so they will be able to use a large vocabulary when they write. "A story is no place to exhibit the extent of your education and vocabulary" (Boles, 1984, p. 33). Vocabulary development is an appropriate element in writing because the best writing uses the right words for the right reasons. The words are only responses to the need; they aren't themselves the need. Words represented the need when the purpose was high scores on the Scholastic Aptitude Test so we could attend the college of our choice. For writing, we learn words so we have the right ones when the need arises.

Usable and Unusable Words

What kinds of words respond to the need? Boles (1984) characterizes words in two categories: *usable words* and *unusable words*. Usable words add texture to the writing and feel natural in the context. We know, for example, that some people are especially perspicacious about word selection. Now doesn't that "p" word just about shatter any possibility of meaning flow we had going in this paragraph? *Perspicacious* is a perfectly good word that expresses the intended meaning precisely, but it's out of kilter for the context. After fourteen chapters, our readers aren't expecting that kind of word, so when one pops up, it startles many of them.

It's the startling words that Boles refers to when he characterizes words as unusable. Those are the ones, Boles says, that writers drag in to show off. *Perspicacious* means insightful, and there certainly are writers whose perspicacity shows in their word selection. Their insight shows in their word selection too, and *insight* fits our context better and tells the same story.

Learning Words

To be useful in writing, a word must be learned, retained in memory, and retrieved automatically when it's needed to serve a particular need (Crowder, 1976). Notice the details of what makes a word useful in writing. The procedural details of learning represent only part of what makes a word useful in writing. That is why so few of the words on vocabulary development exercises in school ever find their way into young writers' writing.

Learned words have to be stored in such a way that they can be accessed when they're needed. This is called expressive vocabulary. *Expressive vocabulary,* Kameenui, Dixon, and Carnine (1987) suggest, demands that writers produce a word or label for a particular meaning context; and as Crowder (1976) indicated, that label or word has to be accessed from memory.

There are two parts to access. First, for the access to memory to be automatic and useful in writing, it has to occur in the form learners used when they learned the words. Typically young writers learn to associate meanings with words, and the words are stored in memory that way: as words with meanings. But in writing, it's the other way around. When we write, we don't think of words and their meanings; we think of meanings first and only then the words that will express them. In typical vocabulary development activities, words are learned and stored for accessing on tests that begin with the word and ask for the meaning. But writers begin with the meaning and then access words. The two processes have very different implications for access, and the differences explain why young writers can do very well on vocabulary activities and tests but rarely use those words when they write.

Second, there is still more interference from some instruction. Even a cursory look at vocabulary development activities shows that learners learn words by associating target words with meanings, where both words and meanings are readily available. Vocabulary development activities and tests usually look very much like variations on standardized tests: the learner matches a given meaning with one of four or five given words. (*She is an insightful person. beautiful - coifed - perspicacious - tall.*) A student can perform the activity perfectly and not be able to think of *perspicacious* when writing a sentence that calls for it. The student didn't store or remember a word in the form through which she can retrieve it for writing, so retrieval, if it occurs at all, cannot be automatic. And the word was learned and stored as a connection with its definition, which the student can recognize on demand. But in writing, the memory demand is recall, not recognition. Word selection in writing isn't one of merely recognizing an accurate match between meaning and word. Writers must reproduce words. They must go into their memory, find words that fit their need, and reproduce them on the page—and all of this automatically. That is a very different kind of memory operation from picking out a word from among several when confronted with a definition.

Crowder (1976) provides an important way to think about vocabulary instruction for writing. We have to teach the words in a way that young writers can use when they write, and that is not the same as traditional vocabulary activity and test protocol. Certainly it is important for there to be multiple exposures to words, as Harmon (1998) points out, if those words are to begin appearing in writing, but it is more than just multiple exposures. The key is multiple exposures in the context in which word thinking occurs in writing and in the way writers use words when they write.

That contextualized word learning might include the following kinds of learning activities:

- Learn words that respond to meanings. ("What are some words we can use when we write about how cold it is outside?")
- Learn those words to automaticity. ("Write sentences in which *chilly* appears in the first position, the second, the third, the fourth, the fifth, and the sixth. Write a sentence that uses the words *chilly* and *warm*.)
- Test recall memory, not recognition memory, on activity sheets and tests. ("The damp wind blew down the street, rustling leaves and making the traffic light sway. Our thermometer had dipped below 40 overnight. We walked quickly toward school. It wasn't exactly cold that morning, but we all shivered in the _____ weather.")

REVIEW AND REFLECTION

1. With a partner, discuss the difference between recognition memory and recall memory. Then discuss the relevance of the difference for vocabulary development.
2. If it's true, as Boles suggests, that the story is not the place for showing off expansive vocabulary, what is the reason for learning new words?

Teaching and Learning Vocabulary

We know a good bit about vocabulary development, and from what we know, we can make decisions about how to teach vocabulary for various purposes. Clearly we know how to teach lots of words so students will achieve high scores on tests that measure the ability to match words with definitions. We also know how to teach vocabulary in order to increase the probability that what young writers learn will appear in what they write. The rest of this chapter concentrates on how to connect young writers with words, so they will be able to select the right words for the right reasons.

Effective vocabulary instruction rests on several basic teaching principles:

- *Multiple experiences.* Multiple experiences with connections between meanings and words, where those connections feature both oral and written contexts with applications throughout the curriculum, are important.
- *Authentic or natural use.* It is also important for instruction to ensure that young writers use their words in as natural a manner as possible (Beck & McKeown, 1991).
- *Connections with students' prior knowledge.* Multiple-exposure and contextualized instruction should be associated with students' prior knowledge about contexts and related words (Johnson & Rasmussen, 1998).

- *Definitional instructions.* While definitional instruction alone does not establish natural, automatic, or accurate use of words in writing, for the several reasons noted above, definitional instruction, along with contextual knowledge and applications, is productive (Dole, Sloan, & Trathen, 1995).
- *Active engagement.* Learners should actively engage with target words and have a strong sense as to why they are learning those words (Dole et al., 1995). If vocabulary instruction occurs in writing context, the answer to the "why" question will be self-evident.
- *Instructional variety.* Variety in vocabulary instruction is important (Kameenui & McKeown, 1982; Stahl, 1983). Among the possibilities are semantic feature analysis (Anders, Bos, & Filip, 1984), connections to context (Gipe, 1978–1979), semantic relatedness (McKeown et al., 1985), writing (Duin & Graves, 1987), and definitions and contexts (Stahl, 1983).

The remainder of this chapter describes classroom applications of vocabulary development in the spirit of those five basic principles of vocabulary instruction: multiple experiences, connections with students' prior knowledge, definitional instruction, active engagement, and instructional variety. As you read, notice how the patterns of effective vocabulary instruction for writing emerge from the activities.

REVIEW AND REFLECTION

1. Everyone remembers definitional instruction from when they were in school. With a partner, discuss what made those definitional activities helpful for learning new words.
2. How many of the words you studied in school do you remember specifically beginning to use when you wrote? What would have made those activities more useful in your writing?
3. There are several terms in the short material above that are critical to vocabulary instruction. Find two synonyms for the word *context.* Find a definition for *semantic,* and write a sentence that uses the idea without using the word.
4. Make a list of examples of what *active engagement* can mean in vocabulary development.

Contexts and Connections

When we read discussions in the literature about continua and matrices in vocabulary development, we note the consistent use of descriptors such as "schema, organization, connections, and contexts" (Adams & Collins, 1979; Anders & Bos, 1986; Anderson & Pearson, 1984; Johnson & Pearson, 1984; Just & Carpenter, 1987; Smith, 1990).

Vocabulary Continua

Word continua are about associations between and among words that explore concepts. For example, temperature is a concept. Let's go into Mr. Lytle's second grade and see how he uses a vocabulary continuum in the context of temperature.

INSTRUCTIONAL SCENARIO

In the Classroom with Vocabulary Continua

Teacher: We were reading about Little Willy and Searchlight [in Gardiner's *Stone Fox*, 1988]. I want you to think about where Little Willy and Searchlight live, and I want someone to tell us something about the temperature there. Alma?

Alma: It's cold.

Teacher: Why do you say that, Alma? What makes you think it's cold in the story about Little Willy and Searchlight?

Alma: There's snow, and he's going to race Searchlight with a sled so he can win some money.

Teacher: Yes, Alma, there is snow, and that probably means it's cold. I want to put your word on the board Alma. What is your temperature word?

Alma: *Cold.*

Teacher: Good. I'll write your word right here on the board, and I will put a number 1 right above it. Let's call Alma's temperature word a 1-word. Now way over here [at the other end of the board], I'm going to write the number 3. If Alma's word is a 1-word, what do you think might be a 3-word? Oh my goodness, so many good word thinkers. Nicole?

Nicole: *Hot.*

Teacher: That's a good word for what we are going to do today. I will write Nicole's word right under the number 3. We'll call Nicole's word a 3-word. Now we have a 1-word and a 3-word. I need another 1-word. Holly?

Holly: *Freezing.*

Teacher: That works. How about another 3-word? Carola?

Carola: *Boiling.*

Teacher: You're all very good at this. Another 3-word? Jason?

Jason: *Burning.*

Teacher: Lorena, do you have a 1-word or a 3-word?

Lorena: A 1-word, and it's *ice.*

Teacher: Good. Now we have six words: three over here with *cold* and three over here with *hot.*

COMMENTARY

The children are thinking about words and associating what they already know with the lesson. Their teacher hasn't said anything about opposites, and he won't, at least not today. If someone were to notice the opposites and say something, he'd reinforce the noticing, but the agenda right now is to get temperature words on the board along a line. This portion of the lesson could go on a long time with the purpose of getting as many as a half-dozen to a dozen words at each end of the continuum. But Mr. Lytle has a different purpose today, especially given that the children are second graders and can't come up with a dozen words for each end of the continuum.

BACK TO THE CLASSROOM

Teacher: We have some 1-words and some 3-words. Now I want you to think of something you might not have thought of before. I want you to think about what might be a 2-word. What is a word that can go right in here, in the middle, right between 1-words and 3-words? Flora?

Flora: *Warm.*

Teacher: I think *warm* can go there as a 2-word. How about another 2-word? Anthony?

Anthony: Maybe *cool?*

Teacher: Do you think that is between *hot* and *cold?*

Anthony: But it's more closer to *cold.*

Teacher: Anthony has a good idea here. If he is right that *cool* is closer to *cold* than to *hot,* maybe it shouldn't be right in the middle. Maybe we should have 1-words such as *cold,* and then we should call the words over here with *hot* 4-words. That way we can have 2-words that are closer to *cold* and 3-words that are closer to *hot.* What do you think? Good idea? Good. So we can make Anthony's word a 2-word and Flora's word a 3-word. Now we have cold words, then cool, then warm, and over here are hot words. Now you need to think of another 2-word—a word that isn't *cold* but it's closer to *cold* than *hot,* and it's like *cool.* What do you think? Alma?

Alma: *Chilly?*

Teacher: Is that a question, Alma? Do you think *chilly* is closer to *cold* than it is to *warm?*

Alma: Yes. *Chilly* is a 2-word.

COMMENTARY

Notice how Mr. Lytle is talking about the words (e.g., "This word is closer to that word than it is to this word over here"). The concept is temperature. There are various words for the concept, but the words have various meanings within the concept. Furthermore, all of the words in the concept category have meanings of their own that paint for readers and writers, listeners and speakers, slightly different images and ideas. All of them nonetheless fit one concept: temperature.

This is a concept in vocabulary development that is fundamentally important for learners to construct. The concept is multiple words for single concepts where each word makes its own concept. That concept cannot be taught, but it can be learned from learners' directly experienced need. Let's go back to Mr. Lytle's second grade and watch what that need looks like and how Mr. Lytle responds to it.

BACK TO THE CLASSROOM

Teacher: We have four kinds of temperature words here, boys and girls. Let me see. Brent, do you agree that cool means not quite cold, but not warm either?

Brent: Yes, and so is *chilly*.

Teacher: That is correct, Brent. Now I have one more word I want you to put on our lists. I want another 3-word. You have *warm* there as a 3-word. What is another 3-word? No hands? This is a hard one. This will be a word that isn't *cold* or even *chilly*, but it isn't *hot* either. It's like *warm*. It's another word we could use instead of *warm*. Elisa?

Elisa: *Lukewarm*?

Teacher: That works. We use that term that way. I'll put Elisa's word here as a 3-word. Now I have one that can be a 3-word. When I say it, you think about it and decide if it really is a 3-word. My word is *toasty*. What do you think? Teresa?

Teresa: I think it's a 3-word because it isn't *hot,* and it's what my sister says in bed in the morning when we don't want to get up. She says it's toasty in bed.

Teacher: So I can put *toasty* as a 3-word? Good. How about a sentence that contains the word *toasty*? Alicia?

Alicia: *It's toasty in front of the fire when it's chilly outside.*

Teacher: Oh, that's a good one, and you have two of our words in the same sentence. How about another sentence?

COMMENTARY

Mr. Lytle established the need by calling for a word along the temperature continuum, a word for which there already was one word they all knew and understood, but it was the only word they had. So the need was real. Then he filled the void with a word they probably knew in a different context but didn't think of for this one. He put the word into a well-known context and asked his second graders to think in sentences that contain the word. The word now will be used several times in second graders' sentences along a line that contains variations on temperature definitions. We can expect the word to begin appearing in these learners' oral and written language, and if it appears in their reading, they'll recognize it immediately.

Now suppose that one of the second graders thinks of a word that is possibly new for everyone else.

BACK TO THE CLASSROOM

Teacher: Brent, do you agree that *cool* and *chilly* are not warm, but not cold either?

Brent: Yes, and I know another one too. It's *bricks*. My mom says it sometimes when we have to go outside and get the paper. She says it bricks outside.

Teacher: Do you mean *brisk*?

Brent: Oh. That's it. *Brisk*.

Teacher: Good, Brent. We'll put *brisk* here as a 2-word. Brent, explain to everyone what your word means. What is it like outside when it's brisk?

Brent: It's like it's not cold because you can go outside and get the paper in your pajamas, and you can't do that when it's cold and there's snow. But it's windy and if you stay outside too long, you'll get cold. It's chilly, but my mom calls it brisk.

Teacher: Brent, think of a sentence that contains the word *brisk.*

Brent: *It is brisk when my mom goes outside and gets the paper.*

Teacher: Good, Brent. Everyone, think of a sentence that contains the word *brisk.* Oh, so many hands. I think I will change the rules. I want you to think of a sentence that contains the word *brisk* plus a 4-word. Now think, and write the sentence in your mind. I will give you ten seconds. [Pause.] Carola?

Carola: *It is hot in the summer when we go swimming, but at Halloween, it's brisk.*

Wendy: *I like it when it's brisk, not hot, because I can wear my school clothes.*

Nicole: *It can't be hot if it's brisk.*

Teacher: I'm going to put the word *brisk* on our Word Wall, and I want to begin seeing that word in your writing and hearing it when you talk. It's a good word. Thank you, Brent.

The temperature continuum in Mr. Lytle's second grade is about schema, connections, organization, and contexts. The continuum is a figural image of the temperature *schema,* or *mental construction.* In the temperature mental construction are the words, all organized in categories, with each category connected to all other categories by the common thread that runs through the temperature context.

In daily applications of vocabulary continua, what other schema or mental constructions can be shown along a line for second, fifth, and ninth graders? (What about words that tell about speed, noise, colors, truth, and freedom?)

Vocabulary Matrices

Vocabulary matrices are also associations between and among words that explore larger concepts. They are like vocabulary continua in that they feature schema, connections, organization, and contexts, but in a different form from continua. Vocabulary matrices allow Mr. Lytle to capitalize on the good aspects of vocabulary study with not only different daily activities, but different kinds of daily activities.

It is now late in the third month of school. Mr. Lytle's second graders have been working on vocabulary continua for a full school month. The Word Wall has been changed three times to accommodate words that come out of the continua activities, which Mr. Lytle conducts twice each week, sometimes for as long as twenty minutes if the children are engaged in word and sentence thinking. Mr. Lytle has prepared the following overhead projection to present to his second graders:

Our Taste and Feeling Matrix

	sour	sweet	hard	bland	cold	hot	soft	salty	pungent
potatoes									
ice cream									
lima beans									
raspberries									
cake									
tea									
celery									
sauerkraut									
peanuts									
spaghetti									
cilantro									
milk									
cream cheese									
pizza									

INSTRUCTIONAL SCENARIO

In the Classroom with a Vocabulary Matrix

Teacher: Boys and girls, if I served you a chocolate bar right now, how would you describe it? What words would you use to describe the taste of the chocolate bar? Nicole?

Nicole: Umm. *Sweet.*

Carola: It would be very sweet and good.

Teacher: Suppose it were a chocolate bar I had just taken out of the freezer? Then what would you say? Nicole?

Nicole: It would be cold and hard. Freezing.

Teacher: Still sweet?

Nicole: Yes. It would melt in your mouth.

Teacher: So we can describe what we eat with several words. Maybe many words. I have something to show you on the overhead screen. I have most of it covered so you will read just the top line. What does it say on the top line? Holly?

Holly: It says "Our Taste and Feeling Mat . . ."

Teacher: Our Taste and Feeling Matrix. Matrix. Everyone, say the word. *Matrix.* A matrix is a way to show how things relate to each other. Let's look at the first row of the matrix on the screen. Here is *potato*. Where would we put an X across the row? Is a potato sour? Sweet? Hard? Bitter? Cold? Hot? Soft? Salty? [The children agree on hot and soft.] That makes two Xs for *potato*. What about that last word? Who can read it? Do you want to give it a try, Antonio?

Antonio: I never saw it before. It's pun . . . pug . . . I don't know.

Teacher: You had a good start, Antonio. Everyone listen because this is not a word you are going to see very often, but it is a terrific word, and when you know it, you'll be able to use it. So here it is: *pungent. Pungent.* Listen: *pungent.* Everyone say it. Good, *pungent.* It means strong. Something has a pungent smell if its smell is strong. A skunk has a pungent smell. A rotting animal in the woods has a pungent smell. Some things have a pungent taste. There is a leafy green plant used in Mexican food. It's called cilantro. Cilantro can have a pungent taste. If it's in your food, you know it. The smell and taste are good, but they're strong too. So look at the foods down the side of the matrix and see if any of them have a pungent taste. Jackie?

Jackie: Cilantro, and I know about sauerkraut. That's pungent because it has a really strong smell and taste. I don't like it, but my father loves it. Our whole house smells when my mom makes it for him, and no one else eats it.

Teacher: I guess we could make a list of pungent foods. Maybe we'll do that tomorrow.

COMMENTARY

Mr. Lytle established the idea of the matrix with his second graders, and he introduced a new word. They will make lists of pungent food and sour food and hard food too. The vocabulary matrix is about associations, connections, and contexts, all of them around one concept. That dynamic is very important. We said earlier that a literature review on vocabulary development showed that direct vocabulary instruction tends not to put words into the natural writing of young writers because it is all definitional. Most direct vocabulary instruction focuses on starting with words and finding definitions. The vocabulary matrix begins with a need or a concept, and learners find and learn associations.

In the case of the matrix on Mr. Lytle's board and overhead, the concept is words that describe the taste and feel of what we eat. Those are describing words. The children connected words they knew with one another to form associations that can be directly useful when they're thinking of words they need to express ideas and images when they write. They are using the words and making them work.

There are many possibilities for vocabulary matrices. The two in Figures 15.1 and 15.2 can be used immediately with primary learners and older learners and English-language learners.

	living room	bedroom	kitchen	garage
sofa				
table				
TV				
car				
chair				
tools				
toaster				
lamp				
stove				

FIGURE 15.1   Vocabulary Matrix

Concept Wheel

The *concept wheel* (Rupley et al., 1998–1999) is another way for young writers to think about vocabulary in contexts. The wheel itself is a circle divided into quarters. One quadrant is reserved for a word that names, describes, or otherwise encompasses attributes in the other three quadrants. Another quadrant is reserved for a description of what the word means. The teacher never says that the second quadrant is for definitions because she wants young writers to describe meanings rather than merely find and copy them. The teacher has found that by assigning descriptions rather than definitions, young writers are more likely to transform dictionary definitions into contexts they can own and use.

	fruit	vegetable	dairy	grain
bread				
apple				
corn				
cheese				
celery				
wheat				
yogurt				
mango				
artichoke				

FIGURE 15.2   Vocabulary Matrix

INSTRUCTIONAL SCENARIO

In the Classroom with Concept Wheels

One morning Lorena, a fourth grader, used a word to name what monarch butterflies do in their annual travels from Central and South America to the central California coastal region. She found the word in her social studies book, and she wrote it in a sentence: *The migration puts millions of butterflies in the central coastal region every year.* The teacher called for the attention of everyone in the room when Lorena read that sentence during their weekly 1-on-1 conference, a time when the teacher meets with individual children to discuss their writing.

Teacher: Lorena wrote a sentence that contains a very good word, and she'd like to share it with you.

Lorena: *The migration puts millions of butterflies in the central coastal region every year.*

Teacher: Lorena and I talked about the word *migration*, and she explained that it meant that butterflies come to central California every year. Lorena and I need some help on this. Angela?

Angela: It's what all sorts of animals do when they all go places together. I saw a National Geographic special where the wildebeests in Africa all stampede every year to get food and water. They go hundreds of miles to the same place every year. It's migration.

Teacher: What do you think of that, Lorena? The butterflies and the wildebeests both migrate, but only one migration is in California.

Lorena: The whales migrate from Mexico to Alaska every year, and they go back to Mexico again to have their babies.

Teacher: Thank you, boys and girls. You may go back to work. Lorena, when we're finished here, I'd like you to make a concept wheel for your word and put it on the board in the Writing Center.

COMMENTARY

Lorena had a good word, the right word for her purpose, and she had a sense of what it meant. But it was a *copy word*—a word she read and understood in the context where she found it but not in the broader context. She needs that broader context if she is going to use it in writing on her own terms. That students understand a word every time they read does not mean at all that they can use it when they write. Readers have to recognize a word by making connections between prior knowledge and the context offered by text already written. Writers have to recall a word that names or describes a situation in the context they are constructing. The two levels of word knowledge, and of word memory, are very different.

A concept wheel will help Lorena understand the word well enough to use it again, in writing. She will use one of the 12-inch-diameter blanks in the Writing Center, each divided into quarters. In the upper left quadrant, she writes the word *migration*. She may also choose to write variations on the word in the upper left quadrant (*migrate, immigrate, immigration*). In the lower left quadrant, she will write a word or phrase that describes what the word means (*animals and people move*). In the upper right and lower right quadrants, she will write examples of migrations (*whales, butterflies, wildebeests, people, swallows, turtles, salmon,* and so forth). Lorena's concept wheel appears in Figure 15.3.

REVIEW AND REFLECTION

1. As you read about the continua and the matrices, what do you think young writers are learning most about vocabulary?
2. What is the difference between continua and matrices?
3. How do you see yourself using vocabulary continua and matrices in your teaching?
4. Can you think of vocabulary continuum words and vocabulary matrix words that would apply to fifth graders' vocabulary needs?

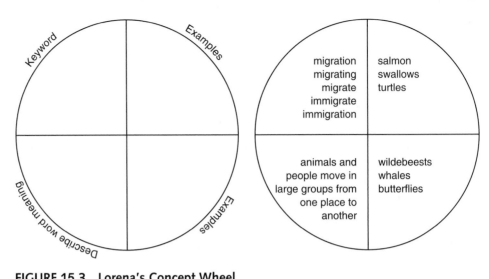

FIGURE 15.3   Lorena's Concept Wheel

Words, Parts, and Meanings

Because so much of authentic vocabulary development depends on what young writers do to satisfy their need for words, a fair amount of the vocabulary development process in a classroom should depend on young writers and their efforts. Furthermore, the words young writers need when they write are the words that satisfy the demands they place on themselves when they write. If, for example, a young writer never writes about erecting chain-link fence, she doesn't need to know words for the pipe at the top of the line, the fencing itself, and the wire that maintains tightness along the line. We can teach "top rail" and "tension wire" if we like, and we can do it well, but neither of those terms is likely to appear in her writing because she doesn't write about the subject matter. We should emphasize word searches that are designed to place the responsibility for finding and using words on young writers' shoulders.

Searching for Words and Meanings

Among the least expensive books available for classroom use are collections of words: a dictionary and a thesaurus. Put an inexpensive dictionary and a thesaurus on each student's desk and instruct everyone on Monday that the task for the week is to read in both books randomly for five minutes each during the week. It may be useful for the first several weeks to set aside reading time. Call it "select-a-word" (SAW) time. Provide five minutes on Tuesday for the dictionary and five minutes on Wednesday for the thesaurus. After several weeks, merely remind the students each morning to remember their SAW time responsibility for the week.

Everyone is to select a word during the week about which they can make a contribution during the Friday's Word Faire, a time when students share the word, the context in which a writer could use the word, forms of the word, and the reasons that that word was appealing to the student. Such discussion points emphasize reasons for student selection (Towell, 1997-1998). On Friday, just after morning recess, begin the Word Faire. Select a student with whom to begin, and give the direction. In the beginning, of course, select someone you know will provide a good model.

INSTRUCTIONAL SCENARIO

In the Classroom with Word Faires

Teacher: Delia, tell us about the word you learned this week.

Delia: It's *grave,* but not the one where people are buried when they die. I found out that *grave* can mean what people feel when something's really serious or sad. Like when there is bad news, but we could say it's grave news. The news was grave.

Teacher: Why did you select that word, Delia?

Delia: I saw the other *grave* first, the one about burial, and then I saw there was another meaning.

Teacher: So you read the other meaning.

Delia: Uh-huh. It's like my grandmother. She was gravely sick before she died.

Teacher: It's a very serious word for you. It sounds as though it's a word you will remember and use. Derrick, you're next. Tell us about a word you learned this week.

COMMENTARY

The teacher will work around the room that way for about twenty to thirty minutes, soliciting additional insights in some cases (as she did with Delia), asking for words in sentences, for similar words and opposites, and for contexts ("Where might a word like that appear?"). Twenty-seven words will be shared in the Word Faire. During the session, everyone should be encouraged to write every word shared. This is a good use for vocabulary journals.

At the end of the Word Faire, the teacher asks students to select several words they think might be useful in their own writing, and circle them in their vocabulary journal. Then the teacher asks the class about words for the Word Faire Bulletin Board, where she will post a 4- by 6-inch card for each word they agree should go up as a reminder of a good word for everyone to know. The class agrees on eight words (or seven or ten). The Word Faire Bulletin Board is off to a good start with the eight self- and then class-selected words.

The following Friday there is another Word Faire, twenty-seven more words self-selected, and some of those selected by the group for posting on the Word Faire Bulletin Board. It isn't long before there's no room to post more words, so some come down.

BACK TO THE CLASSROOM

Teacher: You want me to post seven more words, but there isn't room for seven more. I have to take some down. Which ones should come down? Jessica?

Jessica: Take down the first ones you put up.

Teacher: I don't remember which ones they were.

Delia: You can take mine down. I already know mine, so I don't need them on the bulletin board.

Caralou: Maybe we should get words we like. I see two words I'd like: *sample* and *identical*.

Teacher: Well, Caralou, if you want those words, and no one else has any objection, you may have them.

COMMENTARY

When several students select words they'd like to have and the individual index cards are given to them, there is room on the board for the new words. The Word Faire goes on each week. The children read randomly in their dictionary and thesaurus each week; they select words that appeal to them; they have words on the board near them; and they claim words from the board to have as their own.

Students need to start noticing the words around them that are not in the word books too. Those words pop up when they listen to adults, and even peers, talk. They pop up in television commentary, their content-area reading, reading material around the house, and specialty discussions they hear taking place among adults (insurance, politics, taxes, and so forth).

In the vocabulary journal, students can also write words they hear or read that aren't clear to them. The teacher can have triad word conferences of perhaps five minutes each day. If the conferences occur in triads and there are thirty students in the room, there would be ten conferences—two per day—each week. The conferences would look very much like the Word Faire where students share the new words they wrote in their journal. In conversation with the teacher, they clarify what the words mean, their contexts, how they function in sentences, and how they might use the words in their own writing.

INTO THE WORD CONFERENCE

Teacher: Do you have any words in your vocabulary journal that you aren't clear about?

Spencer: My dad said the word *evidently*. He told me it means "apparently" or something like he wasn't sure but that's how it seems. He said the dog evidently got out of the garage when we opened it to take out the trash.

Teacher: You can use the word *evidently* in your father's sentence about the dog. Are you saying that you don't understand the word well enough to use it in a sentence of your own?

Spencer: Yeah. If I hear it, I know what it means. But I'm not sure how to say it.

Teacher: Evidently you haven't used it enough to understand it for yourself. But evidently you know what it means.

Spencer: It means that I don't really know something for sure, but something seems this way.

Teacher: You don't really know, but the evidence suggests . . .

Spencer: Oh, evidence. Is that what it means? So my dad didn't know how the dog got out, but there was evidence she got out when we took out the trash.

Teacher: That's a terrific idea. Spencer, a man carrying a gasoline can is walking alone on a country road. What can you say about the picture? And use your word.

Spencer: He evidently ran out of gas.

COMMENTARY

The teacher has about five minutes with Spencer and Kendra. The interaction with Spencer took about thirty seconds. There is plenty of time to have an informal conversation about their self-selected words, all along helping the children clarify the words, contextualize them, feel the words in their own mind and their own world, and on their own tongue. Perhaps there is some dictionary or thesaurus time in the conference. Perhaps the children write a sentence or two. But most of the time is committed to discussion of the words.

Another word search is embedded in the various kinds of texts that young readers read and from which young writers acquire so much of their word sense. In the face of considerable evidence against definitional instruction alone, Mc-Keown (1993) makes the point that in proper context and from proper sources, definitional instruction can be quite effective. McKeown suggests that young readers and writers can learn definitions when they are applied in narrative and expository texts that students find interesting. Identifying words and their meanings in word books such as a dictionary and thesaurus is very different from using a real text as the source of meaning. The difference between those sources is important because the massive vocabulary growth between grades 3 and 7 (Jenkins & Dixon, 1983) certainly isn't attributable to looking up words in the dictionary, and it doesn't come from conversations with adults and peers, which also occurred prior to grade 3. What happens between grades 3 and 7 is reading; the act of reading itself is a rich source of vocabulary growth.

Using guided reading, Ms. Foster, a fifth-grade teacher, reads aloud the opening paragraph from the unabridged *Narrative of Sojourner Truth* (1997) as it appeared in the original in 1850:

> The subject of this biography, Sojourner Truth, as she now calls herself, but whose name originally was Isabella, was the daughter of James and Betsey, slaves of one Col. Ardinburgh, Hurley, Ulster County, N.Y. Sojourner does not know in what year she was born, but she knows she was liberated under the act of 1817, which freed all slaves who were forty years old and upward. Ten thousand slaves were then sent to liberty. Those under forty years of age were retained in servitude ten years longer, when all were emancipated. (p. 1)

Guided reading, from the perspective of a student, can be likened to the experience of a newcomer to the Van Gogh Museum in Amsterdam. It isn't that the visitor cannot tour the museum alone and benefit greatly from the experience; but under the guidance of a docent (or an audiotape guide), the visitor can be more efficient in that first visit, looking at the most important paintings in the right order and having them explained. The initial guidance can make all subsequent Van Gogh Museum visits more interesting and productive. In fact, having been guided at this museum, the visitor is likely to learn a good bit about how to benefit from museum visits in general; and a tour of the Louvre, Philadelphia's Franklin Institute, or Berkeley's Lawrence Hall of Science might be more effective because of the Van Gogh guidance.

Guided reading works that way. Its effect can be to help young readers understand how to think when reading a passage. One of those strands of guidance is how to look at and think about words and their effect on readers' construction of meaning from text. These questions would be useful for a discussion of Sojourner Truth's memoir:

- What does it mean to be *liberated*?
- What does it mean to be *set to liberty*?
- What does Sojourner Truth mean when she says that those under forty years of age were *retained* ten years longer?
- What happened after ten years, and what does the word *emancipation* mean?
- Before we get to the document, itself, what do you think is contained in the Emancipation Proclamation?
- What does *proclamation* mean?

INSTRUCTIONAL SCENARIO

In the Classroom with Guided Reading for Vocabulary Development

Teacher: [Reading from *Narrative of Sojourner Truth*:] "... but knows she was liberated under the act of 1817." Oh, there is a word I would like us to know. Listen as I read that part again. She "knows she was liberated." She was liberated, boys and girls. What do you think that might mean? Genille?

Genille: They freed her. She was a slave, and they set her free.

Teacher: That's right, of course, Genille. How did you know that?

Genille: I read a book last year about slavery, and I talked to my father about it. He said the right word for freeing the slaves was *liberate* because they got liberty when they were freed. When they were slaves, it was like they were in prison, and they didn't have any liberty, and then when they were freed, they got their liberty.

Teacher: So if you have a person in prison, and his time in prison is finished, he gets liberated?

Genille: I guess. Sure.

Teacher: Someone, think of a sentence that contains the idea of old man and the word *liberated*. Germain?

Germain: *The old man was liberated from the cell where he lived for forty years.*
Teacher: And what happened to him, Germain?
Germain: He got out of jail.
Teacher: Did he just get liberated? Genille?
Genille: No. Somebody has to liberate him.

COMMENTARY

Read that interchange and check how long it takes to read the lines. On the audiotape from which the transcription was made, the time was sixty-three seconds. It took sixty-three seconds to define and put the word into two contexts, listen to two fifth graders talk about it, listen to one fifth grader's sentence, and call for and get a clarifying remark. If the teacher does something similar with three more words in the opening paragraph of Sojourner Truth's narrative, the vocabulary clarification will take about four minutes and the paragraph reading itself about twenty seconds.

Having worked through the paragraph that way, having guided the children through the vocabulary, the teacher reads the paragraph again, without hesitation and interruption, and moves to the second, third, and fourth paragraphs. That will finish the first page of the narrative and the section called "Her Birth and Parentage." It will also reinforce one of the habits good readers have: to notice words and what they mean both in the context of the print they're reading and in general use.

Harkening back to the Given Word Sentence (see Chapter 4), the teacher will pose the following tasks right before morning recess:

"Write a six-word sentence in which *liberate* appears in the fourth position."

"Write a five-word sentence in which *retain* appears in the third position."

"Write a seven-word sentence in which *retention* appears in the fifth position."

"Write a six-word sentence in which *liberation* appears in the second position, and the first word must have at least four letters." [The second part of that prompt when the target word is in the second position eliminates *the* as the automatic first word.]

Such an activity requires that young learners function like writers as they apply their word knowledge to the construction of images and ideas. The four sentences are their ticket to recess. Everyone gives the teacher a paper. Justin's paper has only one sentence on it. His teacher thanks him, and he runs off to play. For Justin, one sentence in four minutes is an achievement every bit as dramatic as Genille's four. The teacher has a rule of thumb in teaching: "There is nothing so unequal as the equal treatment of unequals." (She thanks Thomas Jefferson for her rule of thumb.)

ESL
This guided reading through a trade book has implications too for vocabulary development for young writers whose native language is not English. Trade books can increase the vocabulary and reading comprehension for English-language learners, according to Cho and Krashen (1994), because these learners can associate their reading with prior knowledge gained in previous readings. In addition, the vocabulary in trade books is repeated and contextually reinforced.

Ms. Foster also knows that the Spanish-speaking children in her class use their prior knowledge of Spanish to help them understand words in English (Nagy, Garcia, Durgunoglu, & Hancin-Bhatt, 1992). She uses cognates, words descended from the same language or form, whenever possible to support students' vocabulary development. Many English and Spanish words are made up of Latin words and affixes. These words appear in slightly different forms in the two languages. For example, in English, such words as *edification, consternation,* and *vindicate* have Spanish cognates: *edificación, consternación,* and *vindicar.* Bilingual Spanish speakers can identify words in English through their knowledge of cognate stems with English suffixes. In English, words such as *reality, agility,* and *ability* have Spanish counterparts with different suffixes: *realidad, agilidad,* and *abilidad.* Of course, students who are best able to identify a cognate in English are those with a strong vocabulary in Spanish.

It's important to realize that cognates do not always have the same meaning or usage. The English word *brilliant* means bright or fantastic, while in French *brillante* means hopeful. In English, a library is a place from which to borrow books. In Spanish, *libreria* has a slightly different meaning; it's a bookstore. In spite of the fact that cognates are not always synonymous, a cognate approach to vocabulary development helps students see similarities between languages and construct meaning by transferring knowledge from their first language to the second. ■

Word Parts and Meanings

There has always been considerable vocabulary development attention on word parts, on the assumption that as young writers understand how words are constructed, their vocabulary power will increase. Therefore, it is useful to focus some vocabulary development attention on affixes, roots, and various derivations of words and meanings.

All of that is called *derivational generalization.* For example, we have taught the meaning of prefixes such as *ir-* and *non-* on the assumption that when the young learners understand those nullification prefixes, they will generalize their understanding to a host of words to which the nullifiers are attached. And we have assumed that when we teach a word such as *melancholy,* young writers will be able to recognize *melancholia* when they see it. In fact, there is evidence that young writers can make such morphological generalizations early in elementary school (Nicol & Graves, 1990; White, Sowell, & Yanagihara, 1989; Wysock & Jenkins, 1987).

Devine (1981) refers to such focused word study as "building word power." The goal is not merely to learn words; the power is in learning how words and meanings are constructed. Devine suggests that young writers might focus their attention on three attributes in word study: the root, the meaning, and one or more examples. Such a word study focus could work from Devine's chart, a sample of which follows:

Affixes	Meaning	Examples
anthro	man	anthropology
bio	life	biology, biosphere
cardio	heart	cardiac, cardiology
demo	people	democracy
geo	earth	geology, geography
magni	great	magnify, magnificent
mono	one	monorail, monolithic
ortho	straight	orthodox, orthodontist
anti	against	antidote
auto	self	automatic
micro	small	microscopic
poly	many	polygamy
pro	first	prototype
ade	a thing made	lemonade
ana	collection of	Americana
arian	person who	librarian
gram	something written	telegram
less	without	fatherless
wright	worker	playwright

REVIEW AND REFLECTION

1. The teacher read through a paragraph of Sojourner Truth's narrative and then led her fifth graders through a specific word study session on that paragraph. Discuss the impact of that specific word study in two contexts: on reading the text and on learning new words.
2. Describe the role of guided reading in direct vocabulary instruction.
3. With one or two partners, discuss how to help young writers learn the essential concepts in the "root and meaning" chart above.

Focused Word Study

There is merit in suggesting to young writers that there might be words they hadn't thought about before that they might find useful if they knew them. After all, school is a place where students are confronted with things they don't already know.

There will always be words for young writers to learn. The question, then, is how to increase the probability that students will begin to use those words when they write. The probability increases as young writers:

- Work with the words many times.
- Work with the words in a variety of ways.

- Have clear contexts for the words.
- Use the words.

Word Maps

In a traditional vocabulary activity, students write the definition and a sentence that contains the word. The definition comes from a dictionary, and the student characteristically copies the dictionary entry. The student then writes a sentence that may or may not characterize an authentic style and may or may not capture the word's meaning in proper perspective. Nancy refers often to her middle school student who wrote the definition of *ferocity* as fierce or savage, then wrote: "The ferocity lion killed the antelope." The student had only one instance of attention to the word (dictionary definition) before writing with it. She worked with the word in only one way (dictionary definition) before writing with it. The student may have had a context (wild animal), but she wasn't clear with respect to variations on the word. And the student used the word only once, and that use didn't require that she understand how the word works. There has to be a better way to learn words.

A *word map* is another way. A word map offers a variety of ways for young writers to look at a word, and it helps young writers construct a context for a word. Under "Word Parts and Meanings" above, we used the word *nullification.* Write the word on a separate sheet of paper. You'll need about a half-page. (Go ahead, write it. Your participation will help you understand the activity.) Think of what the word reminds you of, if anything. Where have you heard or read the word before, if anywhere? What would you suspect is a reasonable context for the word. Now write what it reminds you of. (You might have to look in a dictionary or thesaurus.) Here are other things to do:

- Write a synonym for *nullification.*
- Write another synonym for *nullification.*
- Write an antonym for *nullification.*
- Write a sentence that contains a meaning, a definition, for *nullification,* but do not use the word itself.
- Write a sentence that includes a variation on, or a different form of, the word *nullification.*

You had to work with the key word six times—four times before writing anything—and neither piece of writing used the word itself. This single piece of writing depended entirely on your knowledge of the word's meaning, and the other allowed only a form of the key word. The activity in its entirety serves to help you construct a context for the key word, where the context includes similar words, opposite words, a different form of the word, and a connection between you and the word. If young writers did that with their assigned words, we could expect to begin seeing some of the words from vocabulary lists show up in their writing.

Set up word map activity sheets—one for homework each of four nights and one for independent time in the classroom on each of five days. That will give the students an opportunity to work with nine words each week. Here is an example of a word map activity sheet:

Word Map Activity Sheet

Word: _____   This word reminds me of: _____

_____

Synonym: _____   Antonym: _____

Synonym: _____   Antonym: _____

Write a sentence that includes the meaning of the word without using the word.

_____

Write a sentence that includes a different form of the word. _____

_____

There are additional tasks that could be substituted, mixed and matched, on the word map activity sheet:

- "Write a six-word sentence in which the key word is in the fourth position." [This variation requires young students to pay explicit attention to the word's meaning and how it works in the context that the writer constructs.]
- "Write three synonyms and one antonym" [or three antonyms and one synonym].
- "Write a sentence that contains one of the synonyms, one of the antonyms, two of the synonyms, or one of the synonyms plus the key word."
- "Find a sentence in your literature book that contains the word. Write the sentence, and explain what the word means in the sentence."
- "Find a sentence in your social studies or science textbook that contains the word. Write the sentence, and explain what the word means in the sentence."
- "Study the origins of the word. Where does the word come from? How did it get into contemporary English usage?"

The key to focused word study is to pose a variety of ways for young writers to engage with words and to promote engagement every day. Also, remember that most of focused word study should reinforce people's tendency to claim words. People tend to identify with words they like, words that fit their needs. Focused word study therefore can be largely individual to give young writers daily opportunities to claim words from among those that the teacher selected for study.

Geocabulary

Young writers can work together on focused word study, cooperatively constructing definitional and usage contexts for selected words. There is a word in common use among young people, and it has lost its power because it has become routine. Larry McMurtry uses the word in his biography of Crazy Horse (1999), the Oglala Sioux warrior born around 1840 in what is now South Dakota. McMurtry writes of Spotted Tail, thought to be Crazy Horse's uncle, and his sense of the futility of directly engaging the white invaders: "Spotted Tail was so awed by the power of white weaponry that he later came to Fort Laramie and turned himself in; he served two years in jail and was probably the first of the major Sioux leaders to conclude that the Sioux could not hope to win in sustained conflict with the whites" (p. 39).

What was Spotted Tail's reaction to white weaponry? He was awed by it. He thought it awesome. He looked upon it with awe. Here is a man of the early to middle nineteenth century, a man dressed in skins who hunted for a living and whose most fearsome sense of weaponry was a bow and arrow, a lance, and a knife. And he faced an invading force of enormous numbers, all on horseback, all carrying weapons that could kill from distances of fifty yards or more, and some setting up with automatic weapons that could fire hundreds of rounds or large balls of iron and fire. He found that awesome. It didn't surprise him, or trouble him, or irritate him; it left him stunned, amazed, filled with wonder. In a word, he was awestruck. The word doesn't describe getting a good night's sleep after a concert. It doesn't describe the concert or the new shirt one wears to the concert. *Awesome* is a reference to something so compelling, so staggering, that it will live a lifetime. We have never seen a shirt that deserves the label.

Put fourth graders Marcy, Allan, and Anita into a triad. Give them a flat model of a cube, one of Plato's perfect geometric solids. (There are five: cube, tetrahedron, octahedron, dodecahedron, and icosahedron. In each solid geometric shape, all faces are the same size and shape. That's what makes them perfect.) There are six faces on a cube. The triad writes its key word (*awesome*) on one of the faces, perhaps in red marker. That leaves five faces on which to write. The teacher has prepared directions for them:

- Write a dictionary definition.
- Write a synonym.
- Find a sentence that contains the word or a form of the word in a book. Write the sentence.
- Write a sentence that contains the sense of the meaning of the word without using the word.
- Write a sentence that contains the word.

Marcy, Allan, and Anita cooperate in finding and writing the five entries on each of the remaining five faces of the flat model of the cube. When they've finished, they fold the cube together, tape the edges tight, and hang the cube from the ceiling in the writing center. It's a context cube for *awesome*. The activity is called *geocabulary* (Fearn, 1978).

Two of the five Platonic solids work better than the other three for geocabulary purposes. The octahedron with eight faces, dodecahedron with twelve, and especially the icosahedron with twenty faces have to be as big as volleyballs for the faces to be big enough to write on. The cube with six faces and the tetrahedron with four work well by providing multiple looks at words on models that young writers can handle. And it all can be done cooperatively.

Two- and three-inch cubes and tetrahedrons are a good size because they can be read while they're swaying on thread from the ceiling just out of reach. The flat models for the cube and tetrahedron are shown below:

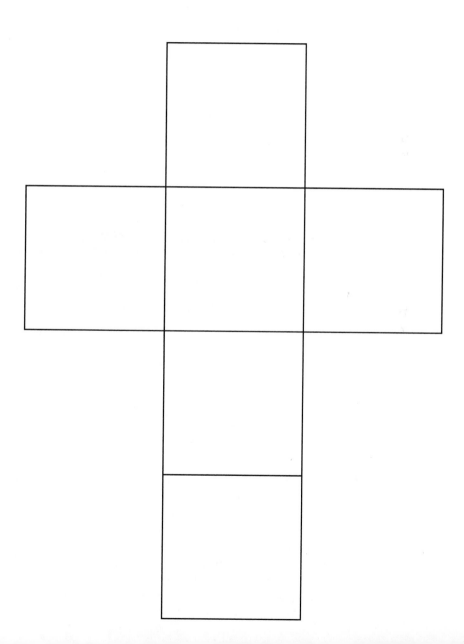

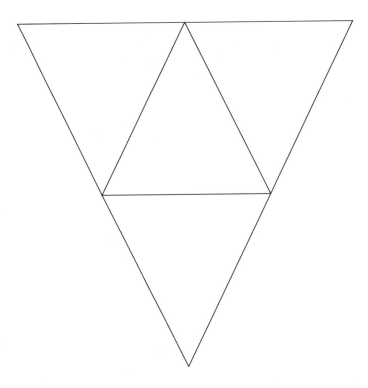

1. What do word maps and geocabulary have in common for purposes of focused word study?
2. What is the relationship between learning new words and helping young writers write more effectively?
3. What is the difference between vocabulary development for reading and vocabulary development for writing?
4. How does word selection affect meaning construction in writing and reading?
5. What can you conclude from what is known about vocabulary development that can inform your teaching?

A Summary: Teaching Vocabulary

The purpose of vocabulary instruction is to equip young writers with an increasingly rich array of words they can use when they write. Young writers need more and more words to express their increasingly complex ideas, and the result of vocabulary instruction must be student ownership of that increasingly rich array of words. Ownership is evident when young writers recall words and use them when they write.

The matter of recall is crucial in vocabulary development for the writing purpose. A recognition vocabulary is appropriate for reading and listening because word knowledge in those language skills requires only a connection between a word heard or read and the definitional context. In writing (and talk), on the other hand, mere recognition is insufficient because the young writer creates the definitional context and the words within it. Young writers must recall and construct words; young writers need only to recognize words in contexts that writers have already created for them. The knowledge demand is very different, so the teaching procedures have to be different as well.

There are hundreds of thousands of words in the English language, only a small portion of which tend to appear in any one writer's work. Writers recognize many more words than they can recall when they write. For writing, we tend to gravitate toward words that satisfy our writing needs. We learn words to satisfy our curiosity about words and ideas. We learn words in conceptual categories. We learn more words as we learn how words are constructed and how they come into common use.

We tend not to learn words, however, by searching for definitions for assigned words. The evidence shows that definitional instruction is more effective the other way around: begin with contexts (definitions) and find words that name and explain.

This chapter emphasizes active and contextual engagement with words, engagement that features relationships between and among words, and multiple exposures to words in multiple contexts. The more that young writers actively study words and contexts, the higher the probability is that they will own the words they study. The more they study relationships between and among words and relationships between words and contexts, the higher the probability is that they will use the words they study when they write. Finally, the more often and the more regularly they study words and contexts, the higher the probability that they will own the words they study.

16 MaxiLessons: Highlighting Writing and the Interactive Language Arts

The Argument We've Made

The difference between causing writing and teaching so that young writers learn to write well is enormous. It often happens that good teachers cause a lot of self-selected and authentic writing; the quantity of many students' writing increases, but the quality of it doesn't seem to improve noticeably. Although many students' authentic writing is interesting to teacher readers and student writers, the writing itself doesn't become clear and detailed, organized, and textured merely from producing a lot of authentic writing. Often the result of causing a lot of writing is that young writers make permanent the way they write. And because many of these young writers aren't very skilled at writing, they habituate, through practice, not-so-skilled writing throughout the year. The skills and attitudes necessary to produce exacting writing tend not to emerge through a lot of self-selected authentic writing alone.

Occasionally teachers at a school site agree on the skills and attitudes that eventuate in better writing. They agree on how they will teach writing, what young writers will be held responsible for each month of every year, and how writing will be used throughout the curriculum. They also plan for teachers and students to know weekly, monthly, and annually how they are doing and what they have to work on to write better. That's when young writers' writing performance becomes noticeably more effective every year. That's the difference between causing writing and teaching writing.

The Basic Premise of the Argument

In this book we have described instruction that ensures that young writers learn to write well. We've based intentional writing instruction on the premise that instruction has to ensure that everyone learns to write increasingly better every week, every month, and every year. We've described what that means in our discussions of teaching the craft, the processes, and the relationship between form and function (the genres). We've also described how to measure "increasingly well" by assessing writing performance. We assess for the purposes of monitoring progress and informing instruction.

Writing Is the Reason

We've shown that writing instruction can be a natural foundation of the language arts program. By "foundation" we mean teaching spelling and vocabulary through the lens of the writing-spelling and writing-vocabulary interactions and the natural and necessary interaction of writing with reading. This book features an absolute commitment to the proposition that everyone can be an effective writer and can, through the language arts' interactions, improve the ability to use effective vocabulary, spelling, and reading.

The key theme in this book, the instructive concept, has been the interactive nature of the language arts, with writing at the center of the instructional context. The interactions are many and powerful. Writing is the gateway to reading, for children learn about sounds and print as they produce them in their earliest temporary spellings. As reading and writing interact, the reading shows young writers what good writing is supposed to look like and what words look like when they're spelled correctly. Writing records ideas and images, and spelling supports conventionality in writing. Vocabulary provides the words that enhance or add texture to the images and ideas, and words and word selection interact with both reading (recognizing meanings) and writing (recalling words that reveal meanings). These are all interactive relationships. The interactions are observable and fundamental to effective learning.

The Mind Is the Organ

Because the interactive language arts function together in the construction of meaning, the concept of construction is central to curricular thinking and planning. Construction, as we talk about it in this book, is mental. Construction of meaning is what people do when they think. Every sentence is a meaning construction. Every relationship between and among sentences is a meaning construction, more expansive and perhaps more complex than the meaning construction in a single sentence. Every larger whole piece of writing (such as description, story, set of directions) is a meaning construction. The interactive nature of the language arts, as described throughout this book, promotes the construction of meaning by ensuring that young writers do the following:

- Commit active attention to literacy tasks.
- Make meaning of what occurs around them.
- Retain meanings that they acquire.

- Construct concepts from what they learn about literacy.
- Transfer what they learn about literacy to new situations.

Furthermore, because writing is, by definition, a creative activity and because creativity is essentially about making connections that produce new or different perspectives, the nature of creativity is a fundamental aspect of teachers' instructional planning and students' learning in the language arts. That is why there has been so much attention in these chapters on interactions (that is, connections) between and among the language arts. The language arts are synergistic. The craft, processes, and form-function relationship (genres) are all interconnected, and in the book we've described those connections in a systematic way. Nothing occurs in isolation because everything is interrelated. Creativity is a way to capture the connections, the interactions, in language arts instruction. Creativity is a way of perceiving the world of literacy.

Simply Said . . .

The interactive language arts foundation rests on three pillars: (1) the craft writers use when they write, (2) the processes writers use when they perform writing, and (3) the relationships writers build between their purposes (functions) and the forms they use to achieve their purposes. Philosophically, as well as linguistically, we teach young writers to write well largely to the extent that we help them:

- Craft the language precisely.
- Approach writing willingly.
- Perform writing fluently.
- Use interactions between form and function in each genre.

Teaching Writing, Now!

We've written the argument. We've presented the evidence. We've explained everything in a variety of ways. We've woven in instructional scenarios and shown what young writers do when the explanations are used in the classroom. We've also written plan book pages. If the argument works, the evidence is persuasive, the instructional scenarios are informative, and the plan book pages are instructive, why not end the book here?

In fact, we're very close to stopping. But this is similar to what the long-distance runner faces after the twenty-fifth mile with one more and change to go. The runner is tired too, but the next eighteen hundred or so yards more clearly define the day than does any mile run so far. In the race, now is the time to do it! Now is also the time to begin teaching writing as well. So what's going to happen tomorrow morning at 9:20?

MaxiLessons

It is impossible to teach the language arts properly in small, intermittent or periodic, sometimes disjointed instructional moments that occur primarily in response to the teacher's perception of need displayed in students' writing. As with any other comprehensive learning focus, the language arts require maximum, not minimum, instructional and learning commitment.

The language arts are among the foundational building blocks of a comprehensive curriculum. They must receive sufficient time for which teachers plan carefully and which students use efficiently. Teachers' and students' time is most efficient when the language arts are interactive and when teachers and students pursue language learning objectives based on whole written productions. Through the process of writing whole pieces, we build on and develop students' language arts skills and insights. When there is maximum instructional and learning commitment, students are more likely to have learning experiences that build on what they know about using language. The meaning of maximum commitment can be understood as lesson designs. The lesson designs for maximum commitment are called **MaxiLessons.**

Writing MaxiLessons

Every MaxiLesson is fundamentally about writing a whole piece of language. In the process, most MaxiLessons feature intentional instruction in elements of the craft and processes associated with writing the whole piece. Each MaxiLesson also includes one or more of the language arts interactions (spelling, vocabulary, and/or reading). It is rare, therefore, for a MaxiLesson to be planned for less than forty-five minutes daily after the third grade and thirty minutes in the third grade and before. MaxiLessons use a whole piece of writing (short fiction, for example) as the playing field on which young writers practice the craft, the processes, and the language arts interactions. There is nothing minimal about teaching writing.

A MaxiLesson may be based, for instance, on writing a description. Perhaps the cue or prompt is, "Write a word picture of the desert after I read *Mojave* [Siebert, 1988] without showing you the illustrations." Here is what the Maxi-Lesson might look like:

- Read-aloud (5–8 minutes): The writing-reading interaction occurs in constructing a word picture from a read-aloud. Without benefit of the book's illustrations, young writers must form the images from the print and then describe their mental image with their own print. The premium is explicitly on the quality of their writing.
- Sentence writing (10–12 minutes): Immediately following the read-aloud, the teacher asks for words that describe the desert scene. From the brain-

stormed words on the board, the teacher selects one as the first cue in a Single Sentence Session (see Chapter 4) that progresses through two and maybe three sentences. The teacher calls attention to main ideas at the single-, double-, and triple-sentence levels of text development.

- Drafting (8–10 minutes): The whole piece of writing is the word picture, the description.
- Vocabulary development (5–10 minutes): Among the words that appear in the first several pages of *Mojave* and might be useful for vocabulary discussion and instructional activity are these: *canyon, sandstone, outspread, arroyo, sudden, thrust, feature, violent, appear,* and *swirl.*
- Opening and closing sentence writing (5–8 minutes): When students' earliest descriptive pieces have been drafted and several are read aloud, the teacher encourages the young writers to write opening and closing sentences for their draft. The teacher calls attention to beginnings and endings as organizational devices, where in this case organization means beginnings, middles, and ends.
- Writers' Workshops (8–12 minutes) and revisions (10–12 minutes): The MaxiLesson will lead to Writers' Workshops (see Chapter 8), where young writers receive feedback on their descriptions, and on the basis of that feedback, they revise.

This prototype MaxiLesson takes sixty to sixty-five minutes of contiguous instruction in and after the fifth grade. Before the fifth grade, the MaxiLesson will take up to ninety minutes spread over three days. In this time frame, the learners engage in reading, drafting, vocabulary, organization, craft (sentences), publication (Writers' Workshop), and revision. We teach those elements in the language arts program anyway, so it isn't as though we need to find extra time. In this MaxiLesson, the language arts activities interact to satisfy a whole language (not Whole Language) purpose: a descriptive piece of writing.

We plan MaxiLessons around whole pieces of writing (genres, modes of discourse, and Short Cues; see Chapter 10). We include in them intentional instruction in the craft and processes of writing as well as interactions with one or more of the language skills: reading, vocabulary, and spelling. We schedule one or more MaxiLessons each week, teach them intentionally, and in the process ensure that every young writer experiences the whole interactive language arts program regularly.

Prototype MaxiLessons

Each of the three prototype MaxiLessons that follows has been taught in the elementary and middle grades.

MAXILESSON: AUTOBIOGRAPHICAL INCIDENT AS FINAL PRODUCT

The objective of this MaxiLesson is to increase students' ability to write autobiographical incidents. After the second grade, the MaxiLesson should always produce a written autobiographical incident. During the primary years, it can produce written, oral, and dictated autobiographical incidents. We know from experience that young writers can write autobiographical incidents for their writing portfolio at the rate of two to four per month (see Chapter 10).

Approximately one week is allotted for this MaxiLesson. It has been completed in a single sixty-five-minute session in the sixth grade and two thirty-five-minute sessions in the fourth.

This MaxiLesson is directed at using sentences, paragraphs, and analytic thinking to write autobiographical incidents. After the preliminary thinking and writing, we highlight the iterative writing process (see Chapter 7) for purposes of organization, further drafting, and revision.

As part of the planning in this MaxiLesson, you will develop Single, Double, and Triple Sentence Session activities, and Paragraph Completion activities that will prompt students' autobiographical thinking and writing according to the attributes of a good autobiographical incident.

As writers, students arrange their sentences and paragraphs in an order that they think responds to what makes a good autobiographical incident. They think about what else they have to do to complete this piece of writing. They write the rest of their autobiographical incident. It is important to reserve time at the end of the week for public readings and audience feedback for as many as six students. If more want to participate and have their peers listen to their writings, conduct Writers' Workshops (see Chapter 8).

During the MaxiLesson, include Sentence Sessions and Paragraph Completion activities that focus on the kinds of details that make good autobiographical incidents (see Chapter 10). While it is possible, depending on grade level and allotted time for language arts, for young writers to work through a MaxiLesson on the autobiography in less than a week, it is reasonable to expect each student to prepare a completed product in a week. After the first MaxiLesson, young writers will need progressively less leadership on this particular genre, so by about midyear, a MaxiLesson on autobiographical incidents can be fifty to seventy-five minutes long, perhaps stretched over a couple of days.

WRITING-READING INTERACTION

It's language arts time. Open a selected autobiography and read aloud to students for several paragraphs. Begin a discussion based on two questions:

1. "What did you notice in the reading?"
2. "What does the reading remind you of?"

On subsequent days, read from other autobiographies likely to appeal to the children. You can select autobiographical subjects about the people who are part of the social studies, the sciences, and the literature studies in your curriculum. Pose discussion questions that highlight the elements in good autobiographical incidents:

• What did the writer do to catch our interest? In other words, how did the writer introduce the autobiographical incident?

- What did you notice about how the writer made the reader understand the significance of an incident in his or her life?
- What did you notice about how the writer revealed details about the incident that bring readers into the incident?
- What did you notice about how the writer included other people in the incident to make the incident clearer or more human?
- How did the reading make you feel? What did the writer do to make you feel that way?

CUE FOR WRITING AN AUTOBIOGRAPHICAL INCIDENT

- *Something I know how to do.* (See Chapter 10 for additional cues.)

SENTENCE ACTIVITIES (SINGLE, DOUBLE, AND TRIPLE SENTENCE SESSIONS, CHAPTER 4)

- Write a sentence that contains an idea or image that reveals what you know how to do. Example: *I know how to fix an electric plug by taking off the one that's burned out and putting in a new one.*
- Write two related sentences that contain an idea or image that reveals what you know how to do. Make the two sentences reveal one idea or image. Example: *I know how to fix a burned-out electric plug and put in a new one. I learned it from my brother who is taking a class on home repairs in school.*
- Write three related sentences that contain an idea or image that reveals what you know how to do. Example: *I learned how to fix a burned-out electric plug from my brother who is taking a home repair course in school. It isn't very hard to do if someone shows you how and you get to practice two or three times. My brother taught me because he said it would be easy for me to learn.*

PARAGRAPH ACTIVITIES (PARAGRAPH COMPLETION, CHAPTER 6)

- What is the utility of what you know how to do? What is it good for? What is its significance? Why is it important to be able to do this?
- The main idea of this paragraph completion activity is the importance of what you know how to do. Read the sentence stems that I am going to give you, and think about how you can use them to write a paragraph about the importance or significance of what you know how to do. You do not have to use the sentence stems exactly, but you may. Your paragraph must contain at least four sentences.

Sentence Stems

It is important to be able to . . . If you have to . . . Sometimes people . . . I have already found that . . . It makes me proud . . .

See Chapter 6 for more examples of the Paragraph Completion activity and ideas for developing Paragraph Completion cues or prompts that will fit any whole piece of writing.

ANALYSIS

- Explain to a reader precisely what you are able to do. Tell the steps or process necessary to do this. Tell what is complicated about it, what is hard to learn, what requires your attention. You may tell it in steps or stages. (See Chapter 6.)

Example: *Sometimes an electric plug burns out. I'm not sure why that happens, but when it does burn out, I can fix it. First, I take off the cardboard cover on the plug and unscrew the screws that hold the wires onto the plug. Then I pull the old plug off and push the wires into the new plug. With a pocket knife, I strip the wires so they're clean, and I wrap one wire around one screw and the other wire around the other screw. Then I tighten the two screws and put the cardboard cover back on. That's what my brother taught me to do.*

ITERATIVE WRITING PROCESS

- Think about what you are trying to tell in this autobiographical incident. What are you trying to accomplish in this piece of writing? Read what you have written. What have you accomplished so far? Where are you now? What do you have to do yet to finish what you think would be a good autobiographical incident?

See Chapter 10 for the attributes of a good autobiographical incident.

MAXILESSON: PERSUASIVE WRITING AS FINAL PRODUCT

The objective of this MaxiLesson is to produce the first example of persuasive writing for the fourth-grade school year. You will want to reserve up to three thirty-minute time frames, but typically not more than one five-day week's worth of twenty-minute instructional sessions.

This MaxiLesson will take young writers through sentence and paragraph thinking and writing activities as they work with their first persuasive writing in the school year. They will also read and discuss examples of persuasive writing and reflect on their writing processes for purposes of organization, further drafting, and revision.

WRITING-READING INTERACTION

Having prepared an overhead transparency of the first two paragraphs of an editorial from a recent issue of the local newspaper, project the first paragraph only on the screen. Read the paragraph aloud as the children follow along. Let them know that you will ask about what they noticed after a second reading aloud. Then read it aloud again, and pose the question: "What did you notice about the paragraph?" After several student contributions, pose another question: "What does the first paragraph tell you? What do you know?" Finally, pose the third question: "What do you think comes next in the editorial?"

On subsequent days, read significant paragraphs from editorial commentary in the daily newspaper, and ask what the young learners notice in the paragraph and what they learn from it. The readings and discussions help them begin to understand the nature of persuasive text. We recommend using the newspaper because that is where authentic editorial commentary appears. It doesn't matter that some or many of the children can't read it on their own. They're constructing meanings from read-aloud. (After several read-alouds, most children are able to read it successfully, if only from memory.)

During discussions of the readings, mention the purpose of persuasive writing and what makes good persuasive writing (see Chapter 10). It is best, certainly in this first MaxiLesson in the fourth grade, not to post characteristics of good persuasive writing on the wall. But a posting can evolve as the learners read and write more and more persuasive pieces. The wall chart should emerge from discussions about the purpose of persuasive writing and how best to organize the writing to fulfill the purpose.

PERSUASIVE WRITING CUE

- *Should there be homework on every school night in the fourth grade?* (See Chapter 10.)

SENTENCES (SENTENCE COMBINING, CHAPTER 4)

- Read the two sentences below, and rewrite them into one sentence:
  Homework is important for learning.
  Homework is when students practice what they learned that day in school.
- Read the two sentences below, and rewrite them into one sentence:
  Homework sometimes takes an hour of my time.
  Homework can even take more than one hour on some nights.
- Read the three sentences below, and rewrite them into two sentences:
  Some students work hard all day in school.
  They do most of their homework during the day.
  They don't have much homework to do at home.

PARAGRAPHS (PARAGRAPH SENTENCE CARDS, CHAPTER 6)

- Arrange the following sentences in sequence. Then explain what the main idea of the paragraph is:

  In addition to the lessons in school, students have to practice what they learn in school.
  Homework is their chance to practice at home.
  Usually it takes more than one lesson to learn things that are important.
  Often students have to practice at home too.
  It is hard to really learn something from one lesson.
  Sometimes teachers help their students practice during the school day.

  Invite several students to read their sequence aloud, and discuss how the various arrangements affect the quality of the paragraph. Ask them to consider whether there is a sequence that is right.

POWER WRITING

On the second day of the MaxiLesson (or after the students have participated in sentence combining and arranging paragraph sentence cards), take them through three rounds of Power Writing (see Chapter 8). After each round, which lasts one minute, students count their words, and their word counts are entered on the Power Writing board chart.

- Round 1: Select one of the two following ideas. In one minute, write as much as you can as well as you can about the idea you selected.
  Homework is good for learning.
  Homework keeps me from doing other important things.
- Round 2: Select one of the two following ideas. In one minute, write as much as you can as well as you can about the idea you selected.
  Homework keeps me from doing other important things.
  I can usually plan my time so I can do homework and other important things.
- Round 3: Select one of the two ideas. In one minute, write as much as you can as well as you can about the idea you selected.
  School is what children do for work, so doing homework every night isn't unreasonable.
  Children should have time to just play when the school day is finished.

ITERATIVE WRITING PROCESS

As the result of the writing they have already done, some of the children will know what they want to write in their persuasive piece. Some will need additional guidance. Conduct a discussion with them about what persuasive writing is supposed to achieve and what they want to put in their persuasive piece.

Everyone in the class should look at everything they have written to see what they have already written and what they still need to write. Discuss with the students the following questions after they have read over their sentences, their paragraph, and their power writes. (We learned these kinds of "quick-conference" questions from a Donald Graves demonstration many years ago.)

- What do you think you would like to persuade your readers about in this piece?
- What do you think you have so far?
- What else do you think you need for your writing to be persuasive?

When the young writers have drafted as much as one or two paragraphs, conduct Writers' Workshops (see Chapter 8), or direct selected young writers to read their work aloud for feedback (see "Process Pieces," Chapter 6). Young writers use the feedback they receive from the peer audience as the catalyst for more drafting or for revision.

After the third or fourth day of persuasive writing, ask them to write their persuasive piece as well as they can, perhaps so it is good enough to display on the refrigerator door. The first persuasive piece in the fourth grade is often confusing for young writers. (So is long division, but we don't stop teaching it.) Wait a week, and conduct another MaxiLesson on persuasive writing. By the end of the year, fourth graders can be writing persuasive pieces in two days.

MAXILESSON: SETTING DESCRIPTION AS FINAL PRODUCT

The objective of this MaxiLesson is to increase the quality of young writers' short fiction by developing their ability to describe the settings where their stories are played out. Young writers will write a setting description in this MaxiLesson and a whole story for any young writer whose setting description promotes a story line.

This MaxiLesson is planned to take approximately two twenty-minute language arts sessions in the second grade. It is important to conduct MaxiLessons on both setting description and character description until young writers routinely put sensory detail in their settings and give their characters a measure of life. Of course, we're referring to reasonable expectations for second graders here. As young writers learn more about textured settings and how to make characters live, we increase the level of expectation.

The MaxiLesson uses sentences, paragraphs, and description, as well as the writing-reading connection and the writing-vocabulary connection, to help young writers think and write their settings and characters. They will also use their writing processes to organize and revise as they draft.

WRITING-READING INTERACTION

Read aloud several examples of well-described settings and follow the readings with questions about what the students noticed. For example, Gary Paulsen does an especially good job describing his story setting in *The Winter Room* (1989). Three paragraphs beginning with, "'Swooosh,' father says when he opens the door of the barn on a spring morning"

(p. 8), put readers into the images and smells of an old Minnesota farm where they raise cattle.

Ask second graders after reading the three paragraphs, "What did you notice about what the farm looks like?" "What does it smell like there?" Then follow students' descriptions with questions about how the writer, Gary Paulsen, helped readers see those images and smell those smells.

During each day of the MaxiLesson, read aloud examples of well-described settings and debrief the readings with a discussion similar to the one described above. The writing-reading interaction helps young writers begin to accumulate the prior knowledge on which subsequent writing will rest.

Because the writing-reading interaction is powerful in read-aloud sessions, the examples do not have to come from a second-grade reading list. Clearly the Paulsen example is not second-grade reading material, but second graders can see and smell the barn. We have had first graders draw pictures of the sodbuster in Sandburg's "Who Was That Early Sodbuster in Kansas," knowing nothing at all about Kansas, sodbusters, the westward movement, or, for that matter, farmers.

SETTING DESCRIPTION CUE

- *Make a word picture of what the inside of a supermarket looks like.* (See Chapter 10.)

SENTENCES (SENTENCES FROM OBSERVATION, CHAPTER 4)

- Close your eyes and see the inside of a supermarket, a food store, the store where you buy your groceries. Think about what it looks like, what you hear when you're there, what it smells like.

Make lists on the board of what the children report seeing. The young writers write oral, then scribal, sentences by using items from the lists on the board. Example: *It's cool in the supermarket, and I can smell the bananas when we go over there. The bananas smell really yellow and fresh.*

On each day of the MaxiLesson, young writers think in and write sentences, both orally and scribally, that describe the grocery store (or a forest, the living room, the inside of a car, a Little League field, and so forth). Encourage them to make their sentences as sensory as possible.

PARAGRAPHS

As the young writers share their sentences, write them on the board. When there are several sentences on the board, pose a question: "If we were going to describe a grocery store and could use only the sentences on the board, which of the sentences would come first? Which would come next?" If there are more than about a half-dozen sentences, make two clusters of sequenced sentences. Then ask what the main idea is in each cluster (or in the one cluster if there are only four or five sentences). (See Chapter 6 for how to help young writers understand main idea.)

DESCRIPTION

When we describe something, we draw attention to size, movement, feelings, and so forth. (See Chapter 6 for the elements of description.) For the grocery store description, ask the students to write a sentence about the movement in the store:

- Who is moving?
- Where does movement take place?
- What is going on that produces movement?

Then ask them to write a sentence about the size of the store, the size of the produce department, or the dimensions of the bread shelves.

ITERATIVE WRITING PROCESS

At this point in the MaxiLesson, young writers have written sentences and paragraphs about the grocery store, and they have sequenced some of the sentences. Now tell them there is an elderly woman in the store pushing a cart, and in the cart is her cat, leashed so it cannot get away. Using what they have already written about the store and by adding their own description of the character, ask them to write a description of the grocery store with the character in it.

In the second grade, especially early in the year, this MaxiLesson may take several days, or maybe even several days stretched over two weeks. It is important for almost everyone to write the setting description with the character in it, even if the description is a sentence or two long. Later in the second-grade year, the descriptions will become increasingly detailed, and through such practice, the settings in their young writers' stories will become increasingly detailed. The detail won't come from the use of more modifiers; it will come from better use of the elements of description.

Implementing MaxiLessons in the Interactive Language Arts

Imagine that what we're going to do tomorrow morning is read aloud. We've selected a passage that introduces a whole piece of writing on which students will work for anywhere from a day to even five days. We will read aloud each day of the MaxiLesson. The children will write sentences and concentrate on relationships between and among sentences. They will also write paragraphs and think about relationships between and among paragraphs. They will write in the modes of discourse and the Short Cues. When the MaxiLesson is completed, almost everyone in the class will have worked on the relationship between form and function to produce a whole written product in a specific genre.

There are thirty-six weeks in the school year. If every MaxiLesson takes a full five-day week, and most will take two or three days, almost every third grader will have participated in the following experiences:

- Thirty-six whole pieces of writing, each in a specific genre
- Specific lessons on sentence and paragraph thinking and writing
- Specific lessons on elements of mechanical control critical to sentence writing
- Writing processes that are idiosyncratic to the writer and the genre in the MaxiLesson
- Organization of sentences, paragraphs, and other portions of MaxiLesson writing into whole pieces of writing

If we believe that effective practice is important in learning any complex human behavior, we have to believe that thirty-six instances of attentive work with the craft, the processes, and the genres in writing will influence third graders' growth in writing and literacy. We also have to believe that thirty-six more in the fourth grade, built on the third-grade foundation, will help make fourth graders even better writers. After the fourth grade, there are two more years of MaxiLessons. If it all started in the second grade, young writers at the end of the sixth grade will have participated in and organized 180 whole pieces of writing. They will have written in specific genres 180 times. They will have had 180 specific instructional experiences with sentences, paragraphs, and mechanical control. They will have grappled with their writing processes 180 times. Some will have more than 180 because some teachers will begin in the first grade.

Some teachers will conduct two MaxiLessons during some weeks: one in interactive language arts and one in social studies. But in most schools, many children aren't in attendance every year because they move, so there are lots of young writers who wouldn't get 180 MaxiLessons through the elementary years. Someone might miss a year and get only 144, but then they might go to a school where teachers are conducting MaxiLessons in interactive language arts. It's like the reading and mathematics program. We don't stop teaching as systematically and specifically as we can just because everyone in the room didn't get the lessons last year on which this year's lessons are planned. We adjust to the realities of their lives, just as they do.

Contents of MaxiLessons in Interactive Language Arts

MaxiLessons in interactive language arts encompass specific experiences for young writers:

- Attentive work on the craft of writing
- The iterative processes of writing
- The production of a whole piece of writing in a specific genre that results from organizational thinking
- The interactions of writing with reading, vocabulary, and spelling

MaxiLesson teachers teach young writers to write well. Perhaps MaxiLesson teachers are not purely "sages on the stage," but they are definitely not "guides on the side." MaxiLessons implement direct instruction. Teachers know with a high degree of certainty what is going to happen in the lesson, how it will happen, to whom it will happen, for how long, and with what result. They believe that they are professionally responsible for nothing short of that.

Interactions in the Language Arts: Making It Happen

In this book, we have defined what an interactive perspective on the language arts means. We have described and shown, often using instructional scenarios, a systematic perspective on curriculum for writing instruction. We have described and shown the interactions between and among writing, reading, spelling, and vocabulary. We have revealed how young writers write in the instructional strategies we have described. We have offered several kinds of implementation plans.

We've done what we're supposed to do when we write a textbook. But that's the same as walking out of a first-grade classroom and saying that we taught the way we're supposed to when we're first-grade teachers. That isn't good enough. The first graders have to have learned from our instruction, and our readers have to have been influenced by our textbook.

We've been talking at you for all these pages. Now it's your turn. We want to hear about what worked when you taught what you learned from one or more of the instructional scenarios. We want to know what happened when you planned and taught a MaxiLesson. We want to know if you learned something about spelling that helped someone in your class become more effective. We want to hear about what you did with vocabulary development that made the words begin to appear in your students' writing. When you scored your students' writing analytically, then taught interactive language arts, and then scored another writing sample, we want to know the difference in scores.

We want to know about where this book has missed the mark as well. What did we describe that might have been clearer? What did you do in a classroom from what we suggested that didn't turn out the way you expected? What problems are you having that you might like to discuss?

What do you think you could do better the next time if it were discussed again? Do you have a question about interactive language arts that you think we could answer for you in an e-mail message? We'd like the interactions to extend beyond the pages of this book. E-mail us at college_educ.hmco.com.

Dear readers, thank you for listening. The ball's in your court now.

RESOURCES FOR FURTHER INVESTIGATION

Writers on Writing

Asimov, I. (1979). *In Memory Yet Green: The Autobiography of Isaac Asimov, 1920–1954*. New York: Avon Books.

> *This first volume of Asimov's autobiography takes readers from the early days in his father's Brooklyn candy store, where he read the magazines sold there, to becoming the father of the golden age of science fiction. What is clear is that his science fiction comes from his voracious interest in and curiosity about science, plus his considerable educational background in science.*

Asimov, I. (1980). *In Joy Still Felt: The Autobiography of Isaac Asimov, 1954–1978*. Garden City, NY: Doubleday.

> *The second volume of Asimov's autobiography is a textbook of the "daytimer" approach to autobiographical writing. It also chronicles the precision with which Asimov approached writing, down to counting the words in every piece he wrote.*

Brohaugh, W. (Ed.). (1987). *Just Open a Vein*. Cincinnati, Ohio: Writer's Digest Books.

> *Red Smith, the dean of twentieth-century sports writers, said, "Writing isn't that hard. All you have to do is open a vein." This collection of writers' comments from autobiographical writing and interviews reveals how they experience writing. This and similar collections are very important because students need to understand that what they experience as young writers is not different from what adult writers experience.*

Chamberlain, M. (1988). *Writing Lives: Conversations Between Women Writers*. London: Virago Press.

> *Maya Angelou talks with Rosa Guy, Elizabeth Hardwick talks with Helen McNeil, and Eudora Welty talks with Hermione Lee. Those are three of the twenty conversations in Mary Chamberlain's collection. The book takes readers inside to listen to practicing writers in conversation.*

Cowley, M. (Ed.). (1958). *Writers at Work: The Paris Review Interviews.* New York: Viking Press.

> *This book contains selected* Paris Review *interviews that Cowley collected. There are draft pages from the work of Robert Penn Warren, James Thurber, Truman Capote, and more of the premier writers of the twentieth century. Their commentary about writing is revealing, maybe especially to young writers.*

Dillard, A. (1989). *The Writing Life.* New York: Harper and Row.

> *Annie Dillard takes readers into her life as a writer. Particularly revealing are peeks into her early life as a reader. Reading Dillard's writing about her writing life is as much a treat as is reading her stories.*

Gallo, D. R. (Ed.). (1993). *Speaking for Ourselves, Too.* Urbana, IL: National Council of Teachers of English.

> *There are eighty-nine writers' comments about writing in this collection. Gallo writes of the lessons they provide. "Any fool can write when they're inspired," Phillip Pullman says. "I love guessing why people do what they do," says Suzanne Newton. The writing classroom, then, might be a place where young writers write even when they aren't motivated and where they understand others' motives.*

Kenyon, O. (1989). *Women Writers Talk: Interviews with 10 Women Writers.* New York: Carroll and Graf Publishers.

> *These interviews are described as beneficial reading for any aspiring writer of either gender. Kenyon characterizes the collection as descriptive of how women write, why, and how they read other women writers. The writers' self-reports are insightful and revealing, especially for novice writers and their teachers, for the voices of practicing writers are critical in the instructional mix.*

Lamb, B. (1997). *Booknotes: America's Finest Authors on Reading, Writing, and the Power of Ideas.* New York: Random House.

> *Contemporary writers share their ideas about writing under the direction of Barry Lamb. These are edited versions of the popular cable television interviews. Lamb is as expert at selecting revealing snippets as he is at asking the right questions.*

Lloyd, P. (1987). *How Writers Write.* Portsmouth, NH: Heinemann.

> *The self-reports that Pamela Lloyd offers all come from the people who write books that children read: Beverly Cleary, Robert Cormier, Max Dann, Jack Prelutsky, Madeleine L'Engle, and many others. As the children read the books, they have an opportunity to listen to the authors tell how and why they write.*

Murray, D. (1983). *Writing for Your Readers: Notes on the Writer's Craft from the Boston Globe.* Chester, CT: Globe Pequot Press.

> *There are thirty questions to produce leads, a list of the writer's ten commandments, a commentary on the five W's, and a description of two writing styles. In and around those are interview questions and answers, tips for science writers, and how to start at the end.*

Any writer can learn from this book, written with journalism in mind, and any teacher can gain years' worth of insight from the writer's perspective.

Murray, D. (1985). *A Writer Teaches Writing.* Boston: Houghton Mifflin.

Donald Murray has made a successful life as a writer and as a writing teacher. He writes here about how the writer views writing instruction.

Murray, D. M. (1990). *Shoptalk: Learning to Write with Writers.* Portsmouth, NH: Boynton/Cook Publishers, Heinemann.

Murray's collection of writers' insights and advice is arranged by category: Why Write, The Writing Habit, and Recognizing Form. Over five hundred writers are represented. This book provides especially rich insights into the world in which writers live and work.

Plimpton, G. (Ed.). (1989). *The Writer's Chapbook: A Compendium of Fact, Opinion, Wit, and Advice from the 20th Century's Preeminent Writers.* New York: Viking.

George Plimpton, a primary interviewer for the Paris Review, *arranged anecdotes from those interviews into this compendium about writers and writing.*

Ruas, C. (1984). *Conversations with American Writers.* London: Quartet Books Limited.

This is a very reader-friendly volume of interviews with writers we all recognize, from Eudora Welty at the beginning, to Scott Spencer at the end. In between there are Gore Vidal, Norman Mailer, E. L. Doctorow, and Toni Morrison. Do you want to know what the writer had in mind when she wrote The Bluest Eye? *It's in here.*

Safire, W., and Safire, L. (Eds.). (1992). *Good Advice on Writing: Great Quotations from Writers Past and Present on How to Write Well.* New York: Simon & Schuster.

William Safire and his late brother collected practical advice about writing from writers. Kathleen Norris, for example, advises that fiction writers should "get a girl in trouble, then get her out again." Of course, it isn't the girl; it's the trouble. And Elmore Leonard is quoted on the back cover of the book: "When you write, try to leave out the parts the readers skip." Teachers can use Norris' advice in a fiction unit and Leonard's as a key in revision.

Steinbeck, J. (1969). *Journal of a Novel: The "East of Eden" Letters.* New York: Penguin Group.

As he wrote East of Eden, *Steinbeck wrote daily "letters" to his editor. The letters reflected his thoughts, fears, and, perhaps most important, his processes as he developed the book and crafted what became one of the great novels in American literature.*

Steinbeck, J. (1989). *Working Days: The Journals of "The Grapes of Wrath."* New York: Penguin Group.

Readers are invited into Steinbeck's world as he developed and crafted The Grapes of Wrath, *in much the same way readers have an opportunity to understand the processes that characterized the writer's work in* East of Eden.

Strickland, B. (Ed.). (1989). *On Being a Writer*. Cincinnati, OH: Writer's Digest Books.

> *This could become a classroom treasure. More like a coffee table book than any other on this list, its advice comes clothed in inspiration. Read the piece on Marsha Norman, if no other. Assign it as basic reading for adolescent writers.*

On the Writing Act

Biagi, S. (1989). *How to Write and Sell Magazine Articles*. New York: Prentice Hall Press.

> *This is a book about writing that works, where "works" is defined as selling your writing. The author covers it all, from knowing the magazine industry, to creating, drafting, and finishing the article, and identifying the right market. It's about writing, but it's also about the business. If writing teachers don't know the business, instruction can lack realism.*

Boles, P. D. (1984). *Storycrafting*. Cincinnati, OH: Writer's Digest Books.

> *Boles' book is useful for teachers if only because it adds so much to the standard teacherism: "Write what you know." Yes, because that's all you can do, but Stephen Crane never saw Civil War combat and J. R. R. Tolkien's hobbits "walked out of his head." If we believe in imagination, to write what you know is a stifling limitation.*

Edelstein, S. (1999). *100 Things Every Writer Needs to Know*. New York: Berkley Publishing Group.

> *There are ninety-six things in addition to the following four: Write what you'd enjoy reading. Write what you care about. Each person's writing process is unique. Never throw away anything you write.*

Fry, D. (Ed.). (1988). *Best Newspaper Writing 1988*. St. Petersburg, FL: Poynter Institute for Media Studies.

> *This is the best of what newspaper writing can look like. The winning categories include Non-Deadline and Deadline writing, Commentary, Editorials, and Obituaries. Each selection is followed with questions and comments about the winning piece.*

Gardner, J. (1983). *On Becoming a Novelist*. New York: Harper & Row.

> *Mihaly Csikszentmihalyi wrote* Flow: The Psychology of Optimal Experience *in 1990. John Gardner wrote about flow in 1983, dynamically, specifically, and precisely. This is a book about the writer who doesn't leave a half-written try at a novel in the bureau drawer. This is about the writer who finishes it and what it takes to do it. Teachers who teach fiction should read John Gardner.*

Gardner, J. (1984). *The Art of Fiction: Notes on Craft for Young Writers*. New York: Knopf.

> *This is one of the more important guidelines for novice and experienced fiction writers by the late John Gardner. Gardner writes clearly about the "fictional dream," which is the writer's primary purpose in writing fiction.*

Gordon, K. E. (1993). *The Deluxe Transitive Vampire: The Ultimate Handbook of Grammar for the Innocent, the Eager, and the Doomed.* New York: Pantheon Books.

> *A relentlessly elegant little book about the English sentence that William Safire calls a book you can sink your fangs into. We add that in the tearing and chewing, you can marvel at how needlessly painful it is for so many students to learn how sentences work.*

Gordon, K. E. (1993). *The New Well-Tempered Sentence: A Punctuation Handbook for the Innocent, the Eager, and the Doomed.* Boston: Houghton Mifflin.

> *Edwin Newman said of this book, "It is Karen Gordon's notion that punctuation is at least as inevitable as death and taxes, so it might as well be learned and enjoyed. Her little book enables us to do both."*

Gordon, K. E. (1998). *Out of the Hound of Darkness: A Dictionarrative.* New York: Pantheon Books.

> *Through delightful narrative peopled with outlandish characters, Gordon takes readers through the "finesses of usage" to discover when one is "disinterested" and when "uninterested," the difference between "prescribe" and "proscribe," and when one might be described as "imperious" and "imperial." In addition, she offers a lexicon full of interesting words and phrases, such as "caveate," "non sequitur," and "vitiate."*

Halberstam, D. (Ed.). (1999). *The Best American Sports Writing of the Century.* Boston: Houghton Mifflin.

> *Some of the best writing occurs on the sports pages of the nation's newspapers. To read selections of the best sports writing of the century is to have a road map of how good writing is supposed to read.*

McCormack, T. (1988). *The Fiction Editor, the Novel, and the Novelist.* New York: St. Martin's Press.

> *McCormack's little book is to fiction what Biagi's is to magazine writing. One of the things most enlightening about this book is the discussion of craft. The author's distinction between instinct and craft—that instinct can tell readers that something is wrong, but only craft can tell what it is and what to do about it—might be useful to teachers.*

Mogilner, A. (1992). *Children's Writer's Word Book.* Cincinnati, OH: Writer's Digest Books.

> *Alijandra Mogilner has offered to children's book writers lists of graded word lists they can use in any attempt to ensure their books are appropriate for their readers. Her research is impressive. Teachers can use her book for vocabulary development, spelling, and as a literature selection criterion.*

Parini, J. (Ed.). (1999). *The Norton Book of American Autobiography.* New York: Norton.

> *To teach autobiography presupposes knowing how autobiography is constructed. There are sufficient autobiographies in this volume to give readers a good image of the autobiography in all of its permutations.*

Peterson, R. (2000). *Real World Research*. Boston: Houghton Mifflin.

> *This book contains everything that students need to research and write careful, thoughtful, and compelling documented papers. It includes advice on conducting electronic research and using the Internet; all of the major documentation styles (with sample papers); chapters on argumentation and alternative media presentations; interviews with professionals in the arts, sciences, business, law, and government; and advice on researching and choosing internships and careers.*

Progoff, I. (1975). *At a Journal Workshop: The Basic Text and Guide for Using the Intensive Journal*. New York: Dialogue House Library.

> *The journal is a staple in what many teachers call their writing "program." To write journals is far more than merely writing what happened recently. Progoff's book is a text for the journal writer and teacher.*

Raines, A. (1999). *Keys for Writers* (2nd ed.). Boston: Houghton Mifflin.

> *This is a popular tabbed handbook designed to provide easy access to information. It contains advice on the writing process, using and documenting sources, style, common sentence problems, punctuation and mechanics, a special section for multilingual/ESL writers, and glossaries of usage and grammatical terms.*

Raines, A. (2000). *Pocket Keys for Writers*. Boston: Houghton Mifflin.

> *As the title states, this is a pocket version of Raines'* Keys for Writers, *containing all of the same information as its parent handbook in a briefer format.*

Webber, E., and Feinsilber, M. (1999). *Merriam-Webster's Dictionary of Allusions*. Springfield, MA: Merriam-Webster.

> *The book cover calls these by the term "hidden meanings." Elsewhere, they're called cultural literacy. These are shorthand references that writers use on the assumption that readers know the big picture. "Quisling," for example, refers to "traitor" or collaborator. In the big picture, there was a man in Norway named Quisling who functioned as an advance man for Hitler's invasion of his country.*

Welty, E. (1990). *The Eye of the Story*. New York: Vintage International.

> *Welty writes nonfiction too. Here, this gentle giant of American literature comments on a variety of writers, writing, and her own stories. For readers of "The Worn Path," she includes an essay titled, "Is Phoenix Jackson's Grandson Really Dead?"*

Willis, M. S. (1984). *Personal Fiction Writing: A Guide to Writing from Real Life for Teachers, Students, and Writers*. New York: Teachers and Writers Collaborative.

> *If a teacher is going to "teach" short fiction and is inclined toward story starters, it's time to read Willis on place, people, action, and dialogue. Willis teaches about inventing the story, not filling the blanks opened by story starters.*

Wills, K. J. (Ed.). (1990). *The Pulitzer Prizes: Our History in the Making, 1990.* New York: Simon & Schuster.

> One of the more important things a writing teacher needs is a good grasp of what excellence looks like. What better place to look for excellence in writing than in a collection of Pulitzer Prize winners?

Teaching Writing and the English Language Arts

Bryson, B. (1990). *The Mother Tongue: English and How It Got That Way.* New York: Morrow.

> In a very readable book, Bryson charts the history of the language we teach, mostly at the level of the word. Well researched and humorously written, the book answers questions about the origins of English, its march through the ages, the seeming inconsistencies, good and bad, old and new, swearing, and the future.

Burke, J. (1999). *The English Teacher's Companion: A Complete Guide to Classroom, Curriculum, and the Profession.* Portsmouth, NH: Boynton/Cook Publishers, Heinemann.

> If novice English teachers were to read this book and carry it with them through the first several years of teaching, the novice life would be a whole lot less trying, and the novice would be a whole lot more confident as he or she learned how to be a good teacher.

Caplan, R., and Keech, C. (1980). *Showing-Writing: A Training Program to Help Students Be Specific.* Berkeley: University of California, Berkeley, Bay Area Writing Project.

> There aren't many people in the field of writing instruction who are known for intentional instruction, but they do exist. Rebekah Caplan is one of them, and has been for a long time. In her case, intentional instruction focuses on the distinction between telling and showing. She describes instruction in the first portion of the book and reports on its effectiveness in the second portion.

Cramer, R. L. (1998). *The Spelling Connection: Integrating Reading, Writing, and Spelling Instruction.* New York: Guilford Press.

> There are several very good books about spelling and teaching spelling, but Cramer's is excellent. It's reader friendly, teacher specific, and very practical.

Fearn, L., and Farnan, N. (1998). *Writing Effectively: Helping Children Master the Conventions of Writing.* Boston: Allyn and Bacon.

> The thirty high-frequency and highest-utility capitalization and punctuation conventions are calibrated to begin with awareness and lead to eventual mastery. Each convention is described and modeled, then explained instructionally in writing, not editing, context. Conventions are taught through youngsters' own writing.

Fearn, L., and Farnan, N. (1999). *Get Writing!!* San Antonio, TX: ECS Learning Systems.

> *A series of six instructional books (K–5) that explore balanced writing instruction. Included in the series are lessons on sentences, paragraphs, relationships between and among sentences and paragraphs, vocabulary, spelling, and genres.*

Peterson, R. (1995). *The Writing Teacher's Companion.* Boston: Houghton Mifflin.

> *This user-friendly guide offers no-nonsense advice on how to succeed as a new composition instructor. It includes advice on everything from course plans to assessment, classroom management to textbook selection.*

r * w * t (Reading, Writing, Thinking), ECS Learning Systems, Inc., P.O. Box 791437, San Antonio, TX 78279-1437 [www.educyberstor.com].

> *This magazine for writing teachers is the only one of its kind. It is explicitly teacher friendly in its various practical articles and interviews with the writers, teachers, and researchers who define how we teach writing.*

What Writers Read

Merlyn's Pen Magazine

> *"Fiction, Essays, and Poems by America's Teens." This is the description on the colorful cover of* Merlyn's Pen, *a unique publication of writing by secondary students. Approximately ten thousand students submit yearly to this publication. Some are published; all receive a response. Visit their Web site at www.merlynspen.com.*

Paris Review, 171st Place, Flushing, NY 11358. [www.parisreview.com]

> *Known by many for containing excellent interviews with the premier writers of the twentieth century, the* Paris Review *is primarily a literary magazine. It would be a terrific subscription for any middle-level or secondary English classroom.*

Publishers' Weekly, 245 West 17th Street, New York, NY 10011. [www.publishersweekly.com]

> *The international news magazine of book publishing and selling,* PW *also contains excellent articles about writing and publishing. The Web site contains an archives on best sellers, author appearance schedules, and articles from the magazine.*

The Writer, 120 Boylston Street, Boston, MA 02116-4615. [www.channel1.com/the writer]

> *Founded in Boston in 1887, this is the oldest writers' magazine. It includes interviews with writers, how-to articles, and tips on how to sell manuscripts.*

Writer's Digest, 1507 Dana Avenue, Cincinnati, OH 45207

> *A recent issue reviews 101 best web sites for writers and an article about writers' conferences. The magazine prides itself with being the insider's guide to the writing scene. [email: writersdig@fwpubs.com].*

Writers' Market, Writer's Digest Books, Cincinnati, OH 45207.

> *Updated annually, the 2000 edition lists the names of eight thousand editors of publishing houses and magazines, along with what they publish and how to submit manuscripts. Among the entries, forty-eight are for young writers. Also included are excellent articles about writing.*

Using Technology and the Internet

Carbone, N. (2000). *Writing Online: A Student's Guide to the Internet and World Wide Web* (3rd ed.). Boston: Houghton Mifflin.

> *This is a pocket-sized guide to everything that writing students need to know about the Internet and World Wide Web. Topics covered include e-mail, writing and designing Web sites, evaluating Internet sources, and documenting Web sources.*

Wepner, S. B., Valmont, W. J., and Thurlow, R. (Eds.). (2000). *Linking Literacy and Technology: A Guide for K–8 Classrooms.* Newark, DE: International Reading Association.

> *An informative text with practical ideas that focus on how to begin using technology; using technology in reading, writing, and literacy development; and technology for content-area learning. This book takes readers into up-to-the-minute classrooms where technology connects to teaching and learning.*

National Writing Project   http://nwp.berkeley.edu

> *This is the National Writing Project web site. Visit the national network of university-based, teacher-centered programs whose mission is to "improve the teaching of writing and learning in the nation's schools." There are links to various publications and to a comprehensive bibliography on teacher action research.*

Guide to Grammar and Writing   http://www.go.to/grammar

> *This "Guide to Grammar and Writing" is full of definitions and examples of effective sentences, capitalization and punctuation conventions, and paragraphing. There's a link to Principles of Composition, PowerPoint presentations, Online Resources for Writers, and quotations from eminent writers and thinkers. Readers can also ask and access frequently asked questions about writing. Visit the site's Trophy Cabinet to see the nearly forty awards for excellence it has received.*

Inkspot: The Writer's Resource   http://www.inkspot.com/

> *This site offers "a resource and community for writers of all ages and levels of experience." This young authors' resource center has a link to pages for young writers age eighteen and under that includes a chat room for young writers, stories to read and critique, free on-line writing classes, a question-and-answer section on writing, and a monthly column just for young writers. Also, there's a Teaching Writing link that includes a wealth of information for teachers and is worth checking out.*

KidPub WWW Publishing   http://www.kidpub.org/kidpub/intro.html

On our latest visit to this site, we were visitor 1,126,110, and on that date we had access to "more than 36,000 stories written by kids from all over the planet!" There is a "new stories" category and "oldies but goodies." Find out how the publisher's nine-year-old daughter provided inspiration for KidPub, how to publish in KidPub, and how to sign up for keypals. Read children's stories as varied as "The Alien from Hale-Bopp" and "Egg Rap," and visit schools where classrooms have published on the site.

National Council of Teachers of English   http://www.ncte.org/

This is the web site of the largest subject matter organization in the world (nearly eighty thousand members), the National Council of Teachers of English, "dedicated to improving the teaching and learning of English and the language arts at all levels of education." Visit the link to SyllabusSite, where teachers have posted syllabi on assessment in writing. You'll find addresses for listservs where teachers "chat" about writing and other literacy topics. It's a large site, so plan to spend some time here.

The Write Environment   http://www.writeenvironment.com/

This site offers writing software and has links to Education Resources, Online Writing Labs, and Resources for Writers Writing in Special Fields. For example, there is excellent material on technical writing. The user must be discriminating, for there are also electronic workbooks (punctuation, for example).

GLOSSARY

Analytic mode of discourse Communication that emphasizes logical explanations and systems for understanding complex matters. It expresses problem-solving processes and procedures for understanding complexity.

Attention A gating mechanism in learning. Learners commit *deliberate* attention to unpracticed stimuli and *automatic* attention to practiced stimuli. Learners decide to attend because the stimuli are compelling to them.

Automaticity The ability to do something while focusing deliberately on something else. Experienced writers focus on constructing their big ideas while they commit automatic attention to elements of craft, such as capitalizing and using end punctuation. Automaticity emerges from practice.

Balanced writing instruction Comprehensive instruction that encompasses objectives, activities designed to meet the objectives, and assessments used to determine growth and inform subsequent instruction. Places primary emphasis on intentional instruction (as opposed to promotion) and the balance among craft, processes, and relationships between form and function (genres).

Cognition Associated with knowing, recognizing. When we see a four-legged animal with a saddle on its back and think "horse," we cognize the idea of horse.

Cohesion In writing, the glue that binds one sentence to another or one paragraph to another. Invariably the result of something transitional, the connections provide readers with a language flow through a piece of writing.

Compare/contrast mode of discourse Communication that features similarities and differences. In a compare/contrast piece of writing, the writer shows how two things are both alike and different and often concludes on the basis of the similarities and differences.

Competence theory Theory based on the proposition that to be competent means to be sufficient or able.

Complex sentence A syntactic structure made of one or more dependent clauses supported by one or more independent clauses.

Compound sentence A syntactic structure made of two or more independent clauses connected by coordinating conjunctions.

Conceptualization What learners do when they construct concepts, which are relationships between and among ideas. Concepts come from the process of conceptualization.

Convention (mechanics) In this book refers to punctuation conventions—that is, a conventional way to punctuate the language so everyone can communicate effectively; also, statements on which people agree. *Convention* is a better term

than *rule*, which presupposes something that is inherently right.

Craft Refers to how writers handle the language. Craft encompasses the sentence, relationships between and among sentences, paragraphs, relationships between and among paragraphs, and mechanics.

Creative writing The term often associated with certain genres, most characteristically fiction and poetry. A clear sense of what creativity is makes all writing creative.

Criticize/persuade mode of discourse Communication whose purpose is to influence how readers think and perceive. It seeks to define for readers how they should view images and ideas.

Curiosity The creative thinking skill most often associated with pondering and wondering. The typical curiosity question is, "What would happen if . . . ?"

Descriptive mode of discourse Communication designed to clarify ideas and images. Description shows how an image can be sensed or how an idea can be understood.

Direct (intentional) instruction Instruction intended to teach selected content intentionally, that is, on purpose. Direct instruction looks more like "sage on the stage" than "guide on the side."

Discourse networks On-line conversational links through e-mail, including listservs, discussion groups, and chat rooms.

Diversity Variety with regard to thoughts, feelings, and behaviors and to the variety of cultures, ethnicities, social classes, and genders. Diversity is thought to enrich interactions among peoples.

Elaboration The creative thinking skill most often associated with embellishment, or adding onto. Sentence expanding is elaborative.

English as a second language The phrase used to label the English language when it is learned and used by speakers of a native language other than English. English is learned and used as the second language. *See also* Second-language learners.

Flexibility The creative thinking skill most often associated with the ability and the inclination to view things from alternative perspectives. Directing young writers to move an idea they have made the subject of their sentence to the end of their sentence can promote flexible thinking.

Fluency The creative thinking skill most often associated with producing many ideas, where the criterion is an emphasis more on quantity than quality. A typical fluency direction is, "Make a list of. . . ."

Form and function Closely associated with genre studies, where *form* refers largely to text structures and *function* to purpose and audience. Genres are crafted most effectively as they emerge from thoughtful, careful attention to how form and function interrelate. *See also* genre.

Fragment (sentence) A nonsentence; usually an introductory or dependent clause without the independent clause that finishes the sentence (e.g., "After the show.").

Free writing To write without regard for quality or convention for a specified period of time for the single purpose of getting writing on paper.

Genre The designation of the form/function relationship writers use when they write. Short fiction is a genre, as are persuasion, poetry, and report of information. Each has its own function, and readers expect that the text will be arranged in a way that they associate with the genre as a certain type of writing.

Grammar A way to understand how language can be organized. Although characteristically associated with parts of speech in English class, grammar is nearly synonymous with *taxonomy*. Basic biological terminology (phylum, class, and so forth) is the grammar of biology, that is, a way to understand how biology can be organized. Another example is the Periodic Table of Elements, which is a taxonomy, or grammar, for chemistry.

Hypermedia Electronic text in which pages are linked in various ways, such as in the World Wide Web. Text that includes graphics/pictures and sound.

Hypertext An electronic form of text in which pages are linked through words or images to one another. The World Wide Web comprises both hypertext and hypermedia.

Intentional instruction Purposeful, systematic instruction that is driven by the expectation of improved learner performance. Nearly synonymous with *direct instruction*.

Interactions Symbiotic relationships where each part is inextricably related to every other part. Interactions in this book are relationships between and among elements in writing and among writing and reading, spelling, and vocabulary.

Language arts The elements—actually, the arts—of language use. The language arts typically are oral language, listening, reading, and writing. Because of the interactive nature of the language arts in this book, writing also includes spelling and vocabulary.

Learning Learning is change; the change is improvement. Improved writing performance indicates learning.

Literacy A measure of competence in a field (e.g., mathematical literacy, cultural literacy). Here we refer to literacy in the language sense, that is, the ability to read and write, to use language effectively.

Mastery Age-appropriate and earned competence.

MaxiLessons A way to plan and conduct writing instruction so the craft, the processes, and a genre, in addition to interactions with reading, spelling, and vocabulary, all occur intentionally and systematically in the same instructional plan.

Meaning markers The special parts of writing that guide readers' meaning making, for example, paragraph divisions, word order, and word selection. Meaning markers typically called "mechanical" are capital letters and punctuation marks.

Mechanics Meaning markers (mainly capitalization and punctuation), spelling, and the use of words and word forms. Mechanical control is the writer's ability to use effectively the mechanics of writing. *See also* Convention; Meaning markers.

Memory The storage of meanings and access to those meanings. *Active memory* means holding a stimulus very briefly before evaluating it for storage); *short-term memory* is holding a stimulus for short-term use; and *long-term memory* is storing a stimulus for immediate or future access (or both). Also included in discussions of memory are recognition and recall. *See also* Recognition.

Modes of discourse Ways by which writers inform readers. There are four modes of discourse (forms for communicating through writing): description, analysis, compare/contrast, and criticize/persuade.

Modification An adjustment or enhancer for emphasis. For example, adjectives are modifiers to enhance nouns in a sentence.

Motivation A person's sense of wanting or desire to do something. It is best seen in the inclination to approach a task willingly as opposed to seeking ways to avoid it.

Nonsentence Any string of language that does not satisfy either of the sentence descriptors. *See also* Sentence.

Onset rime Most clearly associated with phonemic awareness and young readers' ability to sense the construction of words in word families. Phonemically aware children, for example, can make the *-ake* spelling pattern into a variety of words. The teacher voices a phoneme (sound) *r*, and the student returns, *ake*. The *onset* is the consonant before the first vowel in a word. In the word *ask*, there is no onset. In the word *task*, the onset is *t*.

Organization A creative thinking skill (classically referred to as *organization of chaos*) that entails finding patterns that clarify and shape meaning; often it means finding patterns in messes.

Originality Uniqueness in a creative thinking skill context. An idea need not be unique for all time and in all fields to be original. Originality can be determined within a smaller sample. For example, an idea can be original in a particular classroom because only one child in that room thought of it.

Paragraph A segment of text separated from text that comes before or after by virtue of its controlling or main idea. A paragraph is a thoughtful way to arrange or organize ideas.

Parts of speech The definitions and roles of words and word clusters in oral and written language. The parts of speech help linguists understand how the language works by naming the pieces and defining their relationships between and among other pieces.

Perception Making meaning. People perceive because they have made meaning of an instance of stimuli. They must attend to perceive, and that which they perceive, they store in memory. Concep-

tualization is based on organizing perceptions.

PowerPoint A software program designed for the creation of presentations.

Power Writing A structured free-write where the objective is quantity alone. It is timed in three one-minute cued rounds, and students' word count is recorded on the chalkboard. Power Writing helps young writers understand their ability to get black on white.

Practice The mediator between deliberate and automatic attention. Practice makes permanent; only perfect practice makes perfect.

Precision Using only the right words for exactly the right reasons, and no more than necessary to fulfill the writer's purpose. Precision is associated with brevity, for when the prompt or purpose demands brevity, the right word for the right reason becomes the writer's primary objective. Precision is a major objective in writing well.

Précis A French term that means compilation of important facts or information. It captures the essential meaning in a piece of writing.

Prior knowledge What people know when they approach a learning task. It is the knowledge that learners use to construct meaning from new stimuli.

Process Pieces Two-minute image or idea writes that accomplish two purposes: (1) because they are whole pieces of writing, they mobilize all the writer's writing processes; (2) the debrief of the writing focuses on writers' process self-reports, as well as audience feedback and subsequent revision.

Process Reflection A writer's expression of how he or she did the writing. To reflect on writing process is to self-report on how the writing was done.

Process As used in writing, to describe how writers, both novice and experienced, approach and perform writing. Self-reported processes explain how writers write.

Recognition The form of memory that makes a connection between sensory stimuli and memory. We recognize (re cognize) a horse, for example, because we see a four-legged animal with a long face and a saddle on its back and connect it to a similar image we have stored in long-term memory. To exercise recall memory, on the other hand, we have to reproduce the meaning and image of the horse.

Reliability When tests, or instructional processes, produce the same results every time, even with different examiners or teachers, if the procedures are followed properly.

Related sentences Two or more sentences that are connected, clearly run one after another to make one larger meaning or main idea, and are related by transitional devices.

Run-on sentence Extended strings of syntax that should be broken into more than one sentence to accomplish greater readability and comprehensibility. A run-on is not necessarily a long sentence or several independent clauses held together with coordinating conjunctions. (*See also* fragment.)

Scaffolding Bridges from what students know and can do to what they need to know and do; what good teachers do to help learners achieve breakthroughs. A scaffold might be understood as what teachers do when they arrange instruction in successive approximations from where students are at the beginning of a lesson to where teachers want students to be at the end of a lesson.

Second-language learners Students engaged in learning a language other than their native or primary language. In schools in the United States, second-language learners are typically those whose native or primary language is not English, and they are learning English in school as a second language. If they are learning English, they are often called *English-language learners* (ELL). *See also* English as a second language.

Self-concept The image or concept one has of one's self. Self-concept can be connected specifically to ability, as in self-concept of ability, or specifically the self-concept of writing ability or the self-concept of ability in writing. Self-concept is about the sense of competence, the sense of being able to do something.

Self-esteem The value one associates with oneself as an artifact of one's competence. A person can have a good self-concept of visual art ability, but if visual art is not valued in the society that the person values, the person's self-esteem may not be influenced by this visual arts competence.

Self-report What people do when they report on what they are doing. Writers' self-reports tell what they do when they write.

Semantics Refers to meaning in language. When there is a semantic difference between two speakers, the difference is over what words mean. When we observe, "They're only arguing semantics," what we're saying is that the persons do not agree on what the words mean.

Sentence The smallest whole piece of written language that carries an idea or image. Connected discourse bounded by an initial capital letter and a terminal mark; a piece of written language that can stand alone.

Short Cues Short (by time or by word limit) pieces of writing that fall into six categories: précis, direction writing, Power Writing, Process Pieces, Word Limiters, and cues for writing to learn. The premium is brevity, precision, and experience with whole writing processes.

Special needs Children who in the past were labeled by their special characteristics—for example, nonsighted, mentally handicapped, or gifted. In an educational sense, they have special needs.

Subaudible The sense of sound a reader or writer "hears" while reading and writing. Subaudible speech has no sound audible to anyone other than the reader or writer.

Transfer The ability to apply what we have learned under one circumstance to another circumstance. Often referred to as generalization.

Transitions (transitional devices) Words or phrases, or even ideas or images, that help hold pieces of writing together so readers can move from one point to another. For example, when one sentence names an old man, the pronoun *he* in the next sentence is a transitional device.

Usage The way in which native speakers use the language. In writing, the collection of social agreements that designate correctness and respect for readers.

Validity As applied to measurement, the trustworthiness of an instrument. The basic validity question is, "Does the test actually test what it purports to test or measure?"

Whole written language A piece of writing that is at least one sentence in length. Less than a sentence (e.g., prepositional phrase, dependent clause, noun phrase) is less than a whole piece of written language.

Word Limiters Short, whole pieces of writing cued by a main idea and with a word length limitation (e.g., "Describe a rose in not fewer than fifteen or more than eighteen words").

Word Wall A surface in a classroom on which words are displayed for word study, as spelling reminders, or to record words the students have been studying recently.

Writers' Roundtable A hypothetical gathering of writers who discuss their writing.

Zone of proximal development Lev Vygotsky's way of labeling the developmental space between a child's developmental level and his or her potential development. Typically, that space is informally determined by experienced teachers. It can also be formally determined with sophisticated measures of behavior and potential.

REFERENCES

Ackerman, D. (1991). *The moon by whale light: And other adventures among bats, penguins, crocodilians, and whales.* New York: Random House.

Adams, M., & Collins, A. (1979). A schema-theoretic view of reading. In R. Freedle (Ed.), *New directions in discourse processing.* Norwood, NJ: Ablex.

Aliki. (1981). *Digging up dinosaurs.* New York: Crowell.

Aliki. (1985a). *Dinosaurs are different.* New York: Crowell.

Aliki. (1985b). *My visit to the dinosaurs.* New York: Harper & Row.

American Heritage Dictionary of the English Language. (1996). (3rd ed.). Boston: Houghton Mifflin.

Anders, P., & Bos, C. (1986). Semantic feature analysis: An interactive strategy for vocabulary development and text comprehension. *Journal of Reading, 29,* 610–616.

Anders, P. L., Bos, C. S., & Filip, D. (1984). The effect of semantic feature analysis on the reading comprehension of learning disabled students. In J. A. Niles & L. A. Harris (Eds.), *Changing perspectives on research in reading/language processing and instruction* (pp. 162–166). Rochester, NY: National Reading Conference.

Anderson, G. K., Buckler, W. E., & Veeder, M. H. (Eds.). (1979). *The literature of England.* New York: Harper-Collins.

Anderson, J. R. (1980). *Cognitive psychology and its implications.* San Francisco: Freeman.

Anderson, R. C., & Nagy, W. E. (1993). *The vocabulary conundrum* (Tech. Rep. No. 570). Champaign: University of Illinois at Urbana-Champaign, Center for the Study of Reading. (ERIC Document Reproduction Service No. ED 354 489)

Anderson, R. C., & Pearson, P. D. (1984). A schema-theoretic view of basic processes in reading comprehension. In P. D. Pearson (Ed.), *Handbook of reading research* (pp. 255–291). New York: Longman.

Andrews, R. (1995). *Teaching and learning argument.* London: Cassell Wellington House.

Ashton-Warner, S. (1963). *Teacher.* New York: Simon & Schuster.

Asimov, I. (1975). *Of matters great and small.* New York: Doubleday.

Asimov, I. (1979). *In memory yet green: The autobiography of Isaac Asimov, 1920–1954.* New York: Avon Books.

Asimov, I. (1980). *In joy still felt: The autobiography of Isaac Asimov, 1954–1978.* New York: Doubleday.

Atwell, N. (1987). *In the middle: Writing, reading, and learning with adolescents.* Portsmouth, NH: Boynton/Cook.

Bandura, A. (1986). *Social foundations of thought and action: A social cognitive theory.* Englewood Cliffs, NJ: Prentice Hall.

Bangert-Downs, R. L. (1993). The word processor as an instructional tool: A meta-analysis of word processing in writing instruction. *Review of Educational Research, 63,* 69–93.

Barron, F. (1976). The psychology of creativity. In A. H. Rothenberg & C. R. Hausman (Eds.), *The creativity question.* Durham, NC: Duke University Press.

Beach, R., & Lundell, D. (1998). Early adolescents' use of computer-mediated communication in writing and reading. In D. Reinking, M. C. McKenna, L. D. Labbo, & R. D. Kieffer (Eds.), *Handbook of literacy and technology: Transformations in a post-typographic world* (pp. 98–112). Mahwah, NJ: Erlbaum.

Bear, D. R., Templeton, S., Invernizzi, M., & Johnston, F. (1996). *Words their way: Word study for phonics, vocabulary, and spelling instruction.* Columbus, OH: Merrill.

Beck, I. L., & McKeown M. G. (1991). Conditions of vocabulary acquisition. In R. Barr, M. Kamil, P. Mosenthal, & P. D. Pearson (Eds.), *Handbook of reading research* (Vol. 2, pp. 789–814). White Plains, NY: Longman.

Bellack, A. A., Kliebard, H. M., Hyman, R. T., & Smith, F. I., Jr. (1966). *The language of the classroom.* New York: Teachers College Press.

Bell-Villada, G. H. (1981). *Borges and his fiction: A guide to his mind and art.* Chapel Hill: University of North Carolina Press.

Bereiter, C., & Scardamalia, M. (1987). *The psychology of written composition.* Hillsdale, NJ: Erlbaum.

Boles, P. D. (1984). *Story-crafting: A master storyteller teaches the art and craft of writing fine short stories.* Cincinnati, OH: Writer's Digest Books.

Boyle, C. (1996). *Efficacy of peer evaluation and effects of peer evaluation on persuasive writing.* Unpublished master's thesis, San Diego State University, San Diego, CA.

Britton, J. (1970). *Language and learning.* Coral Gables, FL: University of Miami Press.

Brock, C. H. (1997). Exploring the use of Book Club with second-language learners in mainstream classrooms. In S. I. McMahon & T. E. Raphael (Eds.), *The Book Club connection: Literacy learning and classroom talk* (pp. 141–158). New York: Teachers College Press, and Newark, DE: International Reading Association.

Brohaugh, W. (1987). *Just open a vein.* Cincinnati, OH: Writer's Digest Books.

Brown, R., & Bellugi, U. (1964). Three processes in the child's acquisition of syntax. *Harvard Educational Review, 34,* 133–151.

Bruce, B., Michaels, S., & Watson-Gegeo, K. (1985). How computers change the writing process. *Language Arts, 62,* 143–149.

Bryson, B. (1990). *The mother tongue: English and how it got that way.* New York: Morrow.

California. State Department of Education. (1988). *History-social science framework.* Sacramento: Author.

California. State Department of Education. (1991). *Literature for history-social science: Kindergarten through grade eight.* Sacramento: Author.

Calkins, L. M. (1980). When children want to punctuate: Basic skills belong in context. *Language Arts, 57,* 567–573.

Carey, J. (Ed.). (1987). *Eyewitness to history.* New York: Avon Books.

Carr, E. H. (1961). *What is history? The George Macaulay Trevelyan Lectures delivered at the University of Cambridge, January–March 1961.* New York: Vintage Books.

Cho, K. S., & Krashen, S. (1994). Acquisition of vocabulary from the Sweet Valley Kids series: Adult ESL acquisition. *Journal of Reading, 37,* 662–667.

Chomsky, C. (1976, May). *Approaching reading through invented spelling.* Paper presented at the Conference on Theory and Practice of Beginning Reading Instruction. University of Pittsburgh, Learning and Research Development Center. (ERIC Document Reproduction Service No. 15 56 30)

Clark, R. (1971). *Einstein: The life and times.* New York: Avon Books.

Clark, R. P. (1982). *Best newspaper writing 1982.* St. Petersburg, FL: Modern Media Institute.

Clay, M. M. (1966). *Emergent reading behavior.* Unpublished doctoral dissertation, University of Auckland, New Zealand.

Clay, M. M. (1975). *What did I write?* Portsmouth, NH: Heinemann.

Clay, M. M. (1991). *Becoming literate: The construction of inner control.* Portsmouth, NH: Heinemann.

Cochran-Smith, M., Kahn, J., & Paris, C. L. (1990). Writing with a felicitous tool. *Theory into Practice, 29,* 235–247.

Cochran-Smith, M., Paris, C. L., & Kahn, J. L. (1991). *Learning to write differently.* Norwood, NJ: Ablex.

Colvin, C., & Schlosser, L. K. (1997–1998). Developing academic confidence to build literacy: What teachers can do. *Journal of Adolescent and Adult Literacy, 41,* 272–281.

Connolly, P., & Vilardi, T. (Eds.). (1989). *Writing to learn: Mathematics and science.* New York: Teachers College Press.

Cowley, M. (Ed.). (1958). *Writers at work: The Paris Review interviews.* New York: Penguin Books.

Cox, C. (1999). *Teaching language arts: A student- and response-centered classroom.* Needham Heights, MA: Allyn & Bacon.

Cramer, R. L. (1998). *The spelling connection: Integrating reading, writing, and spelling instruction.* New York: Guilford Press.

Cramer, R. L., & Cipielewski, J. F. (1995). Research in action: A study of spelling errors in 18,599 written compositions of children in grades 1–8. In *Spelling research and information: An overview of current research and practices* (pp. 11–52). Glenview, IL: Scott-Foresman.

Crawford, L. W. (1993). *Language and literacy learning in a multicultural classroom.* Needham Heights, MA: Allyn & Bacon.

Crosby, A., Jr. (1972). *The Columbian exchange: Biological and cultural consequences of 1492.* Westport, CT: Greenwood Press.

Crowder, R. G. (1976). *Principles of learning and memory.* Hillsdale, NJ: Erlbaum.

Csikszentmihalyi, M. (1996). *Creativity: Flow and the psychology of discovery and invention.* New York: HarperCollins.

Cullinan, B. (1989). *Literature and the child* (2nd ed.). San Diego: Harcourt Brace.

Cunningham, A. E., & Stanovich, K. E. (1998, Spring–Summer). What reading does for the mind. *American Education,* 8–14.

Cunningham, P. M. (1991). *Phonics they use: Words for reading and writing.* New York: HarperCollins.

Cunningham, P. M., & Cunningham, J. W. (1992). Making words: Enhancing the invented spelling-decoding connection. *Reading Teacher, 46,* 106–113.

Dahl, K. L., & Farnan, N. (1998). *Children's writing: Perspectives from research.* Newark, DE: International Reading Association.

Daiute, C. (1986). Physical and cognitive factors in revising: Insights from studies with computers. *Research in the Teaching of English, 20,* 141–159.

Daniels, H. (1994). *Literature circles: Voice and choice in the student-centered classroom.* York, ME: Stenhouse.

De Montaigne, M. (1958). *Essays.* London: Penguin Books.

Devine, T. G. (1981). *Teaching study skills.* Needham Heights, MA: Allyn & Bacon.

Dickinson, D. K. (1986). Cooperation, collaboration and a computer: Integrating a computer into a first-second grade writing program. *Research in the Teaching of English, 20,* 357–378.

Dole, J., Sloan, C., & Trathen, W. (1995). Teaching vocabulary within the context of literature. *Journal of Reading, 38,* 452–460.

Dressel, J. H. (1990). The effects of listening to and discussing different qualities of children's literature on the narrative writing of fifth graders. *Research in the Teaching of English, 24,* 397–414.

Duin, A. H., & Graves, M. F. (1987). Intensive vocabulary instruction as a prewriting technique. *Reading Research Quarterly, 22,* 311–330.

Eckhoff, B. (1983). How reading affects children's writing. *Language Arts, 60,* 607–616.

Eeds, M. (1985). Book words: Using a beginning word list of high-frequency words from children's literature, K–3. *Reading Teacher, 38,* 418–423.

Elbow, P. (1981). *Writing with power: Techniques for mastering the writing process.* New York: Oxford University Press.

Emig, J. (1971). *The composing processes of twelfth graders.* Urbana, IL: National Council of Teachers of English.

Esbensen, B. J. (1990). *Great northern diver: The loon.* Boston: Little, Brown.

Farnan, N., & Fearn, L. (1992). *Deliberate attention and spelling.* Paper presented at the Washington Organization for Reading Development Conference, Seattle, WA.

Farnan, N., & Fearn, L. (1993a). Writers' workshops: Middle school writers and readers collaborating. *Middle School Journal, 24,* 61–65.

Farnan, N., & Fearn, L. (1993b, September). The big picture: The writing program in action. *Writing Teacher. 7,* 31–34.

Farnan, N., & Romero, A. (1989). Literature and writing in the English/language arts classroom. In D. Lapp, J. Flood, & N. Farnan (Eds.), *Reading in the content areas: Instructional strategies* (pp. 209–226). Needham Heights, MA: Allyn and Bacon.

Fearn, L. (1975). "The maligned wolf." In L. Fearn, R. E. McCabe, & G. Ball (Eds.), *Human development program supplementary idea guide.* La Mesa, CA: Human Development Training Institute.

Fearn, L. (1976). Individual development: A process model in creativity. *Journal of Creative Behavior, 10,* 55–64.

Fearn, L. (1978). Geocabulary cards. San Diego: Kabyn Books.

Fearn, L. (1980). *Teaching for thinking.* San Diego: Kabyn Books.

Fearn, L. (1981). Teaching writing by teaching thinking. *Academic Therapy, 17,* 173–178.

Fearn, L. (1983a). *Developmental writing in the elementary and middle school.* San Diego: Kabyn Books.

Fearn, L. (1983b). *The fear.* San Diego: Kabyn Books.

Fearn, L. (1983c). *Writing a story: A story writer's self-report.* San Diego, CA: Kabyn Books.

Fearn, L. (1983d, July). The art of brevity. *Writers West,* 3–5.

Fearn, L. (1985). *Process pieces.* San Diego: Kabyn Books.

Fearn, L. (1996). The writing program in action: Discussion of quality. *Writing Teacher, 9,* 21–23.

Fearn, L. (1999). The teacher and the writer in the classroom. *California English, 4,* 6–7.

Fearn, L., & Farnan, N. (1993). Writers' Workshops: Middle school writers and readers collaborating. *Middle School Journal, 24,* 61–65.

Fearn, L., & Farnan, N. (1998a). *Get writing!! Book 1, grades 4–5.* San Antonio, TX: ECS.

Fearn, L., & Farnan, N. (1998b). *Writing effectively: Helping children master the conventions of writing.* Boston: Allyn and Bacon.

Fearn, L., & Farnan, N. (1999a). *Get writing!! Book 1, grades 2–3.* San Antonio, TX: ECS.

Fearn, L., & Farnan, N. (1999b). *Get writing!! Paragraphs and forms of writing, book 2, grades 2–3.* San Antonio, TX: ECS.

Fearn, L., & Farnan, N. (1999c). *Get writing!! Main ideas in paragraphs, book 2, grades 4–5.* San Antonio, TX: ECS.

Fearn, L., & Foster, K. (1979a). *The writing kabyn: Assessment and editing.* San Diego: Kabyn Books.

Fearn, L., & Foster, K. (1979b). *The writing kabyn: Products.* San Diego: Kabyn Books.

Fearn, L., & Rowland, M. (1983). *Deliberate attention: Acquisition and retention in spelling.* Unpublished manuscript. San Diego: San Diego State University.

Felder, D. G. (1996). *The 100 most influential women of all time.* Secaucus, NJ: Citadel Press.

Findlay, C. S., & Lumsden, C. J. (1988). The creative mind: Toward an evolutionary theory of discovery and innovation. In C. S. Findlay & C. J. Lumsden (Eds.), *The creative mind.* San Diego: Harcourt Brace.

Flesch, R. F. (1955). *Why Johnny can't read—and what you can do about it.* New York: Harper.

Flower, L. (1979). Writer-based prose: A cognitive basis for problems in writing. *College English, 41*, 19–37.

Flower, L., & Hayes, J. R. (1980). The cognition of discovery: Defining a rhetorical problem. *College Composition and Communication, 31*, 21–32.

Flower, L., & Hayes, J. R. (1981). The pregnant pause: An inquiry into the nature of planning. *Research in the Teaching of English, 15*, 229–244.

Forbes, E. (1943). *Johnny Tremain.* Boston: Houghton Mifflin.

Francis, W. N. (1958). *The structure of American English.* New York: Ronald Press.

Frank, L. A. (1992). Writing to read: Young writers' ability to demonstrate audience awareness when evaluated by their readers. *Research in the Teaching of English, 26*(3), 277–298.

Fulwiler, T. (1985). Research in writing. In M. Schwartz (Ed.), *Writing for many roles.* Upper Montclair, NJ: Boynton/Cook.

Gardiner, J. R. (1980). *Stone fox.* New York: Crowell.

Gardner, J. (1983). *The art of fiction.* New York: Knopf.

Garraty, J. (1957). *The nature of biography.* New York: Knopf.

Gearhart, M., Herman, J. L., Baker, E. L., & Whittaker, A. K. (1992). *Writing portfolios: Potential for large-scale assessment.* Los Angeles: National Center for Research on Evaluation, Standards, and Student Testing. (ERIC Document Reproduction Service No. ED 350 312)

Gentry, J. R. (1997). *Council Chronicle,* NCTE, 6, 7.

Gentry, J. R., & Gillet, J. W. (1993). *Teaching kids to spell.* Portsmouth, NH: Heinemann.

Gere, A. R. (1987). *Writing groups: History, theory, and implications.* Carbondale: Southern Illinois University Press.

Gibbons, G. (1987). *Dinosaurs.* New York: Holiday House.

Gill, J. T. (1992). Focus on research: Development of word knowledge as it relates to reading, spelling, and instruction. *Language Arts, 69*, 444–453.

Gipe, J. P. (1978–1979). Investigating techniques for teaching word meanings. *Reading Research Quarterly, 14*, 624–645.

Goldman, L., & Farnan, N. (1985). *Developing writers in grades 7–12.* San Diego: Kabyn Books.

Gopen, G. D., & Smith, D. A. (1989). What's an assignment like you doing in a course like this? In P. Connolly and T. Vivaldi (Eds.), *Writing to learn: Mathematics and science* (pp. 209–230). New York: Teachers College, Columbia University.

Gould, J. D. (1980). Experiments on composing letters: Some facts, some myths, and some observations. In L. W. Gregg & E. R. Steinberg (Eds.), *Cognitive processes in writing* (pp. 97–127). Hillsdale, NJ: Erlbaum.

Grabe, M., & Grabe, C. (2000). *Integrating the Internet for meaningful learning.* Boston: Houghton Mifflin.

Grattan, K. W. (1997). They can do it too! Book Club with first and second graders. In S. I. McMahon & T. E. Raphael (Eds.), *The Book Club connection: Literacy learning and classroom talk* (pp. 267–283). New York: Teachers College Press, and Newark, DE: International Reading Association.

Gray, J. (1995). Why large-scale testing fails. *California English, 1*, 11.

Groff, P. (1975). Does negative criticism discourage children's compositions? *Language Arts, 52*, 1032–1034.

Guilford, J. P. (1950). Creativity. *American Psychologist, 5*, 444–454.

Guilford, J. P. (1962). Factors that aid and hinder creativity. *Teacher's College Record, 63*, 380–392.

Haas, C. (1989). Does the medium make a difference: Two studies of writing with computers. *Human Computer Interaction, 4*, 149–169.

Haas, C. (1990). Composing in technological contexts: A study of note-making. *Written Communication, 7*, 512–547.

Halberstam, D. (1999). *The best American sports writing of the century.* Boston: Houghton Mifflin.

Harmon, J. M. (1998). Vocabulary teaching and learning in a seventh grade literature-based classroom. *Journal of Adolescent and Adult Literacy, 41*, 518–529.

Harris, T. L., & Hodges, R. E. (Eds.). (1995). *The literacy dictionary: The vocabulary of reading and writing.* Newark, DE: International Reading Association.

Hart, M. H. (1978). *The 100: A ranking of the most influential persons in history.* Secaucus, NJ: Citadel Press.

Hartman, K., Neuwirth, C. M., Kietler, S., Sproull, L., Cochran, C., Palmquist, M., & Zubrow, D. (1991). Patterns of social interaction and learning to write. *Written Communication, 8*, 57–78.

Hawisher, G. (1986). Studies in word processing. *Computers and Composition, 4*, 6–31.

Hawisher, G., & Selfe, C. (1999). Reflections on research in computers and composition studies at the century's end. In J. Hancock (Ed.), *Teaching literacy using information technology: A collection of articles from the Australian Literacy Educator's Association* (pp. 31–47). Newark, DE: International Reading Association.

Hayes, J. R., & Flower, L. (1980). Identifying the organization of writing processes. In L. W. Gregg & E. R. Steinberg (Eds.), *Cognitive processes in writing.* Hillsdale, NJ: Erlbaum.

Hayes-Roth, B., and Hayes-Roth, F. (1979). A cognitive model of planning. *Cognitive Science, 3*, 275–310.

Heath, S. B. (1982). What no bedtime story means: Narrative skills at home and school. *Language in Society, 11*, 49–76.

Heller, M. F. (1995). *Reading-writing connections: From theory to practice* (2nd ed.). New York: Longman.

Henderson, E. H. (1990). *Teaching spelling* (2nd ed.). Boston: Houghton Mifflin.

Herman, J. L., & Winters, L. (1994). Portfolio research: A slim collection. *Educational Leadership, 52,* 48–55.

Hidi, S., & Anderson, V. (1986). Producing written summaries: Task demands, cognitive operations, and implications for instruction. *Review of Educational Research, 56,* 473–493.

Hillocks, G. (1986). *Research on written composition: New directions for teaching.* Urbana, IL: National Council of Teachers of English.

Hillocks, G., Jr. & Mavrogenes, N. (1986). Sentence combining. In G. Hillocks, Jr. (Ed.), *Research on written composition: New directions for teaching* (pp. 142–146). Urbana, IL: Educational Resources Information Center and National Council on Research in English.

Hillocks, G., & Smith, M. J. (1986). Grammar. In *Research on written composition: New directions for teaching* (pp. 134–141). Urbana, IL: Educational Resources Information Center and National Council on Research in English.

Hirsch, E. D. (1987). *Cultural literacy: What every American needs to know.* Boston: Houghton Mifflin.

Holdaway, D. (1979). *The foundations of literacy.* New York: Ashton Scholastic.

Hopkins, L. B. (1995). *Good rhymes, good times.* New York: HarperCollins.

Hopkins, L. B. (1998). *Pass the poetry, please!* (3rd ed.). New York: Harper-Collins.

Horn, E. (1926). *A basic vocabulary of 10,000 words most commonly used in writing.* Iowa City: Iowa City University.

Horn, T. D. (1967). Spelling. In R. I. Ebel (Ed.), *Encyclopedia of educational research* (4th ed.) (pp. 1228–1299). New York: Macmillan.

Hyman, R. (1964). Creativity and the prepared mind: The role of information and induced attitudes. In C. Taylor (Ed.), *Widening horizons in creativity.* New York: Wiley.

International Reading Association. (1988). *New directions in reading instruction.* Newark, DE: Author.

Invernizzi, M., Abouzeid, M., & Gill, T. (1994). Using students' invented spellings as a guide for spelling instruction that emphasizes word study. *Elementary School Journal, 95,* 155–167.

Ivins, M. (1993). *Nothin' but good times ahead.* New York: Random House.

Jenkins, J. R., & Dixon, R. (1983). Learning vocabulary. *Contemporary Educational Psychology, 8,* 237–260.

Johnson, A. P., & Rasmussen, J. B. (1998). Classifying and super word web: Two strategies to improve productive vocabulary. *Journal of Adolescent and Adult Literacy, 42,* 204–207.

Johnson, D., & Pearson, P. D. (1984). *Teaching reading vocabulary* (2nd ed.). New York: Holt, Rinehart & Winston.

Johnson, N. L. (1995). *The effect of portfolio design on student attitudes toward writing.* Unpublished master's thesis, San Diego State University, San Diego, CA.

Jones, I., & Pellegrini, A. D. (1996). The effects of social relationships, writing media, and microgenetic development of first-grade students' written narratives. *American Educational Research Journal, 33,* 691–718.

Just, M. A., & Carpenter, P. A. (1987). *The psychology of reading and language comprehension.* Needham, MA: Allyn & Bacon.

Kameenui, E. J., Carnine, D. W., & Freschi, R. (1982). Effects of text construction and instructional procedures for teaching word meanings on comprehension and recall. *Reading Research Quarterly, 17,* 367–388.

Kameenui, E. J., Dixon, D. W., & Carnine, D. W. (1987). Issues in the design of vocabulary instruction. In M. G. McKeown & M. E. Curtis (Eds.), *The nature of vocabulary acquisition* (pp. 129–145). Hillsdale, NJ: Erlbaum.

Kelly, P. R., & Farnan, N. (1994). Literature: The ART in language arts. *New Advocate, 7,* 169–183.

Knoblach, C. H., & Brannon, L. (1983). Writing as learning through the curriculum. *College English, 45,* 465–474.

Koch, K. (1970). *Wishes, lies, and dreams: Teaching children to write poetry.* New York: Chelsea House.

Koch, K. (1973). *Rose, where did you get that red? Teaching great poetry to children.* New York: Vintage Books.

Kridel, C. (Ed.). (1998). *Writing educational biography.* New York: Garland.

Kroll, B. (1985). Rewriting a complex story for a young reader: The development of audience-adapted writing skills. *Research in the Teaching of Writing, 19*(2), 120–139.

Kuhl, P. (1993). *Life language.* Seattle: University of Washington Press.

Laden, N. (1998). *When Pigasso met Mootisse.* San Francisco: Chronicle Books.

Lamb, B. (1997). *Booknotes: America's finest authors on reading, writing, and the power of ideas.* New York: Random House.

Langer, J. A., & Applebee, A. N. (1987). *How writing shapes thinking.* Urbana, IL: National Council of Teachers of English.

Lashley, K. S. (1974). In search of the engram. In D. G. Stein & J. J. Rosen (Eds.), *Learning and memory.* New York: Macmillan.

Latham, E. C. (Ed.). (1966). *Interviews with Robert Frost.* New York: Holt, Rinehart & Winston.

LeBlanc, P. (1993). *Writing teachers/ writing software: Creating our place in the electronic age.* Urbana, IL: National Council of Teachers of English.

Lewis, R. B., Ashton, T., & Kieley, C. (1996). Word processing and individuals with learning disabilities: Overcoming the keyboard barrier. In *Eleventh Annual Conference of Technology for People with Disabilities.* Northridge, CA: California State University.

Little, J. (1990). *Hey, world, here I am!* New York: Harper Trophy.

Lloyd, P. (1987). *How writers write.* Portsmouth, NH: Heinemann.

Lowry, L. (1989). *Number the stars.* Boston: Houghton Mifflin.

Marshall, J. (1994). Of what does skill in writing really consist? The political life of the writing process movement. In L. Tobin & T. Newkirk (Eds.), *Taking stock: The writing process movement in the '90s.* Portsmouth, NH: Heinemann.

Lund, D., & Sanderson, D. A. (1999). From printed page to multimedia: Evolution of a second-grade class newspaper. *Reading Online.* Available at: http://readingonline.org/articles.

McCarrier, A., Pinnell, G. S., & Fountas, I. (1999). *Interactive writing: How language and literacy come together, K–12.* Portsmouth, NH: Heinemann.

McGrady, H. G., & Olsen, D. A. (1970). Visual and auditory processing in normal children and children with specific learning disabilities. *Exceptional Children, 36,* 581–589.

McKenzie, M. G. (1985). Shared writing: Apprenticeship in writing. *Language Matters, 1–2,* 1–5.

McKeown, M. G. (1993). Creating effective definitions for young word learners. *Reading Research Quarterly, 28,* 16–33.

McKeown, M. G., Beck, I. L., Omanson, R., & Perfetti, C. A. (1983). The effects of long-term vocabulary instruction on reading comprehension: A replication. *Journal of Reading Behavior, 15,* 3–18.

McKeown, M. G., Beck, I. L., Omanson, R., & Pople, M. T. (1985). Some effects of the nature and frequency of vocabulary instruction on the knowledge and use of words. *Reading Research Quarterly, 20,* 522–535.

McMahon, S. I., & Raphael, T. E. (Eds.). (1997). *The Book Club connection: Literacy learning and classroom talk.* New York: Teachers College Press, and Newark, DE: International Reading Association.

McMurtry, L. (1999). *Crazy Horse.* New York: Penguin-Putnam, Inc.

Meeker, M. N. (1969). *Structure of intellect: Its interpretation and uses.* Columbus, OH: Merrill.

Miller, G. A. (1956). The magic number seven, plus or minus two: Some limits on our capacity for processing information. *Psychological Review, 63,* 81–97.

Moffett, J. (1994). Coming out right. In L. Tobin & T. Newkirk (Eds.), *Taking stock: The writing process movement in the '90s.* Portsmouth, NH: Heinemann.

Moffett, J., & Wagner, B. J. (1992). *Student-centered language arts, K–12* (4th ed.). Portsmouth, NH: Boynton/Cook Publishers, Heinemann.

Mogilner, A. (1992). *Children's writer's word book.* Cincinnati, OH: Writer's Digest Books.

Montaigne, M. de. (1958). *Essays.* London: Penguin Group.

Moore, P. (1999). Reading and writing the Internet. In J. Hancock (Ed.), *Teaching literacy using information technology: A collection of articles from the Australian Literacy Educator's Association* (pp. 48–66). Newark, DE: International Reading Association.

Morocco, C. (1987). *Final report to the US Office of Education.* Washington, DC: Special Education Programs, Educational Development Center.

Morocco, C., Dalton, B., & Tivnan, T. (1992). The impact of computer-supported writing instruction on 4th grade students with and without learning disabilities. *Reading and Writing Quarterly: Overcoming Learning Disabilities, 8,* 87–113.

Mowat, F. (1959). *The desperate people.* Toronto: McClelland and Stewart-Bantom Limited.

Mowat, F. (1963). *Never cry wolf.* Boston: Little, Brown.

Mowat, F. (1975). *The desperate people.* Toronto: Seal Books.

Muir, J. (1985). Water ouzel. In J. Moffett, (Ed.), *Points of departure: Anthology of nonfiction* (pp. 349–362). New York: New American Library.

Murray, D. M. (1985). *A teacher teaches writing* (2nd ed.). Boston: Houghton Mifflin.

Murray, D. M. (1990). *Shoptalk: Learning to write with writers.* Portsmouth, NH: Boynton/Cook.

Nagy, W. E., & Anderson, R. C. (1984). How many words are there in printed school English? *Reading Research Quarterly, 19,* 303–330.

Nagy, W. E., Garcia, G. E., Durgunoglu, A., & Hancin-Bhatt, B. J. (1992). *Cross–language transfer of lexical knowledge: Bilingual students' use of cognates* (Tech. Rep. No. 207). Urbana-Champaign, IL: University of Illinois. (ERIC Document Reproduction Service No. ED 350 869)

Nagy, W. E., & Herman, P. A. (1987). Breadth and depth of vocabulary knowledge: Implications for acquisition and instruction. In M. G. McKeown & M. E. Curtis (Eds.), *The nature of vocabulary acquisition.* Hillsdale, NJ: Erlbaum.

Nathenson-Mejia, S. (1989). Writing in a second language: Negotiating meaning through invented spelling. *Language Arts, 66,* 516–527.

National Assessment of Educational Progress. (1998). *Report in brief: NAEP 1996 trends in academic progress.* Available at: http://nces.ed.gov/nationsreportcard/96report/97986.shtml.

National Council of Teachers of English/International Reading Association. (1966). *Standards for the English language arts.* Urbana, IL: National Council of Teachers of English, and Newark, DE: International Reading Association.

Nelson, N., & Calfee, R. C. (Eds.). (1998). *The reading-writing connection: Ninety-seventh yearbook of the National Society for the Study of Education, part II.* Chicago: University of Chicago Press.

Newell, G. E. (1998). Writing and learning. In N. Nelson & R. C. Calfee (Eds.), *The reading-writing connection: Ninety-seventh yearbook of the National Society for the Study of Education, part II* (pp. 178–202). Chicago: University of Chicago Press.

Nicol, J. E., & Graves, M. F. (1990). *Building vocabulary through prefix in-*

struction. Unpublished manuscript, University of Minnesota.

Novas, H. (1995). *The Hispanic 100: A ranking of the Latino men and women who have most influenced American thought and culture.* New York: Carol Publishing Group.

Nystrand, M. (1986). *The structure of written composition.* Orlando, FL: Academic Press.

Oates, S. B. (1991). *Biography as history.* Waco, TX: Mankham Press Fund.

O'Flahaven, J., & Blassberg, R. (1992). Toward an embedded model of spelling instruction for emergent literates. *Language Arts, 69,* 409–417.

Ogle, D. (1986). The K-W-L: A teaching model that develops active reading of expository text. *Reading Teacher, 45,* 298–306.

Osgood, C. (1991). *The Osgood files.* New York: Putnam.

Owston, P. D., Murphy, S., & Wideman, H. H. (1992). On and off computer writing of eighth grade students experienced in word processing. *Computers in the Schools, 8,* 249–276.

Pany, D., & Jenkins, J. R. (1978). Learning word meanings: A comparison of instructional procedures and effects on measures of reading comprehension with learning disabled students. *Learning Disabilities Quarterly, 1,* 21–32.

Parnes, S. (1972). *Creativity: Unlocking human potential.* Buffalo, NY: Creative Education Foundation.

Partridge, E. (1973). *Usage and abusage: A guide to good English.* Middlesex, England: Penguin Books.

Patterson, N. G. (1999). Making connections: Hypertext and research in a middle school classroom. *English Journal, 89,* 69–73.

Paulsen, F., & Paulsen, P. (1994). *A guide for judging portfolios.* Portland, OR: Multnomah Educational Service District.

Paulsen, G. (1989). *The winter room.* New York: Dell.

Petty, W. T., Herold, C. P., & Stoll, E. (1968). *The state of knowledge about the teaching of vocabulary.* Champaign, IL: National Council of Teachers of English.

Pinnell, G. S., & McCarrier, A. (1994). Interactive writing: A transition tool for assisting children in learning to read and write. In E. Heibert & B. Taylor (Eds.), *Getting reading right from the start: Effective early literacy interventions* (pp. 149–170). Needham, MA: Allyn & Bacon.

Pinsky, R., & Dietz, M. (Eds.). (1999). *Americans' favorite poems: The Favorite Poem Project anthology.* New York: Norton.

Plimpton, G. (Ed.). (1989). *The writer's chapbook.* New York: Viking.

Potter, B. (1951). *The tale of Peter Rabbit.* New York: F. Warne.

Prelutsky, J. (1984). *The new kid on the block.* New York: Greenwillow.

Random House. (1996). *Webster's encyclopedic unabridged dictionary of the English language.* New York: Author.

Read*write*now! summer programs underway. (1998, August–September). *Reading Today.*

Reinking, D. (May 1997). Me and my hypertext: A multiple digression analysis of technology and literacy. *Reading Online.* Available at: http://www.readingonline/articles/hypertext.

Rood, R. (1971). *Animals nobody loves.* New York: Bantam Pathfinder Books.

Rosenblatt, L. M. (1978). *The reader, the text, the poem: The transactional theory of the literary work.* Carbondale: Southern Illinois University Press.

Rosenshine, B., Meister, C., & Chapman, S. (1996). Teaching students to generate questions: A review of the intervention studies. *Review of Educational Research, 66,* 181–221.

Rosenthal, W. S. (1974). *The role of perception in child language disorders: A theory based on faulty signal detection strategies.* Paper presented at the American

Speech and Hearing Convention, Las Vegas, NV.

Rupley, W. H., Logan, J. W., & Nicols, W. D. (1998–1999). Vocabulary instruction in a balanced reading program. *Reading Teacher, 52,* 336–346.

Salley, C. (1993). *The black 100: A ranking of the most influential African-Americans, past and present.* New York: Carol Publishing Group.

Savage, J. F. (1998). *Teaching reading and writing: Combining skills, strategies, and literature.* New York: McGraw-Hill.

Scarry, R. (1970). *Best Mother Goose ever.* New York: Golden Press.

Schoephoerster, H. (1962). Research into variations of the test-study plan of teaching spelling. *Elementary English, 39,* 460–462.

Sebranek, P., Meyer, V., & Kemper, D. (1990). *Write Source 2000.* Burlington, WI: Write Source.

Siebert, D. (1988). *Mojave.* New York: Crowell.

Silverstein, S. (1974). *Where the sidewalk ends.* New York: Harper & Row.

Silverstein, S. (1996). *Falling up.* New York: HarperCollins.

Simon, S. (1980). *Einstein Anderson: Science sleuth.* New York: Viking.

Simon, S. (1982). *The smallest dinosaurs.* New York: Crown.

Simon, S. (1986). *The largest dinosaurs.* New York: Macmillan.

Smith, C. (1990). Vocabulary development in content-area reading. *Reading Teacher, 43,* 508–509.

Smith, F. (1983). Reading like a writer. *Language Arts, 60,* 558–567.

Snyder, I. (1999). Integrating computers into the literacy curriculum. In J. Hancock (Ed.), *Teaching literacy using information technology: A collection of articles from the Australian Literacy Educator's Association* (pp. 11–30). Newark, DE: International Reading Association.

Soto, G. (1990). *A fire in my hands.* New York: Scholastic.

Spandel, V., & Stiggins, R. J. (1997). *Creating writers: Linking writing assessment to instruction* (2nd ed.). New York: Longman.

Spinelli, J. (1990). *Maniac Magee.* Boston: Little, Brown.

Stahl, S. A. (1983). Differential word knowledge and reading comprehension. *Journal of Reading Behavior, 15*(4), 33–50.

Stahl, S. A., & Fairbanks, M. M. (1986). The effects of vocabulary instruction: A model-based meta-analysis. *Review of Educational Research, 56,* 72–110.

Stanovich, K. (1986). Matthew effects in reading: Some consequences of individual differences in the acquisition of literacy. *Reading Research Quarterly, 21,* 360–407.

Steinbeck, J. (1969). *Journal of a novel: The East of Eden letters.* New York: Penguin.

Storeyard, J., Simmons, R., Stumpf, M., & Pavloglou, E. (1993). Making computers work for students with special needs. *Teaching Exceptional Children, 26,* 22–24.

Strong, W. (1993). *Sentence combining: A composing book* (3rd ed.). New York: McGraw-Hill.

Strunk, W., and White, E. B. (1979). *The elements of style* (3rd ed.). New York: Macmillan.

Stull, W. L. (1983). *Combining and creating: Sentence combining and generative rhetoric.* New York: Holt, Rinehart & Winston.

Taba, H. (1967). *Teacher's handbook for elementary social studies.* Reading, MA: Addison-Wesley.

Tangel, D. M., and Blachman, B. A. (1992). Effect of phoneme awareness instruction on kindergarten children's invented spelling. *Journal of Reading Behavior, 24,* 233–261.

Taylor, B. M. (1992). Text structure, comprehension, and recall. In S. J. Samuels & A. E. Farstrup (Eds.), *What research has to say about reading instruction* (pp. 220–235). Newark, DE: International Reading Association.

Templeton, S. (1996). Spelling: The foundation of word knowledge for the less proficient reader. In M. L. Putnam (Ed.), *How to become a better reading teacher: Strategies for assessment and intervention* (pp. 317–329). Columbus, OH: Merrill.

Templeton, S. (1997). *Teaching the integrated language arts.* Boston: Houghton Mifflin.

Templeton, S., & Morris, D. (1999). Questions teachers ask about spelling. *Reading Research Quarterly, 34,* 102–112.

Terman, L. M. (1925). *The mental and physical traits of 1000 gifted children (genetic studies of genius).* Stanford, CA: Stanford University Press.

Tobin, L. (1994). Introduction: How the writing process was born—and other conversion narratives. In L. Tobin & T. Newkirk (Eds.), *Taking stock: The writing process movement in the '90s.* Portsmouth, NH: Heinemann.

Tompkins, G., & Hoskisson, K. (1991). *Language arts: Content and teaching strategies.* New York: Merrill.

Torrance, E. P. (1965). *Rewarding creative behavior: Experiments in classroom creativity.* Englewood Cliffs, NJ: Prentice-Hall.

Torrance, E. P. (1970). *Encouraging creativity in the classroom.* Dubuque, IA: William Brown.

Towell, J. (1997–1998). Fun with vocabulary. *Reading Teacher, 51,* 356–358.

Uchida, Y. (1993). *The bracelet.* New York: Philomel.

Van Doren, C. (1991). *A history of knowledge: Past, present, and future.* New York: Ballantine Books.

Viorst, J. (1980). *Alexander and the terrible, horrible, no good, very bad day.* New York: Atheneum.

Vygotsky, L. S. (1978). *Mind in society: The development of higher mental psychological processes.* Cambridge, MA: Harvard University Press.

Vygotsky, L. S. (1986). *Thought and language* (rev. ed.). (A. Kozulin, Trans. & Ed.). Cambridge, MA: MIT Press.

Walberg, H. J., & Tsai, S. (1983). Matthew effects in education. *American Educational Research Journal, 20,* 359–373.

Wallas, G. (1926). *The art of thought.* New York: Harcourt Brace.

Weaver, C. (1996). *Teaching grammar in context.* Portsmouth, NH: Heinemann.

Wentz, G., & Jurus, B. A. (1992). *Men in green faces.* New York: St. Martin's Press.

White, R. (1957). Adler and the future of ego psychology. *Journal of Individual Psychology, 13,* 112–124.

White, T. G., Sowell, J., & Yanagihara, A. (1989). Teaching elementary students to use word-part cues. *Reading Teacher, 42,* 302–308.

Whitman, R. S. (1973). *The development of the curriculum in secondary English to 1960.* (ERIC Document Reproduction Service No. ED 094 422)

Williams, F. E. (1972). *Classroom ideas for encouraging thinking and feeling.* Buffalo, NY: Dissemination of Knowledge.

Wood, A. (1988). *Elbert's bad word.* San Diego: Harcourt Brace.

Wysock, K., & Jenkins, J. R. (1987). Deriving word meanings through morphological generalization. *Reading Research Quarterly, 22,* 66–81.

Yagelski, R. P. (1994). Who's afraid of subjectivity? The composing process and postmodernism or a student of Donald Murray enters the age of postmodernism. In L. Tobin & T. Newkirk (Eds.), *Taking stock: The writing process movement in the '90s.* Portsmouth, NH: Heinemann.

Yopp, H. K. (1995). A test for assessing phonemic awareness in young children. *Reading Teacher, 49,* 20–29.

Zinn, H. (1998). *The twentieth century: A people's history.* New York: Harper Perennial.

Zutell, J. (1994). Spelling instruction. In Purves, A., Papas, L., and Jordan, S. (Eds.), *Encyclopedia of English studies and language arts* (Vol. 2) (pp. 1098–1100). New York: Scholastic.

INDEX

Instructional Scenarios Feature

Found in all chapters in Part II, **Instructional Scenarios** provide extended descriptions of authentic classroom practices relevant to the chapter's content. The scenarios take you directly into classrooms, illustrating how the instructional ideas presented in a chapter look when they are applied with young learners.

INSTRUCTIONAL SCENARIO

In the Classroom Using Power Writing for Writing Process Awareness

Teacher: Well, girls and boys, you may relax now. Look at how the numbers on the chart go up in each round. It looks as though you are able to write a lot in only one minute. Yes, Leo?

Leo: But it isn't very good. Mine got worse each time.

Teacher: I should guess so! You were trying to write as much as you could.

Leo: Sure, but I didn't try to make it so anyone could read it.

Teacher: I didn't ask you to write so someone could read it. I asked you to write as much as you can as well as you can. Did you do that?

Leo: But I could write it better.

Teacher: Could you write as much as you did and write it better too?

Leo: No, I had to go so fast I couldn't write it any better.

... I asked you to do. Leo, now that we're talking about how you ... Think about that last round. How did you do that?

INSTRUCTIONAL SCENARIO

In the Classroom with Power Writing

Teacher: You are to write as much as you can as well as you can. Write for the whole minute. Don't stop. I will write two words on the board. You pick one. Use the word you pick as the idea you will write about. Here are the words: *pony* and *mountain.* Now, when I say "Go," you begin to write, and write for the whole one minute. Go.

COMMENTARY

While the young writers are writing, the teacher draws the following chart on the board.

	Round 1	Round 2	Round 3
46–50			
41–45			
36–40			
31–35			
26–30			
21–25			
16–20			
11–15			
6–10			
0–5			

After one minute, the teacher calls "Stop."